Guide to TREES Introduced into Southern Africa

Hugh Glen & Braam van Wyk

Published by Struik Nature
(an imprint of Penguin Random House South Africa (Pty) Ltd)
Reg. No. 1953/000441/07
The Estuaries No. 4, Oxbow Crescent, Century Avenue, Century City, 7441
PO Box 1144, Cape Town, 8000 South Africa

Visit **www.randomstruik.co.za**
and join the Struik Nature Club for updates,
news, events and special offers.

First edition 2016

1 3 5 7 9 10 8 6 4 2

Publisher: Pippa Parker
Managing editor: Helen de Villiers
Editor: Emsie du Plessis
Project manager: Colette Alves
Designer: Gillian Black
Typesetter: Deirdré Geldenhuys
Proofreader: Marthina Mössmer

Reproduction by Hirt & Carter Cape (Pty) Ltd
Printed in China by RR Donnelley Asia Printing Solutions Ltd

Print 978 1 77584 125 8
ePub 978 1 77584 470 9
ePDF 978 1 77584 471 6

Front cover, main photograph: *Jacaranda mimosifolia* (Braam van Wyk); insets (left to right): *Carica papaya* (Ton Rulkens), *Ravenala madagascariensis* (cephoto, Uwe Aranas, Wikimedia Commons, CC BY SA 3.0), *Ficus carica* (Richard Peterson, shutterstock.com), *Hura crepitans* (Cerlin Ng), *Acer saccharum* (Quercus1981, Wikimedia Commons, CC BY SA 3.0). Title page: *Plumeria rubra* (Braam van Wyk). Contents page: *Eucalyptus saligna*. Back cover, top row (left to right): *Eugenia uniflora* (Braam van Wyk), *Araucaria columnaris* (Geoff Nichols), *Calliandra haematocephala* (Braam van Wyk), *Aesculus hippocastanum* (Hugh Glen), *Caesalpinia spinosa* (Ryno Naude); middle: *Aesculus* × *carnea* (Daderot, Wikimedia Commons, public domain); bottom row (left to right): *Butea monosperma* (wie146, Wikimedia Commons, CC BY SA 3.0), *Bauhinia variegata* (Braam van Wyk).

FSC www.fsc.org
MIX
Paper from responsible sources
FSC® C101537

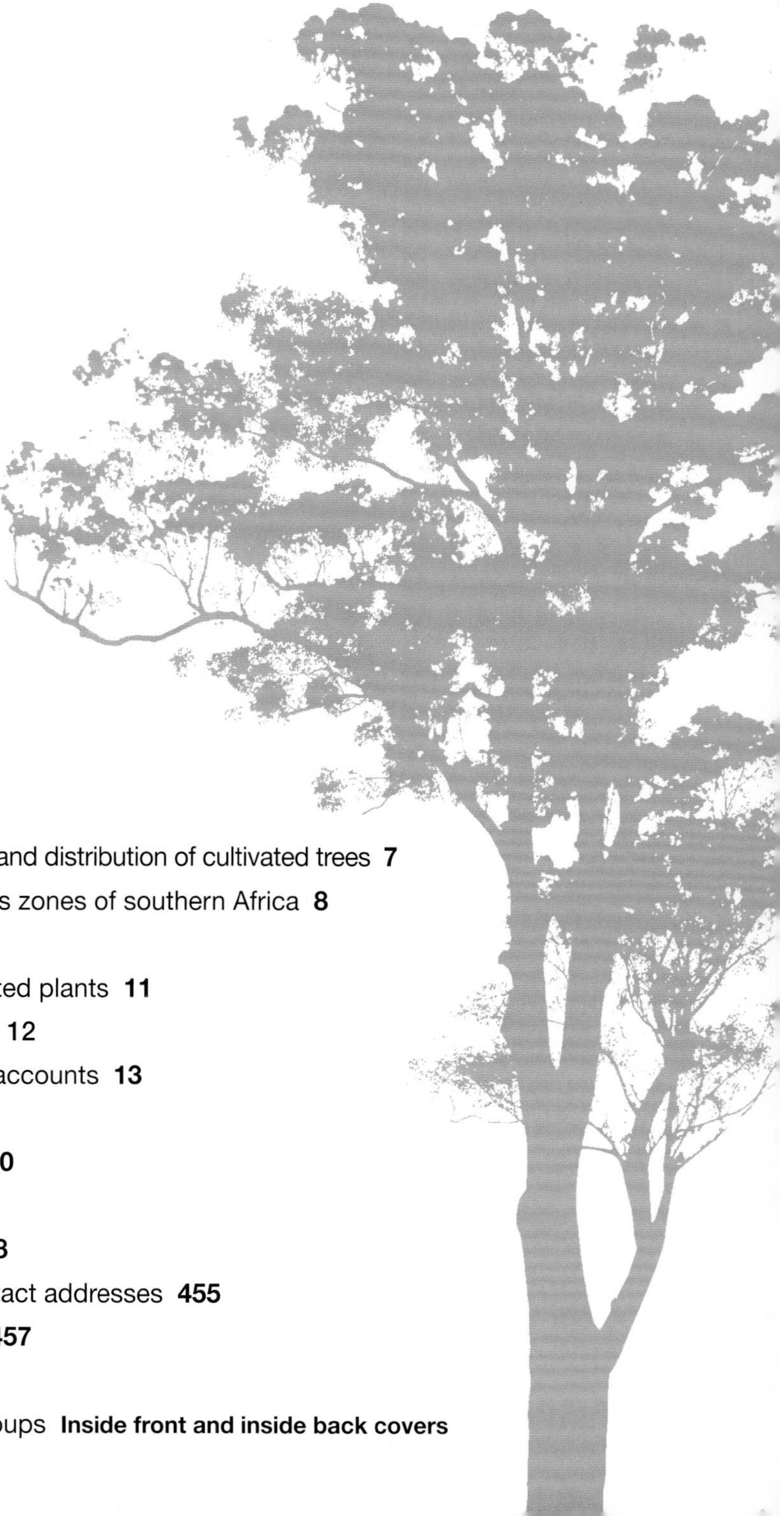

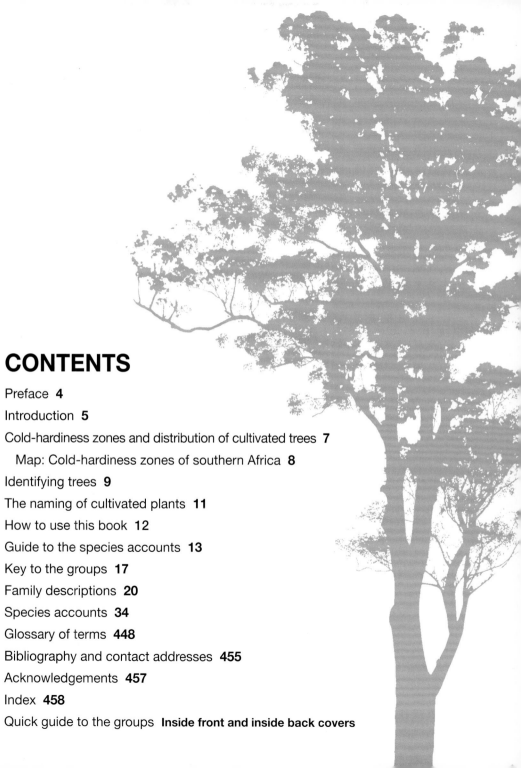

CONTENTS

PREFACE

This book is intended primarily as a manual to identify cultivated alien trees in southern Africa. Such non-native trees are predominantly associated with places of human habitation, notably home gardens, parks and other open spaces in towns and cities. This guide has been compiled as a companion volume to *Field Guide to Trees of Southern Africa* (2013, Struik Nature), one of the most popular books for the identification of trees native to the subcontinent. Hence the present book follows the same easy-to-understand group recognition approach adopted in the former. Readers familiar with using one of the two books will therefore be able to switch between them with ease. For both field guides, there is the added advantage of a complementary volume that presents the background botanical information required for tree identification, namely *How to Identify Trees in Southern Africa* (2007, Struik Publishers).

With southern Africa's exceptionally rich native tree flora of about 2,100 species, most tree identification books for the subcontinent have hitherto neglected the identification of those cultivated trees introduced from other parts of the world. However, it is estimated that at least 2,000 alien tree species are being cultivated in the region. By far the majority were introduced because they possess one or more properties valued by humans. For example, several tree species from cool-temperate parts of the northern hemisphere have been introduced to compensate for the general lack of native trees that can tolerate the extreme winter cold on the South African Highveld. Since the 1970s, efforts to promote the preferential cultivation of trees indigenous to southern Africa have to some extent overshadowed the immense importance of alien trees. In any case, so-called indigenous trees in cultivation are strictly speaking also aliens if they are grown outside their natural range, as is often the case.

Alien trees in general have unfortunately also acquired a bad reputation in our region because of the invasive tendencies of a relatively small number of species. In South Africa, several trees once popular in gardens have been declared alien invaders and are now subject to legal control and various restrictions. However, trying to curb the spread of most of the more common naturalised alien species through legislation is, in our opinion, a futile if not unjust (towards land owners) exercise. Once naturalised in a new region, alien plants become part of the local biodiversity and can still be immensely useful by providing a range of ecological services. Some people even dub the disdain with which these species are viewed as 'green xenophobia'. Perhaps the best long-term solution for containing the spread of well-established alien invaders is to put in place specific biological control measures for each species to ensure that numbers are being kept in check.

We present this book to our readers with the hope that it would help to open for them a whole new world of hitherto neglected tree diversity present within their midst. Being able to identify the many cultivated alien trees makes it possible to retrieve information from the literature or the internet, not only on their biology and cultivation requirements, but also on both their valuable and potentially undesirable properties. Alien trees are a permanent feature of our surroundings. In environments radically modified by human action, alien trees should be seen as forming an integral part of the local ecosystem, in most instances immensely useful to humans, birds and a range of other organisms. May this book help to foster a greater appreciation of alien trees, thus ensuring that they take their rightful place along native trees as important contributors to biodiversity, to the economy and to our quality of life.

Hugh Glen
Braam van Wyk
January 2016

INTRODUCTION

The Royal Horticultural Society journal *The Garden* reported in a news item in January 2013 that 'Cultivated plants … including other socio-economically as well as culturally valuable species' have for the first time been deemed important enough to be included in the United Nations' Strategic Plan for Biodiversity 2011–2020. It is therefore fitting that this book about trees cultivated in southern Africa should appear at this time.

The reasons for growing trees are much the same here as anywhere else: for timber, paper, food, flavourings, shade, shelter and aesthetics would make a good start to a list. Certainly all of these reasons are to be found in the trees shown here. The question is, why grow alien trees? Some people contend that the safest rule when it comes to planting is 'nothing but indigenous'. But that seems an absurd limitation. Consider just fruit trees: to be sure, there are marulas *(Sclerocarya birrea)* in southern Africa, though it is possible to argue that even they were carried here out of their natural range in prehistoric times. But what if you really need an apple or a peach? They do not grow on marula trees, even for the most dedicated 'only-indigenous' fanatics. And why should residents of cold places be denied summer shade because 'it's not indigenous'? To insist that cool-temperate trees should not be grown under such circumstances seems unnecessarily prescriptive.

This book includes trees that please the palate and the eye, and others that offer protection to scarce indigenous resources by providing a product so similar to the indigenous one as to be indistinguishable, but grown under controlled conditions and ready in half the time. Our indigenous forests have a history of over-exploitation stretching back almost to Van Riebeeck's arrival in 1652, when a 'timber boom' lasting more than 200 years resulted in irreversible damage to this natural resource. Redressing this destruction has driven the import of alien trees for timber, firewood and more.

This cannot be claimed to be a *complete* guide to introduced trees; if it were, it would be at least three times the size of the present volume. Records indicate that in the century or so following the appointment of the country's first professional forester, Count Médéric de Vasselot de Regné, to the Cape Colonial Forest Department in 1880, a great variety of trees was tested to determine which species would make the best contribution to South Africa's economy. In many cases we know the identity of the subjects that failed, although no trees of those species survive in cultivation here. A long list of other 'lost species' could be generated of trees once popular and sold in nurseries, but which have gone out of fashion, leaving no living trace.

Then there are the specialist enthusiasts, who import seeds of a vast assortment of species and raise sometimes as many as half a dozen individual trees to maturity in their own, private gardens. These trees are almost always inaccessible to tree-lovers who only want to see and learn about their favourite plants.

And so we have selected 588 species out of the 2,000 or more possible contenders. Instead of the 80-odd rather similar pines that could have confused beginner and expert alike, we have included 16. You will find an even smaller number of the 300-odd eucalypts that have been grown here; they are harder to tell apart. And of the many palms grown by the worthy members of the Palm Society (difficult to tell how many, as the number grows continually), we include no more than 31.

For the purposes of this book, mainly those introduced trees most likely to be seen by the general public have been described and illustrated. Among these are trees commonly encountered in gardens and parks, as well as those being cultivated

Ravenala madagascariensis (p.64)

commercially for timber, shelter, fodder or food. Undoubtedly we have omitted some trees that are accessible to the public at large. And a handful of trees that are not yet widely grown have been included to inform readers about their existence and horticultural or crop potential.

At the time of writing (2015) more than half of the world's population lives in cities. This means that it takes effort and usually money for those whose interest in trees is just awakening to visit even the commonest wild trees, but cultivated trees can be seen almost without effort on the street, at the shopping mall or in the neighbour's (or one's own) garden. And so we have included commonly grown trees, described in simple terms that still enable accurate identification.

Of course, a number of weeds and invaders are included: these started out as cultivated trees and are probably still cultivated in some places. However, they account for only some two per cent of all the trees ever imported here.

A count of the trees in this book shows that Asia and the Americas are the most important sources of imported trees, with Europe, Africa and Australia lagging some way behind. Although the statistics here refer mostly to trees featured in this book, not to all trees ever grown in southern Africa, totals for the larger group would probably not be wildly different from those presented here. Note that, in the table below, species coming from more than one area are counted separately in each, so the numbers add up to more than the number treated in the book.

Europe and Mediterranean Basin	**71**
Sub-Saharan Africa	**87**
Asia north of Himalayas (cooler)	**155**
Asia south of Himalayas (warmer)	**182**
Australasia	**119**
North America	**145**
South America	**150**
Pacific islands	**59**

That southern Asia is the source of more trees than anywhere else may be partly due to the fact that much of this book was prepared referring to the Durban Botanic Garden, which still shows the effect of the contacts that South African botanist John Medley Wood, arguably the most important Curator (1882–1915), had with the rest of the British Empire, especially India. In addition, in the early days the Cape Colonial Forestry Department looked to India before going elsewhere. North Asian (mostly Chinese, Korean and Japanese) trees have been bred for millennia because they are both beautiful and useful.

Salix babylonica (p.188)

In our region, the North Asian trees are desirable because they are tolerant of the cooler climates found inland. Much the same could be said of North American trees, albeit with a much shorter history of scientific exploration, cultivation and breeding. South America includes areas with almost every possible climate, from subantarctic ice to the driest desert on Earth and steamy equatorial rainforests. It is hardly surprising, then, that trees from there are desirable for timber, food, drugs and aesthetics. Unfortunately, too many do all too well away from their natural pests and predators, and so South America is a major source of plants that have become weedy in our region. Too many Australian trees pose the same problem when introduced here, although others remain useful and attractive without becoming pestilential. (It is worth noting that Australia has the same problem with our indigenous plants.) Despite the fact that South Africa was mainly colonised from northwestern Europe, the European–Mediterranean contribution is relatively minor. A factor here is that most of the flora of Europe north of the Alps was driven to extinction by the Ice Ages that ended only about 10,000 years ago and so the total tree flora of Europe north of the Alps comprises only 66 species. Similarly, the remote islands of the Pacific have relatively limited floras and those trees generally require the warmest and wettest climates our area can provide.

Part of the reason for the small number of tropical African trees here is the difficulty of disentangling indigenous from alien (a tree naturally common in Zimbabwe is definitely alien in the Western Cape, for example).There have also been difficulties in bringing living material from our northern neighbours due to access problems (such as Congo rainforests being a war zone) and differing export regulations and requirements. Species that survive into cultivation may be difficult to identify and there is a risk of accidentally introducing a major weed or pathogen along with some desirable tree.

COLD-HARDINESS ZONES AND DISTRIBUTION OF CULTIVATED TREES

It is common knowledge that most plants can be successfully grown only in certain parts of the world. The survival of trees under cultivation is dependent on interactions between their genetic potential and the environment in which they are being grown. In its natural habitat, each plant species is genetically optimally adapted for growth under the prevailing environmental conditions, the principal one of which is climate. For perhaps the majority of trees, rainfall (water) and temperature are the two most limiting climatic components. Rainfall is the easiest to modify under conditions of cultivation. Hence trees adapted to a high average annual rainfall can often be grown successfully in regions with a lower rainfall, provided supplementary irrigation is provided. Trying to simulate more arid conditions in a high-rainfall region can be quite tricky, but is possible. Temperature, on the other hand, is the one essential factor that is particularly difficult to manipulate when alien trees are grown in the open, that is, outside a greenhouse equipped with climate control. No wonder that temperature is generally considered to be the most limiting factor for the cultivation of trees outside their natural range.

The ability of trees to endure low-temperature extremes, commonly referred to as cold hardiness, varies widely among species. In some plants the freezing point of plant sap, because of its solute content, usually lies several degrees below 0°C. This is particularly the case in trees that are native to temperate parts of the world. However, many trees of tropical affinity are injured by exposure to temperatures that are low but yet above the freezing point. It requires just a single cold snap that exceeds the lower temperature limits of a tree for it to be killed. Hence the extreme minimum temperature experienced in a particular part of the world is a good indication of the kinds of introduced trees that can be cultivated successfully under local conditions. To this end, the United States Department of Agriculture (USDA) has developed a cold-hardiness zone map for the USA by which gardeners and growers can determine the plants that are most likely to thrive at a given location. It is known as the 'USDA Plant Hardiness Zone Map', with the various geographically defined zones based on the average annual *extreme* minimum winter temperature measured over a period of about 30 years, divided into ten-degree Fahrenheit zones (Daly *et al.* 2012). There are 13 zones, each of which has been given a standard number. For example, Zone 1, which is at the lowest temperature limits for tree growth, is characterised by an annual average extreme winter temperature of -60 to -50°F (-51 to -46°C), whereas Zone 13, the warmest, is distinguished by an average extreme winter temperature of 60 to 70°F (16 to 21°C).

Although originally developed for the USA, the USDA hardiness zones have subsequently also been adopted elsewhere as a standard to indicate where a plant species can be cultivated outdoors. Although low temperature is not the only determinant of plant survival (factors such as high summer temperature, humidity and soil type may be equally important), the USDA hardiness zones have proved to be particularly useful in the case of woody perennials, notably trees. Based on information obtained from the South African Weather Service and the available meteorological literature, supplemented by our own personal experience, we have compiled the accompanying map depicting the USDA hardiness zones for southern Africa. Considering that localised microclimates can result in warmer or colder pockets, even within the same garden, the map should at best serve as a broad guide only. Five such cold-hardiness zones are recognised in our region, namely Zones 8 to 12. For each tree species treated in this book we give a map showing the hardiness zone(s) to which it is best adapted. These are also the areas in which cultivated specimens of the particular species are most likely to be encountered.

Malus sylvestris (p.170)

COLD-HARDINESS ZONES OF SOUTHERN AFRICA

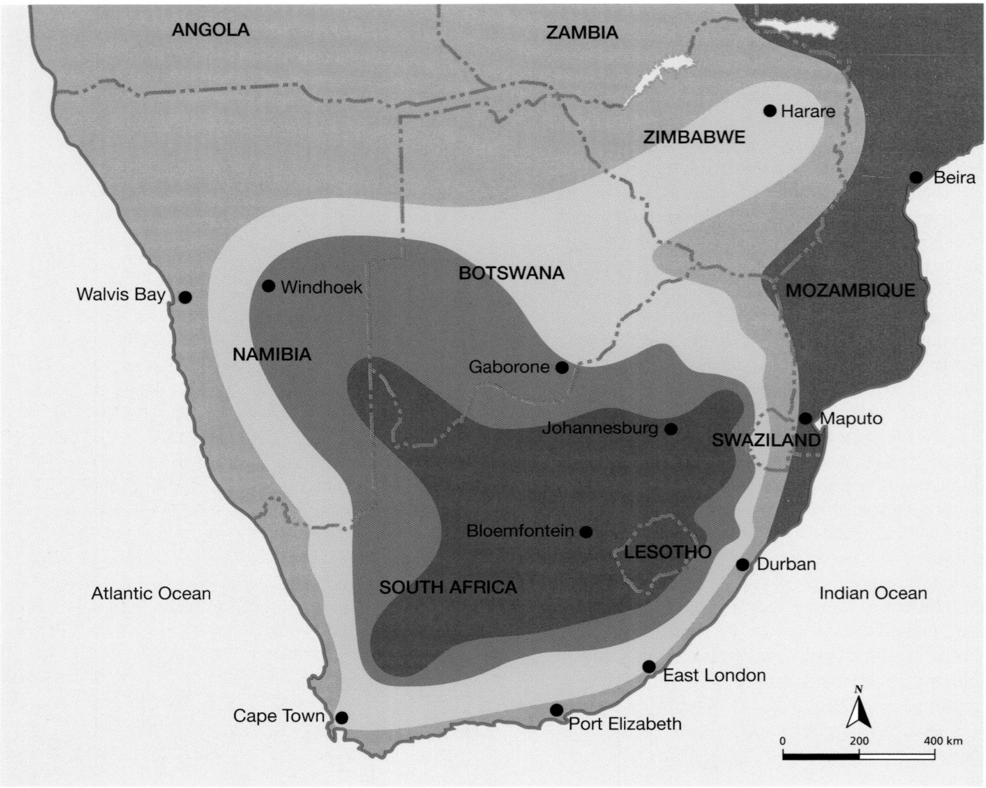

Average Annual Extreme Minimum Temperature

Temp (°C)	Zone	Temp (°F)
-12 to -7	8	10 to 20
-7 to -1	9	20 to 30
-1 to 4	10	30 to 40
4 to 10	11	40 to 50
10 to 16	12	50 to 60

Above: Map showing the five USDA cold-hardiness zones recognised for southern Africa, and referred to in this book. These zones are based on the average annual extreme minimum winter temperature measured over a period of about 30 years. For the purposes of this book, southern Africa is defined as the mainland region of the African continent **south** of the Kunene, Okavango and Zambezi rivers. It comprises Namibia, Botswana, Zimbabwe, South Africa, Swaziland, Lesotho and that part of Mozambique south of the Zambezi River.

IDENTIFYING TREES

By observing the many and various identifying tree features, or characters, listed below, you will be able to build a composite picture of and arrive at a name for the particular plant you are observing. Turn to the 'Glossary of terms' (pp.448–454) if you are unsure of some of the technical terms (the numbers that appear in square brackets in this section refer to the appropriate Glossary illustrations). *How to Identify Trees in Southern Africa* (Van Wyk & Van Wyk 2007) provides the background knowledge essential for tree identification. It is strongly recommended that you acquire this guide (also available in Afrikaans; Van Wyk & Van Wyk 2008) and use it in conjunction with this book.

Apart from the book itself, your most valuable items of equipment are a pair of sharp eyes, a retentive mind, and a small notebook and pencil. A 10x handlens or a magnifying glass can also be a great help when studying a small object. Alternatively, reverse a pair of binoculars and look though the 'wrong' end. Binoculars are also useful in identifying leaf details, flowers and fruit in the upper parts of trees (and for bird-spotting). A pair of small secateurs and a plastic bag can come in handy when collecting material for later study.

However, you should really accumulate as much information about the tree as you can while you are in the field. Certain characters can only be reliably observed in living specimens (for example, the presence or absence of latex). Positive identification of most trees requires physical handling of the plant material, so do not be afraid to touch and smell as well as look.

Tree size, shape and foliage colour, texture: Note the size and shape of the tree, as well as the colour and texture of the crown. Basic tree shape is genetically determined; each species has a specific tree architecture, though one that can be modified, within limits, by environmental and physiological conditions. Shape, colour and texture are the most useful features for identifying trees from a distance. These attributes are also used to help form a search image to locate other individuals of an identified tree in the same general area.

BRAAM VAN WYK

Populus fremontii (p.172)

Bark: Note the bark of the tree. Every species has its own characteristic mature bark pattern. Mature trees with a flaky or rough and thick covering usually have thin, smooth bark when young. Therefore you should examine only mature specimens when attempting to identify trees by their bark characters.

Branches and twigs: Note the surface texture and colour of branches and twigs. Young twigs are often marked with small, light-coloured pustules called lenticels [45]. Check whether twigs and older branches are round, flattened or more or less square in cross section. In deciduous species, thick twigs tend to indicate compound leaves. Record the presence of any spines or thorns, and note their arrangement.

Latex: Test for the presence of latex [53, 54]. Any abundant liquid exudate, whether watery (clear), cloudy, milky, or otherwise coloured, is here referred to as such. Pick a healthy green leaf, preferably one from an actively growing shoot; break it off at the point where the stalk (petiole) is attached to the stem, and check immediately whether any liquid oozes out at the broken end or from the scar on the stem. The exudate needs to be fairly copious, preferably forming a drop that completely covers the wound. If no latex is detected, check a few other leaves from different parts of the tree to confirm the fact.

Leaf samples: Always examine a variety of leaves, preferably from the canopy of the tree, to determine characters such as size, shape, colour, texture and degree of hairiness. A single leaf can be misleading. Leaves on coppice shoots may differ substantially from those in the canopy.

Simple and compound leaves: Determine at the outset whether the leaves are simple (undivided) [1, 2] or compound (that is, made up of separate leaflets/pinnae) [3–8]. If in doubt, look for the axillary bud to determine whether the leaf is really compound or not. There is a small bud (which can develop into a leafy shoot, or a flower) in the axil between the stem and the petiole, but not between the rachis and stalk of a leaflet (pinna). Moreover, in a compound leaf there is no growing tip at the end of the rachis.

Leaf arrangement: Note how the leaves are arranged on the stem [9–12]. Are they alternate, opposite, or whorled? In compound leaves, these characters refer to the leaves themselves, not the individual leaflets. Clustered leaves are nearly always alternate, unless the clusters themselves are arranged in opposite pairs.

Leaf texture and hairiness: Touch the leaves on both sides. Are they smooth or rough, thin or leathery, woolly, hairless, or sticky?

External glands: Check for the presence of external glands on the leaf. These are often located at the point where the petiole is attached to the blade in simple leaves, or on the petiole or rachis in the case of compound leaves [55, 56].

Leaf margins: Are the leaf edges smooth, toothed, scalloped, wavy, lobed or rolled under? [35–38]

Venation: Note the venation pattern. Is there a single midrib, or several veins from the base of the blade? Are the veins prominently raised or obscure on one or both surfaces? Are the lateral veins more or less parallel and terminating at the margin without forming an intramarginal vein? Check for the presence of domatia [57, 58] in the axils of the principal lateral veins.

Secretory cavities: Test for the presence of these cavities in the leaf blade [59]. Hold the leaf up to the sun (other light sources are invariably not bright enough) and look for translucent dots. These are extremely small (the size of pinpricks) and uniformly scattered all over the blade (here, the use of a handlens is recommended). Practise looking at a leaf known to contain them (for instance, any citrus or eucalypt species).

Bacterial nodules: These nodules [60] are also detected by holding the leaf up to the sun. These structures should be sought only in plants with opposite leaves and interpetiolar stipules [50]. They are much larger than secretory cavities, dark-coloured, not translucent and are easily visible although often confined to a specific area of the blade, particularly towards the midrib.

Odour: Crush the leaf and check its smell. Leaves with secretory cavities are usually strongly aromatic, but not all aromatic leaves have secretory cavities.

Stipules: Check for the presence of stipules at the base of the petiole [1, 46–49]. This is best done with young leaves near the tips of actively growing shoots. These structures can be very small and, again, a handlens is recommended. Stipules are often deciduous or shrivelled in mature leaves and, if the stipules have been shed, a distinct scar is usually left on the stem. In the case of opposite leaves, look out for the presence of interpetiolar stipules [50, 51].

Flowers: Look carefully for flowers [39], which, on many trees, are small and inconspicuous. Although we have tried to limit the use of floral technicalities in this book, four easy-to-observe characters are particularly useful (especially for family recognition), namely: flowers regular or irregular [43, 44]; petals free or united; stamens many (more than 10) or very few (4 or fewer); ovary superior or inferior [41, 42].

Fruit: Examine the tree carefully to establish whether the mature fruit is dry (pod, capsule, nut) or fleshy (berry, drupe). If you don't see any fruit, look on the ground directly beneath the tree: one can often find old pods, capsules, nuts and seeds (in this way, even the leaves of deciduous species can be studied). Make sure you understand the difference between a fruit and a seed; the two concepts are often confused.

Collecting material: It is always worthwhile collecting one or more twigs with a number of leaves attached (a single leaf does not show the leaf arrangement) together with any other fertile material that might be present, for more leisurely examination. These samples may be kept for several days in a moist plastic bag, provided that it is kept cool and not exposed to direct sunlight. If your attempts to identify the tree are unsuccessful, the material can be pressed and dried as a specimen, which you could then submit to an individual expert or herbarium (see 'How to use this book', p.12).

Terminalia catappa flowers (p.238)

THE NAMING OF CULTIVATED PLANTS

Common names of plants can be confusing, because they are quite variable. For example, in a recent internet discussion about a well-known edible plant, three different names arose: egg-plant, aubergine and brinjal – all referring to the same plant, because English speakers in different places use different names for the same thing. But botanists the world over, from any language group, can pinpoint the species by referring to its unambiguous scientific name, in this case *Solanum melongena*. (And they will know it is not a tree, so not discussed further in this book.)

Confusion can also arise because different plants can be called by the same name in different places: no fewer than six unrelated plants are known to share the Afrikaans name *kanniedood*. And so, to limit confusion, in this book scientific names appear first, followed by as many common names as could be found; many of those in different languages had to be phonetically translated for local accessibility.

Scientific names of plants are governed by two rule books, a situation less confusing than it sounds: the *International Code of Nomenclature for Algae, Fungi and Plants* (ICN), referred to in older works as the *International Code of Botanical Nomenclature* (McNeill *et al.* 2012), and the *International Code of Nomenclature for Cultivated Plants* (ICNCP) (Brickell *et al.* 2009, edition 8; edition 9 is in preparation at the time of writing). Clearly, the first deals with plants in their wild or natural state and the second with plants that have attracted the attention of breeders or marketers. Where is the boundary between the codes? The ICN states quite clearly that a wild plant brought into cultivation is named under that code and ICNCP only comes into play when an identifiable selection or hybrid is made. The first article of ICNCP agrees, with different and generally more detailed wording.

This sounds clear enough, but what about plants that have been in cultivation and so subject to artificial rather than natural selection for so long that all natural populations have disappeared? That description covers several of our most ancient crops, such as lentils and potatoes, and one or two trees mentioned in this book. In such cases groups of plants corresponding to wild species are named under ICN (*Lens culinaris* and *Solanum tuberosum*, for example) and individual strains, of which there may be thousands, are named under ICNCP.

The general structure of scientific species names for wild plants, with a genus name and specific modifier (specific name or epithet), is well covered in many guides and will not be repeated here. Interested readers are referred to Meg Coates Palgrave's excellent one-page summary in her account of southern African trees (Coates Palgrave 2002). Things become a little more complicated with cultivated plants.

Consider the black poplar, *Populus nigra*. The wild form of this tree has a spreading form with a relatively short, branched trunk. A commonly seen form, however, has a tall, essentially unbranched trunk and very erect twigs and small branches. Nurserymen and gardeners have bred and propagated this form for centuries and it is widely known to English speakers as a Lombardy poplar. It also has a name under ICNCP, *Populus nigra* 'Italica'. The last word is the cultivar name and the rules of ICNCP stipulate that cultivar names are written between single quotes and in normal, not italic, type. This is a rather old name and so the Latin form is allowed; ICNCP states that more recent cultivar names may be in any language other than Latin, or in some cases (most notably roses and agricultural crops) a partially numeric code is allowed. Cultivar names in non-alphabetic scripts are allowed and ICNCP gives guidance on transcribing these into Roman letters. One of the examples in that code concerns the transcription of three names of Korean cultivars of *Hibiscus syriacus* (the species is covered in this book) from Hangeul to Roman characters.

There are ways in which ICNCP is more forgiving than ICN. For example, there is only one scientific name for the grape, *Vitis vinifera*. But there are three permitted ways of referring to any particular cultivar in that species, and so the following examples are all legitimate: *Vitis vinifera* 'Pinotage'; *Vitis* 'Pinotage'; Grape 'Pinotage'.

In this book, for the sake of brevity (among other reasons), we have rarely mentioned individual cultivars. The study of cultivated plants in our region is in its infancy and undoubtedly many more described cultivars are grown here than are recorded or known to the authors. Finally, it is not always easy to distinguish among them – the requirement for distinctness is sometimes met more in the eye of the breeder than on the ground!

An excellent guide for anyone who wants to know more about the naming of plants is Spencer, Cross & Lumley's *Plant Names: A Guide to Botanical Nomenclature* (Spencer *et al.* 2007).

HOW TO USE THIS BOOK

Probably the greatest difficulty when trying to identify trees associated with places of human habitation in southern Africa is deciding whether a particular species is native to the region, or was introduced from elsewhere in the world. This is an unavoidable consequence of having separate tree books for predominantly native and predominantly alien trees. Both native and alien trees are widely grown in gardens, parks and other urban environments. There is no easy solution to this dilemma. If a tree bears cones, it is most probably a gymnosperm and an alien. Otherwise, for trees in an urban setting, first consult the present book and if the species cannot be found, then the tree may well be native and you would have to consult *Field Guide to Trees of Southern Africa* (Van Wyk & Van Wyk 2013).

Once you have examined the tree carefully (see 'Identifying trees', p.9), and have material in hand, you are ready to begin the identification process. The following steps will enable you to narrow down the possible species to which a sample may belong.

1. The trees in this book have been classified into most of 43 groups based on easy-to-observe vegetative features. More details on the groups are supplied by Van Wyk & Van Wyk (2007). Begin with the key on page 17. This key consists of pairs of choices (leads) and employs easily seen vegetative characters, some of which are illustrated in the 'Glossary of terms' (pp.448–454). Start at the first choice and establish which description matches your plant. At the end of each choice, there is either the name of a group or a line leading to the next pair of choices. After arriving at the name of a group, turn to that particular section in the book.

Each group starts with a concise statement of its diagnostic characters. This statement is essentially a summary of the most important choices you have made in the key. However, it takes just one incorrect choice to arrive at the wrong group. So it is important to verify the group's identification by checking that it agrees with the group characters. If there is any discrepancy you must, at some point in the key, have gone astray.

In addition, the icon accompanying each group is a pictorial representation that summarises some of the group's diagnostic features. With a little practice you should be able to recognise the group simply by looking at the icons – which will save you having to work through all the choices. For convenience, all these icons are reproduced, in the form of a quick guide, on the inside front and back covers of the book.

BRAAM VAN WYK

Platycladus orientalis female cones (p.96)

2. Having established the group in which your plant falls, the cold-hardiness zones (see p.8) become the next clue to its identity (unless, of course, you know its family; see further on). Each species entry in the main section of this book has a map depicting the cold-hardiness zone(s) to which it is best adapted. Concentrate initially only on those species likely to occur in the hardiness zone from which your plant comes. Bear in mind that these are not plant distribution maps. The map merely indicates the area in which a species is most likely to be encountered. However, perhaps most species will occasionally be found in localised sites outside the zones mapped as being optimal, temperature-wise, for its cultivation.

3. Compare your plant carefully with the photographs of those species with a relevant hardiness zone distribution. Once you have found a picture that seems to match the material in hand, compare it carefully with the accompanying description. Pay particular attention to those diagnostic features that are highlighted in bold. Check the specimen against the family description (pp.20–33). If you cannot find a matching picture, check the cross references listed at the beginning of some of the groups.

If you cannot identify the species, don't be disheartened. With so many different cultivated trees, both native and alien, in southern Africa, even seasoned botanists are quite often totally baffled. Remember also that this book does not feature every cultivated alien tree in the region. Ask a local expert, or try some of the books listed in the bibliography (p.455). If the tree lacks fertile material, revisit it during a different season. You can also send your material to a herbarium that undertakes the naming of plants. Always contact the institution to ask if it would be willing to help (contact addresses are listed at the back of this book). Establish whether there are any costs involved. Some herbaria charge a so-called handling fee, whereas others provide a free service. Make sure you send your plants in the form of good, properly dried, properly packed herbarium specimens, together with all the relevant data you have.

Knowing the family to which your plant belongs will obviously be a considerable help to speed up the identification process, but family recognition requires some experience and botanical knowledge and, in any event, it should be possible to identify most specimens without the use of family features. Nevertheless, novices are advised to familiarise themselves with the diagnostic characters of the principal tree families of alien trees in southern Africa (see pp.20–33). Mastering this skill, indeed, is an essential step towards becoming truly competent in the field of plant identification. Naturally it will involve practice, but you might be surprised how quickly you will be able to recognise families on sight. Most of our trees belong to a relatively small number of families, and it is of course much easier to recall the names of families than those of species.

GUIDE TO THE SPECIES ACCOUNTS

In this section the layout of the main text is briefly explained. The species entries, or accounts, contain a wealth of information, presented in concise and consistent fashion. To get the most out of the book, it is essential to understand the meaning of all the various components numbered in the miniaturised sample spread shown below and described under a matching number.

1. GROUP The species described in this book are arranged in most of 43 groups based on easy-to-observe leaf and stem characters. Each group has a number, as well as a common name derived from one of its constituent genera native to southern Africa or from an outstanding character of that group. For a key to the groups, see page 17. Diagnostic group characters are summarised at the start of each of the 43 sections and should be used to confirm the options offered in the key. For more detailed information on group identification, see Van Wyk & Van Wyk (2007, 2008).

2. GROUP ICON Each of the 43 groups has its own icon, which appears as an identification and reference aid on every text page. An icon is a pictorial representation of a plant, or a stem with leaves, and it summarises a group's

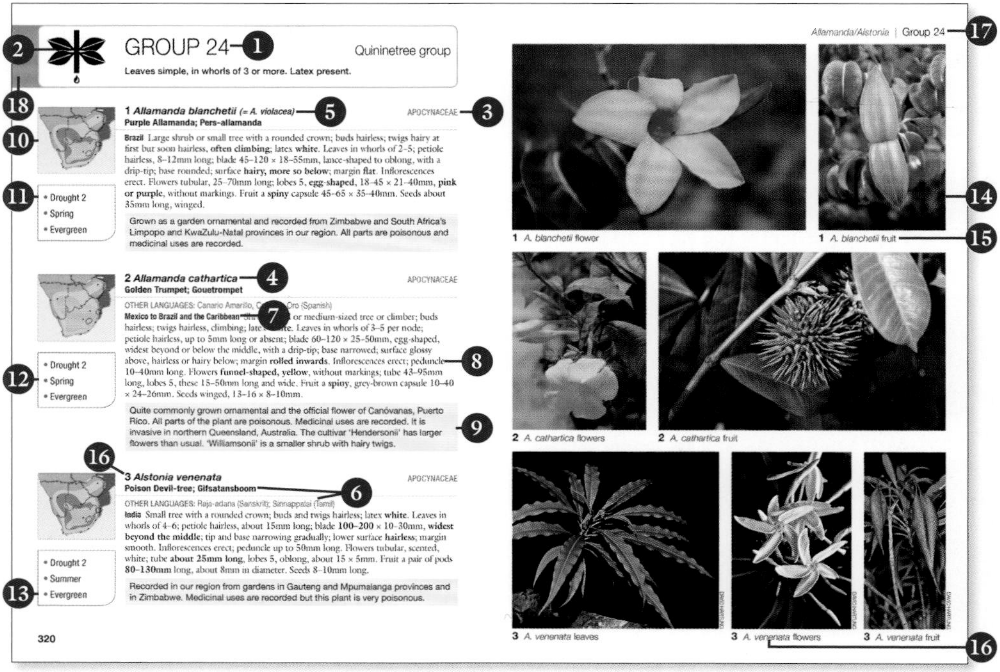

diagnostic characters. As a quick guide to the groups, all the icons are repeated, arranged together, on the inside front and back covers of the book.

3. FAMILY NAME Just as species are brought together in inclusive units called genera, so genera are arranged in families. Four of the families represented in this book may also be referred to by an alternative name. These families and their alternative names are, respectively, the Compositae/Asteraceae, Labiatae/Lamiaceae, Palmae/Arecaceae, and Guttiferae/Clusiaceae; in each case we have used the second name. We have treated the legumes as a single inclusive family, the Leguminosae/Fabaceae (broadly defined). Some authors (including Van Wyk & Van Wyk 2013) separate the legumes into three different families: the Mimosaceae, Caesalpiniaceae and the Fabaceae (narrowly defined; also referred to as Papilionaceae).

4. SCIENTIFIC SPECIES NAME Within the 43 groups into which the main part of this book is organised, species appear alphabetically. A species name is made up of two parts. The first part is the genus name (e.g. *Quercus*; comparable to a person's surname). The second part is the specific epithet (e.g. *robur*; comparable to a first name). The name of subspecies or varieties (which are variants within a species) consists of the name of the species in which it is classified, followed by a word indicating its rank (subsp. or var.), then the subspecific or varietal epithet. For the most part we have followed the scientific names accepted by *The Plant List* (www.theplantlist.org). For reference purposes and as a source of historical information, scientific names are often followed by one or more personal names, sometimes abbreviated. These so-called authority citations are of little use to laypeople and they have been omitted in this book (but are supplied by *The Plant List*).

BRAAM VAN WYK

Ailanthus altissima fruit (p.382)

5. SYNONYMS The names under which a plant was previously known, or are alternatively referred to, are its synonyms. Many people find name changes perplexing and even downright annoying, so it is worth outlining briefly why plant names change, or why at any one time a species may have more than one name.

Plants often have to be reclassified following the discovery of new information. As a result, a species may be transferred from one genus to another, or a single species may be split into two or more species. By the same token, two or more species may be combined into a single one, or what has previously been considered a subspecies or variety may be given specific rank. In certain circumstances a name may also change if an older published name is found.

Botanists also differ in their choice of classification systems, and this sometimes means that a single species bears two or more alternative and equally valid names, each one correct within its own particular system. The same applies to the grouping of species into families. One classification system may, for example, emphasise the genealogical sharing of a hypothetical recent common ancestor between certain species regardless of morphological specialisation and so tend to lump them together (phylogenetic approach). Another may emphasise not only common descent, but also morphological specialisation and other structural and behavioural differences between the same species, splitting them up into different entities (evolutionary approach).

Synonyms are preceded by an equal sign (=) and placed in brackets. In this book we supply very few synonyms and then only from fairly recent name changes. Synonyms may facilitate cross-referencing between this book and other publications on trees, particularly older ones. When searching the literature to find out more about a particular tree species, you should not only use its currently accepted correct name, but also its synonyms.

6. COMMON NAMES Common names are often confusing. The same name may apply to two or more different species, or the same species may have more than one common name. To provide a measure of stability, recommended common names in English and Afrikaans are proposed for each species and these are given first and in bold, often followed by one or more other options in grey. Common names in English or Afrikaans were taken from various sources and in a few cases new ones had to be invented where no existing ones could be found. Preference was given to the English common names used internationally (and/or in the trees' home ranges) rather than creations by local authors. But there are the odd cases of a well-known local name used in preference, e.g. 'naartjie' rather than 'mandarin' and 'pawpaw' rather than 'papaya'. In this book we are following, with a few exceptions, the English and Afrikaans common names recommended by Von Breitenbach (1989), National Terminology Services *et al.* (1991), and for southern African trees, Van Wyk *et al.* (2011).

In the case of internationally well-known species, common names are also supplied in other languages.

7. ORIGIN Cultivated alien trees in southern Africa have been introduced from all over the world. Here we record the principal countries and/or regions covered by the species' natural range. For a breakdown of the main regions from where our alien species came from, see under 'Introduction' (p.6).

8. DESCRIPTIVE TEXT The text for each species begins with an indication of the growth form (habit). Salient features of the bark, branchlets, leaves, inflorescence, flowers and fruit are then described. Particularly significant diagnostic characters are printed in bold. These characters, in combination, are normally essential for the positive identification of a species. Although we have tried to use language that can be readily understood by the layperson, some botanical terminology has been unavoidable (see 'Glossary of terms', p.448). Background information on tree identification terminology is provided by Van Wyk & Van Wyk (2007).

9. NOTEWORTHY INFORMATION (shaded panel)
Plant usage Cultivated trees are significant not only for their aesthetic qualities in horticulture or their spiritual importance for particular cultures, but also have immense practical value as food, fodder, medicine, tools, timber, building materials, shade, shelter, hedges, donga reclamation and fuel. Selective mention is made of specific uses for some of the species. Also mentioned are various other aspects of potential interest, e.g. historical trees, diseases (of the tree), toxicity and allergenic pollen. This feature has often had to be kept very short because of space constraints. Many of the healing properties ascribed to tree parts have not yet been scientifically proven, and potentially negative side-effects have often not been established. We have therefore refrained from mentioning specific medicinal usages.

Alien invasive species A few alien trees introduced into southern Africa from other parts of the world have become naturalised – that is, capable of reproducing and spreading without human agency. Some of these species have a negative impact on the native vegetation,

BRAAM VAN WYK

Manihot grahamii female flower (p.402)

biodiversity and water sources, and have been declared alien invaders. In South Africa, landowners are legally responsible for the control of invasive alien plants on their properties. Under the *Alien and Invasive Species Regulations* (AIS), promulgated under the *National Environmental Management: Biodiversity Act* (NEMBA), declared weeds and invaders have been divided into four categories, namely:

Category 1a species may not occur on any land and must be combated and eradicated. Any form of trade or planting is strictly prohibited.

Category 1b species must be controlled and, wherever possible, removed and destroyed. Any form of trade or planting is strictly prohibited.

Category 2 species are commercially important and may be grown in demarcated areas, such as commercial plantations, provided a permit has been obtained and steps are taken to prevent their spread.

Category 3 species are ornamentals that may no longer be planted, propagated or traded, although existing plants may remain, except within the flood line of watercourses and wetlands.

Cultivars For a few entries, one or more cultivar names are listed, especially if particular ones are being planted in our region. For more information on cultivar names, see 'The naming of cultivated plants' (p.11). A cultivar refers to an assemblage of plants that has been selected for a particular attribute or combination of attributes and that is clearly distinct, uniform and stable in these characters and that when propagated by appropriate means retains those characters (Hawksworth 2010). In the local nursery trade, cultivars are often informally referred to as 'varieties', a practice that should be discouraged. A multiplication sign as part of a name (e.g. *Citrus* × *paradisi*) indicates that the plant is of hybrid origin.

Similar species Where appropriate, the names of closely related species and their diagnostic characters are provided. The diagnostic characters of easily confused species are also given.

10. COLD-HARDINESS MAPS The cold hardiness of a tree is generally measured by the lowest temperature it can withstand, which largely determines where it can be cultivated outdoors at a particular location. For each tree in this book we supply a map with a grey neutral background on which is depicted in colour the cold-hardiness zone(s) to which it is best adapted. These maps are based on the map of USDA cold-hardiness zones for southern Africa (see p.8). For background information on the cold-hardiness zones, see 'Cold-hardiness zones and distribution of cultivated trees' (p.7). These maps tell you the zones where a species will do well in cultivation and is most likely to be found, as well as the zones from which it will most probably be absent. Colours used, and the USDA hardiness zone numbers (based on the average annual extreme winter temperature) they represent, are as follows:

Grey	Temperature not optimal for a species, therefore unlikely to be encountered in this area.	
Blue	**Zone 8:**	-12 to -7°C (10 to 20°F)
Green	**Zone 9:**	-7 to -1°C (20 to 30°F)
Yellow	**Zone 10:**	-1 to 4°C (30 to 40°F)
Orange	**Zone 11:**	4 to 10°C (40 to 50°F)
Red	**Zone 12:**	10 to 16°C (50 to 60°F)

11. DROUGHT HARDINESS Drought tolerance refers to the degree to which a plant is adapted to arid or drought conditions, an important consideration in plant selection for especially arid or drought-prone regions. A rather arbitrary three-point scale is used to indicate drought hardiness:
1 = somewhat resistant; **2** = moderately resistant;
3 = very resistant.

12. FLOWERING TIME In a few tree species the peak flowering time occurs within fairly narrow limits. In many others, however, it may vary significantly from year to year and even between two trees of the same species growing next to each other. We have therefore decided to give seasonal indicators rather than specific months. Our seasonal concepts are intended as a rough guide only: **spring** = August–November; **summer** = November–March; **autumn** = March–May; **winter** = May–August. Fruiting logically follows directly on flowering (except in the case of male trees of unisexual species).

VLADYSLAV SIABER / FOTOLIA.COM

Cydonia oblonga fruit (p.208)

13. DURATION An indication of duration, that is whether predominantly **deciduous, evergreen** or **semi-evergreen**, is given for each species.

14. COLOUR PHOTOGRAPHS Each species description is accompanied, on the facing page, by one or more photographs. Thus all pertinent information relating to a tree appears on one spread. Illustrations showing features that are particularly helpful in identification (whole trees, flowers, fruit, vegetative characters) have been selected. Bark patterns have been included only if they are especially diagnostic.

15. CAPTIONS Label captions give the scientific name for the species, and the part(s) illustrated.

16. ENTRY NUMBERS The number adjacent to each species entry corresponds with the number of the species illustration(s) on the opposite page.

17. RUNNING HEADS These itemise the genera that feature on the spread, and the group in which they fall.

18. THUMB INDEXES The colour of these corresponds with the colour of the relevant group panel appearing in the key to the groups (pp.17–19) and in the quick guide on the inside front and back covers.

KEY TO THE GROUPS: DIAGRAM A

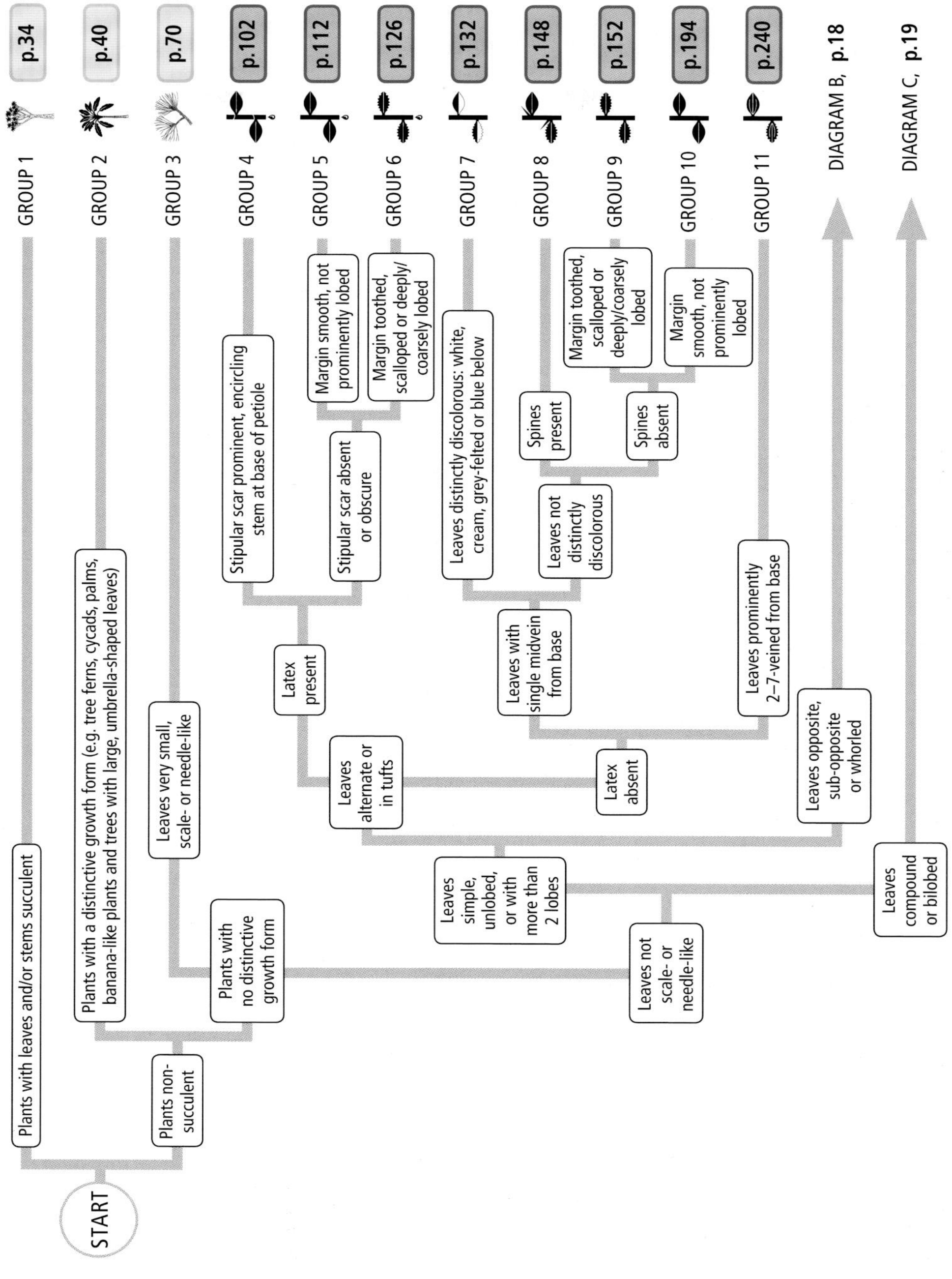
START
Plants with leaves and/or stems succulent
Plants non-succulent
Plants with a distinctive growth form (e.g. tree ferns, cycads, palms, banana-like plants and trees with large, umbrella-shaped leaves)
Plants with no distinctive growth form
Leaves very small, scale- or needle-like
Leaves not scale- or needle-like
Leaves simple, unlobed, or with more than 2 lobes
Leaves compound or bilobed
Leaves alternate or in tufts
Leaves opposite, sub-opposite or whorled
Latex present
Latex absent
Stipular scar prominent, encircling stem at base of petiole
Stipular scar absent or obscure
Margin smooth, not prominently lobed
Margin toothed, scalloped or deeply/coarsely lobed
Leaves with single midvein from base
Leaves prominently 2–7-veined from base
Leaves distinctly discolorous: white, cream, grey-felted or blue below
Leaves not distinctly discolorous
Spines present
Spines absent
Margin toothed, scalloped or deeply/coarsely lobed
Margin smooth, not prominently lobed
GROUP 1 p.34
GROUP 2 p.40
GROUP 3 p.70
GROUP 4 p.102
GROUP 5 p.112
GROUP 6 p.126
GROUP 7 p.132
GROUP 8 p.148
GROUP 9 p.152
GROUP 10 p.194
GROUP 11 p.240
DIAGRAM B, p.18
DIAGRAM C, p.19

KEY TO THE GROUPS: DIAGRAM B

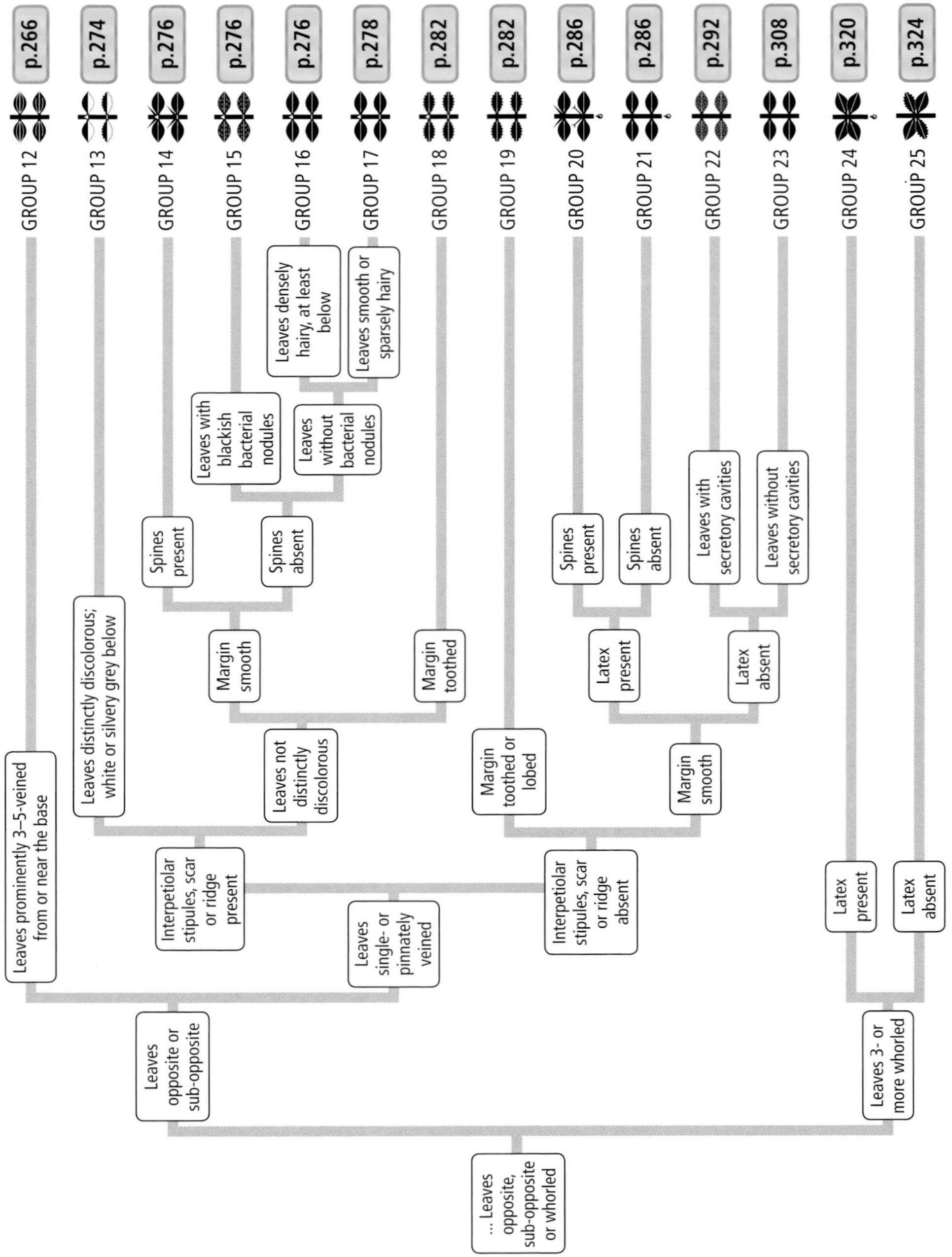

... Leaves opposite, sub-opposite or whorled
Leaves opposite or sub-opposite
Leaves 3- or more whorled
Leaves prominently 3–5-veined from or near the base
Leaves single- or pinnately veined
Interpetiolar stipules, scar or ridge present
Interpetiolar stipules, scar or ridge absent
Leaves distinctly discolorous; white or silvery grey below
Leaves not distinctly discolorous
Margin smooth
Margin toothed
Spines present
Spines absent
Leaves with blackish bacterial nodules
Leaves without bacterial nodules
Leaves densely hairy, at least below
Leaves smooth or sparsely hairy
Margin toothed or lobed
Margin smooth
Latex present
Latex absent
Spines present
Spines absent
Leaves with secretory cavities
Leaves without secretory cavities
Latex present
Latex absent
GROUP 12 p.266
GROUP 13 p.274
GROUP 14 p.276
GROUP 15 p.276
GROUP 16 p.276
GROUP 17 p.278
GROUP 18 p.282
GROUP 19 p.282
GROUP 20 p.286
GROUP 21 p.286
GROUP 22 p.292
GROUP 23 p.308
GROUP 24 p.320
GROUP 25 p.324

KEY TO THE GROUPS: DIAGRAM C

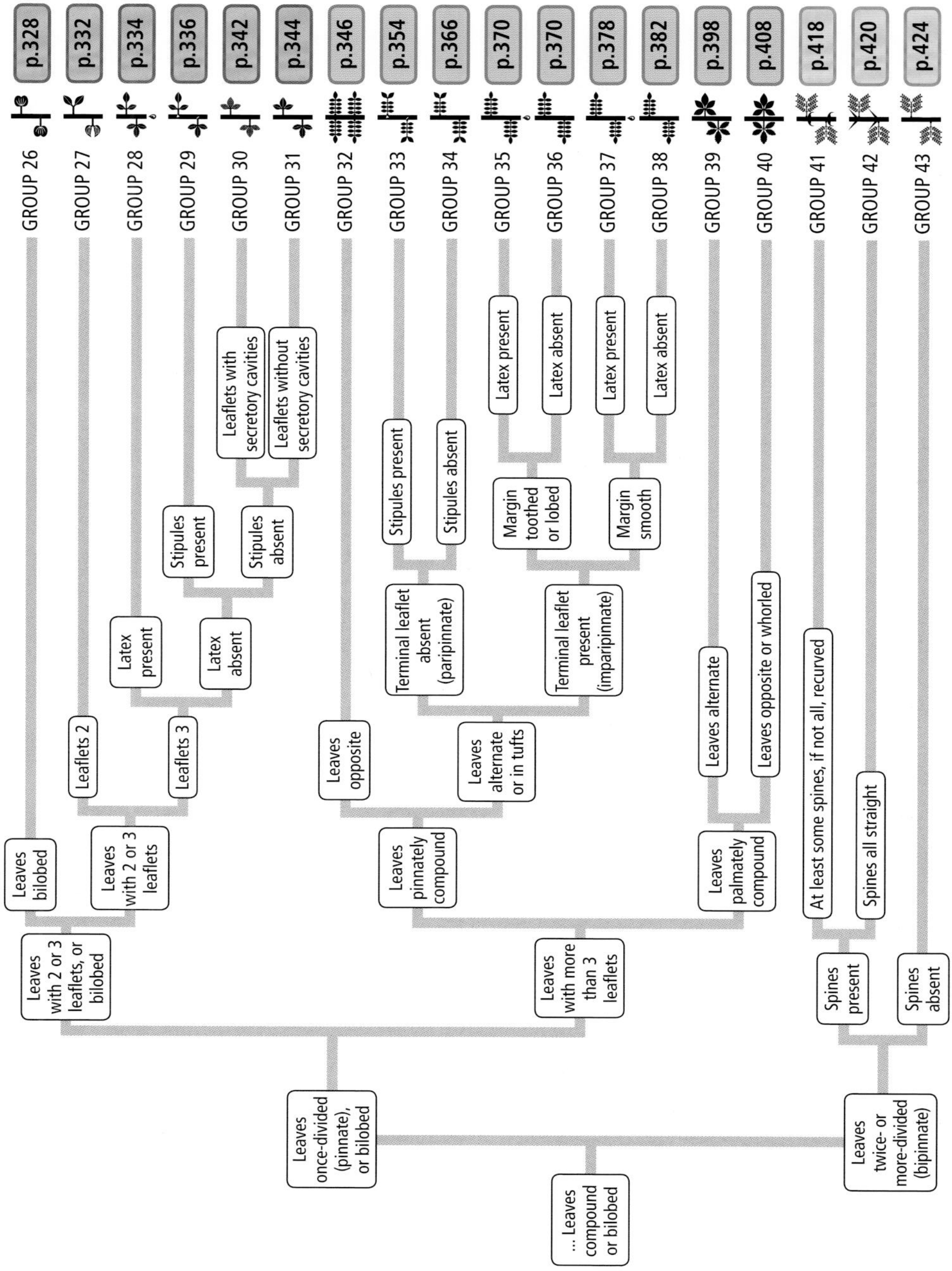

FAMILY DESCRIPTIONS

When identifying trees, much time can be saved if one is familiar with the most important plant families in an area, especially as botanical keys – the formally accepted analytical devices for the determination of plant names – tend to be rather long and difficult to use. Therefore anyone interested in cultivated alien trees should be able to recognise, on sight, members of such prominent families as the Fabaceae (broadly defined), Myrtaceae, Arecaceae, Rosaceae, Malvaceae (broadly defined), Moraceae, Pinaceae, Bignoniaceae, Fagaceae, Euphorbiaceae, Cupressaceae, Apocynaceae, Oleaceae, Proteaceae, Rutaceae, Aceraceae, Anacardiaceae and Rubiaceae. Together these 18 families, which we have ranked in descending order of importance, account for almost 68 per cent of the tree species included in this book. We do not believe that including all trees that have ever been recorded as cultivated in southern Africa would materially alter either the rankings or the proportion of all trees included in the top few families.

Each family entry appearing below begins with a brief summary of the features that distinguish its members in southern Africa. In the case of statistics on diversity, infraspecific taxa such as subspecies and varieties have been counted as 'species'. As the technical floral characters by which most plant families are defined are so obscure and esoteric (usually involving a determination of ovule number, placement and orientation), the emphasis here is on the more easily observed features that could assist in field identification. This section is followed by examples of the most important economic plants in each family, with the emphasis on those species and products that are known worldwide and with which readers might be familiar. Numerous examples of local usage are mentioned in the main section of this book. Please note that a few of the smallest families have been omitted from these descriptions due to space constrictions.

Aceraceae narrowly defined (maple family) A relatively small, north-temperate zone family of two genera and some 150 species of which almost all belong to the genus *Acer* (maples) and about 25 are grown in our region; often included in Sapindaceae. The leaves are opposite and usually palmately lobed, rarely pinnately compound or simple; they are nearly always deciduous and in many species are noted for their autumn colours. Fruits are 1-winged nuts, borne in pairs; the angle between the outer edges of the wings is often diagnostic for species. ◆ Many fine timber trees, and one species (*A. saccharum*, sugar maple) is the source of real maple syrup. (Groups 12, 23, 32)

Anacardiaceae (mango family) A pantropical family of some 70 genera and 600 species, of which over 50 are grown in our region. Unfortunately, though, it is rather a difficult family to distinguish. Several members have alternate, imparipinnate leaves with watery rather than milky latex (technically resin). Stipules are absent. Crushed leaves usually have a strong turpentine-like or resinous odour. Flowers are small, unisexual and inconspicuous. The genera are much easier to recognise. *Searsia* (= *Rhus*), for instance, has 3-foliolate leaves with a resinous smell; and the leaves of *Ozoroa*, *Protorhus* and *Heeria* are simple, with numerous more or less parallel side veins and watery or milky latex. The family can be confused with the latex-containing Burseraceae, but the latter often has bark that flakes in papery pieces. The pinnate leaves are also reminiscent of Sapindaceae and Meliaceae, which both lack any kind of milky latex. ◆ Common edible fruit and seeds are the mango *(Mangifera indica)*, pistachio nut *(Pistacia vera)* and cashew nut *(Anacardium occidentale)*. The resinous exudate is poisonous in many species, causing severe irritation of the skin, as in poison ivy *(Toxicodendron radicans*; = *Rhus radicans)* and the indigenous *Smodingium argutum* and *Trichoscypha ulugurensis.* The pepper tree *(Schinus molle)* from South America is widely planted for shade and ornament, particularly in arid regions. Wax tree *(Toxicodendron succedaneum)* has brilliant autumn colours, but is invasive around Durban. (Groups 5, 9, 37)

Annonaceae (custard-apple family) A large family of mainly tropical trees and shrubs, with 132 genera and 2,300 species, some 20 of which are grown in our area. All its members have simple, entire, aromatic leaves arranged in two ranks and without stipules. The flowers, which tend to be greenish and inconspicuous, are usually bent to one side and downwards (nodding). They are very distinctive, with the perianth in two whorls of three, and with numerous, peculiar, short, thick stamens and usually several separate carpels instead of a single ovary. The separate carpels, which have almost no style, are most prominent during fruiting, often developing into clusters of several fleshy fruits radiating from the tip of the original pedicel (flower stalk). ◆ Numerous species produce edible fruits, which for the most part are consumed locally rather than marketed for profit, and which are sometimes collectively known as 'custard-apples' (from the custard-like flavour of many of them). Oil of ylang-ylang, one of the principal ingredients of French perfume, is distilled from the flowers of *Cananga odorata* and *Artabotrys odoratissimus.* (Group 10)

Apocynaceae narrowly defined (oleander family) A woody plant family that is easy to recognise, with about 355 genera and 3,700 species, over 50 of which are grown in the region. The combination of opposite or whorled leaves and milky or watery latex is definitive. In some of the succulent or semisucculent genera, though, the leaves are alternate or in terminal tufts *(Adenium, Pachypodium, Plumeria)*. All members have flowers with 5 petals, which are fused into a tube and twisted when in bud. Clusiaceae has a similar leaf arrangement, but the latex tends to be yellowish. Nowadays usually broadly defined to include Asclepiadaceae and Periplocaceae, which include few trees. ◆ The family is rich in alkaloids and several members are toxic or are used medicinally. Ornamentals include the oleander *(Nerium oleander)*, Madagascar periwinkle *(Catharanthus roseus)*, both which have become naturalised in the region, and the frangipani *(Plumeria rubra)*. (Groups 1, 5, 10, 21, 24)

Aquifoliaceae (holly family) A widespread family of trees and shrubs, represented by a single genus (*Ilex*, holly) with over 400 species, some 20 of which are grown in our region. Family characters are therefore unimportant in the context of this book. ◆ European holly *(Ilex aquifolium)*, with its attractive spiny foliage and bright red berries, has become a basic ingredient of Western-style Christmas decorations. (Groups 9, 10)

Araliaceae (cabbagetree family) Closely related to the Apiaceae (carrot family), but predominantly woody; with about 50 genera and 1,150 mostly tropical species, some 30 of which are grown in our region. Plants are usually conspicuous because of their large, palmately or pinnately lobed/compound leaves. The latter are alternate and have stipules. The flowers have an inferior ovary and are usually borne in umbels or spikes, which are often further compounded into large and complex umbels, racemes or panicles. ◆ Cultivars of ivy *(Hedera helix)* are widely grown as ornamentals. Ginseng, a popular traditional medicine, is obtained from the roots of *Panax quinquefolius* and *P. pseudoginseng*. (Groups 2, 39, 43)

Araucariaceae (monkey-puzzle family) A small family of three genera and 41 species from South America and Australasia; about a third of the species grown in our region. Branches often whorled, secondary branches mostly deciduous. Leaves alternate, often 2-ranked, relatively broad. Cones large and heavy, many falling intact from the tree; scales 1-seeded. ◆ Valuable timber trees; in addition, the resin of *Agathis* (kauri) is highly prized and is sold as gum dammar. *Araucaria* (monkey-puzzle, bunya-bunya) is often grown for ornament. (Groups 3, 11)

Arecaceae/Palmae (palm family) A distinctive, iconically tropical (also subtropical and warm-temperate) family with an unmistakable habit, with some 200 genera and 2,800 species. An estimate of 300 species grown in our region in the early 1990s is now almost certainly seriously low, as there is a very active Palm Society continually importing novelties. However, many of these are seldom seen in public and so this book discusses only 31 species. The leaves are very large, palmately or pinnately, rarely twice pinnately, divided (simple in Musaceae) and spirally arranged or 3- or 5-ranked (2-ranked in Strelitziaceae). ◆ Important economic products include coconuts *(Cocos nucifera)*, dates *(Phoenix dactylifera)*, sago (starch from the stem pith of *Metroxylon* spp., notably *M. sagu*), fibres (coir from husks of coconut; raffia from leaflets of *Raphia*) and rattan cane (stems of *Calamus* spp.). *Elaeis guineensis* (African oil palm) is one of the world's most important sources of edible and soap-making oils. Palm leaves are among the oldest known flowering-plant fossils. (Group 2)

Betulaceae (birch family) An ancient, mostly northern-hemisphere family dating back to the Cretaceous (145–66 million years ago), with six genera and 125–200 species, some two dozen of which are grown in our region. The leaves are alternate and undivided, with distinctive toothed margins and stipules that often fall early. The drooping inflorescences (catkins) are composed of all-male or all-female flowers, but the two occur on the same tree. The fruit is a small nut. ◆ Members of this family have various uses, such as timber (*Betula* spp., the birches), food (*Corylus* spp., hazelnuts and filberts) and ornament (all members grown in our region). (Group 9)

Bignoniaceae (jacaranda family) A very distinctive family of woody shrubs, trees and lianas, with about 113 genera and 800 species, mostly in the New World; of these, about 80 are grown in our region. The leaves are pinnately or palmately compound, opposite or whorled and without stipules. Flowers are large, bell- or funnel-shaped and very showy. In several species the fruit is dehiscent and resembles a long, narrow pod, usually with winged seeds. ◆ Ornamental trees and shrubs include trumpet trees (*Tabebuia* spp.), Cape honeysuckle *(Tecomaria capensis)*, yellow bells *(Tecoma stans)*, jacaranda *(Jacaranda mimosifolia)* and the African flame tree *(Spathodea campanulata)*. Many garden creepers with showy flowers – including golden shower *(Pyrostegia venusta)*, trumpet vine *(Campsis radicans)*, Chinese trumpet vine *(C. grandiflora)*, cat's claw *(Macfadyena unguis-cati)* and scarlet trumpet vine *(Distictis buccinatoria)* – belong to the family. (Groups 10, 31, 32, 40, 43)

Bixaceae (annatto family) A Caribbean family of one genus comprising a single species. The leaves are large and heart-shaped, and the pale pink flowers and softly spiny fruits, which remain on the plant all year if not removed, are distinctive. ◆ Annatto (*Bixa orellana*, the only species) is a highly decorative small tree or large shrub. The red juice of the seeds is a dye and flavouring used in Caribbean cooking, cheddar cheese and lipstick, among other things. (Group 11)

Boraginaceae (borage family) A predominantly herbaceous family with some 117 genera and 2,400 species, about 40 of which are grown in the region. The leaves are alternate, simple, without stipules and are often harsh (sandpapery) to the touch. Twigs tend to be round. The flowers are regular, with 5 united petals and 5 stamens arising from the corolla tube. The sepals are often persistent in fruit. ◆ Many members of the family are used as garden ornamentals, among them forget-me-not *(Myosotis)*; also used in traditional medicine, including comfrey *(Symphytum officinale)* and borage *(Borago officinalis)*, the latter also featuring as a herb in cookery and drinks such as Pimm's Cup. (Group 10)

Brexiaceae (mfukufuku family) One genus of 11 species, sometimes included in Celastraceae. Only one species, *Brexia madagascariensis* (mfukufuku), is known to be cultivated. The leaves are alternate to almost opposite, dark glossy green above and much paler below. The flowers are creamy-white and quite large. ◆ Trees of apparently limited usefulness and so only seen as specimens in botanical gardens. (Group 10)

Buddlejaceae (sagewood family) A small family of 6–10 genera and some 150 species, most belonging to the genera *Buddleja* and *Nuxia*; 15–20 species grown in our region. *Buddleja* is easily recognised by the opposite or 3-whorled leaves, often with star-shaped hairs. Interpetiolar stipules, or a stipular ridge, are usually present (particularly in *Buddleja*) between the petioles. Leaf margins are often toothed, distinguishing them from the Rubiaceae. The flowers have 4 petals, united into a short tube, and 4 free stamens. Formerly often included in Loganiaceae, sometimes now included in Scrophulariaceae. ◆ Certain species of *Buddleja* are used as garden ornamentals. (Groups 7, 13)

Buxaceae (boxwood family) A small family of six genera of evergreen shrubs and trees of some 50 species, mostly from the warm parts of the Old World, six grown in our region. These are vegetatively indistinct, with opposite, leathery leaves, without stipules. The flowers are inconspicuous, unisexual, with 3-chambered ovaries, the latter developing into very distinct capsules tipped by 3 slender horns. ◆ A few species are grown as foliage plants, often as hedges or border edgings. The wood of *Buxus sempervirens* (boxwood) is used for engravings and printing blocks (woodcuts) and, because of its hardness and dimensional stability, was used to make rulers and other instruments in the past. Jojoba oil, a potential biofuel, is made from *Simmondsia chinensis.* (Group 23)

Cactaceae (cactus family) A large, unmistakable but taxonomically difficult family of about 100 genera and 1,200–1,800 species of mainly leafless stem succulents, almost exclusively confined to the semidesert regions of North, Central and South America. Many species are grown in our region; it is difficult to be specific because of continual importation by enthusiasts and because of taxonomic uncertainty. Most species have spines, often with tufts of tiny barbed hairs, which arise from cushions or areoles. Some resemble species of *Euphorbia*, but lack milky latex. The ovary is inferior, 1-chambered and many-seeded. ◆ Prickly pears (*Opuntia)* are grown commercially for their fruit. Many species are valued as ornamentals, but several are also invasive. (Group 1)

Caricaceae (pawpaw/papaya family) A small family of three genera and some 30 species, two of which are grown in our region. The trunks are almost unbranched, with milky sap and a crown of large, palmately lobed leaves. ◆ The pawpaw (papaya, *Carica papaya*) is grown for fruit throughout the tropics and subtropics. *Carica* × *heilbornii* (papaya babaco) was grown in Mpumalanga for a year or two in about 2000, but was a commercial failure. (Group 2)

Casuarinaceae (beefwood family) A small family of four genera and 90 species of almost leafless, woody flowering plants from Australasia and Southeast Asia, with about a dozen species in our region. Characterised by peculiar jointed branchlets (which function as leaves), superficially resembling pine needles. Represented by introduced species of *Casuarina* and *Allocasuarina* in the region. ◆ The wood of several species is extremely hard and is valued for furniture. Several species are grown as sand binders and have become invasive. (Group 3)

Celtidaceae (white-stinkwood family) A woody family of seven genera and about 150 species of trees and shrubs; about 10 species grown in our region. Leaves are alternate, simple, with toothed margins, an often unequal-sided base, and stipules. The flowers are mostly unisexual (male and female on the same plant), greenish and inconspicuous, yet very characteristic in having 1 stamen opposite each sepal (petals absent) and 2 divergent styles; the fruit is a fleshy drupe. Alternatively classified as subfamily Celtidoideae under a broadly defined Ulmaceae. ◆ Species of *Celtis* are valued as ornamental trees. (Group 11)

Chenopodiaceae (saltbush family) A large, mainly herbaceous family of 104 genera and about 1,500 species, many of which can grow in saline soils, often in arid regions; about 30 species grown in our region. They are all rather similar looking, with small, reduced leaves and inconspicuous flowers. ◆ Different cultivars of *Beta vulgaris* (beetroot, sugar beet, spinach beet, chard) and *Spinacia oleracea* (spinach) are of major agricultural importance. A number of species, notably the saltbushes *(Atriplex)*, are cultivated as fodder in arid areas. (Group 10)

Clusiaceae/Guttiferae (mangosteen family) A family of 45 genera and just over 1,000 species, seven of which are grown in our region. They have opposite (rarely whorled), entire leaves, with very distinctive yellow or orange latex in some genera. In some species of *Garcinia* the leaves have many conspicuously parallel secondary and intersecondary veins. Flowers have 4–12 usually showy, yellow, white or pink petals and many stamens. The fruits are fleshy and often good eating. ◆ The mangosteen *(G. mangostana)*, a delicious fruit from Southeast Asia, is probably the best-known family member. Gamboge, a yellow pigment used in watercolour paints, is prepared from the latex of *G. hanburyi* or *G. xanthochymus.* It has been used for centuries in the Far East as a dye to colour the orange-brown silk robes of Buddhist monks and priests, and is a classic artists' pigment. Timber and medicines are derived from various lesser-known species. (Group 21)

Cochlospermaceae (silk-cotton family) A family of three genera and 25 species of small trees with smooth bark and palmately lobed leaves; one species grown in our region. The flowers are yellow; otherwise plants are similar to Bixaceae. ◆ *Cochlospermum vitifolium* (silk-cotton tree) is occasionally grown for ornament. (Group 6)

Combretaceae (bushwillow family) A pantropical family of 20 genera and some 600 species, mostly woody, with some lianas; 40 species grown in our region. The leaves are entire, alternate or opposite and are without stipules. *Combretum*, the region's largest genus, has opposite leaves that remind one of Rubiaceae, but it lacks the characteristic stipules of the latter. Members of the second-largest genus, *Terminalia*, often have a very distinctive pagoda-like tree architecture, known as Aubréville's Model. The main stem produces whorls of horizontal lateral branches. Each lateral branch is made up of a succession of branchlet units, each with the tip turned up and a cluster of leaves at its apex. The flowers are usually inconspicuous, small, greenish or yellowish white, clustered in axillary heads or spikes. The ovary is inferior, elongated and is easily mistaken for the pedicel (flower stalk). Fruits of *Combretum* are usually 4-winged. In most other members the fruit is surrounded by a single wing. ◆ A few species, notably *T. catappa* (Indian almond), are occasionally planted for ornament in the coastal regions of KwaZulu-Natal. The Rangoon creeper *(Quisqualis indica)* is widely grown for its attractive flowers. (Groups 7, 10, 23)

Convolvulaceae (morning-glory family) A large family of 59 genera and about 1,800 species, over 50 of which are grown in our region. Most members of the family are herbs or twiners and very few reach tree size. The leaves are alternate and unlobed or pinnately or palmately divided. The flowers have joined petals and almost always have crease-marks in the shape of a 5-pointed star with narrow rays. ◆ Sweet potato *(Ipomoea batatas)*, a food plant with a fascinating archaeological history, belongs here. Other economically important members of the family include several noxious weeds, a few species that produce poisonous alkaloids and many garden ornamentals. (Group 5)

Cornaceae (dogwood family) A mostly north-temperate family of six genera and some 78 species, about a dozen of which are grown in our region. The leaves are opposite, without stipules and with smooth margins. The flowers are in small to inconspicuous heads, each with 4 showy, petal-like bracts in the species likely to be seen in cultivation in our region. ◆ In ancient times the hard wood could be used to make spears and daggers; the name 'dogwood' is derived from an older form 'dag[ger]-wood'. Today these trees are grown for ornament. (Group 23)

Cunoniaceae (wild-alder family) A family of 26 genera and about 240 species of trees and shrubs, mainly from Australasia; half a dozen grown in our region. Leaves are opposite, 3-foliolate or pinnately compound, the leaflets having toothed margins. Stipules are present, often large and united in pairs over the growing tip. ◆ The family is of little economic importance. (Group 29)

Cupressaceae (cypress family) A family of about 30 genera with about 120 species of conifers (gymnosperms), usually with scale-like mature leaves arranged in opposite pairs or in whorls; over half of the species grown in our region. Juvenile leaves tend to be needle-like. The female cones are more or less globose, with the scales arranged in opposite pairs. ◆ Timber is obtained from many species. The family also yields resins and flavourings. Some members are cultivated as ornamentals, including many cultivars of hardy, dwarf conifers with bluish, golden or variegated foliage. (Group 3)

Cyatheaceae (scaly treefern family) There are about five genera and over 600 species in this pantropical family, half a dozen of which are grown in our region. Tree ferns are unmistakable, having large, much-divided leaves, which unfurl from a coiled tip and usually have scales and/or prickles, but not hairs, at the base of the petiole. Plants reproduce by means of spores, which are borne in fertile parts (sori) near the midribs on the lower surface of the leaflets. ◆ A few species are grown as ornamentals; the family is otherwise of little economic importance. (Group 2)

Dicksoniaceae (Australian treefern family) An ancient family of five genera and about 50 species, arising in the Triassic (245–208 million years ago); one species grown in our region. Trees in this family are very similar to indigenous tree ferns in the family Cyatheaceae, but the main axis (stipe) of the leaf has hairs, not scales, and the sori are always solitary, borne on the leaflet margin, not the midrib. ◆ One or two species are grown for ornament and *Dicksonia antarctica* (Tasmanian tree fern) is naturalised on the Cape Peninsula. (Group 2)

Didieriaceae (Madagascar-ocotillo family) A small family of five genera and about 15 species, until recently thought to be confined to Madagascar; almost all species can be found in specialist succulent collections. Recent DNA evidence suggests that the South African *Portulacaria* (spekboom) belongs here too. The family is distinguished by succulent or semisucculent stems and small, equally succulent, often paired, oval leaves widest beyond the middle. Plants have masses of tiny flowers. ◆ Spekboom is increasingly commonly planted in our region for stock feed and carbon sequestration, and here and elsewhere for ornament. Other members of the family are curiosities sought after by succulent collectors. (Group 1)

Dilleniaceae (simpur family) A moderate-sized family of 10 genera and 400–500 species, mostly of North America and Australasia; two species grown in our region. The leaves are alternate, with toothed margins and 'herringbone' secondary veins. Flowers are large, with 5 sepals, 5 petals and many stamens. ◆ A few species are occasionally grown for ornament. (Group 9)

Dracaenaceae (dragontree family) A distinct monocot family of nine genera and about 230 species of large, perennial herbs or small trees, with about 20 grown in our region. The leaves are long and tapering, parallel-veined and often clustered in dense terminal rosettes. The flowers are very similar to those of the Asphodelaceae. Formerly classified under Agavaceae; sometimes placed in Convallariaceae. ◆ Ornamentals include species of *Sansevieria* (mother-in-law's tongue), *Cordyline* and *Dracaena* (dragon trees). (Group 2)

Ebenaceae (ebony family) A woody, pantropical family with three or four genera and some 500 species, about 20 of which are grown in our region. Vegetatively rather indistinct, with simple, entire leaves without stipules. The two major genera are much easier to recognise: *Euclea* has hard, leathery leaves that tend to be opposite and often have undulate margins; *Diospyros* has alternate leaves and fruits that are subtended or enclosed by the persistent and enlarged calyx. ◆ Commercial ebony is the hard, black heartwood of certain species of *Diospyros*. The best-known fruits are the persimmons (among others *D. kaki* and *D. virginiana*). (Group 10)

Elaeocarpaceae (quandong family) A family of two to six genera and about 550 species, mostly from Australasia and the Western Pacific; about 10 species grown in our region. The leaves are alternate or opposite, with toothed margins and a swelling at each end of the petiole. Flowers often have fringed petals and the fleshy fruits are often blue. ◆ The fruits of some species of *Elaeocarpus* (bhadrasey) are edible and are made into pickles in India. Several species are grown for ornament. (Group 9)

Ericaceae (heather family) A family with about 125 genera and over 4,000 species in mostly temperate areas of both hemispheres; almost 100 species grown in our region, possibly more by enthusiasts. Readily recognised by the leathery, alternate leaves that lack stipules. The flowers are small, with 4 or 5 united petals and 8 or 10 stamens. The anthers, which open with pores to release the pollen, are distinctive. The family can be confused with narrow-leaved members of the Rosaceae (with stipules) and Thymelaeaceae (with tough, fibrous bark). ◆ The azaleas *(Rhododendron)* are popular garden ornamentals. Blueberries, cranberries and bilberries are obtained from species of *Vaccinium. Arbutus unedo* (strawberry tree) is often cultivated in gardens. (Groups 9, 10)

Euphorbiaceae narrowly defined (euphorbia family) With over 200 genera and more than 6,000 species, this is among the largest of flowering-plant families; about 100 species grown in southern Africa. Rather heterogeneous, the vegetative and floral structures showing great variation. The vast majority of its species can be readily recognised by combinations of milky or watery latex, simple alternate leaves, a pair of glands at the petiole apex or base of the leaf blade and the presence of stipules or stipule scars. However, there are exceptions to each one of these. In most cases the fruit is characteristically 3-lobed (3-chambered) and often crowned by the 3 persistent stigmas. Each fruit chamber contains 1 ovule (compare Phyllanthaceae). The combinations of stem succulence and milky latex, and of toothed leaf margins and milky latex, are definitive for the family. Succulent members are also characterised by specialised inflorescences (cyathia) that mimic flowers. Formerly usually broadly defined so as to also include Phyllanthaceae, Picrodendraceae and Putranjivaceae. ◆ Most of the world's natural rubber is obtained from *Hevea brasiliensis.* Cassava or tapioca (starchy tubers of *Manihot esculenta*) is a staple food in many tropical countries. Many members are poisonous and/or have medicinal uses, including castor oil *(Ricinus communis)*. The poinsettia *(Euphorbia pulcherrima)* is widely grown in gardens. (Groups 1, 5, 6, 11, 24, 28, 39)

Fabaceae/Leguminosae broadly defined (pea family) A cosmopolitan family of over 600 genera and 18,000 species, almost 800 of which are cultivated in southern Africa. Divided into three subfamilies, sometimes (as in Van Wyk & Van Wyk 2013) regarded as separate families, but intermediates are known and recent work suggests that the treatment adopted here is more appropriate. An outstanding vegetative feature is the pulvinus, a conspicuous thickening at the base of each petiole and petiolule.

Fabaceae – Caesalpinioideae (flamboyant group) About 120 species of this, the most primitive subfamily, are grown in our region. The leaves are alternate and characteristically paripinnate with opposite leaflets, 2-foliolate or deeply 2-lobed. A few species have imparipinnate or bipinnate leaves. Stipules are always present, at least in young growth, and are rarely spiny. The flowers are relatively large and showy, slightly irregular, with 10 or fewer stamens. ◆ Garden ornamentals include several species of *Bauhinia*, *Caesalpinia*, *Cassia* and *Senna* and the flamboyant *(Delonix regia)*. Various alkaloids, including the purgative senna, are obtained from species of *Cassia* and *Senna*. (Groups 3, 26, 27, 33, 38, 41, 43)

Fabaceae – Mimosoideae (thorntree group) About 150 species of this subfamily are cultivated in southern Africa. The subfamily is easily recognised by the bipinnate leaves, usually with petiolar or rachis glands. Stipules (or a stipular scar) are always present and are often modified into thorns or spines *(Vachellia)*. The flowers are small, regular, with numerous exserted stamens, and are arranged into dense capitate or spicate inflorescences. Many species have leaflets that fold up at night (so-called sleeping movements). ◆ Various commercial products are obtained from *Acacia*, *Vachellia* and *Senegalia* (tan-bark, wood, gums) and the family also produces a few ornamentals, including *Calliandra* (powder-puff), *Acacia* and *Albizia*. Gum arabic (from *Senegalia senegal* and *Vachellia seyal*) is used to thicken many convenience foods, pharmaceuticals and cosmetics, and is sometimes a component of watercolour paints and printing inks. Pods of mesquite trees *(Prosopis)* are an important stock feed in arid areas. Most members have root nodules containing nitrogen-fixing bacteria, playing a significant role in the nitrogen enrichment of soils. Several species of *Acacia* from Australia (so-called wattles) have become serious invader weeds in southern Africa. The latter are nearly all spineless. (Groups 11, 42, 43)

Fabaceae – Papilionoideae (pea group) Almost 500 species are grown in our region. The alternate leaves are usually imparipinnate or 3-foliolate, but sometimes simple. Stipules are always present, although deciduous with age in some species. Easily recognised by the very characteristic butterfly-like flower type. The petals are unequal, with the uppermost (standard or banner) the largest, the two side ones (wings) small and stalked and the two basal ones united into a boat-shaped structure (keel). ◆ Seeds and pods of many of the herbaceous species are sources of human food, including garden pea *(Pisum sativum)*, various types of beans *(Glycine, Phaseolus, Vicia)* and the peanut *(Arachis hypogaea)*. The cowpea *(Vigna unguiculata)*, clover *(Trifolium)* and lucerne *(Medicago sativa)* are widely used as forage plants. Liquorice is obtained from the dried roots and rhizomes of several *Glycyrrhiza* species. Garden ornamentals include lupin *(Lupinus)*, broom *(Cytisus)*, sweet pea *(Lathyrus)*, blue rain *(Wisteria)* and several coral trees *(Erythrina)*. Most members have root nodules containing nitrogen-fixing bacteria and play an important role in the nitrogen enrichment of soils. (Groups 29, 33, 38)

Fagaceae (oak family) A mostly northern-hemisphere family of nine genera and some 700–800 species, over 50 of which are grown in our region. The genus *Nothofagus* (southern beech) occurs in southern South America, New Zealand and Tasmania; Von Breitenbach (1989) claims this genus is cultivated in our region, but we can find no evidence to support this. The leaves are usually but by no means always deciduous, often with dramatic autumn colours; they are alternate, with smooth, toothed or lobed margins. The minute flowers are wind-pollinated; males and females are borne separately on the same tree. The fruits are nut-like and always enclosed, at least partly, by a cup-like structure. ◆ The family is notable for many kinds of highly desirable timber, including oak *(Quercus)*, chestnut *(Castanea)* and beech *(Fagus)*. The fruits of *Castanea* are sought after as food (chestnuts) and those of *Fagus* (beech-nuts) are traditionally fed to pigs, but are also eaten by humans. The bark of *Q. suber* (cork oak) is the classic source of closures for wine bottles, acoustic tiles and other items. Oak galls (result of insect activity on species of *Quercus*) were formerly used to make high-quality ink. (Groups 7, 9, 10)

Flacourtiaceae narrowly defined (Kei-apple family) A family of some 84 genera and 850 species of woody, often spiny plants, found mainly in tropical and subtropical places; 24 or more species grown in southern Africa. This is a difficult family to distinguish, particularly vegetatively. Plants have leaves that are always simple and usually alternate. The flowers (which are often unisexual) tend to have 5 free petals, numerous free stamens and a superior, 1-chambered ovary (later a 1-chambered fruit). Formerly broadly defined so as to also include Gerrardinaceae and Kiggelariaceae; alternatively classified under a broadly defined Salicaceae. ◆ The fruit of several species are eaten locally (notably the Kei-apple, *Dovyalis caffra*), but otherwise the family contains few plants of economic importance. (Group 9)

ASHLEY WHITFORTH / FOTOLIA.COM

Liquidambar styraciflua autumn colours (p.254)

Ginkgoaceae (maidenhair-tree family) One genus with a single species survives of a family that was very diverse and widespread before the age of the dinosaurs (known from fossils dating back 270 million years). The fan-shaped leaves, which may or may not be bilobed to various degrees, are distinctive and a tree in leaf (they are deciduous) cannot be confused with anything else. Male and female cones are borne on separate trees. The female cones are fleshy and inclined to smell unpleasant; for this reason they are seldom seen in the West. ◆ Trees are widely grown for ornament and the female cones (seeds) are eaten in China and Japan. (Group 26)

Gnetaceae (eru family) A small, anomalous family of two genera and 29–35 species mostly from tropical Asia; one species grown in our region. Most species are lianas and have opposite leaves with a conspicuous interpetiolar ridge and smooth margins, like members of the Rubiaceae. However, the reproductive parts are small male and female cones borne on separate plants. Although the leaves and wood anatomy resemble those of flowering plants, DNA evidence suggests that this family is a gymnosperm distantly related to the conifers. ◆ Several species have edible seeds and leaves. (Group 17)

Hamamelidaceae (witch-hazel family) A woody family of 30 genera and 120 species, discontinuously distributed in temperate and subtropical areas and vegetatively rather indistinct; about a dozen species are cultivated in southern Africa. The flowers in some species (including all those native to our region) are clustered in dense heads and have very characteristic, ribbon-shaped petals. ◆ Storax, a fragrant gum used in perfumery and medicine, is derived from certain species of *Liquidambar*. This genus also yields excellent timber (American sweet gum or red gum). *Liquidambar styraciflua* (sweet gum) is often cultivated for its ornamental autumn foliage.

Loropetalum chinense (Chinese fringe flower) is a shrub or small tree with, depending on the cultivar, attractive white or bright pink flowers. Witch hazel lotion, from *Hamamelis virginiana*, is widely used to treat cuts and bruises. (Group 11)

Hippocastanaceae (horse-chestnut family) A small family of three genera and 15 species, mostly New World, sometimes included in Sapindaceae; four species grown in our region. The leaves are opposite and palmately compound, with parallel secondary veins and usually toothed margins. The flowers are white, pink or both and are held in erect spikes looking, in some species, like Christmas-tree candles. ◆ Horse-chestnut *(Aesculus hippocastanum)* is widely grown in cool-temperate areas as an ornamental. English children traditionally use the seeds to play conkers, a game as incomprehensible to the uninitiated as cricket. (Group 40)

Hypericaceae (St. John's-wort family) A cosmopolitan family of nine genera and 540 species; about 25 grown in our region. The leaves are opposite and not divided, with clear or black secretory cavities and smooth margins. The flowers have 4 or 5 petals and many stamens, often in as many bundles as petals. ◆ Some species of St. John's-wort *(Hypericum)* are grown for ornament and some (occasionally the same) are noxious weeds. Some, possibly the same as the above, have medicinal uses. (Group 21)

Juglandaceae (walnut family) A mainly north-temperate family of eight genera and 59 species with centres in East Asia and eastern North America; 10 species grown in our region. The trees are aromatic and resinous, with pinnately compound leaves. Male and female flowers are separate, the males in hanging catkins, the females in erect clusters. The fruits are nuts, often enclosed in leathery husks. ◆ Despite its relatively small size, this family is very important for timber (walnut, *Juglans*; hickory, *Carya* and possibly others), food (walnuts, *J. regia* and other species; pecans, *C. illinoinensis*) and ornament (various genera). (Groups 36, 38)

Lamiaceae/Labiatae (sage family) A large, cosmopolitan, predominantly herbaceous family of 260 genera and some 7,000 species, almost 250 of which are grown in our area. Usually one of the easier families to identify; the opposite (rarely whorled), aromatic leaves with margin usually toothed, more or less 4-angled stems, markedly 2-lipped flowers and distinctly 4-lobed ovary are particularly diagnostic for the bulk of the members. The calyx is persistent and often enlarges in fruit. On the other hand, identification of some of the woody members can be quite tricky. Several of the woody species have an unlobed ovary and the flowers are not so pronouncedly tubular as in the herbaceous ones. *Vitex* is rather anomalous in having opposite, palmately compound leaves, making the group particularly easy to identify. ◆ Because of their aromatic properties, many species are extensively used as culinary (e.g. to flavour food) and medicinal herbs, as well as in the perfume industry, for example *Lavandula* (lavenders), *Mentha* (mint, spearmint, peppermint), *Ocimum basilicum* (basil), *Origanum* (oregano, marjoram), *Rosmarinus officinalis* (rosemary), *Salvia officinalis* (sage) and *Thymus* (thymes), to name but a few. Also many decorative garden and popular house-plants such as *Coleus* (painted nettles), *Phlomis fruticosa* (Jerusalem sage), *Plectranthus* (spurflowers) and *Salvia* (sages). (Groups 12, 23, 25, 40)

Lauraceae (laurel family) An almost exclusively woody family of 31 genera and 2,500 species, best represented in tropical forests; about 20 species grown in our region. Vegetatively rather indistinct, with alternate (opposite in *Dahlgrenodendron*), non-2-ranked, simple, entire leaves and no stipules. A useful diagnostic leaf character is the very fine reticulum of tertiary veins (as in Rhamnaceae). Twigs are usually green and without prominent lenticels. Leaves contain oil cells (very small and not visible against the light unless magnified) and are usually aromatic when crushed. The flowers are small, inconspicuous, with 6 tepals and unmistakable anthers, which dehisce by flap-like valves. ◆ Economic products include cinnamon and camphor *(Cinnamomum)*, bay leaves *(Laurus nobilis)*, timber *(Ocotea)* and the avocado *(Persea americana)*. (Groups 7, 10, 11)

Lecythidaceae (brazilnut family) A family of 17 genera and about 280 species of tropical trees centred in South America, with about half a dozen species grown in southern Africa. The leaves are alternate, large and simple, usually without stipules. Most species have large, showy but very short-lived flowers. These have a fluffy appearance due to the numerous stamens. Fruits are usually hard and woody, with a lid through which the seeds are released. ◆ Brazil or pará nuts are the seeds of *Bertholletia excelsa*. (Group 10)

Lythraceae (pride-of-India family) A mainly tropical family of 25 genera and some 460 species of herbs, trees and shrubs; about two dozen grown in our area. Leaves are opposite or whorled, unlobed, with smooth margins and generally without stipules. The flowers are often showy, with 6 petals; the fruit is a capsule. ◆ Henna, a reddish brown dye, is obtained from *Lawsonia inermis*. Cultivars of pride-of-India *(Lagerstroemia indica)* are hardy trees with attractive flowers. *Cuphea* species are small shrublets often grown in gardens. (Groups 10, 23)

Magnoliaceae (magnolia family) A northern-hemisphere family of seven genera and 200–220 species, mainly from warm parts of East Asia and eastern North America; some two dozen grown in our area. The leaves of *Liriodendron* (tulip tree) have a distinctive shape, with 4 lobes and an indented tip, but those of *Magnolia* are undistinguished, being undivided with smooth margins. The flowers have an indefinite number of tepals, which are spirally arranged, as are the stamens and ovaries. In *Magnolia* the fruits are pods (winged nuts in the tulip tree), arranged in a banana-like column; the seeds are attached to the pod by elastic threads. ◆ This is considered to be one of the most ancient and primitive families of flowering plants. The timber of both magnolia and tulip tree is sought after for cabinet work and species of both are esteemed garden ornamentals. (Group 10)

Malvaceae broadly defined (hibiscus family) A cosmopolitan family of some 200 genera and over 2,300 species of herbs, shrubs and trees; over 150 species grown in our area. In this book we differ from Van Wyk & Van Wyk (2013) by including Bombacaceae, Tiliaceae and Sterculiaceae here, as family distinctions break down in many South American species, several of which are included here. Leaves are alternate, simple, often lobed and are 3- or more-veined from the base, with stipules and star-shaped hairs. The flowers are very distinctive, with 5 free petals and numerous stamens united into a tube around the style, often subtended by an epicalyx (lower calyx whorl). ◆ Cotton (seed fibres of *Gossypium*) is the most important product. Okra is a common vegetable in tropical regions (young fruit of *Hibiscus esculentus*); other comestibles include cacao (used in the manufacture of chocolate, cocoa powder and cocoa butter), extracted from the seeds (cacao beans) of *Theobroma cacao*, and cola (used in popular beverages) from seeds of *Cola nitida* and *C. acuminata*. The durian *(Durio zibethinus)* is an extremely popular edible fruit in Southeast Asia but is banned from many public places because of its odour. Kapok is derived from the fruit of silk-cotton trees *(Bombax* spp., *Ceiba pentandra)*. *Ochroma pyramidale* is the source of balsa wood. Brazil kapok *(Ceiba speciosa* or *Chorisia speciosa)* is an attractive flowering tree in tropical gardens. The family produces many garden ornamentals, notably species of *Hibiscus* and hollyhocks *(Althaea)*. (Groups 7, 10, 11, 39)

Melastomataceae, including Memecylaceae (rose-apple family) A mainly tropical family of over 240 genera and 3,300 species, especially common in South America; about 15 species grown in our region. Twigs are more or less 4-angled, with simple, glossy and rather leathery, entire leaves. Some are vegetatively easily confused with Myrtaceae but can be distinguished by the lack of secretory cavities. However, all the cultivated species are more commonly distinguished by 3 or more main veins from the leaf base and the often rather rough, hairy leaf surface. The ovary is inferior, resulting in a fruit tipped by the persistent calyx. ◆ Several of the herbaceous members and a few woody ones *(Dissotis, Medinilla, Tibouchina)* are cultivated for their showy flowers. (Group 12)

Meliaceae (mahogany family) A large, tropical, woody family with 51 genera comprising some 550 species, about two dozen of which are grown in our region. Vegetatively rather diverse, with both simple (not in cultivated trees) and pinnately compound leaves. These are always alternate and without stipules. Species with compound leaves can be distinguished from the rather similar Anacardiaceae by the lack of latex. They also resemble pinnate-leaved members of the Sapindaceae, but the latter tend to have an aborted rachis apex. The flowers, however, are very distinct, with 5 free petals, and 8–10 stamens, which are united into a cylindrical tube around the style. ◆ A very important tropical timber family. True mahogany is derived from species of *Swietenia* and sapele from *Entandrophragma cylindricum*. The family contains certain bitter-tasting chemical compounds, many of which have insecticidal properties. Langsat *(Lansium domesticum)* is a popular edible fruit in Southeast Asia. *Melia azedarach* is widely cultivated for shade and ornament and has now become a troublesome invader weed in our region. (Groups 34, 36, 37, 38, 43)

Melianthaceae narrowly defined (honeyflower family) A small family of two genera and about 35 species, endemic to Africa and perhaps best known from the herbaceous genus *Melianthus*; scarcely half a dozen grown in our area. *Bersama* is an exclusively woody genus. This is the only family in our region with alternate, pinnately compound leaves, with intrapetiolar stipules. ◆ Species of *Melianthus* are grown as garden ornamentals. *Bersama* bark is widely used in traditional medicine. (Group 36)

Moraceae (fig family) This family of 40–54 genera encompassing 1,100–1,500 species (about 75 grown in our region) is well represented in warmer, frost-free parts of the region, particularly so by the genus *Ficus*, which has more than 50 tree species grown in southern Africa. The family is easily recognised by the combination of alternate leaves, milky latex and a distinctive conical stipule that covers the apical bud. The stipule is deciduous and leaves an obvious circular or semicircular scar on falling. Flowers of all Moraceae are tiny, inconspicuous and clustered into often complicated inflorescences – for example a 'fig', which is a hollow, vase-like receptacle containing numerous tiny flowers. ◆ Edible fruit include breadfruit and jackfruit *(Artocarpus)*, figs *(Ficus)* and mulberries *(Morus)*. Timber is obtained from *Chlorophora* (iroko-wood or fustic). Several species of *Ficus* are grown for ornamental purposes. The rubber plant *(F. elastica)* and weeping fig *(F. benjamina)* are common indoor and outdoor container plants in southern Africa. (Groups 4, 5, 6)

Moringaceae (horseradish-tree family) A small family of one genus and about 13 species of pale-barked, deciduous trees, four of which are grown in our region. All have graceful leaves, which are 2 or 3 times pinnate. The fruit is a long, pod-like capsule. ◆ Ben oil, used in salads and soap, comes from *Moringa oleifera* seeds; it is also cultivated locally as a major leaf vegetable crop. (Group 43)

Musaceae (banana family) Three genera and 40-odd species of tropical monocots with an unmistakable habit; five or more species grown in southern Africa. All species have large, oblong or oblong-elliptic leaf blades, borne spirally at the end of a pseudostem formed by the tightly overlapping leaf sheaths. The leaves resemble those in tree forms of Strelitziaceae, but the latter has true stems and leaves arranged in a single plane. ◆ The banana and the plantain (both bred in Southeast Asia from *Musa acuminata* and *M. balbisiana* and most easily grouped under *M.* × *paradisiaca*, though their ancestry is vastly complicated) are major food crops. (Group 2)

Myoporaceae (manatoka family) Seven mostly Australian genera and about 250 species, sometimes included in Scrophulariaceae; about 10 species grown in our region. New growth is clothed in unusual (often star-shaped or glandular) hairs, the leaves are alternate and undivided with smooth or toothed margins and the flowers are irregular and tubular, with 5 corolla lobes and 4 stamens. The fruits are fleshy. ◆ A few species are grown as ornamentals, but in our region they are more noted for being noxious weeds. (Group 10)

Myrsinaceae (Cape-myrtle family) A rather indistinct, almost cosmopolitan, evergreen woody family of some 33 genera and 1,000 species, about five of which are grown in our region. Leaves with secretory cavities and/or ducts (appearing as dots or streaks) containing an often brownish, yellowish or blackish contents. It is nevertheless much easier to familiarise oneself with the diagnostic features of individual species than to try and recognise the family. ◆ Members of *Ardisia* are grown in gardens for their bright red fruit, but are becoming weedy in our region. Otherwise the family is of little economic importance. (Group 9)

Myrtaceae (myrtle family) A predominantly woody family, mostly tropical and subtropical, which is represented by some 120–150 genera and 3,000–4,000 species, over 360 of which are grown in our region. Easily recognised in the region by the combination of opposite, simple, entire leaves with secretory cavities. The flowers tend to have many showy stamens and the ovary is invariably inferior, resulting in fruit tipped by the remains of the calyx. The introduced eucalypts *(Eucalyptus)* are unusual in having mature leaves that are apparently alternate. ◆ The eucalypts (which are almost all Australian) yield valuable timber and many species are grown in commercial plantations. Important spices produced by the family include allspice or pimento *(Pimenta dioica)* and cloves (the dry flower buds of *Syzygium aromaticum*; what appears to be a stalk, is the inferior ovary). The guava *(Psidium guajava)* is probably the most popular edible fruit. Garden ornamentals include the bottlebrushes *(Callistemon* and *Melaleuca)* and tea bushes *(Leptospermum)*. (Groups 3, 10, 11, 22)

Oleaceae (olive family) A mainly woody family with 25–29 genera and about 600 species in most parts of the world; about 75 species grown in our area. Rather indistinct vegetatively, with both simple or pinnately compound leaves. These are always opposite, entire-margined and lack stipules. Branchlets almost always have at least a few small, whitish, raised lenticels. The flowers are regular, with 4, 5 or more united petals and 2 stamens arising from the petals. ◆ The family contains several genera of economic or horticultural importance, among them *Olea* (olive), *Fraxinus* (ash), *Jasminum* (jasmine), *Ligustrum* (privet, liguster) and *Syringa* (lilac). The best baseball bats are made from the wood of the ash. (Groups 19, 23, 32)

Oxalidaceae (wood-sorrel family) A cosmopolitan family of six genera and some 775–900 species, 10 of which are known to be cultivated here, but possibly many more in specialist collections. Nearly all species are herbaceous, but a few are woody. The leaves are usually 3-foliolate or rarely pinnately compound and show sleep movements. Flowers are bisexual, regular and often showy; fruits are usually capsules, rarely fleshy. ◆ Carambola or bilimbi *(Averrhoa carambola)* is grown for its edible fruit and some species of *Oxalis* are grown for ornament. Others (sheep-sorrel, wood-sorrel and more) are noxious weeds. (Group 38)

Phyllanthaceae (potatobush family) A large and diverse family of about 60 genera and 2,000 species, about 12 of which are grown in our area. These were formerly usually included in a broadly defined Euphorbiaceae, but are rather difficult to recognise as a family. Members differ from Euphorbiaceae (narrowly defined) in rarely being succulent and in never having latex or foliar glands. The relatively small flowers may have 3-lobed ovaries (2–5-chambered) as in Euphorbiaceae, but a key character is that they have 2 (instead of 1 as in Euphorbiaceae) ovules per chamber, though only 1 may develop into a seed. ◆ Considering the diversity of the family, it is of surprisingly little economic significance, although many species are of local importance for their edible fruit *(Antidesma, Phyllanthus, Uapaca)*, timber and medicinal properties. (Groups 5, 10)

Phytolaccaceae (pokeweed family) A mostly New World family of 14 genera and about 100 species, with some half a dozen grown in our area. Few species are woody. The leaves are alternate and undivided, with smooth margins. Flowers are minute, bisexual and borne in spikes. The fruits are fleshy and deeply coloured, staining anything they come in contact with. ◆ A few species such as *Phytolacca dioica* (belhambra) are grown as ornamentals and others such as *Rivina humilis* (pigeonberry) are noxious weeds. (Group 10)

Pinaceae (pine family) The largest family of conifers, comprising 10 genera and some 220 species, about half of which are grown in our area. Readily distinguished by the relatively long, needle-shaped leaves borne in small clusters. Female cones are woody and conspicuous. ◆ This is the most economically important gymnosperm family, providing the bulk of the world's requirements for soft-wood timber and wood pulp. It also yields various oils and turpentine. Species of *Pinus* are extensively grown in commercial plantations in the high-rainfall areas of southern Africa. (Group 3)

Pittosporaceae (cheesewood family) A medium-sized family of nine genera and 250–350 species of evergreen trees and shrubs, with its greatest diversity in Australia and Southeast Asia; about 15 species grown in southern Africa. Crushed leaves have a resinous smell, but otherwise a rather indistinct family. ◆ *Hymenosporum flavum* (sweet cheesewood) and several species of *Pittosporum* (cheesewood) are cultivated as garden ornamentals. (Groups 7, 10)

Platanaceae (plane-tree family) A very small, north-temperate family of a single genus with six to nine species, more than half of which are grown in our region. The base of the petiole is swollen and completely covers the axillary buds; leaves are generally lobed and have unusual hairs shaped like tiny Christmas trees. These are highly irritant, even allergenic, to sensitive individuals. The flowers are minute and unisexual, males and females occurring on the same tree. They are held in ball-shaped clusters and the number of these found together is a good way of distinguishing species. The fruits are nutlets, surrounded by the bristly remains of the flower and often remaining for months in the balls in which they were formed. ◆ Almost all species and quite a few hybrids in this family are grown for timber and ornament. (Group 11)

Polygonaceae (buckwheat family) A mostly north-temperate family of 15–46 somewhat ill-defined genera and 800–1,100 species, about 30 of which are grown in our region. Few of these are woody and fewer reach tree size. The leaves are undivided, with smooth margins; the base of the petiole is hidden by a stipule-like outgrowth called an ocrea. Individual flowers are generally small and inconspicuous but are often massed into attractive inflorescences. Most fruits are winged. ◆ Buckwheat *(Fagopyrum esculentum)* is one of the staple foods of Russia and is widely grown elsewhere. Rhubarb *(Rheum × hybridum)* is another widely grown food plant. Other members of the family yield timber, charcoal or tannins, or are ornamentals or noxious weeds. (Groups 5, 10)

Proteaceae (protea family) An ancient, woody, southern-hemisphere (Gondwana) family of some 80 genera and 1,800 species, over 100 of which are grown in our region. The leaves are simple, alternate, entire, leathery and without stipules (*Brabejum stellatifolium*, with leaves whorled and toothed, is a notable exception). The flowers, which are usually congested in showy heads or spikes, are very characteristic. Each has 4 petal-like sepals with reflexed tips and 4 stamens that are opposite and fused to the sepals, often with only the anthers free or with very short filaments. The ovary is superior, with a long style. ◆ Plants are cultivated mainly for ornament and cut flowers (e.g. *Banksia*, *Grevillea* and *Protea*). The wood is very distinctive: it has broad rays and makes beautiful furniture *(Grevillea, Faurea)*. The macadamia nut *(Macadamia integrifolia)* is the only significant commercially grown food crop. (Groups 3, 9, 10, 11, 25, 36)

Punicaceae (pomegranate family) A very small family of a single genus of two species thought to originate in subtropical Asia and sometimes included in Lythraceae; one species widely cultivated. Very young twigs of these small, shrubby trees are 4-winged, but the wings fall early. Leaves are opposite, undivided, with smooth margins. The flowers are showy, with 5–7 petals and an inferior ovary. The fleshy fruits have a woody rind and contain many red, pearl-like seeds. ◆ Cultivated pomegranates *(Punica granatum)* have had religious significance around the Mediterranean for millennia and are grown for food and ornament in many places around the world. (Group 23)

Rhamnaceae (buffalo-thorn family) A woody family with about 50 genera and 900 species, about 40 of which are grown in our area. Members are often thorny, with simple, glossy leaves. The venation tends to be diagnostic – particularly the tertiary one, which forms a very fine and regular reticulum of minute squares or rectangles. In this respect the family resembles the Lauraceae. The flowers are usually inconspicuous, with a prominent disc and 5 reduced petals very characteristically borne opposite to, and often embracing, the 5 stamens. Flowers of Celastraceae also have a well-developed disc, but the petals alternate with the stamens. ◆ The family includes few plants of economic value. *Ceanothus* contains many attractive flowering shrubs, which are widely cultivated. Many species are used locally in traditional medicine. (Groups 7, 11, 19)

Rosaceae (rose family) A family that is at its most abundant in temperate regions of the northern hemisphere, with about 90–100 genera and 2,000–3,000 species; over 225 species and a vast number of hybrids and cultivars grown in southern Africa. The leaves are alternate, simple or compound, usually with toothed margins (needle-shaped in some species of *Cliffortia*). Stipules are present and often conspicuous. The flowers are showy, regular, with 5 free, short-stalked petals, numerous free stamens and an often inferior ovary (superior in *Prunus*). ◆ Economically an extremely important family, yielding many fruit crops. Among these are *Prunus* (almond, apricot, cherry, nectarine, peach, plum, prune), *Pyrus* (pear), *Fragaria* (strawberry), *Eriobotrya* (loquat), *Malus* (apple), *Cydonia* (quince), *Rubus* (blackberry, raspberry). The family also produces many garden ornamentals, most notably the rose *(Rosa)* itself. Rose oil is one of the world's most valuable oils, used as the base for most perfumes; the principal centre of production is Bulgaria. (Groups 7, 9, 10)

Rubiaceae (gardenia family) This family comprises over 600 genera and 10,000 species and is extremely easy to recognise by its opposite leaves and interpetiolar stipules; about 100 species grown in our region. The leaves are always entire and often have domatia in the axils of the side veins. Interpetiolar stipules occur between the opposite petiole bases and often fall off at an early stage, leaving a distinct line or scar connecting the opposite petioles. The ovary is inferior, the fruit therefore crowned by either the persistent remains of the calyx or by a circular scar. Inconspicuous interpetiolar stipules or lines are also found in Acanthaceae, Rhizophoraceae and Buddlejaceae, but these families usually have toothed leaf margins. Many species of *Combretum* (Combretaceae) also have opposite, simple leaves with entire margins, but they lack stipules. ◆ The family is rich in alkaloids and is widely used medicinally. Coffee (mainly from *Coffea arabica* and *C. canephora*), quinine *(Cinchona)* and ipecacuanha *(Psychotria)* are the best-known products. Coffee is said to be one of the highest revenue earners among the world's natural products. Ornamental plants include species of *Gardenia*, *Hamelia*, *Ixora*, *Pentas*, *Rondeletia* and *Serissa*. (Group 17)

Rutaceae (citrus family) About 150 genera and 900–1,800 species belong to this family; about 70 species and hybrids grown in the region. An easy family to recognise vegetatively: trees with undivided, palmate, 3-foliolate or pinnate leaves with secretory cavities in the blade are usually members of Rutaceae. Crushed leaves, typically, have a pungent, often citrus-like odour. Flowers of Rutaceae usually have 10 or fewer stamens and a superior ovary, whereas those of Myrtaceae have numerous stamens and an inferior ovary. ◆ The family is of great economic importance, yielding commercial citrus fruits such as lemons, oranges, naartjies, limes and grapefruit (all species of *Citrus*). Rue *(Ruta graveolens)* is widely grown in herb gardens as a medicinal plant. Numerous species are cultivated for their essential oils (among them bergamot oil) used in perfumes. Some forest species yield attractive, often yellowish wood that is used for furniture. (Groups 8, 9, 30, 36, 38, 39)

Salicaceae narrowly defined (willow family) A mainly temperate northern-hemisphere family of three genera and some 530 species of deciduous trees and shrubs; about 50 species and hybrids grown in our region. The leaves are alternate, narrow, toothed and stipulate. Flowers, which lack sepals and petals, are inconspicuous, clustered into erect or pendulous spikes. ◆ Willows *(Salix)* and poplars *(Populus)* provide timber and are also grown for ornament, shade and shelter. Willow wood (*Salix alba* 'Caerulea') is used in the making of cricket bats; poplar wood is used for matches. (Groups 7, 9, 11)

Sambucaceae (elder family) A family of one genus *(Sambucus)* and about nine species (but with many subspecies) of robust herbs or small trees mostly confined to temperate regions of the northern hemisphere. One species is commonly grown in our area. In the past often classified in Caprifoliaceae, from which it differs in having compound leaves, a corolla without nectaries, partially inferior ovaries and a stigma borne directly on the ovary (style absent). The leaves are opposite, usually pinnately compound, the leaflets always with toothed margins. ◆ The flowers and fruit of members of *Sambucus* (elders) are the source of a number of alcoholic beverages and the fruit is also used as food. The group has many medicinal properties and is widely cultivated as ornaments. (Group 32)

Santalaceae (sandalwood family) A family of 40–45 genera and 900–950 species of herbs, shrubs and trees, most of which are hemiparasites on the roots of other plants; two species grown in our area. Members often have bluish green, simple, entire leaves with obscure secondary and tertiary veins. The flowers are inconspicuous, with inferior ovaries. The family is closely related to some of the mistletoes (Loranthaceae). ◆ The sandalwood tree *(Santalum album)* is probably the best-known member of the family. It yields sandal oil and a fragrant timber. (Group 23)

Sapindaceae (litchi family) A predominantly woody family of some 130–150 genera and 1,500–2,300 species, about 30 of which are grown in the region. The leaves are always alternate and lack stipules. They are usually 3-foliolate, paripinnate or imparipinnate, rarely simple *(Dodonaea* and *Pappea)* or 2-foliolate *(Lepisanthes)*. *Allophylus*, with 3-foliolate leaves, resembles species of *Searsia*, but the leaves lack the resinous smell of those of the latter when crushed. Pinnate leaves often have the rachis ending in a very diagnostic aborted rachis apex (resembling an inactive terminal growth tip). Flowers in local species are small and inconspicuous and the seeds are often surrounded by a fleshy aril. ◆ The fleshy arils of many species are edible (the best-known example being the litchi, *Litchi chinensis*). *Koelreuteria paniculata* (golden rain) is a popular garden ornamental. (Groups 34, 36, 38, 43)

Sapotaceae (milkwood family) A predominantly woody, pantropical plant family with about 53 genera and 1,100 species, about two dozen of which are grown in this region. Members are easily recognised by the combination of milky latex and simple, entire, alternate leaves, which lack large stipules or conspicuous stipular scars (as in Moraceae). Young growth often has a rusty or brownish colour. All local members have fleshy fruit and the seeds are shiny, brown, with a broad scar at the point of attachment. ◆ The latex of some species was once a source of various rubber-like substances – used, for example, in golf balls (gutta-percha) and as the elastic component of chewing gum. The coating of top-quality golf balls is currently made from balata rubber, prepared from the latex of trees belonging to the genus *Manilkara*. (Group 5)

Scrophulariaceae broadly defined (snapdragon family) A predominantly herbaceous family, with some 220 genera and 3,000 species; over 120 species, hybrids and selections grown in our region. Easily recognised by a combination of vegetative and floral features. Leaves opposite or whorled, simple, without stipules. Stems 4-angled. Flowers irregular, 2-lipped, with 5 united petals, 4 stamens (2 longer than the others) attached to the petals. The fruits are many-seeded. ◆ The family produces many garden ornamentals, among them snapdragons *(Antirrhinum)*, beard tongues *(Penstemon)* and slipper flowers *(Calceolaria)*. The drugs digitalin and digoxin are obtained from *Digitalis*. The family is rich in hemiparasitic plants, including a few troublesome weeds *(Striga*, *Alectra)*, but these members are often classified in a separate family, Orobanchaceae. (Group 12)

Simaroubaceae (tree-of-heaven family) A pantropical family of some 25 genera and 150 species, four of which are grown in our area. Plants are mostly woody, with pinnately compound leaves. Bitter quassinoid triterpenes are characteristic compounds of the family. The flowers are usually unisexual, with males and females on different trees. Fruits are usually winged nuts. ◆ Tree-of-heaven *(Ailanthus altissima)* is a widely cultivated ornamental and an invasive in many places, not only in our region. (Group 38)

Solanaceae (potato family) A cosmopolitan, vegetatively diverse family of some 75–100 genera and 2,500–3,000 species; over 100 species and a vast number of cultivars grown in our region. The leaves are simple, alternate, without stipules, often with an unpleasant scent when crushed. They are often spiny in members of *Solanum*. The flowers are regular, with 5 united petals and 5 stamens (often coherent, but not fused in *Solanum*). The fruit is either a many-seeded berry or a capsule. ◆ Food plants include potato *(S. tuberosum)*, egg plant *(S. melongena)*, tomato *(Lycopersicon esculentum)* and peppers *(Capsicum)*. The family is rich in poisonous alkaloids, producing, among others, the nicotine in tobacco *(Nicotiana tabacum)*. Many species are used in traditional medicine. *Datura ferox* and *D. stramonium* (thorn-apples) are troublesome weeds. (Groups 7, 8, 10)

Strelitziaceae (strelitzia family) A small family of four genera, 250 species of banana-like plants, about 10 of which are grown in our area. They are easily recognised by their crowns of alternate, large, simple and distinctly stalked leaves arranged in a fan (2-ranked). The flowers are borne in large, boat-shaped bracts. ◆ Several species are grown as ornamentals, notably *Strelitzia reginae* (crane flower or bird-of-paradise flower) and lobster's claw *(Heliconia)*. (Group 2)

Tamaricaceae (tamarisk family) A small family of three or four genera and about 110 species of trees and shrubs, characterised by slender branches with alternate, small, scale-like leaves; about 10 species grown in our area. Many species (halophytes) can tolerate saline soils. The flowers are minute and either pink or white. ◆ Several species of *Tamarix* (tamarisk) are grown for ornament. Manna is an edible, white, sweet, gummy substance secreted by a scale insect, *Trabutina mannifera*, associated with tamarisk in the Middle East; it accumulates when attending ants are absent. (Group 3)

Theaceae (tea family) A tropical and subtropical family of 28 genera and some 500 species, most diverse in the Americas and Asia; about 10 species grown in our area. Members of this family are evergreen trees or shrubs with alternate, leathery leaves with toothed margins and without stipules. The flowers are solitary, usually large, showy and scented. Fruits are large, often woody capsules with few, large, short-lived seeds. ◆ Pre-eminent among this family's claims to economic fame is the beverage tea, which is made from the leaves of *Camellia sinensis*. Other species in the family are grown as ornamentals; especially poignant among these is *Franklinia alatamaha*, the Franklin tree, which is extinct in the wild. An ornamental *Camellia* (*C. japonica* or a similar species) is significant in the novel *La Dame aux Camélias* by Alexandre Dumas fils; this novel in turn provided the story for the Verdi opera *La Traviata*. (Group 9)

Ulmaceae (elm family) A mostly north-temperate family of six genera and 40 species, closely related to Celtidaceae; about 12 species and cultivars grown in our area. Leaves have an oblique base, as in Celtidaceae, but differ in that there is only one main vein and the secondary veins run out to the toothed margin. The fruits are dry, flat and winged, unlike the round berries of Celtidaceae. ◆ The timber of species of *Ulmus* (elm) has limited use in furniture-making. Elms and *Zelkova* (Caucasian elm) are grown for ornament, but *U. parvifolia* (Chinese elm) is invasive in Gauteng. (Group 9)

Verbenaceae narrowly defined (verbena family) Vegetatively a rather indistinct family, with about 35 genera and 1,000 species, about 35 of which are grown in the region. Most species formerly placed in this family have been transferred to Lamiaceae. The leaves are opposite and simple. Crushed leaves are usually strongly aromatic and the twigs tend to be 4-angled. The flowers have 5 united petals and are more or less irregular (2-lipped), with 4 stamens arising from the corolla. ◆ A number of species are cultivated for ornament, including the lemon verbena *(Aloysia citrodora)*, purple wreath *(Petrea volubilis)* and various species of *Verbena*. *Lantana camara* is a serious alien invader weed in southern Africa. (Groups 19, 23)

Viburnaceae (snowball family) A family of one genus *(Viburnum)* and about 150 species, widespread in northern temperate and tropical regions, with centres of diversity in China and the Americas. Superficially similar to Rubiaceae (coffee family); several mainly shrubby species grown in our region, with only one commonly encountered as a small tree. The leaves are opposite, usually simple and always without interpetiolar (as in Rubiaceae) stipules. In some species the outermost flowers of the many-flowered flat-topped or rounded inflorescences are highly modified, sterile, with a much enlarged corolla. The corolla of fused petals is tubular to funnel-shaped, white to pink and the style is very short or absent. In the past, *Viburnum* has often been included in the Caprifoliaceae, but it now seems to be more closely related to Sambucaceae. ◆ Many species of *Viburnum* are cultivated in temperate regions as garden ornamentals. Among these are *V. lantana* (wayfaring tree) and *V. opulus* (guelder rose). (Group 19)

GROUP 1

Succulent group

Plants with leaves and/or stems succulent.

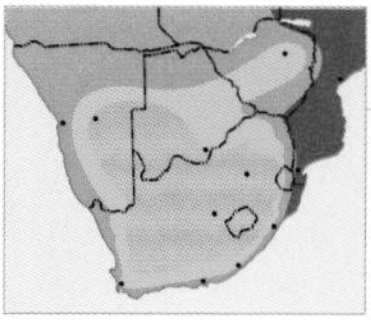

1 *Alluaudia procera*

DIDIERIACEAE

Madagascar Ocotillo; Madagaskarvalskaktus

OTHER LANGUAGES: Fantsiholitra (Malagasy)

Madagascar Medium-sized, **columnar** or (in very large, old individuals) vase-shaped tree; bark whitish or grey, smooth, **with vertical or spiral rows of paired, short, straight, sturdy thorns**. Leaves alternate or in tufts, without petiole; blade 7–25 × 4–12mm, egg-shaped to oblong, **aligned vertically**; tip rounded; base narrowed; surface glossy; margin smooth. Stipules absent. Inflorescences erect, crest-like, on tops of trunks; males and females on separate trees. Flowers individually very small. Fruit a 3-angled nut.

- Drought 3
- Intermittent
- Deciduous

Grown with increasing frequency as an ornamental in succulent collections, both public and private.

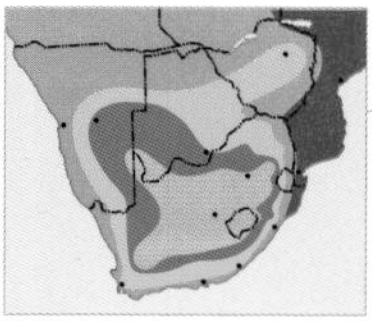

2 *Cereus jamacaru* (= *C. peruvianus*)

CACTACEAE

Queen of the Night, Tree Cactus; Nagblom, Bobbejaanpaal, Boomkaktus

Brazil and Guyana Small vase-shaped tree; bark green, brown or grey, smooth; branches hairless, stout, dull, green, **permanently leafless**; mucilage watery; stems **6–10-ribbed**, with **up to 20 straight thorns on an areole**. Inflorescences an erect, single flower **up to 250mm long**. Flowers with many free, linear to oblong parts, white, rarely green, without markings. Fruit a spiny but hairless, ellipsoid berry, red outside but with white flesh. Seeds black.

- Drought 3
- Spring–Summer
- Leafless

Introduced as an ornamental in succulent collections, it is now a declared Category 1b invader in South Africa. It is also invasive in East Africa.

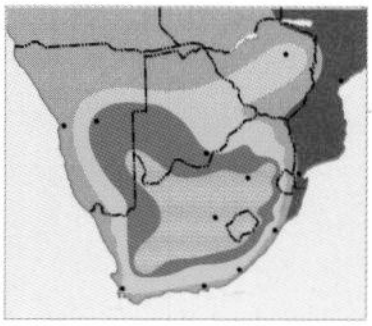

3 *Euphorbia stenoclada*

EUPHORBIACEAE

Silver Thicket; Ruigtenaboom

Madagascar Small tree with a rounded to spreading crown, often much narrower in cultivation; bark grey, deeply fissured or rough; twigs **hairy**, stout, green with **golden orange hairs**, permanently **leafless**; latex **white**; stems **flattened**, unarmed. Flowers inconspicuous, in stalkless clusters at the tip of branches; males and females separate but in the same cluster. Fruit a roundish capsule.

- Drought 3
- Intermittent
- Leafless

Occasionally grown in botanical gardens and specialist succulent collections, specifically noted in Gauteng and Mpumalanga.

1 *A. procera*

1 *A. procera* leaves

1 *A. procera* fruit

2 *C. jamacaru*

2 *C. jamacaru* flowers

2 *C. jamacaru* fruit

3 *E. stenoclada*

3 *E. stenoclada* branch tips

3 *E. stenoclada* fruit

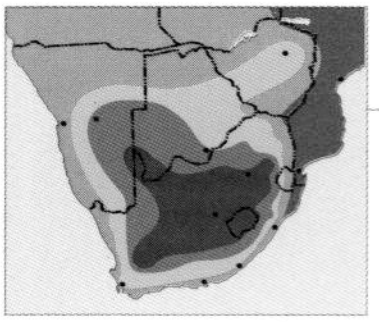

- Drought 3
- Intermittent
- Leafless

1 *Opuntia ficus-indica* (= *O. megacantha, O. occidentalis*) CACTACEAE
Sweet Prickly-pear; Boereturksvy

OTHER LANGUAGES: Kermus ennsara (Arabic); Chardon d'Inde (French); Feigenkaktus (German); Figo de Cacto (Portuguese); Cardón de México (Spanish)

Mexico Spreading small tree or large shrub; bark brown, smooth or narrowly fissured; stems **flattened into pads** 300–600 × 60–150mm, with tufts of straight thorns and watery sap. Leaves absent but stems green. Inflorescences an erect, single flower on the edge of a pad. Flowers yellow to brown. Fruit a hairless, ellipsoid, red or yellow berry about 70 × 35mm, with areoles of bristles. Seeds about 5mm long.

Invasive in many warm, dry countries and one of the worst weeds in the Eastern Cape, Karoo and elsewhere. It is a declared Category 1b invader in South Africa. Originally introduced for stock feed and the edible fruits. Many cultivars of *Opuntia* have this species in their ancestry; at least 28 are known from South Africa.

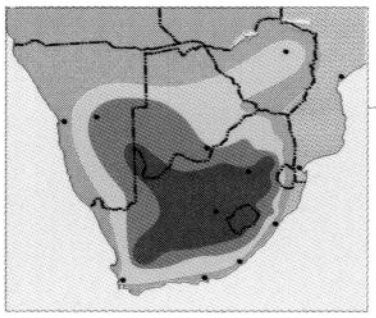

- Drought 3
- Intermittent
- Quickly deciduous

2 *Opuntia imbricata* (= *O. arborescens*) CACTACEAE
Imbricate Cactus, Chain-link Cactus; Kabelturksvy

Southwestern USA and adjacent parts of Mexico Shrub or small tree with an upright to spreading crown; bark brown, narrowly fissured; stems **round with a braided appearance**, green, with **8–30 straight thorns** and almost invisible hairlike spines (glochids) on each areole. Leaves soon falling, alternate, without petiole; blade 10–20mm long, awl-shaped; tip pointed; base squared; surface glossy; margin entire. Inflorescences an erect, single flower. Flowers magenta. Fruit a spiny, ellipsoid, red or yellow berry about 50mm long. Seeds yellow, about 3 × 3mm.

Seriously invasive in Europe, Africa, Australia and southern South America and a declared Category 1b invader in South Africa. Grown as a garden ornamental but birds spread the seeds.

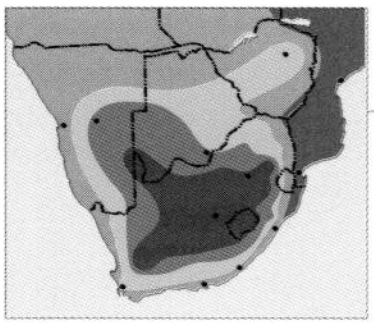

- Drought 3
- Intermittent
- Leafless

3 *Opuntia monacantha* (= *O. vulgaris*) CACTACEAE
Sour Prickly-pear, Barbary Fig; Suurturksvy

Brazil to Argentina Spreading shrub or small tree; bark brown, smooth or narrowly fissured; watery sap present; stems flattened into **thin, often drooping pads** 100–350 × 75–125mm, with **1–3 grey or brown spines** per areole. Leaves minute, soon falling. Inflorescences an erect, single flower, on the edge of a pad. Flowers yellow or red, 75–100mm long. Fruit a bristly, narrowly egg-shaped, red to purple berry about 60mm long. Seeds midbrown, 2mm long.

Invasive in Australia, the USA and southern and East Africa and a declared Category 1b invader in South Africa. Originally introduced for stock feed and ornament. The variegated cultivar 'Josephs Coat' is recorded from South Africa.

1 *O. ficus-indica* pad

BRAAM VAN WYK

1 *O. ficus-indica* flowers

BRAAM VAN WYK

1 *O. ficus-indica* fruit

2 *O. imbricata* stem

GEOFF NICHOLS

2 *O. imbricata* flowers

GEOFF NICHOLS

2 *O. imbricata* fruit

3 *O. monacantha* pad

GEOFF NICHOLS

3 *O. monacantha* flower

3 *O. monacantha* fruit

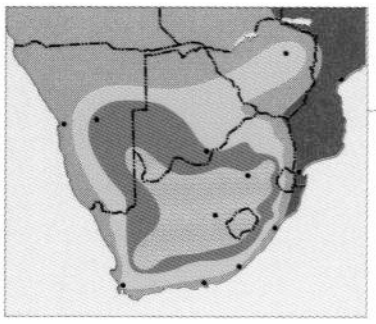

1 *Pachypodium geayi*

APOCYNACEAE

Madagascar Bottle Tree; Madagaskarbottelboom

OTHER LANGUAGES: Vontaka (Malagasy)

Madagascar Succulent, small to medium-sized tree with few branches; new growth and spines **hairy**; spines **in 3s**, persistent, straight; latex **clear**. Leaves with petiole **hairy**, 10–40mm long; blade 60–430 × 10–35mm, strap- to egg-shaped, **grey**; tip pointed to rounded; base narrowed; lower surface minutely hairy; margin smooth, **rolled inwards**. Inflorescences erect, 100–220mm long; peduncle 25–110mm long. Flowers tubular, **white**, tube 11–16mm long, lobes 5, egg-shaped, 12–22 × 8–12mm. Fruit **a pair of spindle-shaped**, brown or dark green pods 140–160mm long, about 20mm in diameter.

- Drought 3
- Spring
- Deciduous

Grown as a curiosity in succulent collections.

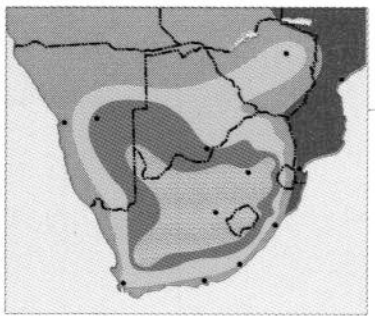

2 *Pachypodium lamerei*

APOCYNACEAE

Madagascar Palm; Valshalfmens

OTHER LANGUAGES: Pachypodium de Madagascar (French); Madagaskarpalme (German); Votasitry (Malagasy)

Madagascar Succulent, small, rarely branched tree; new growth and spines **hairless**; spines **in 3s**, persistent, straight; latex **clear**. Leaves with petiole **hairless**, 12–60mm long; blade 90–410 × 24–110mm, egg-shaped or oblong, **green**; margin smooth, **bent inwards**. Inflorescences erect, 90–220mm long; peduncle 20–120mm long. Flowers tubular; throat red inside and green outside, tube 26–60mm long, **white**, lobes 25–68 × 17–41mm, white. Fruit **a pair of brown, woody, spindle-shaped** pods 90–260 × 25–55mm. Seeds buff, with straw-coloured hair-tuft, 14–15 × 4–6 × 3mm.

- Drought 3
- Spring
- Deciduous

Grown for its sculptural form and seen in this capacity with increasing frequency. Young plants sometimes mistaken for *P. namaquanum* (halfmens), a species native to arid parts of South Africa and Namibia but much rarer in cultivation.

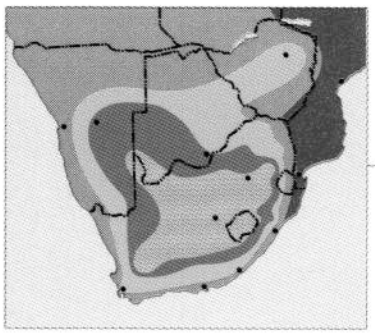

3 *Pereskia grandifolia* (= *Cactus grandifolius, Rhodocactus grandifolius*)

CACTACEAE

Strawberry Cactus, Rose Cactus; Aarbeikaktus

Brazil Large shrub or small tree with a vase-shaped to spreading crown; bark grey, narrowly fissured; twigs hairless, with clear sap and many **long, straight, black thorns** on each areole. Leaves alternate; petiole hairless, 5–15mm long; blade 60–300 × 30–90mm, lance-shaped to elliptic, **thick and succulent**; tip bluntly pointed; base bluntly narrowed; surface glossy; margin smooth. Inflorescences stiffly angled downwards, 50–150mm long; peduncle 15–60mm long. Flowers pink or purple; petals many, oblong, 15–32mm long. Fruit an egg-shaped, **angled**, yellow berry 50–100 × 30–70mm. Seeds 5–7 × 3.6–5.4mm.

- Drought 3
- Intermittent
- Evergreen

Grown as specimen trees in Durban Botanic Gardens and elsewhere. Recorded from Gauteng and the Western and Eastern Cape as well. The leaves are edible and medicinal uses are recorded.

1 *P. geayi* (right)

ANDREW HANKEY

1 *P. geayi* leaves

1 *P. geayi* flower

NAAMAN ABREU / SHUTTERSTOCK.COM

2 *P. lamerei*

ETTORE BALOCCHI

2 *P. lamerei* flowers

2 *P. lamerei* fruit

BRAAM VAN WYK

3 *P. grandifolia* stem

MOKKIE, WIKIMEDIA COMMONS, CC BY SA 3.0

3 *P. grandifolia* flowers

BRAAM VAN WYK

3 *P. grandifolia* fruit

GROUP 2

Palm group

Plants with a distinctive growth form, usually unbranched or only sparsely branched. Leaves large, sometimes umbrella-shaped, usually in terminal clusters.

See also Group 4: *Cecropia peltata* (p.104); Group 39: *Schefflera actinophylla* (p.404) and *Tetrapanax papyrifer* (p.406).

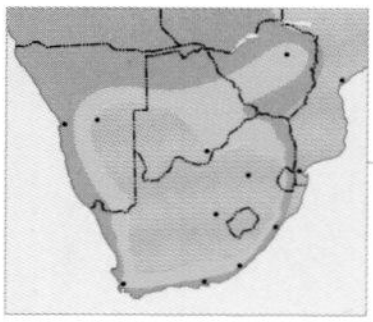

- Drought 2
- Summer
- Evergreen

1 *Acrocomia aculeata* (= *A. mexicana, A. sclerocarpa* and about 30 others)

ARECACEAE

Grugru Palm, Macaw Palm; Kalanderpalm

OTHER LANGUAGES: Acrocome (French); Coyol (Spanish)

The Caribbean, Mexico and South America Single-stemmed palm; bark grey, rough, ringed with leaf scars and **sharp, black spines** about 100mm long. Leaves **pinnate**; petiole with **toothed margin**; rachis flattened above, rounded below; leaflets 2-ranked, evenly spaced, about 1m long, 20–40mm wide; lower surface **hairy**. Inflorescences between the leaves, hanging, branched, about 1.5m long. Flowers small. Fruit hard, woody, brown, 35–45 × 35–45mm, containing a single seed each.

Most if not all described species of *Acrocomia* are now considered to be variations of this species, not worthy of formal taxonomic recognition. The word 'grugru' in the common name is the American Spanish for the large edible worm-like larva of a weevil, *Rhynchophorus palmarum*, that infests this palm. Grown in botanical gardens and enthusiasts' collections. The sap can be fermented into an alcoholic beverage and the fruits have been suggested as a source of biodiesel.

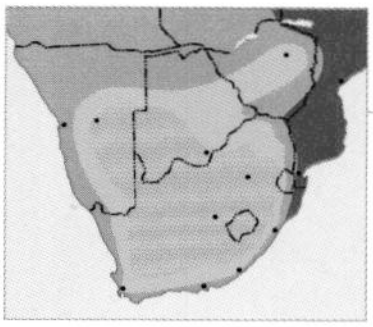

- Drought 2
- Summer
- Evergreen

2 *Adonidia merrillii* (= *Veitchia merrillii*)

ARECACEAE

True Manila Palm; Ware Manilapalm

OTHER LANGUAGES: Palmier de Manille (French); Weihnachtspalme (German); Palma de Navidad (Spanish); Bunga de Jolo (Tagalog); Maak nuan (Thai)

The Philippines Small, single-trunked palm; bark grey, ringed with leaf scars; trunk with a conspicuous **green or rarely yellowish crownshaft**. Leaves **pinnate**; petiole **unarmed**; rachis flattened and round; leaflets 2-ranked, **hanging**, evenly spaced, single-fold, fold up, 350–750 × 4–50mm, lance-shaped; tip **trifid to ragged**; surface glossy. Inflorescences below the leaves, erect to ascending, 400–500mm long. Flowers small. Fruit pear-shaped, red, 15–30 × 13–20mm.

In our region, grown as a specimen tree in botanical gardens and enthusiasts' collections. In the USA this is a popular plant at Christmas time on account of the fruits. Alexandra Palm (p.42) is sometimes sold there as this species.

1 *A. aculeata*

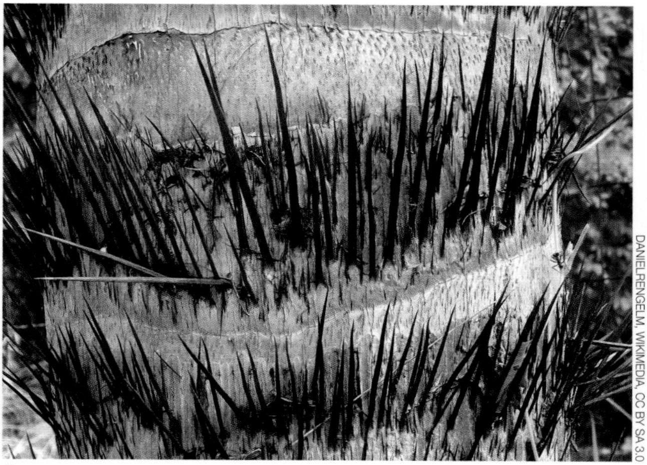

1 *A. aculeata* stem with spines

1 *A. aculeata* fruit

2 *A. merrillii* flowers

2 *A. merrillii*

2 *A. merrillii* fruit

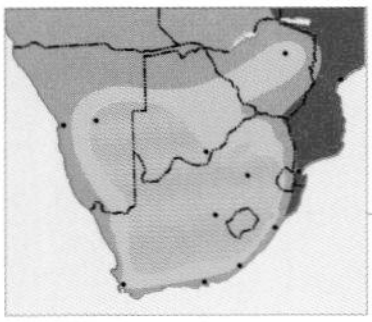

- Drought 2
- Summer
- Evergreen

1 *Archontophoenix alexandrae* (= *A. alexandrae* var. *beatriciae*, *Ptychosperma alexandrae*)

ARECACEAE

Alexandra Palm, Club-foot King Palm, Ring-step King Palm; Klompvoetkoningpalm, Ringtrapkoningpalm

OTHER LANGUAGES: Palmier Alexandre (French); Alexandrapalme (German); Palma Alejandra (Spanish)

Australia Tall, **slender**, single-stemmed palm; bark grey, rough, ringed with leaf scars and sometimes stepped; trunk with **a lime-green crownshaft**. Leaves **pinnate**; petiole unarmed; rachis flat above, rounded below; leaflets 2-ranked, stiff, single-fold, fold up, up to 800 × 30–50mm; tip bifid; lower surface **silvery**. Stipules absent. Inflorescences below the leaves, hanging, 400–800mm long. Flowers small. Fruit red, fibrous, pear-shaped, 8–14 × 8–11mm.

Can be confused with *A. cunninghamiana* (= *Ptychosperma cunninghamiana*) (king palm), which is grown by enthusiasts. Grown in botanical gardens and specialist collections.

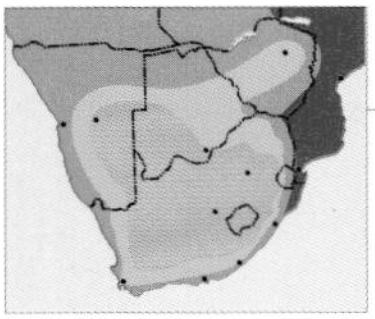

- Drought 2
- Intermittent
- Evergreen

2 *Arenga pinnata* (= *A. saccharifera*)

ARECACEAE

Sugar Palm, Areng Palm, Black-fibre Palm, Gomuti Palm; Suikerpalm

OTHER LANGUAGES: Aren, Gomuti (Bahasa Indonesia); Sha tang ye zi (Chinese); Zuckerpalme (German)

Indonesia Medium-sized, single-stemmed palm; bark grey, rough with leaf scars. Leaves **pinnate**; petiole unarmed, up to 1.5m long; rachis flattened above, rounded below; leaflets 2-ranked, single-fold, fold down, 1.2–1.6m long, 50–90mm wide; tip **ragged**; base sometimes eared; lower surface **silvery**. Inflorescences between the leaves, hanging, 2m or longer, monocarpic. Flowers small. Fruit 3-angled, dark purple, up to 70 × 60mm.

The sap can be processed into a form of sugar, or used as a beverage. In parts of Indonesia the fruits are cooked and eaten and old trees nearing the end of their lives can be cut and a form of sago extracted from the pith. The growing point can be used as palm hearts. Traditional Javanese roofs are often made of the fibre surrounding the leaf base, which can also be made into cordage. The hard outer sheath of the stem can be used for barrels and flooring. In our region, grown as a specimen tree in botanical gardens and enthusiasts' collections.

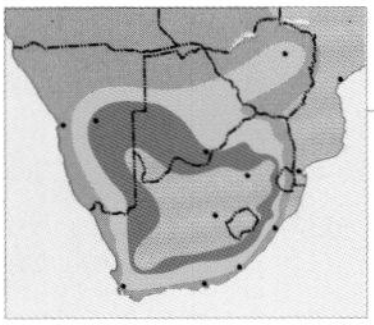

- Drought 2
- Summer
- Evergreen

3 *Beaucarnea recurvata* (= *Nolina recurvata*)

ASPARAGACEAE

Ponytail Palm, Bottle Palm, Elephant-foot Tree; Poniestert

OTHER LANGUAGES: Monja, Palma Culona (Spanish)

Mexico Small tree with a **conspicuous swollen** base and one or a few trunks, unbranched or with few branches, each topped with a **'mop'** of leaves. Leaves spirally arranged, without petiole, angled up near the base but then **drooping**, up to 1.8m long, 25mm wide, flat, **strap-shaped**; tip pointed. Inflorescences seldom seen and only formed on large adult trees, erect to horizontal. Flowers white to yellowish, inconspicuous. Fruit an elongated capsule about 10mm long.

Popular garden plant in all urban areas in our region, often seen as a juvenile scarcely a metre tall. Although shown on the map as being suitable for USDA Zones 9–12, the ponytail palm can be grown indoors in colder areas if it is given shelter. If planted in a container, take care to allow enough space for the expanding stem base. Despite the name, it is not related to the true palms.

KAHUROA, WIKIMEDIA, PUBLIC DOMAIN

1 *A. alexandrae*

ALEJANDRO BAYER TOMAYO, WIKIMEDIA COMMONS, CC BY SA 2.0

1 *A. alexandrae* fruit

MMCKNIGHT4, WIKIMEDIA COMMONS, PUBLIC DOMAIN

1 *A. alexandrae* flowers

2 *A. pinnata*

W.A. DJATMIKO, WIKIMEDIA COMMONS, CC BY SA 3.0

2 *A. pinnata* flowers

W.A. DJATMIKO, WIKIMEDIA COMMONS, CC BY SA 3.0

2 *A. pinnata* fruit

3 *B. recurvata*

3 *B. recurvata* leaves

FOREST AND KIM STARR

3 *B. recurvata* flowers

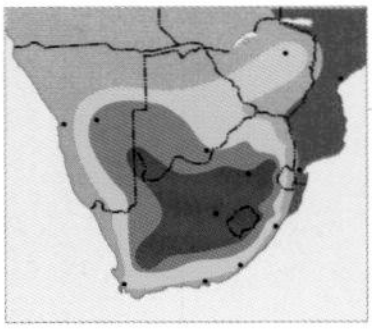

1 *Butia capitata* — ARECACEAE

Jelly Palm, Wine Palm; Jelliepalm

- Drought 2
- Intermittent
- Evergreen

OTHER LANGUAGES: Geleepalme (German)

Brazil and Uruguay Short, thick-stemmed palm; bark whitish, brown or grey, **rough with old leaf bases**. Leaves **pinnate**; petiole **spiny** with teeth up to 40mm long; rachis flattened above, rounded below, **arched almost back to the trunk**; leaflets 2-ranked, stiff, evenly spaced, single-fold, 600–750 × 15–25mm, grey-green; tip single or bifid; lower surface silvery. Inflorescences between the leaves, hanging like a horse's tail, about 1m long. Flowers small. Fruit orange, 24–30 × 20–27.5mm. Seeds buff.

Fruits edible and can be fermented or used for jelly. More cold-resistant than most palms, this is becoming more widely grown than it once was.

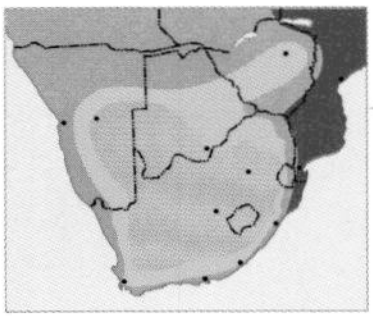

2 *Carica papaya* (= *Papaya carica*) — CARICACEAE

Pawpaw, Papaya; Papaja

- Drought 2
- Spring
- Evergreen

OTHER LANGUAGES: Papaya (Bahasa Indonesia); Papayer (French); Papayabaum (German); Papaeira (Portuguese); Papayero (Spanish)

Tropical America Small tree, rarely branched, with leaves **at top of the trunk**; bark yellowish to brown, smooth; buds hairless; lenticels smooth but conspicuous. Leaves with petiole hairless, 0.3–1.05m long; blade **400–700 × 100–200mm, kidney-shaped to round**, deeply **palmately 7–13-lobed**, lobes **pinnately lobed**; tip drawn out; base **heart-shaped**, with **7–13 main veins** from the base; surface glossy above, dull below. Stipules absent. Inflorescences erect or bent downwards; males and females on separate trees, males 0.5–1.0m long; peduncle 100–200mm long in males and 30–40mm long in females. Flowers white to creamy, tubular, 12–70 × 15–25mm. Fruit a yellow, ellipsoid to ovoid berry 100–300 × 60–100mm, with pink or orange flesh. Seeds black, 5–7mm long.

Widely grown for its fruit in the warmer parts of our region and recorded from Namibia, South Africa and Zimbabwe. The ripe fruit is eaten raw or consumed as juice. The less ripe fruit contains an enzyme that can act as a meat tenderiser in a marinade. Medicinal uses of the seeds are recorded. The common name 'pawpaw' is also used for members of the unrelated genus *Asimina* (Annonaceae), a group of trees and shrubs native to eastern North America.

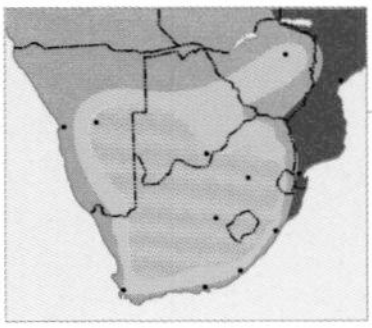

3 *Carpentaria acuminata* — ARECACEAE

North Australian Feather Palm, Carpentaria Palm; Noord-Australiese Veerpalm

- Drought 1
- Intermittent
- Evergreen

OTHER LANGUAGES: Palmier de Darwin (French)

Northern Territory, Australia Medium-sized to **tall, slender**, single-stemmed palm; bark grey, ringed with faint leaf scars; **crownshaft green**. Leaves **pinnate**; petiole unarmed, about 300mm long; rachis flattened above, rounded below; leaflets 2-ranked, stiff, evenly spaced, single-fold, fold up, 200–300 × **20–40mm, narrowly oblong**; tip ragged; surface glossy. Inflorescences below the leaves, **stiff, horizontal**, about 1m long; peduncle 100–200mm long. Flowers small. Fruit red, about 10–20 × 18mm.

Widely used in the tropics as an accent plant in public gardens. In our region, grown as a specimen tree in botanical gardens and enthusiasts' collections.

1 *B. capitata*

TRIANGULATED TRUTH

1 *B. capitata* fruit

2 *C. papaya*

TON RULKENS

2 *C. papaya* flowers (male)

MARCO SCHMIDT, WIKIMEDIA COMMONS, CC BY SA 2.5

2 *C. papaya* fruit

KYLE WICOMB

3 *C. acuminata*

3 *C. acuminata* flowers

FOREST AND KIM STARR

3 *C. acuminata* fruit

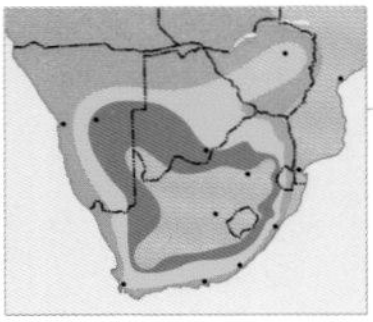

1 *Caryota mitis* ARECACEAE

Clustered Fish-tail Palm, Burmese Fish-tail; Boskasievisstertpalm

- Drought 2
- Monocarpic
- Evergreen

OTHER LANGUAGES: Sarai (Bahasa Indonesia); Duan sui yu wei ku (Chinese); Caryote doux (French); Fischenschwanzpalme (German); Cola de Pescado (Spanish)

Southeast Asia Small to medium-sized, **clustering** palm; bark green, later grey, ringed with prominent leaf scars. Leaves **bipinnate** in adult palms, once-pinnate in juveniles; petiole unarmed, 0.6–2m long; rachis channelled above, rounded below; leaflets 2-ranked, evenly spaced, multifold, central fold **down**, 110–170mm long, about 50mm wide, **triangular**, widest at ragged tip; base narrowed; lower surface silvery. Inflorescences between, later ones below the leaves, hanging like a horse's tail, 250–850mm long; stems monocarpic. Flowers small. Fruit black, egg-shaped, 7–12 × 12–20mm.

Fruit contains irritant crystals of calcium oxalate. An edible starch can be extracted from the stem and the sap used to prepare jaggery, an unrefined sugar. The palm heart is edible. Quite often grown in larger gardens in the warm parts of our region.

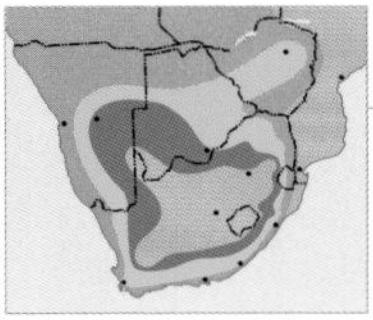

2 *Caryota urens* ARECACEAE

Common Fish-tail Palm; Gewone Visstertpalm

- Drought 2
- Monocarpic
- Evergreen

OTHER LANGUAGES: Kongque yezi (Chinese); Caryot brûlant (French); Brennpalme (German); Palmeira de Vinho, Rabo-de-Peixe, Cariota (Portuguese); Koonthalpanai (Tamil)

India, Sri Lanka, Myanmar and Malaysia Small to large, **single-trunked** palm; bark grey, ringed with prominent leaf scars. Leaves **bipinnate**; petiole unarmed, 500–600mm long; rachis channelled above, rounded below; leaflets 2-ranked, evenly spaced, multifold, central fold down, 100–200 × **70–100mm**, triangular, widest at ragged tip; base squared; surface dull, hairless. Inflorescences between, later ones below the leaves, hanging like a horse's tail, **1.5–3m long**, monocarpic. Flowers small. Fruit 3-angled, red, egg-shaped, 15–25 × 15–25mm. Seeds black.

Fruit contains irritant crystals of calcium oxalate. This is one of the more commonly grown ornamental palms and has been memorably described as being suitable for planting around shopping centres because its short lifespan is about as long as the mean time between centre remodellings. Medicinal uses have been recorded.

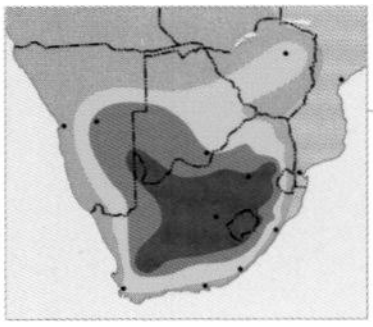

3 *Chamaerops humilis* ARECACEAE

European Fan Palm; Europese Waaierpalm

- Drought 2
- Summer
- Evergreen

OTHER LANGUAGES: Dôm (Arabic); Palmier nain (French); Zwergpalme (German); Palma nana, Ciafagghiuni (Italian); Palma vassoureira (Portuguese); Palma de escoba (Spanish)

Southern Europe and North Africa Small, clumping, thick-stemmed palm; trunks **angled to prostrate**; bark grey to black, ringed with prominent leaf scars. Leaves **palmate**; petiole up to 800mm long, with 1–7mm long spines 7–11mm apart; rachis flattened above, round below; leaflets stiff, evenly spaced, single-fold, fold down, 230–800mm long, about 7mm wide; tip bifid; surface glaucous or green. Inflorescences between the leaves, erect to ascending. Flowers small; males and females usually on different trees. Fruit brown or yellow, round to egg-shaped, 12–40 × 12–40mm.

Leaves are used in basket work and medicinal uses are recorded. In our region, occasionally planted in parks, botanical gardens and enthusiasts' collections.

1 *C. mitis*

ITDO / SHUTTERSTOCK.COM

1 *C. mitis* flowers

BERNARD DUPONT

1 *C. mitis* fruit

MAURO HALPERN

2 *C. urens* leaves

MAURO HALPERN

2 *C. urens* fruit

ZINGARO, WIKIMEDIA COMMONS, CC BY SA 2.5

3 *C. humilis*

HANS HILLEWAERT, WIKIMEDIA COMMONS, CC BY SA 3.0

3 *C. humilis* fruit

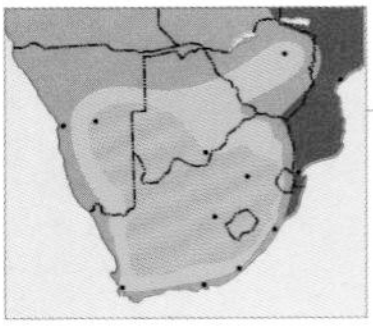

- Drought 2
- Summer
- Evergreen

1 *Chambeyronia macrocarpa* ARECACEAE

Blushing Palm, New Caledonia Red-leaved Palm; Rooiblaarpalm

OTHER LANGUAGES: Palmier de Houailou (French); Rotblattpalme (German)

New Caledonia Medium-sized to tall, solitary palm with **a crownshaft**; bark green, ringed with prominent leaf scars. Leaves **pinnate**; petiole unarmed, 125–450mm long; rachis flattened above, rounded below; leaflets 2-ranked, evenly spaced, stiff, single-fold, 110–1,500mm long, **10–73mm wide**, strap-shaped; tip bifid; surface glossy above, dull below, **coppery when young**. Inflorescences below the leaves, erect to ascending, about 300mm long; peduncle 150–175mm long. Flowers small. Fruit red, ellipsoid, 40–60 × 24–30mm.

National tree of New Caledonia. In our region, grown as specimen trees in botanical gardens and specialist collections.

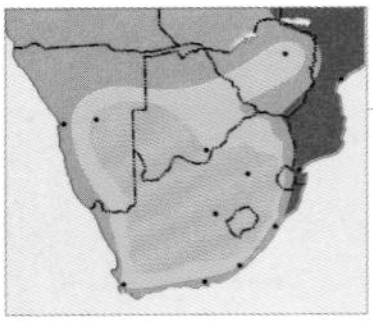

- Drought 1
- Summer
- Evergreen

2 *Cocos nucifera* ARECACEAE

Coconut Palm; Kokospalm

OTHER LANGUAGES: Nargil, goz al hindi (Arabic); Kelapa (Bahasa Indonesia); Daab (Bengali); Nargil (Farsi); Noix de Coco (French); Kokos (German); Naariyal (Hindi); Narikeli (Sanskrit); Cocotero (Spanish); Tengai (Tamil); Maphrao (Thai)

Possibly Micronesia or Central America, now throughout the tropics Short to tall, solitary palm; trunk **often ascending**, or erect in formal situations; bark grey, smooth or ringed with leaf scars. Leaves **pinnate**; petiole unarmed, **up to 2m long**; rachis channelled above, rounded below; leaflets 2-ranked, stiff, evenly spaced, single-fold, fold up, up to 1m long, 20mm wide; tip bifid; surface glossy. Inflorescences between the leaves, but below them in fruit, hanging, up to 1m long; peduncle up to 400mm long. Flowers with sepals 3, yellow or white; petals 3, creamy, 13–25 × 4–25mm. Fruit **3-angled, orange-yellow**, fibrous and woody, **up to 250** × 200mm. Seeds midbrown, 100–150mm wide.

All parts of this palm have multiple uses and this is said to be both the world's most cultivated palm and one of the world's most useful trees. Grown in plantations in Mozambique and as a street tree in parks and gardens in the warmer parts of our region.

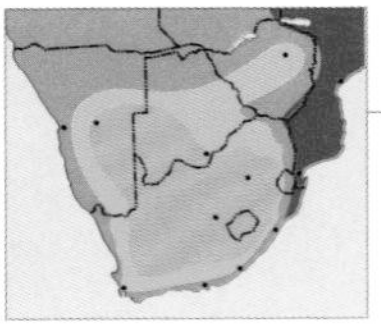

- Drought 2
- Summer
- Evergreen

3 *Copernicia prunifera* ARECACEAE

Carnauba-wax Palm, Leaf-wax Palm; Brasiliaanse Waspalm

OTHER LANGUAGES: Carnaubeira (Portuguese); Palma blanca (Spanish)

Brazil Medium-sized, solitary palm; trunk erect; bark grey, **covered with old leaf bases in a distinctive spiral pattern**. Leaves **palmate**; petiole 1–1.5m long, with **straight spines** up to 10mm long, 20–80mm apart; rachis flattened above, rounded below; leaflets stiff, evenly spaced, single-fold, 600–930mm long; tip bifid; surface **glossy green to grey-blue**. Inflorescences between the leaves, hanging, 1.5–2.7m long. Flowers small. Fruit black, egg-shaped, up to 27 × 22mm.

Carnauba wax (food additive E903, also used in polishes) is derived from the waxy coating of the leaves. Fruits and pith are eaten and the wood is used in construction. In our region, grown as specimen trees in botanical gardens and private collections.

BENOÎT HENRY

1 *C. macrocarpa*

1 *C. macrocarpa* flowers

1 *C. macrocarpa* fruit

PETER RIBTON / IMAGES OF AFRICA

2 *C. nucifera*

GEOFF NICHOLS

2 *C. nucifera* flowers

TUTUH, WIKIMEDIA COMMONS, CC BY SA 3.0

2 *C. nucifera* fruit

3 *C. prunifera*

3 *C. prunifera* flowers and leaves

GEORGE REBELO

3 *C. prunifera* fruit

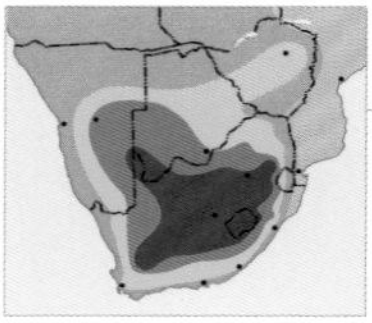

1 *Cyathea australis* CYATHEACEAE

Rough Tree Fern; Skurweboomvaring

Eastern Australia Small to medium-sized tree fern; trunk 150–400mm in diameter, with **many persistent leaf bases** near the top, these brown, not crumbling with time. Leaves **almost 3-pinnate**, almost whorled; petiole with **short spines below**, with **dark brown** scales; leaflets (secondary pinnae) 100–120mm long, up to 25mm wide, deeply scalloped, 1 or more lowest pair(s) of lobes completely separate; secondary leaflet stalks (costae and costules) with scales and fine hairs easily rubbed off.

- Drought 2
- All year (spores)
- Evergreen

Grown in public and private gardens for ornament and there less demanding than the indigenous *C. dregei*. The cultivated tree ferns are easily confused.

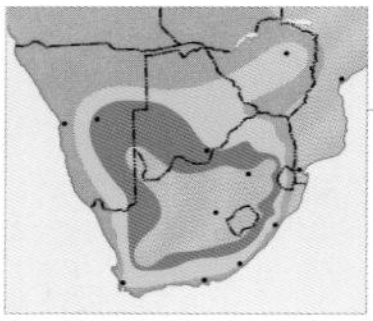

2 *Cyathea brownii* CYATHEACEAE

Smooth Tree Fern, Norfolk Tree Fern; Gladdeboomvaring

Norfolk Island Medium-sized to large tree fern; trunk with **scars where dead leaves have dropped**. Leaves **fully 3-pinnate**; petiole **unarmed**, but covered with **pale sandy brown** scales; secondary pinnae 70–130 × 15–22mm; leaflets completely separate, 8–15 × 2–4mm, shallowly scalloped; costae and costules without scales but with felted hairs.

- Drought 2
- All year (spores)
- Evergreen

The world's largest tree fern, grown as an accent plant in both public and private gardens.

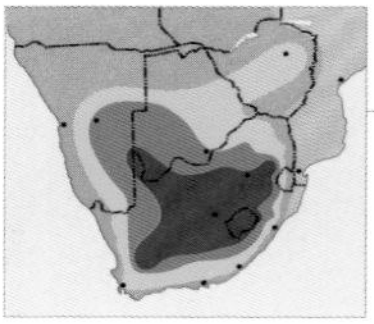

3 *Cyathea cooperi* CYATHEACEAE

Lacy Tree Fern, Australian Tree Fern; Australiese Boomvaring

Eastern Australia Small tree fern; trunk up to 150mm in diameter, but broader near the base because of adventitious roots, with **scars where dead leaves have dropped**. Leaves **almost 3-pinnate**, well separated; petiole **vertical for a short distance** before fronds start to spread, **warty but not spiny below**, scales mid- to dark brown; leaflets (secondary pinnae) up to 120 × 25mm, scalloped to toothed; costae and costules with scattered, branched, hair-like scales. Sori about **16** per leaflet, in two rows.

- Drought 2
- All year (spores)
- Evergreen

Widely grown as a garden ornamental and recorded as naturalised in the Western Cape and KwaZulu-Natal.

PETER WOODARD

1 *C. australis*

RÉMIH, WIKIMEDIA COMMONS, CC BY SA 3.0

1 *C. australis* leaflets

2 *C. brownii*

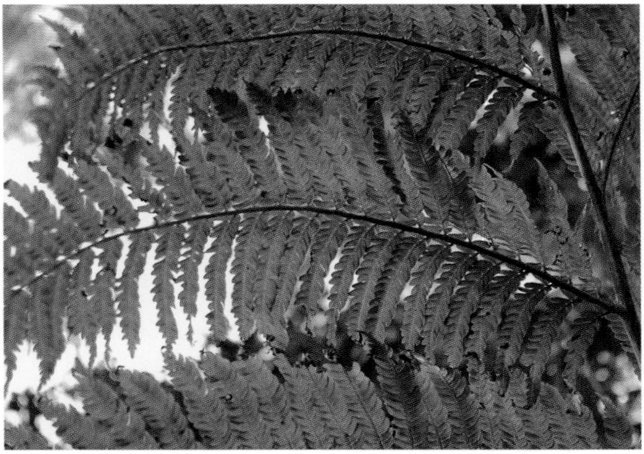

2 *C. brownii* leaflets

P. GARIN

3 *C. cooperi*

NEIL CROUCH

3 *C. cooperi* leaflets

NEIL CROUCH

3 *C. cooperi* sori

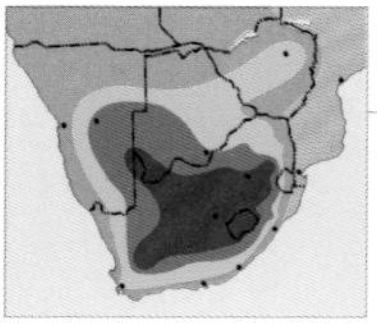

- Drought 2
- All year (spores)
- Evergreen

1 *Dicksonia antarctica*

DICKSONIACEAE

Tasmanian Tree Fern; Tasmaniese Boomvaring

Eastern Australia Small tree fern; trunk broad to narrow, hidden by many adventitious roots; bases of old leaves **persisting and crumbling** with time. Leaves **fully 3-pinnate**; petiole smooth, unarmed, with **red-brown hairs but not scales**; sterile leaflets flat, oblong, with toothed margin; fertile leaflets partly wrapped around the **single** sorus, with margin deeply incised.

Often grown as an accent plant in woodland gardens, both public and private, in our region.

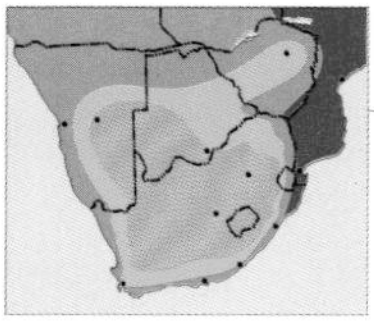

- Drought 2
- Summer
- Evergreen

2 *Dictyosperma album*

ARECACEAE

Princess Palm; Prinsespalm

OTHER LANGUAGES: Palmiste Blanc (French)

Mauritius and Réunion Medium-sized, solitary palm; trunk erect, straight, with **a small basal swelling**; bark grey, ringed with prominent leaf scars; **crownshaft brownish white**. Leaves **pinnate**; petiole unarmed, 150–300mm long; rachis flattened above, rounded below; leaflets 2-ranked, hanging, evenly spaced, single-fold, fold up, 180–750 × 5–47mm, narrowly lorate; tip bifid; surface glossy. Inflorescences below the leaves, erect to ascending, 0.4–1m long; peduncle 40–70mm long. Flowers small. Fruit purple or brown, egg-shaped, 16–18 × 8–10mm. Seeds buff.

The palm heart is a highly regarded luxury food and so this species is almost extinct in nature. In our region, it is grown as specimen trees in botanical gardens and enthusiasts' collections.

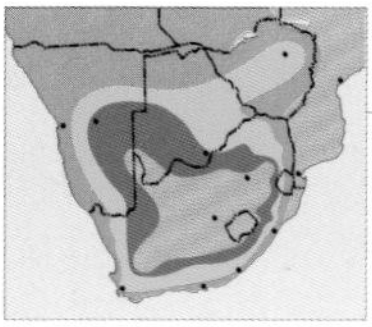

- Drought 2
- Spring
- Evergreen

3 *Dracaena draco*

DRACAENACEAE

Dragon Tree; Drakeboom

OTHER LANGUAGES: Long xue shu (Chinese); Dragonnier des Canaries (French); Drakonovo derevo (Russian); Drago de Canarias (Spanish)

Canary Islands, Azores, Morocco, Cape Verde Islands and Madeira Small to medium-sized tree with a dense, umbrella-shaped crown. Leaves **spirally arranged, without petiole**; blade 500–600 × 35–50mm, **lance-shaped**, blue-grey-green, with a sharp tip. Inflorescences dense, erect, up to 650mm long. Flowers white or green, without markings. Fruit fleshy, yellow to red or brown, round, hairless, up to 15 × 15mm.

Cut leaves and stems ooze a red resin, which is sold as 'dragon's blood' and used in folk medicine. These trees are quite often grown for ornament and can be seen in botanical gardens in Cape Town, Grahamstown, Durban, Harare and probably elsewhere.

1 *D. antarctica*

1 *D. antarctica* leaflets

1 *D. antarctica* sori

2 *D. album*

3 *D. draco*

3 *D. draco* leaves

2 *D. album* flowers

3 *D. draco* flowers

3 *D. draco* fruit

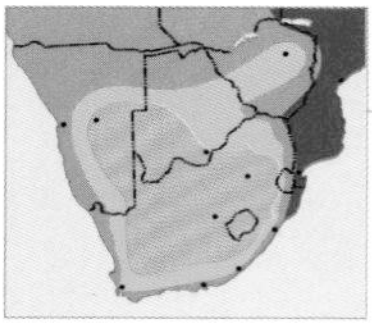

1 *Dracaena steudneri* DRACAENACEAE

Northern Large-leaved Dragon-tree; Noordelike Grootblaardrakeboom

- Drought 2
- Spring
- Evergreen

Tropical Africa Small to medium-sized, **sparsely branched** tree; bark pale brown or grey, smooth. Leaves alternate, without petiole; blade **0.4–1.3m long, 40–160mm wide, lance-shaped or oblong**; tip sharply pointed; base squared; veins parallel, with a distinct midrib; surface glossy; margin smooth. Inflorescences **erect**, 0.3–1m long, rarely up to 2m, branches **orange**. Flowers scented, only opening at night, lobes 6, white or green, narrow, 5–18 × 0.5–1mm. Fruit a round, red or black berry 12–30 × 12–30mm. Seeds whitish, about 10 × 10 × 10mm.

A garden ornamental widely grown in Zimbabwe, rather less so further south.

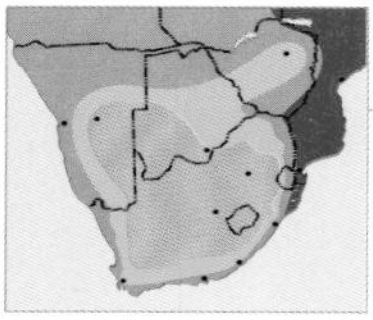

2 *Dypsis decaryi* (= *Neodypsis decaryi*) ARECACEAE

Triangle Palm, Brown Bamboo Palm; Driehoekpalm, Bruinbamboespalm

- Drought 2
- Spring
- Evergreen

OTHER LANGUAGES: Palmier Triedre (French); Dreieckspalme (German); Palmeira-três-quinas (Portuguese); Palmeira triangular (Spanish)

Madagascar Small to medium-sized, **solitary** palm; trunk ringed with leaf scars, slightly swollen at the top; bark brown to grey. Leaves **3-ranked, pinnate**; petiole unarmed, base split; rachis flattened above, rounded below; leaflets 2-ranked, evenly spaced, hanging, 350–750 × 10–25mm, single-fold, fold up; surface **grey**. Inflorescences below the leaves, horizontal. Flowers small. Fruit grey-green at first, black when ripe, 15–20 × 15–20mm.

Increasingly grown as an ornamental in public and private gardens in our region. The leaves are used in Madagascar for roofing and the fruits are eaten by children and stock.

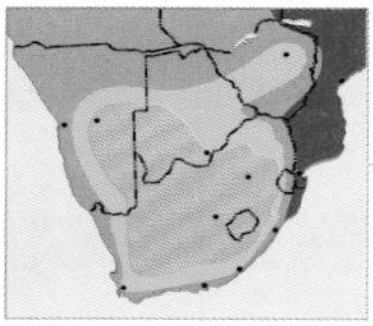

3 *Dypsis madagascariensis* (= *Chrysalidocarpus lucubensis, C. madagascariensis*) ARECACEAE

Madagascar Bamboo Palm; Madagaskarbamboespalm

- Drought 2
- Spring
- Evergreen

Madagascar Small to medium-sized palm; trunks **usually in clusters of 2–4**, sometimes solitary; bark green or grey, ringed with leaf scars; **crownshaft green**. Leaves **3-ranked, pinnate**; petiole unarmed, 300–500mm long; rachis flattened below, rounded above; leaflets several-ranked, grouped, hanging, 650–950 × 19–35mm, strap-shaped, with 1–3 folds each; tip bifid; surface green, glossy. Inflorescences between the leaves, hanging, 1m long and more; peduncle about 450mm long. Flowers small. Fruit green at first, later purple, egg-shaped, 12–15 × 6–8mm.

Widely and commonly grown as a garden ornamental. In Madagascar the trunks, which are very hard, are used for flooring in houses. The palm heart and fruits are edible.

BRAAM VAN WYK

1 *D. steudneri*

1 *D. steudneri* flowers

1 *D. steudneri* fruit

2 *D. decaryi*

2 *D. decaryi* flowers

FOREST AND KIM STARR

2 *D. decaryi* fruit

3 *D. madagascariensis*

GEOFF NICHOLS

3 *D. madagascariensis* fruit

3 *D. madagascariensis* flowers

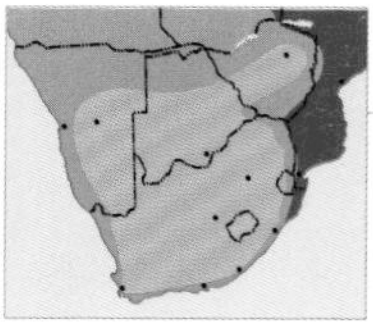

- Drought 2
- Spring
- Evergreen

1 *Elaeis guineensis* ARECACEAE

Oil Palm; Oliepalm

OTHER LANGUAGES: Nakhlet ez zayt (Arabic); Kelapa sawit (Bahasa Indonesia); Palmier à Huile (French); Ölpalme (German); Maslichnaia pal'ma (Russian); Palma de Aceite (Spanish); Mchikichi (Swahili)

West Africa Small to large, solitary palm; trunk **stout**, covered with old leaf bases for a long time; exposed bark grey, with prominent discontinuous leaf scars. Leaves **pinnate**; petiole with **spines up to 35mm long and about 10mm apart**; rachis flattened above, rounded below; leaflets 2- to several-ranked, **hanging, grouped**, 0.7–1.2m long, 30–80mm wide, strap-shaped, usually single-fold, fold up; tip undivided; surface glossy; old leaflets **becoming spines**. Inflorescences between the leaves, erect to ascending. Flowers small. Fruit pear-shaped, 3-angled, red to black, 30–55 × 20–30mm. Seeds black, about 30mm long.

The fruits are the main source of palm oil and the seeds give palm kernel oil. In addition to the obvious applications in cookery and soap-making, palm oil can be used to make explosives and biodiesel. In some tropical areas, oil palm plantations have caused considerable environmental damage but in our region these trees are apparently only grown as specimens in private and public gardens.

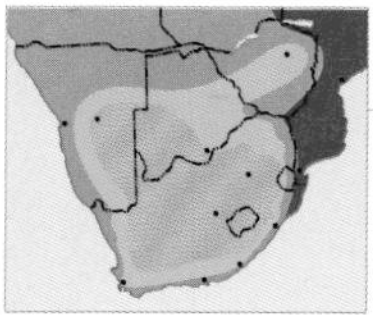

- Drought 2
- Spring
- Evergreen

2 *Howea forsteriana* *(= Kentia belmoreana)* ARECACEAE

Sentry Palm, Thatch Palm; Skildwagpalm

OTHER LANGUAGES: Howea frisé (French); Curly-palme (German)

Lord Howe Island Medium-sized, **solitary, erect** palm; bark green or grey, ringed with prominent leaf scars. Leaves alternate, **pinnate**; petiole unarmed, 1–1.67m long; rachis flattened above, rounded below; leaflets 2-ranked, evenly spaced, hanging, single-fold, 300–600 × 20–40mm; midrib **yellowish**; tip ragged. Inflorescences below the leaves, hanging, like a horse's tail, of 3–8 spikes, 0.7–1.25m long; peduncle 30–50mm long. Flowers small. Fruit dark brown to red, 30–50 × 12–20mm.

Classed as vulnerable in its natural home, this is one of the world's commonest house-plants. In our region it is less often seen outdoors but where it is, it makes a fine avenue plant.

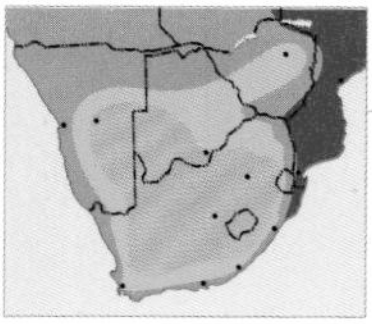

- Drought 2
- Spring
- Evergreen

3 *Hyophorbe lagenicaulis* *(= Mascarena lagenicaulis)* ARECACEAE

Bottle Palm; Bottelpalm

OTHER LANGUAGES: Palmiste Gargoulette (French); Flaschenpalme (German)

Mauritius Small, solitary palm with a **distinctively swollen** trunk; crownshaft green, deeply split; bark green or grey, ringed with prominent leaf scars. Leaves 3-ranked, **pinnate**; petiole unarmed, 100–150mm long; rachis flattened above, rounded below; leaflets 2-ranked, stiff, evenly spaced, single-fold, fold up, 170–600 × 15–43mm, **lance-shaped**; tip not split; surface dull, glabrous. Inflorescences below the leaves, hanging, about 770mm long; peduncle 150–240mm long. Flowers small. Fruit round, orange to black, about 20–25 × 18mm.

Although very rare in nature, this species' survival is assured by its popularity and large numbers of plants in cultivation throughout the tropics and subtropics.

CRAIG, WIKIMEDIA COMMONS, PUBLIC DOMAIN

1 *E. guineensis*

WK1003MIKE / SHUTTERSTOCK.COM

1 *E. guineensis* fruit

1 *E. guineensis* flowers (male)

2 *H. forsteriana*

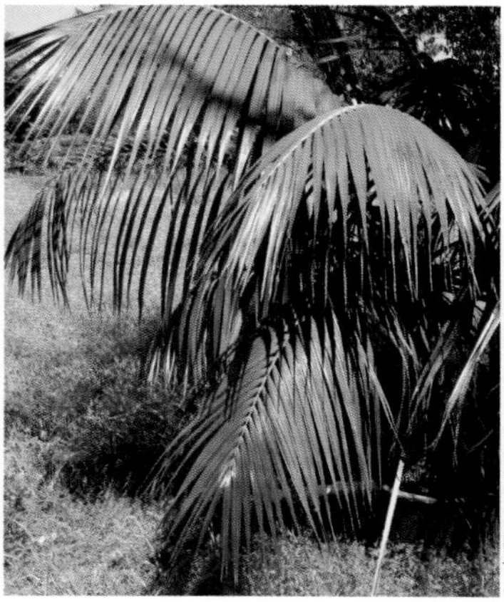

COURTESY OF GRUBB & NADLER, INC

2 *H. forsteriana* leaves

2 *H. forsteriana* fruit

FOREST AND KIM STARR

3 *H. lagenicaulis*

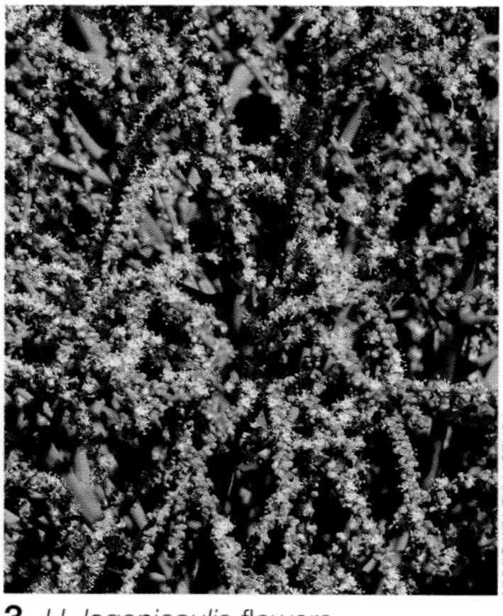

FOREST AND KIM STARR

3 *H. lagenicaulis* flowers

GEOFF NICHOLS

3 *H. lagenicaulis* fruit

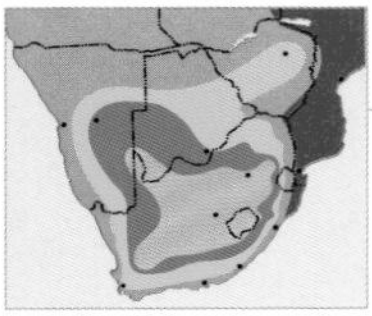

- Drought 2
- Spring
- Evergreen

1 *Livistona chinensis* ARECACEAE

Chinese Fountain Palm, Chinese Fan Palm, Chinese Fringe Palm; Chinese Fonteinpalm

OTHER LANGUAGES: Serdang Cina (Bahasa Indonesia); Pu kui (Chinese); Latanier de Chine (French); Chinesische Fächerpalme (German); Leque-chines, Palmeira-chapariz, Palmeira-ventarola (Portuguese)

Japan, China and Bonin Islands Medium-sized, solitary palm; bark grey, with discontinuous leaf scars; old leaf bases remaining at top of trunk. Leaves **palmate**; petiole 1–1.8m long, with **spines 6–10mm or longer**, 5–15mm apart; rachis flattened above, rounded below; leaflets stiff, evenly spaced, single-fold, **fold up**, 400–900 × 10–15mm, lance-shaped; tip bifid; surface glossy. Inflorescences between the leaves, hanging, 1–1.2m long. Flowers small. Fruit grey-blue, egg- to pear-shaped, 15–25 × 10–20mm.

In our region, grown as a garden ornamental. However, there are records of it becoming naturalised in Zululand, Florida (USA) and the Caribbean.

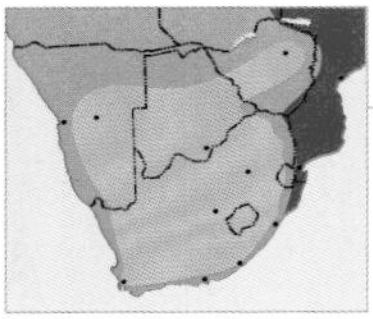

- Drought 2
- Spring
- Evergreen

2 *Musa* × *paradisiaca* MUSACEAE

Banana; Piesang

OTHER LANGUAGES: Moz (Arabic); Pisang (Bahasa Indonesia); Ye jiao (Chinese); Banane (French, German); Kadali (Hindi); Banana (Italian, Portuguese, Spanish); Banan (Russian); Ndizi (Swahili)

India Giant herb achieving the height of a small tree; pseudostems (tightly overlapping leaf bases) cylindrical, **not thickened at base**, dying off after flowering but plant **suckering from base**. Leaves **simple** (not compound), often torn by wind; petiole large, vertical; blade up to 2.7m long, 600mm wide; tip rounded or hooded; base rounded or squared; midrib **green**. Inflorescences growing up through centre of pseudostem, then hanging. Flowers hidden by showy, purple bracts. Fruit up to 300mm long, almost cylindrical, curved or straight, yellow but usually picked green, fleshy, **seedless**.

The taxonomy and nomenclature of the edible banana are complex and the name used here may well be no more than a convenient 'catchall' hiding a very difficult group. The bananas grown commercially in our area are of the eating cultivar 'Dwarf Cavendish' though cooking-banana cultivars, sometimes called 'plantains', are known to be grown in private gardens.

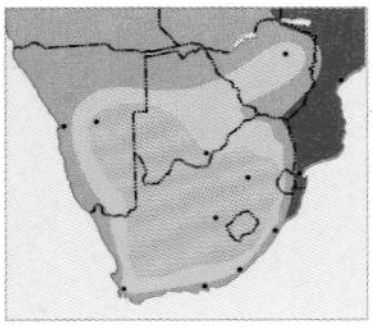

- Drought 1
- Summer
- Evergreen

3 *Pandanus utilis* PANDANACEAE

Common Screw-pine; Gewone Skroefpalm

OTHER LANGUAGES: Vacoa (French); Biyou tako no ki (Japanese); Pandano (Spanish)

Madagascar, Mauritius and Seychelles Small tree with a **strongly pyramidal** crown and **prominent stilt-roots**; bark grey, horizontally ridged with old leaf scars. Leaves in a **3-ranked spiral**, without petiole, 0.5–2m long, 60–100mm wide, strap-shaped, channelled, stiff or with tip hanging; tip pointed; surface glossy green; lower midrib **spiny**; margin with **reddish spines**. Flowers with males and females on different trees, males ephemeral, fragrant, females long-stalked, hanging. Fruit a ball of individual woody fruits, 150–200mm in diameter.

There are about 600 species of *Pandanus* in the Indopacific region. All are so similar as to be almost indistinguishable without considerable effort. The leaves of our species are used in making products such as ropes, mats, hats and thatching; fruits are reportedly edible after cooking. Quite commonly grown in warm coastal areas from Mozambique to the Eastern Cape in South Africa.

1 *L. chinensis*

EVA KRÖCHER, WIKIMEDIA COMMONS, GFDL 1.2

1 *L. chinensis* flowers

FOREST AND KIM STARR

1 *L. chinensis* fruit

2 *M.* × *paradisiaca*

2 *M.* × *paradisiaca* flowers

2 *M.* × *paradisiaca* fruit

3 *P. utilis*

B. NAVEZ, WIKIMEDIA COMMONS, CC BY SA 3.0

3 *P. utilis* flowers (male)

JESÚS CABRERA

3 *P. utilis* fruit

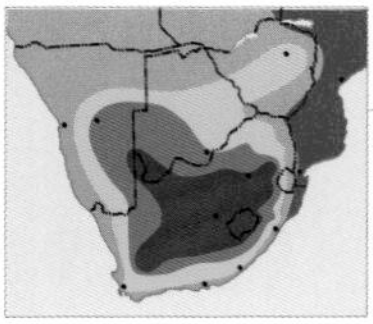

1 *Phoenix canariensis*

ARECACEAE

Canary Date Palm; Kanariese Dadelpalm

OTHER LANGUAGES: Palmier dattier des Canaries (French); Kanarischer Dattelpalme (German)

Canary Islands Medium-sized, solitary, usually straight palm with a **very stout** trunk; bark brown, with prominent leaf scars. Leaves **pinnate**; petiole **unarmed**; rachis flattened above, rounded below; leaflets 2-ranked, stiff, single-fold, **fold down**, 400–500mm long, lowest ones **reduced to sharp prickles**; tip sometimes bifid; surface **glossy, green**. Inflorescences between the leaves, hanging. Flowers small; males and females on separate trees. Fruit fleshy, brown or yellow, about 20 × 10–15mm.

- Drought 2
- Spring
- Evergreen

Provincial tree of the Canary Islands. Very commonly grown as a garden ornamental and street tree. Fruit is edible and tastes like dates but the flesh is so thin that it is hardly worth the effort. The prickles at the base of each leaf are sharp and dangerous and the wounds they cause often become septic. Invasive in New Zealand.

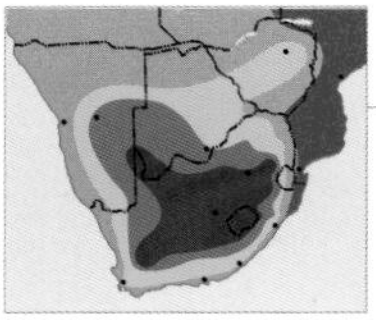

2 *Phoenix dactylifera*

ARECACEAE

Real Date Palm; Egte Dadelboom

OTHER LANGUAGES: Nakhl, Tamar (Arabic); Palmier Dattier (French); Dattelpalme (German); Kajoor (Hindi); Datileiro (Spanish); Mtende (Swahili); Ton inthaphalam (Thai); Hurma (Turkish)

Western Asia and North Africa Medium-sized to tall, solitary, straight palm; trunk **slightly less stout** than in *P. canariensis* (above); bark with prominent leaf scars. Leaves **pinnate**; petiole **unarmed**; leaflets 2-ranked, stiff, evenly spaced, single-fold, fold down, 150–300 × 9–20mm; tip undivided; surface **blue-green, waxy**. Inflorescences between the leaves, **erect to ascending**, hanging in fruit; peduncle up to 600mm long. Flowers small; males and females on separate trees. Fruit pale brown, fleshy, **40–70 × 20–30mm**.

- Drought 2
- Spring
- Evergreen

Archaeological evidence suggests that dates have been grown in Iraq for the last 8,000 years. At present they are grown commercially in the driest parts of the Northern Cape in our region and are occasionally seen as garden ornamentals and street trees in Namibia. The fruits are well known and where craft traditions survive, all parts of the palm have uses. The date palm features in the coat of arms of Saudi Arabia.

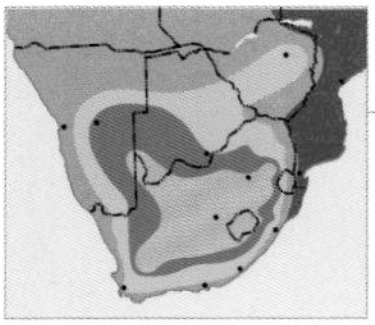

3 *Phoenix roebelenii*

ARECACEAE

Dwarf Date Palm; Dwergdadelboom

OTHER LANGUAGES: Palmier dattier miniature (French); Zwergdattelpalme (German); (Vietnamese)

Laos Small, usually single-stemmed palm; trunk medium-stout, usually erect, upper part **covered in black fibres**; bark brown, grey or black, with prominent leaf scars; old leaf bases **persisting longer than in other species of *Phoenix***. Leaves **pinnate**; petiole unarmed; rachis flattened above, rounded below; leaflets 2-ranked, single-fold, fold down, 200–400 × 7–12mm; tip bifid or not; surface glossy, green; lowest leaflets reduced to spines. Inflorescences between the leaves, hanging, about **300mm long**. Flowers white to creamy; males and females on separate trees. Fruit fleshy, black, 15–18 × 6–7mm.

- Drought 2
- Spring
- Evergreen

Often grown as an ornamental or house-plant in private and public places. The spines at the base of the leaves are very sharp and wounds from them often go septic and need surgery. The fruits are edible but have little flesh.

1 *P. canariensis*

BIDGEE, WIKIMEDIA COMMONS, CC SA BY 3.0

1 *P. canariensis* flowers

WOUTER HAGENS, WIKIMEDIA COMMONS, PUBLIC DOMAIN

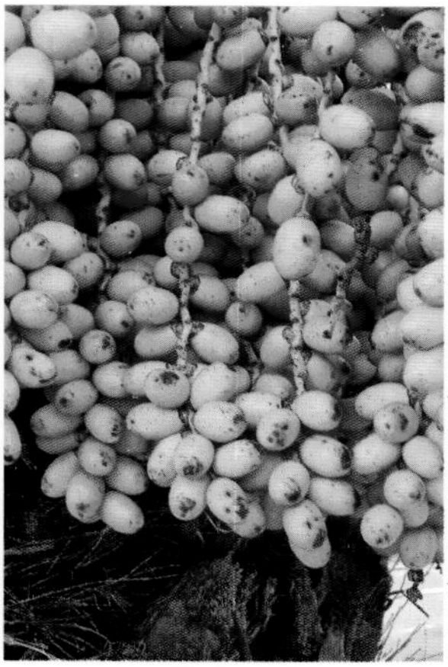

1 *P. canariensis* fruit

FRANK VINCENTZ, WIKIMEDIA COMMONS, GDFL 1.2

2 *P. dactylifera*

PAL MEIR / FLICKR

2 *P. dactylifera* leaves and fruit

B SIMPSON, WIKIMEDIA COMMONS, CC BY SA 3.0

3 *P. roebelenii*

FOREST AND KIM STARR

3 *P. roebelenii* flowers

MMCKNIGHT, WIKIMEDIA COMMONS, PUBLIC DOMAIN

3 *P. roebelenii* fruit

FOREST AND KIM STARR

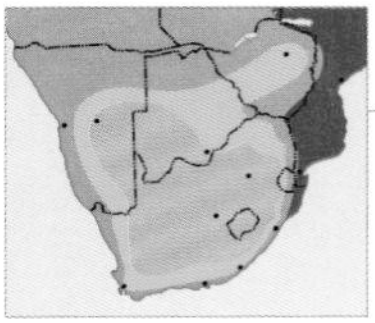

- Drought 2
- Spring
- Evergreen

1 *Pinanga coronata*

ARECACEAE

Ivory Cane Palm; Ivoorbamboespalm

OTHER LANGUAGES: Pinang (Bahasa Indonesia)

Sulawesi Small to medium-sized, clustering palm; trunk **slender**, erect; bark green, ringed with prominent leaf scars; crownshaft green, yellow or brown. Leaves **pinnate**; petiole unarmed; rachis flattened above, rounded below; leaflets 2-ranked, stiff, evenly spaced, with **5–7 folds each**, central fold up, up to 450 × 90mm, lance-shaped; tip undivided. Inflorescences below the leaves, hanging. Flowers small. Fruit black on red stalks, 10–14 × 7–8mm.

Grown in our region as an ornamental in public and private collections.

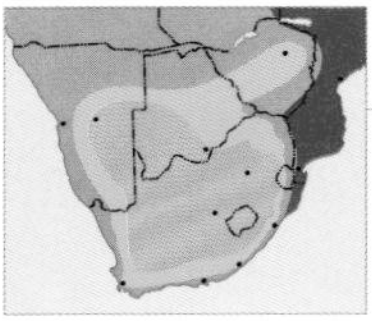

- Drought 2
- Spring
- Evergreen

2 *Ptychosperma elegans*

ARECACEAE

Solitaire Palm; Solitêrpalm

OTHER LANGUAGES: Solitairepalme (German)

Australia Medium-sized, solitary palm; trunk erect, 75–100mm in diameter; **crownshaft deeply split**, grey or greenish; bark grey, ringed with prominent leaf scars. Leaves **pinnate**; petiole unarmed, 200–300mm long; rachis channelled above, rounded below; leaflets **several-ranked, drooping, grouped**, single-fold, fold up, 540–940 × 45–80mm, narrowly lance-shaped; tip ragged; surface glossy. Inflorescences below the leaves, drooping, 600–900mm long; peduncle about 70mm long. Flowers small. Fruit 6-angled, egg-shaped, red, 8–15 × 7–10mm.

Grown in our region as an ornamental in public and private collections.

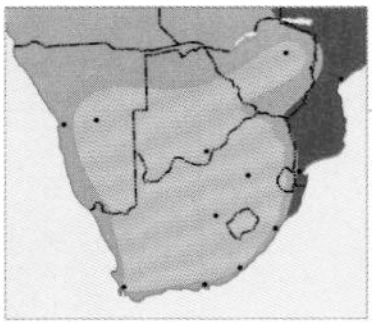

- Drought 2
- Spring
- Evergreen

3 *Ptychosperma lineare*

ARECACEAE

Black-fruit Cluster Palm; Swartvrug-trospalm

Papua New Guinea Medium-sized, erect, **clustering** palm with a slender trunk; bark green, ringed with leaf scars. Leaves **pinnate**; petiole unarmed; rachis flattened above, rounded below; leaflets 2-ranked, stiff, 110–530 × 25–30mm, strap-shaped; tips **ragged**; surface glossy. Inflorescences below the leaves, horizontal or drooping, 440–800mm long; peduncle 35–60mm long. Flowers small. Fruit purple or black, egg-shaped, 11–15 × 7–8mm.

Grown in our region as an ornamental in public and private collections.

PAUL CRAFT

1 *P. coronata*

KENPEI, WIKIMEDIA COMMONS,GFDL 1.2, CC BY SA 3.0

1 *P. coronata* flowers

1 *P. coronata* fruit

2 *P. elegans*

SCOTT ZONA

2 *P. elegans* flowers

FOREST AND KIM STARR

2 *P. elegans* fruit

3 *P. lineare*

3 *P. lineare* flowers

PAUL CRAFT

3 *P. lineare* fruit

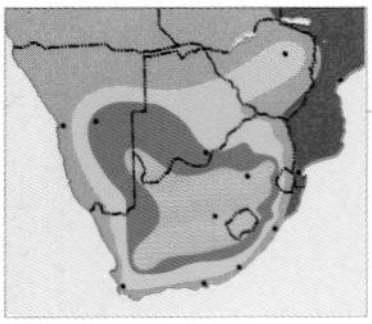

- Drought 2
- Spring
- Evergreen

1 *Ravenala madagascariensis* STRELITZIACEAE

Traveller's Tree; Waaierpiesang

OTHER LANGUAGES: Arbre du Voyageur (French); Baum der Reisenden (German); Árbol del Viajero (Spanish)

Madagascar Medium-sized to large tree with a single trunk; bark grey, fissured, only seen in large specimens. Leaves in **a fan** in one plane; petiole **up to 3m** long; blade oblong, **up to 3 × 1m**, often torn by wind; tip bluntly pointed; base squared; surface glossy green. Inflorescences erect, of **4–10 green, *Strelitzia*-like spathes** each arising from within the one below, facing in the opposite direction to its neighbours. Flowers creamy white, 220–260mm long. Fruit a pale brown, woody capsule. Seeds black, kidney-shaped, 10–12 × 7–8mm, with a **tuft of blue hairs (aril)**.

Highly iconic of Madagascar, featured in the national emblem and the Air Madagascar logo. Intermittently available from nurseries in the warmer, moister parts of our region, this slow-growing plant is seen as a spectacular ornamental in larger gardens. The fan of leaves is said to orientate itself approximately north-south.

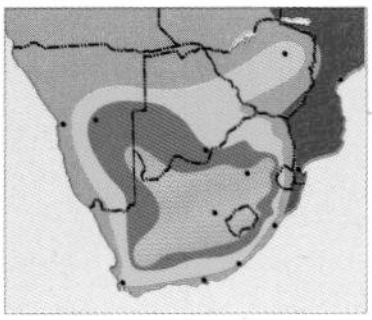

- Drought 2
- Spring
- Evergreen

2 *Rhapis excelsa* ARECACEAE

Japanese Peace Palm, Large Lady Palm; Japanese Vredespalm

OTHER LANGUAGES: Zong zhu (Chinese); Palmier éventail (French); Steckenpalme (German); Gwan eum jook (Korean)

Southern China Small to very small, **clustered** palm with erect stems **resembling bamboo**; trunk green, ringed with leaf scars. Leaves **palmate**; petiole unarmed, about 200mm long; rachis flattened above, rounded below; leaflets in a single plane, stiff, with 5 folds each, 250–350 × 40–80mm; tip ragged; surface glossy. Inflorescences between the leaves, **horizontal**. Flowers small; males and females often on different trees. Fruit yellow, egg- to pear-shaped, up to 10 × 6–8mm.

One of the few palms that is easier to propagate by suckers than by seed. Grown for ornament in public and private gardens; makes a good hedge or screen in a tropical or subtropical area.

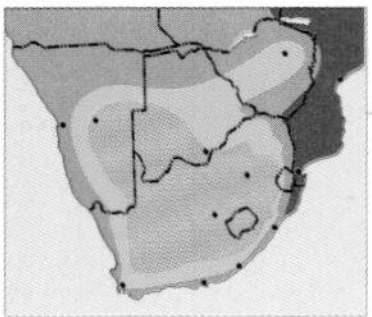

- Drought 2
- Spring
- Evergreen

3 *Roystonea regia* *(= Oreodoxa regia, R. elata, R. ventricosa)* ARECACEAE

Cuban Royal Palm; Kubaanse Rojaalpalm

OTHER LANGUAGES: Nakhl rokhan, nakhl melouki (Arabic); Palmier royal de Cuba (French); Palmeira Real (Portuguese); Palma Real (Spanish)

Cuba and Honduras to Florida, USA Medium-sized to tall, solitary palm; trunk erect, **swollen at the top**; **crownshaft obscured by hanging leaves**; bark grey, almost smooth. Leaves **pinnate, ascending to drooping**; petiole unarmed, 60–600mm long; rachis flattened above, rounded below; leaflets **several-ranked**, stiff and drooping, evenly spaced, single-fold, fold up, 400–900 × 10–30mm; surface glossy. Inflorescences below the leaves, drooping, up to 1m long. Flowers small. Fruit round to egg-shaped, red or orange, 8–13 × 8–10mm.

National tree of Cuba. A classic avenue tree and found in large numbers throughout the tropics. The leaves are used for thatch and the wood for construction. Medicinal uses are recorded.

1 *R. madagascariensis*

1 *R. madagascariensis* flowers

1 *R. madagascariensis* fruit

2 *R. excelsa*

2 *R. excelsa* flowers

2 *R. excelsa* fruit

3 *R. regia*

3 *R. regia* flowers and young fruit

3 *R. regia* fruit

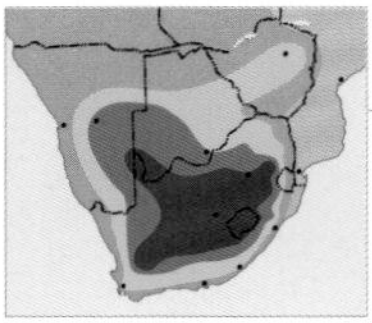

- Drought 1
- Summer
- Evergreen

1 *Sabal palmetto* ARECACEAE

Common Palmetto, Blue Palmetto; Gewone Palmetto

OTHER LANGUAGES: Chou palmiste (French); Palmettopalme (German); Sabal de Carolina (Spanish)

USA and the Caribbean Robust, small to medium-sized palm; trunk erect; old leaf bases **soon falling**; bark ringed with prominent leaf scars. Leaves **palmate**; petiole unarmed, **extending into the lamina as a well-defined 'axis' or costa (costapalmate)**; leaflets single-fold, glossy, **500–800** × 30–40mm; tips **bifid**. Inflorescences between the leaves, more or less erect. Flowers small. Fruit black, egg-shaped, **8–12** × 9–12mm.

In our region, grown in enthusiasts' collections and as specimen tree in a few botanical gardens. In other regions it is noted for its resistance to salt and cold. The palm heart is edible but extracting it kills the tree.

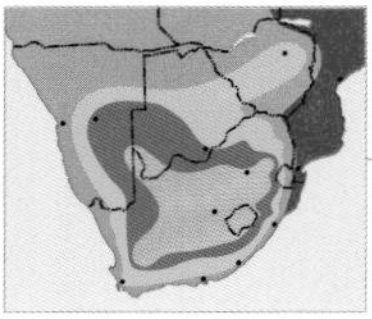

- Drought 2
- Spring
- Evergreen

2 *Syagrus romanzoffiana* (= *Arecastrum romanzoffianum, Cocos plumosa, C. romanzoffiana*) ARECACEAE

Queen Palm; Koninginpalm

OTHER LANGUAGES: Brejauba, Coco de Sapo, Pindo (Portuguese); Pindo de Misiones, Palma del Monte (Spanish)

Brazil to Argentina Small to medium-sized solitary palm with an erect trunk, top **clad with boat-shaped bases of old leaves**; bark grey, faintly ringed with leaf scars. Leaves **pinnate**; petiole unarmed, about 1m long; rachis flattened above, rounded below; leaflets **several-ranked, grouped, drooping**, single-fold, 400–840 × 30–40mm; tip bifid; surface glossy. Inflorescences between the leaves, drooping, 1–2m long. Flowers small. Fruit yellow to orange, egg-shaped, 22–28 × 18–19mm.

A commonly grown ornamental, which has become invasive in Queensland (Australia) and Florida (USA).

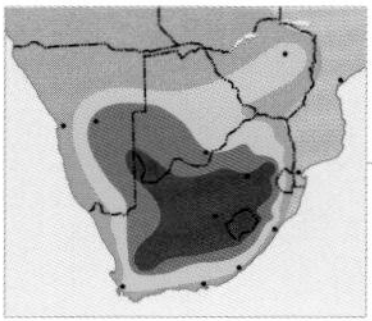

- Drought 2
- Spring
- Evergreen

3 *Trachycarpus fortunei* ARECACEAE

Chinese Windmill Palm, Chusan Palm, Hemp Palm, Windmill Palm; Egte Houtpalm, Houtpalm

OTHER LANGUAGES: Zong lü (Chinese); Palmier de Chusan (French); Echte Hanfpalme (German); Cânhamo de China (Portuguese); Palma de jardín (Spanish)

Myanmar and China Small to medium-sized, solitary palm; trunk erect, clad with **dark grey to black fibres**; bark grey, with prominent leaf scars. Leaves **palmate**; petiole **spiny**, up to 600mm long; rachis flattened above, rounded below; leaflets evenly spaced, usually stiff, single-fold, fold up, 0.5–1.2m long, about 30mm wide; surface glossy above, **almost silvery below**. Inflorescences between the leaves, erect to ascending, 700–900mm long. Flowers small; males and females on different trees. Fruit black, kidney-shaped, up to 9 × 14mm.

Because of its frost tolerance, greater than that of all other commonly grown palms, this is a popular ornamental in cold places. The fibre around the trunk can be woven into coarse, strong cloth or spun into rope. Medicinal uses are recorded.

FOREST AND KIM STARR

1 *S. palmetto*

1 *S. palmetto* leaves

MMCKNIGHT4, PUBLIC DOMAIN

1 *S. palmetto* flowers

1 *S. palmetto* fruit

MAURO HALPERN

2 *S. romanzoffiana*

JOÃS MEDEIROS, WIKIMEDIA COMMONS, CC BY SA 2.0

2 *S. romanzoffiana* flowers

MAURO HALPERN

2 *S. romanzoffiana* fruit

3 *T. fortunei*

3 *T. fortunei* flowers

ISTOCKPHOTO.COM / GARYSFRP

3 *T. fortunei* fruit

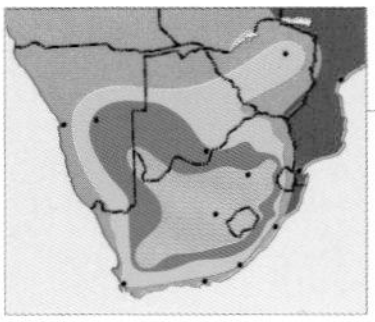

1 *Trevesia palmata* ARALIACEAE

Snowflake Aralia; Sneeuvlok-aralia

- Drought 2
- Spring
- Evergreen

OTHER LANGUAGES: Citongcao (Chinese)

India to southern China and Indochina Small tree with a vase-shaped crown, or a single tuft of leaves in young trees; bark whitish, smooth, with **scattered triangular prickles**; twigs hairy. Leaves alternate; petiole hairless, **prickly**, 300–900mm long; blade **600–900mm long, overall 600–900mm wide**, round in outline, young leaves deeply palmately 5–9-lobed, **in older trees palmately compound with a shallowly-lobed basal 'frill' surrounding the top of the petiole**; tip pointed; base heart-shaped, base of leaflets rounded; upper surface glossy; margin **variously toothed and indented**. Stipules attached to petiole. Inflorescences, erect, complex, up to 450mm long; peduncle 40–170mm long. Flowers white, small. Fruit fleshy, egg-shaped, 10–18mm in diameter.

An ornamental grown in our region as a specimen tree in botanical gardens and very few private collections. The intricately palmately lobed leaves resemble a snowflake under magnification, hence the common names.

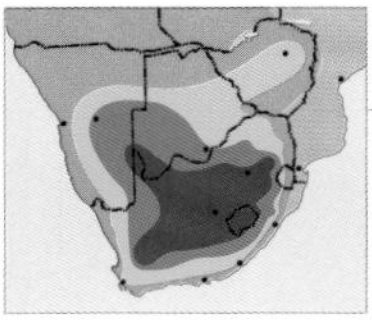

2 *Washingtonia filifera* ARECACEAE

Cotton Palm, Desert Fan Palm, Petticoat Palm; Katoenpalm

- Drought 2
- Spring
- Evergreen

OTHER LANGUAGES: Palmier évantail de Californie (French)

Southwestern USA and Mexico (Baja California) Medium-sized to tall palm with **a 'petticoat' of dead leaves** at the top of the single trunk **over 1m in diameter**. Leaves **palmate**; petiole hairless, up to 2m long, with **toothed** margins; blade 1.5–2.0m long, strap-shaped; tip split, each half very narrowly pointed; margins apparently splitting off long, pale brown fibres. Inflorescences hanging between the leaves. Flowers white, inconspicuous. Fruit fleshy, dark brown, egg-shaped, about 8–13 × 6mm.

The trunk of this palm is significantly thicker than that of *W. robusta* (1–1.5m as opposed to 800mm in diameter). Widespread cultivation of both species has led to a significant southward range expansion of the African Palm-swift *(Cypsiurus parvus)* in South Africa. These birds use the skirt of hanging dead leaves as roosts and also as nesting sites. For this reason it is advisable not to remove the dead leaves as is the usual practice in other cultivated palms.

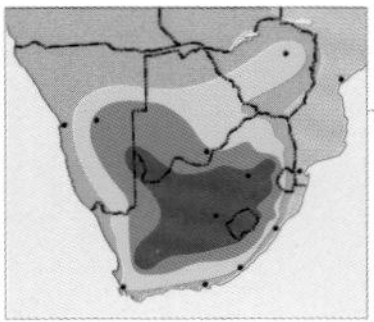

3 *Yucca gloriosa* ASPARAGACEAE

Spanish Dagger, Palm Lily; Spaanse Dolk

- Drought 2
- Spring
- Evergreen

Southeastern USA Small tree; trunks **unbranched, forming clumps at ground level**. Leaves **without petiole**; blade 0.4–1.0m long, 35–60mm wide, lance-shaped with a sharp, pointed tip and **smooth** margins. Inflorescences erect, 1.4–2.7m long; peduncle 0.9–1.5m long. Flowers 40–50mm **long**, white or creamy, without markings, **hanging** on pedicels up to 20mm long. Fruit dry, 6-angled, not springing open, 25–80mm long.

Spanish dagger is sporadically seen in private and public gardens and is known from localities as widely scattered as Cape Town, Port Edward and Bloemfontein (and doubtless elsewhere). The Spanish bayonet, *Y. aloifolia*, is almost as commonly seen. That species has branched trunks and leaves that sometimes have toothed margins. The flowers are not known to set fruit in our region because of the absence of the '*Yucca* moths', the obligate pollinators of the *Yucca* plants.

VOJTECH ZAVADIL

1 *T. palmata* young leaf

STICKPEN, WIKIMEDIA COMMONS, PUBLIC DOMAIN

1 *T. palmata* fruit

2 *W. filifera* young trees

FLORIAN BOYD, WIKIMEDIA COMMONS, CC BY SA 3.0

2 *W. filifera* older trees

FOREST AND KIM STARR

2 *W. filifera* flowers

3 *Y. gloriosa*

3 *Y. gloriosa* leaves

3 *Y. gloriosa* flowers

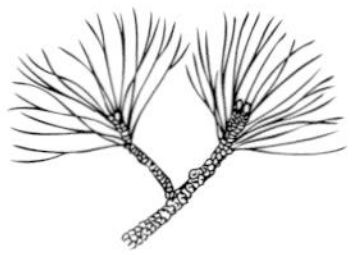

GROUP 3

Cedar group

Leaves very small, scale- or needle-like.

See also Group 10: *Melaleuca armillaris* (p.228) and *M. ericifolia* (p.228); Group 22: *M. cuticularis* (p.296) and *M. decora* (p.296); Group 23: *Buxus sempervirens* (p.310).

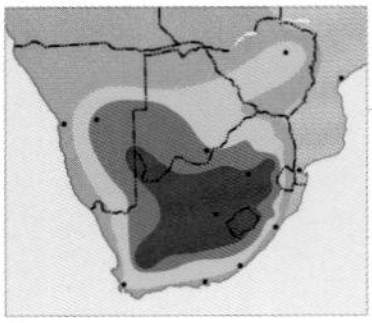

- Drought 2
- Autumn
- Evergreen

1 *Allocasuarina torulosa* (= *Casuarina torulosa*)

CASUARINACEAE

Forest Oak, Rose Sheoak; Bosperdestertboom

Eastern Australia Small to large tree with an irregularly pyramidal to rounded crown; bark brown, deeply fissured, forming broad ridges; twigs hairless, slender, green, **square when young**. Leaves whorled, minute, triangular, appearing as rings of **4 or 5 whitish teeth** on the green twigs. Inflorescences with males and females on different trees, males 5–30mm long, erect or flexible, narrow, females 15–33 × **12–25mm**; peduncles 8–30mm long. Seeds **mid- to dark brown**, 7–10mm long.

Timber is valued in Australia for making small items such as turnings or knife handles but because of severe shrinkage it is very difficult to dry and obtain a useful piece of wood. Grown in our region as specimen trees in botanical gardens from the Western Cape to KwaZulu-Natal.

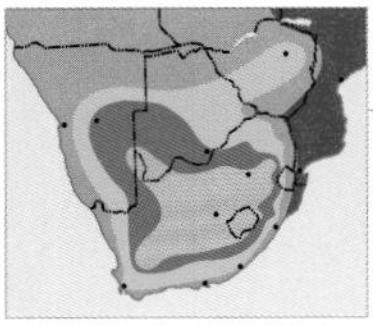

- Drought 2
- Spring
- Evergreen

2 *Araucaria columnaris* (= *A. cookii*)

ARAUCARIACEAE

New Caledonian Pine, Captain Cook's Pine; Nieu-Caledoniese Den

New Caledonia Tall tree with a **narrowly columnar** crown and a **distinct kink in the trunk** near the base; bark grey-brown, **peeling in thin flakes**; twigs hairless. Leaves without petiole; blade 2–6 × 0.8–1.3mm, linear; tip pointed; base squared. Cones with males and females on the same tree, males up to 4 together, 20–70mm long, females solitary, elliptic, about 150 × 110mm, scales with 1 seed each.

New Caledonian pine is a good ornamental for large gardens in warm-temperate to tropical areas and is resistant to the stresses of living on the coast. It is no surprise to see it often in the environs of Durban but it is also recorded from elsewhere in coastal southern and tropical Africa. The wood is very attractively figured and can be used to make beautiful furniture and turned items.

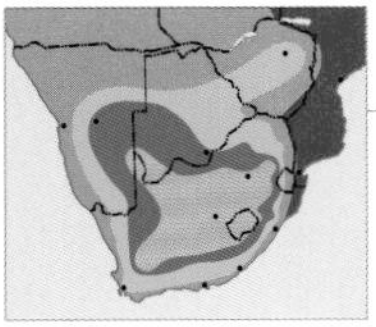

- Drought 2
- Spring
- Evergreen

3 *Araucaria cunninghamii*

ARAUCARIACEAE

Hoop Pine, Moreton Bay Pine; Hoepelden

OTHER LANGUAGES: Nan yang shan (Chinese); Kolonialkiefer (German); Yau (Portuguese)

Australia and New Guinea Tall tree with an **egg-shaped to pyramidal** crown; bark brown, **rough, adhering**; twigs hairless. Leaves without petiole; blade 6–15mm long, **awl-shaped**, incurved; lower (outer) surface **keeled**. Cones with males and females on the same tree, males 1–4 together, not stalked, cylindrical, 20–35 × 5–7mm, females solitary, stalked, egg-shaped, 50–100 × 50–70mm, with many scales, each bearing 1 seed.

Planted in scattered localities in our region for ornament and for timber, which is of high quality, being used for plywood, furniture, boat-building and more.

1 *A. torulosa* stems

1 *A. torulosa* flowers (male)

1 *A. torulosa* fruit

2 *A. columnaris*

2 *A. columnaris* cones (male)

2 *A. columnaris* cone (female)

3 *A. cunninghamii* cone (male)

3 *A. cunninghamii* cones (female)

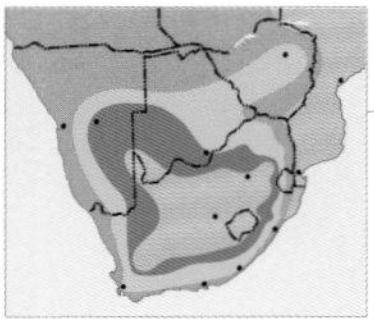

- Drought 2
- Spring
- Evergreen

1 *Araucaria heterophylla* (= *A. excelsa*) ARAUCARIACEAE
Norfolk Island Pine; Norfolkeiland-den

Norfolk Island, Australia Tall tree with a pyramidal to columnar crown, whorls of branches **well spaced**; bark grey, peeling in **small flakes**; twigs hairless. Leaves without petiole; blade awl-shaped, at an angle to twig, 6–12mm long **in juveniles**, egg-shaped to triangular, clasping the twig, 5–9 × 3–6mm in **adults**. Cones with males and females on the same or different trees, solitary, males cylindrical, 40–50 × 10–13mm, females elliptic, 80–120 × 70–110mm, with many scales, 35–40mm long. Seeds elliptic, 25–30 × 13–15mm.

Usually planted for ornament but the wood is used for turned items and can be made into plywood. Probably the most often grown species of the genus in our area, where it is widespread. CAUTION: All araucarias shed their female cones whole. These cones are spiky, fall from a considerable height and can weigh up to 20kg.

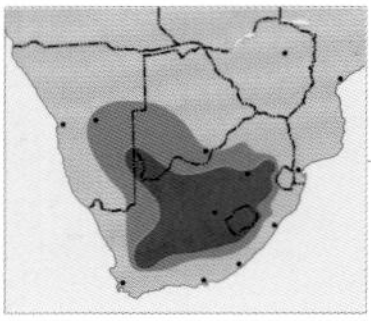

- Drought 2
- Spring
- Evergreen

2 *Calocedrus decurrens* (= *Heyderia decurrens, Libocedrus decurrens, Thuja gigantea*) CUPRESSACEAE
Incense-cedar; Wierookseder

OTHER LANGUAGES: Arbre de la Vida (Catalan); Kalifornische Flusszeder (German); Cedro-de-incenso (Portuguese); Cedro de incienso (Spanish)

Western USA Tall tree with a very narrow, **conical** crown; bark brown, deeply fissured, fibrous, forming ridges; twigs hairless, **flattened**, striped, green. Leaves **opposite or whorled**; blade 3–14mm long, **triangular to awl-shaped**; tip pointed and spine-tipped; surface glossy; margin smooth. Cones with males and females on the same tree, males cylindrical, 6–8mm long, females oblong to egg-shaped, 20–35 × 6–8mm, with 6 scales, each bearing 2 seeds. Seeds buff, 14–25mm long.

The classic tree for making wooden pencils. Grown in our region as a specimen tree in public and private collections. Recorded from Gauteng, the Free State, Western and Eastern Cape.

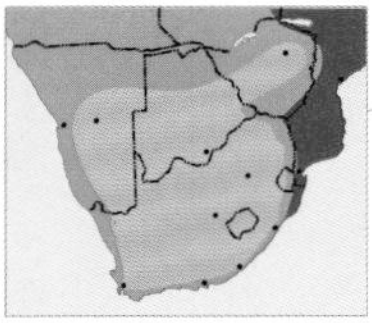

- Drought 2
- Spring
- Evergreen

3 *Casuarina equisetifolia* CASUARINACEAE
Horsetail Tree, Coastal Beefwood, Shingle Tree; Perdestertboom

OTHER LANGUAGES: Filao (French, Creole)

Australia and Southeast Asia Medium-sized to tall tree with a pyramidal to rounded crown; bark brown or grey to black, narrowly fissured, forming small ridges; twigs **hairy**, slender, dull, green, with **sharp ridges**. Leaves whorled, minute, triangular, appearing as rings of 7 or 8 whitish teeth on the twigs. Inflorescences with males and females on the same tree, males erect or flexible, narrow, 7–40mm long, females erect, cone-like, 10–24 × **9–13mm**; peduncle 3–12mm long. Seeds **6–8mm long**.

Invasive in Japan, Réunion, the USA, the Caribbean, Brazil, Polynesia and South Africa, where it is a declared Category 2 invader. Grown as a sand binder, street tree or bonsai. The wood is used for roof shingles, firewood and other purposes.

1 *A. heterophylla* leaves

TAMARA KULIKOVA / SHUTTERSTOCK.COM

1 *A. heterophylla* cone (female)

2 *C. decurrens* cones (male)

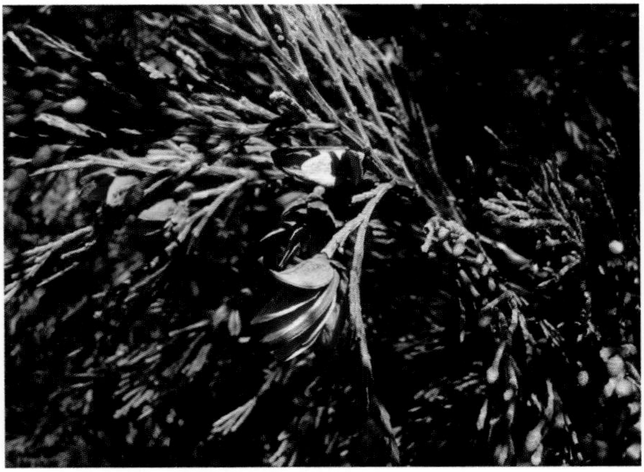

2 *C. decurrens* cones (female)

FOREST AND KIM STARR

3 *C. equisetifolia* stems

B. NAVEZ, WIKIMEDIA COMMONS, CC BY SA 3.0

3 *C. equisetifolia* flowers (male)

ATAMARI, WIKIMEDIA COMMONS, CC BY SA 3.0

3 *C. equisetifolia* inflorescences (female)

GROUP 3 Cedar group

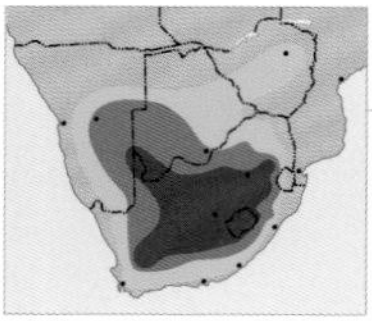

1 ***Cedrus atlantica*** *(= C. africana)* PINACEAE

Atlas Cedar, Atlantic Cedar; Atlasseder

- Drought 2
- Spring
- Evergreen

OTHER LANGUAGES: Al arz alatalsi (Arabic); Atlas-Zeder (German); Cedro del Atlas (Spanish)

North Africa Tall to very large tree with a pyramidal to rounded crown, leader drooping in old specimens; bark grey, deeply fissured and rough, forming broad ridges; twigs **hairy**. Leaves in tufts, needle-like, about 10–30 × 1mm, **blue-green**; tip **pointed but not sharp**; margin smooth. Cones with males and females separate but on the same tree, males 30–50 × 10–15mm, females cylindrical, 50–80 × **30–50mm**, with many scales, each bearing 2 seeds. Seeds about 12mm long.

An essential oil distilled from the wood is used in perfumery and as an insect repellent. The timber is aromatic and prized for use in joinery and veneer. Grown as an ornamental in parks and large gardens; a magnificent specimen is to be seen at Harold Pearson's grave in Kirstenbosch, Cape Town. Also recorded from the Eastern Cape and Gauteng in South Africa and from Zimbabwe.

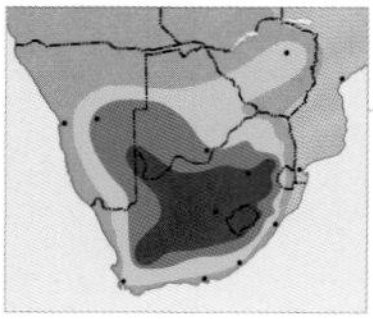

2 ***Cedrus deodara*** *(= C. indica)* PINACEAE

Deodar, Himalayan Cedar, Indian Cedar; Deodaar, Heilige Seder

- Drought 2
- All year
- Evergreen

OTHER LANGUAGES: Sanawbar hindi (Arabic); Xue song (Chinese); Himalaya-Zeder (German); Devdar (Hindi, Sanskrit); Cedro del Himalaya (Spanish)

Himalayas Medium-sized to very large tree with a **pyramidal, later rounded** crown, leader drooping in old specimens; bark grey, narrowly fissured; twigs **hairless**. Leaves alternate or in tufts, needle-like, 25–50 × 1–1.5mm, **blue-green**; tip drawn out and **spine-tipped**; margin smooth. Cones with males and females separate but on the same tree, males cylindrical, 40–60mm long, females conical to elliptic, 70–120 × **50–90mm**, with many scales, each 25–40mm long and bearing 2 seeds. Seeds about 10mm long.

National tree of Pakistan. A common ornamental in our region and one of the most frequently encountered Christmas trees. The wood is aromatic and an essential oil used in perfumery and as an insecticide is extracted from it. It is also used for construction both on land and water (houseboats, for example). Medicinal uses are recorded.

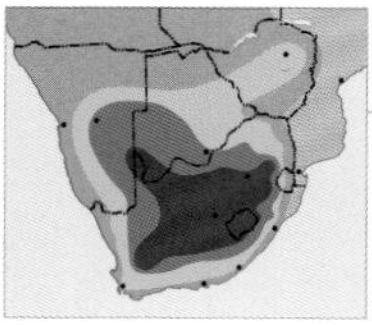

3 ***Chamaecyparis lawsoniana*** *(= Cupressus lawsoniana)* CUPRESSACEAE

Lawson Cypress, Port Orford Cedar; Lawsonsipres

- Drought 2
- Spring
- Evergreen

OTHER LANGUAGES: Lawsons Scheinzypresse (German); Cedro-branco (Portuguese); Ciprés de Lawson (Spanish)

Western USA Medium-sized to very large tree with a **pyramidal** crown; bark reddish brown, smooth or narrowly fissured, peeling; twigs hairless, **flattened**, green. Leaves **opposite**, each pair at right angles to its neighbours; adult leaves triangular, scale-like, about 1mm long, juveniles up to 8mm long; tip **pointed**; surface dull, **silvery below**; margin entire. Cones with males and females on the same tree, males oblong to egg-shaped, females round, 8–10mm in diameter, with **8 scales**, each bearing 2–4 seeds.

Of the several known cultivars of this species, three ('Aurea', with yellowish leaves; 'Pottenii', a semidwarf tree with grey-green leaves; and 'Wisselii', a full-size tree with very blue leaves) are regularly grown in southern Africa. The wood is ginger-scented and favoured in Japan for making arrows, coffins and temples.

1 *C. atlantica* leaves

1 *C. atlantica* cones (male)

1 *C. atlantica* cone (female)

2 *C. deodara*

2 *C. deodara* cones (female)

2 *C. deodara* cones (male)

3 *C. lawsoniana* cones (female)

3 *C. lawsoniana* cones (male)

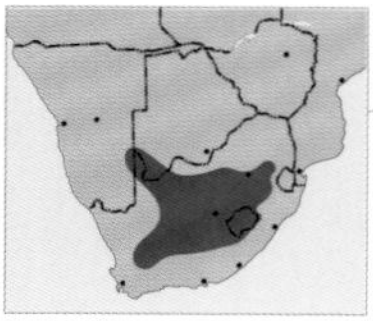

- Drought 2
- Spring
- Evergreen

1 ***Chamaecyparis obtusa*** (= *Cupressus obtusa*) CUPRESSACEAE
Hinoki Cypress; Hinoki-sipres

OTHER LANGUAGES: Ri ben bian bai (Chinese); Hinoki-Scheinzypresse (German)

Japan and Taiwan Large tree with a **pyramidal**, rarely irregular crown; bark reddish brown, narrowly fissured, shredding; twigs hairless, slender, somewhat flattened, green. Leaves opposite, each pair at right angles to its neighbours; adult leaves triangular, scale-like, blade 1–3mm long; tip **rounded**; margin **white, forming X-patterns** on twigs. Cones with males and females on the same tree, males elliptic, about 3mm long, females round, 10–12 × 10–12mm, with **4–6 scales**, each bearing 2–5 seeds. Seeds reddish brown, round to obovoid, 3–3.5 × 3–3.5mm.

Three cultivars ('Aurea', with yellowish leaves; 'Filicoides' and 'Lycopodioides', both with fine leaves) are grown in southern Africa. The wood is lemon-scented, with a straight grain, and is used in Japan for building palaces and temples and for making such things as table-tennis bats and also boxes for measuring quantities of food. In Japan the pollen is a major cause of hay fever.

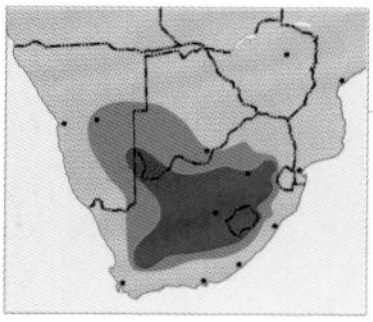

- Drought 2
- Spring
- Evergreen

2 ***Chamaecyparis pisifera*** CUPRESSACEAE
Sawara Cypress; Sawarasipres

OTHER LANGUAGES: Ri ben hua bai (Chinese); Sawara-Scheinzypresse (German); Sawara (Japanese)

Japan Tall tree with a **pyramidal**, rarely rounded crown; bark reddish brown, smooth or narrowly fissured; twigs hairless, flattened, dull, green. Leaves opposite, of two forms; adults 1mm long, triangular, juveniles 8mm long, awl-shaped; tip pointed, **spine-tipped**; margin smooth, white, **patterns irregular or inconspicuous**. Cones with males and females on the same tree, males egg-shaped to oblong, females round, 5–6mm in diameter, with **10–12 scales**, each bearing 2 seeds.

Sold occasionally as an ornamental in nurseries in our region and recorded from Limpopo, Gauteng and KwaZulu-Natal. In Japan, the pale, lemon-scented wood is prized for constructing temples and palaces and for making coffins.

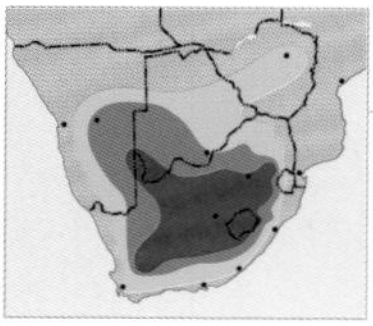

- Drought 2
- Spring
- Evergreen

3 ***Cryptomeria japonica*** CUPRESSACEAE
Japanese Cedar, Japanese Red Cedar; Japanse Seder

OTHER LANGUAGES: Ri ben liu shan (Chinese); Japanische Sicheltanne (German); Sugi (Japanese); Cedro-japonés (Portuguese); Cedro rojo japonés (Spanish)

China and Japan Medium-sized to tall tree with a narrowly **pyramidal or columnar** crown and bronze colour if cold enough; bark reddish brown, fibrous, shredding in long narrow strips; twigs hairless, glossy, green. Leaves **alternate**, without petiole; blade 4–20 × 0.8–1.2mm, **awl-shaped**; tip pointed to rounded; surface glossy; margin smooth. Cones in hanging sprays or clusters; males and females on the same tree, males 6–35 together, cylindrical to oblong, 2–8 × 1.3–4mm, females 1–6 together, conical to elliptic, 10–25 × 10–25mm, with 20–30 scales each, surface **irregularly warty**, scales with 2–6 seeds each. Seeds mid- to dark brown, 4–6.5 × 2–3.5mm.

National tree of Japan but sugi pollen is a major cause of hay fever there. Often grown in our region for shelter or to demarcate property boundaries. Twigs can be burned as incense. The wood is aromatic, very resistant to rot, easy to work and so has many uses. Medicinal uses are recorded.

1 *C. obtusa* leaves

1 *C. obtusa* cones (female)

2 *C. pisifera* leaves

2 *C. pisifera* leaves and cones (female)

3 *C. japonica* cones (male)

3 *C. japonica* cones (female)

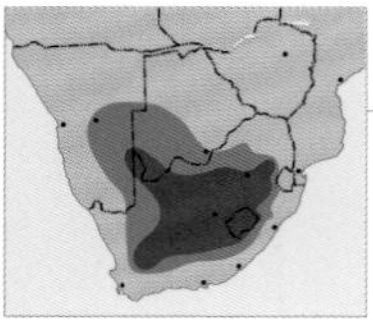

- Drought 2
- Spring
- Evergreen

1 *Cunninghamia lanceolata* CUPRESSACEAE

Chinese Fir; Chinese Den

OTHER LANGUAGES: Shan mu (Chinese); Chinesische Spiesstanne (German); Sa moc (Vietnamese)

China Tall to very tall tree with a **conical** crown; branches **horizontal, layered**; bark brown to grey, deeply fissured, flaking irregularly; twigs hairless. Leaves **alternate**, without petiole; blade 8–65 × 1.5–5mm, very narrowly triangular; tip **pointed**, sometimes with a soft spine; surface glossy above, dull below; margin smooth. Cones with males and females on the same tree, hanging, males many together, elliptic, 10–12 × 10–12mm, on peduncles 2–4mm long, females stalkless, round to ovoid, 12–45 × 8–40mm, scales many, 10–15mm long, with 3 seeds each. Seeds dark brown, about 5–6 × 4mm.

In autumn, whole branches turn bronze and are shed. The wood is aromatic and prized for construction in China. Grown as an ornamental in public and private gardens in many parts of our region but not commonly. Medicinal uses are recorded.

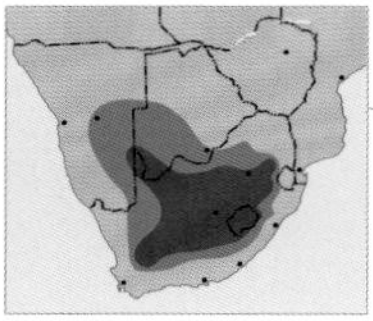

- Drought 2
- All year
- Evergreen

2 *Cupressus arizonica* (= *C. glabra*) CUPRESSACEAE

Arizona Cypress, Blue Cypress; Arizonasipres, Blousipres

OTHER LANGUAGES: Xiprer blau (Catalan); Arizona-Zypresse (German); Cipreste-do-Arizona (Portuguese); Ciprés de Arizona (Spanish)

Southwestern USA and adjacent Mexico Tall tree with a **conical or oval-conical** crown; bark grey to brown, smooth, forming **long shreds**; twigs hairless. Leaves **opposite**, each pair at right angles to its neighbours, without petiole; blade 1–2mm long, triangular; tip pointed; surface **blue-grey**. Cones with males and females on the same tree, males elliptic, about 2–5 × 2mm, females **elliptic**, 20–30 × **20–25mm**, usually with 6 scales, each bearing 6–20 seeds. Seeds buff to dark brown, 4–6mm long.

Widely grown as an ornamental in our region and elsewhere. The cones open to release seeds only after fire. Uses of the wood include construction and fuel.

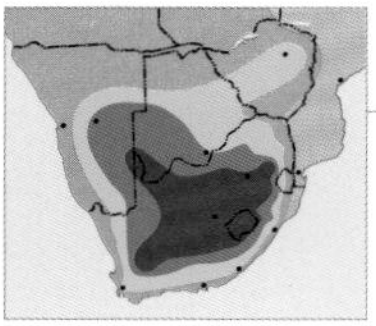

- Drought 2
- All year
- Evergreen

3 *Cupressus funebris* (= *Chamaecyparis funebris*) CUPRESSACEAE

Weeping Cypress, Mourning Cypress; Treursipres

OTHER LANGUAGES: Sarû mustahh (Arabic); Xiprer Fúnebre (Catalan); Bai mu (Chinese); Trauer-Zypresse (German); Ciprés llorón (Spanish)

China Large tree, crown usually **conical**, sometimes spreading; bark grey, with narrow fissures; twigs **drooping**. Leaves **opposite**, each pair at right angles to its neighbours, without petiole; adult leaves triangular, 1mm long, juveniles awl-shaped, up to 8mm long; tip pointed; surface **green**. Cones with males and females on the same tree, males elliptic, 2.5–5mm long, females round, **8–15mm in diameter**, scales 6–8, with **3–5 seeds** each; peduncle 3–6mm long. Seeds buff, 2.5–3.5mm long.

Grown in several parts of our region and beyond as a specimen tree in public and private gardens. The wood is used for construction and medicinal uses are recorded.

1 *C. lanceolata* leaves

1 *C. lanceolata* cones (male)

1 *C. lanceolata* cone (female)

2 *C. arizonica* leaves

2 *C. arizonica* cones (male)

2 *C. arizonica* cone (female)

3 *C. funebris* leaves and cones (male)

3 *C. funebris* cone (female)

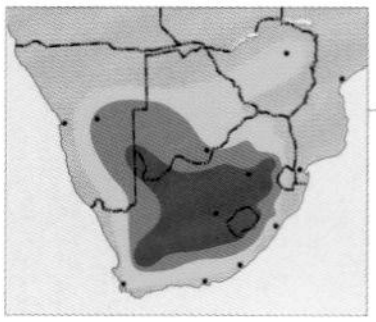

- Drought 2
- All year
- Evergreen

1 *Cupressus macrocarpa* CUPRESSACEAE

Monterey Cypress, Black Cypress, Macrocarpa; Swartsipres

OTHER LANGUAGES: Xiprer de Califòrnia (Catalan); Monterey-Zypresse (German); Cipreste-de-Monterey (Portuguese); Ciprés de Monterrey (Spanish)

California Medium-sized to large tree with a pyramidal to spreading crown; bark brown or grey, narrowly to deeply fissured; twigs green. Leaves **alternate or opposite**, without petiole; blade 1–2 × 0.3–0.7mm, triangular; tip pointed; surface **grey-green**; margin entire. Cones with males and females on the same tree, males elliptic to oblong, 4–6 × 2.5–3mm, females **barrel-shaped**, 20–50 × **20–35mm**, scales 8–14, with 8–20 seeds each. Seeds dark brown, 5–6mm long.

Widely grown for windbreaks, shelter or to mark property boundaries. The wood is decorative and is used to build furniture, boats and other items. The foliage is toxic to stock and medicinal uses are recorded.

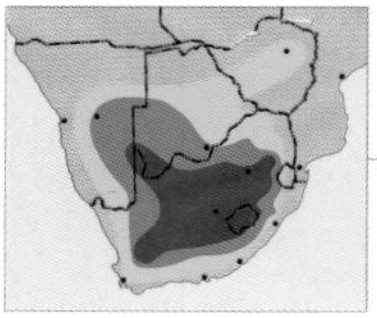

- Drought 2
- All year
- Evergreen

2 *Cupressus sempervirens* CUPRESSACEAE

Churchyard Cypress, Funeral Cypress, Italian Cypress, Pencil Cypress; Kerkhofsipres, Italiaanse Sipres

OTHER LANGUAGES: Sarû (Arabic); Xifrer baix, Xiprer comú (Catalan); Mittelmeer-Zypresse (German); Cipreste-dos-cemitérios (Portuguese); Ciprés de los cementerios (Spanish)

Southern Europe to Southwestern Asia Tall to very tall tree with a **pencil-slim** to narrowly pyramidal crown; bark brown to grey, narrowly fissured; twigs dull, green. Leaves **opposite**, each pair at right angles to its neighbours; blade 0.5–1mm long, narrowly triangular; tip **rounded**; surface dark green. Cones with males and females on the same tree, males 4–8mm long, females **round to oblong**, 25–40 × 20–30mm, with 8–14 scales, each bearing 8–20 seeds.

The family of one of us (HG) refers to these as 'semitrees', because they are so often grown in cemeteries. It has also been grown for timber, which is attractive, scented and insect-repellent, and for building, furniture-making and other purposes; it can be seen in the doors of St. Peter's Basilica, Vatican City. Medicinal uses are recorded.

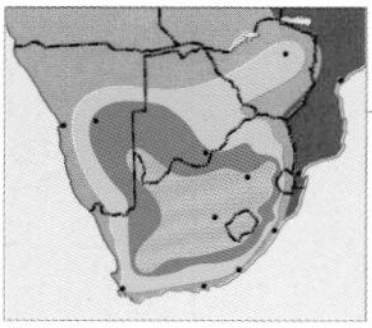

- Drought 2
- Winter–Spring
- Evergreen

3 *Hakea drupacea* (= *H. pectinata, H. suaveolens*) PROTEACEAE

Sweet Hakea; Soethakea

Western Australia Large shrub or small tree with a spreading crown; bark grey, smooth; twigs **hairy**. Leaves **alternate**, sometimes pinnate, without petiole; blade 30–130 × 1–1.6mm, **round in section**, spine-tipped; surface glossy or hairy. Inflorescences erect. Flowers curled, tubular, white or pink. Fruit a hairless, egg-shaped, rough, woody pod 20–25 × 16–19mm, **without horns**, opening after fire. Seeds 16–20mm long.

A declared Category 1b invader in South Africa; also invasive in New Zealand. Formerly grown in the Western Cape for dune reclamation and ornament.

FOREST AND KIM STARR

1 *C. macrocarpa* cones (male)

ROSS GORDON HENRY / SHUTTERSTOCK.COM

1 *C. macrocarpa* cones (female)

BRAAM VAN WYK

2 *C. sempervirens*

2 *C. sempervirens* cones (male)

2 *C. sempervirens* cone (female)

MICHAEL WOLF, WIKIMEDIA COMMONS, GDFL 1.2

3 *H. drupacea* leaves

MELBURNIAN, WIKIMEDIA COMMONS, CC BY SA 2.5

3 *H. drupacea* flowers and fruit

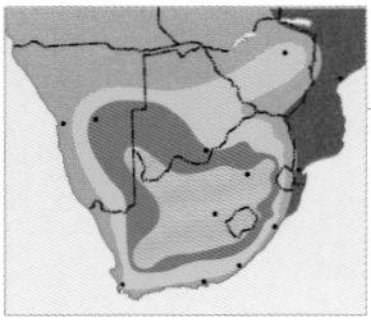

- Drought 2
- Spring
- Evergreen

1 *Hakea sericea* *(= H. acicularis, H. tenuifolia)* PROTEACEAE
Silky Hakea; Silwerhakea

Southeastern Australia Large, spreading shrub or small tree, **very spiny**; bark brown, narrowly fissured; twigs hairy, becoming **hairless with age**. Leaves alternate, without petiole; blade 13–72 × 0.7–1.3mm, awl-shaped, spine-tipped; surface dull, hairless or velvety. Inflorescences erect; peduncle 0.5–1.5mm long. Flowers tubular, curled, white or pink. Fruit a hairless, ellipsoid, warty, woody, grey-purple pod 20–40 × 15–30mm, **tipped with 2 horns**, opening after fire. Seeds black, 16–31 × 6–11.5mm.

Invasive in our region, New Zealand and Portugal. A declared Category 1b invader in South Africa. Formerly grown in several provinces for dune reclamation, ornament and hedging.

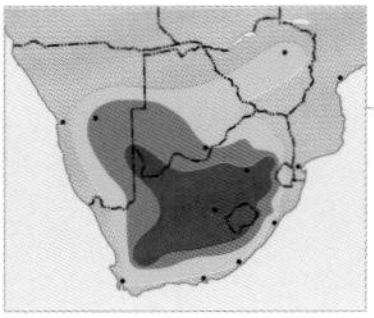

- Drought 2
- Spring
- Evergreen

2 *Juniperus cedrus* CUPRESSACEAE
Canary Island Juniper; Kanariese Seweboom

OTHER LANGUAGES: Genévrier des îles Canaries (French); Cedro (Spanish, Portuguese); Sabina (Spanish)

Canary Islands and Madeira Formerly a large tree, now mostly small to medium-sized, with a rounded crown; bark orange-brown, narrowly fissured, shedding in long shreds; twigs hairless, green to grey. Leaves **in whorls of 3**, without petiole; blade 1–12 × 1–1.5mm, narrowly triangular or awl-shaped; tip pointed; surface dull above, glossy below. Cones with males and females on the same tree, males cylindrical to round, 4–7mm long, females round, **fleshy**, scales **3 per cone**, each bearing 1 seed.

Formerly over-harvested for the very desirable timber and now endangered in nature but recovering with good conservation. Grown experimentally in Mpumalanga, KwaZulu-Natal and the Western Cape by the former Forestry Department. There are trees of this species in Tokai Arboretum, Cape Town.

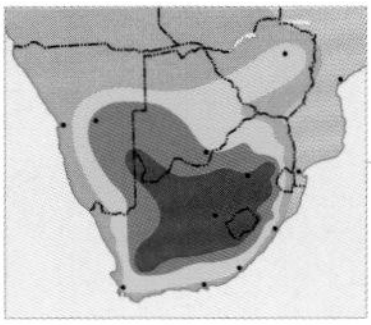

- Drought 2
- Spring
- Evergreen

3 *Leptospermum scoparium* (= *L. scoparium* var. *nichollii*) MYRTACEAE
Manuka Myrtle, Crimson Tea Tree, Manuka, Manuka Tea Tree, New Zealand Tea Tree; Manukamirt

New Zealand Large shrub or small tree with a rounded crown; bark grey, narrowly to deeply fissured; twigs hairy or hairless. Leaves **alternate**; petiole **0–2mm long**, hairless; blade 8–20 × 2–6mm, narrowly lance-shaped, with **secretory cavities**; tip pointed and **spine-tipped**; base somewhat narrowed; surface dull, hairless; margin smooth. Inflorescences an erect, single flower. Flowers with petals 5, white or pink, 4–7mm long. Fruit a woody, brown, egg-shaped capsule 6–9mm in diameter.

Commonly grown as an ornamental and can be used as a hedge. The leaves can be used as a tea substitute and the wood is red, elastic and strong, suitable for cabinet work and inlay, if large enough pieces can be found.

1 *H. sericea* leaves

1 *H. sericea* flowers

BRAAM VAN WYK

1 *H. sericea* fruit

P. GARIN

2 *J. cedrus*

2 *J. cedrus* leaves

P. GARIN

2 *J. cedrus* cones (female)

FOREST AND KIM STARR

3 *L. scoparium* flowers

FOREST AND KIM STARR

3 *L. scoparium* fruit

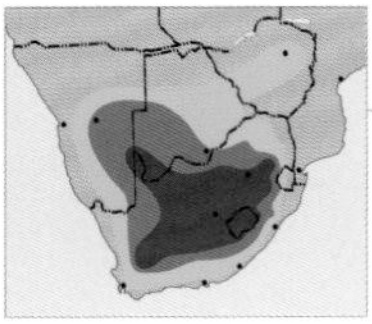

1 *Metasequoia glyptostroboides* CUPRESSACEAE

Dawn Redwood; Oerrooihout

- Drought 2
- Spring
- Deciduous

OTHER LANGUAGES: Shui shan shu (Chinese)

China Large tree with a **columnar to pyramidal** crown and **bronze autumn colours**; bark brown to grey, deeply fissured; twigs hairless, green, shed whole in autumn. Leaves **opposite**, without petiole; blade 8–15 × 1–2mm, strap-shaped; tip rounded and sometimes hair-tipped; surface dull, blue-green above, pale green below; margin smooth. Cones with males and females on the same tree, males egg-shaped, 2.5–5.5 × 2–3.8mm, females in 3s, cylindrical to round, 14–25 × 15–23mm, with **16–24 scales**, each bearing 5–9 seeds; peduncle about 3mm long. Seeds widest beyond the middle, about 5 × 4mm.

A 'living fossil', grown as specimen trees in botanical gardens in the Western Cape and Gauteng in South Africa and in Zimbabwe. Some reports indicate that the wood is too brittle to be useful.

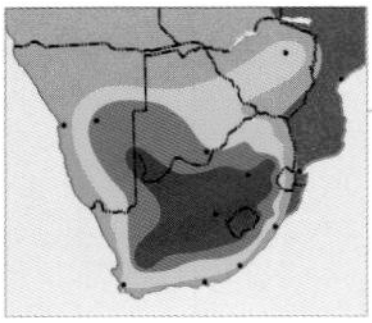

2 *Parkinsonia aculeata* FABACEAE

Jerusalem Thorn, Ratama; Mexikaanse Groenhaarboom

- Drought 2
- Spring
- Deciduous

OTHER LANGUAGES: Jerusalemdorn (German); Espinho de Jerusalem (Portuguese); Palo verde (Spanish)

Southern USA and adjacent Mexico Small, thinly leaved tree or large shrub with a vase-shaped to spreading crown; bark brown, narrowly fissured; buds hairy; twigs hairless, yellow-brown or greenish yellow; stems with **paired thorns** (modified stipules). Leaves alternate, **twice-pinnate, drooping**; petiole hairless; rachis flattened, **ending in a spine**; leaflets 2–6 × 1–2mm, elliptic; tip rounded and tapering to an abrupt point; base obliquely narrowed; surface dull, hairless; margin smooth. Inflorescences erect, up to 200mm long. Flowers with petals 5, yellow, 8–14mm long. Fruit a papery, brown, flattened pod 30–120 × 5–8mm. Seeds 5–9 × 4–6 × 1.5–2.5mm.

Invasive in Australia, Africa, Pakistan and the Pacific islands and a declared Category 1b invader in South Africa. Grown for fodder; the pulp of the pods is edible and sweet. Timber is too small for sawn wood but is used for fuel and poles. There are reports that the foliage is poisonous. Medicinal uses are recorded.

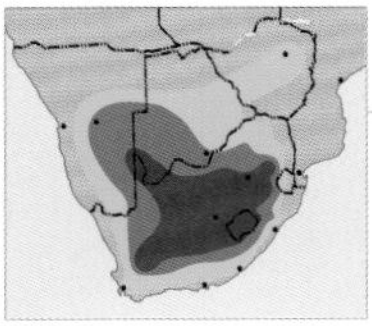

3 *Picea smithiana* PINACEAE

Himalayan Spruce; Himalaja-spar

- Drought 2
- Spring
- Evergreen

OTHER LANGUAGES: Himalaya-Fichte (German)

Western Himalayas Tall tree with a **pyramidal** crown; bark pale brown, forming plate-like scales; twigs hairless, brown or grey; short shoots **absent**. Leaves **single**, without petiole; blade 25–110 × 1.3–1.8mm, **strap-shaped**; tip drawn out; surface **dull**; margin smooth. Cones with males and females on the same tree, males cylindrical, females cylindrical, 100–180 × 45–50mm, with many scales, about 30mm long. Seeds dark brown or grey, 5–6mm long, elliptic to more or less rectangular.

Grown as specimen trees in botanical gardens and rarely privately in the Western Cape, Eastern Cape and KwaZulu-Natal. Some parts are edible. The bark is waterproof and used for roofing and water pipes. The wood is used for construction and other purposes.

1 *M. glyptostroboides* leaves

1 *M. glyptostroboides* cones (male)

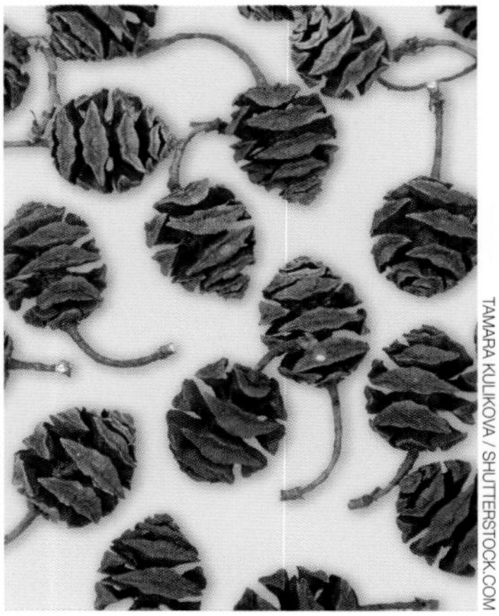

1 *M. glyptostroboides* cones (female)

2 *P. aculeata* flowers

2 *P. aculeata* fruit

3 *P. smithiana* cones (male)

3 *P. smithiana* cones (female)

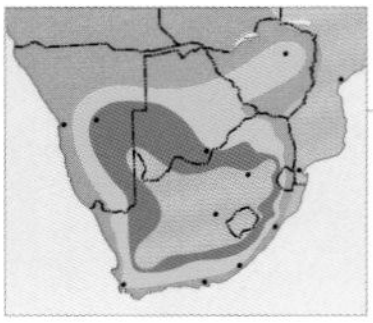

- Drought 2
- All year
- Evergreen

1 *Pinus arizonica* (= *P. ponderosa* var. *arizonica*) PINACEAE

Arizona Pine; Arizona-den

OTHER LANGUAGES: Pino de Arizona (Spanish)

USA Large tree with a more or less rounded crown; bark brown to grey, deeply fissured, forming large slabs; twigs stout, brown. Leaves in **bundles of 3–5**, on short shoots; needles 80–250mm long, **triangular in section**; tip pointed; surface glossy. Cones with males and females on the same tree, males cylindrical, about 15–20 × 5mm, females stalked, egg-shaped to round, **50–140** × 35–60mm, with 90–140 scales, each bearing 2 seeds. Seeds buff, 3–4mm long.

Grown experimentally in various parts of South Africa and Zimbabwe and still seen in Tokai Arboretum, Cape Town. Used in its native area for construction and firewood.

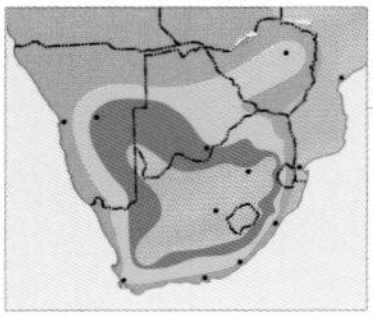

- Drought 2
- All year
- Evergreen

2 *Pinus canariensis* PINACEAE

Canary Pine, Canary Island Pine; Kanariese Den

OTHER LANGUAGES: Pi de Canàries (Catalan); Pino canario (Spanish)

Canary Islands Medium-sized tree with an open, **pyramidal to rounded** crown; bark brown, rough, deeply fissured, forming large slabs; twigs stout, dull, yellow; resin clear. Needles **in 3s** on short shoots, spirally arranged, 150–300 × 1–2mm, triangular in section, **spine-tipped**; surface glossy. Cones with males and females on the same tree, males cylindrical, about 10mm long, females stalked, cylindrical or elliptic, **100–220** × 50–130mm, scales many, with 2 elliptic seeds each.

Widely grown for its timber, which is among the best in the genus, but invasive in Australia and South Africa, where it is a declared Category 3 invader.

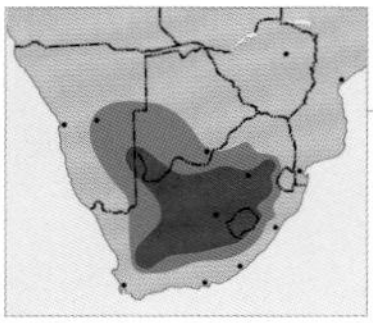

- Drought 2
- All year
- Evergreen

3 *Pinus coulteri* PINACEAE

Bigcone Pine, Coulter Pine; Grootkeëlden

OTHER LANGUAGES: Pi de pinyes grosses (Catalan); Pin à pommes géantes (French); Coulters Kiefer (German); Pino de piñas grandes (Spanish)

USA Medium-sized tree with a **pyramidal** crown; bark brown to black, deeply fissured, forming broad ridges; terminal bud **15–30mm long**; twigs stout, violet-brown. Needles **in 3s**, 150–350mm long, about 2mm wide; tip **drawn out**; surface dull; margin minutely saw-toothed. Cones with males and females on the same tree, males cylindrical to conical, up to 25mm long, females solitary, cylindrical, 200–350 × 125–175mm, with many scales, each with a **sharp, downward point** and bearing 2 seeds; peduncle up to 30mm long. Seeds dark brown, 15–22mm long.

Grown occasionally in scattered localities as a specimen tree. This species has the heaviest cones of all pines and the *Flora of North America* advises 'one who seeks its shade should wear a hardhat'. The wood is of poor quality but the seeds are edible and medicinal uses are recorded.

1 *P. arizonica* cones (male)

1 *P. arizonica* cone (female)

2 *P. canariensis* cone (female)

2 *P. canariensis* cones (male)

3 *P. coulteri* leaves

3 *P. coulteri* cones (male)

3 *P. coulteri* cone (female)

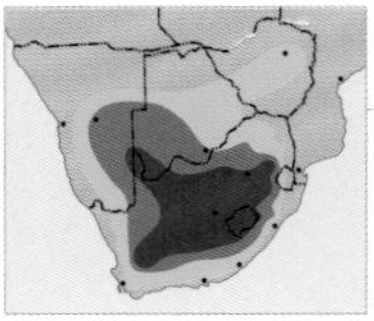

1 *Pinus elliottii*

PINACEAE

Slash Pine; Basden

OTHER LANGUAGES: Pin à aiguilles longues (French); Elliotts Kiefer (German); Pino tea (Spanish)

USA Medium-sized tree with a conical, rounded or spreading crown atop a tall bole; bark brown to grey, deeply fissured, forming **large slabs**; terminal bud 15–20mm long; scales brown; twigs orange- or greyish brown. Needles **in pairs or 3s, straight**, stiff, 150–250 × 1.2–1.5mm; tip pointed; surface glossy; margin smooth. Cones with males and females on the same tree, 1 or 2 together, males cylindrical, 30–40mm long, females conical, 60–200mm long, peduncle up to 30mm long, scales many, each tipped with a **blunt grey prickle** and bearing 2 seeds. Seeds elliptic, dark brown, 6–7mm long.

- Drought 2
- All year
- Evergreen

This pine is widely grown commercially in our region and has escaped, now being a declared Category 1b invader in South Africa, Category 2 in the case of sterile specimens. The wood is used for construction and pulp.

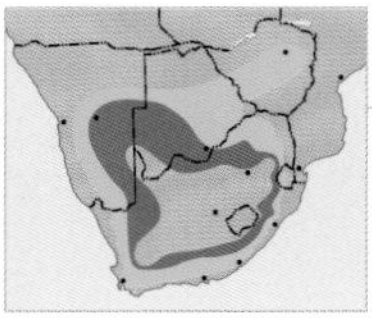

2 *Pinus engelmannii* (= *P. apacheca*)

PINACEAE

Apache Pine; Apache-den

OTHER LANGUAGES: Pin de l'Arizona à longues feuilles (French); Apachen-Kiefer (German); Pino prieto (Spanish)

Arizona and Mexico Medium-sized tree with an open, oval crown; bark reddish brown, widely fissured and rough, forming large slabs; twigs stout, brown. Needles usually **in 3s, straight or drooping**, 200–400 × 1.5–2mm; tip pointed; surface glossy. Cones with males and females on the same tree, males cylindrical, females stalked, 1–5 together, conical to oblong, 80–150 × 60–100mm, with 100–140 scales, each with a **stout spine** and bearing 2 seeds. Seeds buff to grey, 18–25 × 7–10mm.

- Drought 2
- All year
- Evergreen

Grown experimentally as a potential source of construction timber in several countries. Trees can still be seen in Tokai Arboretum, Cape Town.

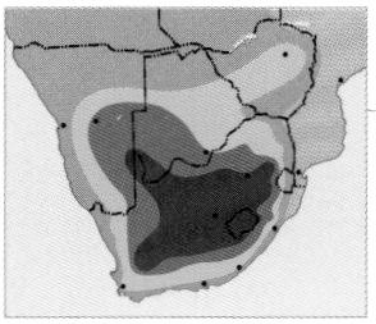

3 *Pinus halepensis*

PINACEAE

Aleppo Pine; Aleppo-den

OTHER LANGUAGES: Sanawbar el hhalab (Arabic); Pi Blanc (Catalan); Pin Blanc (French); Seekiefer (German); Pevki halepios (Greek); Oren Yrushalayim (Hebrew); Pinheiro-de-Aleppo (Portuguese); Pino blanquillo (Spanish)

Eastern Mediterranean Medium-sized to large tree with a conical to open crown; bark grey, smooth to deeply fissured, forming large slabs; terminal bud about 8mm long; twigs **hairy**, stout, brown or grey. Needles in **bundles of 2, stiff, grey-green to yellow-green**, 40–150mm long; tip pointed; surface glossy. Cones with males and females on the same tree, males cylindrical, females drooping, conical, 50–120mm long, 20–40mm in diameter at base, peduncle 10–20mm long, scales many, **smooth or with a faint crossways ridge** and bearing 2 seeds each. Seeds elliptic, reddish brown or black, 6–7mm long.

- Drought 2
- All year
- Evergreen

Widely grown for shelter, poles and firewood; the resin is used in Greece to give characteristic flavour to *retsina* wine and the seeds are often eaten. Has become invasive in the USA, Australia and Argentina and is a declared Category 3 invader in South Africa's Western Cape, Eastern Cape and Free State provinces.

GEOFF NICHOLS

1 *P. elliottii* cones (male)

BRAAM VAN WYK

1 *P. elliottii* cones (female)

ROB YOUNG, WIKIMEDIA COMMONS, CC BY SA 2.0

2 *P. engelmannii* cones (male)

2 *P. engelmannii* cone (female)

BRAAM VAN WYK

3 *P. halepensis* cones (male)

BRAAM VAN WYK

3 *P. halepensis* cone (female)

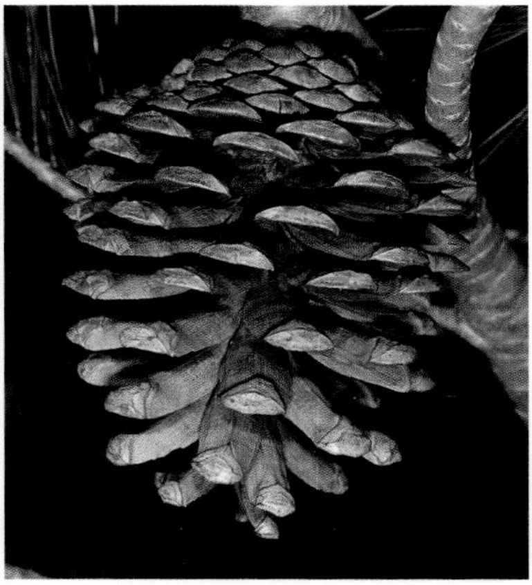

BRAAM VAN WYK

3 *P. halepensis* cone (dehisced female)

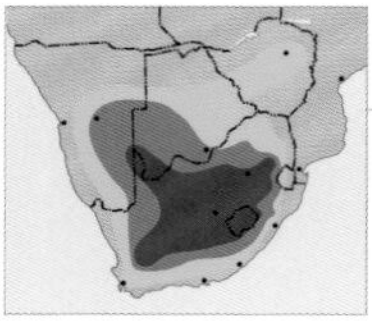

- Drought 2
- All year
- Evergreen

1 *Pinus muricata* PINACEAE
Bishop Pine; Bishop-den

OTHER LANGUAGES: Pin d'évêque (French); Bischofskiefer (German); Pino del obispo (Spanish)

California Medium-sized to large tree with a pyramidal to rounded crown; bark brown to grey, rough, deeply fissured, forming broad ridges; terminal bud 10–25mm long; twigs stout, brown. Needles **in pairs**, erect, 75–175 × 1.2–2mm; tip pointed; surface glossy; margin minutely saw-toothed. Cones with males and females on the same tree, males elliptic, up to 5mm long, females **asymmetrically** conical, 40–90mm long, peduncle up to 10mm long, scales many, each **ending in a hooked claw** and bearing 2 seeds. Seeds elliptic, dark brown to black, 6–7mm long.

Grown experimentally in southern and tropical Africa; trees are still to be seen in Tokai Arboretum, Cape Town. The seeds are edible but the wood is inferior. The most important product of this species is turpentine, which has industrial and medicinal uses.

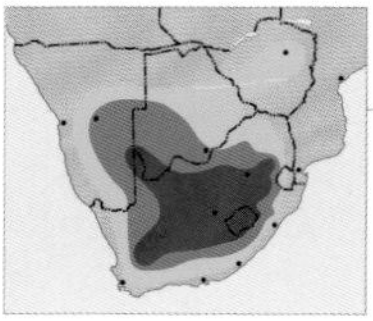

- Drought 2
- All year
- Evergreen

2 *Pinus palustris* (= *P. australis*) PINACEAE
Longleaf Pine; Langblaarden

OTHER LANGUAGES: Pi melis (Catalan); Pitchpin du sud (French, Canada); Pino del sur (Spanish)

Southeastern USA Large tree with a columnar to narrowly spreading, open crown; bark brown, deeply fissured, forming large slabs; bud scales white; terminal bud **30–45mm long**; twigs stout, red-brown. Needles **in 3s, arched, twisted**, 200–450mm long, about 1.5mm wide; tip pointed; surface glossy. Cones with males and females on the same tree, males cylindrical, 30–80mm long, females 1 or 2 together, **lance-shaped, 150–250mm long**, with many scales, each with a **small, hooked spine** and bearing 2 seeds. Seeds buff, 9–12mm long.

State tree of Alabama. Grown experimentally in several countries of southern and tropical Africa and now seen in botanical gardens and arboreta. Today used for timber and pulp but formerly a source of naval stores (turpentine, pitch, resin etc.).

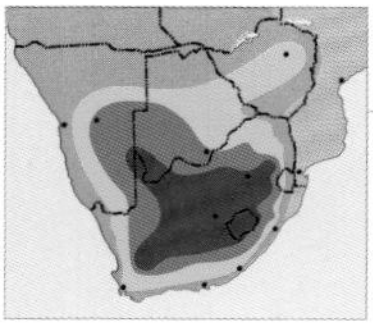

- Drought 2
- All year
- Evergreen

3 *Pinus patula* PINACEAE
Patula Pine, Mexican Pine, Weeping Pine; Treurden

OTHER LANGUAGES: Pin à feuilles étalées (French); Mexikanische Kiefer (German); Pino ocote (Spanish)

Mexico Large to very tall tree with a pyramidal crown in open situations, or a small rounded crown in plantations; bark brown to grey, rough, deeply fissured, forming broad ridges; terminal bud 10–20mm long; twigs stout, brown. Needles **in 3s or 4s, drooping**, 120–300mm long; tip pointed; surface glossy; margin very finely saw-toothed. Cones with males and females on the same tree, males cylindrical, females 3–5 together, stalked, 75–120 × 30–40mm, with many scales, each with a **minute, deciduous prickle** and bearing 2 seeds. Seeds elliptic, reddish brown or black, about 8 × 20mm including wing.

Commonly grown commercially for timber and is the pine planted most extensively for this purpose in our region. It is naturalised in many tropical and subtropical areas and is a declared Category 2 invader in South Africa.

1 *P. muricata* cones (male)

1 *P. muricata* cone (female)

WILL STUART

2 *P. palustris* cones (young male)

STACEY LYNN PAYNE / SHUTTERSTOCK.COM

2 *P. palustris* cone (female)

BRAAM VAN WYK

3 *P. patula* leaves

BRAAM VAN WYK

3 *P. patula* cones (male)

BRAAM VAN WYK

3 *P. patula* cone (female)

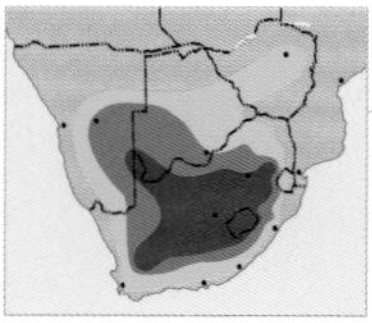

- Drought 2
- All year
- Evergreen

1 *Pinus pinaster* (= *P. maritima*)

PINACEAE

Cluster Pine, Maritime Pine; Trosden, Mannetjiedenneboom, Pinasterden

OTHER LANGUAGES: Al sanawbar alsahlî (Arabic); Pinastre (Catalan); Pin Maritime (French); Strand-Kiefer (German); Pino marittimo (Italian); Pino Gallego (Spanish)

Western Mediterranean and Italy to Morocco Medium-sized to large tree with a rounded to spreading crown on a tall bole in plantations, irregular in invasive trees; bark grey, deeply fissured, forming large slabs; terminal bud 20–37mm long; scales brown; twigs becoming hairless, stout, reddish brown. Needles **in pairs, stiff**, 80–240mm long, about **2mm wide**; tip pointed; surface glossy; margin very finely saw-toothed. Cones stalked, conical, 80–220 × 50–80mm, scales many, each with a **prominent ridge ending in a short, curved point** and bearing 2 seeds. Seeds elliptic, greyish brown, about 10mm long.

Grown commercially for timber. Naturalised in England, Australia and a declared Category 1b invader (with some exceptions) in South Africa. The cones are often sold for Christmas decorations.

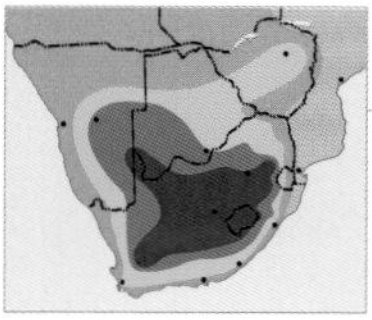

- Drought 2
- All year
- Evergreen

2 *Pinus pinea*

PINACEAE

Stone Pine, Umbrella Pine; Sambreelden, Kroonden, Wyfiedenneboom

OTHER LANGUAGES: Khashab' azizi (Arabic); Pi Campaner (Catalan); Pin â Pignons (French); Italienische Steinkiefer (German); Pevke koukounaria (Greek); Oren hasela (Hebrew); Pino da Pínoli, Pinocchio (Italian); Pinheiro-manso (Portuguese); Pino Piñonero (Spanish); Çam fıstık ağac (Turkish)

Northern Mediterranean Medium-sized to large tree with a **spreading** crown; bark reddish brown to grey, deeply fissured, forming large slabs; terminal bud 6–12mm long; scales brown; twigs stout, brown or yellowish green. Needles **in pairs**, stiff, 50–200mm long; tip pointed; surface glossy; margin finely saw-toothed. Cones stalked, conical to elliptic, 80–150 × 50–110mm, scales many, each with a **bulbous tip bearing a short, curved spine** and 2 seeds. Seeds elliptic, reddish brown, 10–15 × 7–11mm.

Grown since prehistoric times for its edible seeds; brought to our region in the 17th century by the French Huguenots and here used for both food and ornament. Naturalised in the Western Cape and proposed as a Category 3 invader.

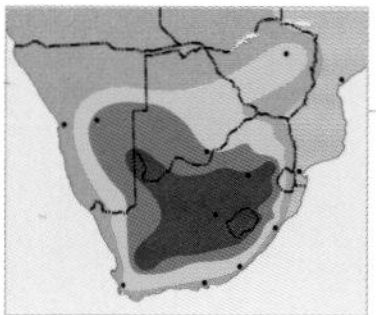

- Drought 2
- All year
- Evergreen

3 *Pinus radiata* (= *P. insignis*)

PINACEAE

Monterey Pine, Radiata Pine; Radiata-den

COMMON NAMES: Pi insigne (Catalan); Pin de Monterey (French); Monterey-Kiefer (German); Pinheiro-de-Monterey (Portuguese); Pino de Monterrey (Spanish)

Monterey Peninsula, California Medium-sized to large tree with a narrow, columnar or conical crown in plantations but broad and open when invasive; bark dark brown to grey, deeply fissured, forming large slabs; terminal bud about 15mm long; twigs stout, brown. Needles usually **in 3s**, stiff, 60–150 × 1.3–2mm; tip pointed; surface glossy; margin finely saw-toothed. Cones **several together**, conical to elliptic, 70–170mm long, peduncle up to 10mm long, scales many, with tip **slightly hooked and spineless**, bearing 2 seeds each. Seeds elliptic, black, about 6mm long.

The commonest commercial pine in the Western Cape but invasive wherever it has been planted in the southern hemisphere and a declared Category 1b invader (with some exceptions) in South Africa. Used for timber ('South African Pine') and pulp.

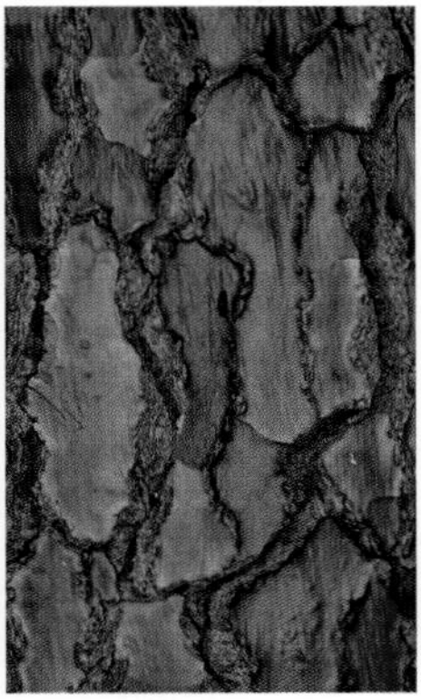
BRAAM VAN WYK

1 *P. pinaster* bark

BRAAM VAN WYK

1 *P. pinaster* cones (male)

BRAAM VAN WYK

1 *P. pinaster* cones (dehisced female)

BRAAM VAN WYK

2 *P. pinea* nuts and empty shells

2 *P. pinea* cones (male)

BRAAM VAN WYK

2 *P. pinea* cone (female)

BRAAM VAN WYK

3 *P. radiata* cones (male)

BRAAM VAN WYK

3 *P. radiata* cones (female)

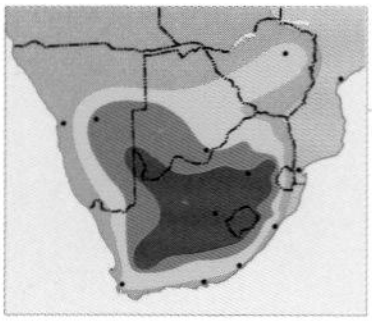

1 *Pinus roxburghii* (= *P. longifolia*)

PINACEAE

Chir Pine, Indian Longleaf Pine; Tjirden

- Drought 2
- All year
- Evergreen

OTHER LANGUAGES: Xu mi chang ye song (Chinese); Pin de l'Inde à longues feuilles (French); Chirkiefer (German); Chir (Hindi); Pinheiro-indiano-de-folha-larga (Portuguese); Pino de la Himalaya (Spanish); Paari-bhadra (Urdu)

Himalayas Medium-sized to large tree with a conical to spreading crown; bark grey, deeply fissured, forming large slabs; twigs stout, brown or grey. Needles **in 3s, arched**, 200–325mm long, about 1.5mm wide; tip pointed; surface glossy; margin finely saw-toothed. Cones with males and females on the same tree, males cylindrical, females stalked, **solitary**, conical, 100–240 × 50–90mm, scales many, tip **strongly hooked**, with 2 seeds each. Seeds elliptic, midbrown or grey, 8–15mm long.

Grown for timber in southern and tropical Africa and invasive in Gauteng. It is a declared Category 2 invader in South Africa.

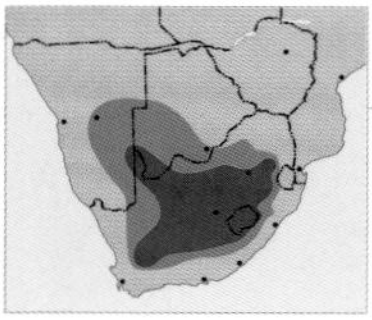

2 *Pinus taeda*

PINACEAE

Loblolly Pine, Shortleaf Pine; Loblollyden

- Drought 2
- All year
- Evergreen

OTHER LANGUAGES: Pi de Carolina de Nord (Catalan); Pin à encens (French); Amerikanische Terpentinkiefer (German); Pinho-teda (Portuguese); Pino del incienso (Spanish)

Southeastern USA Tall tree with a narrow, oval, open crown; bark reddish brown, deeply fissured, forming large slabs; terminal bud 6–20mm long; scales red-brown; twigs yellowish brown. Needles **in 3s**, stiff, 100–225 × 1–2mm; tip pointed; surface glossy; margin finely saw-toothed. Cones with males and females on the same tree, males cylindrical, 20–40mm long, females 2–5 together, cylindrical to conical, 60–170 × 20–60mm, scales many, **ending in a sharp, 7mm-long prickle** and bearing 2 seeds each. Seeds elliptic, midbrown, 5–6mm long.

Grown for timber and pulp but has escaped plantations and is now a declared Category 2 invader in South Africa.

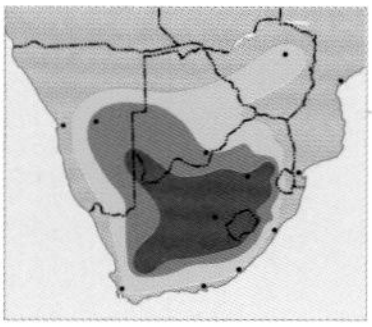

3 *Pinus thunbergii*

PINACEAE

Japanese Black Pine; Japanse Swartden

- Drought 2
- All year
- Evergreen

OTHER LANGUAGES: Hei song (Chinese); Pin noir du Japon (French); Japanische Schwarzkiefer (German); Kuro matsu (Japanese); Pino negro de Japón (Spanish)

Japan and South Korea Medium-sized to large tree with an open, spreading, irregular crown, sometimes shaped by careful pruning; bark grey to black, deeply fissured or rough; terminal bud **often white**; twigs brown. Leaves **in pairs**, stiff, 60–110mm long, **spine-tipped**; surface dark green. Cones with males and females on the same tree, males up to 60 together, females 1 or 2 together, stalked, narrowly egg-shaped, 40–60 × 25–40mm, scales many, **ending in a small prickle** and bearing 2 seeds each. Seeds elliptic, grey-brown, 5–7 × 2–3.5mm.

This pine is characteristic of Japanese gardens and bonsai. The timber is among the most important species in Japanese architecture. In our region, it is seen in Japanese-themed sections of public gardens.

BRAAM VAN WYK

1 *P. roxburghii* cones (male)

BRAAM VAN WYK

1 *P. roxburghii* cones (female)

G.J. BLICK

2 *P. taeda* bark

RROR, WIKIMEDIA COMMONS, CC BY SA 3.0

2 *P. taeda* cones (male)

ALICIA PIMENTAL, WIKIMEDIA COMMONS, CC BY SA 3.0

2 *P. taeda* cone (female)

KENPEI, WIKIMEDIA COMMONS, GFDL 1.2, CC BY-SA 3.0

3 *P. thunbergii* cones (male)

TANELI MIELIKÄINEN, WIKIMEDIA COMMONS, CC BY-SA 2.0

3 *P. thunbergii* cones (female)

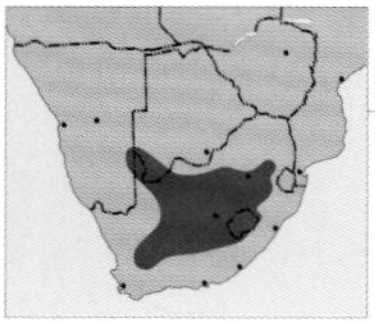

- Drought 2
- All year
- Evergreen

1 *Pinus wallichiana* PINACEAE
Bhutan Pine; Bhutan-den

OTHER LANGUAGES: Qiao song (Chinese); Pin bleu (French); Tränenkiefer (German); Cirā (Hindi); Pinheiro do Himalaia (Portuguese); Pino llorón del Himalaya (Spanish)

Himalayas Tall to very tall tree with a **cylindrical or narrowly conical** crown; bark dark brown to grey, rough; twigs slender, glossy, green. Leaves in **5s, drooping**, 60–200 × 0.7–1mm; tip pointed; surface glossy; margin minutely saw-toothed. Cones with males and females on the same tree, hanging, females cylindrical, 100–300 × 30–70mm (50–90mm when open), peduncle 25–40mm long, scales many, 30–50mm long, **spineless**, each bearing 2 seeds. Seeds dark brown to black, 3–9 × 4–6mm.

Grown experimentally in several parts of our region and seen rarely in public and private collections. A source of high-quality turpentine, the wood is very resinous and emits acrid smoke when burned.

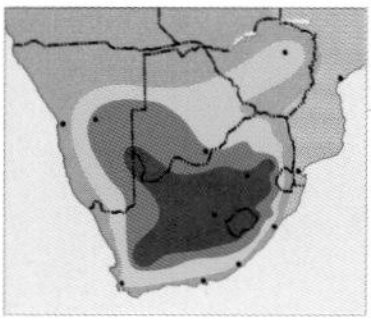

- Drought 2
- Spring
- Evergreen

2 *Platycladus orientalis* (= *Biota orientalis, Thuja orientalis*) CUPRESSACEAE
Chinese Arborvitae, Oriental Arborvitae; Lewensboom

OTHER LANGUAGES: Ce bai (Chinese)

Northern China Medium-sized tree, crown cylindrical to conical when young, becoming rounded with age; bark brown, narrowly fissured, flaking, forming **long strips**; twigs glossy, green, **spreading out in flat, vertical planes**. Leaves **opposite**, each pair at right angles to its neighbours, with **a distinctive aroma**; blade 1–3mm long, triangular; surface glossy. Cones with males and females on the same tree, males ovoid, 2–3mm long, females round, 15–25 × 10–18mm, with **6–8 horned scales** each, lowest pair bearing 2 seeds each, upper pair 1 seed each. Seeds elliptic, dark greyish or purplish brown, 5–7 × 3–4mm.

Grown in our region as an ornamental in private and public gardens. The wood is used for building, particularly Buddhist temples, and for making furniture. Wood chips are used in the Far East for incense. An essential oil has several uses, including medicinal.

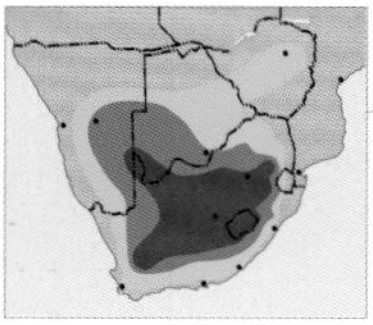

- Drought 2
- Spring
- Evergreen

3 *Pseudotsuga menziesii* PINACEAE
Douglas Fir, Oregon Pine; Douglas-den

OTHER LANGUAGES: Sapin de Douglas (French); Douglasie (German); Pino real (Spanish)

Western USA and Canada Very tall tree with a columnar to conical crown; bark red-brown, deeply fissured, forming broad ridges; terminal bud 6–12mm long; twigs **hairy**, brown. Leaves alternate; blade 20–35 × 0.7–1mm, **strap-shaped**; tip **rounded**; surface glossy above, dull below. Cones with males and females on the same tree, males cylindrical, females stalked, egg-shaped, 50–100 × 20–35mm, with many blunt, smooth scales bearing 2 seeds each and **distinctive 3-pointed bracts** between scales. Seeds ovoid, 6mm long.

Grown experimentally in several places and to be seen as a specimen tree in Arderne Gardens, Cape Town, but much more often as imported timber. Wood is among the world's most important timbers, used for construction, flooring, furniture and much else. Many other uses, including medicinal, are recorded.

1 *P. wallichiana* cones (male)

1 *P. wallichiana* cone (female)

2 *P. orientalis*

2 *P. orientalis* cones (male)

2 *P. orientalis* cones (female; see also p.12)

3 *P. menziesii* cones (male)

3 *P. menziesii* cones (female)

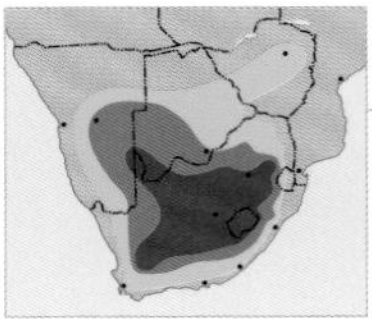

1 *Sequoia sempervirens* CUPRESSACEAE

Californian Redwood, Coast Redwood; Kaliforniese Rooihout

- Drought 2
- Spring
- Evergreen

OTHER LANGUAGES: Mammutbaum (German); Árbol mamut (Spanish)

California and Oregon Among the tallest living trees, crown columnar, on a tall bole where this has had time to develop; bark brown, **spongy**, deeply fissured, flaking, forming broad ridges; twigs hairless, stout, dull, green. Leaves alternate, **irregularly 2-ranked**; blade 8–20 × 1.3–3mm, oblong; tip pointed; surface glossy above, dull below; margin smooth. Cones with males and females on the same tree, males egg-shaped to round, 2–5mm long, females elliptic, 20–30 × 12–15mm, with **14–20 scales**, each bearing many seeds. Seeds buff, 1.5–6mm long.

Grown as specimen trees in botanical and some private gardens; suitable only for the largest spaces on account of its size. In its native area, one of the most important timbers and apparently somewhat fire-retardant. The bark is used as insulation, soil conditioner and for paper-making. Medicinal uses are recorded.

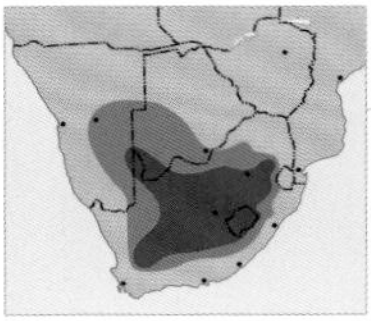

2 *Sequoiadendron giganteum* (= *Sequoia wellingtoniana*) CUPRESSACEAE

Giant Redwood, Mammoth Tree, Sierra Redwood; Mammoetboom

- Drought 2
- Spring
- Evergreen

OTHER LANGUAGES: Mammutbaum (German); Árbol mamut (Spanish)

California World's largest tree by volume but not quite as tall as *Sequoia sempervirens* (above), crown columnar to conical; bark reddish brown, deeply fissured, **fibrous**, forming broad ridges; twigs glabrous, slender, dull, brown or green. Leaves **spirally arranged**, waxy blue to green, 10–15mm long, **awl-shaped**; tip pointed. Cones with males and females on the same tree, males egg-shaped to round, 4–8mm long, females egg-shaped, 40–90 × 30–55mm, with **25–45 scales**, each bearing 3–9 seeds. Seeds elliptic, buff, 3–6mm wide.

Grown as specimen trees in botanical gardens; suitable only for the largest spaces on account of its size. Less important than *Sequoia* in its native area because of its brittleness and rarity. Used for roof shingles and other purposes.

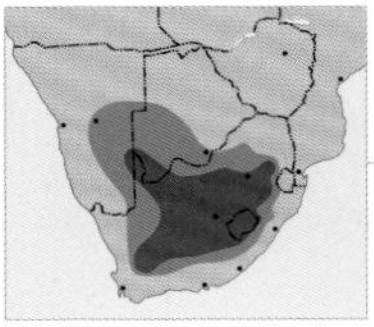

3 *Tamarix chinensis* (= *T. amurensis, T. elegans, T. japonica, T. plumosa*) TAMARICACEAE

Chinese Tamarisk; Chinese Tamarisk

- Drought 2
- Spring
- Evergreen

OTHER LANGUAGES: Cheng liu (Chinese)

China and Japan Small, often shrubby, rounded tree; bark brown or **black**, narrowly fissured, forming plate-like scales; twigs hairless, slender, brown or green. Leaves alternate, 1.5–3mm long, triangular; tip **narrowly pointed**; surface blue-green; margin smooth. Inflorescences arched, 20–60mm long. Flowers white or pink; petals 5, **egg-shaped**, about 2mm long. Fruit a small, conical, hairless capsule.

Widely naturalised in drier areas and a declared Category 1b invader in South Africa. Tolerant of wind and salt and formerly used for shelter. Medicinal uses are recorded.

1 *S. sempervirens* leaves

1 *S. sempervirens* cone (male)

1 *S. sempervirens* cones (female)

2 *S. giganteum* cones (male)

2 *S. giganteum* cones (female)

3 *T. chinensis* leaves

3 *T. chinensis* flowers

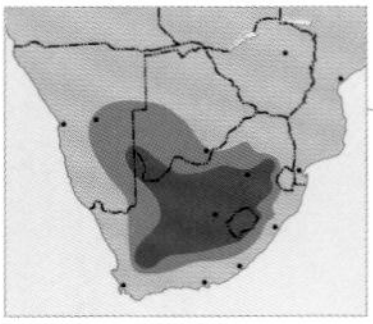

1 *Tamarix ramosissima* (= *T. pentandra*) TAMARICACEAE
Pink Tamarisk, Salt Cedar, Summer Tamarisk; Perstamarisk

- Drought 2
- Spring
- Evergreen

OTHER LANGUAGES: Duo zhi cheng liu (Chinese)

Central and Southwestern Asia to western China and eastern Europe Small, often shrubby, rounded tree; bark **reddish brown**, narrowly fissured or rough, forming plate-like scales; twigs hairless, slender, green. Leaves alternate, 1.5–3.5mm long, lance-shaped; tip **long drawn out**; surface green to blue-green; margin smooth. Inflorescences arched, 15–70mm long. Flowers with petals 5, usually pink, 1–1.75mm long, **widest beyond the middle**. Fruit a conical, papery capsule 3–4mm long.

Invasive in the USA and Australia. A declared Category 1b invader in South Africa. Formerly used as a sand binder in various countries.

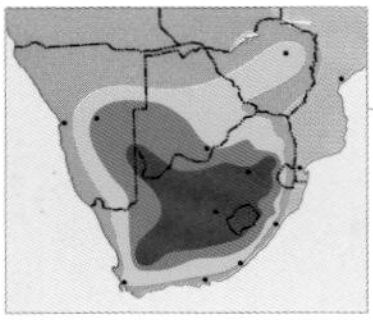

2 *Taxodium distichum* CUPRESSACEAE
Swamp Cypress, Bald Cypress, Deciduous Cypress; Moerassipres, Herfssipres

- Drought 2
- Spring
- Deciduous

OTHER LANGUAGES: Xiprer dels pantans (Catalan); Sumpfzypresse (German); Ciprés de los pantanos (Spanish)

Southeastern USA Tall tree with a conical crown and **russet autumn colours**; trunk often swollen and buttressed at base, forming **'knees' in waterlogged situations**; bark brown, narrowly fissured, forming plate-like scales; twigs slender, brown, smallest ones shed whole in autumn. Leaves alternate, **2-ranked**, about 5–17 × 1mm, **strap-shaped**, spine-tipped; surface glossy above, dull below; margin smooth. Cones with males and females on the same tree, hanging, males stalked, egg-shaped, 2–3mm long, females round, 15–40 × 13–30mm, scales 5–10, bearing 2 seeds each, rarely 1. Seeds triangular, reddish brown to midbrown, 12–26 × 5–23mm.

State tree of Louisiana and often grown as an ornamental in our region. Timber is used for construction, roof shingles and other purposes. Medicinal uses are recorded.

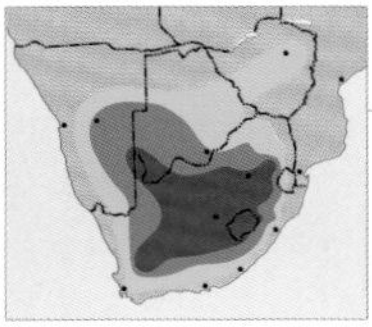

3 *Taxus baccata* TAXACEAE
Common Yew; Gewone Taksisboom

- Drought 2
- Spring
- Evergreen

OTHER LANGUAGES: Zarnab (Arabic); Teix (Catalan); Eibe (German); Melos (Greek); Teixo (Portuguese); Tejo (Spanish)

Europe, North Africa and Western Asia to Iran Medium-sized tree with a rounded to spreading crown, often modified by pruning; bark whitish grey or brown, smooth, **flaking**; twigs slender, green. Leaves alternate, often **2-ranked, dark green**, 10–30 × 1.5–2mm, narrowly oblong; tip **horny**, pointed; surface glossy above, dull below. Cones with males and females on different trees, males round, females elliptic, with 1–4 **red, fleshy scales**, each bearing 1 seed. Seeds ovoid, 6–7mm long.

All parts of the tree are poisonous. Nevertheless, the timber is excellent for making furniture and is the classic raw material for making longbows. In mediaeval, renaissance and baroque times it was the most prized wood for making lutes. Horticulturally, a classic topiary and hedge plant. Medicinal uses are recorded. Grown in public and private gardens in the Western Cape and Gauteng but toxicity makes the choice questionable.

1 *T. ramosissima* leaves and flowers

1 *T. ramosissima* flowers

2 *T. distichum* cones (male)

2 *T. distichum* cones (female)

3 *T. baccata* cones (male)

3 *T. baccata* cone (female)

GROUP 4

Fig group

Leaves simple, alternate or in tufts, not bilobed. Stipular scar prominent, encircling stem at base of petiole. Latex present.

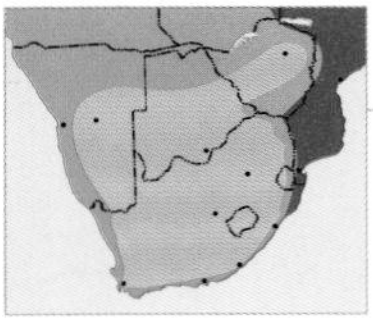

- Drought 1
- Spring
- Semi-deciduous

1 *Artocarpus altilis* (= *A. incisus*)

MORACEAE

Breadfruit Tree; Broodvrugboom

OTHER LANGUAGES: Kulor (Bahasa Indonesia); Mian bao shu (Chinese); Arbre à pain (French); Brotfruchtbaum (German); Fruta-pão (Portuguese); Nagadamani (Sanskrit); Árbol del pan (Spanish); Rimas (Tagalog); Saake (Thai)

Indonesia and New Guinea Large tree with a pyramidal to rounded crown; bark grey, smooth, adhering; twigs hairy or hairless; **latex white**. Leaves with petiole hairless; blade **50–250 × 35–120mm**, lance-shaped to elliptic, **pinnately 3–11-lobed**; tip pointed; base rounded; surface **glossy above**, dull below; margin smooth. Inflorescences hanging. Flowers individually minute, insignificant; males and females separate but on the same tree. Fruit a **round** aggregate of berries **150–300mm in diameter**, rind warty, leathery, yellow-green.

Fruits are a staple diet in much of the Pacific and Caribbean. The light, durable timber is used to build houses and canoes and the latex is used to caulk boats. The leaves and flowers have many uses. Medicinal uses are recorded. Grown in our region as specimen trees in botanical gardens in Mozambique and South Africa's KwaZulu-Natal. Closely related to the jack fruit, *A. heterophyllus* (below).

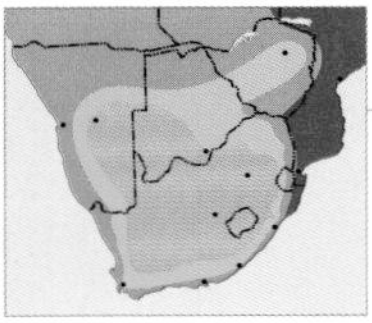

- Drought 1
- Spring
- Evergreen

2 *Artocarpus heterophyllus* (= *A. integrifolius*)

MORACEAE

Jack Fruit, Jak-fruit Tree; Nangkaboom

OTHER LANGUAGES: Bo luo mi (Chinese); Jacquier (French); Jackfrucht (German); Kathal (Hindi); Jaca (Portuguese); Panasah (Sanskrit); Árbol del Pan, Jaqueiro (Spanish); Fenesi (Swahili); Palaa (Tamil); Khanun (Thai)

India Medium-sized tree with a rounded crown; bark yellowish brown or grey, narrowly fissured, **flaking**; twigs hairless; terminal **bud and enclosing stipule constricted at base**; latex white. Leaves with petiole hairless, up to 50mm long; blade 50–250 × 35–120mm, more or less elliptic; tip usually rounded; base narrowed; surface glossy above, dull below; margin smooth, sometimes wavy. Inflorescences hanging, **on old wood**. Flowers inconspicuous; males and females separate but on the same tree. Fruit fleshy, oblong, yellow, **300–1,000** × 250–600mm, rough. Seeds whitish.

National fruit of Bangladesh and the Indian state of Kerala. Fruits edible, widely used in Indian cookery and so grown on the east coast of our region and in Malawi, Zambia, Zimbabwe and Cape Verde Islands. The wood is used for construction, musical instruments and other purposes. Medicinal uses are recorded. Closely related to the breadfruit tree, *A. altilis* (above).

1 *A. altilis* leaves and fruit

FOREST AND KIM STARR

1 *A. altilis* flowers and fruit

1 *A. altilis* fruit

2 *A. heterophyllus* leaves

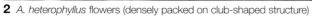

2 *A. heterophyllus* flowers (densely packed on club-shaped structure)

2 *A. heterophyllus* fruit

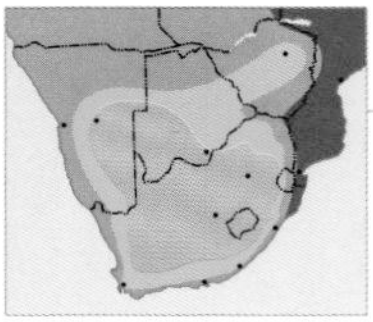

- Drought 2
- Spring
- Evergreen

1 *Cecropia peltata*

URTICACEAE

Trumpet Tree; Trompetboom

Mexico to Venezuela Small to medium-sized tree with a columnar to vase-shaped, open crown; bark grey, horizontally ribbed; twigs hairless; lenticels warty, conspicuous; latex **white**. Leaves alternate; petiole hairy, with enlarged base; blade **300–500mm long and wide**, round, **deeply palmately 7–11-lobed**; tip **rounded**; base **surrounding attachment of petiole**; surface **rough** above, **white-hairy** below; margin smooth. Stipules attached to petiole. Inflorescences erect, 100–150mm long; peduncle 70–100mm long; males and females on separate trees. Fruit an aggregate of berries.

Grown as a specimen tree in botanical gardens in our region. On the IUCN list of the world's 100 worst invasives but apparently contained in our region. The soft, weak wood is used to make insulation board, matchsticks, pulp and other products. Hollow stems have various uses and the corrosive, astringent latex has medicinal uses.

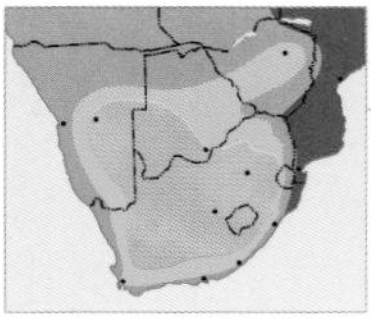

- Drought 2
- Summer
- Evergreen

2 *Ficus aspera* (= *F. cannonii, F. parcellii*)

MORACEAE

Clown Fig; Harlekynvy

OTHER LANGUAGES: Higueira abigarrada (Spanish)

New Hebrides Small tree with a broadly columnar or vase-shaped crown; bark grey; twigs hairy or hairless, red or green; lenticels warty, conspicuous. Leaves with petiole **hairy**, 10–20mm long; blade 100–350 × 50–180mm, egg-shaped, with a long drip-tip; base **obliquely** heart-shaped; surface **variegated**, dull, smooth or rough above, hairy below; margin wavy. Inflorescences erect; peduncle 10–20mm long. Fruit a round, red or **variegated green and white**, hairy fig 18–25 × 18–25mm.

Rarely grown for ornament or as a specimen tree in botanical gardens in our area.

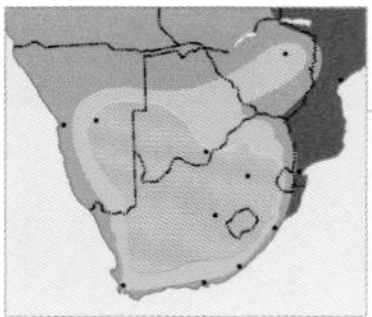

- Drought 2
- Summer
- Evergreen

3 *Ficus benghalensis* (= *F. indica, Urostigma benghalensis*)

MORACEAE

Banyan Tree, Banyan Fig; Baniaanboom, Waringinboom

OTHER LANGUAGES: Bar (Hindi); Nyagrodha (Sanskrit); Aalamaram (Tamil); Ni khrot (Thai)

Himalayan foothills of India and Bangladesh Medium-sized to large strangler fig, whose spreading crown is supported by **numerous aerial roots**; bark grey, smooth; buds hairy; twigs **hairy**, brown or grey; lenticels warty or smooth, conspicuous. Leaves with petiole **hairy**, 20–70mm long; blade 65–250 × 35–170mm, egg-shaped or triangular; tip broadly pointed; base squared to heart-shaped; margin smooth. Inflorescences erect; peduncle absent. Fruit a round, red, hairy fig about 18mm in diameter.

National tree of India; grown in scattered places in South Africa and Zimbabwe. The shade of this tree is of little use in our area, as specimens seen here have subsidiary trunks too close together to park a car or sit between. The typical variety is more often seen but var. *krishnae* (Krishna's cup), in which the leaf bases are bent and fused to form a cup, is occasionally encountered. Shellac is made from the secretions of various insects living on this tree. The wood is hard, durable and used to make furniture. Medicinal uses are recorded.

1 *C. peltata*

GÉRARD HAUTBOIS

1 *C. peltata* flowers

JIM CONRAD, WIKIMEDIA COMMONS, PUBLIC DOMAIN

1 *C. peltata* fruit

2 *F. aspera* leaves

JESÚS CABRERA

2 *F. aspera* figs

3 *F. benghalensis*

3 *F. benghalensis* figs

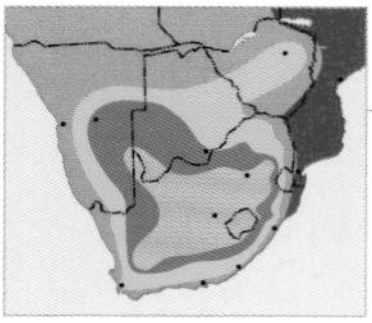

- Drought 2
- Summer
- Evergreen

1 *Ficus benjamina* (= *F. nitida, Urostigma benjamina*)

MORACEAE

Weeping Fig, Benjamin, Java Fig, Weeping Laurel; Treurvy, Waringin

OTHER LANGUAGES: Beringin (Bahasa Indonesia); Chui ye rong (Chinese); Birkenfeige (German); Pukar (Hindi); Samii (Nepalese); Árbol Benjamín (Spanish); Sai yoi (Thai); Cây sanh (Vietnamese)

India to southern China and Australia Small to medium-sized tree with a columnar to spreading crown; bark grey, smooth; branches **weeping**; buds hairless; terminal bud 9–30mm long; twigs **hairless**; lenticels warty, conspicuous. Leaves with petiole hairless, 7–25mm long; blade 40–100 × 20–50mm, elliptic to oblong, with a **long drip-tip**; base narrowed to rounded; surface glossy, sometimes dull; margin smooth. Inflorescences erect. Fruit a round, warty, red fig 8–12 × 8–12mm. Seeds whitish.

This is most often seen as an office plant, with three stems plaited together. A cultivar with variegated leaves ('Starlight') is sometimes seen. The very aggressive root system makes it inadvisable to plant this tree in open ground.

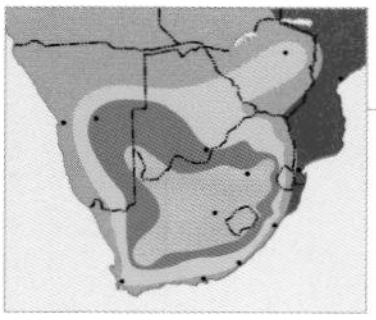

- Drought 2
- Summer
- Evergreen

2 *Ficus binnendijkii* (= *F. peracuta*)

MORACEAE

Narrow-leaved Fig, Long-leaved Fig; Smalblaarvy

Java, Borneo and the Philippines Small tree with a rounded crown; bark smooth or rough, pale grey-brown; branches **arched to drooping**; twigs hairless, obscurely angular. Leaves with petiole hairless, 5–20mm long; blade 30–150 × 10–15mm, **narrowly oblong**, leathery, with a long drip-tip; base narrowed; margin **flat or bent downwards near the base**. Fruit an egg-shaped to round, yellow fig about 8mm in diameter, single or paired.

Introduced as an indoor plant in the 1980s, and now seen occasionally both indoors and out in warmer areas. It is considered to be a replacement for *F. benjamina* (above).

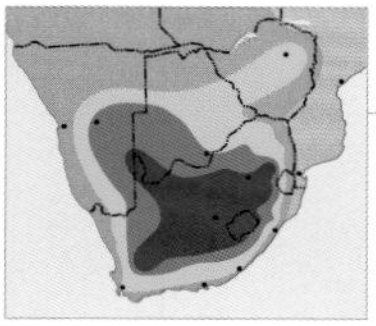

- Drought 2
- Summer
- Deciduous

3 *Ficus carica*

MORACEAE

Common Fig, Edible Fig, Fig; Makvy, Vy

OTHER LANGUAGES: Teen barchomi (Arabic); Figuier Comun (French); Echte Feige (German); Anjeer (Hindi); Figueira (Portuguese); Higueira (Spanish); Anjeer (Urdu, Farsi)

Mediterranean region and Western Asia Small, spreading tree or large shrub; bark grey, smooth; terminal bud up to 12mm long; twigs hairy, green or grey. Leaves with petiole hairless, 25–120mm long; blade 100–300 × 90–270mm, **deeply palmately 3–5-lobed**, with **3–5 main veins from the base**; tip bluntly pointed to rounded; base heart-shaped; surface dull; margin smooth. Peduncle about 10mm long. Fruit a hairless, egg-shaped, **purple, brown or green fig up to 60mm in diameter**. Seeds whitish.

Many cultivars are known, some with separate male and female trees and others producing fruit without fertilisation; all grown in southern Africa belong to the latter group. These can only be reproduced by cuttings. Has been grown for fruit for at least the last 10,000 years; the wood is of minimal value. Medicinal uses are recorded.

1 *F. benjamina*

1 *F. benjamina* leaves

GEOFF NICHOLS

1 *F. benjamina* figs

FOREST AND KIM STARR

2 *F. binnendijkii*

KENRAIZ, WIKIMEDIA COMMONS, GFDL 1.2, CC BY SA 3.0

2 *F. binnendijkii* leaves

KENRAIZ, WIKIMEDIA COMMONS, CC BY SA 3.0

2 *F. binnendijkii* figs

3 *F. carica* leaves

RICHARD PETERSON / SHUTTERSTOCK.COM

3 *F. carica* figs

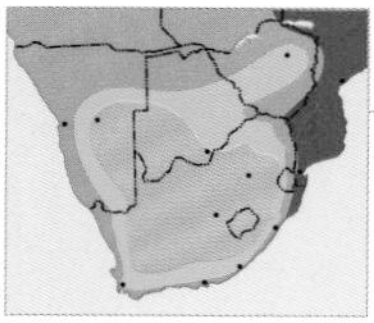

1 *Ficus elastica*

MORACEAE

Rubber Fig, India Rubber Tree; Rubbervy

OTHER LANGUAGES: Bor (Bengali); Arbre á Caoutchouc (French); Gummibaum (German); Attaabor (Hindi); Borracheira da India (Portuguese); Árbol del caucho (Spanish); Yang india (Thai); Đa búp đỏ (Vietnamese)

Southern Himalayas through Indochina to Java Medium-sized to large, spreading tree (much smaller as a house-plant) with aerial roots; bark grey; terminal bud **up to 40mm long**, covered by a **pinkish** sheath (stipule); twigs hairless, glossy. Leaves with petiole hairless, 30–90mm long; blade 110–300 × 50–150mm, elliptic, with a drip-tip; base narrowed to rounded; lower surface **hairless**; margin smooth. Inflorescences erect; peduncle **absent**. Fruit a hairless, yellow to purple or black, **ellipsoid fig 10–15** × 8–10mm.

- Drought 2
- Summer
- Evergreen

At least seven cultivars are known to be grown for ornament in southern Africa. In the 19th century, the latex of this species was in great demand as a source of India rubber.

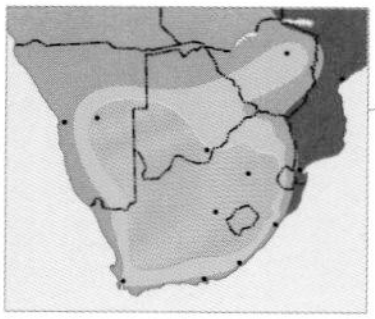

2 *Ficus lyrata*

MORACEAE

Fiddle-leaved Fig, Banjo Fig, Lyrate-leaved Fig; Vioolblaarvy

OTHER LANGUAGES: Geigenfeige (German)

Cameroon to Sierra Leone Medium-sized, spreading tree (smaller as a house-plant); bark grey, smooth or narrowly fissured, forming thin scales; twigs hairless; lenticels warty, conspicuous. Leaves with petiole hairless, about 50mm long; blade 120–450 × 50–300mm, **violin-shaped**; tip **rounded and indented**; base heart-shaped or eared; margin sometimes wavy. Inflorescences erect; peduncle absent. Fruit a **round**, warty, green, hairless fig 40–60 × 40–60mm.

- Drought 2
- Summer
- Evergreen

Grown for ornament in the warmer parts of our region; may survive in slightly cooler areas as a house-plant.

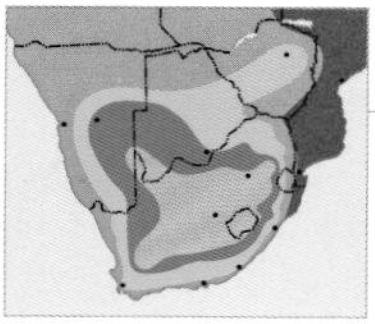

3 *Ficus macrophylla*

MORACEAE

Moreton Bay Fig, Australian Banyan; Australiese Baniaan

OTHER LANGUAGES: Australischer Gummibaum (German); Permite (Portuguese); Higueira australiana (Spanish)

Eastern Australia Large, spreading tree, sometimes with aerial roots; bark brown, smooth or narrowly fissured, forming small ridges; buds hairy; twigs hairy. Leaves with petiole hairy or hairless, 40–150mm long; blade 110–230 × 50–125mm, elliptic to oblong; tip pointed; base rounded to squared; lower surface **rusty-hairy**; margin smooth. Inflorescences erect; peduncle **up to 15mm long**. Fruit a **round, red**, hairless fig **13–25** × 13–25mm.

- Drought 2
- Summer
- Evergreen

Grown in our region for shade and ornament, with limited use as a street tree. However, its aggressive root system makes this use questionable, as can be seen in the avenue of these figs at Kirstenbosch. The wood is of poor quality but has been used to make boxes.

VASILYEV / SHUTTERSTOCK.COM

1 *F. elastica* leaves

GEOFF NICHOLS

1 *F. elastica* figs

CASLIBER, WIKIMEDIA COMMONS, CC BY SA 3.0

2 *F. lyrata* leaves and figs

CERLIN NG

2 *F. lyrata* figs

3 *F. macrophylla* leaves

FOREST AND KIM STARR

3 *F. macrophylla* figs

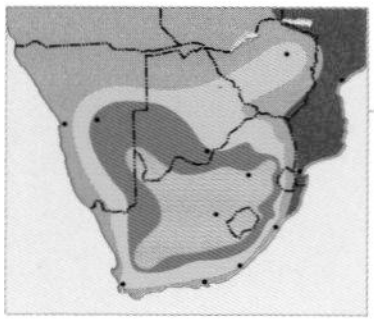

- Drought 3
- Summer
- Evergreen

1 *Ficus microcarpa* MORACEAE

Malay Banyan; Maleise Baniaan

OTHER LANGUAGES: Jawi-jawi, jejawi (Bahasa Indonesia); Rong shu (Chinese); Chinesische Feige (German); Kamarup (Hindi); Jaamu (Nepalese); Kal-ichchi (Tamil); Sai yoi (Thai); Cây gừa (Vietnamese)

India to southern China, Australia and the Pacific Medium-sized to large, widely spreading tree; bark grey, smooth; twigs hairless, **stiff**, green to grey. Leaves with petiole hairless, 8–20mm long; blade 27–110 × 15–60mm, egg-shaped to elliptic; tip **pointed or with a short, broad drip-tip**; base **obliquely** narrowed; margin smooth. Inflorescences erect; peduncle absent. Fruit a round, red or yellow, hairless fig 7–15 × 7–15mm. Seeds whitish.

Widely grown for ornament in our region.

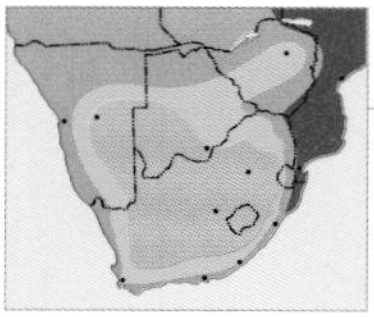

- Drought 2
- Summer
- Semi-deciduous

2 *Ficus religiosa* MORACEAE

Peepul, Bo Tree, Bodhi, Sacred Fig, Tree of Enlightenment; Stertblaarvy

OTHER LANGUAGES: Pu ti shu (Chinese); Figuier des Pagodes (French); Bobaum (German); Pipal (Hindi); Ashvattha (Sanskrit); Aracu (Tamil); Pho si maha pho (Thai); Peepal (Urdu); Cây đề (Vietnamese)

India to southern China, Vietnam and Thailand Medium-sized to large tree with a rounded to widely spreading crown, **without aerial roots**; bark brown, smooth; terminal bud 8–45mm long; twigs hairless; lenticels warty, conspicuous. Leaves with petiole hairless, 60–100mm long; blade 65–175 × 50–120mm, egg-shaped to triangular, **clattering in the wind**, with a **long drip-tip**; base squared to heart-shaped; margin smooth. Inflorescences erect; peduncle absent. Fruit a red to purple, ellipsoid fig about 7 × 10–14mm.

Grown in the warmer, wetter parts of our region, usually for religious reasons; the species is sacred to Hindus, Jains and Buddhists. Trees can be destructive to buildings because of their aggressive roots and are unfortunately planted too close to them too often. Numerous medicinal uses are recorded. *F. rumphii* is similar, but the leaf tips are shorter.

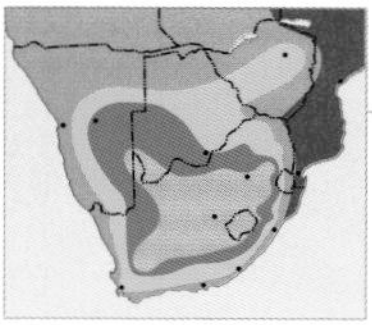

- Drought 3
- Summer
- Evergreen

3 *Ficus rubiginosa* (= *F. australis*) MORACEAE

Port Jackson Fig; Port Jacksonvy

Eastern Australia Medium-sized (large overseas) tree with a rounded to spreading crown; bark grey, smooth; buds **hairy**, terminal bud 15–40mm long, green; twigs **hairy**, brown; lenticels warty, conspicuous; stems angled or round. Leaves with petiole hairy, 6–40mm long; blade 42–170 × 20–75mm, egg-shaped to elliptic; lower surface **rusty-hairy**; margin smooth. Inflorescences erect; peduncle up to 10mm long. Fruit a yellow, sparsely hairy to hairless, round fig 13–15 × 13–15mm.

Widely but not commonly grown for ornament in our region.

1 *F. microcarpa* leaves

1 *F. microcarpa* figs

2 *F. religiosa* leaves

2 *F. religiosa* figs

3 *F. rubiginosa* leaves

3 *F. rubiginosa* figs

GROUP 5

Milkplum group

Leaves simple, alternate or in tufts, not bilobed; margin smooth, not prominently lobed. Stipular scar absent or obscure. Latex present.

See also Group 4: *Cecropia peltata* (p.104); Group 11: *Liquidambar styraciflua* (p.254); Group 39: *Manihot esculenta* (p.400) and *M. glaziovii* (p.402).

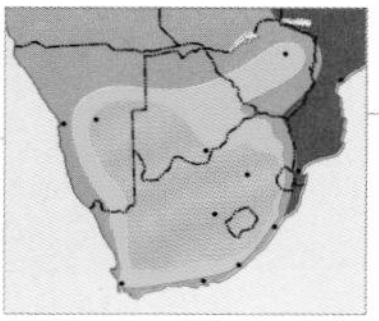

- Drought 2
- Summer
- Evergreen

1 *Aleurites moluccanus* (= *A. trilobus*) — EUPHORBIACEAE

Candlenut Tree; Kersneutboom

OTHER LANGUAGES: Buah keras (Bahasa Indonesia); He shi li (Chinese); Bankoelnoot (Dutch); Bancoulier des Moluques (French); Candlenuss (German); Jangli akhrot (Hindi); Noz-molucana (Portuguese); Calumbán (Spanish); Phothisat (Thai); Lai (Vietnamese)

Tropical East Asia Medium-sized to small tree with a narrow to rounded crown and **watery sap**. Leaves with petiole 60–220mm long, densely hairy, with **2 small green-brown glands** at the junction with the blade; blade 70–240 × 40–200mm, **shallowly palmately 1–5-lobed**, with **3–5 main veins** from the narrowed, squared or heart-shaped base; lower surface sparsely to moderately hairy. Inflorescences erect, 100–160mm long; pedicels stellate-hairy; males 7–10mm long, females 3–4.5mm long. Flowers white, small but attractive; perianth of a calyx and corolla; males and females on the same tree. Fruit fleshy, **3-angled** and egg-shaped, greenish, about 40 × 40–55mm. Seeds midbrown, mottled whitish to cream, about 2.5 × 2.75 × 2.25mm.

The seeds are used in Indonesian cookery but must be prepared carefully as they are poisonous when raw. Several parts of the plant have been used in traditional medicine in areas where it is native. Candlenut oil derived from the seeds is sometimes used like castor oil. Trees are grown as specimens and for ornament in the warmer parts of South Africa and Zimbabwe. Compare *Reutealis trisperma* (p.260).

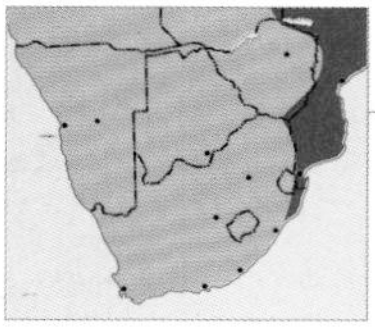

- Drought 2
- Spring
- Evergreen

2 *Anacardium occidentale* — ANACARDIACEAE

Cashew, Cashew Nut; Kasjoe, Kasjoeneut

OTHER LANGUAGES: Kaju (Arabic); Yao gu (Chinese); Acajou à pommes (French); Kaschubaum (German); Kaaju (Hindi); Cajueiro (Portuguese); Marañon (Spanish); Kallarma (Tamil)

Northeastern Brazil Small to medium-sized tree with a **widely spreading** crown; buds hairy; twigs hairless; latex **watery**, flow inconsistent. Leaves with petiole hairless, 3–25mm long; blade 70–240 × 34–120mm, **widest beyond the middle**; tip **rounded**; base narrowed or rounded. Inflorescences erect, 110–290mm long; peduncle 10–60mm long; pedicels hairy, **swollen (receptacle) in fruit**. Flowers white to pale green with red lengthways stripes, tubular, 8–13mm long. Fruit a **kidney-shaped** nut partly embedded in a fleshy receptacle (swollen pedicel); nut grey-brown, hairless, 20–30 × 10–20mm, receptacle fleshy, thin-skinned, yellow to red, 50–200 × 20–80mm.

An important food crop – both the seed and the expanded stalk (receptacle, or so-called apple) are edible, the latter being popular in areas where the trees are grown. This stalk can be eaten fresh or made into beverages. In Mozambique, it is distilled into *agua ardente*. The 'shells' of the nuts (actually the outer layers of the fruit) are poisonous, being filled with an irritant oil that has over 200 known uses, including as insecticide, jet-engine lubricant and a component in epoxy composites. The tree is said to be naturalised in South Africa but it will only grow in the warmest frost-free parts of the country such as Maputaland in northeastern KwaZulu-Natal.

1 *A. moluccanus* leaves and flowers

1 *A. moluccanus* flowers

1 *A. moluccanus* fruit

2 *A. occidentale* leaves

2 *A. occidentale* flowers

2 *A. occidentale* fruit

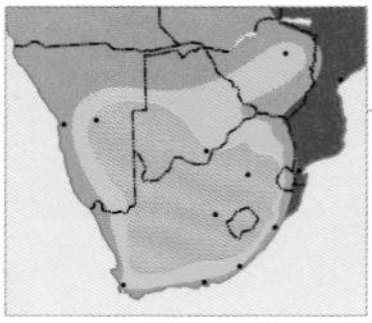

- Drought 2
- Summer
- Evergreen

1 *Chrysophyllum cainito* (= *Achras cainito*)

SAPOTACEAE

Star Apple; Sterappel

OTHER LANGUAGES: Goudblad Boom (Dutch); Caïnitier (French); Sternapfel (German); Ajara (Portuguese); Cainito (Spanish)

USA (Florida), the West Indies, Mexico to Peru and Brazil Large tree with an upright to rounded crown and white latex. Leaves with petiole **hairless**, 8–23mm long; blade 100–160 × 50–80mm, not lobed; base narrowed to a point; surface glossy above, **brownish hairy below**; margin smooth. Inflorescences erect fascicles; pedicels hairy, 5–16mm long in flower. Flowers white, yellow or red, small. Fruit **round**, fleshy, **yellow to purple**, 30–100mm in diameter. Seeds 10–25 × 4–7mm.

The fruits are reported to be delicious when eaten fresh and are best served chilled. In the warmer parts of the New World, star apple is often grown as a garden ornamental and as a support for epiphytic orchids; in our region only in KwaZulu-Natal.

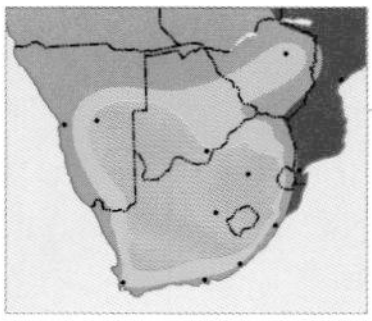

- Drought 2
- Summer
- Evergreen

2 *Hura crepitans*

EUPHORBIACEAE

Sandbox Tree, Monkey No-climb, Possumwood; Sandstrooierboom

OTHER LANGUAGES: Jabillo (Spanish)

Costa Rica to Bolivia Large to very large tree; bark **spiny**; lenticels **conspicuous** (on young twigs). Leaves with petiole hairless, up to 150mm long; blade 100–150 × 60–120mm, ovate, with a drip-tip and heart-shaped base, with **two conspicuous glands** on the **underside** of the leaf where it joins the petiole. Inflorescences erect; males in a spike 20–50mm long, on a peduncle up to 110mm long, females solitary. Flowers without petals; males and females **separate** but on the same tree, sepals in females red, conspicuous. Fruit hairless, pumpkin-shaped, dark brown, about 40 × 30–80mm, **splitting explosively**. Seeds midbrown, about 22 × 20 × 4mm.

The wood is used for furniture, under the commercial name *hura*. The milky sap is caustic and has been used to poison fish and to make arrow poison. In the days of quill pens, unripe fruits were sawn in half to make decorative boxes for the sand used to dry ink before the common use of blotting paper. Invasive in Tanzania but rarely grown in our region.

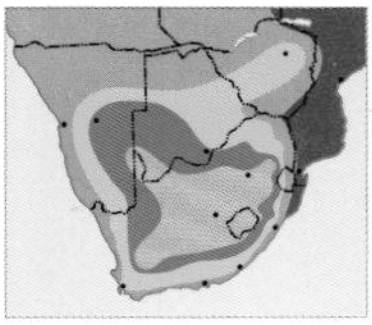

- Drought 2
- Spring
- Deciduous

3 *Ipomoea arborescens*

CONVOLVULACEAE

Morning-glory Tree, Tree Convolvulus; Eendagskoonboom, Boomakkerwinde

OTHER LANGUAGES: Palo del Muerto (Spanish)

Jamaica and Mexico Small tree with a sparse, spreading crown and **semisucculent branches**; twigs **hairy**, brown. Leaves with petiole **hairy**, 10–90mm long; blade 90–190 × 60–90mm, lance- to egg-shaped, with a drip-tip; base **heart-shaped**; surface sparsely hairy above, **densely so below**. Inflorescences a single flower or spike, 10–140mm long, appearing **before** the leaves; stalk 3–10mm long. Flowers **white**, tubular, 40–60mm long. Fruit a greenish, densely hairy, egg-shaped capsule 17–25mm long, brown inside. Seeds midbrown, 13–15 × 14–16 × 14–16mm.

Occasionally grown in warm areas as a garden ornamental. In nature, the flowers are visited by bats, birds and bees for nectar.

1 *C. cainito* leaves

CERLIN NG

1 *C. cainito* flowers

RICHARDERNESTYAP / SHUTTERSTOCK.COM

1 *C. cainito* fruit

CERLIN NG

2 *H. crepitans* flowers (male)

2 *H. crepitans* flower (female)

BARRY STOCK INSET: CHIEN-TI CHAO

2 *H. crepitans* fruit; inset: dried fruit

WICKI, WIKIMEDIA COMMONS, PUBLIC DOMAIN

3 *I. arborescens*

WICKI, WIKIMEDIA COMMONS, PUBLIC DOMAIN

3 *I. arborescens* flowers

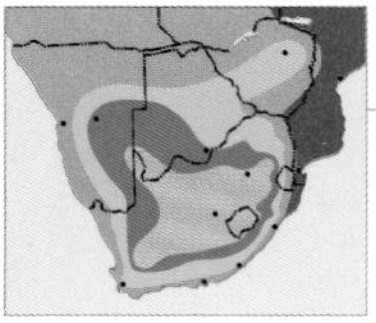

- Drought 2
- Spring
- Evergreen

1 *Ipomoea carnea* CONVOLVULACEAE

Pink Morning Glory; Pienk-akkerwinde

OTHER LANGUAGES: Canudo-de-pita (Portuguese); Gloria-de-mañana (Spanish)

Mexico to Florida (USA), Brazil and Peru Large straggling shrub; buds and twigs **hairless**. Leaves with petiole **hairless**, 20–100mm long; blade 100–250 × 35–70mm, egg-shaped to triangular, with a drip-tip; base squared to heart-shaped; surface **appearing hairless**. Inflorescences a single flower or sprays; stalk 60–150mm long. Flowers **pink to lilac**, tubular, 50–90mm long. Fruit an egg-shaped to round capsule about 20 × 10–15mm.

Invasive in many places and seen as such in our region far more often than cultivated, for which reason it is now a declared Category 1b invader. The plant is poisonous and all parts should be regarded as deadly. All the plants in southern Africa belong to subsp. *fistulosa*.

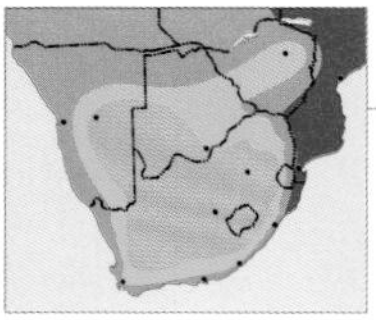

- Drought 2
- Spring
- Evergreen

2 *Jatropha curcas* EUPHORBIACEAE

Physic Nut; Purgeerboontjie

OTHER LANGUAGES: Pignon d'Inde, Purghère (French); Purgiernussbaum (German); Pinhão-de-purga (Portuguese); Árbol de los pinones de Indias (Spanish); Mbono kaburi (Swahili)

Mexico to South America Small tree with a spreading crown, shape often much modified by pruning; bark pale brown or greyish olive green, smooth, peeling; buds hairy; twigs hairless; latex **watery or cloudy**. Leaves alternate; petiole hairless, 90–200mm long; blade 50–150mm long and wide, egg-shaped to **pentagonal, shallowly palmately 1–5-lobed**; tip pointed; base heart-shaped, with **7–9 main veins** from the base; surface glossy above, dull below; margin smooth. Stipules soon falling. Inflorescences erect, 100–250mm long; peduncle 40–100mm long. Flowers small, greenish yellow; males and females separate but in the same inflorescence. Fruit a smooth to rough, leathery or woody, green, **3-angled**, ellipsoid capsule 25–30 × 20–25mm. Seeds black, 15–17 × 9–10 × 7–8mm.

Naturalised in southern Africa and a declared Category 2 invader in South Africa. Oil extracted from the seeds is a promising source of biodiesel and can be processed into jet fuel. All parts of the plant are poisonous, containing hydrogen cyanide. Medicinal uses are recorded.

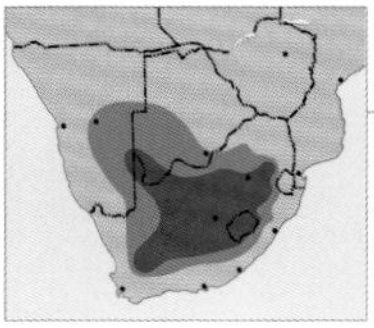

- Drought 3
- Spring
- Deciduous

3 *Maclura pomifera* (= *M. aurantiaca*) MORACEAE

Osage Orange; Indiaanse Soetlemoen

OTHER LANGUAGES: Bois d'arc (French)

USA Medium-sized tree with a pyramidal or rounded crown, which can be shaped by pruning, and **yellow-green to golden autumn colours**; buds with **stiff hairs on the margin of scales**; twigs hairy or not; branchlets with **short, stout spines**. Leaves with petiole hairy, 10–37mm long; blade 35–110 × 20–60mm, egg-shaped to elliptic, with a long drip-tip; lower surface hairy. Inflorescences hanging balls; males and females on separate trees, males whitish, females green, both inconspicuous. Fruit a **round, yellow-green**, hair-like (when young) cluster of berries **50–100mm in diameter**, rind with furrows like a brain. Seeds buff, 8–12 × 5–6mm.

The fruits are *not* edible but the seeds are said to be edible by both rodents and humans. The tree can be grown as an ornamental, though the fruits are messy, and trees can be used for hedges and shelter-belts. Medicinal uses are recorded.

1 *I. carnea* leaves

BRAAM VAN WYK

1 *I. carnea* flower

1 *I. carnea* fruit

BRAAM VAN WYK

BRAAM VAN WYK

2 *J. curcas* flowers; inset: flower detail

JOLOEI / SHUTTERSTOCK.COM

2 *J. curcas* fruit

LLEZ, WIKIMEDIA COMMONS, CC BY SA 3.0

3 *M. pomifera* flowers (female)

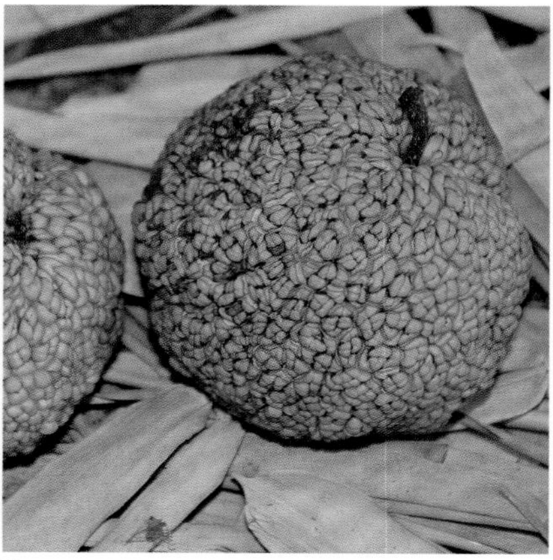

3 *M. pomifera* fruit

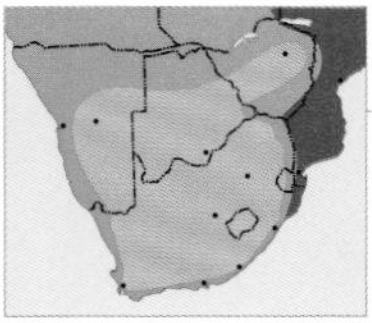

1 *Mangifera indica* ANACARDIACEAE

Mango; Mango, Veselperske

- Drought 2
- Spring
- Evergreen

OTHER LANGUAGES: Manga (Bahasa Indonesia); Mang guo (Chinese); Manguier (French); Mangobaum (German); Am chur (Hindi); Aamra (Sanskrit); Mwembe (Swahili); Āmpiram (Tamil)

India and Myanmar Medium-sized to large tree with a columnar to rounded crown; buds minute, hairless; twigs stout, hairless; latex **watery**, flow inconsistent. Leaves with petiole hairless, 15–60mm long, its base **swollen**; blade 150–300 × 35–70mm, oblong, with an ill-defined drip-tip; base narrowed; margin sometimes wavy; new growth **red**. Inflorescences stiff to hanging, 200–350mm long. Flowers small, dirty-white; petals 3–5 × 1–2mm. Fruit fleshy, elliptic or kidneyshaped, 40–250 × 10–100mm, peel leathery, red and yellow or green, flesh orange, juicy, often **fibrous**. Seeds large, buff.

Mangoes have been grown for their fruit in India for about 4,000 years. Fruits are consumed fresh, preserved in various ways or cooked. The fruits, juice and sap may cause contact dermatitis in sensitive individuals. Mango is the national fruit of India, Pakistan and the Philippines and the national tree of Bangladesh. It is sacred in Hindu custom. Locally naturalised in South Africa.

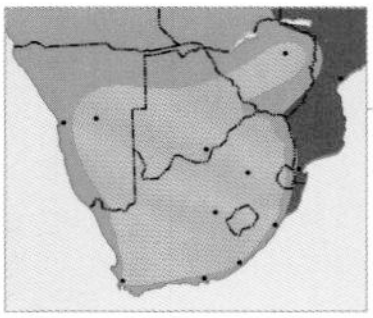

2 *Manilkara zapota* (= *Achras zapota, Sapota achras*) SAPOTACEAE

Sapodilla, Chicle, Noseberry; Sapodilla

- Drought 2
- Summer
- Evergreen

OTHER LANGUAGES: Nèfle d'Amérique (French); Breiapfel, Kaugummibaum (German); Sapote, Zapote, Zapotillo (Spanish)

Mexico to Nicaragua Medium-sized tree with a compact to rounded crown and **hairy twigs**. Leaves with petiole hairless, 6–30mm long; blade 30–130 × 15–50mm, lance-shaped to oblong; tip and base pointed to rounded; surface hairless throughout; margin smooth. Inflorescences **hanging downwards** (pendent), a single flower or clusters; stalk hairless. Flowers brown outside, white inside, generally 5–8mm long. Fruit fleshy, hairless, brown or yellow, 40–70 × 40–70mm, with a rough, leathery peel. Seeds black, about 25mm long.

The latex of this tree was used to make the original chewing gum, though most gum sold at present is derived from other sources of latex, some synthetic. However, the latex harvested from these trees is still so valuable that in Mexico it is illegal to fell a tree of this species. The ripe fruit is delicious and is eaten raw or made into jam, ice cream and other delicacies. The wood was once used as beams and lintels in Maya temples and these survive to the present day.

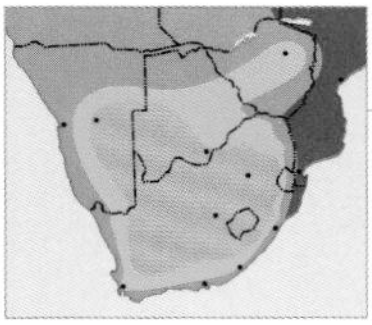

3 *Mimusops commersonii* SAPOTACEAE

Mauritius Milkberry; Mauritiusmelkbessie

- Drought 2
- Summer
- Evergreen

OTHER LANGUAGES: Varanto (Malagasy); Abricó da Praia (Portuguese)

The Mascarenes Small tree with a rounded crown. Leaves with petiole hairless, 10–15mm long; blade 70–150mm long, up to 110mm wide, ovate to oblong; tip **indented**; base narrowed; surface hairless; margin smooth, inrolled. Inflorescences **a single**, hanging **flower**; peduncle hairless, 50–80mm long. Flowers brown outside, white inside, 10–13mm long. Fruit **round**, hairless, fleshy, 30–45 × 30–45mm, **yellow**.

The fruit is edible, with a flavour compared to 'mashed potato and pineapple'. By all accounts, this is not the world's most palatable fruit. In our region, known with certainty only from KwaZulu-Natal.

FOREST AND KIM STARR

1 *M. indica* flowers

GEOFF NICHOLS

1 *M. indica* fruit

WIE146, WIKIMEDIA COMMONS, CC BY SA 3.0

2 *M. zapota* flowers

HK ARUN, WIKIMEDIA COMMONS, CC BY SA 3.0

2 *M. zapota* fruit

3 *M. commersonii* leaves

GEOFF NICHOLS

3 *M. commersonii* flower

CARL LEWIS

3 *M. commersonii* fruit

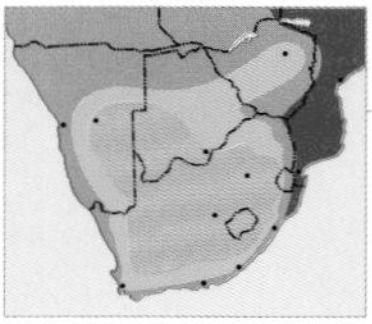

- Drought 2
- Autumn
- Deciduous

1 *Plumeria alba* APOCYNACEAE

White Frangipani; Witfrangipani

OTHER LANGUAGES: Frangipanier à Fleurs Blanches (French); Gulchin (Hindi)

Central America and the Caribbean Small tree with an open, upright to spreading crown; twigs very stout; latex white. Leaves crowded at ends of branches; petiole **hairless**, 30–50mm long; blade **200–300 × 20–60mm**, lance-shaped; tip drawn out to a point; surface **flat**, glossy above; margin rolled inwards. Inflorescences erect; peduncle 100–250mm long. Flowers tubular, scented; tube 15–20mm long, **white, with a yellow throat**, lobes 30–35mm long. Fruit **a pair** of pods up to 150mm long, not often seen.

Widely grown as an ornamental and naturalised in South and Southeast Asia. Flowers in all species of *Plumeria* are most fragrant at night. They are pollinated by hawk moths. However, this is pollination by deceit because the flowers offer no nectar as reward.

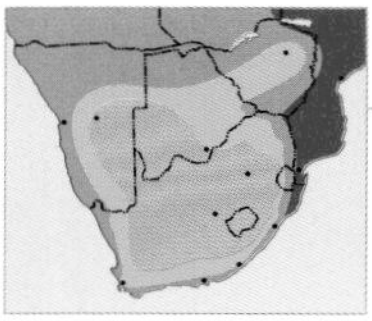

- Drought 2
- Summer
- Deciduous

2 *Plumeria rubra* *(= P. acutifolia, P. tricolor)* APOCYNACEAE

Frangipani, Nosegay, Red Frangipani; Frangipani, Rooifrangipani

OTHER LANGUAGES: Ji dan hua (Chinese); Lal Gulachin (Hindi); Cacaloxochitl (Nahuatl); Champaka (Sanskrit); Nela Sampangi (Tamil)

Mexico, Central America to Brazil and Paraguay Small tree with a spreading, candelabra-like crown; bark **rough**; twigs **very stout**, **dull**, hairless, pale brown; latex white. Leaves **crowded** at ends of branches; petiole **hairless**, 30–110mm long; blade 200–500 × **70–100mm**, widest at or beyond the middle, with a drip-tip; base narrowing gradually; surface dull, hairless. Inflorescences erect. Flowers scented, **white, yellow or pink**, with a **yellow** throat; tube up to 25mm, lobes 25–40 × 15–20mm. Fruit rarely set, **a pair** of pods up to 250 × 20–30mm, spindle-shaped.

Grown as a garden ornamental, with the same uses as other species of the genus. The most widely encountered frangipani in our region. Frangipanis are readily propagated by cuttings of branches taken in cooler months and left to dry for a week or more before planting.

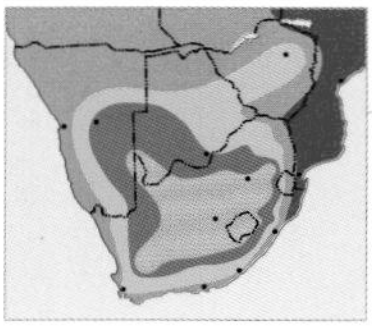

- Drought 2
- Summer
- Evergreen

3 *Pouteria campechiana* *(= Lucuma nervosa)* SAPOTACEAE

Yellow Sapote, Canistel, Eggfruit; Geelsapoot

OTHER LANGUAGES: Gelbe Sapote (German); Zapote Amarillo, Zapote de Niño (Spanish)

Mexico to Panama Usually a small tree but can become quite tall, crown **narrow**, up to 25m tall. Leaves with petiole **densely hairy**, 10–25mm long or longer; blade 80–250 × 27–70mm, rarely up to 330 × 150mm, lanceolate or elliptic; apex narrowed to rounded; base narrow; surface **hairless throughout**; margin smooth, **not rolled**. Inflorescences **erect**; pedicels hairy, 8–11mm long. Flowers greenish, inconspicuous, 7.5–13.5mm long. Fruit fleshy, almost hairless, 25–70mm long, yellow to orange. Seeds 20–38mm long.

The fruits are good eating when fully ripe and can be prepared in various ways. Various parts of the plant have medicinal uses in the area where it grows naturally. The timber is fine-grained and strong and so is valued for construction work. Grown in Mpumalanga and KwaZulu-Natal.

1 *P. alba* flowers

KS-ART / SHUTTERSTOCK.COM

1 *P. alba* flowers

2 *P. rubra* leaves; inset: fruit

BRAAM VAN WYK

BRAAM VAN WYK

2 *P. rubra* flowers

3 *P. campechiana* flowers

3 *P. campechiana* fruit

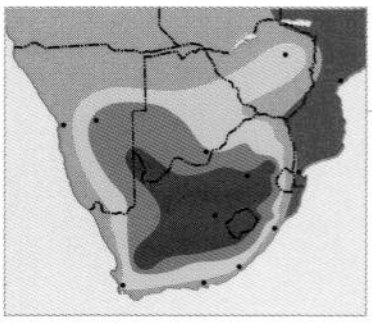

- Drought 2
- Summer
- Deciduous

1 *Sapium sebiferum* EUPHORBIACEAE
Chinese Tallow Tree; Chinese Kersvetboom

China and Taiwan Small tree with a spreading crown and **yellow, orange or red autumn colours**. Leaves with petiole hairless, 25–40mm long; blade 30–70 × 25–65mm, **rhombic to ovate** with a drip-tip; base rounded to heart-shaped; surface hairless throughout; margin smooth. Inflorescences **erect**, 25–100mm long; males and females separate but on the same spike. Fruit a **triangular capsule** about 12 × 10–15mm, brown-black when ripe. Seeds whitish, about 8 × 6 × 5mm.

This is a highly decorative tree for areas with wide temperature differences between summer and winter. The oil in the seed has industrial applications but is toxic; the waxy outer covering of the seed is used in soap-making. However, the tree is known to be invasive in the USA and Australia. It should only be planted in places where its seeds are rigorously contained or removed and where neither seeds nor root fragments can pose a threat to the natural vegetation. The sap is toxic and must be avoided.

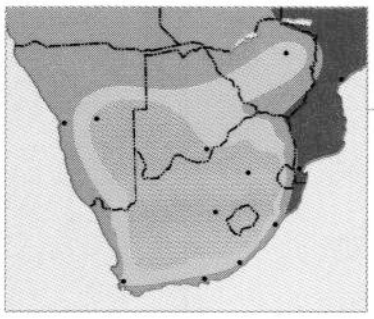

- Drought 2
- Spring–Summer
- Deciduous

2 *Semecarpus anacardium* ANACARDIACEAE
Marking Nut, Dhobi Nut; Merkneut

OTHER LANGUAGES: Noix à marquer (French); Ostindischer Merkfruchtbaum (German); Bhilawan (Hindi); Anacárdio oriental (Portuguese); Anacardio oriental (Spanish); Cen-kottai (Tamil); Bhilavan (Urdu)

India Small tree with a rounded to spreading crown; buds and twigs **hairy**; latex **white, drying black**. Leaves with petiole hairy, up to 40mm long; blade 200–350 × 80–150mm, widest beyond the middle, **stiff-textured**; veins hairy below. Inflorescences erect, up to 200mm long. Flowers green, inconspicuous; males and females on different trees. Fruit a **kidney-shaped** nut about 20 × 25mm, **shiny black**, borne on a **fleshy, yellow-orange** receptacle.

Because the nuts yield a water-insoluble substance that is used as an ink, Indian washermen *(dhobi-wallahs)* traditionally use them to mark the clothes in their care. The bark yields a resin that can be made into a varnish. A lubricant and preservative oil is expressed from the nuts. Parts of the tree have uses in Ayurvedic medicine.

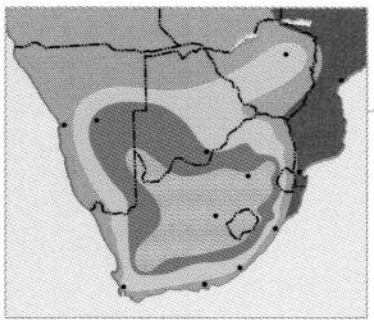

- Drought 2
- Summer
- Evergreen

3 *Sideroxylon foetidissimum* *(= Mastichodendron foetidissimum)* SAPOTACEAE
False Mastic; Valsmastiekboom

OTHER LANGUAGES: Acomat (French); Tortuga Amarillo (Spanish)

USA (Florida), Mexico to Guatemala, and the West Indies Medium-sized to large, potentially fast-growing tree with a rounded crown. Leaves with petiole hairless, **20–45mm long**; blade 75–145 × 33–77mm; tip and base broad; surface hairless throughout; margin smooth. Inflorescences **erect**; pedicels hairless, 4–8mm long. Flowers **yellow**, inconspicuous but **smelling of cheese**. Fruit fleshy, round, hairless, 15–26 × 15–26mm, **orange**. Seeds 13–20mm long.

The fruits are edible but very sticky with latex and so are more attractive to birds than to humans. This tree is rare in nature, because it has been over-exploited for boat-building. The heartwood is attractive, yellow-orange in colour.

1 *S. sebiferum* flowers

TATIANA GERUS

1 *S. sebiferum* fruit

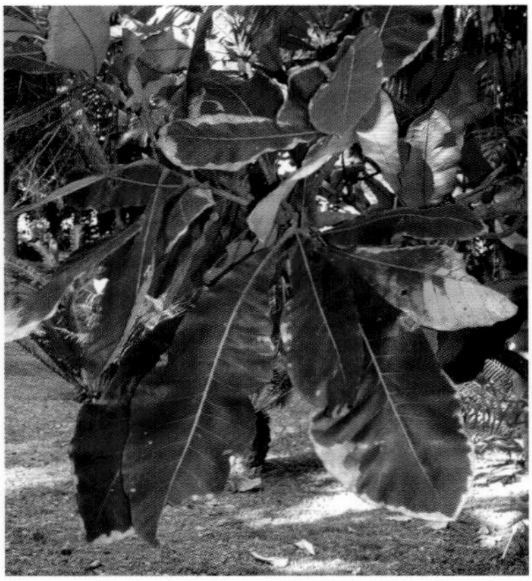

2 *S. anacardium* leaves

J.M. GARG / WIKIMEDIA COMMONS, 1.2 CC BY SA 3.0

2 *S. anacardium* flowers

LLEZ, WIKIMEDIA COMMONS, CC BY SA 3.0

2 *S. anacardium* fruit

KAREN BLIX / FLICKR

3 *S. foetidissimum* leaves and flowers

LEON LEVY NATIVE PLANT PRESERVE

3 *S. foetidissimum* fruit

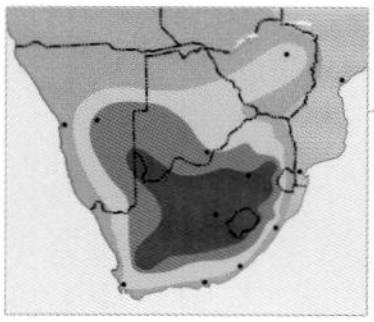

1 *Thevetia peruviana* *(= Cascabela thevetia, T. neriifolia, T. yccotli)* APOCYNACEAE

Yellow Oleander, Lucky Nut; Geelselonsroos, Geel-oleander

- Drought 2
- Spring–Autumn
- Evergreen

OTHER LANGUAGES: Laurier jaune des Indes (French); Loendro amarelo (Portuguese); Adelfa amarilla (Spanish)

Southern Mexico and Central America Large shrub or small tree with a rounded crown; buds hairless; twigs hairless, **brown or grey**; lenticels **smooth**, **conspicuous**; latex white. Leaves with petiole hairless, 3–5mm long; blade 75–120 × **4–13mm**, strap-shaped; tip and base **long drawn out**; lower surface **hairless**. Inflorescences an erect, single flower. Flowers **yellow to orange**, without markings; tube 10–25mm long, lobes 35–45mm long. Fruit fleshy, red or black, 18–27 × 25–33mm. Seeds 1–3mm long and wide.

All parts of the plant are deadly poisonous and it would seem for this reason alone that its popularity in gardens is unfortunate. However, it is also invasive and has been declared a Category 1b invader in South Africa and may not be grown.

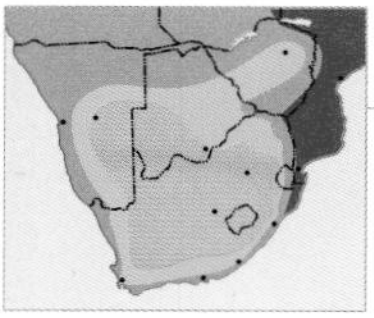

2 *Triplaris americana* POLYGONACEAE

Ant Tree, Long Jack; Triplaris

- Drought 2
- Spring
- Deciduous

OTHER LANGUAGES: Palo Santo (Spanish)

Panama to Brazil Medium-sized to tall tree with a narrow to pyramidal crown; buds and twigs hairless. Leaves with petiole hairy or hairless, 10–40mm long, with **watery latex** forming a drop when fresh petiole is broken; blade 200–400 × 80–180mm, oblong; tip **rounded with a small point**; base rounded; lower surface sometimes hairy; texture **leathery**. Inflorescences erect, up to 300mm long; males and females on different trees. Flowers individually small; males white, females red and persistent. Fruit a small nut 6–10 × 4–6mm, **surrounded by the chaffy remains of the flower**.

This species is becoming naturalised in Durban and is already a declared Category 1a invader in South Africa. The timber can be used for construction and flooring but the hairs of the flowers can cause dermatitis. Medicinal uses are recorded. Compare *T. weigeltiana* (p.238).

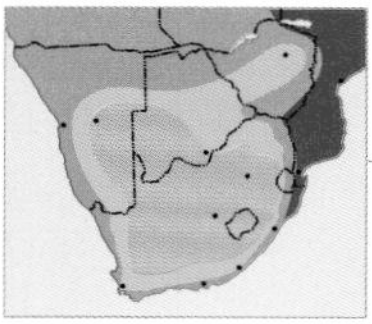

3 *Uapaca kirkiana* PHYLLANTHACEAE

Mahobohobo (fruit), Muzhanje (tree), Masuku, Wild Loquat; Mahobohobo (vrug), Muzhanje (boom)

- Drought 2
- Summer
- Evergreen or semi-deciduous

OTHER LANGUAGES: Musuku (Bemba, Lozi); Mahobohobo (fruit), Muzhanje (tree) (Shona); Mkusu (Swahili)

Tropical Africa Medium-sized tree with a rounded crown, hairy twigs and **clear latex**. Leaves clustered at ends of branches; petiole hairless, 5–20mm or longer; blade large, **thick-textured**, 100–300 × 70–170mm, **ovate to round**; tip and base rounded; surface, especially veins, hairy below; margin **wavy**. Inflorescences erect; peduncle 4–20mm long. Flowers yellow, inconspicuous; males and females **on separate trees**. Fruit fleshy, round, hairless, 30–40 × 30–40mm, brown or yellow to orange. Seeds midbrown, about 15 × 8 × 5mm.

The edible fruits are sought after in the native range of this tree. In addition to being consumed fresh, they can be used to make wine, jams and sweetmeats. Horticulturally, the tree is an ornamental shade tree. Around villages, the dry, fallen leaves rustle relatively loudly when trodden on, so betraying any attempt at a stealthy approach. Fresh seeds remain viable for only about three weeks.

GEOFF NICHOLS

1 *T. peruviana* leaves

BRAAM VAN WYK

1 *T. peruviana* flowers

LLEZ, WIKIMEDIA COMMONS, CC BY SA 3.0

1 *T. peruviana* fruit

TATIANA GERUS

2 *T. americana* flowers (male)

SCOTT ZONA

2 *T. americana* young fruit

JMK, WIKIMEDIA COMMONS CC BY SA 3.0

2 *T. americana* fruit

3 *U. kirkiana* leaves

NEIL CROUCH

3 *U. kirkiana* fruit

GROUP 6

Tamboti group

Leaves simple, alternate or in tufts, not bilobed; margin toothed, scalloped and/or sometimes deeply or coarsely more than 2-lobed. Stipular scar absent or obscure. Latex present.

See also Group 2: *Carica papaya* (p.44); Group 5: *Jatropha curcas* (p.116).

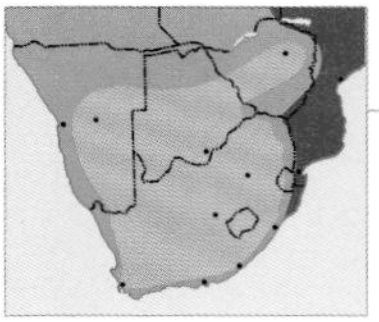

- Drought 2
- Summer
- Deciduous

1 *Chlorophora tinctoria* (= *Maclura tinctoria*)

MORACEAE

Old Fustic, Dyer's Mulberry, Fustic; Fustiekboom

OTHER LANGUAGES: Bois d'Orange (French); Mora amarilla (Spanish)

Northern South America to Mexico and the West Indies Medium-sized to large tree with a narrow to rounded crown and **yellowish latex**. Stems sometimes thorny. Leaves with petiole hairless, 5–10mm long; blade 50–110 × 15–50mm, lance- or egg-shaped to elliptic; apex acuminate; base truncate; surface hairless; margin **usually toothed**. Inflorescences erect, usually 10–30mm long; peduncle 4–12mm long. Flowers inconspicuous; males and females on separate trees. Fruit fleshy, yellow, 12–14mm in diameter.

The wood yields a yellowish brown dye ('old fustic', as opposed to 'young fustic', which is derived from *Cotinus coggygria*, p.162) and is also used for construction, boats, turning, furniture and more. The dye was used to make khaki clothing for US troops in World War I. With different mordants, a range of yellow, brownish and green colours can be obtained. Grown in Mozambique and in KwaZulu-Natal in South Africa.

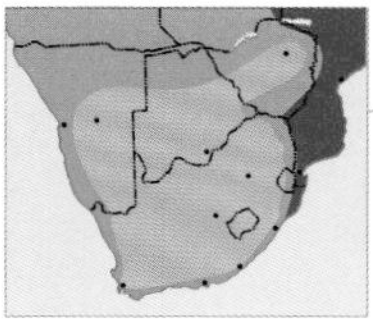

- Drought 2
- Spring
- Deciduous

2 *Cochlospermum vitifolium* (= *Bombax vitifolium*)

COCHLOSPERMACEAE

Shellseed Tree, Silk-cotton Tree; Skulpsaadboom

OTHER LANGUAGES: Carne de perro, Poro-poro (Spanish)

Mexico, Florida and Puerto Rico to Bolivia and Brazil Small tree with a **bowl-shaped crown, often branching close to the ground**; bark grey, narrowly fissured; twigs hairless, stout; latex **yellowish**. Leaves alternate; petiole hairless; blade 250–300 × 150–300mm, oblong or round, deeply **palmately 3–7-lobed**; tip rounded or with a long drip-tip; base heart-shaped; surface glossy above, dull below; margin **toothed**. Inflorescences erect, appearing before the leaves. Flowers **yellow**; petals 5. Fruit a densely hairy, papery, grey-brown capsule up to 80mm long. Seeds dark brown to black, about 5mm long.

Grown in our region as a specimen tree in a few places in KwaZulu-Natal but would make a good ornamental in warmer gardens. The wood is soft and brittle, with little value. The latex can be used as a dyestuff. Medicinal uses are recorded.

1 *C. tinctoria* leaves

ANDRES HERNANDEZ

1 *C. tinctoria* flowers (female)

2 *C. vitifolium*

ROLANDO PÉREZ

2 *C. vitifolium* leaves

2 *C. vitifolium* flower

ROLANDO PÉREZ

2 *C. vitifolium* flowers and fruit

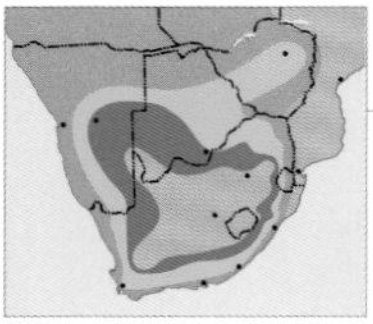

- Drought 2
- Summer
- Deciduous or Evergreen

1 *Euphorbia pulcherrima* (= *Poinsettia pulcherrima*) EUPHORBIACEAE

Poinsettia; Karlienblom

OTHER LANGUAGES: Euphorbe écarlate (French); Weihnachtsstern (German); Flor-de-papagaio (Portuguese); Flor de noche buena (Spanish)

Central America Tree-shrub of indefinite form, with **white latex**. Leaves with petiole hairless, 35–100mm long; blade 50–165 × 25–90mm, of variable shape; base rounded; surface hairless throughout; margin usually very coarsely toothed. Inflorescences erect, 25–50mm long; 'petals' (technically bracts) **spirally arranged, shaped like the leaves, creamy to red**. Flowers yellow, inconspicuous. Fruit a hairless capsule with a smooth wall, rarely seen.

Surely one of the most important horticultural crops, with millions of small individuals sold as pot plants at Christmas time each year. Unfortunately one of the most difficult to reflower after the initial display when purchased. Poinsettias need a period of long, uninterrupted, light-free nights for about two months in early spring to develop flowers. Plants are tolerant of full sun.

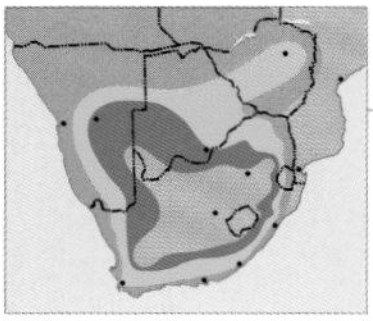

- Drought 2
- Spring
- Evergreen

2 *Jatropha multifida* EUPHORBIACEAE

Coral Bush; Koraalbos

OTHER LANGUAGES: Médicinier espagnol (French); Flor de Coral (Portuguese); Avellano purgante (Spanish)

Central America **Shrub or small tree** with an open, spreading crown; twigs hairless; lenticels warty, conspicuous; latex **cloudy**. Leaves alternate; petiole hairless, up to 200mm long; blade up to 200 × 300mm, **round, deeply palmately 10-12-lobed**; tip narrowly pointed; base heart-shaped, with **10–12** main veins from the base; surface glossy above, whitish below; margin very **coarsely and deeply toothed**. Inflorescences erect, up to 250mm long; peduncle up to 220mm long, **red**. Flowers red; petals 5, these 5–7 × 2–3mm; males and females separate, in the same inflorescence. Fruit a **3-angled**, pear-shaped capsule about 25 × 28mm. Seeds buff, about 17 × 15 × 13mm.

Grown occasionally for ornament or as part of a succulent collection and recorded from Limpopo, Gauteng and KwaZulu-Natal. The plant is poisonous and medicinal uses are recorded.

1 *E. pulcherrima* leaves

1 *E. pulcherrima* flowers

1 *E. pulcherrima* flower detail

BRAAM VAN WYK

2 *J. multifida* leaves and fruit

WENDY CUTLER

2 *J. multifida* flowers (male)

2 *J. multifida* fruit

GEOFF NICHOLS

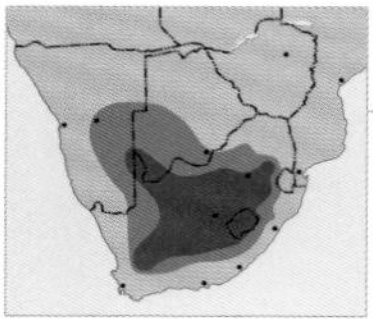

- Drought 2
- Spring
- Deciduous

1 *Morus alba* MORACEAE
White Mulberry; Witmoerbei

OTHER LANGUAGES: El Ttuut (Arabic); Bebesaran (Bahasa Indonesia); Sang (Chinese); Mûrier (French); Maulbeere (German); Aspromouria (Greek); Shahtoot (Hindi); Amoreira (Portuguese); Mora (Spanish); Mfurusadi (Swahili); Mon (Thai)

Central Asia, eastwards to China Medium-sized tree with a rounded crown and **dull yellow autumn colours**; buds and twigs **hairless**; latex watery to cloudy. Leaves with petiole hairless, 12–50mm long; blade 75–200 × 30–150mm, very variable in shape, may be deeply lobed on young trees or water shoots, with **3 main veins** from the **heart-shaped** base; margin **toothed**. Inflorescences erect or hanging, 8–40mm long. Flowers inconspicuous. Fruit **fleshy, cylindrical**, red to black, or white, 12–25mm long, about 10mm in diameter. Seeds 2–3mm long.

One website aptly describes the white mulberry as a 'trash tree' – it suckers, is invasive (declared Category 3 invader in South Africa), serves as host to several serious plant diseases, generally looks untidy and the fruit stains can be very messy indeed. On the positive side, it is the preferred food of silkworms and it is possible that this (and the enthusiasm with which primary-school children keep silkworms) accounts for the fact that it seems to have almost completely replaced the more intensely flavoured and better behaved black mulberry *(M. nigra)* in southern Africa. It is noteworthy for its explosive release of pollen, with grains being released at over 500km/h, or half the speed of sound.

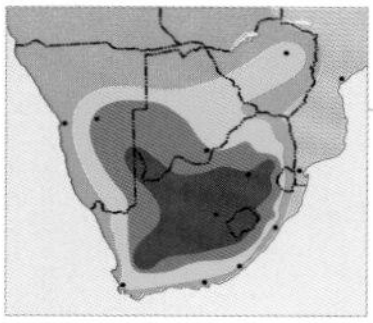

- Drought 2
- Spring
- Deciduous

2 *Morus nigra* MORACEAE
Black Mulberry; Swartmoerbei

OTHER LANGUAGES: Hei sang (Chinese); Mûrier noir (French); Schwarzer Maulbeerbaum (German); Mavri mouria (Greek); Moro nero (Italian); Kuro mi guwa (Japanese); Amoreira negra (Portuguese); Shelkovitsa chernaia (Russian); Morera negra (Spanish)

Southwestern Asia Medium-sized tree with a rounded crown and **dull yellow autumn colours**; buds and twigs **hairy**; latex watery to cloudy. Leaves with petiole hairless, 15–40mm long; blade 60–225 × 50–200mm, egg-shaped to round, **sometimes shallowly lobed**, with 1–3 main veins from the **heart-shaped** base; surface **rough or hairy**; margins toothed. Inflorescences erect, 12–35mm long. Flowers inconspicuous; males and females separate, sometimes on the same tree. Fruit fleshy, cylindrical, 20–25mm long, red, ripening dark purple or black.

This species is much less often seen than the white mulberry (*M. alba*, above), though it was once commoner. Remaining trees in cultivation are widely scattered, usually in private gardens in cooler areas such as the Free State, Gauteng and North West province. It can be distinguished by its rough, more regularly shaped leaves on hairy twigs, and generally larger, darker-coloured fruit. These fruits can be eaten fresh or preserved as jams, or can be fermented into an alcoholic beverage similar to red wine. One of the reasons why it has become unpopular is that trees are quite messy; fallen fruit and the droppings of birds that love feeding on them cause dark purple stains, a particular nuisance near homes with carpets.

1 *M. alba* leaf

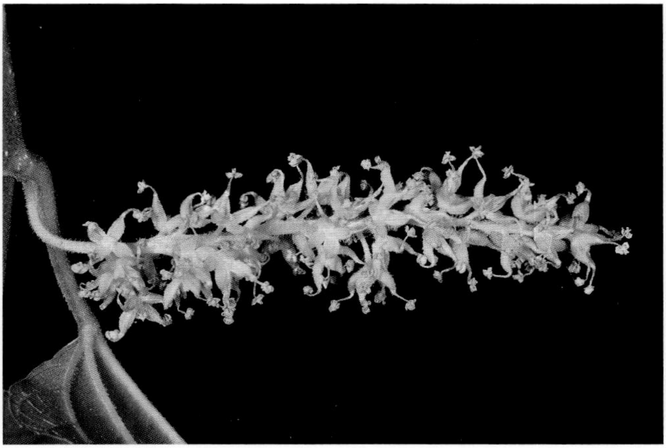

1 *M. alba* flowers (male)

1 *M. alba* fruit

2 *M. nigra* leaves

2 *M. nigra* flowers

2 *M. nigra* flowers (female)

GROUP 7

Silver-oak group

Leaves simple, alternate or in tufts, not bilobed; blade with single midvein from base, distinctly discolorous. Latex absent.

See also Group 10: *Cydonia oblonga* (p.208) and *Magnolia grandiflora* (p.226); Group 11: *Populus* × *canescens* (p.260).

1 *Alphitonia excelsa*

RHAMNACEAE

Red Ash, Soap Tree; Rooi-esseboom

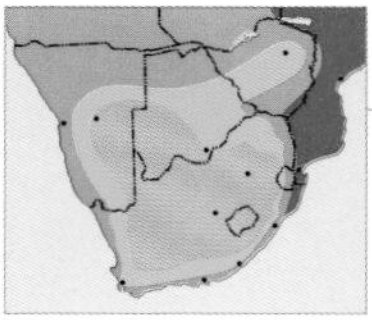

- Drought 2
- Autumn
- Semi-deciduous

Northern and eastern Australia Medium-sized tree with a spreading crown and hairy twigs and buds. Leaves with petiole 6–12mm long; blade 70–120 × 10–25mm; tip pointed; base rounded; margin **smooth, sometimes inrolled**. Inflorescences erect, large and showy. Flowers small, **creamy white**, numerous. Fruit fleshy, **black**, 6–11mm in diameter. Seeds midbrown.

Trees grow fast in cultivation but are short-lived, rarely exceeding 15 years. It can be used as a street or shelter tree and is also ornamental. The timber is tough and reddish brown and has been used in boat-building and cabinet-making. There are records of its use as fodder for sheep and cattle but in our region it is known only as a specimen tree.

2 *Buddleja alternifolia*

BUDDLEJACEAE

Weeping Butterfly Bush; Chinese Treursalie

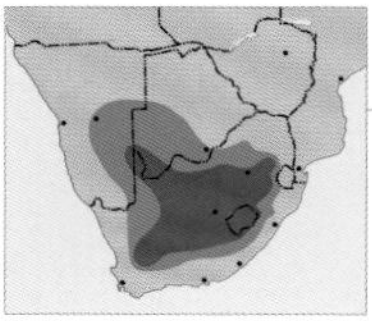

- Drought 2
- Summer
- Evergreen

OTHER LANGUAGES: Huye zuiyucao (Chinese)

China Spreading tree-shrub, often with a **weeping** habit; buds hairy; twigs becoming hairless; stems **square**. Leaves with petiole densely hairy and **up to 3mm long or absent**; blade 37–100 × 6–12mm, narrowly lance-shaped to elliptic; base narrowed; upper surface dull, 'quilted'; margin smooth. Stipules present. Inflorescences **hanging**, 10–45mm long. Flowers creamy, **lilac or purple**, with an orange throat. Fruit a small, inconspicuous capsule about 4–5 × 2mm. Seeds buff, 1.5–2 × 0.4–0.5 × 0.2–0.3mm.

This garden ornamental not only pleases human viewers but also attracts butterflies. In our region it is grown only in cold places.

3 *Conocarpus erectus*

COMBRETACEAE

Buttonwood; Knoophout

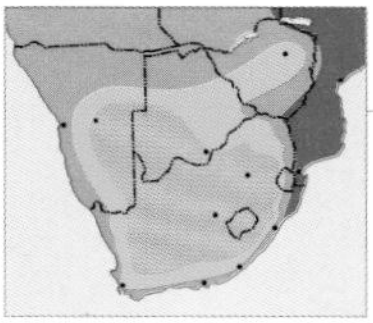

- Drought 1
- Summer
- Evergreen

OTHER LANGUAGES: Palétuvier gris (French); Mangue de Botão (Portuguese); Mangle Blanco (Spanish)

Mexico to West Africa Spreading shrub or tree, rarely reaching medium size; buds hairy; twigs **hairless, brittle**. Leaves with petiole hairless; blade 20–100mm long, with **two salt glands at the base**; margin smooth. Inflorescences an erect ball. Flowers inconspicuous. Fruit a **dense cluster** of red-brown capsules 5–15mm long, bursting when ripe. Seeds dispersed by water.

Unusually for trees with a record of cultivation, buttonwood usually grows in brackish water in nature. However, it can be grown on dry land, where it has a place as a curiosity in botanical gardens. It is also used as an ornamental, especially as a bonsai or a support for epiphytes. There are reports of its being eaten by buffalo in West Africa. The fruit clusters are button-like, hence the common names.

1 *A. excelsa* flowers

1 *A. excelsa* fruit

2 *B. alternifolia* leaves

2 *B. alternifolia* flowers

3 *C. erectus* leaves

3 *C. erectus* flowers

3 *C. erectus* fruit

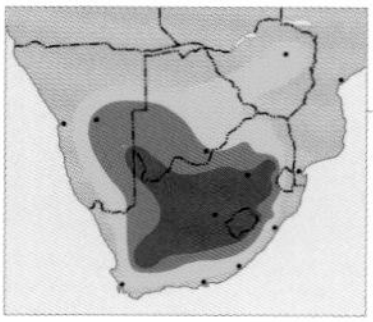

1 *Cotoneaster frigidus* ROSACEAE

Giant Showberry; Reusepronkbessie

- Drought 2
- Spring
- Deciduous or Evergreen

OTHER LANGUAGES: Nai han xun zi (Chinese)

Himalayas Large, spreading shrub or small tree with **unarmed, arching** branches and hairy, angled or round twigs. Leaves with petiole hairy, 4–7mm long; blade **75–125 × 25–50mm**, rarely smaller; margin smooth, sometimes fringed with hairs. Inflorescences **erect**, 40–60mm long. Flowers small, white or pink, on individual pedicels 2–4mm long. Fruit fleshy, **round**, red, 4–5mm in diameter, **crowned with persistent remains of the calyx**.

The cultivar 'Cornubia', which is more compact than the wild form, is recorded from the cold parts of southern Africa. The fruits of this hardy garden ornamental attract birds, which may in due course spread the seeds into natural areas.

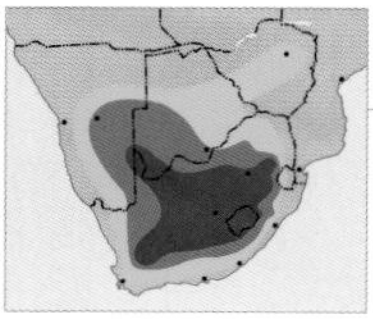

2 *Cotoneaster lacteus* ROSACEAE

Milkflower Cotoneaster; Melkblompronkbessie

- Drought 2
- Summer
- Evergreen

China Large shrub or small tree, 2.5–4m tall, with **unarmed** branches; buds and twigs **hairy**. Leaves with petiole hairy, up to 6mm long; blade **30–55 × 20–30mm**; tip and base pointed; margin smooth. Inflorescences erect. Flowers small, white, numerous. Fruit fleshy, red to orange, **egg-shaped**, about 4.5–6 × 3mm, **crowned with persistent remains of the calyx**.

One report suggests that birds avoid the fruits of this species but others suggest they are attracted by them, as they are by other species. The flowers attract bees and other nectar-feeding insects. As a garden plant, this ornamental is notably resistant to salt, smog and other adversities and is grown in many parts of South Africa and Zimbabwe.

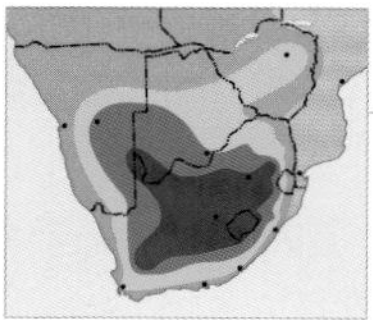

3 *Eriobotrya japonica* *(= Mespilus japonica, Photinia japonica)* ROSACEAE

Loquat; Lukwart

- Drought 2
- Spring
- Evergreen

OTHER LANGUAGES: Pi ba (Chinese); Bibassier (French); Japanische Mispel (German); Lokat (Hindi); Nespolo di Giappone (Italian); Biwa (Japanese); Lokat (Nepalese); Nespereira (Portuguese); Lokva (Russian); Muzhanje (Shona); Níspero del Japón (Spanish); Pi pae (Thai); Nhót tây (Vietnamese)

China and Japan Small tree with a rounded crown; buds and twigs **woolly**. Leaves with petiole **woolly**, 6–10mm long; blade **leathery, 150–300 × 75–125mm**, widest beyond the middle; margin toothed. Inflorescences erect, 75–150mm long. Flowers white to yellow; petals 5–9 × 4–6mm. Fruit fleshy, yellow-orange, hairy or hairless, about 37 × 10–15mm.

Usually grown in gardens for its fruit, eaten fresh or cooked. The wood is pink, hard and close-grained and has been used to make drawing instruments. Leaves are occasionally used as stock fodder and various parts of the tree are used in Asian medicine. The seeds contain hydrogen cyanide (prussic acid, HCN) and are poisonous. The fruits ripen during late winter and spring and act as a bridge for the destructive fruit fly until the summer fruiting of the deciduous fruits industry. Consequently the species is listed as a declared Category 1b invader in the Western Cape.

P. GARIN

1 *C. frigidus* flowers

PAUL SELIGMAN

1 *C. frigidus* fruit

2 *C. lacteus* flowers

2 *C. lacteus* fruit

3 *E. japonica* leaves

TETSUYA ODAKA

3 *E. japonica* flowers

BRAAM VAN WYK

3 *E. japonica* fruit

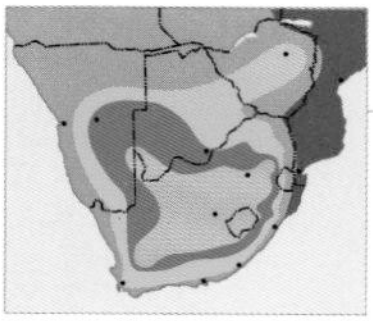

- Drought 3
- Spring–Summer
- Evergreen

1 *Lagunaria patersonia* MALVACEAE

Pyramid Tree, Kangaroo Apple; Piramideboom, Australiese Piramideboom

OTHER LANGUAGES: Hibiscus de l'île Norfolk (French); Weißholz (German); Árbol Pica-pica (Spanish)

Northeastern Australia and Norfolk Island Small to medium-sized tree with a **pyramidal** crown; buds and twigs hairy. Leaves with petiole **hairy**, up to 20mm long; blade 50–100 × 40–50mm; tip rounded; base narrowed; hairs on lower surface rough; margin smooth. Inflorescences an axillary, erect, **single flower**. Flowers erect, pink, **hibiscus-like**, 40–45mm long, up to 25mm across, on pedicels 10–20mm long. Fruit a grey-brown, densely hairy, **5-angled capsule** 30–40 × 20–30mm. Seeds red-orange.

Pyramid tree is a common garden ornamental and street tree with the positive features of attractive flowers and drought resistance. However, the hairs in the fruits and possibly elsewhere on the plant are irritant, making it unsuitable for use in crowded places and near mischievous schoolboys! A report was received from Cape Town of a case where hairs from a tree were blown into washing hanging out to dry on a neighbouring property and the owners of the latter had severe dermatitis as a result. There are occasional reports, mostly from Australia, of its becoming naturalised outside its normal range. The foliage of this species superficially resembles that of *Acca sellowiana* (p.292), whose leaves are opposite and have secretory cavities.

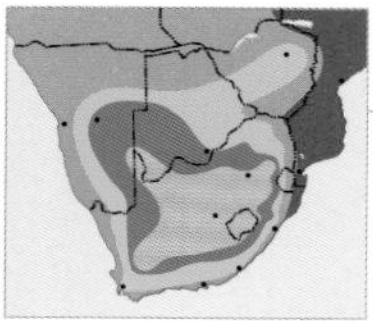

- Drought 2
- Spring
- Evergreen

2 *Persea americana* (= *P. gratissima*) LAURACEAE

Avocado, Alligator Pear, Avocado Pear; Avokado, Avokadopeer

OTHER LANGUAGES: Avocatier (French); Alligatorbirne (German); Ahuacatl (Nahuatl); Abacateiro (Portuguese); Aguacate (Spanish)

Central America Medium-sized to large tree with a narrow to pyramidal crown and hairless twigs. Leaves with petiole hairless, 10–60mm long; blade **60–220 × 30–140mm, blue-green below**, with a hard texture and a **very fine network of tertiary veins**; margin smooth. Inflorescences erect, **much branched**, 40–120mm long; peduncle 10–70mm long. Flowers small, creamy to green. Fruit fleshy, **pear-shaped, black or green when ripe, 100–300 × 50–150mm**, rind rough or smooth, depending on cultivar. Seeds **large, up to 65mm long**, buff.

There are many cultivars known, in two main groups and at least one minor one. The most commonly encountered cultivar in South Africa is 'Fuerte'. South Africa ranked 17th in the FAO's (United Nations Food and Agriculture Organization) list of major producers of avocados in 2011. The fruits are an important source of mono-unsaturated fats and are also a good source of potassium and some vitamins. In Spanish-speaking South America and many other places, avocado fruits are eaten as a savoury but in other places, such as tropical Asia and Brazil, the flesh is sweetened and forms part of a variety of desserts. Home growers may need to know that trees are not self-fertile and will not bear unless there is a second tree, preferably of a cultivar belonging to a different group, nearby. The trees are stressed by cold, drought and salt, all of these reducing the yield. Seeds only remain viable for a few weeks after ripening.

The leaves, bark, fruit flesh, peels and pits contain persin, a potentially toxic compound. If consumed in large quantities, persin is known to be harmful, even fatal, to many mammals and birds. It is generally harmless to humans, although negative effects may be seen in allergic individuals.

1 *L. patersonia* leaves

GEOFF NICHOLS

1 *L. patersonia* flowers

IGOR MAKUNIN

1 *L. patersonia* fruit

2 *P. americana* leaves

GEOFF NICHOLS

2 *P. americana* flowers

2 *P. americana* fruit

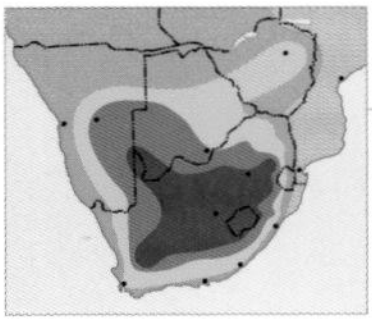

1 *Pittosporum crassifolium* PITTOSPORACEAE

Stiff-leaved Cheesewood, Karo; Styweblaarkasuur

- Drought 2
- Spring
- Evergreen

OTHER LANGUAGES: Kaikaro (Maori)

New Zealand Small tree or large shrub with a rounded crown, shape dependent on pruning; buds and twigs **hairy**. Leaves with petiole densely hairy, 4–14mm long; blade 30–80 × 10–30mm, **widest beyond the middle**; base gradually tapering; upper surface **hairy at first, later glossy**; lower surface white-woolly; margin **rolled under**. Inflorescences erect. Flowers **red to purple**; petals 10–16 × 3–5mm. Fruit a woody capsule 10–30 × 10–30mm. Seeds black.

The cultivar 'Variegatum' has a creamy margin to the leaves and is sometimes seen in southern Africa. This cheesewood is particularly useful as a hedge at the coast. Reports of other uses are rare but include a note that the wood has been used for inlay. In South Africa, the species is a declared Category 3 invader.

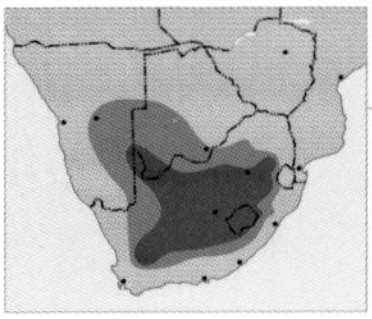

2 *Populus alba* SALICACEAE

White Poplar, Abele; Witpopulier

- Drought 1
- Summer
- Evergreen

Eurasia and North Africa Medium-sized, **often suckering** tree with a narrow to rounded crown and **yellow autumn colours**; twigs and buds hairy. Leaves with petiole hairy, 12–37mm long; blade 40–120mm long, sometimes **shallowly 3-5-lobed**, with **5 main veins** from the squared base; margin toothed, sometimes wavy. Inflorescences **hanging**, 60–100mm long. Flowers inconspicuous; males and females on separate trees, only females known in southern Africa. Fruit a hairless capsule 3–5mm long (not set in southern Africa).

Formerly planted in many parts of the region as a source of cheap, soft lumber and for shelter, this species is a declared Category 2 invader in South Africa. It is said to be dispersed by seed in its native area but in the absence of seed in our region, local plants spread vegetatively through root suckering.

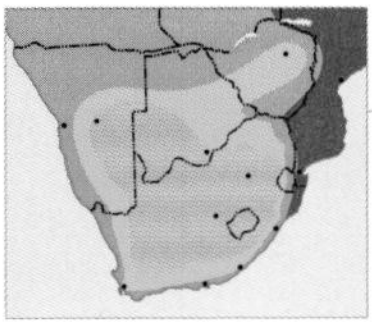

3 *Pterospermum semisagittatum* MALVACEAE

Mukua Tree; Makuaboom

- Drought 2
- Summer
- Evergreen

India and Myanmar Small to medium-sized tree with an erect to spreading crown and **hairy** twigs. Leaves with petiole hairy, 3–5mm long; blade 120–270 × 20–50mm; tip **drawn out into a long point**; base **oblique**, rounded to eared; margin smooth. Stipules **relatively large**. Inflorescences a hanging, single flower; stalk about 5mm long. Flowers white; petals 45–55 × 8–12mm. Fruit a **hairless**, brown capsule 70–80 × 30–35mm.

The wood is heavy and durable, making it suitable for use in construction. There are records of bark fibre being used for rope-making. In South Africa, it is seen as an ornamental specimen tree in botanical gardens.

1 *P. crassifolium* flowers

PHILLIPPA FLANNERY

1 *P. crassifolium* fruit

KURT STUEBER, WIKIMEDIA COMMONS, GFDL 1.2

2 *P. alba* leaves

2 *P. alba* flowers (male)

2 *P. alba* flowers (female)

DIMITAR NAIDENOV, WIKIMEDIA COMMONS, CC BY SA 3.0

3 *P. semisagittatum* flowers; inset: stipules

3 *P. semisagittatum* flruit (cut open)

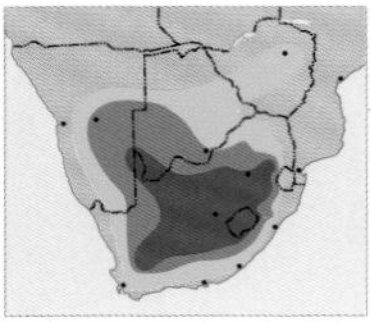

- Drought 2
- Spring–Summer
- Evergreen

1 *Pyracantha angustifolia* (= *Cotoneaster angustifolia*) ROSACEAE

Yellow Fire-thorn; Geelbranddoring, Geelvuurdoring

OTHER LANGUAGES: Zhai ye huo ji (Chinese)

Western China Rounded tree-shrub with **single thorns**; buds and twigs hairy. Leaves with petiole hairy, 2–6mm long; blade 12–55 × 3–12mm; tip **indented, lower surface woolly**; margin **smooth**. Inflorescences erect. Flowers small, white, almost stalkless. Fruit fleshy, roundish, hairy or hairless, red to orange, 6–10 × 5–8mm, **crowned with the persistent remains of the calyx**.

Pyracantha is most easily distinguished from often very similar members of the genus *Cotoneaster* by the presence of thorns at the ends of older branches. This species is also characterised by the very narrow leaves (about 4 or 5 times as long as wide). All parts of the plant contain hydrogen cyanide (prussic acid, HCN) and so are bitter. A declared Category 1b invader in South Africa.

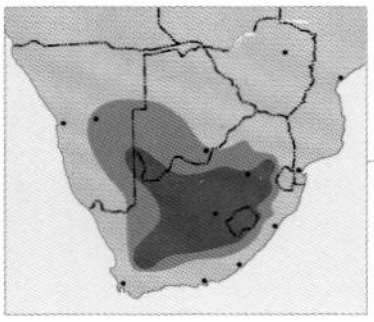

- Drought 2
- Summer
- Semi-evergreen

2 *Pyracantha coccinea* (= *Cotoneaster pyracantha, Crataegus pyracantha*) ROSACEAE

Red Fire-thorn; Rooibranddoring, Rooivuurdoring

OTHER LANGUAGES: Divlja trnovina (Croatian); Buisson ardent (French)

Southeastern Europe and Caucasus Open tree-shrub with **erect** to irregularly arching, thorny stems and coppery late autumn colours in very cold places; buds hairless; twigs hairy. Leaves with petiole hairy, up to 8mm long; blade 20–50 × 6–20mm; tip **pointed to rounded**; lower surface **at most sparsely hairy**; margin **usually toothed**. Inflorescences erect. Flowers small, white, numerous. Fruit fleshy, round, red (orange in some cultivars), hairless, about 6mm in diameter, **crowned with the persistent remains of the calyx**.

Pyracantha is distinguished from similar members of the genus *Cotoneaster* by having thorns at the ends of older branches. All parts of the plant contain hydrogen cyanide and are bitter. However, birds eat the fruits and spread the seeds. The flowers and fruit are attractive and plants can withstand strong winds but not salt spray. Bees are attracted to the flowers, which they pollinate. The cultivar 'Lalandii' (orange firethorn; *oranjebranddoring, oranjevuurdoring*) is recorded from southern Africa and, like the wild-type species, is a declared Category 1b invader in South Africa.

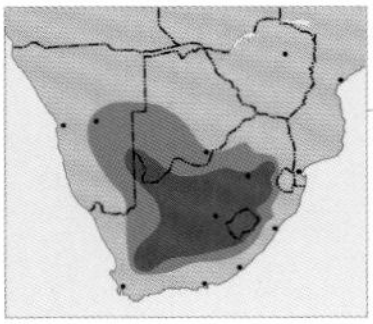

- Drought 2
- Spring
- Deciduous

3 *Quercus acutissima* (= *Q. serrata*) FAGACEAE

Bristle Oak, Chinese Oak; Stekeleik

OTHER LANGUAGES: Ma li (Chinese); Chêne à dents de scie (French); Gesägte Eiche (German); Roble del Himalaya (Spanish)

Himalayas to Japan Medium-sized to large tree with a pyramidal, later rounded crown and **yellow autumn colours**; buds and twigs **generally hairless**. Leaves with petiole 15–40mm long; blade 75–180 × 20–60mm; tip **pointed and hair-tipped**; margin with **hair-tipped teeth**. Flowers yellow-green, small, inconspicuous; males and females separate on the same tree, males in hanging spikes, females hanging, solitary. Fruit a hairless acorn 15–20 × 17–22mm, in a **spiky** cup.

The leaves are very similar to those of a chestnut (*Castanea*; p.158) but the fruits are quite different. Bristle oak is a good street and shade tree and is resistant to urban pollution. It is commonly and widely planted.

1 *P. angustifolia* flowers

1 *P. angustifolia* fruit

2 *P. coccinea* flowers

2 *P. coccinea* fruit

3 *Q. acutissima* leaves

3 *Q. acutissima* flowers (male)

3 *Q. acutissima* fruit

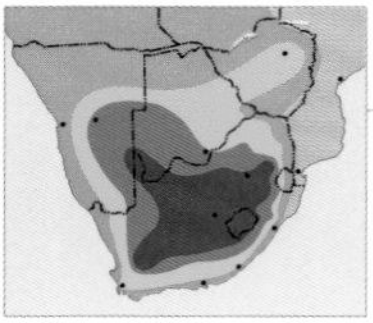

1 *Quercus ilex* FAGACEAE

Holm Oak, Holly Oak; Holmeik, Hulseik, Steeneik

- Drought 2
- Spring
- Evergreen

OTHER LANGUAGES: Alzinera (Catalan); Chêne vert (French); Grüneiche (German); Aria (Greek); Leccio (Italian); Azinheira (Portuguese); Dub kamennyi (Russian); Encina (Spanish); Pırnal meşe (Turkish)

Mediterranean region Large tree, crown columnar at first but later rounded; buds and twigs hairy. Leaves with petiole **hairy**, 3–15mm long; blade 35–75 × 12–30mm; tip **pointed**; base rounded; margin smooth or toothed. Flowers greenish yellow, inconspicuous; males and females separate but on the same tree, males in hanging spikes, females solitary. Fruit a **purplish brown**, bullet-shaped acorn 15–20mm long, in a **scaly, greyish** cup.

The seeds are edible, though some strains contain a bitter tannin that needs to be leached out before eating. The trees are a major host of truffles and are grown for that purpose. The wood can be used in construction and for making tools, wheels, wine casks and other items. It is also a source of charcoal. In addition to being widely grown garden ornamentals, these trees can be used to make windbreaks. Insect galls formed on the trees have medicinal uses.

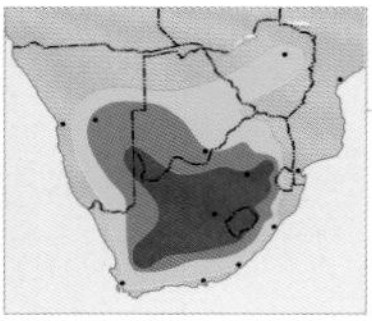

2 *Quercus leucotrichophora* (= *Q. incana*) FAGACEAE

Hairy Oak, Bluejack Oak; Harige Eik

- Drought 2
- Spring
- Evergreen

OTHER LANGUAGES: Chêne de l'Inde (French); Banjh (Hindi)

Himalayas Large tree with a columnar to pyramidal crown; buds and twigs hairy. Leaves with petiole hairy, 8–15mm long; blade 60–150 × 25–50mm; tip **drawn out to a long point**; base rounded; margin **toothed**. Flowers greenish yellow, inconspicuous; males in spikes, females solitary. Fruit a brown acorn up to 15mm long, **half or more hidden by the scaly cup**.

The timber is not much used, being inclined to warp and split. However, the wood is used as fuel and in the tree's native range foliage is well used for fodder. It is widely but not commonly grown in our region.

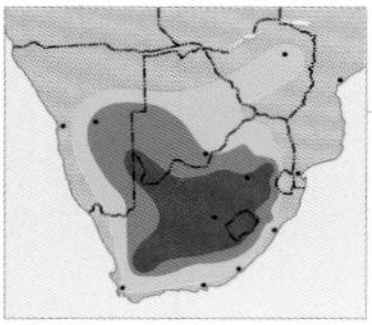

3 *Quercus rugosa* (= *Q. reticulata*) FAGACEAE

Evergreen Oak; Immergroeneik

- Drought 2
- Spring
- Evergreen

OTHER LANGUAGES: Avellana, Encino cuero (Spanish)

Southwestern USA and Mexico Small tree (rarely shrubby or medium-sized) with a pyramidal to rounded crown and **hairless buds**. Leaves with petiole hairy, **short**, 4–12mm long; blade 40–170 × 20–90mm, **widest beyond the middle**; tip **rounded to squared, with a bristle**; base **squared to heart-shaped**; margin coarsely toothed. Flowers greenish yellow, inconspicuous; males in spikes, females solitary. Fruit an acorn 9–28 × 7–14mm, a third covered by a scaly cup, **on a long stalk**.

This species seems to have no recorded use other than as a garden ornamental and in our region it is widely but not particularly commonly grown. Like all oaks, the seeds lose viability after a few months at most.

WOLFGANG KATZ

1 *Q. ilex* flowers (male)

1 *Q. ilex* fruit

2 *Q. leucotrichophora* leaves and flowers (male)

2 *Q. leucotrichophora* fruit

P. GARIN

3 *Q. rugosa* leaves

3 *Q. rugosa* flowers (male)

3 *Q. rugosa* fruit

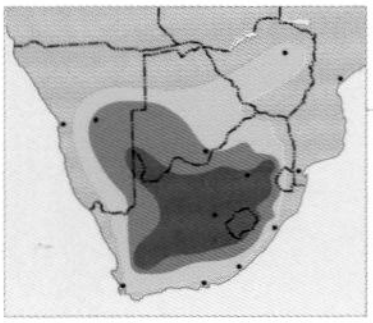

1 *Quercus stellata* FAGACEAE
Post Oak; Paaleik

- Drought 2
- Spring
- Deciduous

OTHER LANGUAGES: Chêne à lobes obtus (French); Roble estrellado (Spanish)

Southeastern USA Medium-sized tree with a rounded crown, usually **without autumn colours**; bark grey, narrowly fissured, forming chunky scales; buds and twigs hairless; lenticels warty, conspicuous. Leaves alternate; petiole hairy, 3–30mm long; blade 70–200 × 45–125mm, **deeply pinnately 5-lobed**; middle lobes **square or shallowly lobed**; tip rounded; base narrowed; surface dull, hairless above, with **dense star-shaped hairs** below; margin smooth. Stipules soon falling. Inflorescences a hanging, single flower or string of multiple flowers, appearing after the leaves; males and females separate, on the same tree. Flowers individually inconspicuous. Fruit an acorn 10–20 × 8–20mm, about **one third enclosed in a rough, brownish cup**.

Grown in our region as specimen trees in Tokai Arboretum, Cape Town. The wood is hard, heavy and durable, like most oaks, but is seldom available in wide pieces and is most used for fence posts, hence the common names.

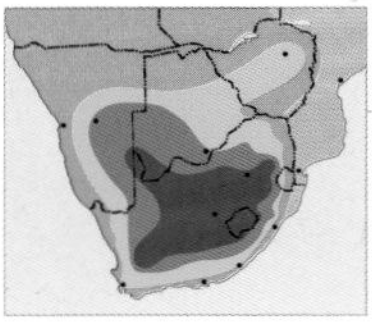

2 *Quercus suber* FAGACEAE
Cork Oak; Kurkeik

- Drought 2
- Spring
- Evergreen

OTHER LANGUAGES: Alzina surera (Catalan); Plutnjak (Croatian); Chêne liège (French); Korkeiche (German); Fellodrys (Greek); Sughera (Italian); Sobreiro (Portuguese); Sorbreiro (Spanish)

Mediterranean region Medium-sized to large tree with a rounded crown; bark **thick, corky**; buds and twigs hairy. Leaves with petiole hairy, 6–15mm long; blade 25–70 × 15–40mm, egg-shaped; margin **toothed**. Flowers greenish yellow, inconspicuous; males in spikes, females solitary. Fruit a **purplish brown** acorn 20–30mm long, in a **loose, scaly cup**.

In its home range the bark of this tree has had many uses for at least 2,000 years, ranging from Roman sandals to modern closures for bottles of wine and oil. Cork forests are also valuable for several reasons, providing mushrooms, hunting (and therefore a refuge for biodiversity) and honey. In our region, trees are seen as specimens in large parks and gardens, especially Johannesburg Botanic Gardens. Trees grow well here but the bark grows too fast to make saleable cork.

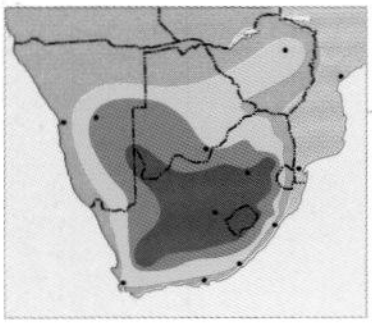

3 *Quercus virginiana* FAGACEAE
Live Oak; Lewenseik

- Drought 2
- Spring
- Evergreen

OTHER LANGUAGES: Chêne des sables (French); Lebens-Eiche (German); Roble de Virginia (Spanish)

Southeastern USA Medium-sized to large tree with a rounded to spreading crown; buds **hairless**; twigs hairy. Leaves with petiole hairy, 1–15mm long; blade 20–120 × 8–20mm, elliptic to oblong; tip **rounded**; base narrowed; margin smooth or toothed. Inflorescences hanging. Flowers inconspicuous; males and females in different catkins on the same tree. Fruit an acorn 15–25 × 8–15mm, in a **rough cup**.

In our region, a specimen tree in botanical gardens. The wood is heavy, hard, tough and difficult to work. In the past it was highly valued for making the ribs of ships and it still finds use anywhere that requires a hardwearing material. In nature it provides food and shelter for wildlife, including moths and butterflies. In cultivation the tree is very long-lived and 500-year-old specimens are not unknown.

1 *Q. stellata* leaves

1 *Q. stellata* fruit

2 *Q. suber* bark

2 *Q. suber* flowers (male)

2 *Q. suber* fruit

3 *Q. virginiana* leaves and young fruit

3 *Q. virginiana* fruit

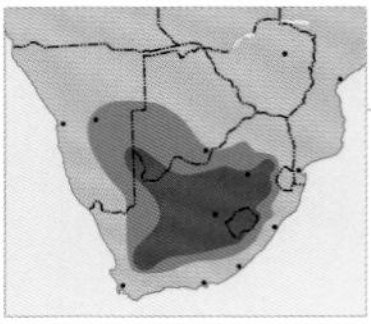

- Drought 2
- Spring
- Deciduous

1 *Salix caprea* SALICACEAE

Goat Willow, Pussy Willow, Sallow; Bokwilger

OTHER LANGUAGES: Safsaf al mi'za (Arabic); Vrba jíva (Czech); Osier cendré (French); Palmweide (German); Gidoïtiá (Greek); Salice delle capre (Italian); Salgueiro (Portuguese); Iva koz'ja (Russian); Salce cabruno (Spanish); Keçi söğüdü (Turkish)

Europe Small to medium-sized tree with a columnar-spreading crown and **yellow autumn colours**; buds hairless; twigs hairy. Leaves with petiole **hairy**, up to 6mm long; blade 50–160 × 10–80mm; tip and base pointed; lower surface **velvety**; margin toothed, sometimes wavy. Inflorescences **erect**, 15–95mm long. Flowers with males and females on different trees. Fruit a capsule up to 10mm long. Seeds grey, about 1 × 0.4mm.

This tree yields very poor-quality wood, whose only recorded use is in making charcoal. The form of the inflorescences signifies prosperity and abundance in Chinese custom and so the tree is widely grown for the cut-flower industry. Young stems can be used in basketry and there is a recorded use of the bark as a leather substitute. As with most willows, the bark has been used medicinally.

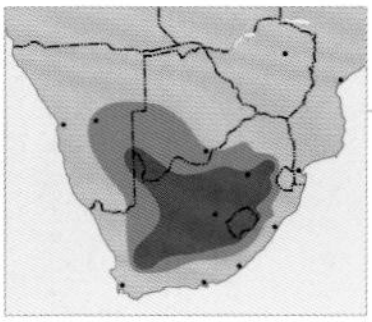

- Drought 2
- Spring
- Deciduous

2 *Salix matsudana* (= *S. babylonica* var. *pekinensis*) SALICACEAE

Peking Willow, Hankow Willow; Pekingwilger

OTHER LANGUAGES: Han liu (Chinese); Pekin yanagi (Japanese)

Northern Asia Medium-sized tree with an upright crown, **corkscrew-twisted**, weeping young branches and slightly yellow autumn colours; buds and twigs hairless. Leaves with petiole hairy, 5–8mm long; blade 50–100 × 10–15mm, narrowly lance-shaped and **often twisted**; tip pointed; base rounded; lower surface **blue-green to white**, hairless; margin **indented**. Inflorescences erect, 15–30mm long. Flowers with males and females on separate trees. Fruit a hairless capsule.

Very similar to the ordinary weeping willow (*S. babylonica*, p.188) and some experts consider them to be forms of the same species. However, the distinctions mentioned above are easily seen in cultivation; in addition, Peking willow is much shorter-lived than weeping willow, rarely exceeding an age of 15 years. The twisted, contorted leaves and stems emphasised above are a distinguishing character of the cultivar 'Tortuosa', the only one grown in southern Africa.

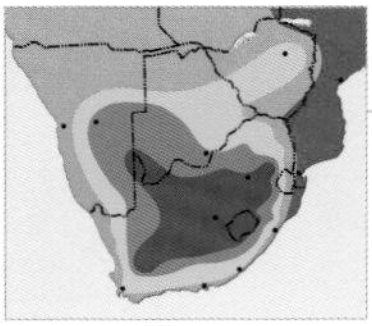

- Drought 3
- Spring
- Evergreen

3 *Solanum mauritianum* SOLANACEAE

Bugweed, Bug Tree; Luisboom

OTHER LANGUAGES: Fona de Porco (Portuguese)

Brazil, Argentina, Paraguay and Uruguay Large, spreading shrub or small tree with an open crown, **covered throughout with star-shaped hairs**. Leaves with petiole hairy, 30–90mm long; blade 120–250 × 50–100mm, elliptic, **strong-smelling** when crushed; tip and base **narrowed**. Stipules ear-like and **conspicuous** at base of petiole. Inflorescences **erect at ends of branches**, 80–270mm long; peduncle up to 150mm long. Flowers purple. Fruit a roundish, densely hairy berry 10–12 × 10–15mm, green at first, ripening yellow. Seeds 1–1.5 × 1–1.5mm.

A declared Category 1b invader in South Africa and a pest in many other places. All parts are poisonous to humans but birds can eat the fruits with impunity. Although it has been a garden subject in the past, this plant has no place in modern cultivation.

1 *S. caprea* flowers (female); inset: male

1 *S. caprea* fruit

2 *S. matsudana* leaves

2 *S. matsudana* flowers (female)

3 *S. mauritianum* leaves

3 *S. mauritianum* flowers

3 *S. mauritianum* fruit

GROUP 8

Spikethorn group

Leaves simple, alternate or in tufts, not bilobed; blade with single main vein from base, not distinctly discolorous. Spines present. Latex absent.

See also Group 9: *Crataegus laevigata* (p.162), *C.* × *lavallei* (p.164) and *C. pubescens* (p.164).

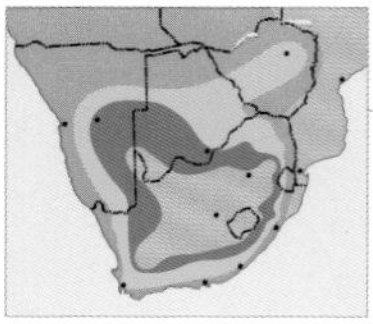

- Drought 2
- Spring
- Evergreen

1 *Citrus aurantifolia* (= *Limonia aurantifolia*)

RUTACEAE

Lime; Lemmetjie

OTHER LANGUAGES: Jeruk nipis (Bahasa Indonesia); Lai meng (Chinese); Limettier (French); Liimuu (Hindi); Lima (Italian); Limão galêgo (Portuguese); Matulunga (Sanskrit); Manao (Thai); Limu (Urdu); Chanh ta (Vietnamese)

Indonesia Small shrubby tree of indefinite shape; buds and twigs hairless. Leaves aromatic; petiole **winged**, hairless, 6–12mm long; blade 50–80 × 17–53mm, with numerous minute **secretory cavities** when viewed against the sun; tip and base rounded; surface glossy; margin **scalloped**. Thorns single, straight. Inflorescences erect, often a single flower. Flowers white to palest pink; petals 8–12 × 2.4–4mm. Fruit fleshy, roundish, green to yellow, **aromatic**, 30–80 × 30–60mm.

Limes, and probably most citrus, in southern Africa are usually grown on rootstocks of *Poncirus trifoliata* (p.342), which promotes resistance to cold and disease. Occasionally a shoot from the rootstock below the graft may be seen, confusing attempts at identification. Trees are grown commercially and domestically for their fruit, which has many uses.

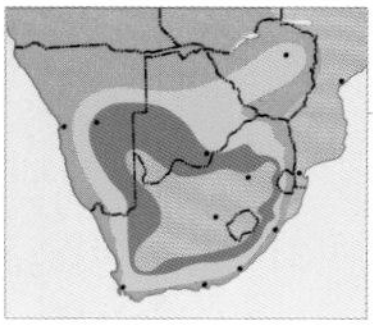

- Drought 2
- Spring
- Evergreen

2 *Citrus aurantium*

RUTACEAE

Seville Orange, Bitter Orange; Sevillelemoen, Bitterlemoen

OTHER LANGUAGES: Burtuqâl (Arabic); Suan cheng (Chinese); Bittere Sinaasappel (Dutch); Orange amère (French); Bitterorange (German); Neratzia (Greek); Khushkhash (Hebrew); Narangii (Hindi); Arancio amaro (Italian); Laranja-azeda (Portuguese); Naranja ácida (Spanish); Kiccilippal̲am (Tamil); Som kliang (Thai)

Southeast Asia Small tree with a spreading crown but **more erect and compact** than sweet orange (*C. sinensis*, p.160); buds and leaves hairless. Leaves aromatic; petiole **wingless**, hairless, 20–30mm long; blade up to 100 × 25–65mm, with numerous minute **secretory cavities** when viewed against the sun; tip and base pointed or rounded; surface glossy; margin **smooth**. Thorns single, straight. Inflorescences erect, usually a single flower. Flowers white, aromatic; petals, about 7–8 × 5mm. Fruit round, orange, aromatic, up to 75mm in diameter.

Less often seen than it once was, the Seville orange provides rootstocks for the more tender sweet orange (*C. sinensis*, p.160). The flowers are used to make orange flower water. The fruits are used in making liqueurs and in cookery. It is the correct fruit for the classic French *sauce bigarade* (for duck), among many other dishes. One of us (HG) vividly recalls his mother maintaining that this was the best if not the only fit orange for making marmalade and major family expeditions were made to the Rustenburg area to buy the necessary. Some medicinal uses are recorded but with serious side effects.

1 *C. aurantifolia* flowers

1 *C. aurantifolia* fruit

1 *C. aurantifolia* leaves

2 *C. aurantium*

2 *C. aurantium* leaves

2 *C. aurantium* fruit

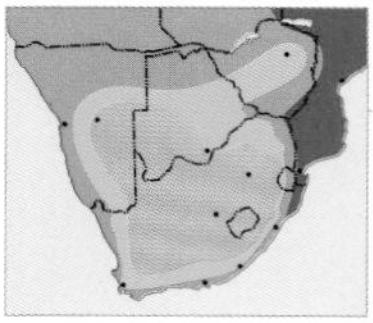

1 *Citrus hystrix* RUTACEAE
Makrut Lime; Makrutlemmetjie

- Drought 2
- Spring
- Evergreen

OTHER LANGUAGES: Jeruk Obat (Bahasa Indonesia); Jian ye cheng (Chinese); Citron Combera (French); Indische Zitrone (German); Cambuyao (Tagalog); Kolumiccai (Tamil); Ma kruut (Thai); Chanh sác (Vietnamese)

India to the Philippines and Indonesia Small tree or shrub of irregular shape; buds and twigs hairless. Leaves with petiole hairless, **broadly winged**, 12–32mm long, so that **blade appears doubled lengthways**; blade 18–40 × 11–28mm, with numerous minute **secretory cavities** when viewed against the sun; tip **indented**; base rounded to squared; margin scalloped. Inflorescences erect. Flowers white. Fruit fleshy, green, hairless, 40–50mm in diameter, with characteristic **warty, rough skin**.

Leaves, with their strong citrus flavour, are essential in Thai, Indonesian and other Indochinese cooking. The juice and peel are used in Indonesian folk medicine and the Indonesian name can be translated as 'medicine citrus'. Trees can be grown easily anywhere warm enough, either in open soil or in containers.

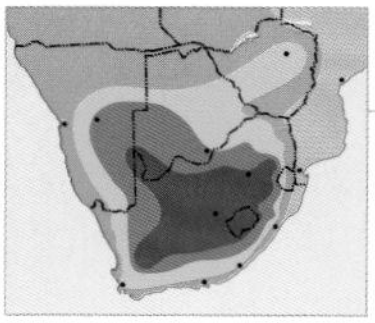

2 *Citrus limon* *(= C. limonium)* RUTACEAE
Lemon; Suurlemoen

- Drought 2
- Spring
- Evergreen

OTHER LANGUAGES: Laymûn (Arabic); Ning meng (Chinese); Citroen (Dutch); Limoo khagi (Farsi); Citronnier comun (French); Zitrone (German); Lemoni (Greek); Nimbu (Hindi); Limoeiro azedo (Portuguese); Limón (Spanish); Elumicchai (Tamil); Manao farang (Thai); Limun (Urdu); Chanh tây (Vietnamese)

Possibly Southeast Asia, but not known with certainty Shrub or small tree with a rounded to spreading crown; buds hairless; twigs **glossy, green**. Leaves aromatic; petiole wingless, hairless, 3–7mm long; blade 50–100 × 30–60mm, with numerous minute **secretory cavities** when viewed against the sun; tip and base pointed; lower surface **dull**; margin scalloped and toothed. Inflorescences erect. Flowers aromatic; petals about 20mm long, white inside, **purple outside**. Fruit fleshy, aromatic, **ellipsoid** green to yellow, 65–125mm long. Seeds whitish to buff, about 9.5mm long.

Lemons are widely grown and used in cookery and the preparation of drinks of various kinds. Less well known, possibly, is the use of lemon juice as a cleaning agent. Various other medicinal, domestic and other uses have been recorded.

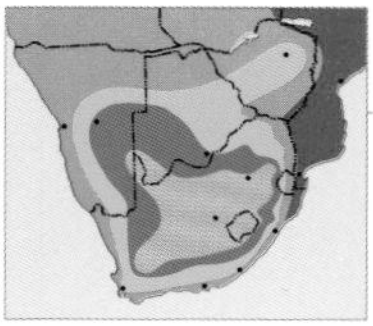

3 *Solanum macranthum* SOLANACEAE
Potato Tree; Aartappelboom

- Drought 2
- Spring
- Evergreen

OTHER LANGUAGES: Arbre Patate (French)

Brazil **Small** tree with a pyramidal to spreading crown; bark grey, smooth; twigs hairy; stems **prickly**, with **single, straight or hooked** thorns. Leaves alternate; petiole hairy, 50–75mm long; blade up to **350 × 225–250mm**, egg-shaped to elliptic in outline, deeply or shallowly **pinnately 7-9-lobed**; tip bluntly pointed; base rounded; surface with star-shaped hairs; margin smooth. Inflorescences a hanging, single flower or spikes 75–125mm long; stalk up to 25mm long. Flowers tubular, **purple or blue**; lobes 5. Fruit a round, **yellow** berry.

An ornamental tree, grown in our region as a specimen in Durban Botanic Gardens and in Mpumalanga.

1 *C. hystrix* leaf

1 *C. hystrix* flowers

1 *C. hystrix* fruit

2 *C. limon* flowers

2 *C. limon* fruit

3 *S. macranthum* flowers

3 *S. macranthum* fruit

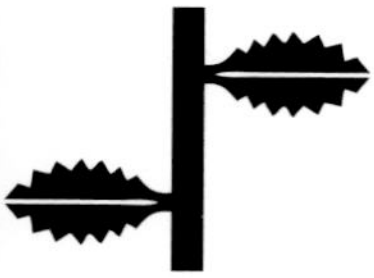

GROUP 9

Wild-plane group

Leaves simple, alternate or in tufts, not bilobed; blade with single midvein from base, not distinctly discolorous; margin toothed, scalloped and/or sometimes deeply or coarsely more than 2-lobed. Spines absent. Latex absent.

See also Group 7: *Quercus stellata* (p.144); Group 8: *Solanum macranthum* (p.150); Group 10: *Liriodendron tulipifera* (p.222).

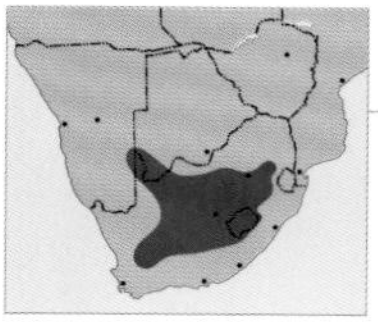

- Drought 1
- Spring
- Deciduous

1 *Alnus glutinosa* (= *A. communis, A. rotundifolia, A. vulgaris*) — BETULACEAE

Black Alder; Swartels

OTHER LANGUAGES: Joha (Croatian); Verne (French); Erle (German); Ontano (Italian)

Europe and Southwestern Asia Medium-sized to large tree up to 20m tall. Leaves with petiole hairless, 10–30mm long; blade 30–90 × 30–80mm, round or widest beyond the middle; tip rounded, squared or indented; margin **twice-toothed**. Males 40–130mm long, females shorter, wider, woody like small conifer cones. Fruit a 2-winged nut about 2 × 1mm.

The soft wood is white when fresh but oxidises to a reddish shade with an attractive figure. Trees can be grown as windbreaks in damp areas but in South Africa it is most obviously seen as a specimen tree in botanical gardens in cooler areas. It is invasive in New Zealand and parts of the northeastern USA.

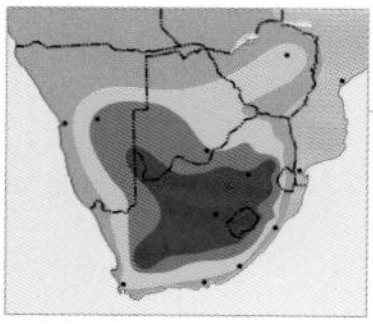

- Drought 2
- Spring
- Deciduous

2 *Alnus rubra* (= *A. oregona*) — BETULACEAE

American Red Alder; Amerikaanse Rooiels

Western USA Medium-sized to large tree with a pyramidal to rounded crown; buds **stalked**; twigs **distinctly triangular, hairy in first year**, green at first, red after first winter, later grey. Leaves with petiole hairless, about 25mm long; blade 60–160 × 30–110mm; margin **twice-toothed, rolled inwards**. Inflorescences drooping catkins; males 35–140mm long, females woody, 8–12mm long. Fruit a 2-winged nut about 1.5 × 1mm.

Red alder has been considered 'trash timber' in the past but it is now gaining popularity as an affordable, easily worked and finished wood for making furniture and musical instruments. In nature, the roots of these trees act as host to nitrogen-fixing bacteria and so they may be of use in cultivation on poor soils. Trees are sporadically grown in cool, moist parts of our region.

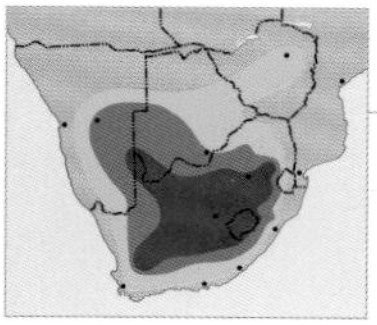

- Drought 2
- Spring
- Evergreen

3 *Arbutus unedo* — ERICACEAE

Strawberry Tree; Aarbeiboom

OTHER LANGUAGES: Al ginâ' el ahlmar (Arabic); Arbousier commun (French); Erdbeerbaum (German); Albatro, Fragola Arborea (Italian); Ervedeiro (Portuguese); Madroño (Spanish)

Ireland to Western Asia Large shrub or small tree, shape dependent on pruning but essentially rounded, with **hairy** twigs. Leaves with petiole hairless, about 6mm long; blade 50–100 × 12–45mm, egg-shaped, **hard** and glossy; tip and base pointed to rounded; margin **scalloped**. Inflorescences hanging, up to 50mm long. Flowers urn-shaped, greenish white or rarely pink, up to 6mm long. Fruit fleshy, **red**, **rough-skinned**, about 20mm in diameter.

Primarily a garden ornamental, this plant also attracts bees (for honey) and birds. The fruits are made into jams and liqueurs and the tree has been used in folk medicine. In our region, it is sporadically grown over a wide area.

1 *A. glutinosa* leaves and unripe fruit

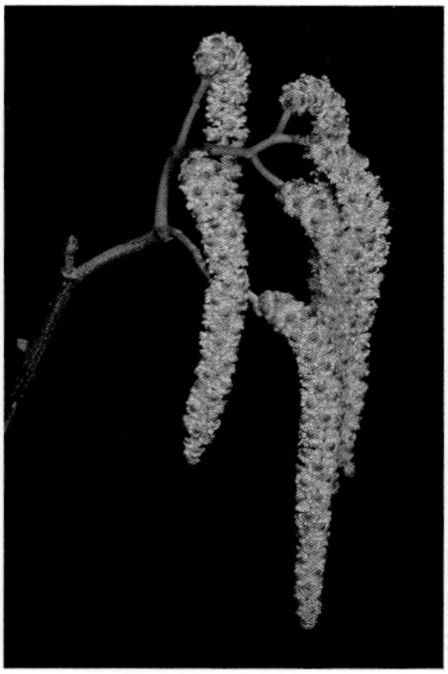

1 *A. glutinosa* flowers (male)

1 *A. glutinosa* fruit

2 *A. rubra* leaves

2 *A. rubra* flowers (male)

2 *A. rubra* fruit

3 *A. unedo* flowers; inset: leaves

3 *A. unedo* fruit

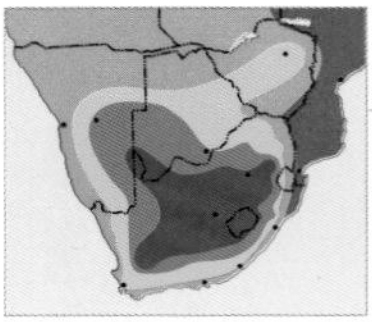

- Drought 2
- Spring
- Evergreen

1 *Ardisia crenata* MYRSINACEAE

Coralberry Bush, Hen's Eyes; Koraalbessiebos

OTHER LANGUAGES: Zhushagen (Chinese)

India, Indochina, China, Japan, the Philippines and Indonesia Erect shrub up to 2m tall, with red or brown twigs. Leaves with petiole hairless, 6–10mm long; blade 60–210 × 10–40mm, **narrowly elliptic to oblong**; tip and base pointed; surface **glossy**; margin **scalloped**. Inflorescences hanging, 20–40mm long. Flowers small, white or pink. Fruit a **round**, **red** berry 5–8mm in diameter.

Coralberry is invasive in coastal KwaZulu-Natal and in parts of the USA and Australia. In South Africa, it is now a declared Category 1b invader. It has been widely planted as a garden ornamental and a few medicinal uses are recorded.

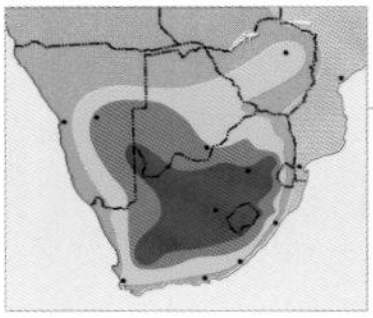

- Drought 2
- Spring
- Evergreen

2 *Banksia serrata* PROTEACEAE

Blue Banksia; Bloubanksia

Eastern Australia Small, columnar to spreading tree or large shrub; bark **very thick**, rough; twigs hairless. Leaves with petiole very short, hairless; blade 100–200 × 20–40mm, **oblong or widest beyond the middle**; tip rounded; base narrowed; surface dull; margin **coarsely toothed**. Stipules absent. Inflorescences **broad, erect, 100–150mm long**. Flowers creamy, up to 40mm long. Fruit a woody, yellow-brown capsule 25–35mm long, **half hidden** in the remains of old flowers.

Mainly a garden ornamental in scattered parts of this region but recommended as a street tree, especially under service lines, in Australia. The flowers attract birds and bees.

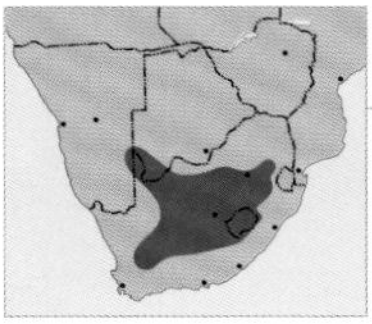

- Drought 2
- Spring
- Deciduous

3 *Betula pendula* (= *B. alba* partly, *B. verrucosa*) BETULACEAE

Silver Birch, White Birch; Silwerberk

OTHER LANGUAGES: Breza (Croatian); Bouleau (French); Birke (German)

Europe Small to medium-sized tree with **drooping shoots** and **yellow autumn colours**; bark **silver-white**; buds and twigs hairless. Leaves with petiole hairless, 10–15mm long; blade up to 60 × 50mm, **triangular**; tip drawn to a point; base rounded to heart-shaped; margin **twice-toothed**. Inflorescences catkins; males and females on the same tree, males **hanging**, up to 60mm long, females **erect**. Fruit a 2-winged nut about 2 × 1mm.

This is the national tree of Finland and it is no surprise that it requires frosty winters to survive. Trees planted when this species was fashionable in Johannesburg in the 1990s should be reaching maturity at the time of writing. Silver birch should therefore be sought as a specimen tree in parks, gardens and sidewalk plantings. Among the fungi associated with this tree is *Amanita muscaria* (fly agaric), the classic toadstool illustrated in innumerable children's books. CAUTION: despite its use in folklore and shamanistic religion, fly agaric is poisonous and can be DEADLY!

1 *A. crenata* flowers

1 *A. crenata* fruit

2 *B. serrata*

2 *B. serrata* flowers

2 *B. serrata* fruit

3 *B. pendula* flowers (male)

3 *B. pendula* flowers (female)

3 *B. pendula* bark

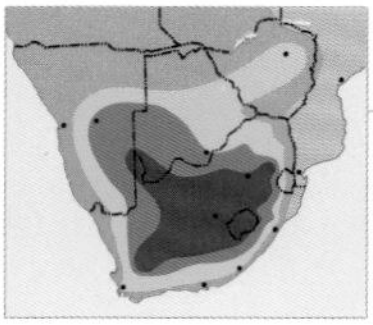

1 *Camellia japonica* THEACEAE

Common Camellia, Japanese Camellia; Gewone Kamelia, Kamelia

- Drought 2
- Spring
- Evergreen

OTHER LANGUAGES: Shancha (Chinese); Camélia du Japon (French); Japanische Kamelie (German); Housan tsubaki (Japanese); Camélia (Portuguese); Camelia (Spanish)

Japan, Korea, China and Taiwan Pyramidal to spreading large shrub or small tree; bark **grey-brown, peeling**; buds and twigs hairless, apical and axillary buds **rather elongate**. Leaves with petiole hairless; blade 50–110 × 25–50mm, rather **stiff and leathery, glossy**, with a **drip-tip**; margin **saw-toothed**. Inflorescences an erect, single, stalkless flower. Flowers usually **double or semidouble** in cultivated forms, **relatively large**; petals white, pink or red, without markings or with white lengthways stripes. Fruit a round, hairless capsule. Seeds 20–25mm long.

Ornamental cultivars of common camellia have been bred in China since at least the Song Dynasty (960–1273 AD) and at present over 2,000 are known. They are all garden ornamentals and need a frost-free, well-watered position in semishade. These conditions are found in many parts of our region.

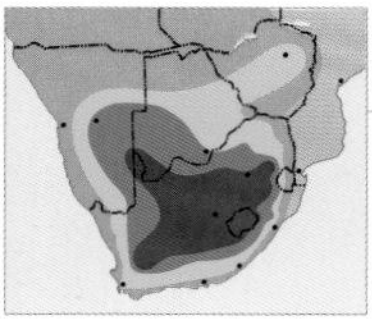

2 *Camellia reticulata* THEACEAE

Yunnan Camellia; Yunnan-kamelia

- Drought 2
- Spring
- Evergreen

OTHER LANGUAGES: Dianshan cha (Chinese); To-tsubaki (Japanese)

China: Guizhou, Sichuan and Yunnan Small tree or large shrub; bark **dark brown, adhering**; buds and twigs hairless. Leaves with petiole hairless; blade 80–110 × 30–55mm; tip **pointed to rounded**; base rounded; margin **saw-toothed**. Inflorescences an erect, single, apparently stalkless flower. Flowers **up to 200mm in diameter**, usually **double** in cultivated forms; petals pink to red, without markings. Fruit a **flattened**, hairless, brown capsule about 36 × 46mm.

Floral emblem of Yunnan, China, where it is grown for seed oil; some cultivars date back at least to the Ming Dynasty (1368–1644 AD). Yunnan camellia is much used in the West as an ornamental and is said to have the largest flowers of any camellia.

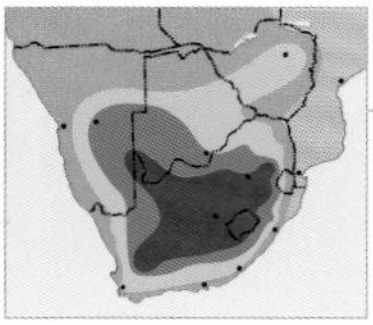

3 *Camellia sinensis* THEACEAE

Tea; Tee

- Drought 2
- Spring
- Evergreen

OTHER LANGUAGES: Shay (Arabic); The (Bahasa Indonesia); Cha (Chinese); Teestruik (Dutch); Arbre à Thé (French); Teestrauch (German); Chaay (Hindi); Cha no ki, Cha (Japanese); Chá (Portuguese); Árbol de Té (Spanish)

China, India, Japan, Korea and Indochina Dense shrub or open-crowned tree; bark **grey, adhering**; buds and twigs hairless. Leaves with petiole hairless; blade 40–144 × 16–50mm, **lance-shaped** to elliptic; tip pointed; base rounded; surface hairless, but Indian teas have leaves with hairy veins on the lower surface; margin **saw-toothed**. Inflorescences an erect, single flower; stalk **up to 12mm long**. Flowers **white, relatively small**, 25–40mm in diameter. Fruit a round, brown, hairless capsule up to 20mm in diameter. Seeds black.

Usually pruned to a height of about a metre in commercial plantations, in our area it can only be seen in its natural shape in a few botanical gardens. In our region, plantations are mostly in Limpopo and Mpumalanga provinces of South Africa and in Zimbabwe. Because of their small flowers, tea bushes are not used as ornamentals.

SKYPRAYER2005 / SHUTTERSTOCK.COM

1 *C. japonica* leaves and buds

BRAAM VAN WYK

1 *C. japonica* flowers

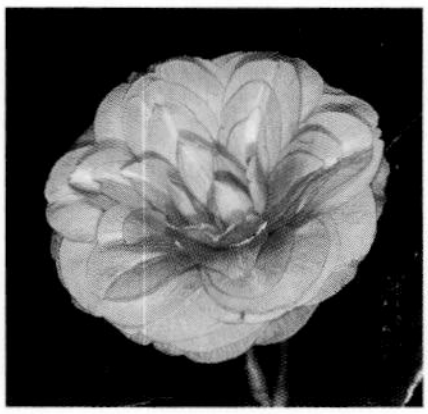

BRAAM VAN WYK

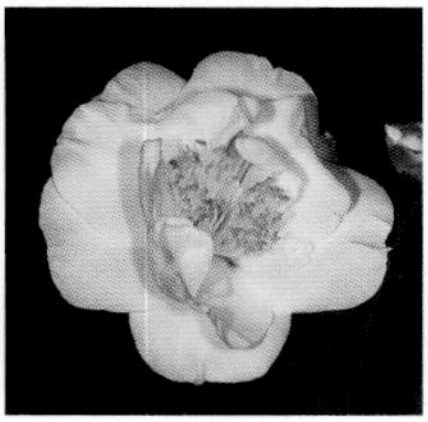

BRAAM VAN WYK

1 *C. japonica* flowers

2 *C. reticulata*

2 *C. reticulata* leaves

2 *C. reticulata* flower

BRAAM VAN WYK

3 *C. sinensis* flower

FOREST AND KIM STARR

3 *C. sinensis* fruit

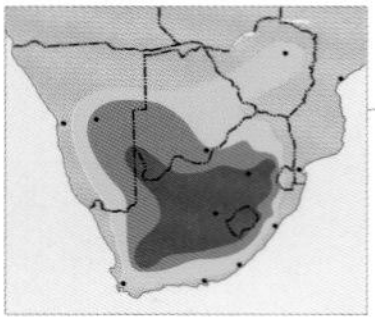

- Drought 2
- Spring
- Deciduous

1 *Carpinus betulus* BETULACEAE

Common Hornbeam; Gewone Hagebeuk

OTHER LANGUAGES: Grab (Croatian); Charme (French); Hainbuche (German)

Europe to Iran Medium-sized to large tree with a rounded crown; trunk becoming **fluted with age**; buds hairless; twigs hairy at first, hanging. Leaves with petiole **hairy**, 7–15mm long; blade 40–60 × 24–36mm, with **oblique base**; margin twice-toothed. Inflorescences hanging catkins; males and females on the same tree, males up to 50mm long, females up to 75mm. Fruit a nut 7–8mm long, surrounded by a **3-pointed bract** 25–40mm long.

Hornbeam is usually grown as an ornamental. In our area it is seen in the Western Cape and KwaZulu-Natal midlands, with uses as shade, street and specimen trees, and as windbreaks and hedges. The timber is pale, tough and dense, used for flooring, musical instruments, veneer, fuelwood and other purposes.

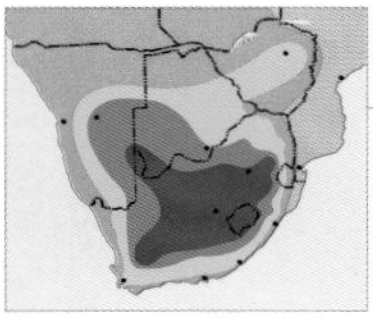

- Drought 2
- Spring
- Deciduous

2 *Castanea dentata* FAGACEAE

American Chestnut; Amerikaanse Kastaiing

OTHER LANGUAGES: Châtaignier américain (French); Castaño americano (Spanish)

Eastern USA Large to very large tree with a columnar to rounded crown; buds and twigs **hairless**. Leaves with petiole hairless, 10–35mm long; blade 90–300 × 30–100mm; tip **drawn out to a point**; base **narrowed and rounded, lower surface hairless**; margin **coarsely toothed**. Infloresecences **hanging** catkins, 150–200mm long. Flowers white to yellow; males and females separate, but on the same catkin. Fruit a spiny, brown, 3-seeded capsule ('burr') 50–70mm in diameter. Seeds reddish brown, 18–25 × 18–25mm.

In its native home, this tree has been almost completely destroyed by a fungus disease, chestnut blight (*Cryphonectria parasitica*). This blight does not appear to have hit chestnut trees in southern Africa, yet. The seeds of this and even more the next tree (*Castanea sativa*) are magnificent eating but chestnut trees are messy and not ideal for planting near a house or other relatively high-traffic areas. In our region this species seems only to be grown in the cooler parts of KwaZulu-Natal.

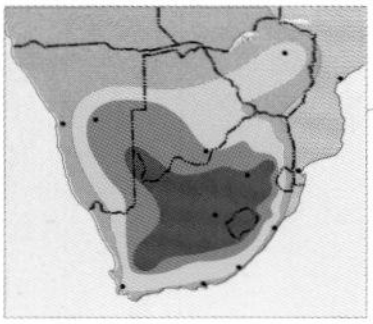

- Drought 2
- Spring
- Deciduous

3 *Castanea sativa* FAGACEAE

Sweet Chestnut, Spanish Chestnut; Soetkastaiing, Spaanse Kastaiing

OTHER LANGUAGES: Abu farwa (Arabic); Châtaignier Commun (French); Echte Kastanie (German); Castagno Comune (Italian); Castanheira (Portuguese); Castaño Regoldo (Spanish))

Southern Europe and Southwestern Asia Large, columnar tree; buds hairless; twigs **hairy**. Leaves with petiole hairless, 12–25mm long; blade 125–225 × 100–140mm; tip pointed; base **rounded to heart-shaped**; lower surface **at least sparsely hairy**; margin toothed. Inflorescences **stiff** catkins, **100–200mm long**. Fruit a **spiny**, brown, 2–4-seeded capsule ('burr') 37–50mm in diameter. Seeds reddish brown, 20–40mm wide.

Seeds of this and the previous species (*C. dentata*) need to be cooked and peeled (seed coat removed) before being eaten but the effort involved is more than repaid by the delicious flavour of the result. The (European) sweet chestnut seems to be resistant to chestnut blight but it is still not a friendly tree for small gardens. The timber is resistant to rot and so can be used outdoors for purposes such as fencing; indoors it can be used to make furniture, barrels and roof beams. Grown in many, scattered, cooler places in our region.

1 *C. betulus* leaves

RADIO TONREG, WIKIMEDIA COMMONS, CC BY SA 2.0

1 *C. betulus* flowers

PIXELJOY / SHUTTERSTOCK.COM

1 *C. betulus* fruit

2 *C. dentata* flowers

2 *C. dentata* fruit

FLAVIANO FABRIZI / SHUTTERSTOCK.COM

3 *C. sativa* flowers

3 *C. sativa* fruit

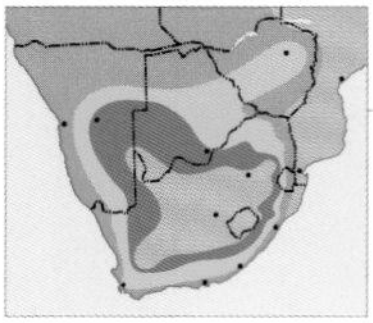

- Drought 2
- Spring
- Evergreen

1 *Citrus × paradisi* (= *C. maxima × C. sinensis*) RUTACEAE

Grapefruit, Pomelo; Pomelo, Bitterlemoen

OTHER LANGUAGES: Limau gedang (Bahasa Indonesia); Pu tao you (Chinese); Pampelmousse (French); Pampelmusenbaum (German); Pomelo (Spanish); Toronja (Spanish, Tagalog)

A garden hybrid raised in the 18th century in Barbados Small tree with a spreading crown; buds and twigs hairless. Leaves with petiole hairless, **wingless**, 7–27mm long; blade 30–125 × 12–72mm, with a **drip-tip** and numerous minute **secretory cavities** when viewed against the sun; margin **smooth or scalloped**. Inflorescences erect clusters. Flowers white; perianth of a calyx and corolla, petals about 50mm long. Fruit fleshy, **round, yellow**, hairless, **100–150mm in diameter**, flesh off-white or pink.

Grown for its fruit. In 2007, South Africa was the third largest producer after the USA and China. Fruits are consumed fresh or processed in many ways, including marmalade and juice. CAUTION: there appear to be many interactions between grapefruit and prescription medications, not all of them beneficial.

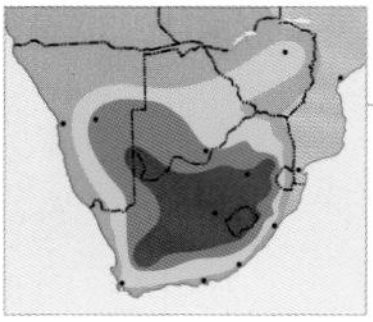

- Drought 2
- Spring
- Evergreen

2 *Citrus reticulata* (= *C. deliciosa*) RUTACEAE

Naartjie, Clementine, Mandarin, Tangerine; Nartjie

OTHER LANGUAGES: Mandarinier (French); Mandarinenbaum (German); Santaraa (Hindi); Mandarino (Italian, Spanish); Ponkan (Japanese); Mandarina (Portuguese); Kamalā (Tamil); Som Khlao Waan (Thai)

Southeast Asia and the Philippines Small tree with a spreading crown; buds and twigs hairless. Leaves with petiole hairless, 6–21mm long; blade 43–95 × 18–45mm, **lance-shaped**, with numerous minute **secretory cavities** when viewed against the sun; tip **pointed**; margin smooth or scalloped. Inflorescences erect. Flowers white. Fruit fleshy, **flattened-round, orange**, hairless, 40–75 × 50–100mm, with **loose peel**. Seeds whitish.

Grown commercially and in gardens for its fruit, which is usually eaten fresh. Dried naartjie peel is used as a flavourant in cooking and baking and is the main flavour ingredient of Van der Hum liqueur. In Canada, naartjies are traditional Christmas-time stocking fillers and in Chinese custom, naartjies at New Year (Chinese New Year is usually in February) are traditional symbols of abundance and good fortune.

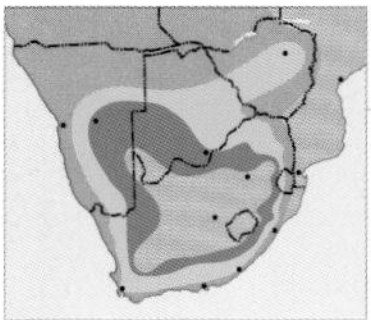

- Drought 2
- Spring
- Evergreen

3 *Citrus sinensis* (= *C. aurantium* var. *sinensis*) RUTACEAE

Sweet Orange, Orange; Soetlemoen, Lemoen

OTHER LANGUAGES: Tian Cheng (Chinese); Orange douce (French); Apfelsinenbaum (German); Arancio dolce (Italian); Laraanja-doce (Portuguese); Mchungwa (Swahili); Cam ngọt (Vietnamese)

China and Vietnam Small tree with an irregular or spreading crown. Leaves with petiole hairless, 6–19mm long; blade 45–105 × 25–55mm, **egg-shaped to elliptic**, with numerous minute **secretory cavities** when viewed against the sun, and with a **drip-tip**; base narrowed; margin smooth or scalloped. Inflorescences erect. Flowers white. Fruit fleshy, **round, orange**, hairless, 65–95mm in diameter, with **firmly attached peel**. Seeds whitish.

Oranges have been grown in China for almost 5,000 years, since before the Xia Dynasty (2070–1600 BC, the first recorded Imperial dynasty). South Africa exports many tons of oranges each year and they are also commonly consumed domestically. The fruits are eaten fresh or consumed as juice; this species is not as successful in marmalade as the Seville orange. Orange blossom is the state flower of Florida, USA. Orange trees are good bee plants, yielding an attractive honey.

1 *C.* × *paradisi* leaves

1 *C.* × *paradisi* flowers

1 *C.* × *paradisi* fruit

2 *C. reticulata* flowers

2 *C. reticulata* fruit

3 *C. sinensis* flower

3 *C. sinensis* fruit

1 *Corylus avellana* BETULACEAE

Hazel, Cobnut; Haselaar

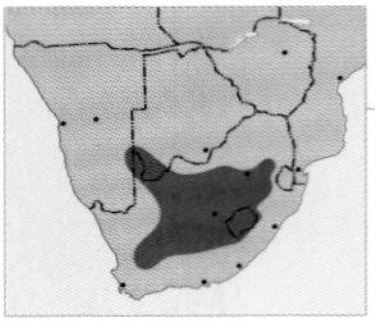

- Drought 2
- Spring
- Deciduous

OTHER LANGUAGES: Ou zhen (Chinese); Noisetier commun (French); Gewönlicher Hasel (German); Fountoukia (Greek); Nocciuolo (Italian); Aveleira (Portuguese); Leščina obyknovennaja (Russian); Avelaneira (Spanish); Adi fındık (Turkish)

Eurasia Large shrub or small tree with rounded to pyramidal habit; buds **stalked**, hairless; twigs with **glandular hairs**. Leaves with petiole hairy, 6–15mm long; blade 50–100 × 40–70mm, **widest beyond the middle**; tip rounded; base **heart-shaped**; veins hairy below; margin twice-toothed. Inflorescences hanging (males) or erect (females), up to 60mm long, on the same tree. Fruit an egg-shaped nut 15–20mm long.

Important in our region (where it is grown in several scattered areas) for the nuts and as a minor garden ornamental in cold places. Elsewhere hazels are regularly coppiced and the stems are used for construction of farm fences and crude (wattle-and-daub) walls. In Britain, hazels form the core of traditional field hedges. A purple-leaved cultivar, 'Fuscorubra', is known.

2 *Cotinus coggygria* (= *Rhus cotinus*) ANACARDIACEAE

Smoke Tree, Venetian Sumach, Wig Tree; Rookboom

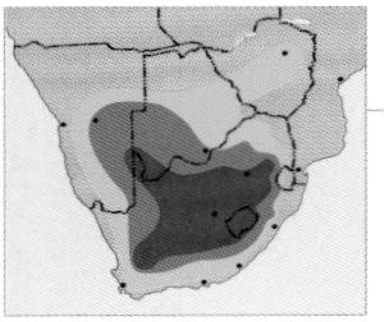

- Drought 2
- Spring
- Deciduous

OTHER LANGUAGES: Huang lu (Chinese); Pruikenboom (Dutch); Arbre à perruque (French); Europäischer Perückenstrauch (German); Albero della nebbia (Italian); Kasumi no ki (Japanese); Zheltinnik (Russian); Árbol de las pelucas (Spanish); Duman Ağacı (Turkish)

Southern Europe to China Small tree or large shrub of open, rounded to irregular habit and with **yellow, orange or red autumn colours**; buds and twigs hairless. Leaves **blue-green or purple**; petiole hairless, 10–40mm long; blade 30–120 × 30–80mm, round or widest beyond the middle; margin smooth. Inflorescences **erect, much-branched and gauzy, 80–200mm long**. Flowers **inconspicuous**, yellow or pale purple. Fruit inconspicuous, kidney-shaped, fleshy, 3–5 × 3–4mm.

Grown as an ornamental in a few scattered places in South Africa and Zimbabwe, as a single specimen or in small groups or shrub borders. The wood was used in former times to make a yellow dye called 'young fustic'.

3 *Crataegus laevigata* ROSACEAE

English Hawthorn; Engelse Haagdoring, Meidoring, Witdoring

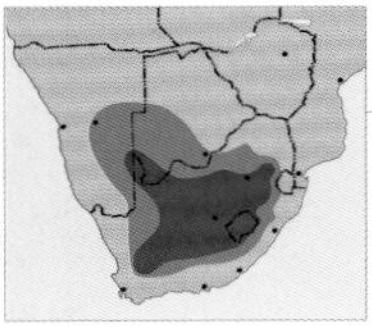

- Drought 2
- Spring
- Deciduous

Europe and Western Asia Small tree or large shrub with a spreading crown often shaped by pruning; bark brown or grey, narrowly fissured and **rough**; buds and twigs **hairless**; lenticels warty, conspicuous; stems round, with **single, straight thorns**. Leaves alternate or in tufts; petiole hairless, 6–20mm long; blade 12–55 × 8–35mm, egg-shaped, shallowly **pinnately 3–5-lobed**, lobes pointing forward; tip pointed to rounded; base **rounded**; surface glossy; margin **toothed**. Inflorescences erect, appearing after the leaves. Flowers small, white. Fruit a fleshy, red, egg-shaped pome up to 20 × 12mm.

Grown in cooler areas as a hedge or windbreak. English hawthorn can be used as a rootstock for fruit trees such as medlar. The wood is hard and heavy but is rarely available in pieces large enough to be worth working. The fruit is edible but needs to be processed in order to become palatable. Medicinal uses are recorded.

1 *C. avellana* leaves

1 *C. avellana* flowers

1 *C. avellana* fruit

2 *C. coggygria* flowers

2 *C. coggygria* fruit

3 *C. laevigata* flowers

3 *C. laevigata* fruit

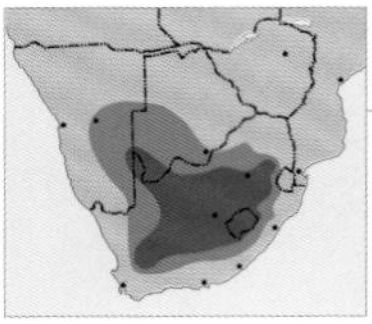

- Drought 2
- Spring
- Deciduous

1 *Crataegus × lavallei* *(= C. crus-galli × C. pubescens)* ROSACEAE

Lavallée Hawthorn; Lavallé-meidoring

Artificial hybrid raised in France Small tree with a pyramidal to rounded crown, may be shaped by pruning, and with **bronze-red autumn colours**; bark grey, **smooth**; twigs **hairy**; lenticels smooth and conspicuous; stems round, with single, **straight branch-thorns**. Leaves alternate; petiole hairy, 6–20mm long; blade 37–150 × 25–62mm, egg-shaped to elliptic, shallowly pinnately 3-lobed or not lobed; tip pointed; base **narrowed**; surface glossy above, **hairy below**; margin toothed. Inflorescences erect. Flowers white; petals 5. Fruit fleshy, **orange-red**, about 20mm in diameter.

In China, the fruits of large-fruited hawthorns such as this are made into delicacies such as stewed fruit, jellies, juices and a form of mebos. All are delicious. Widely grown as an ornamental in cooler parts of our region.

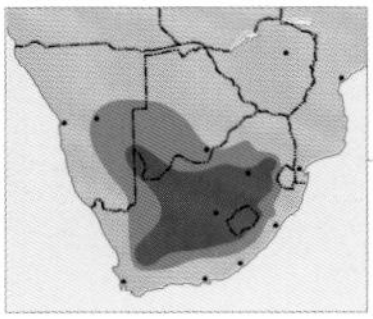

- Drought 2
- Spring
- Semi-deciduous

2 *Crataegus pubescens* *(= C. mexicana)* ROSACEAE

Mexican Hawthorn, Japanese Hawthorn; Skaapvrug, Mexikaanse Haagdoring, Japanse Haagdoring

OTHER LANGUAGES: Manzanita, Tejocotera (Spanish)

Mexico Large shrub or small tree with a narrow to indefinite crown and **red autumn colours**; rarely with single, straight thorns. Leaves with petiole **hairy**, about 8mm long; blade 40–100 × 20–50mm, sometimes shallowly 3-lobed; margin toothed. Inflorescences erect. Flowers white, 7–10mm long. Fruit fleshy, roundish, hairless, **yellow**, about 20 × 15–30mm, **crowned with persistent remains of the calyx**. Seeds midbrown.

In China, the fruits of large-fruited hawthorns such as this are made into delicacies such as stewed fruit, jellies, juices and a form of mebos. All are delicious. In Mexico, the fruits of this species are prepared in various ways and eaten. The wood is hard and compact but is seldom seen in pieces big enough to do more than make tool handles or firewood. In our region, this species is almost always seen as a garden ornamental and the fruits seem to go to waste far too often.

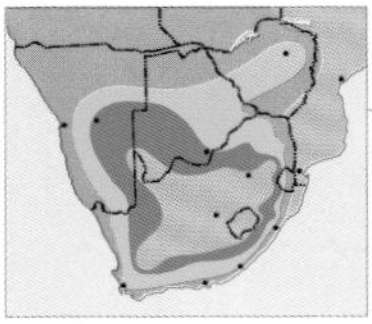

- Drought 2
- Spring
- Evergreen

3 *Dillenia indica* *(= D. speciosa)* DILLENIACEAE

Elephant Apple; Olifantappel

OTHER LANGUAGES: Wuyaguo (Chinese); Chalta (Hindi); Avartaki (Sanskrit)

India to China (Yunnan), Indonesia and Sri Lanka Medium-sized to large tree with a pyramidal crown and hairy twigs. Leaves with petiole hairless, 25–75mm long; blade 150–300 × 60–120mm, oblong; surface **corrugated**; margin **saw-toothed**. Inflorescences a **hanging**, white, **single flower**; stalk 70–80mm long. Flowers with petals 70–90 × 50–65mm. Fruit a hairless, yellow, **egg-shaped aggregate** 80–100mm in diameter.

The flesh of the fruit is edible but fibrous and has limited use in Indian cuisine for making curries, jams and jellies. The sapwood is used for weaving shuttles and the heartwood can be carved and so is used for making a variety of decorative items. Several uses in Ayurvedic medicine are recorded. A few trees were grown experimentally by the South African Forestry Department but now it is seen as specimen trees in Durban, Mbombela and tropical Africa. The large but short-lived flowers may seem to make this a desirable garden subject but the smell of the ripe fruit is overpowering.

NADIATALENT, WIKIMEDIA COMMONS, PUBLIC DOMAIN

1 *C.* × *lavallei* flowers

NADIATALENT, WIKIMEDIA COMMONS, PUBLIC DOMAIN

1 *C.* × *lavallei* fruit

2 *C. pubescens* leaves

BRAAM VAN WYK

2 *C. pubescens* fruit

3 *D. indica* flower

3 *D. indica* fruit

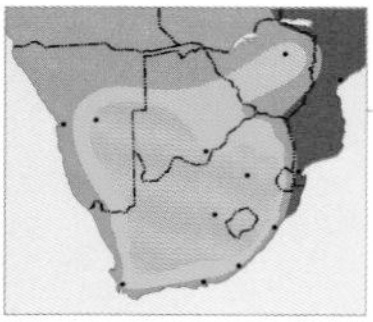

• Drought 2
• Autumn
• Evergreen

1 *Elaeocarpus angustifolius* (= *E. grandis*)

ELAEOCARPACEAE

Silver Quandong, Blue Fig, Giant Blueberry Ash; Reusebloubessie-es

India to Australia Tall tree with a **buttressed** trunk and thin, narrow crown; twigs hairless. Leaves **clustered at ends of branches**; petiole hairless, 10–15mm long; blade 80–120 × 20–30mm, **relatively narrow, turning red before falling**, usually with **distinct pitdomatia** in axils of principal veins below; margin saw-toothed. Inflorescences erect, 50–100mm long. Flowers white; petals **fringed**, about 10–15 × 6mm. Fruit fleshy, round, **blue**, 20–30 × 20–30mm. Seeds about 10mm long.

Timber of this tree is highly regarded. In horticulture, this is a feature tree ideal for parks and large gardens in warmer parts of our region, with year-round interest. Australian animals and birds, including cassowaries, eat the fruit and in Asia the hard seed coats have various uses, including religious significance.

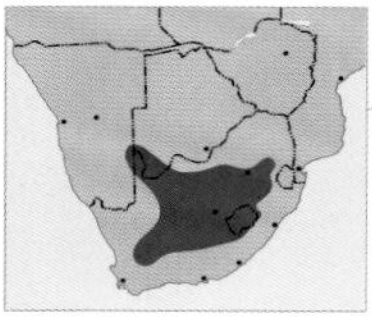

• Drought 2
• Spring
• Deciduous

2 *Fagus sylvatica*

FAGACEAE

European Beech; Europese Beukeboom

OTHER LANGUAGES: Bukva (Croatian); Fayard, Hêtre (French); Buche (German); Faggio (Italian)

Europe and Turkey Large tree with a **pyramidal** crown and **red autum colours**; twigs hairy. Leaves **only shed in spring** (dead leaves remaining over winter); petiole hairy, 6–12mm long; blade 50–125 × 37–100mm; base **obliquely** rounded; margin **scalloped and toothed**. Inflorescences **hanging**. Flowers with males and females in separate spikes on the same tree. Fruit a brown, hairless, **egg-shaped nut** 15–20 × 7–10mm.

Beech nuts ('mast') have for centuries formed part of the diet of hogs raised in Europe; there is evidence that Stone-age people ate them too. The timber is excellent for all indoor uses, especially furniture and parquet flooring. It is an excellent fuelwood and can be used as chips or extract in producing smoked foods, or their substitutes. Minor medicinal uses are recorded. This species makes a magnificent and long-lived garden specimen (only reaching full fruiting in 30 years) and trees can be clipped into hedges and windbreaks.

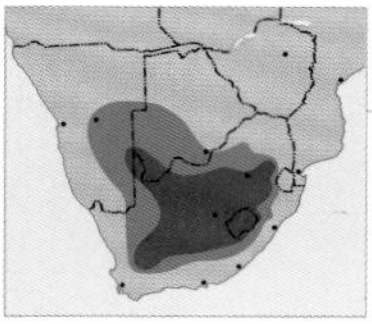

• Drought 2
• Spring
• Evergreen

3 *Ilex aquifolium*

AQUIFOLIACEAE

European Holly, Holly; Europese Huls, Huls

OTHER LANGUAGES: Zelenika (Croatian); Houx (French); Stechpalme (German); Agrifoglio (Italian)

Europe to Western Asia Medium-sized tree or shrub of variable form. Leaves with petiole hairless; blade 25–75 × 20–62mm; tip **ending in a spine**; margin **coarsely toothed**, teeth **spine-tipped**; margin sometimes wavy. Inflorescences erect. Flowers small, white; males and females separate, on the same or different trees. Fruit a **round, red**, hairless **berry** about 6 × 6mm.

Probably no European tree has more folklore attached to it than holly and to this day it is a staple of Christmas decorations. The evergreen leaves and bright red berries have been an assurance 'since always' in the coldest and darkest season that the sun and spring will return. In nature, groves of trees provide shelter for game, and the fruits, which soften after the first frost, attract birds in winter when little other food is available. In the garden, berries are only formed if both male and female flowers are to hand and so two or more trees may be needed.

BRAAM VAN WYK

1 *E. angustifolius* leaf with pit-domatia

MARK MARATHON, WIKIMEDIA COMMONS, CC BY SA 3.0

1 *E. angustifolius* flowers

BRAAM VAN WYK

1 *E. angustifolius* fruit

DER MICHELS, WIKIMEDIA COMMONS, PUBLIC DOMAIN

2 *F. sylvatica* flowers

SCISETTI ALFIO / SHUTTERSTOCK.COM

2 *F. sylvatica* fruit

3 *I. aquifolium* variegated leaves

OLIVIER PICHARD, WIKIMEDIA COOMONS, CC BY SA 3.0

3 *I. aquifolium* flowers

MAYASIMFAN, WIKIMEDIA COMMONS, GFDL 1.2

3 *I. aquifolium* fruit

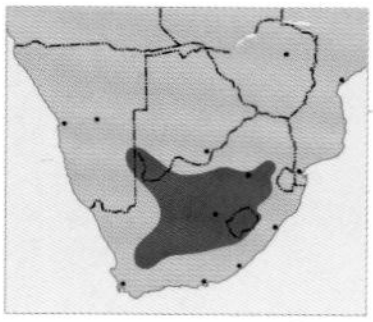

1 *Malus floribunda* ROSACEAE

Japanese Crab-apple, Purple Chokeberry, Showy Crab-apple; **Japanse Blomappel**

OTHER LANGUAGES: Vielblütiger Apfel (German); Kaidouzumi (Japanese)

Japan Small tree with a rounded to spreading crown and **yellow, not showy, autumn colours**; buds hairless; twigs **hairy**. Leaves with petiole **hairy**, 12–25mm long; blade 37–100 × 20–50mm, egg-shaped, with a drip-tip; lower surface **hairy**; margin saw-toothed. Inflorescences hanging. Flowers white to pink; pedicels 20–40mm long. Fruit fleshy, round, **orange**, hairless, 20 × 20mm, **crowned with persistent remains of the calyx**.

- Drought 2
- Spring
- Deciduous

One source claims that this is the best of the flowering crab-apples; it is certainly the commonest in our region. The fruits are edible but not often seen. Where present, they attract animals and birds. Japanese crab-apple is only ever grown as an ornamental.

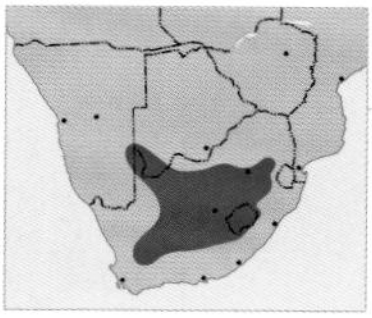

2 *Malus hupehensis* ROSACEAE

Himalayan Crab-apple; Himalajablomappel

OTHER LANGUAGES: Hu bei hai tang (Chinese)

China to India Small to medium-sized tree with a spreading (**'vase-shaped'**) crown and **inconspicuous yellow-green autumn colours**; buds purple. Leaves with petiole hairless, 10–30mm long; blade 50–100 × 25–60mm; tip pointed; lower surface hairless; margin saw-toothed. Inflorescences hanging. Flowers deep pink in bud opening paler pink and fading white; pedicels hairy, 25–60mm long. Fruit fleshy, round, almost hairless, 8–10 × 8–10mm, **yellow with a red blush, crowned with persistent remains of the calyx**.

- Drought 2
- Spring
- Deciduous

Mainly grown as a garden ornamental, recorded only from Gauteng in our area. The leaves can be used as a tea substitute or tisane. The fruits are edible and may attract birds and wildlife. Unusually, the flowers in this species are self-fertile and so a single tree may set fruit.

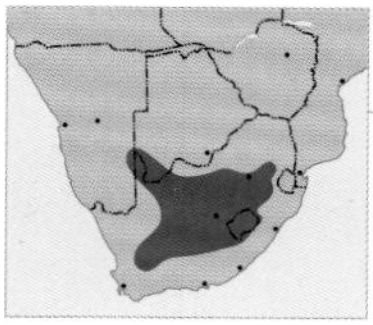

3 *Malus 'Lemoinei'* ROSACEAE

Purple-leaved Crab-apple, Lemoine's Crab-apple; **Persblaarblomappel**

A garden hybrid first made in Nancy, France Small, upright to spreading tree with **yellow to red autumn colours** and hairy twigs. Leaves with petiole **hairy**; blade 80–90mm long, **purple at first, later coppery green**, with a drip-tip; base rounded; lower surface hairy; margin toothed. Inflorescences hanging. Flowers purple or deep pink to pink. Fruit fleshy, round, hairless, **dark purple**, 15–25 × 15–25mm, **crowned with persistent remains of the calyx**.

- Drought 2
- Spring
- Deciduous

Strictly ornamental, commonly seen in parks and private gardens in the cooler parts of our region.

JULIA KUZNETSOVA / SHUTTERSTOCK.COM

1 *M. floribunda* flowers

1 *M. floribunda* fruit

DADEROT, WIKIMEDIA COMMONS, PUBLIC DOMAIN

2 *M. hupehensis* flowers

P. GARIN

2 *M. hupehensis* fruit

3 *M.* 'Lemoinei'

3 *M.* 'Lemoinei' flower

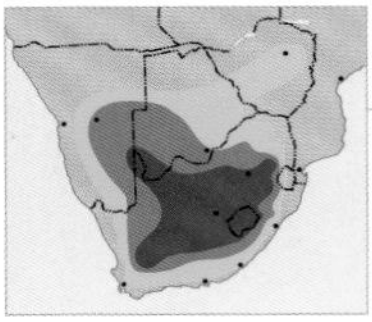

- Drought 2
- Spring
- Deciduous

1 *Malus sylvestris* *(= M. communis, M. pumila, Pyrus malus)* ROSACEAE

Common Apple, Apple; Gewone Appel, Appel

OTHER LANGUAGES: Ping guo (Chinese); Pommier (French); Apfelbaum (German); Seb (Hindi); Seiyou ringo (Japanese); Maceira (Portuguese); Lablonia nizkaia (Russian)

Kazakhstan, Kyrgyzstan and western China Small tree, crown shape determined by pruning, **no autumn colours**; buds and twigs hairy. Leaves with petiole **hairless**, 15–30mm long; blade 40–100 × 30–55mm, **egg-shaped to round**; base **rounded to squared**; lower surface hairy; margin saw-toothed. Inflorescences hanging. Flowers white to pink; petals 15–18mm long. Fruit fleshy, roundish, hairless, green, yellow or red, 20–60 × 20–60mm, **crowned with persistent remains of the calyx**.

The name of the former Kazakh capital, Almaty, can be translated as 'Father of Apples' and it is no surprise that the greatest known variety of wild apples is to be found in the mountains near the city. Over 7,500 cultivars are known, of which about half-a-dozen (such as 'Golden Delicious', 'Granny Smith', 'Starking' and 'Top Red') supply by far the greatest part of the South African crop. Apples feature in the folklore of northern Europe, Greece and the Middle East. The fruits are eaten either fresh or cooked, or juiced and the juice consumed fresh, fermented (cider) or distilled (applejack, Calvados and other spirits).

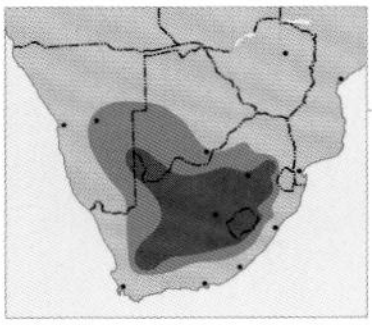

- Drought 2
- Spring
- Deciduous

2 *Ostrya carpinifolia* BETULACEAE

Hop-hornbeam; Hopbeukeboom

OTHER LANGUAGES: Charme-houblon (French); Hopfenbuche (German); Carpinella (Italian)

Southern Europe and Turkey Medium-sized to large tree with a pyramidal or irregular crown; buds and twigs hairless. Leaves with petiole hairless, 5–10mm long; blade 50–100 × 25–50mm, egg-shaped; tip **drawn out to a point**; lower surface hairy; veins **impressed into upper surface**; margin **twice-toothed**. Inflorescences catkins; males and females on the same tree, male ones hanging, 30–75mm long, female ones erect, shorter, but on a longer peduncle. Fruit an egg-shaped nut, 4–5mm long, hidden between **many bracts**.

Useful as an ornamental because it resists most urban adversities. Hop-hornbeam wood is very heavy and hard, making it useful in carpentry. It is also a good fuelwood. Grown occasionally in the Western Cape, Gauteng and north of the Limpopo River.

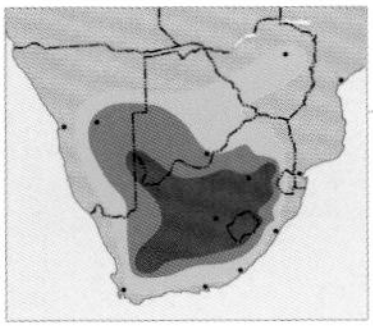

- Drought 2
- Spring
- Evergreen

3 *Photinia serratifolia* *(= P. davidsoniae)* ROSACEAE

Chinese Hawthorn; Chinese Haagdoring

OTHER LANGUAGES: Shi nan (Chinese)

China Large shrub or small to medium-sized tree of irregular form; buds and twigs hairless. Leaves with petiole **20–40mm long, becoming hairless**; blade 75–220 × 30–90mm, **oblong**, with a **drip-tip**; margin smooth or saw-toothed; young leaves **copper-coloured**. Inflorescences erect, 80–120mm long. Flowers white; petals 3–4 × 3–4mm. Fruit fleshy, round, red-purple or brown, hairless, 5–6 × 5–6mm. Seeds midbrown, 2–2.5mm long.

Most often grown as a garden ornamental. Recorded from scattered localities in South Africa and Zimbabwe, where it can be a specimen tree or a hedge. The wood is hard and heavy and suitable for making small items of furniture.

GEOFF NICHOLS

1 *M. sylvestris* flower

1 *M. sylvestris* fruit (see also p.7)

FRANZ XAVER, WIKIMEDIA COMMONS, GFDL 1.2, CC BY-SA

2 *O. carpinifolia* flowers (male)

FRANZ XAVER, WIKIMEDIA COMMONS, CC BY SA 3.0

2 *O. carpinifolia* flowers (female)

2 *O. carpinifolia* fruit

3 *P. serratifolia*

BRAAM VAN WYK

3 *P. serratifolia* leaves

B. MARINER

3 *P. serratifolia* flowers

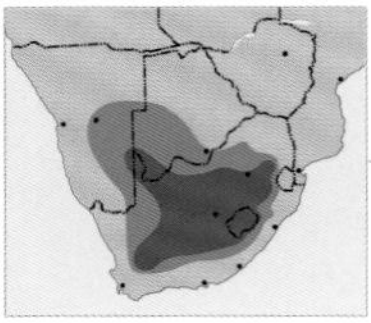

- Drought 2
- Spring
- Deciduous

1 *Populus deltoides* (= *P. canadensis* Michx.f., not of Moench, *P. monilifera*)

SALICACEAE

Match Poplar, Canada Poplar, Cottonwood; Vuurhoutjiepopulier

USA Large tree with a **pyramidal to spreading** crown and yellow autumn colours; buds and twigs hairless. Leaves with petiole hairless, **often vertically compressed**, 30–120mm long; blade 75–200 × 75–125mm, **triangular**; tip drawn to a point; base **squared**; veins **hairy** on lower surface; margin scalloped or toothed. Inflorescences hanging, yellow, inconspicuous catkins, 50–100mm long. Flowers with males and females on separate trees. Fruit a hairless, **oval**, brown capsule 6–8mm long, soon opening to reveal a mass of **white cottony fibres** in which the seeds are hidden.

Cottonwood is the official state tree of Kansas. The flattened petiole means that the leaves tremble in the slightest breeze; this is a diagnostic character. Originally grown in our region for raw material to make matches, this species has become naturalised in cold, wet places. Although it has been grown in parks and gardens for shade, the web page that notes 'Liabilities: too many to mention' has more than a grain of truth.

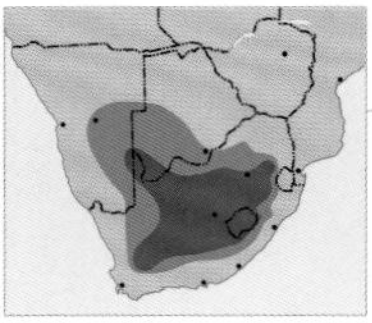

- Drought 2
- Winter/Early Spring
- Evergreen

2 *Populus fremontii*

SALICACEAE

Fremont Cottonwood, Alamo Cottonwood; Vaalhartspopulier

OTHER LANGUAGES: Álamo cimarron (Spanish)

USA and Mexico Medium-sized to large tree with a **columnar to pyramidal** crown and yellow autumn colours; buds hairy, twigs hairless. Leaves with petiole hairless, **round**, 10–90mm long; blade usually 40–80 × 30–100mm, triangular or lance- to kidney-shaped; tip pointed; base usually squared to slightly heart-shaped; surfaces sometimes hairy; margin smooth or scalloped. Inflorescences hanging, inconspicuous, red or green, 50–100mm long, appearing before the leaves. Flowers with males and females on separate trees. Fruit a **round**, hairless capsule 6–11 × 6–11mm, soon opening to reveal a mass of white cottony fibre in which the seeds are hidden.

Very fast growing and commonly planted in the North West province, especially on the Vaal-Harts Irrigation Scheme. In many ways this tree is closely similar to *P. deltoides*, match poplar above. One source mentions that in North America it can be used as a form of 'natural air-conditioning', as in summer it cools the air under the canopy to a remarkable degree.

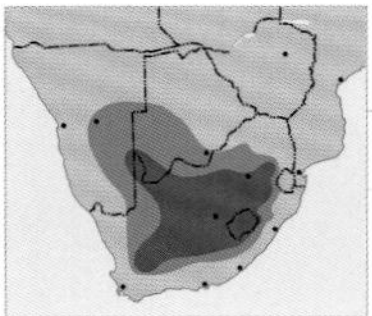

- Drought 2
- Spring
- Deciduous

3 *Populus nigra*

SALICACEAE

Black Poplar, Lombardy Poplar; Swartpopulier

OTHER LANGUAGES: Hei yang (Chinese)

Europe and Asia Large tree with a pyramidal to irregular (wild-type) or **cigar-shaped** ('Italica') crown and yellow autumn colours. Leaves with petiole **round**, hairless, 20–55mm long; blade 40–80 × 40–80mm, **triangular**; tip drawn out to a point; base **broad to squared; veins hairless**. Inflorescences hanging catkins, 50–75mm long. Flowers with males and females on separate trees, only males seen in our region. Fruit a capsule.

The cultivar 'Italica' (Lombardy poplar; *Italiaanse populier, vaarlandspopulier*) is far more often seen than the 'wild-type' form. Often planted in cold, damp places for ornament and as windbreaks. However, it is not without disadvantages, being short-lived, with very invasive root systems and a great capacity for suckering.

1 *P. deltoides* leaves and flowers (female)

1 *P. deltoides* fruit

2 *P. fremontii* bark

2 *P. fremontii* leaves (see also p.9)

2 *P. fremontii* flowers (female)

3 *P. nigra*

3 *P. nigra* flowers (male)

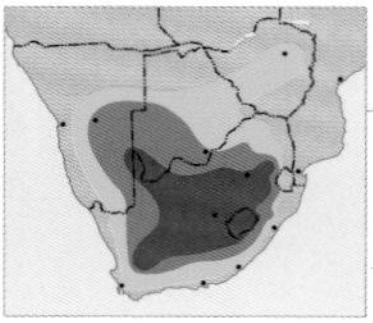

- Drought 2
- Spring
- Deciduous

1 *Prunus armeniaca*

ROSACEAE

Common Apricot, Apricot; Gewone Appelkoos, Appelkoos

OTHER LANGUAGES: Mishmish (Arabic); Xing (Chinese); Zerdalu (Farsi); Abricotier (French); Aprikosenbaum (German); Khuubaanii (Hindi); Seiyou anzu (Japanese); Abrikos (Russian)

Northern China Small, spreading tree with hairless, **purple buds** and **glossy twigs**. Leaves with petiole hairless, **20–35mm long**; blade 50–90 × 40–80mm; tip **pointed**; base **rounded**; margin **saw-toothed**. Inflorescences an erect, single flower. Flowers white or pink, appearing before or with the leaves. Fruit fleshy, **yellow-orange**, egg-shaped to round, hairless, 15–30 × 15–30mm. Seeds midbrown.

Apricots are, and have been for at least 5,000 years, mainly grown for their fruits, which are enjoyed fresh, dried or prepared in various forms. The kernels are occasionally used as a substitute for almonds and are the main flavourant in Italian *Amaretto* liqueurs and *amaretti* biscuits. However, a degree of caution is needed, because like most seeds in the genus *Prunus*, apricot kernels contain a cyanogenic glucoside, which liberates hydrogen cyanide (prussic acid, HCN) as it breaks down.

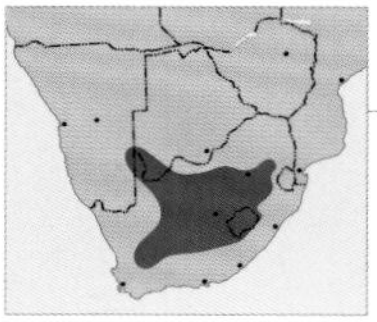

- Drought 2
- Spring
- Deciduous

2 *Prunus avium*

ROSACEAE

Sweet Cherry, Cherry, Gean, Hagberry, Mazzard; Soetkersie, Kersie

OTHER LANGUAGES: Karaz barrî (Arabic); Cerise doux (French); Kirschbaum (German); Gilaas (Hindi); Ciliegia dolce (Italian); Sakuranbo (Japanese); Cerejeira (Portuguese); Ceresera (Spanish)

Europe and western Siberia Medium-sized to large tree with a pyramidal to rounded crown; buds hairless, **brown**; twigs hairless, brown or purple. Leaves with petiole hairless, 20–45mm long, bearing **2 red glands below the base of the blade**; blade 75–150 × 40–70mm; tip drawn out to a point; base rounded; veins **hairy below**; margin saw-toothed. Inflorescences hanging; individual pedicels hairless, 25–45mm long. Flowers white, appearing **after** the leaves. Fruit fleshy, egg-shaped, red to black, hairless, **10–20 × 10–20mm**. Seeds buff, 6–8mm long.

Grown commercially for fruit in the eastern Free State, it can be grown in other areas with cold winters but gardeners may find a reason for the Latin specific name ('of birds') – birds love the fruit. Sweet cherries are eaten fresh or cooked in desserts. The trees are ornamental in flower and the gum from wounds is used as a substitute for chewing-gum. Cabinets, furniture, musical instruments and turned articles are made from the wood, which is also good for smoking meats. Medicinal uses are recorded.

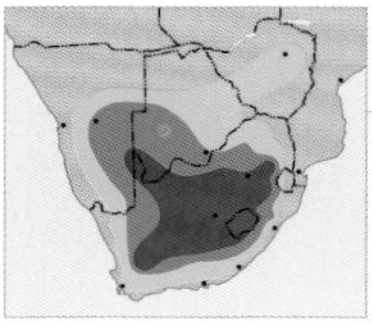

- Drought 2
- Spring
- Deciduous

3 *Prunus campanulata*

ROSACEAE

Cherry Plum, Mirabelle, Myrobalan; Kersiepruim

OTHER LANGUAGES: Zhong hua ying tao (Chinese); Kan hi zakura (Japanese)

Taiwan Small tree with a rounded crown; buds hairless; twigs hairless, dull. Leaves with petiole hairless, **10–20mm long**, and stipules **feathery**; blade 60–100 × 25–45mm, sometimes widest beyond the middle; tip drawn out to a point; base rounded; margin saw-toothed. Inflorescences hanging; peduncle 25–40mm long. Flowers deep pink, appearing **before or with** the leaves. Fruit fleshy, **egg-shaped, red, hairless**, about 15 × 12mm.

Three cultivars are known in South African gardens, where they are grown for their decorative flowers.

MASSIMILIANO PIERACCINI / SHUTTERSTOCK.COM

1 *P. armeniaca* leaves and fruit

BRAAM VAN WYK

1 *P. armeniaca* flowers

1 *P. armeniaca* fruit

DINKUM, WIKIMEDIA COMMONS, PUBLIC DOMAIN

2 *P. avium* leaves and fruit

JOE JENZE, WIKIMEDIA COMMONS, CC BY SA 3.0

2 *P. avium* flowers

4028MDK09, WIKIMEDIA COMMONS, CC BY SA 3.0

2 *P. avium* fruit

3 *P. campanulata* stipules

3 *P. campanulata* flowers

VINCENT IGNACE, WIKIMEDIA COMMONS, CC BY SA 3.0

3 *P. campanulata* fruit

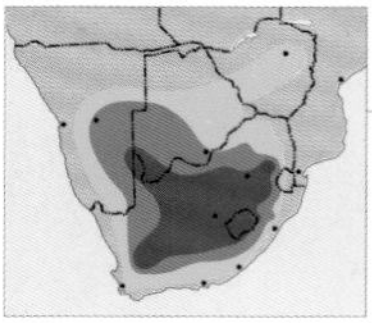

- Drought 2
- Spring
- Deciduous

1 *Prunus domestica* ROSACEAE

Common Plum, Plum; Gewone Pruim, Pruim

OTHER LANGUAGES: Ou zhou li (Chinese); Sliva (Czech); Prunier cultivé (French); Bauernpflaume (German); Alu bukhara (Hindi); Susino (Italian); Abrunheiro (Portuguese); Ciruelo (Spanish)

A natural hybrid arising in Europe and Western Asia Small to medium-sized tree with a spreading crown; bark **purplish brown**; buds and twigs hairless, brown, the latter **glossy**. Leaves with petiole **hairy**, 10–20mm long; blade 40–100 × 25–50mm; tip **rounded**; lower surface **hairy**; margin **saw-toothed**. Inflorescences erect; individual pedicels hairless, 6–12mm long. Flowers white, appearing **after** the leaves. Fruit fleshy, red-purple or yellow, roundish, hairless, 10–25 × 10–25mm. Seeds buff.

Grown for its fruits, which are eaten fresh or cooked, and distilled into plum brandy (slivovitz). Prunes are the dried fruit of several cultivars of plum. Various dyes are made from different parts of the tree and the wood is used to make musical instruments. Medicinal uses are recorded.

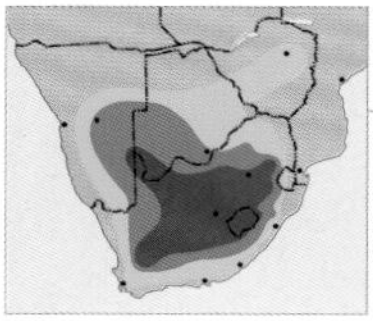

- Drought 2
- Spring
- Deciduous

2 *Prunus dulcis* *(= Amygdalus communis, P. amygdalus, P. communis)* ROSACEAE

Almond; Amandel

OTHER LANGUAGES: Lawz (Arabic); Bian tao (Chinese); Amandier commun (French); Mandelbaum (German); Baadaam (Hindi); Mandorlo (Italian); Amendoeira (Portuguese); Almendrero (Spanish)

Southwestern Asia and North Africa Small tree with a rounded or spreading crown; buds and twigs hairless, the latter **green to purple** in first year. Leaves with petiole hairless, up to 25mm long; blade **narrow**, 75–125 × 20–40mm, **lance-shaped**; tip shortly drawn out; base rounded; veins hairless; margin **saw-toothed**. Inflorescences an erect, single flower or clusters. Flowers white, appearing **before** the leaves. Fruit **leathery, green**, egg-shaped, densely hairy, 30–60mm long. Seeds buff or midbrown to black.

Almonds are believed to be among the first nut trees to be domesticated, about 4,500 years ago. The part of the fruit normally eaten is the seed. The nuts can be eaten fresh, toasted or as part of innumerable dishes both sweet and savoury. They can also be ground into marzipan and nougat. Although the flowers are hermaphrodite, they are obligate outcrossers and two trees of different cultivars must be planted close together to ensure a crop.

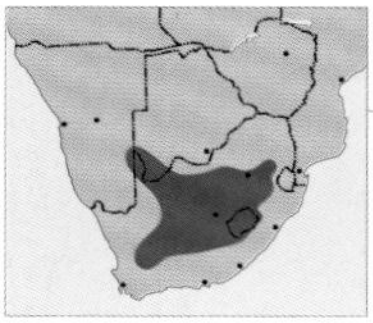

- Drought 2
- Spring
- Evergreen

3 *Prunus laurocerasus* ROSACEAE

Cherry Laurel; Kersielourier

OTHER LANGUAGES: Laurier-cerise (French); Kirschlorbeer (German); Lauroceraso (Italian); Loureiro-cerejera (Portuguese); Lavrovishnia lekarstvennaia (Russian); Lauroceraso (Spanish)

Eastern Europe and Southwestern Asia Large shrub or small tree with a rounded crown; bark **smooth**; buds hairless; twigs **green**, hairless. Leaves with petiole hairless, about 12mm long; blade 75–250 × 30–75mm, **oblong**, leathery, with a small **drip-tip**; base rounded; margin remotely small-toothed, sometimes almost smooth. Inflorescences **erect, spike-like, 75–150mm long**, usually **shorter than the leaves**. Flowers white; petals 3–4mm long. Fruit fleshy, egg-shaped, hairless, purple to black, 12–20 × 12–20mm.

A garden ornamental grown in the cooler, eastern parts of our region for its form and for greenery to use with cut flowers. The fruits are edible when very ripe and attract birds. With this exception, all parts of the plant are poisonous.

1 *P. domestica* flowers

1 *P. domestica* fruit

2 *P. dulcis* flowers

2 *P. dulcis* unripe fruit

3 *P. laurocerasus* flowers

3 *P. laurocerasus* fruit

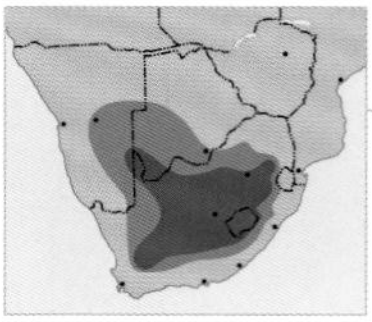

- Drought 2
- Spring
- Deciduous

1 *Prunus mume* ROSACEAE

Japanese Apricot; Japanse Appelkoos

OTHER LANGUAGES: Mei (Chinese); Abricotier japonais (French); Japanischer Aprikosenbaum (German); Ume (Japanese); Damasqueiro da China (Portuguese); Albaricoquero japonés (Spanish)

China and southern Japan Small tree with a rounded to spreading crown; buds and twigs hairless. Leaves with petiole hairless, 12–20mm long; blade 60–100 × 25–50mm, **egg-shaped or elliptic**, with a **drip-tip**; base narrowed; lower surface **hairy**; margin saw-toothed. Flowers single or double, white, pink or red, fragrant, appearing **before** the leaves; petals 9–14 × 8–12mm. Fruit fleshy, **yellow, sometimes with a red blush**.

Chinese growers have been breeding cultivars of this species for at least 1,000 years. The fruits are pickled or consumed as juice or an alcoholic beverage. These are all delicacies in China, Korea and Japan, each form named separately in each country. These preparations are unusual but attractive to the Western palate and deserve to be sought out. Meihua (plum blossom) is the national flower of China.

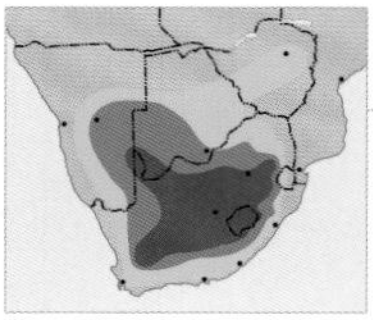

- Drought 2
- Spring
- Deciduous

2 *Prunus persica* *(= Amygdalus persica, Persica vulgaris)* ROSACEAE

Peach, Nectarine; Perske

OTHER LANGUAGES: Tao (Chinese); Pêcher (French); Pfirschenbaum (German); Adoo (Hindi); Ke momo (Japanese); Pessequeiro (Portuguese); Persik (Russian); Pérsico duraznero (Spanish); Peras (Tagalog)

Northern and central China Small tree with an open, spreading crown usually shaped by pruning, sometimes with **yellow autumn colours**; buds **hairy**. Leaves with petiole hairless, 10–20mm long, usually with **two glands** at point of attachment to the blade; blade 75–150 × 20–40mm, **lance-shaped**; tip **sharply pointed**; base oblique; lower surface **hairless**; margin **saw-toothed**. Flowers usually pink, appearing before the leaves; petals 10–17 × 9–12mm. Fruit fleshy, egg-shaped, **hairy (peach) or hairless (nectarine)**, 30–110 × 40–100mm. Seeds (stones) buff, **deeply pitted and furrowed**, 15–20mm long.

Peaches were domesticated in China about 4,000 years ago. Nectarines differ only in having hairless fruits and this appears to be governed by a single gene. The wilted leaves, twigs and seeds are deadly poisonous. Peaches are susceptible to so many pests and diseases that they require constant maintenance to give an acceptable crop. Nevertheless, they have become naturalised in some parts of our region.

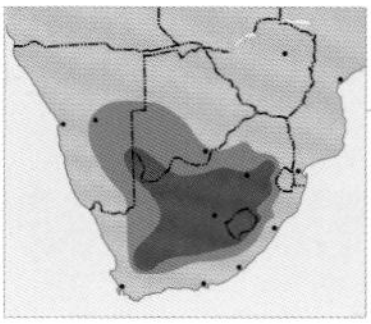

- Drought 2
- Spring
- Deciduous

3 *Prunus serotina* *(= P. capuli)* ROSACEAE

Black Cherry, American Cherry, Mexican Cherry; Swartkersie, Mexikaanse Kersie

OTHER LANGUAGES: Cerisier du Méxique (French); Capolim (Portuguese); Capuli (Spanish)

Canada to Mexico Medium-sized to large tree with an upright to rounded crown and **red autumn colours**; bark of mature trees **almost black**, distinctively **cracked and flaking**. Leaves with petiole hairless, 6–25mm long; blade 50–140 × 25–45mm, lance-shaped to elliptic, sharply pointed; base narrowed; midrib **with a line of brown hairs below**; margin saw-toothed. Inflorescences hanging, at least in fruit, 100–150mm long. Flowers white, appearing **after** the leaves. Fruit fleshy, ellipsoid, **black**, hairless, about 8mm in diameter.

This species has become naturalised in parts of Europe and in South Africa, where it is a declared Category 1b invader. The wood is very desirable for furniture, cabinet-making and other uses where a fine finish is required. Native Americans have used this species medicinally. However, most parts are known to be poisonous.

1 *P. mume* flower

1 *P. mume* fruit

2 *P. persica* leaves

2 *P. persica* flowers

2 *P. persica* fruit

3 *P. serotina*

3 *P. serotina* flowers

3 *P. serotina* fruit

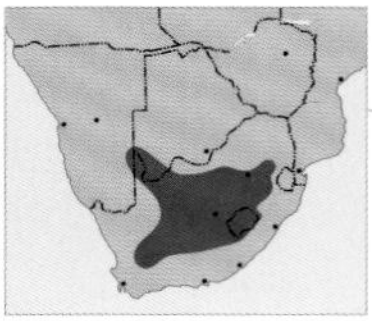

1 *Prunus serrulata* (= *P. sieboldii*)

ROSACEAE

Japanese Flowering Cherry, Oriental Cherry; Japanse Blomkersie

- Drought 2
- Spring
- Deciduous

OTHER LANGUAGES: Shan ying hua (Chinese); Cerisier à feuilles en dents de scie (French); Gesägtblättrige Kirsche (German); Yama Zakura (Japanese)

China, Korea and Japan Small to medium-sized tree with a rounded to vase-shaped crown and **bronzy red autumn colours**; bark **smooth, brown**; buds and twigs hairless. Leaves with petiole hairless, 10–15mm long; blade 50–125 × 30–60mm, **egg-shaped**; tip sharply pointed; base narrowed; margin **saw-toothed**. Inflorescences erect; common peduncle 5–10mm long; individual pedicels up to 40mm long. Flowers white or pink, appearing **before** the leaves. Fruit fleshy, roundish, **black**, hairless, 8–10 × 6–10mm.

Japanese growers have been producing cultivars of this species for at least 1,000 years. Flowers may be single, semidouble or double; these latter forms seldom if ever set fruit. Recorded from scattered localities in the cooler parts of our region.

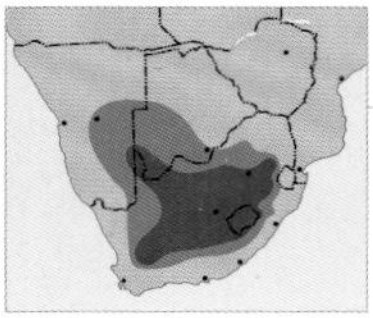

2 *Pyrus calleryana*

ROSACEAE

Chinese Pear, Callery Pear; Chinese Peer

- Drought 2
- Spring
- Deciduous

OTHER LANGUAGES: Dou li (Chinese)

Central and southern China Medium-sized tree with a conical to rounded crown and **orange to purple autumn colours**; bark **brownish**; buds **hairy**. Leaves with petiole hairless, 9–40mm long; blade 45–80 × 35–60mm; base squared to shallowly heart-shaped; veins **hairy** on lower surface; margin **scalloped**. Inflorescences erect. Flowers white, appearing with the leaves; petals about 13 × 10mm. Fruit fleshy, **round, brown, roughish**, hairless, 15–20mm in diameter.

Chinese pear is mainly grown as a garden ornamental in cooler areas, because its compact crown fits well into restricted spaces. Birds eat the fruits and spread the seed; as a result, the tree has become invasive in eastern North America.

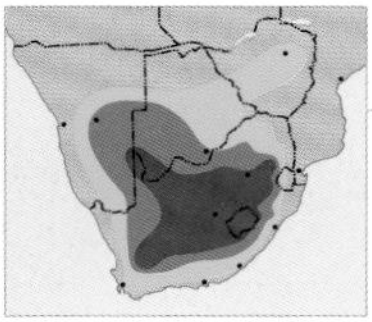

3 *Pyrus communis*

ROSACEAE

Common Pear, European Pear, Pear; Gewone Peer, Peer

- Drought 2
- Spring
- Deciduous

OTHER LANGUAGES: Xi yang li (Chinese); Poirier (French); Birnenbaum (German); Nashpati (Hindi); Pero comune (Italian); Seiyou nashi (Japanese); Pereira (Portuguese); Pera (Spanish)

Europe and Southwestern Asia Medium-sized to large tree with a pyramidal crown, sometimes with bronze autumn colours; bark **grey**; buds and twigs **hairless**. Leaves with petiole hairless, 20–50mm long; blade 25–100 × 15–50mm; base rounded to shallowly heart-shaped; only midrib **hairy** below; margin smooth to toothed. Inflorescences erect; individual pedicels 10–40mm long. Flowers white, appearing **after** the leaves; petals 13–15 × 10–13mm. Fruit fleshy, **distinctively shaped**, green, yellow or brown, sometimes with a reddish blush, smooth or slightly rough, hairless, 30–100 × 15–60mm.

Bartlett pear trees are self-fertile but most, if not all others, need a companion of a different cultivar if they are to set fruit. The fruits can be eaten fresh or cooked, or the juice can be extracted for consumption as is or fermented into a cider analogue called Perry. The wood is hard and fine-grained and is sought after for making furniture, veneer and musical instruments.

1 *P. serrulata* autumn leaves

1 *P. serrulata* flowers

BRAAM VAN WYK

2 *P. calleryana* flowers

ALPSDAKE, WIKIMEDIA COMMONS, CC BY SA 3.0

2 *P. calleryana* fruit

RLEYSE, WIKIMEDIA COMMONS, PUBLIC DOMAIN

3 *P. communis* leaves

3 *P. communis* flowers

BRAAM VAN WYK

3 *P. communis* fruit

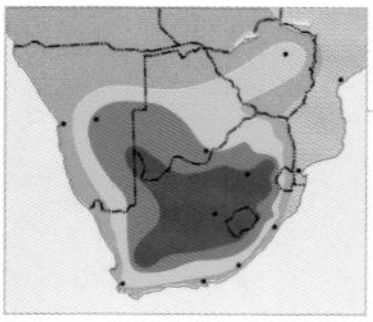

- Drought 2
- Spring
- Semi-deciduous

1 *Quercus canariensis* (= *Q. mirbeckii*)

FAGACEAE

Algerian Oak, Canary Oak; Algeriese Eik

OTHER LANGUAGES: Chêne des Canaries (French); Algerische Eiche (German); Quercia africana (Italian); Carvalho de Monchique (Portuguese); Roble andaluz (Spanish)

Portugal to Tunisia Medium-sized to large tree with a spreading crown; buds hairless. Leaves with petiole **hairy**, 10–30mm long; blade 90–150 × 50–80mm; tip **rounded**; base **rounded to heart-shaped**; margin with **6–12 pairs** of shallow lobes. Male inflorescences hanging catkins on a peduncle up to 20mm long, female flowers solitary. Fruit an ellipsoid acorn nut about 25 × 20mm, in a cup with **hairy, protruding**, pale brown scales.

A large, slow-growing, long-lived tree, therefore suitable as a specimen in parks or very large gardens. Recorded from Gauteng, Mpumalanga, KwaZulu-Natal and Western Cape. The wood of this tree is typical of the genus, valuable for construction and furniture-making. The acorns are used in places to feed pigs.

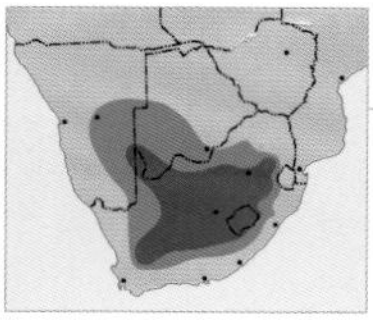

- Drought 2
- Spring
- Deciduous

2 *Quercus cerris*

FAGACEAE

Turkey Oak, Mossy-cup Oak; Turkse Eik, Mos-eik

OTHER LANGUAGES: Cer (Croatian); Cerre (French); Zerr-eiche (German); Alon shasua (Hebrew); Dub turetskii (Russian); Crni Cer (Serbian); Roble Turco (Spanish); Saçlı meşe (Turkish)

Europe and eastern Mediterranean Large tree, crown pyramidal, later spreading, with **red autumn colours**; buds hairless, with **whiskery stipules**; twigs hairy. Leaves with petiole hairless, 8–20mm long; blade **very variable, even on the same tree**, 60–125 × 25–75mm; tip **pointed**; base **narrowed**; lower surface with **star-shaped hairs**; margin **coarsely toothed to deeply lobed**. Inflorescences slender, **hanging**. Fruit an acorn 25–40mm long, about 20mm in diameter, in a **mossy, hairy** cup.

Grown in parks or large gardens for ornament or shade and recorded from scattered places in cooler parts of South Africa. Unusually among oaks, the wood is poor, as it warps and splits during seasoning. Furthermore, it does not weather well and cannot be used for outdoor work. In the Serbian Orthodox Church, this species and *Q. robur* (English oak) are used for Christmas trees.

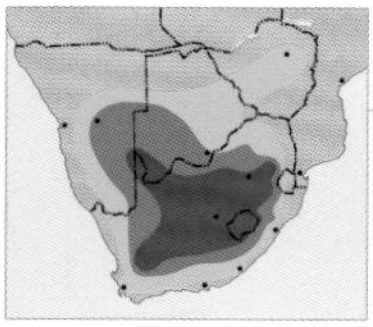

- Drought 2
- Spring
- Deciduous

3 *Quercus macrocarpa*

FAGACEAE

Bur Oak; Grootneuteik

OTHER LANGUAGES: Chêne à gros glands (French); Bur-eiche (German); Roble de frutos grandes (Spanish)

USA Large tree with a rounded crown and **yellow to brown autumn colours**; bark brown to grey, ruggedly fissured; buds hairy or not; twigs hairy; lenticels warty, conspicuous. Leaves alternate; petiole hairy, 10–30mm long; blade 50–310 × 40–160mm, widest at or beyond the middle, **shallowly pinnately 5–7-lobed**; tip **rounded**; base narrowed; surface glossy above, hairy below; margin **scalloped**. Stipules soon falling. Inflorescences a **hanging**, single flower or string of multiple flowers; males and females separate, on the same tree. Flowers individually inconspicuous. Fruit an acorn 15–50 × 10–40mm, three quarters enclosed in a **mossy, hairy**, woody, brown to grey cup.

An important timber tree, the wood used for flooring, shipbuilding, cabinet-making, flooring and more. Formerly grown in scattered cooler places in our region but now apparently only seen at Tokai Arboretum in Cape Town. Medicinal uses are recorded.

1 *Q. canariensis* flowers (male)

JAVIER MARTIN, WIKIMEDIA COMMONS, PUBLIC DOMAIN

1 *Q. canariensis* fruit

2 *Q. cerris* leaves

2 *Q. cerris* fruit

MONGO, WIKIMEDIA COMMONS, PUBLIC DOMAIN

3 *Q. macrocarpa* young fruit

USDA, WIKIMEDIA COMMONS, PUBLIC DOMAIN

3 *Q. macrocarpa* fruit

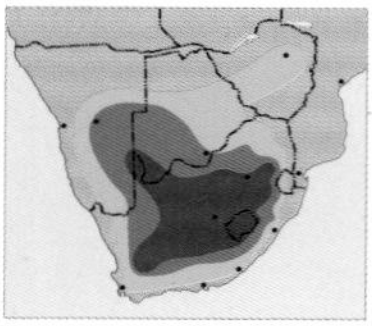

1 *Quercus nigra* *(= Q. aquatica, Q. uliginosa)*

FAGACEAE

Water Oak; Watereik

- Drought 2
- Spring
- Deciduous

OTHER LANGUAGES: Chêne gris (French); Wassereiche (German); Roble de agua (Spanish)

Southeastern USA Medium-sized to large tree with a rounded crown and **yellow-brown autumn colours**; buds **hairy**; twigs **hairless, grey**. Leaves with petiole hairless, 2.5–7.5mm long; blade 40–130 × 12–60mm, **widest beyond the middle**; tip **usually with 3 lobe-like teeth**; base narrowed. Inflorescences hanging. Fruit a roundish acorn 9.5–14 × 9.5–14.5mm, in a flat, brown, shortly papillate cup.

Grown as a specimen tree in botanical and a few private gardens in our region. It is also occasionally seen on golf courses, where it is considered resistant to hits from stray golf-balls. The wood is heavy, hard and close-grained and is used for railway sleepers and for poles. Not being highly valued, it is also used for fuelwood. Medicinal uses are recorded.

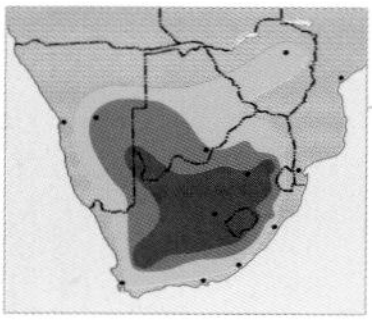

2 *Quercus palustris*

FAGACEAE

Pin Oak; Moeraseik, Naaldeik, Spelde-eik

- Drought 2
- Spring
- Deciduous

OTHER LANGUAGES: Chêne des marais (French); Sumpf-eiche (German); Roble de las marismas (Spanish)

Eastern USA Medium-sized tree with a pyramidal or later **columnar** crown and **red autumn colours**; bark grey, narrowly fissured; buds and twigs hairless. Leaves alternate; petiole hairless, 20–60mm long; blade 50–200 × 50–137mm, egg-shaped, **deeply pinnately 5–9-lobed**; tip pointed and hair-tipped; base narrowed to squared; surface glossy above, **hairless or woolly below**; margin smooth. Stipules soon falling. Inflorescences a hanging, single flower or string of multiple flowers, appearing with the leaves; males and females separate, on the same tree. Flowers individually inconspicuous. Fruit an acorn 10–25 × 9–15mm, in a **shallow, rough** cup.

Widely grown in cooler parts of South Africa and Zimbabwe as an ornamental in parks and gardens. The wood is sold as 'red oak' but is weaker than that species, with many knots. One source suggests that the common name comes from a former use of this tree to make wooden pins used in building construction.

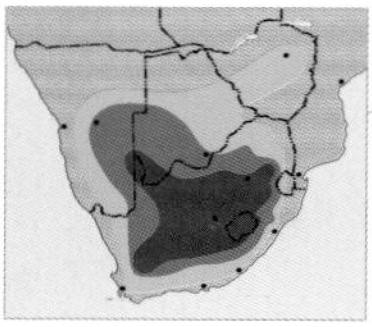

3 *Quercus petraea*

FAGACEAE

Durmast Oak, Sessile Oak; Wintereik

- Drought 2
- Spring
- Deciduous

OTHER LANGUAGES: Chêne rouvre (French); Trauben-eiche (German); Amischos (Greek); Carvalho-branco (Portuguese); Dub skal'nyi (Russian); Roble albero (Spanish); Sapsız meşe (Turkish)

Europe and Western Asia Medium, rarely large, tree with a pyramidal to rounded crown and **purple autumn colours**; bark grey, narrowly fissured; buds and twigs hairless. Leaves alternate; petiole hairless, **10–30mm long**; blade 70–140 × 40–80mm, widest beyond the middle, shallowly **pinnately 7–11-lobed**; tip rounded to squared; base narrowed. Inflorescences a **hanging**, single flower or string of multiple flowers, appearing after the leaves; males and females separate, on the same tree. Flowers individually inconspicuous. Fruit a **stalkless acorn** 20–30 × 10–20mm, in a **shallow, rough** cup.

National tree of Wales and Cornwall, grown in our region in scattered forestry plantations, most easily seen as a specimen tree in Tokai Arboretum, Cape Town. The wood is durable under water as well as dry and is valued for furniture, construction and other uses. Medicinal uses are recorded.

1 *Q. nigra* leaves

1 *Q. nigra* fruit

2 *Q. palustris* leaves

2 *Q. palustris* flowers

2 *Q. palustris* fruit

3 *Q. petraea* flowers (male)

3 *Q. petraea* fruit

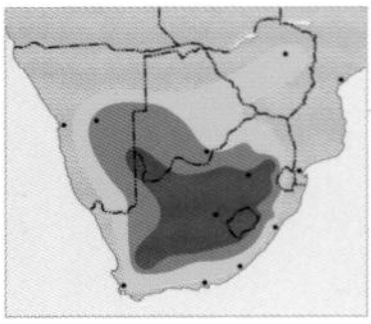

- Drought 2
- Spring
- Deciduous

1 *Quercus robur* *(= Q. pedunculata)* FAGACEAE

English Oak, Oak Tree, Pedunculate Oak; Akkerboom, Europese Eik, Steeleik

OTHER LANGUAGES: Chêne pédonculé (French); Deutsche Eiche (German); Emmischos (Greek); Rovere di slavonia (Italian); Carvalho comum (Portuguese); Encino común (Spanish); Saplı meşe (Turkish)

Europe and Southwestern Asia Medium-sized tree with a rounded crown and **no autumn colours**; bark brown or black, fissured or rough; buds and twigs hairless; lenticels warty or smooth, conspicuous. Leaves alternate; petiole **almost absent** (up to 6mm long); blade 50–200 × 20–100mm, egg-shaped to oblong, **shallowly pinnately 7–13-lobed**; tip rounded and indented; base narrowed. Fruit an acorn 15–35 × 12–20mm, in a **shallow, rough cup on a long stalk**.

The classic oak of legend and of great symbolic value in several European countries. Widely grown in South Africa and Zimbabwe, rarely in Mozambique, for ornament and timber, Van der Stel's oaks in Stellenbosch being particularly noteworthy. The timber is durable both dry and underwater and has the same uses as Durmast oak (p.184). Medicinal uses are recorded.

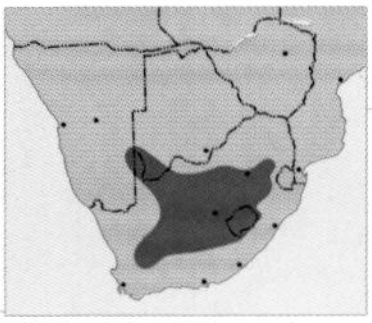

- Drought 2
- Spring
- Deciduous

2 *Quercus rubra* *(= Q. borealis, Q. ambigua)* FAGACEAE

Red Oak; Rooi-eik

OTHER LANGUAGES: Chêne rouge (French); Roteiche (German); Roble rojo (Spanish)

Eastern USA Large tree with a rounded crown and **red, yellow and brown autumn colours**; bark grey to black, narrowly fissured, forming distinctively striped ridges; buds and twigs hairless. Leaves alternate; petiole hairless, 25–50mm long; blade 100–225 × 60–150mm, egg-shaped or oblong, **deeply or shallowly pinnately 7–11-lobed**; tip **pointed and bristle-tipped**; base squared; surface dull, hairless; margin smooth. Stipules soon falling. Inflorescences a **hanging**, single flower or string of multiple flowers, appearing after the leaves; males and females separate, on the same tree. Flowers individually inconspicuous. Fruit an acorn 15–30 × 10–21mm, in a **rough, shallow** cup.

State tree of New Jersey, USA, and provincial tree of Prince Edward Island, Canada. Widely grown for ornament and as a specimen tree in cooler parts of our region. One of the most important timber trees in North America, the wood is used for furniture, interior finishes and veneer, with defective logs making good firewood. Medicinal uses are recorded.

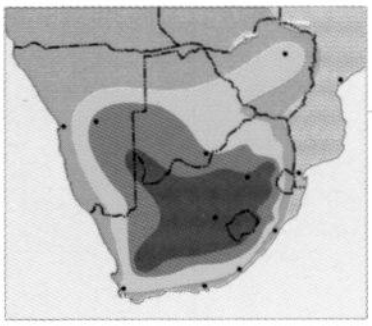

- Drought 2
- Spring
- Evergreen

3 *Rhaphiolepis indica* ROSACEAE

Indian Hawthorn; Indiese Haagdoring

OTHER LANGUAGES: Shi ban mu (Chinese)

China, Japan and Indochina Small, rounded tree, can be grown as a large shrub; twigs hairy. Leaves with petiole hairless, 5–18mm long; blade 30–80 × 15–40mm, **widest beyond the middle**; tip rounded; base narrowed; margin **scalloped**. Inflorescences erect, 50–75mm long. Flowers white or pink; petals 5–7 × 4–5mm. Fruit fleshy, round, hairless, **purple to black, 5–8 × 5–8mm**.

A garden ornamental recorded from several parts of South Africa and Mozambique. It can be shaped into hedges or bonsai. The fruits are edible and can be made into jams and pie fillings. Dyes in various shades of blue and purple can be made from the fruits.

SIMON EUGSTER, WIKIMEDIA COMMONS, GFDL 1.2, CC BY SA 3.0

1 *Q. robur* flowers (male)

GEOFF NICHOLS

1 *Q. robur* fruit

ANGELA HUSTER, WIKIMEDIA COMMONS, PUBLIC DOMAIN

2 *Q. rubra* leaves

ANRO0002, WIKIMEDIA COMMONS, PUBLIC DOMAIN

2 *Q. rubra* flowers (male)

2 *Q. rubra* fruit

BRAAM VAN WYK

3 *R. indica* flowers

BRAAM VAN WYK

3 *R. indica* fruit

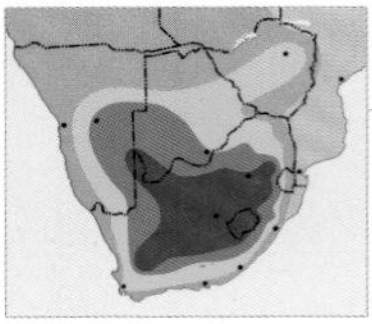

- Drought 2
- Spring
- Evergreen

1 *Rhaphiolepis umbellata* ROSACEAE

Indian Hawthorn, Yedo Hawthorn; Indiese Haagdoring

OTHER LANGUAGES: Hou ye shi ban mu (Chinese)

China and Japan Large, rounded shrub; twigs hairy, dark brown. Leaves with petiole hairless, 5–12mm long; blade 30–100 × 20–60mm, **egg-shaped to elliptic**; tip rounded; base narrowed; margin **scalloped, sometimes rolled under**. Inflorescences erect, 75–100mm long. Flowers white; petals 10–12mm long. Fruit fleshy, roundish, **purple to black, hairless, 7–12 × 7–10mm**.

A garden ornamental, widespread in our region. A brown dye can be made from the bark.

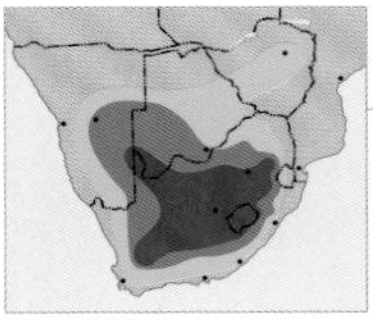

- Drought 2
- Spring
- Deciduous

2 *Salix babylonica* SALICACEAE

Weeping Willow; Treurwilger

OTHER LANGUAGES: Safsaaf baky (Arabic); Chui liu (Chinese); Saule Pleureur (French); Trauerweide (German); Salceiro-chorão (Portuguese); Iva plakuchaia (Russian); Vrba žalujka (Slovenian); Msafsafi wa Babeli (Swahili)

China Medium-sized tree with a spreading, **weeping** crown; buds and twigs usually hairless. Leaves with petiole hairless, 3–6mm long; blade 60–100 × 8–20mm, **narrowly lance-shaped**; tip **drawn out to a point**, base pointed; lower surface **milky green, hairless**; margin toothed. Inflorescences erect, 15–30mm long. Flowers with males and females on separate trees. Fruit a hairless capsule 3–4mm long. Seeds dark brown.

Male trees are hardly ever seen in southern Africa and reproduction of this species here is usually by cuttings or suckers. The young, flexible stems can be used in basket-making. As is the case with most willows, the bark can be used medicinally. Widely grown and naturalised in our region.

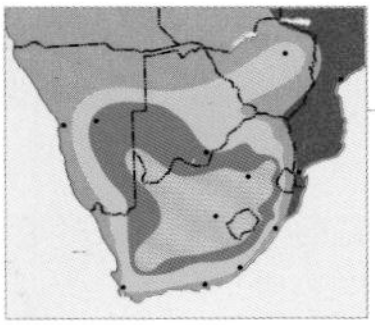

- Drought 3
- Spring
- Evergreen

3 *Stenocarpus sinuatus* PROTEACEAE

Firewheel Tree, Queensland Firewheel Tree; Vuurwielboom

Eastern Australia Medium, rarely large, tree usually with a **columnar** crown; bark grey, smooth; buds hairless; twigs hairy. Leaves alternate; petiole hairless, 10–30mm long; blade **150–600** × 20–50mm, lance-shaped to elliptic in outline, **leathery, pinnately 3–9-lobed**, rarely simple; tip pointed; base narrowed; surface glossy above, dull below; margin **wavy**. Stipules absent. Inflorescences erect; peduncles 40–100mm long. Flowers tubular, narrow, 25–38mm long, bright red, arranged in a **wheel-like** formation. Fruit a **boat-shaped**, woody pod 50–100mm long. Seeds 25–36mm long.

Widely but not very commonly grown ornamental tree seen in many parts of South Africa and Zimbabwe.

1 *R. umbellata* leaves and fruit

1 *R. umbellata* flowers

1 *R. umbellata* fruit

2 *S. babylonica*

2 *S. babylonica* flowers

3 *S. sinuatus* flowers

3 *S. sinuatus* fruit

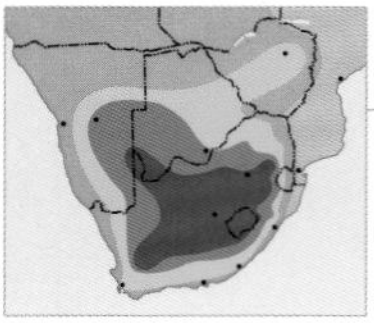

1 *Telopea speciosissima* PROTEACEAE

Common Waratah, Waratah; Gewone Waratah

- Drought 2
- Spring
- Evergreen

Eastern Australia Large shrub or small tree with a pyramidal crown; buds and twigs hairless. Leaves with petiole **winged**, hairless, up to 50mm long; blade 80–280 × 20–65mm, **egg-shaped**; tip rounded; base narrowed; margin toothed, rarely smooth. Inflorescences erect, protea-like heads; bracts **red**, oblong, 50–90mm long; margin smooth. Flowers **red**, tubular, 10–34mm long. Fruit a spindle-shaped, densely hairy capsule 90–140mm long. Seeds whitish.

Grown as a garden ornamental in scattered places in South Africa and Zimbabwe. The flowerheads can be used for cut flowers and last for about 10–14 days. Waratah is the state flower of New South Wales.

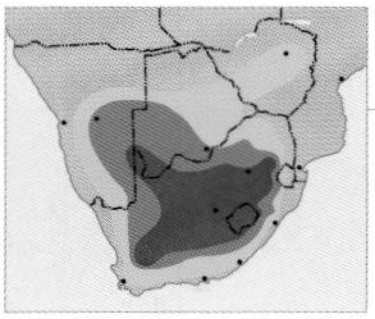

2 *Ulmus carpinifolia* ULMACEAE

European Field Elm; Europese Veldolm

- Drought 2
- Spring
- Deciduous

Europe and Southwestern Asia Large tree with a **pyramidal** crown and **inconspicuous yellow-brown autumn colours**; buds **hairy**; twigs hairless, often with **corky outgrowths**. Leaves with petiole hairless, 5–10mm long; blade 40–100 × 25–50mm; tip pointed; base oblique; surface **glossy** above; veins **hairy** below; margin twice-toothed. Inflorescences erect. Flowers inconspicuous, appearing before the leaves. Fruit a hairless **2-winged nut** 10–15mm long.

Both the typical variety and var. *suberosa*, with corky twigs, are grown in scattered localities in South Africa, Zimbabwe and Mozambique. In addition, the cultivar 'Variegata', with variegated leaves, is sometimes encountered. Field elms are not seen very often in Europe, as most have been destroyed by Dutch elm disease. It is not ideal for gardens because it suckers freely.

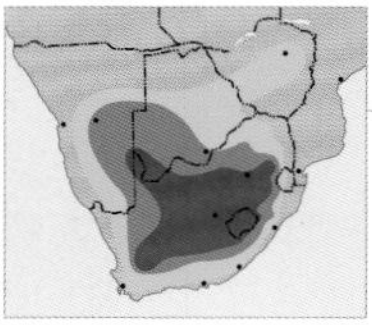

3 *Ulmus parvifolia* *(= U. chinensis)* ULMACEAE

Chinese Elm; Fynblaarolm, Chinese Iep

- Drought 2
- Spring
- Deciduous

OTHER LANGUAGES: Lang yu (Chinese)

China and Korea Small to medium-sized tree with a rounded crown; bark **irregularly flaking**; buds hairless; twigs hairy, **zigzag**. Leaves with petiole hairless, 3–6mm long; blade 15–40 × 10–20mm; tip pointed; base **oblique**; surface **glossy** throughout; margin **once**-toothed. Inflorescences hanging. Flowers inconspicuous, appearing before the leaves. Fruit a hairless **2-winged nut** about 8mm long.

Chinese elm has been recorded as invasive in some parts of the Highveld; there are also records of its becoming naturalised in North America. It is often used as a street tree in Gauteng as it is resistant to Dutch elm disease; it can also be used for bonsai. Internet sources mention the possibility of using it for shelter belts in windy places, a suggestion that seems ill-advised in view of its known invasive tendencies. The timber is the hardest among the elms and is used for purposes such as tool handles, longbows, flooring and others where hardness is important.

BRAAM VAN WYK

1 *T. speciosissima* flowerhead

BRAAM VAN WYK

BRAAM VAN WYK

1 *T. speciosissima* fruit; inset: old dehisced fruit

2 *U. carpinifolia* leaves

HERMANN SCHACHNER, WIKIMEDIA COMMONS, PUBLIC DOMAIN

2 *U. carpinifolia* flowers

HERMANN SCHACHNER, WIKIMEDIA COMMONS, PUBLIC DOMAIN

2 *U. carpinifolia* fruit

3 *U. parvifolia* flowers

MIKE TURNER

3 *U. parvifolia* fruit

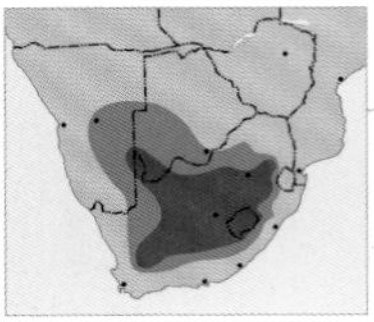

1 *Ulmus procera*

ULMACEAE

English Elm; Skurwe-olm

- Drought 2
- Spring
- Deciduous

England Large tree with a **fan-shaped** or 'figure-eight' crown, **yellow autumn colours**; bark **flaking, sometimes deeply fissured**; buds hairless; twigs hairy, sometimes with corky wings. Leaves with petiole hairless, up to 11mm long; blade 50–95 × 30–60mm, almost round; tip sharply pointed; base **oblique**; surface **very rough** above, hairy below; margin twice-toothed. Inflorescences hanging. Flowers inconspicuous, appearing after the leaves. Fruit a hairless 2-winged nut 10–17mm long.

The English elm rarely, if ever, produces viable seed and Bean (1970) notes that the only practical way of propagating this species is by the root-suckers which are produced in great numbers. Large trees in England are noted for shedding branches without warning and Bean comments that 'this habit makes the elm a very unsuitable tree to plant in crowded thoroughfares'. Elm wood is both tough and beautiful, with no tendency to split. Hollowed elm logs were used as water-pipes on account of their durability, before the introduction of iron pipes. Sadly, the elm has now virtually disappeared from England, as a result of the ravages of Dutch elm disease. Medicinal uses are recorded. In our region it is widespread, showing signs of becoming invasive. A cultivar with leaves marked and edged with creamy white, 'Argenteo-variegata', can be encountered.

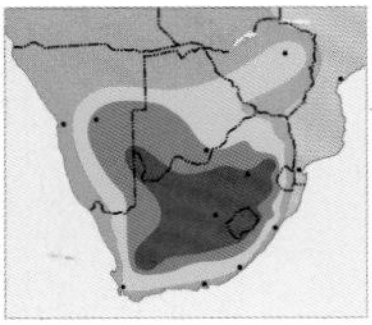

2 *Xylosma congestum*

FLACOURTIACEAE

Shiny Xylosma, Dense Logwood; Blinkblaarxylosma

- Drought 1
- Spring
- Evergreen

OTHER LANGUAGES: Zuomu (Chinese)

China, Korea and Japan Small tree with a rounded crown; buds and twigs **hairless**. Leaves with petiole hairy or hairless, 2–5mm long; blade 20–80 × 15–40mm, more or less egg-shaped; tip pointed; base rounded; upper surface **glossy**; margin toothed. Inflorescences erect, 5–20mm long. Flowers **yellow-green, inconspicuous**. Fruit a round, hairless, red or black berry 4–5mm in diameter.

Grown as a specimen tree in Pretoria, also used for hedges and bonsai in drier areas outside our region.

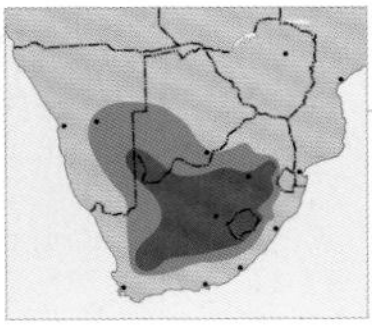

3 *Zelkova carpinifolia*

ULMACEAE

Caucasian Elm; Kaukasiese Olm

- Drought 2
- Spring
- Deciduous

Caucasus Large tree with a **columnar** crown and **yellow autumn colours**; buds and twigs hairless. Leaves with petiole hairless (but **hairy when young**), 1.5–6mm long; blade 20–60 × 15–50mm, egg-shaped; tip **drawn out into a long point**; base oblique; margin **coarsely toothed**. Inflorescences a single flower or clusters. Flowers whitish, inconspicuous. Fruit fleshy, green, hairless, about 4mm in diameter, drying brown with age.

Trees are ornamental and so are grown for decoration and shade both in their native area and elsewhere. However, they are rarely seen in our region, apparently only in the Drakensberg foothills. They are also used for bonsai. Caucasian elm trees yield good timber.

MELBURNIAN, WIKIMEDIA COMMONS, CC BY SA 2.5

1 *U. procera*

1 *U. procera* leaves

2 *X. congestum*

BRAAM VAN WYK

2 *X. congestum* flowers

BRAAM VAN WYK

2 *X. congestum* flowers detail

P. GARIN

3 *Z. carpinifolia* leaves

BEARTOMCAT, J. JOHNSTON

3 *Z. carpinifolia* fruit

GROUP 10

Common group

Leaves simple, alternate or in tufts, not bilobed; blade with single midvein from base, not distinctly discolorous; margin smooth, not prominently lobed. Spines absent. Latex absent.

See also Group 5: *Anacardium occidentale* (p.112), *Mangifera indica* (p.118) and *Uapaca kirkiana* (p.124); Group 7: *Quercus stellata* (p.144) and *Solanum mauritianum* (p.146); Group 8: *Solanum macranthum* (p.150); Group 9: *Quercus macrocarpa* (p.182), *Q. palustris* (p.184), *Q. petraea* (p.184), *Q. robur* (p.186), *Q. rubra* (p.186) and *Stenocarpus sinuatus* (p.188).

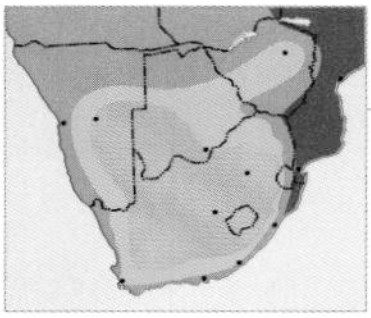

- Drought 2
- Spring
- Evergreen

1 *Agonis flexuosa*

MYRTACEAE

Willow Myrtle, Peppermint Tree; **Wilgermirt**

Western Australia Small tree with a spreading crown of **weeping** branches; bark **fibrous**; buds and twigs hairy. Leaves with petiole about 3mm long; blade 60–120 × 6–10mm, strap-shaped, smelling of **peppermint** when crushed; tip drawn out to a point; base gradually narrowing. Inflorescences erect. Flowers white. Fruit a brown, egg-shaped, hairless capsule.

Ornamental tree but sheds much rubbish. Grown in scattered places in South Africa, Zimbabwe and Kenya.

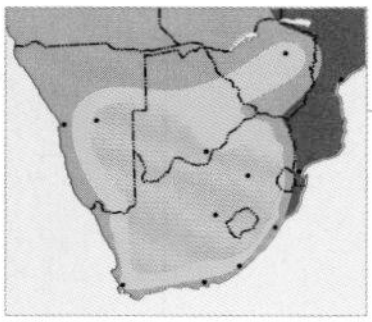

- Drought 1
- Spring
- Evergreen

2 *Annona cherimola*

ANNONACEAE

Cherimoya, Custard Apple; **Vla-appel**

OTHER LANGUAGES: Chérimolier (French); Chirimoyabaum (German); Graviola (Portuguese); Mamón (Spanish)

South America Small tree with a **spreading** crown; twigs with **brownish yellow hair**. Leaves alternate **in two rows**; petiole 6–12mm long; blade 50–150 × 40–100mm, **lance- to egg-shaped**, with a drip-tip; base **rounded**; surface **woolly below**. Inflorescences hanging. Flowers white; petals 15–30mm long, white with a purple basal mark. Fruit fleshy, green, **rough-skinned**, heart-shaped, hairless, 200 × 100mm, flesh white. Seeds black, 15 × 8mm.

A delicious tropical fruit that was once quite commonly sold by greengrocers in the warmer parts of our region but is now seldom seen, though still grown in a few private gardens.

1 *A. flexuosa*

1 *A. flexuosa* leaves

STEVE AND ALISON PEARSON

1 *A. flexuosa* flowers

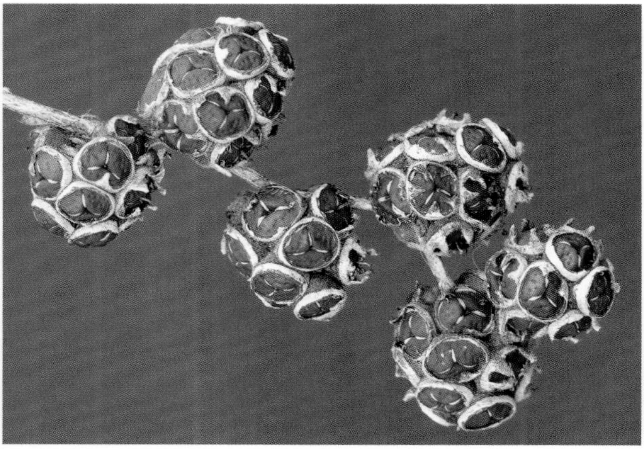

JAMES GAITHER

1 *A. flexuosa* immature fruit

2 *A. cherimola* leaves

GEOFF NICHOLS

2 *A. cherimola* flower

2 *A. cherimola* fruit

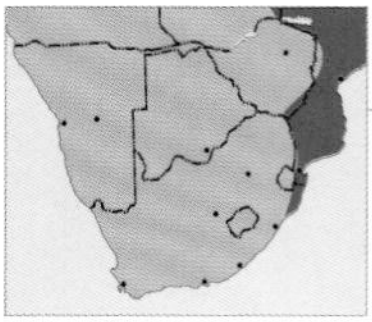

1 *Annona muricata* ANNONACEAE

Soursop; Suursak

OTHER LANGUAGES: Cachiman épineux (French); Sauersack (German); Coração-da-rainha (Portuguese); Catuche (Spanish); Mstafeli (Swahili)

Central America and the West Indies Small tree with an **irregular, upright** crown; buds hairy; twigs **soon becoming hairless**. Leaves alternate **in two rows**; petiole hairless, 5–10mm long; blade 60–250 × 25–80mm, oblong or widest beyond the middle; tip and base variable; lower surface **minutely hairy**; margin **bent back**. Inflorescences a single, hanging flower. Flowers greenish yellow; petals 25–35 × 20–30mm. Fruit fleshy, 150–300mm long, about 100mm in diameter, skin **spiny**, green, flesh white. Seeds dark brown to black, 10–17 × 10mm.

- Drought 2
- Spring
- Evergreen

A seldom seen tropical fruit, with many uses in other warm areas but not well known in our region. It is recorded from South Africa's KwaZulu-Natal and from Mozambique and Tanzania. The seeds, however, are poisonous.

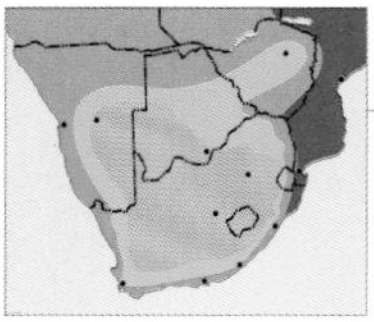

2 *Annona squamosa* ANNONACEAE

Sweetsop; Soetsak

OTHER LANGUAGES: Annone écailleuse (French); Rahmapfel (German); Anona blanca (Spanish)

Central America and the West Indies Small tree with a spreading crown; buds hairy; twigs soon hairless. Leaves alternate **in two rows**; petiole minutely hairy, 5–15mm long; blade 60–150 × 30–50mm, elliptic to oblong; base **oblique**; surface **waxy blue-grey**; veins hairy below; margin entire, bent back. Inflorescences 3 or 4 hanging flowers. Flowers white to yellow or green; petals about 15–25 × 5mm, with a purple basal mark. Fruit fleshy, round, 60–120 × 60–120mm, skin **waxy green, lumpy**, flesh yellowish white. Seeds dark brown to black, 10–13 × 8 × 5mm.

- Drought 1
- Spring
- Semi-deciduous

A tropical fruit tree that deserves to be grown more often in our region where it is recorded from Namibia, South Africa and Tanzania. Fruits are eaten fresh or variously prepared and can be fermented into a wine-like beverage.

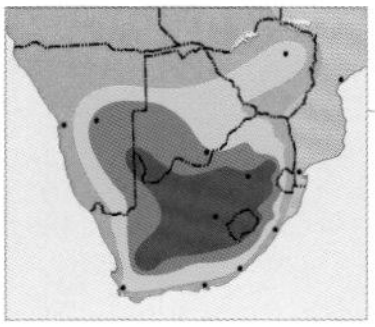

3 *Atriplex nummularia* CHENOPODIACEAE

Old Man Saltbush; Oumansoutbos

Australia Upright, often rather shapeless shrub with hairless twigs. Leaves with petiole hairless, 5–10mm long; blade 20–65 × 10–60mm, **grey, rhombic**, with a **salty taste** when licked; tip rounded. Inflorescences erect, up to 200mm long; males and females usually on different plants. Fruit dry, not opening, 5–20mm long, 3-angled. Seeds midbrown, about 2mm wide.

- Drought 3
- Spring
- Evergreen

Naturalised in the drier parts of southern Africa, where it is grown for stock feed. However, it is now a declared Category 2 invader in South Africa.

1 *A. muricata* leaves

NOPPHARAT46 / SHUTTERSTOCK.COM

1 *A. muricata* flower

1 *A. muricata* fruit

2 *A. squamosa* leaves

2 *A. squamosa* flowers

2 *A. squamosa* fruit

3 *A. nummularia* leaves

BRAAM VAN WYK

3 *A. nummularia* flowers

RUSSELL CUMMING

3 *A. nummularia* fruit

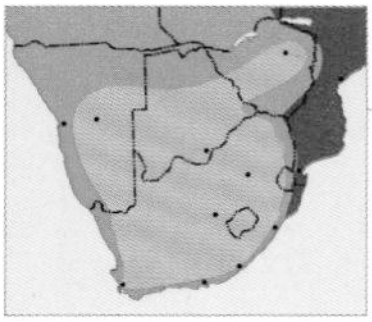

1 *Barringtonia asiatica* (*= B. speciosa, Mammea asiatica*) LECYTHIDACEAE

Asian Barringtonia, Fish Killer Tree; Oosterse Barringtonia

- Drought 1
- Spring
- Evergreen

OTHER LANGUAGES: Binyurui (Chinese); Arbre à Barrette, Bonnet de Prêtre (French); Goban no ashi (Japanese); Putat (Malay); Árbol de los Muertes (Spanish); Chik le (Thai)

Zanzibar to Taiwan and French Polynesia Medium-sized to large tree with a rounded crown; buds and twigs hairless, the latter **green**. Leaves with petiole hairless, up to 5mm long; blade 200–380 × **100–180mm, widest beyond the middle**; tip **indented or spine-tipped**. Inflorescences hanging, 20–300mm long. Flowers with petals white, 55–85 × 25–45mm; stamens **many, 60–120mm long**, white with pink tip. Fruit fibrous, green or buff, square in section, hairless, 85–110 × 85–100mm. Seeds 40–50 × 25–40mm.

Grown in our region as a few specimen trees in Durban Botanic Gardens but worthy of consideration as an ornamental in a warm tropical garden with a high water table. All parts of the plant are poisonous but medicinal uses are recorded. The occasional use of the fruits as fishing floats is recorded from India. The flowers are fragrant and attract bats and moths as pollinators.

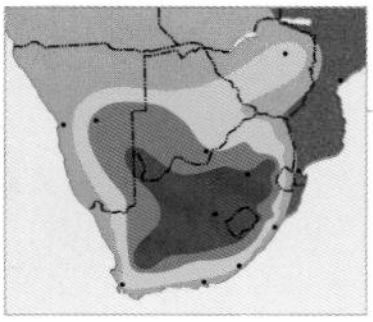

2 *Brachychiton populneus* (*= Sterculia diversifolia*) MALVACEAE

Kurrajong, Bottle Tree, White-flower Kurrajong; Koerajong, Bottelboom

- Drought 3
- Spring
- Deciduous

OTHER LANGUAGES: Kurrajong-Flaschenbaum (German)

Australia Medium-sized tree with an oval to rounded crown; bark grey, narrowly fissured; twigs **hairless**. Leaves with petiole hairless, 50–100mm long; blade 50–100mm long, lance- to egg-shaped, simple or palmately 3–9-lobed; tip **long drawn out**; base **usually rounded**, usually with **1 main vein from the base**; surface glossy; margin smooth. Inflorescences erect. Flowers cup-shaped, yellow-green with reddish spots. Fruit a **boat-shaped**, woody, black pod 50–70mm long. Seeds buff, embedded in **irritant hairs**.

Commonly grown for ornament in Mozambique, Namibia, South Africa and Zimbabwe. The fruits and seeds are edible and string can be made from the bark. The seeds are surrounded in the capsule by irritant hairs and must be collected with great care.

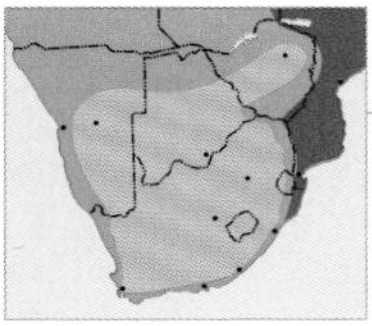

3 *Brexia madagascariensis* CELASTRACEAE (OR BREXIACEAE)

Brexia, Mfukufuku; Brexia

- Drought 2
- Summer
- Evergreen

Tropical Africa, Madagascar and Seychelles Small tree or large shrub with a narrow crown and hairy twigs and buds. Leaves with petiole hairy, 10–20mm long; blade 35–350 × 20–76mm, **widest beyond the middle**; tip **rounded to squared**; base narrowed; surface glossy; margin **inrolled**. Inflorescences erect, 10–90mm long. Flowers green or yellowish white, 12–17 × 9–12mm; stamens 10–18mm long. Fruit fleshy, **ovoid and 5-angled**, 40–100 × 19–30mm. Seeds black, 4.5–7.5 × 3–3.5mm.

It appears that this tree is only cultivated as specimen trees in a few botanical gardens and little, if anything, is known of its uses.

1 *B. asiatica* flower fallen from tree

1 *B. asiatica* fruit

JESÚS CABRERA

2 *B. populneus* flowers

MONOMOYANO, WIKIMEDIA COMMONS, PUBLIC DOMAIN

2 *B. populneus* open fruit

2 *B. populneus* fruit

3 *B. madagascariensis* flowers

GEOFF NICHOLS

3 *B. madagascariensis* fruit

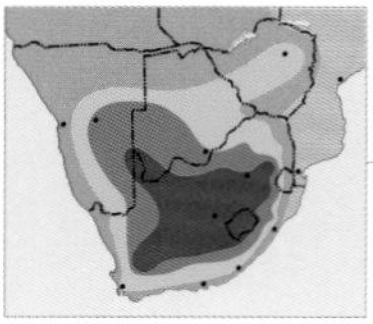

• Drought 2
• Spring
• Evergreen

1 *Brugmansia* × *candida* (= *B. aurea* × *B. versicolor*, *Datura* × *candida*)

SOLANACEAE

Moonflower; Maanblom

OTHER LANGUAGES: Borrachero Buyés (Spanish)

Natural hybrid from tropical South America Large shrub or small, spreading tree; twigs **hairy**. Leaves with petiole **hairy**, up to 60mm long; blade **up to 200 × 80–120mm**, elliptic to oblong; tip pointed; base **narrowed to rounded**; surface **hairy**; margin wavy, sometimes with a few teeth. Inflorescences a hanging, single flower on stalk 30–50mm long. Flowers tubular, colour varying according to cultivar, white fading yellowish, or shades of yellow, pink, orange, green, or red, 250–350mm long. Fruit a spindle-shaped capsule up to 150 × 20mm, rarely formed. Seeds 6–10mm long.

A common garden ornamental. All parts of the plant are poisonous.

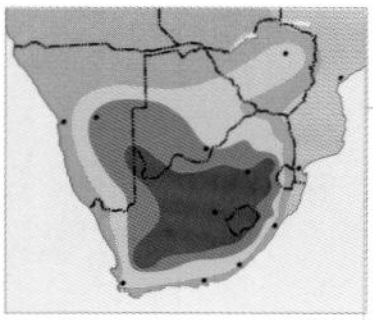

• Drought 2
• Spring
• Evergreen

2 *Brugmansia suaveolens* (= *Datura suaveolens*)

SOLANACEAE

Angel's Trumpet; Engeltrompet

OTHER LANGUAGES: Duftende Engelstrompete (German); Floripondio (Spanish)

Brazil Large shrub or small, rounded tree; twigs sometimes hairless. Leaves with petiole **hairless**, about 4mm long; blade **up to 250 × 110mm**, egg-shaped to elliptic; tip drawn out to a long point; base **heart-shaped**; surface **hairless or nearly so**; margins wavy. Inflorescences a **hanging**, single flower on stalk about 35mm long. Flowers fragrant, tubular, white, often with pink or yellow mouths, tube 250–300mm long. Fruit a spindle-shaped, hairless capsule 100–160mm long, not often seen. Seeds about 8 × 5mm.

Garden ornamental, almost as common as moonflower. All parts of the plant are poisonous.

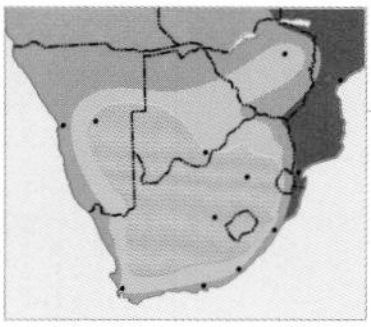

• Drought 2
• Spring
• Evergreen

3 *Bucida buceras* (= *Terminalia buceras*)

COMBRETACEAE

Bullet Tree, Black Olive Tree, Jucaro; Jucaro-boom

OTHER LANGUAGES: Bois gris-gris (French); Cacho de Toro (Spanish)

Central America and the West Indies Medium-sized, spreading tree with tiered, later drooping branches; buds hairy; twigs hairless. Leaves **in tufts**; petiole hairy, 5–10mm long; blade 30–90 × 30–60mm, **widest beyond the middle**; tip rounded; base narrowed; surface hairless but **veins hairy below**. Inflorescences erect, 30–100mm long. Flowers small, yellow-green, inconspicuous. Fruit fleshy, pale brown, silky-hairy, egg-shaped, **5-angled** in section, 8mm long. Seeds midbrown.

Widely planted for shade and ornament in the Caribbean area but only as specimen trees in botanical gardens in our region. It is said to make a good windbreak but is not suitable for places such as car parks, because of the dark, sticky gum it exudes. The wood (trade name 'Jucaro') is heavy and hard to work but takes a fine finish. It is used for flooring, furniture, railway sleepers, ship's timbers and more. The flowers are used by bees making honey.

FOREST AND KIM STARR

1 *B.* × *candida*

1 *B.* × *candida* flower

GEOFF NICHOLS

1 *B.* × *candida* fruit

2 *B. suaveolens* leaves

BRAAM VAN WYK

2 *B. suaveolens* flowers

DADEROT, WIKIMEDIA COMMONS, PUBLIC DOMAIN

2 *B. suaveolens* fruit

3 *B. buceras* leaves

FOREST AND KIM STARR

3 *B. buceras* flowers

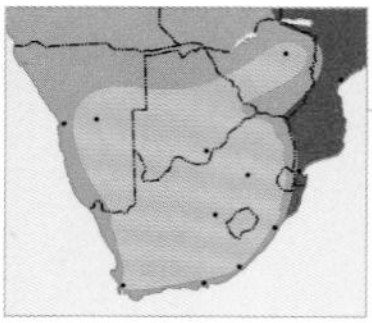

- Drought 2
- Late Summer
- Evergreen

1 *Buckinghamia celsissima* PROTEACEAE

Ivory Curl Flower; Ivoorkrulblom

Northeastern Australia Tall, narrow tree in confined spaces, but shorter and rounded in the open; twigs hairy. Leaves with petiole hairless, 5–20mm long; blade 100–200 × 30–70mm, egg-shaped to elliptic, juvenile leaves sometimes lobed; tip **indented**; base rounded; lower surface sometimes hairy. Inflorescences **erect, 100–200mm long**. Flowers creamy, white or pale pink, 7–10mm long. Fruit an egg-shaped, woody capsule about 20 × 15–20mm.

This beautiful ornamental has been used with success as a street tree in Australia but is extremely rarely seen, only in one or two private collections, in our region. Overseas experience suggests that it has little or no tolerance of frost and high humidity. When in flower, trees may bear a superficial resemblance to some of the macadamia nuts (*Macadamia* spp., Group 25), members of the same family.

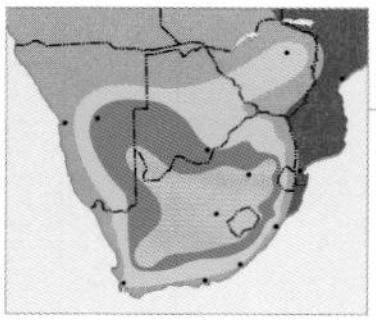

- Drought 2
- Spring
- Evergreen

2 *Callistemon citrinus* (= *C. lanceolatus, Metrosideros citrina*) MYRTACEAE

Lemon Bottlebrush; Lemoenperdestert

Eastern Australia Large upright shrub or small spreading tree, often multistemmed; twigs hairless. Leaves **lemon-scented**, without petiole; blade 35–90 × 3–20mm, strap-shaped to oblong, with numerous minute **secretory cavities** when viewed against the sun; tip and base narrowed; veins **hairy below**. Inflorescences erect, up to 100mm long, initially at the ends of branches, which grow on through them as flowering progresses, so the fruits are **some distance back from the tip**. Flowers red. Fruit a hairless, ellipsoid, brown capsule.

A very popular garden ornamental, which attracts birds and bees. It is not clear whether the dwarf cultivar 'Little John' belongs to this species or to *C. viminalis* (p.204).

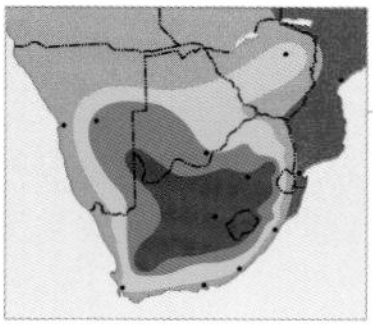

- Drought 2
- Spring–Early Summer
- Evergreen

3 *Callistemon salignus* MYRTACEAE

Willow Bottlebrush, Yellow Bottlebrush; Geelperdestert

Eastern Australia Small tree or large shrub with a narrow crown; bark **whitish, flaking, papery**; new growth hairy, **purplish pink**. Leaves without petiole; blade 50–110 × 12mm, strap- to lance-shaped, with numerous minute **secretory cavities** when viewed against the sun; tip and base pointed; veins hairless throughout. Inflorescences erect, 50–75mm long, initially at the ends of branches, which grow on through them as flowering progresses, so the fruits are **some distance back from the tip**. Flowers white, yellowish or pink. Fruit a brown, hairless capsule 4–5mm in diameter.

A widely grown garden ornamental with many different colour forms. The cultivars 'Red Splendour' and 'Rubra' have red flowers.

RUSELL CUMMING

1 *B. celsissima* flowers

1 *B. celsissima* fruit

2 *C. citrinus* flowers

2 *C. citrinus* leaves and young fruit

3 *C. salignus* leaves

3 *C. salignus* flowers

3 *C. salignus* fruit

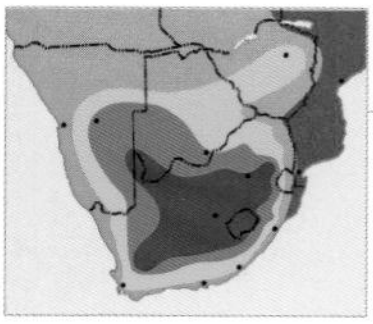

- Drought 3
- Spring–Early Summer
- Evergreen

1 *Callistemon viminalis* MYRTACEAE
Weeping Bottlebrush; Treurperdestert

Eastern Australia Small tree or large shrub with a vase-shaped crown and **weeping** branches; twigs hairless, grey. Leaves with petiole hairless, **up to 2mm long** or absent; blade 30–100 × 3–7mm, strap-shaped or widest beyond the middle, with numerous minute **secretory cavities** when viewed against the sun; tip and base tapering; veins hairless throughout. Inflorescences erect, 40–100mm long, initially at the ends of branches, which grow on through them as flowering progresses, so the fruits are **some distance back from the tip**. Flowers red. Fruit a grey, hairless, ellipsoid capsule 5–6mm in diameter.

One of the most popular bottlebrushes and it does well even in places as dry as Kimberley, Northern Cape. The species is a declared Category 1b invader in the Eastern Cape, KwaZulu-Natal, Mpumalanga and Limpopo, and Category 3 elsewhere in South Africa; sterile cultivars are not declared.

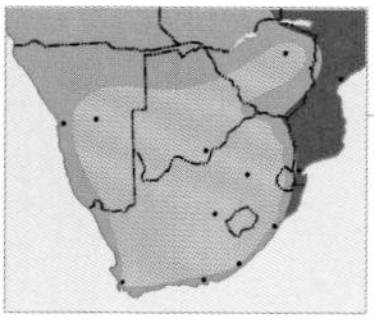

- Drought 2
- Spring
- Evergreen

2 *Cananga odorata* ANNONACEAE
Ylang-ylang; Ilang-ilang

OTHER LANGUAGES: Yi lan (Chinese); Ilang-ilang en arbre (French); Ilang-ilangbaum (German); Kananga (Malay); Ilanga (Portuguese); Ilang-ilang (Spanish, Tagalog)

India to the Philippines Large tree with a narrow crown, but can be kept small by pruning; buds and twigs hairless. Leaves alternate **in two rows**; petiole hairless, 8–20mm long; blade 90–200 × 40–90mm, egg-shaped to elliptic, with a **drip-tip**; base **rounded to squared**; veins **hairy below**. Inflorescences hanging; peduncle up to 10mm long. Flowers **scented**, greenish yellow, on pedicels 20–50mm long; petals 40–90 × 5–12mm, with a purple-brown basal mark. Fruit a **cluster of black berries**, each about 20–25 × 15mm. Seeds buff.

An essential oil, said to be the basis of some classic perfumes, is extracted from the flowers. This oil is one of the main exports of the Comoro Islands. In Micronesia and Tonga, and presumably elsewhere as well, it is an important source of flowers for personal adornment. Birds and mammals eat the fruit in many places and in Malaysia it is used as a street tree. The species is represented in our region by a single tree in Durban Botanic Gardens and colonial records from Mozambique.

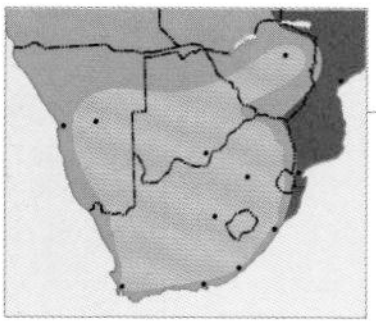

- Drought 2
- Spring
- Evergreen

3 *Cerbera manghas* *(= C. tanghin, C. venenifera)* APOCYNACEAE
Sea Mango, Reva; See-mango

OTHER LANGUAGES: Tanguin (Malagasy); Bintaro (Malay, Bahasa Indonesia)

Seychelles to Polynesia Small to medium-sized tree with a rounded to spreading crown; buds and twigs hairless; latex **white or greenish**. Leaves with petiole hairless, 20–40mm long; blade 100–250 × 20–80mm, lance-shaped, oblong or widest beyond the middle, with a **drip-tip**; base narrowed; surface glossy above, dull below. Inflorescences erect, about 200mm long; peduncle 60–80mm long. Flowers tubular; tube about 30mm long, greenish white, lobes 5, obovate, about 10 × 8mm, pink. Fruit fleshy, **roundish to heart-shaped**, green, yellow, then reddish black, **80–100 × 60–80mm**. Seeds about 25 × 22 × 2mm.

Grown in our region as specimen trees in botanical gardens. The wood is used for carvings, furniture or charcoal. All parts of the plant are very poisonous but medicinal uses are recorded.

1 *C. viminalis* leaves

1 *C. viminalis* flowers

1 *C. viminalis* fruit

2 *C. odorata* leaves

2 *C. odorata* flowers

2 *C. odorata* fruit

3 *C. manghas* flowers

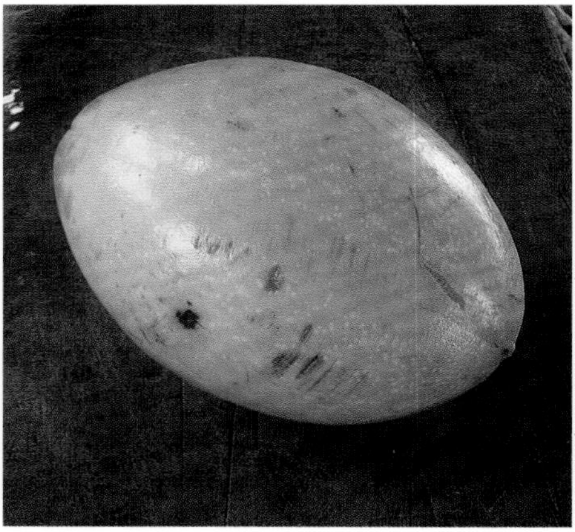

3 *C. manghas* fruit

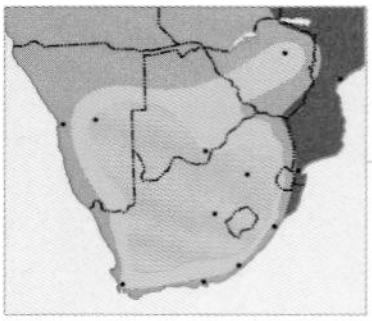

1 *Cordia africana* (= *C. abyssinica, C. holstii*)

BORAGINACEAE

Large-leaved Saucer-berry, East African Cordia, Large-leaved Cordia; Grootblaarpieringbessie

- Drought 2
- Spring
- Evergreen

OTHER LANGUAGES: Faux Teck (French); Makobokobo (Swahili); Mukebu, Mukumari (trade names)

Tropical Africa, just extending into southern Africa Small to medium-sized, rarely large tree with an irregular, rounded or spreading crown. Leaves with petiole hairless, 20–105mm long; blade **60–210 × 40–165mm**, egg-shaped; base rounded to heart-shaped; lower surface **velvety**. Inflorescences erect; pedicels glabrous, up to 1mm long in flower. Flowers white, tubular, 15–22 × 10–14mm; perianth of a calyx and corolla. Fruit fleshy, brown, roundish, hairless, 10–12 × 8–10mm.

Grown as a specimen tree in botanical gardens in our region but would make a good garden ornamental. Fruits are edible and used as famine food in Ethiopia. The timber is easily worked and makes good furniture, doors, drums and other artifacts. The flowers are attractive to bees. Medicinal uses are recorded. See also *C. grandicalyx* in Van Wyk & Van Wyk (2013).

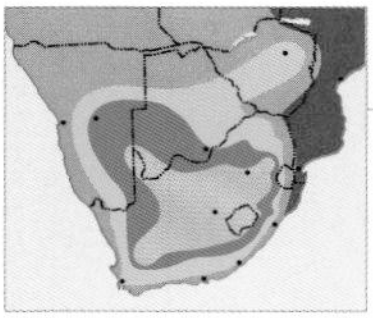

2 *Cordia myxa*

BORAGINACEAE

Indian Saucer-berry, Lasura, Sudan Teak; Indiese Pieringbessie

- Drought 3
- Spring
- Evergreen

OTHER LANGUAGES: Bois Savon (French); Brustbeeren (German); Lasodaa (Hindi); Sebesteira (Portuguese); Bahuvāra (Sanskrit); Ciruelo asirio (Spanish)

Tropical Africa to Iraq Small tree with a pyramidal to spreading crown and hairy buds. Leaves with petiole hairy or hairless, 13–32mm long; blade 40–100 × 40–90mm, **egg-shaped to round**; base **squared to heart-shaped**; lower surface **hairy**. Inflorescences erect, 50–90mm long. Flowers white, tubular, 9–13.5mm long. Fruit fleshy, roundish, yellow, hairless, 19–24 × 19–21mm.

Grown for fruit, which is edible and has applications in Asian medicine. The timber is similar to that of *C. africana* (above).

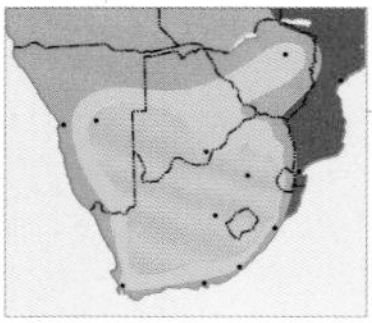

3 *Cordia sebestena*

BORAGINACEAE

Geiger Tree; Geiger-se-pieringbessie

- Drought 2
- Spring
- Evergreen

OTHER LANGUAGES: Bois Râpe (French); Scharlach-Kordie, Sebestenenbaum (German); Sebesteira-verdadeira (Portuguese); Anacahuita, Anaconda (Spanish)

Mexico to Venezuela Small tree with a rounded crown; buds and twigs hairy. Leaves with petiole **hairy**, 10–45mm long; blade 70–220 × 50–140mm, egg-shaped; base rounded to squared; surface **sandpapery**; margin **wavy**, sometimes rolled under. Inflorescences erect. Flowers **orange**, tubular, 25–40mm long. Fruit fleshy, white, hairless, egg-shaped, 20–40 × 15–25mm.

Garden ornamental seen in Durban, South Africa, and in Mozambique, less used than it possibly should be. The common names commemorate one John Geiger, a sea captain who guided John James Audubon, famous ornithologist, around southern Florida in 1832 or soon after.

1 *C. africana* flowers

BART WURSTEN

1 *C. africana* fruit

2 *C. myxa* flowers

2 *C. myxa* fruit

VINAYARAJ, WIKIMEDIA COMMONS, CC BY SA 3.0

3 *C. sebestena* flowers

FOREST AND KIM STARR

3 *C. sebestena* fruit

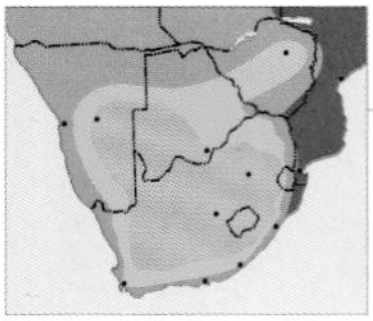

1 *Couroupita guianensis* LECYTHIDACEAE
Cannonball Tree; Boskalbas

- Drought 2
- Mostly Spring
- Evergreen

OTHER LANGUAGES: Calabasse Colin (French); Kanonenkugelbaum (German); Abricó de Macaco, Macacarecuia (Portuguese); Coco de Mono (Spanish)

Guatemala to Peru, Brazil and Puerto Rico Large tree with a narrow crown. Leaves sometimes in tufts; petiole hairless, 5–30mm long; blade **70–440** × 30–100mm, oblong; surface glossy; margin sometimes undulate. Inflorescences erect or hanging, up to 3.5m long, **persistent, on old wood**. Flowers scented, pink, orange or red; petals 30–50mm long, with white markings, surrounding a conspicuous **cluster of 600–700 stamens**. Fruit a **round**, hairless, brown capsule 120–240mm in diameter, **seen all year round**, falling intact. Seeds buff, 115–225mm long.

A spectacular tree for warm gardens but hazardous if planted too close to a path. The flowers attract bees, which visit for the pollen, as there is no nectar. Sacred to Hindus, who consider the flower to resemble the Naga, a group of mythical snake-like creatures. Native Americans have many medicinal uses for this tree.

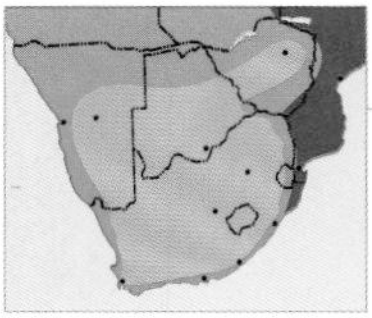

2 *Crescentia cujete* BIGNONIACEAE
Calabash Tree; Kalbasboom

- Drought 2
- Spring
- Evergreen

OTHER LANGUAGES: Cuité (Portuguese); Calabacero, Totumo (Spanish)

Mexico to Bolivia, Brazil and the West Indies Small tree with an irregular, spreading crown; buds and twigs hairless, the latter **very stout**. Leaves **in tufts, without petiole**; blade 40–260 × 10–76mm, usually widest beyond the middle; base **gradually narrowing**. Inflorescences 1 or 2 hanging flowers, **on old wood**. Flowers tubular, brownish yellow, **41–74mm long**, with **purple lengthways stripes**. Fruit dry, not opening, up to 300 × 130–200mm. Seeds 7–8 × 4–6mm.

National tree of St. Lucia, an island in the Caribbean Sea. The flowers are bat-pollinated and only open at night. Dry fruits have a variety of uses, as scoops, cups, containers and maracas. Unfortunately, the tree in Durban Botanic Gardens does not ripen fruit.

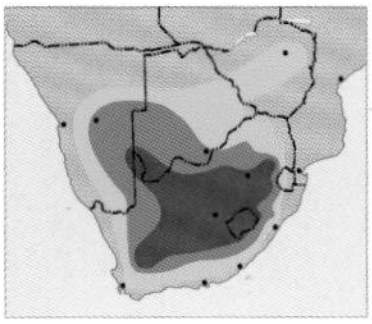

3 *Cydonia oblonga* ROSACEAE
Quince; Kweper

- Drought 3
- Spring
- Deciduous

OTHER LANGUAGES: Supurgillu (Akkadian); Al safarjal (Arabic); Dunja (Croatian); Cognassier (French); Quittenbaum (German); Kydonia (Greek); Cotogno (Italian); Marmelo (Portuguese); Ajva (Russian); Dunja (Serbian); Membrillo (Spanish); Ayva (Turkish)

Wild origin lost in the mists of time, but possibly Western Asia Small, rounded tree, shape determined by pruning; buds and twigs hairy. Leaves with petiole **hairy**, 8–15mm long; blade 60–100 × 45–55mm; base rounded to squared; lower surface **woolly**. Flowers white, pink or red; petals 20–30mm long. Fruit fleshy, apple-like, densely hairy, **yellow**, 70–120 × 60–90mm, **crowned with the persistent remains of the calyx**.

One of the first fruit trees to be domesticated, possibly even before the apple; it is thought that in some early references to ‘apples’ in the Hebrew Bible, quinces are actually meant. Quinces are a useful source of pectin in making jams and marmalade and have several medicinal uses. They may also be grown for ornament and are to be found in scattered, cooler parts of our region.

1 *C. guianensis* leaves

1 *C. guianensis* flowers

1 *C. guianensis* fruit

GIORGIOGLOBE, WIKIMEDIA COMMONS, PUBLIC DOMAIN

2 *C. cujete* flower

BRAAM VAN WYK

2 *C. cujete* fruit

FRANZ XAVER, WIKIMEDIA COMMONS, GDFL 1.2, CC BY SA 3.0

3 *C. oblonga* flowers

MANFRED HEYDE, WIKIMEDIA COMMONS, PUBLIC DOMAIN

3 *C. oblonga* fruit (see also p.16)

BRAAM VAN WYK

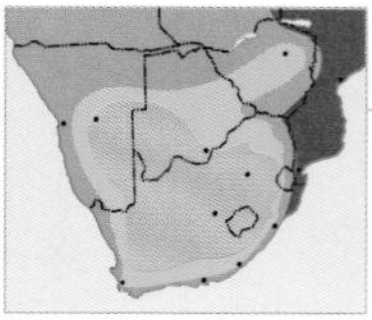

1 *Diospyros digyna* (= *D. ebenaster*) EBENACEAE

Black Sapote; Swartsapoot

- Drought 2
- Spring
- Evergreen

OTHER LANGUAGES: Barbacoa (French); Ébano das Antilhas (Portuguese); Zapote Prieto (Spanish)

Mexico, Central America and Colombia Large tree with an irregular, spreading crown; bark **black**; twigs hairy. Leaves with petiole hairless; blade 130–300 × 50–70mm, elliptic to oblong; tip and base **narrowed**; lower surface **hairless**. Inflorescences an erect, single flower or clusters; stalk about 5mm long. Flowers white, tubular, 9–18mm long; males and females very similar, on separate trees. Fruit fleshy, roundish, **black or yellow**, hairless, 45–125mm in diameter, **flesh almost black**. Seeds reddish to midbrown, about 19–20 × 10 × 5mm.

Ripe fruit edible if peeled, flesh said to be chocolate-flavoured. Timber is yellow with black flecks and probably good, but rarely used. In our region, black sapote is only seen as specimen trees in botanical gardens.

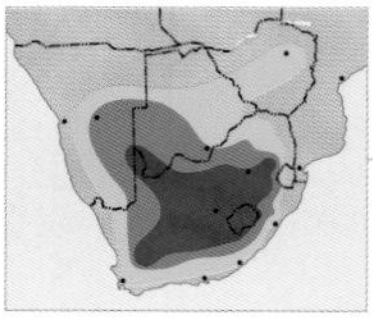

2 *Diospyros kaki* (= *D. chinensis*) EBENACEAE

Chinese Persimmon, Japanese Persimmon, Kaki-fruit, Persimmon, Sharon fruit; Chinese Persimmon, Persimmon, Tamatiepruim

- Drought 2
- Spring
- Deciduous

OTHER LANGUAGES: Shi (Chinese); Kaki, Plaqueminier du Japon (French); Kakinoki (Japanese); Caqui (Portuguese, Spanish); Khurma (Russian); Phlap chin (Thai)

China and Japan Small to medium-sized tree with an upright to rounded crown and red-purple autumn colours; buds and twigs hairy; bark and twigs **brown**. Leaves with petiole hairless, 8–20mm long; blade 50–200 × 26–90mm, **lance- or egg-shaped to elliptic**, with a drip-tip; lower surface **hairy**. Flowers tubular, 10–16mm long, white, yellow or red; males and females very similar, on different trees. Fruit fleshy, roundish or heart-shaped, **orange**, hairless, **35–85mm in diameter**. Seeds dark brown, 13–16 × 7.5–9 × 4–5mm.

Cultivated for over 2,000 years for its fruits, which are occasionally seen for sale. Grown in scattered places in South Africa and Zimbabwe in our region. These fruits should be harvested as late as possible to avoid astringency and can be eaten fresh or cooked. The flesh of unripe fruit is sometimes used as a cosmetic and the wood is used to make fine furniture. Medicinal uses are recorded.

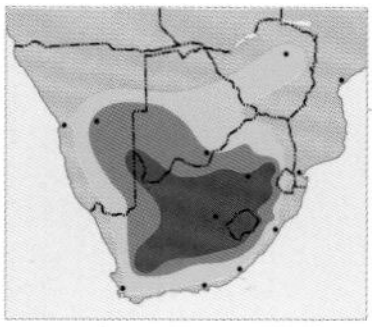

3 *Eucalyptus camaldulensis* (= *E. rostrata*) MYRTACEAE

River Red Gum, Murray Red Gum, Red Gum; Rooibloekom, Bloekom

- Drought 3
- Spring
- Evergreen

Australia Tall tree with a narrow to rounded crown; bark peeling; trunk **smooth above with whitish, grey and ochre patches**, with a rough, **dark 'boot' at the base**; juvenile stems square. Leaves alternate, opposite in juveniles; petiole hairless, 8–33mm long; blade 50–300 × 7–32mm, lance-shaped and **curved**, with numerous minute **secretory cavities** when viewed against the sun; base obliquely narrowed to rounded; surface **blue-green**, hairless. Inflorescences erect, 7- or 9-flowered; peduncle 5–28mm long. Flowers with 'lid' of bud **beaked**. Fruit a hemispherical **capsule 4–10mm in diameter**, rim **raised to vertical**, valves **4, protruding**. Seeds buff to yellow, 1–1.5mm long.

Among the most widespread of the gums, this tree is planted in many countries. The wood takes a fine polish and can be used to make furniture and decorative items. River red gum is an important honey plant and medicinal uses are recorded in Australia. This species is a declared Category 1b invader in some parts of South Africa but the exemptions are many and complex.

1 *D. digyna* flowers

1 *D. digyna* fruit

2 *D. kaki* leaves

2 *D. kaki* flower

2 *D. kaki* fruit

3 *E. camaldulensis* bark

3 *E. camaldulensis* flowers

3 *E. camaldulensis* fruit

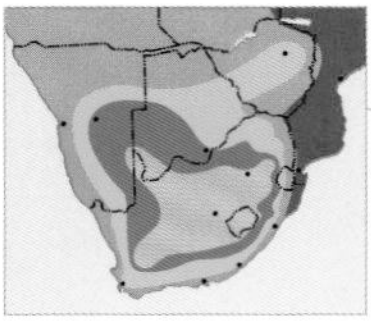

1 *Eucalyptus deglupta* MYRTACEAE

Rainbow Gum, Mindanao Gum; Reënboogbloekom

OTHER LANGUAGES: Amamanit (Filipino); Galang (Bahasa Indonesia)

- Drought 2
- Spring
- Evergreen

Papua New Guinea, Indonesia and the Philippines Tall tree with a narrow crown; bark peeling to the base, underbark **green, orange, maroon and brown**. Leaves alternate; petiole hairless; blade 50–140 × 20–70mm, lance- to egg-shaped, **straight**, with numerous minute **secretory cavities** when viewed against the sun; tip long-pointed; base rounded; surface **olive-green**, hairless. Inflorescences stiff, **clusters of 3–7 flowers** in large sprays. Flowers with 'lid' of bud **conical**. Fruit an egg-shaped capsule about 5mm in diameter, rim thin, valves **4, protruding**.

Arguably one of the most decorative gums because of its attractively coloured bark, this tree has a place in large, warm gardens. Plantation-grown trees are used for pulp and timber. Like *E. camaldulensis* (p.210), it deserves the nickname 'widow-maker', as the wood is brittle and large branches can fall without warning. Grown in a few localities in KwaZulu-Natal.

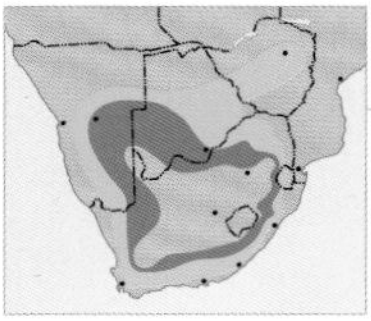

2 *Eucalyptus diversicolor* MYRTACEAE

Karri; Karrie

- Drought 2
- Spring
- Evergreen

Southwestern Australia Very tall tree with a narrow crown; bark peeling to the base, underbark **grey, cream and buff**. Leaves alternate (opposite at lowest nodes in juveniles); petiole hairless, 10–20mm long; blade 70–135 × 15–37mm, lance-shaped, straight, with numerous minute **secretory cavities** when viewed against the sun, with a drip-tip; base **narrowed**; surface **dark green above, paler below**, hairless. Inflorescences erect, **7-flowered**; peduncle slightly flattened, 12–30mm long. Flowers with 'lid' of bud **broadly conical**. Fruit a barrel-shaped, greenish brown capsule 7–10mm in diameter, rim **descending**, valves **3, enclosed**. Seeds grey, 1.2–3mm long.

The wood is very valuable, being hard and taking an excellent finish. It is used for roof joists, flooring and furniture and is the second most important timber tree in Australia. Karri honey is pale in colour, of delicate flavour and much sought after. This species is a declared Category 1b invader in some parts of South Africa but the exemptions are many and complex.

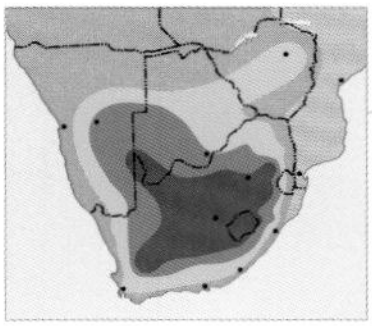

3 *Eucalyptus ficifolia* MYRTACEAE

Red Flowering Gum; Rooiblombloekom

- Drought 2
- Late Summer
- Evergreen

Southwestern Australia Small to medium-sized tree with a rounded crown; bark **fibrous, tan to grey, not shed**. Leaves alternate throughout; petiole hairless, 8–22mm long; blade 70–140 × 25–50mm, **egg-shaped to broadly lance-shaped**, with numerous minute **secretory cavities** when viewed against the sun; base often rounded; surface **dark green, glossy above, paler, dull below**; hairless. Inflorescences erect, 7-flowered; peduncle 15–32mm long. Flowers usually **red, rarely orange or pink**; 'lid' of bud rounded to flattened. Fruit an urn-shaped capsule 20–30mm in diameter, rim **vertically descending**, valves **3, enclosed**.

Used as a street tree in Cape Town, Port Elizabeth and other cities and occasionally as an ornamental in home gardens elsewhere in our region. In Tokai, Cape Town, there is an avenue of the very similar *E. calophylla* (marri), which differs in little more than having white flowers and being somewhat taller.

1 *E. deglupta* bark

1 *E. deglupta* flowers

1 *E. deglupta* fruit

2 *E. diversicolor* flowers

2 *E. diversicolor* fruit

3 *E. ficifolia* flowers

3 *E. ficifolia* fruit

1 *Eucalyptus globulus* MYRTACEAE
Tasmanian Blue Gum; Bloekom

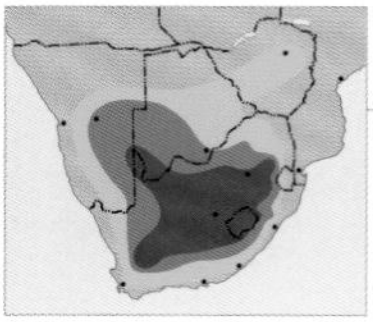

- Drought 2
- Spring
- Evergreen

Southeastern Australia Tall tree with a narrow, rounded crown; bark peeling, **smooth above with whitish and grey patches**; trunk with **a rough, dark 'boot' at the base**; juvenile stems square. Leaves alternate, opposite in juveniles; petiole hairless, 20–35mm long (absent in juveniles); blade 120–300 × 17–30mm, lance-shaped and **curved**, with numerous minute **secretory cavities** when viewed against the sun; surface **glossy green**, hairless. Inflorescences a **solitary** flower; pedicel absent or up to 5mm long. Flowers with buds **strongly 4-ribbed and white-waxy**, 'lids' **flattened and with a central knob**. Fruit a conical capsule, **square in section, 4-ribbed, waxy**, rim **slightly raised**, valves **4 or 5, more or less horizontal**. Seeds black or grey, 2–4mm long.

This gum was the foundation of South African eucalyptus plantations but is now very rare in cultivation, having been essentially eliminated by an indigenous fungus. The wood is used for timber or pulp. An essential oil is distilled from the leaves and the flowers are favoured by bees. This blue gum is the floral emblem of Tasmania.

2 *Eucalyptus grandis* MYRTACEAE
Flooded Gum, Rose Gum, Saligna Gum; Salignabloekom

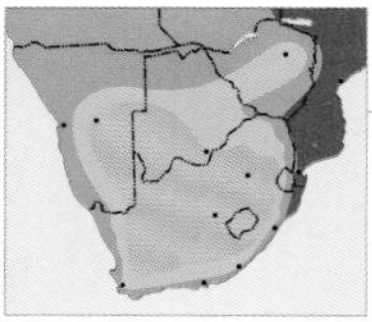

- Drought 2
- Spring
- Evergreen

Eastern Australia Tall tree **without** an underground woody swelling (lignotuber) but with a **rough, flaking, grey 'boot'** at the base of the trunk; bark peeling, underbark **powdery, whitish**. Leaves alternate, but opposite in juveniles; petiole hairless, 10–25mm long; blade 80–180 × 15–40mm, lance-shaped, slightly curved; base rounded; surface glossy green. Inflorescences erect, **7-, 9- or 11-flowered**; peduncle 10–18mm long. Flowers with buds **waxy**, 'lids' **conical or beaked**. Fruit a conical, grey capsule 5–7mm in diameter, rim **descending**, valves **4 or 5, protruding, bent inwards**. Seeds reddish brown, 1–1.7mm long.

Very similar to and often confused with *E. saligna*. Flooded gum lacks a lignotuber and has waxy buds and the valves of the fruit bend inwards. *Eucalyptus saligna* (p.216) has a lignotuber and clear green buds and the fruits always have 4 valves that bend inwards. Grown in many parts of the world for timber and pulp. The flowers attract bees. This species is a declared Category 1b invader in some parts of South Africa but the exemptions are many and complex.

3 *Eucalyptus maculata* MYRTACEAE
Spotted Gum; Gevlektebloekom

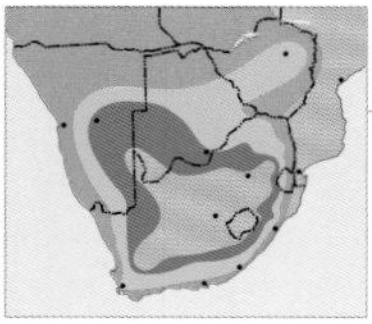

- Drought 2
- Winter
- Evergreen

Eastern Australia Tall tree with a **rounded to pyramidal** crown; bark peeling throughout, **mottled whitish and shades of grey**. Leaves alternate except first 2 or 3 pairs; petiole hairless, 10–25mm long; blade 80–210 × 12–30mm, lance-shaped and curved, with numerous minute **secretory cavities** when viewed against the sun. Inflorescences erect, **3-flowered**. Flowers with 'lid' of bud **rounded, with a small beak**. Fruit a grey-brown, urn- or barrel-shaped capsule 9–13mm in diameter, rim descending, valves **3 or 4, enclosed**.

Grown for timber and pulp, rarely as a garden ornamental. Its flowering time makes it a good source of winter food for bees. There is a tree of the very similar *E. citriodora* (lemon-scented gum) in the KwaZulu-Natal National Botanical Garden, Pietermaritzburg. The latter can be distinguished by its very pale tawny to white bark which is not mottled and by the lemon scent of the crushed, fresh leaves.

ROLF THEODOR BORLINGHAUS

1 *E. globulus* flowers

BILL HIGHAM

1 *E. globulus* flowers

FOREST AND KIM STARR

1 *E. globulus* fruit

2 *E. grandis* leaves

GEOFF NICHOLS

2 *E. grandis* flowers

BARRY M. RALLEY

2 *E. grandis* fruit

3 *E. maculata*

3 *E. maculata* flowers

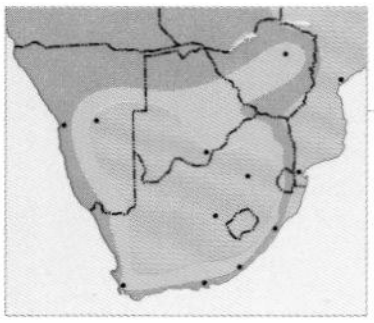

- Drought 2
- Spring
- Evergreen

1 *Eucalyptus paniculata* MYRTACEAE

Grey Ironbark; Grysysterbasbloekom

Eastern Australia Tall tree with a **narrow** crown; bark **grey, deeply fissured, persistent, not fibrous**. Leaves alternate except for the first about 6 pairs; petiole hairless, 9–25mm long; blade 50–180 × 12–30mm, lance-shaped, curved, **glossy above, paler below**, with numerous minute **secretory cavities** when viewed against the sun. Inflorescences **7-flowered,** grouped into sprays at the ends of branches; peduncle 5–15mm long. Flowers with 'lid' of buds **conical**. Fruit grey, hemispherical to cup-shaped, 5–8mm in diameter, rim **descending**, valves **4 or 5, at or below level of rim**.

Timber is very heavy, hard, strong and durable but needs care in drying and can be difficult to work. It is used for railway sleepers, heavy construction and the like.

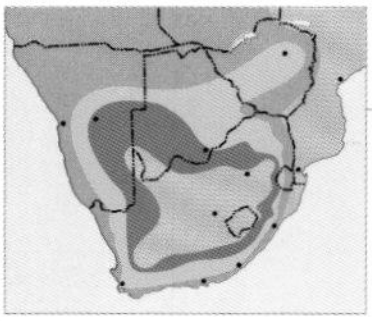

- Drought 2
- Spring
- Evergreen

2 *Eucalyptus saligna* MYRTACEAE

Sydney Blue Gum; Sydneybloekom

Eastern Australia Tall tree **with an underground lignotuber** and a **rough, flaking, grey 'boot'** at the base of the trunk; crown narrow in plantations but rounded where there is space; bark peeling, underbark **powdery, whitish with grey mottles**. Leaves alternate, opposite in first few nodes of juveniles; petiole 15–30mm long; blade 90–190 × 15–40mm, lance-shaped, curved, with numerous minute **secretory cavities** when viewed against the sun. Inflorescences erect, **7-, 9- or 11-flowered**; peduncle 5–15mm long. Flowers with 'lid' of buds **conical or beaked**. Fruit a conical, grey capsule 4–7mm in diameter, rim **descending**, valves **4, protruding, erect or bent outwards**. Seeds brown, 1–2mm long.

A grove of very tall trees of the species that was planted in 1906, has been given the status of Champion Trees by the Department of Agriculture, Forestry and Fisheries. The two tallest of these trees were 79m high when measured by professional tree climbers in 2008. These are officially the tallest trees in Africa and among the tallest planted trees anywhere in the world. Very similar to *E. grandis* (p.214) and not always separable from the latter, *E. saligna* has a lignotuber and clear green buds and the fruits always have four valves that are erect or bent outwards. Grown in many parts of the world for timber and pulp. The flowers attract bees.

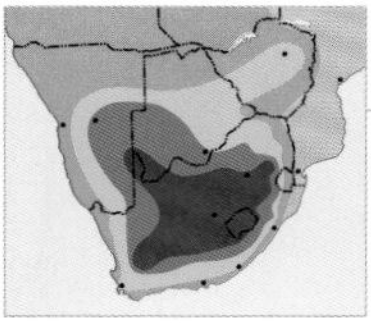

- Drought 2
- Spring
- Evergreen

3 *Eucalyptus sideroxylon* (= *E. leucoxylon* var. *sideroxylon*) MYRTACEAE

Black Ironbark, Mugga, Red Ironbark; Swartysterbasbloekom

Eastern Australia Medium-sized tree with a narrow crown; bark **black, deeply fissured, persistent, not fibrous**. Leaves alternate, except for the first 4–7 pairs on seedlings; petiole hairless, 5–25mm long; blade 50–140 × 10–40mm, lance-shaped, blue-green **on both sides**, with numerous minute **secretory cavities** when viewed against the sun. Inflorescences **clusters of 7 flowers**; peduncle 7–30mm long. Flowers **white to pink**; 'lid' of buds **conical to beaked**. Fruit a cup-shaped, greenish grey capsule 5–10mm in diameter, **rim broad, valves 5, enclosed**.

The wood is hard and dense and is one of the few timbers that will not float. It is used for heavy construction, railway sleepers and similar purposes. Useful gums, usually reddish and known as 'kino' are exuded from wounds in the trunk and an essential oil can be extracted from the leaves. As in the case of all gums, honey from this species is desirable. In our region, black ironbark, like river red gum, has been planted for shade around 19th-century farmhouses.

1 *E. paniculata* flowers

1 *E. paniculata* fruit

2 *E. saligna*

2 *E. saligna* leaves

2 *E. saligna* flowers

3 *E. sideroxylon* bark

3 *E. sideroxylon* flowers

3 *E. sideroxylon* fruit

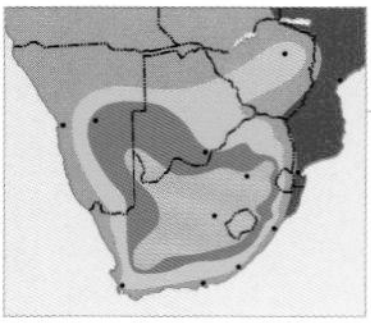

- Drought 2
- Spring
- Evergreen

1 *Grevillea hilliana*

PROTEACEAE

White Silky Oak, White Yiel Yiel; **Witsilwereik**

Eastern Australia Small to large tree with a columnar to pyramidal crown; bark brown, smooth or narrowly fissured; buds and twigs **hairy**. Leaves alternate; petiole hairy; blade 90–240 × 15–60mm, juvenile and intermediate leaves deeply **pinnately 3–10-lobed**, adult leaves simple; tip pointed or rounded; base gradually narrowed; surface glossy above, **velvety below**; margin **smooth**. Stipules absent. Inflorescences **hanging**, 90–220mm long. Flowers white to yellow-green. Fruit a brown, hairless, ellipsoid pod 17–26mm long.

Endangered in New South Wales but less rare in Queensland. Grown in South Africa's Western and Eastern Cape and Gauteng provinces as specimen trees and for ornament.

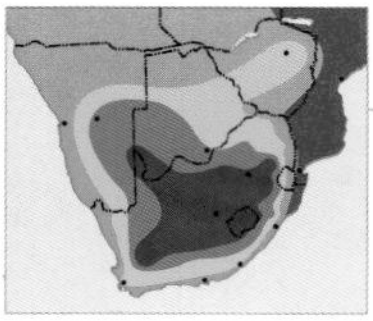

- Drought 3
- Spring
- Deciduous

2 *Hakea salicifolia* (= *H. saligna*)

PROTEACEAE

Willow Hakea; Wilgerhakea

Eastern Australia Large shrub or small tree with a rounded crown; twigs hairless, **pink to brownish**, new growth **reddish**. Leaves **without petiole**; blade 50–125 × 4–25mm, lance-shaped or elliptic; tip and base narrowed; surface **dull, hairless**. Inflorescences erect clusters; pedicels hairless, 4.5–7mm long. Flowers white, tubular. Fruit a hairless, **egg-shaped, warty**, shiny capsule 20–35 × 13–30mm, brown with black spots. Seeds 17–20mm long.

Widely grown in South Africa and Zimbabwe for ornament or hedges. The timber is of use almost only for fuel. Most species of *Hakea* are invasive in our region and this one is a declared Category 1b invader in the Western Cape.

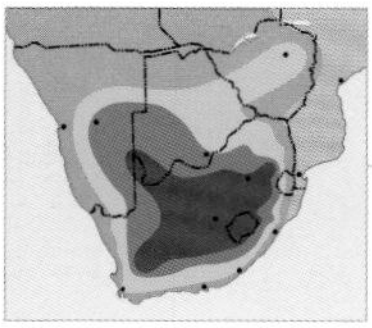

- Drought 2
- Spring
- Evergreen

3 *Hymenosporum flavum* (= *Pittosporum flavum*)

PITTOSPORACEAE

Sweet Cheesewood, Scented Blossom Tree, Sweet Shade; **Soetkasuur,** Basterkasuur, Geeltuit

Australia and New Guinea Medium-sized tree with a **narrow, sometimes pyramidal** crown; buds and twigs hairy. Leaves with petiole hairless, 10–15mm long; blade 55–150 × 15–40mm, **widest beyond the middle**; tip drawn to a long point; base narrowed; surface **glossy above, dull below**. Inflorescences erect, 100–125mm long; peduncle 30–60mm long. Flowers tubular, yellow to white, tube about 25 × 7–10mm, lobes about 15mm long. Fruit a roundish, black capsule about 25 × 23mm. Seeds reddish brown to midbrown, winged, 10–12 × 6–8 × 1mm.

Often seen throughout our region. Grown as a garden ornamental.

1 *G. hilliana* leaves

1 *G. hilliana* flowers

2 *H. salicifolia* young growth

2 *H. salicifolia* flowers

3 *H. flavum* flowers

3 *H. flavum* fruit

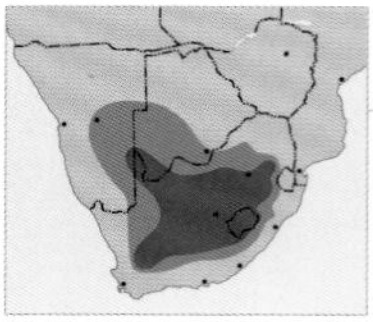

- Drought 2
- Spring
- Evergreen

1 *Ilex cornuta* AQUIFOLIACEAE

Horned Holly, Chinese Holly; Horinghuls, Chinese Huls

OTHER LANGUAGES: Gou gu (Chinese)

China and Korea Large shrub or small tree with a rounded, spreading crown usually (in cultivation) shaped by pruning; twigs hairless, **green or grey**. Leaves with petiole hairless, 4–8mm long; blade 40–90 × 25–75mm, oblong, **spine-tipped**; base rounded; surface glossy above, dull below; margin with **up to 5 spines**. Inflorescences erect. Flowers white, inconspicuous; males and females separate, usually on different trees, males fragrant. Fruit a round, red, hairless berry 8–10 × 8–10mm. Seeds about 7–8 × 5 × 5mm.

'Burfordii', the cultivar almost always seen in our region, has only the one spine at the leaf tip and a smooth leaf margin. It is a garden ornamental recorded from our eastern provinces, the fruits attracting birds. All other parts of the plant (including unripe fruits) are poisonous but medicinal uses are recorded.

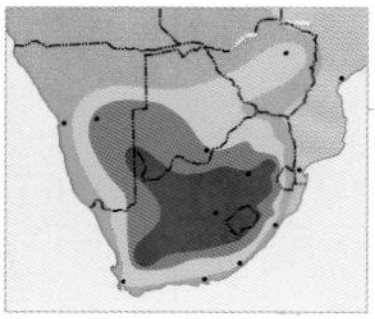

- Drought 2
- Summer
- Deciduous

2 *Lagerstroemia indica* (= *L. chinensis, Murtughas indica*) LYTHRACEAE

Pride-of-India, Crape-myrtle; Prag-van-Indië, Indiese Trots, Skubliesroos

OTHER LANGUAGES: Ziwei (Chinese); Lilas d'été (French); Chinesische Kräuselmyrte (German); Saoni (Hindi); Albero de San Bartolomeo (Italian); Àrvore de júpiter (Portuguese); Árbol de Júpiter (Spanish); Melendres (Tagalog); Dta baek (Thai); Tường vi (Vietnamese)

China, Himalayas, Indochina, Japan, Malaysia, Pakistan and the Philippines Small tree or large shrub with a rounded to spreading crown (can be pruned into other shapes) and coppery red autumn colours; bark **smooth, mottled brown and grey**; buds and twigs **hairless**; new stems sometimes square. Leaves alternate or opposite, **without significant petiole**; blade 30–100 × 20–40mm, elliptic to oblong; veins hairless. Inflorescences erect, 50–200mm long, appearing after the leaves. Flowers white, pink or purple; petals up to 11 × 12mm, **crinkled**. Fruit a roundish capsule about 10 × 8mm.

Pride of India is widely grown as a garden ornamental. The wood is reportedly hard and useful. Medicinal uses are reported. Compare *L. speciosa* (p.312).

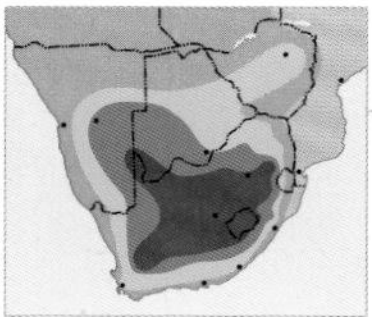

- Drought 2
- Spring
- Evergreen

3 *Laurus nobilis* (= *L. azorica*) LAURACEAE

Bay Laurel, Real Laurel, Sweet Bay; Lourier, Edellourier, Egte Lourier, Griekse Lourier

OTHER LANGUAGES: Laurier (French); Lorbeerbaum (German); Daphne (Greek); Alloro (Italian); Loureiro (Portuguese); Laural (Spanish)

Mediterranean region Large shrub or small to medium-sized tree with a **columnar** crown; buds and twigs hairless. Leaves with petiole hairless, 3–8mm long; blade 50–100 × 20–40mm, **lance-shaped** to oblong; tip and base pointed; surface glossy above, dull below; **crushed leaves aromatic**. Inflorescences erect. Flowers yellowish or white, **small**; males and females on separate trees. Fruit a black, egg-shaped berry 10–15mm in diameter.

Bay laurel is a common garden ornamental in our region and the leaves (bay leaves) are an essential ingredient in Mediterranean and many other styles of cookery. Whole leaves are normally removed before serving, as they do not soften noticeably in cooking. Other products of bay laurel used in cooking are crushed berries, pressed leaf oil and wood for smoking foods. In the garden, bay laurel has applications in topiary and as hedges, among others. The extracted oil is used in the making of Aleppo soap and other medicinal uses are recorded.

1 *I. cornuta* flowers (female)

1 *I. cornuta* fruit

2 *L. indica* flowers

2 *L. indica* fruit (dehisced)

3 *L. nobilis* flowers

3 *L. nobilis* fruit

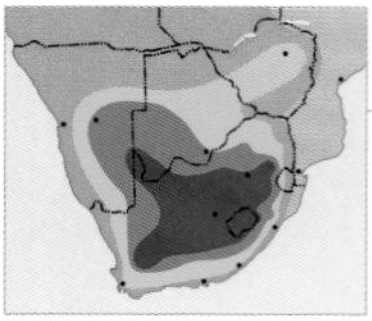

- Drought 2
- Winter–Spring
- Evergreen

1 *Leptospermum laevigatum* MYRTACEAE

Australian Myrtle, Australian Tea Tree; Australiese Mirt

Southeastern Australia Large, spreading shrub or small tree; bark thin, brown, shed in strips. Leaves without petiole; blade 10–30 × 5–8mm, **widest beyond the middle**, with numerous minute **secretory cavities** when viewed against the sun, **eucalyptus-scented** when crushed; tip broad, minutely spine-tipped; surface **sparsely silky-hairy at first**. Inflorescences erect, **paired** flowers. Flowers white; petals 5–8mm long, without markings. Fruit a **flat-topped**, grey-brown, woody capsule 7–8mm in diameter.

Grown in various parts of South Africa and Zimbabwe for ornament and hedging but a declared Category 1b invader in the former.

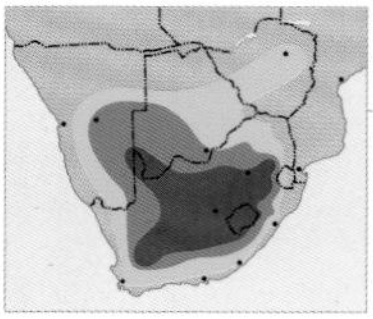

- Drought 3
- Spring
- Deciduous

2 *Liriodendron tulipifera* MAGNOLIACEAE

Tulip Tree, Whitewood; Tulpeboom

Eastern USA **Large to very tall** tree with a cylindro-conical crown and **clear to golden yellow autumn colours**; bark brown to purple, narrowly fissured; buds and twigs hairless; lenticels warty, conspicuous. Leaves alternate; petiole hairless, 50–100mm long; blade 70–150 × 125–185mm, shallowly **pinnately 4–6-lobed**; tip **broadly and characteristically indented**; base **squared**; surface dull, hairless, bright green above, bluish below; margin **smooth**. Stipules soon falling. Inflorescences a single flower, appearing with the leaves. Flowers with 'petals' 9, **green towards the tips, orange-yellow at the base**, 40–60 × 18–30mm. Fruit a head of many pale brown nuts with 1 wing each, 30–55 × 5–10mm.

Grown in botanical and private gardens in scattered places in our region, this tree deserves to be better known than it is but it does require plenty of space. The wood is ideal for building organs and has other uses. Bees use the flowers for honey.

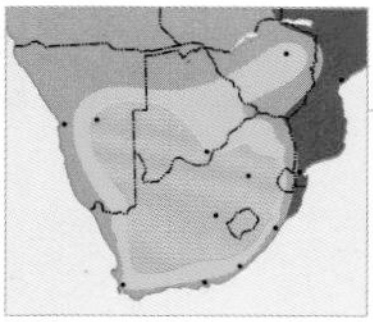

- Drought 2
- Spring
- Evergreen

3 *Litsea glutinosa* (= *L. sebifera*) LAURACEAE

Indian Laurel; Indiese Lourier

OTHER LANGUAGES: Chan gao mu jiang zi (Chinese); Avocat marron (French); Puso-puso (Tagalog)

India and China to the western Pacific islands Medium-sized tree with a rounded crown; buds and twigs hairy. Leaves with petiole hairy, 15–30mm long; blade 70–150 × 30–70mm, egg-shaped to oblong, with a **disagreeable odour** when crushed; tip rounded, with a **minute drip-tip**. Inflorescences erect, 40–50mm long; peduncle 25–30mm long. Flowers whitish, small; males and females on separate trees. Fruit fleshy, round, black, hairless, about 6 × 7mm.

A weed on the KwaZulu-Natal coast and declared a Category 1b invader in South Africa, also grown in Mozambique. Elsewhere the leaves are used for fodder and plaster and the bark is used as an adhesive in making incense sticks. The wood is of poor quality and apparently only used for fuel. Medicinal uses are recorded.

STEPHEN BAIN, WIKIMEDIA COMMONS, CC BY SA 3.0

1 *L. laevigatum* flowers

FOREST AND KIM STARR

1 *L. laevigatum* fruit

PJACOBI, WIKIMEDIA COMMONS, GFDL, CC BY SA 3.0

2 *L. tulipifera* flower and leaves

AMADA44, WIKIMEDIA COMMONS, GDFL, CC BY SA 1.2

2 *L. tulipifera* flower

3 *L. glutinosa* leaves

GEOFF NICHOLS

3 *L. glutinosa* flowers

3 *L. glutinosa* fruit

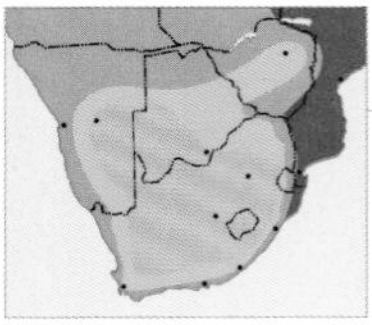

- Drought 2
- Spring
- Evergreen

1 *Magnolia champaca* *(= Michelia champaca)* MAGNOLIACEAE

Champac Magnolia, Joy Perfume Tree, Yellow Jade Orchid Tree; Laventelmagnolia

OTHER LANGUAGES: Huang lan (Chinese); Champa (Hindi); Cempaka (Malay); Chenpakam (Tamil)

Southern China Medium-tall tree with a columnar crown; bark **smooth**; buds hairy, **shortly stalked**; twigs hairy, slender, **brown or grey**. Leaves with petiole hairy, 10–32mm long, **becoming hairless**; blade 50–230 × 20–90mm, widest beyond the middle or oblong, with a **drip-tip**; base narrowed or rounded. Inflorescences a single flower; stalk 7–12mm long. Flowers yellow to orange, strongly scented; petals 12–15, free, 20–45 × 7–9mm, with a purple basal mark. Fruit a head of many woody capsules, whole head 20–150 × 15–30mm. Seeds reddish brown, 9–10 × 6–8 × 2–4mm.

Occasionally grown for garden ornament and shade. The timber is of high quality and is used for construction, furniture and other purposes. Champac flowers yield an essential oil said to be the key ingredient in at least one expensive perfume. The flowers are also worn for adornment and fragrance in the hair by Indian women and floated on bowls of water to perfume a room. This species is sacred to Hindus and Buddhists and is frequently planted around temples and, in southern India, as sacred groves. Medicinal uses are recorded.

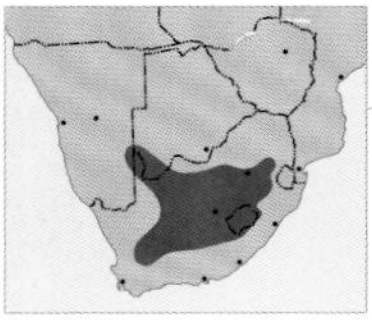

- Drought 2
- Late Winter
- Deciduous

2 *Magnolia denudata* *(= M. heptapeta)* MAGNOLIACEAE

Yulan Magnolia; Yulanmagnolia

OTHER LANGUAGES: Yu lan (Chinese)

Eastern China Small to medium-sized tree with a vase-shaped to rounded crown; bark rough; buds and twigs hairy, the latter **brown to purple**. Leaves with petiole 13–20mm long, **becoming hairless**; blade 55–175 × 45–105mm, widest beyond the middle or oblong; surface hairless or slightly hairy on both sides. Flowers **solitary, white**, appearing **before** the leaves; petals 9, white, 60–120 × 20–60mm. Fruit a head of many reddish brown capsules, whole head 75–150 × 25–50mm. Seeds red, about 9 × 10mm.

Grown for ornament since the Tang Dynasty (about 600 AD), yulan magnolias are considered in China to symbolise purity. The petals can be eaten pickled or fried. Yulan magnolia is the city flower of Shanghai. Seen in scattered places in our area.

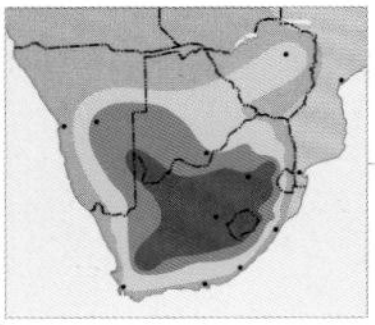

- Drought 2
- Spring
- Evergreen

3 *Magnolia figo* *(= Magnolia fuscata, Michelia figo, Michelia fuscata)* MAGNOLIACEAE

Banana Magnolia, Banana Shrub, Port Wine Magnolia; Piesangmagnolia

OTHER LANGUAGES: Han xiao hua (Chinese)

Southeastern China Large, conical shrub or small tree with a pyramidal crown; buds hairy; twigs hairy, **grey, often zigzag**. Leaves with petiole **absent** or **short**, hairy, up to 5mm long; blade 30–130 × 20–40mm, widest beyond the middle to elliptic, with an ill-defined drip-tip; lower surface **pale**; margin **bent downwards**. Inflorescences an erect, single flower. Flowers usually purple-brown, rarely creamy, **banana-scented**; petals 6, lance-shaped, **18–20 × 6–8mm**, without markings. Fruit a head of many capsules, whole head 10–50mm long.

Grown in South Africa and Mozambique for ornament on account of its scented flowers; can be used to make a tall hedge. Banana magnolia requires partial shade and is suitable for an understorey position in a collection of trees.

1 *M. champaca* flower

1 *M. champaca* fruit

2 *M. denudata* flowers

2 *M. denudata* fruit

BRAAM VAN WYK

3 *M. figo* flower

3 *M. figo* fruit

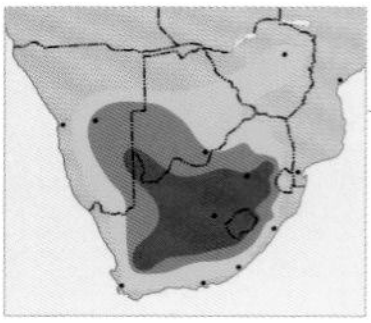

- Drought 2
- Spring
- Evergreen

1 *Magnolia grandiflora* MAGNOLIACEAE

Southern Magnolia, Laurel Magnolia; Louriermagnolia

OTHER LANGUAGES: Him champa (Hindi)

Southeastern USA Large tree with a columnar or pyramidal crown; bark **deeply fissured**; buds and twigs hairy, the latter reddish. Leaves with petiole hairy, 9–27mm long; blade 80–200 × 60–100mm, widest beyond the middle to ovate, with an ill-defined drip-tip; lower surface **minutely woolly**, often **brownish**; margin bent downwards. Inflorescences an erect, single flower; stalk 30–40mm long. Flowers scented; petals 9–12, **creamy white, 75–120 × 50–80mm**, without markings. Fruit a head of many woody, yellow-brown to red-brown capsules, whole head 55–100 × 35–50mm. Seeds red, 12–14 × 5–6 × 2–5mm.

State tree of Mississippi and the state flower of Mississippi and Louisiana; the flower was also the emblem of the Confederate army in the US Civil War. This is a beautiful ornamental for large gardens and is widely planted on university campuses in its natural range; it is resistant to wind but not to salt spray. The wood is used for veneer, furniture, venetian blinds and the like. The flowers are reportedly edible and medicinal uses are recorded. Widely if not very commonly grown in our region.

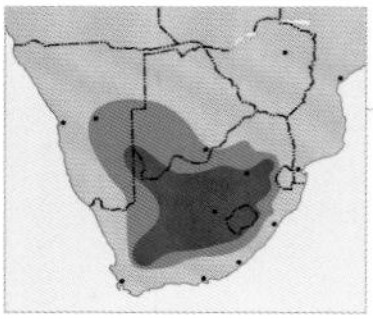

- Drought 2
- Spring
- Deciduous

2 *Magnolia × soulangeana* (= *M. denudata* × *M. quinquepeta*) MAGNOLIACEAE

Purple Magnolia, Saucer Magnolia; Persmagnolia

OTHER LANGUAGES: Er qiao yu lan (Chinese)

A garden hybrid raised in France Small to medium-sized tree or large shrub, with a narrow to spreading crown and inconspicuous autumn colours; buds and twigs **hairless**. Leaves with petiole **hairless**, 7–30mm long; blade 75–165 × 30–125mm, usually widest beyond the middle, with a drip-tip; base narrowed; lower surface hairy. Flowers solitary, appearing **before** the leaves; peduncle 12–14mm long; petals 9, **white inside and purple outside**, without markings, 50–125 × 20–55mm. Fruit a head of many capsules, whole head 50–100mm long, about 30mm in diameter, spindle-shaped.

This hybrid was first raised by Étienne Soulange-Bodin (1774–1846), who had a nursery near Paris. The cultivar 'Candolleana' is recorded from southern Africa, where it is commonly grown in public and private gardens for ornament.

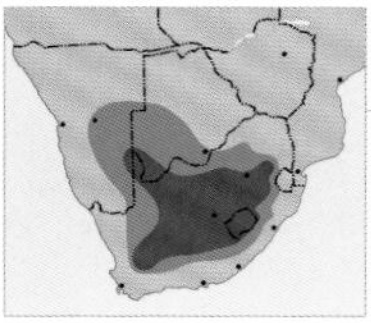

- Drought 2
- Spring
- Deciduous

3 *Magnolia tripetala* MAGNOLIACEAE

Umbrella Magnolia; Sambreelmagnolia

OTHER LANGUAGES: Magnolia parasol (French); Schirm-Magnolie (German)

Eastern USA Small to medium-sized, spreading, often multistemmed tree; buds and twigs hairless. Leaves **clustered at ends of branches**; petiole hairless, 20–35mm long; blade 220–570 × 100–300mm, **widest three quarters of the way along**, with a drip-tip; surface lime-green above, paler below. Flowers solitary, **malodorous**, appearing with the leaves; peduncle 50–75mm long; petals 9–12, greenish white, 80–130 × 25–50mm, without markings. Fruit a head of many **pink** capsules, whole head 60–100 × 20–35mm. Seeds pink to red, 9–12mm long.

Rarely grown as a specimen tree in large gardens in our area but likely to appeal only to collectors.

1 *M. grandiflora* flower

1 *M. grandiflora* fruit

2 *M.* × *soulangeana* leaves

2 *M.* × *soulangeana* flowers

2 *M.* × *soulangeana* fruit

3 *M. tripetala* flower

3 *M. tripetala* fruit

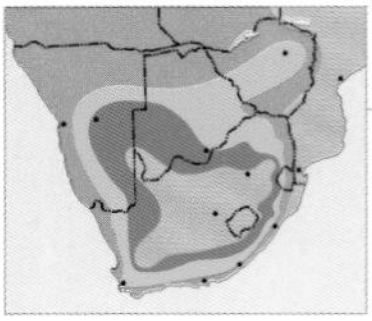

1 *Melaleuca armillaris* MYRTACEAE

Bracelet Honey-myrtle; Armbandheuningmirt

- Drought 2
- Spring
- Evergreen

Southeastern Australia Large shrub or small tree with a rounded crown, often dependent on pruning for shape; bark **pale grey, peeling**. Leaves with petiole **hairless**, 1–2mm long; blade 12–25mm long, strap-shaped, with numerous minute **secretory cavities** when viewed against the sun; tip narrowed; base squared. Inflorescences erect, **30–70mm long**, often with the branch continuing to grow from the end. Flowers white; stamens **conspicuous**, 5–6mm long. Fruit a grey, hairless capsule 3–5mm in diameter.

Grown in several provinces as an ornamental tree but it can be trained as a ground cover. Has become invasive in parts of Australia where it is not native.

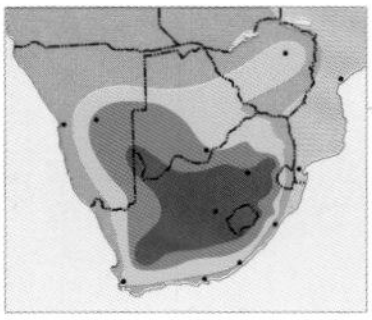

2 *Melaleuca ericifolia* MYRTACEAE

Heath Myrtle, Swamp Paperbark; Heidemirt

- Drought 1
- Spring
- Evergreen

Southeastern Australia Large shrub or small tree with an upright crown, but strongly influenced by pruning; bark **papery, pale, peeling**. Leaves single or in whorls of 3; petiole **almost absent**, hairless; blade 7–15mm long, strap-shaped, with numerous minute **secretory cavities** when viewed against the sun; tip narrowed; base rounded to squared. Inflorescences erect, **7–17mm long**, branch continuing to grow from the end. Flowers white, scented; stamens **conspicuous, 5–7mm long**. Fruit a hairless, grey, woody capsule 2.5–4mm in diameter.

Grown for ornament in places with a high water table or flooded from time to time, salt-tolerant. The essential oil is sometimes used in aromatherapy. Invasive in the Western Cape.

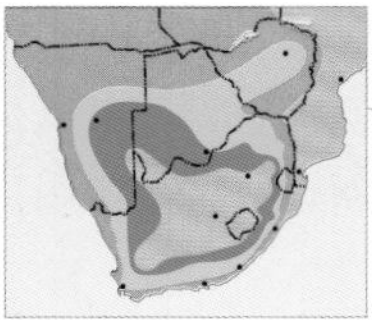

3 *Melaleuca nesophila* MYRTACEAE

Tea Myrtle, Pink Melaleuca, Showy Honey-myrtle; Teemirt

- Drought 2
- Spring–Summer
- Evergreen

Western Australia **Spreading** shrub or small tree; bark pale, peeling; twigs hairless, slender. Leaves **almost without petiole**; blade 15–30 × 5–10mm, **more or less elliptic**, with numerous minute **secretory cavities** when viewed against the sun; tip broad to rounded; base narrowed. Inflorescences erect, about 25mm long, shoots continuing to grow through. Flowers lilac-pink; stamens **conspicuous**. Fruit a brown, woody, hairless capsule.

Grown in scattered parts of South Africa and Zimbabwe for ornament and as a specimen or hedge. Notably drought-resistant once established. Invasive in parts of Victoria, Australia.

1 *M. armillaris* bark

FOREST AND KIM STARR

1 *M. armillaris* flowers

WIKIMEDIA COMMONS, CC BY SA 3.0

1 *M. armillaris* fruit

FOREST AND KIM STARR

2 *M. ericifolia* flowers

JOHN TANN, WIKIMEDIA COMMONS CC BY SA 2.0

2 *M. ericifolia* fruit

DINKUM, WIKIMEDIA COMMONS, PUBLIC DOMAIN

3 *M. nesophila* flowers

3 *M. nesophila* fruit

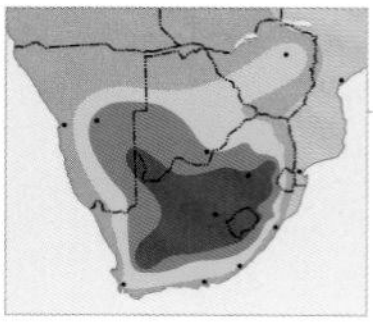

1 *Myoporum insulare* (= *M. serratum*) MYOPORACEAE

Manatoka, Common Boobialla; Manatoka

- Drought 2
- Late Winter–Late Summer
- Evergreen

Southern Australia, from Western Australia to New South Wales Shrub or small tree with a rounded to spreading crown; buds and twigs **hairless**, the latter brown. Leaves thick, **almost succulent**; petiole absent or up to 10mm long, hairless; blade 25–145 × 6–30mm, lance-shaped to elliptic or oblong; surface dull, hairless; margin sometimes with a few teeth towards the tip. Inflorescences erect; pedicels 5–8mm long. Flowers small, **white with purple nectar guides**. Fruit fleshy, **round, purple or black**, hairless, 4.5–8 × 4.5–8mm. Seeds whitish, about 2.2–2.7 × 0.9mm.

Used for hedges, manatoka is salt- and wind-tolerant and fire-resistant. The wood is hard and has been used for turnery and cabinet-making. The fruits are reportedly edible but other members of the genus have toxic fruits. In our region, this species and others in the complex to which it belongs are declared Category 3 invaders in South Africa. Species in this complex are grown in South Africa, Namibia and Zimbabwe.

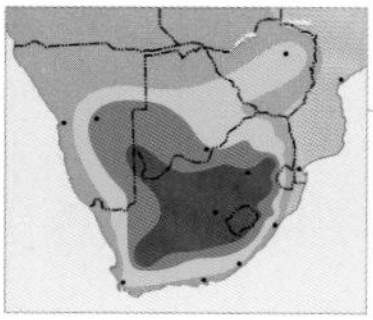

2 *Nicotiana glauca* SOLANACEAE

Wild Tobacco, Tree Tobacco; Wildetabak

- Drought 3
- Spring–Autumn
- Evergreen

OTHER LANGUAGES: Blaugrüner Tabak (German); Tabaco Moro (Spanish)

Argentina and Brazil Straggling small tree or large shrub with an ill-defined crown; buds and twigs hairless. Leaves with petiole hairless, 37–100mm long; blades 37–250 × 25–75mm, **egg-shaped**; tip narrowed; base rounded; surface **blue-green**. Inflorescences **nodding**. Flowers tubular, lobes 5, yellow, 25–45 × 4–10mm, without markings. Fruit a **papery, brown capsule** 7–15mm long. Seeds dark brown or black, about 0.5mm long.

All parts of the plant contain nicotine and are poisonous. Unsurprisingly, the use of this plant as an insecticide is recorded. It is a declared Category 1b invader in South Africa and is widespread in our region.

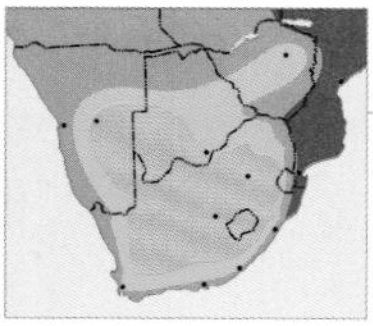

3 *Phyllanthus emblica* (= *Emblica officinalis*) PHYLLANTHACEAE

Emblic, Ambal; Amblaboom

- Drought 2
- Spring
- Deciduous

OTHER LANGUAGES: Yu gan zi (Chinese); Ambla-baum (German); Amla (Hindi); Akara (Sanskrit); Mirobalano (Spanish); Nelikkai (Tamil); Makhaam pom (Thai); Anwla (Urdu); Me Rùng (Vietnamese)

Tropical Asia Small to medium-sized tree with a vase-shaped to spreading crown. Leaves **in two rows**; petiole tiny, hairy, 0.3–0.7mm long; blade 12–20 × 2–5mm, **narrowly oblong**; tip with a **tiny sharp point**; base rounded; leafy branchlet **resembling a compound leaf**. Inflorescences a hanging, single flower. Flowers yellowish, inconspicuous, appearing after the leaves; males and females separate but on the same tree. Fruit a round, greenish yellow berry about 30mm in diameter. Seeds maroon.

Fruits have uses in Ayurvedic medicine and as ink, shampoo and hair oil and dye. They can also be pickled and eaten. The bark is esteemed as a tanning agent due to its high tannin content. Timber is red and flexible, making it suitable for gunstocks and small items of furniture, though it is subject to warping and splitting. Wood chips are used for water purification and whole pieces for crude water pipes.

1 *M. insulare* flowers

1 *M. insulare* fruit

2 *N. glauca* leaves

2 *N. glauca* flowers

2 *N. glauca* fruit

3 *P. emblica* flowers

3 *P. emblica* fruit

3 *P. emblica* fruit

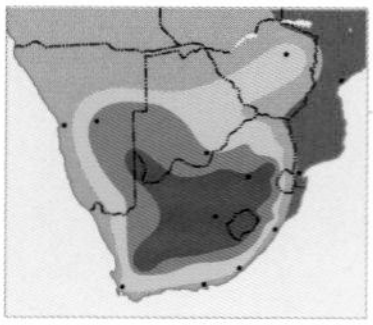

- Drought 3
- Spring
- Evergreen

1 *Phytolacca dioica*

PHYTOLACCACEAE

Belhambra, Pokeberry Tree; Belhambra, Bobbejaandruifboom

OTHER LANGUAGES: Ombu, La Bella Sombra (Spanish)

South America Small to large tree with a rounded to spreading crown and (in adult specimens) a **large, swollen base**; twigs **hairless**. Leaves with petiole hairless, up to 80mm long; blade **50–150 × 50–75mm**, egg-shaped to elliptic; tip narrowed; base rounded. Inflorescences **hanging, 100–150mm long**. Flowers whitish; males and females on different trees. Fruit a cluster of hairless, black berries, each 3–7 × 10–12mm. Seeds black.

Female trees are messy and it comes as no surprise that ink has been made from the fruits. The wood is so soft that it can be cut with a pocket knife and so the tree is a popular subject for bonsai. Full-size trees should not be planted anywhere near buildings as the large basal 'boss' is known to destroy walls as, for example, at Eureka City near Barberton, Mpumalanga. Kudu have been seen browsing leaves, and presumably controlling seedlings, of a solitary tree, believed to be a waif rather than an invader, in Pilanesberg Game Reserve. However, this species is a declared Category 3 invader in South Africa. It is widely grown in South Africa and Zimbabwe.

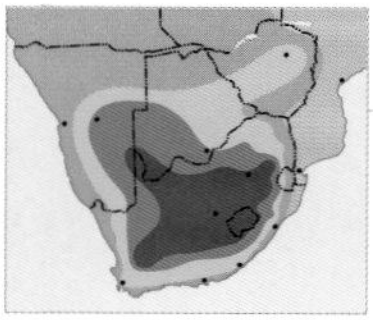

- Drought 2
- Spring
- Evergreen

2 *Pittosporum tobira*

PITTOSPORACEAE

Japanese Cheesewood, Tobira; Japanse Kasuur

OTHER LANGUAGES: Hai tong (Chinese); Tobira (Japanese)

Japan, Korea and China Small tree with a rounded crown, often shaped by pruning; buds and twigs **hairy**. Leaves with petiole hairless, 4–11mm long; blade 30–100 × 20–40mm, **widest near tip, egg-shaped**; tip sometimes indented; base gradually narrowing; lower surface minutely hairy; margin **inrolled**. Inflorescences erect, 15–40mm long. Flowers white to yellow; petals 8–11 × 2–3mm. Fruit a round, **yellow-green capsule** 10–12 × 10–12mm. Seeds **red**, 6–7 × 4–5 × 2–2.5mm.

Grown in scattered localities in our region as a garden ornamental or hedge. The cultivar 'Variegata' has leaves with a creamy margin and is recorded from southern Africa.

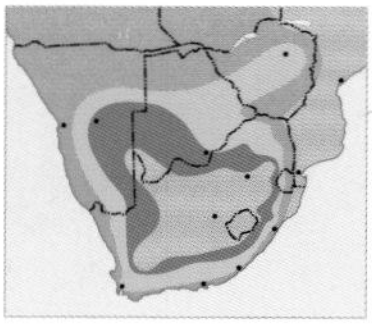

- Drought 2
- Summer
- Evergreen

3 *Pittosporum undulatum*

PITTOSPORACEAE

Australian Cheesewood, Mock Orange, Victorian Box; Australiese Kasuur

Australia Medium-sized tree with a narrow to rounded crown; buds hairy, twigs **hairless**. Leaves with petiole hairless, **11–20mm long**; blade 70–150 × 25–50mm, **widest near tip, egg-shaped**; tip pointed; base gradually narrowing; lower surface hairless; margin **wavy**. Inflorescences about 30mm long; peduncle 7–10mm long. Flowers white to creamy; petals 13.5–15.5 × 4–5mm. Fruit a round, woody, **brown capsule** up to 10mm in diameter. Seeds **reddish brown**, about 3.5 × 2.5 × 1.8mm.

A declared Category 1b invader but nevertheless widely grown in South Africa and a serious pest even in its native Australia.

1 *P. dioica* flowers (male)

1 *P. dioica* flowers (female)

1 *P. dioica* fruit

2 *P. tobira* flowers

2 *P. tobira* fruit

3 *P. undulatum* flowers

3 *P. undulatum* fruit (one dehisced)

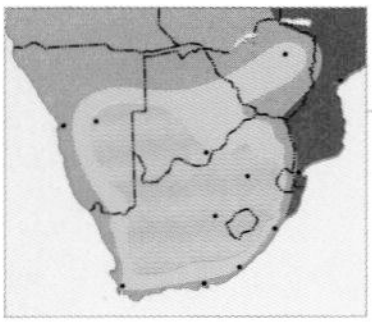

- Drought 2
- Spring
- Evergreen

1 *Polyalthia longifolia* (= *Unona longifolia, Uvaria longifolia*) ANNONACEAE

Indian Mast Tree, False Ashoka; Indiese Masboom

OTHER LANGUAGES: Glodogan tiang (Bahasa Indonesia); Debdaru (Bengali, Hindi); Chang ye an luo (Chinese); Indienbaum (German); Asopalav (Gujarati); AraNamaram (Malayalam); Devadaru (Sanskrit); Nettilikam (Tamil)

India and Sri Lanka Relatively tall tree with a **very narrow, columnar** crown remaining **leafy to the base**; twigs hairy. Leaves with petiole hairy, 3–15mm long; blade 60–120 × 25–35mm, egg-shaped to oblong; tip **drawn out to a long point**; base rounded to heart-shaped; margin **wavy**. Inflorescences hanging, 25–65mm long. Flowers small, white. Fruit a leathery, purple to black, hairless capsule 30–57 × 25–32mm.

Recommended in Florida, USA, as a warm-climate replacement for *Cupressus sempervirens* (churchyard cypress, p.80) in gardens where the latter does not thrive; elsewhere (again in warm places) as a barrier against noise. The wood is flexible and in former times was used to make masts for ships; today it is mainly used for smaller items. Medicinal uses are recorded. In our region, it is apparently only represented by a few specimen trees in Durban.

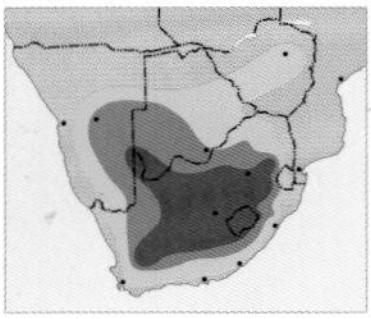

- Drought 2
- Spring
- Deciduous

2 *Quercus phellos* FAGACEAE

Willow Oak; Wilgereik

OTHER LANGUAGES: Chêne à feuilles de saule (French); Roble sauce (Spanish)

Eastern USA Large tree with a pyramidal to rounded crown and **yellow-brown autumn colours**; buds hairless. Leaves with petiole hairless, 2–6mm long; blade 50–137 × 8–25mm, **very narrowly** lance-shaped to oblong; tip **sharply pointed**; base broader to rounded; margin sometimes wavy. Inflorescences **hanging**. Flowers appearing with the leaves, inconspicuous; males and females separate but on the same tree. Fruit an egg-shaped to half-round acorn 8–12 × 6.5–10mm, in a **rough, shallow** cup.

Grown occasionally as an ornamental; represented in our region by specimen trees in Tokai Arboretum, Cape Town. Galls, as in other oaks, produce tannins which have a variety of uses. The timber is of relatively poor quality but has been used for fuel, rough construction and wheel felloes. Medicinal uses are recorded.

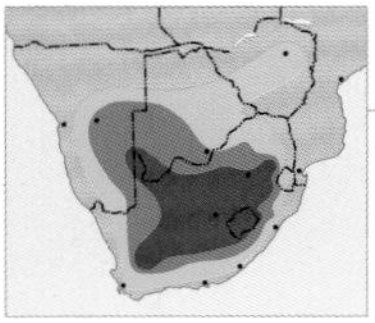

- Drought 2
- Spring
- Evergreen

3 *Rhododendron arboreum* ERICACEAE

Tree Rosebay; Boombergroos

OTHER LANGUAGES: Shuxing dujuan (Chinese); Burans (Hindi); Lali Gurans (Nepali); Billi (Tamil)

Himalayas from India to China, and Sri Lanka, Myanmar and Thailand Small tree or large shrub with a rounded to spreading crown; bark **grey, narrowly fissured**; buds **large, hairy, rounded**; twigs hairless, grey. Leaves with petiole hairy or hairless, 12–20mm long; blade 75–200 × 25–55mm, lance-shaped to oblong; lower surface **hairy**, woolly **or scaly**; margin rolled in. Inflorescences erect. Flowers showy, red, tubular, lobes 5, these 40–50mm long, with a **red to maroon basal mark and spots**. Fruit a hairy to hairless, egg-shaped, papery capsule 10–25mm long, up to 6mm in diameter. Seeds dark brown, 1.2–3mm long.

This is the national flower of Nepal and state tree of Uttarkand (India). The wood seasons badly but is nevertheless used in turnery; it is also used as fuel and to make charcoal. Leaves and flowers are poisonous but have recorded medicinal uses. Sporadically grown in cold places in our region.

1 *P. longifolia*

1 *P. longifolia* flowers

1 *P. longifolia* fruit

2 *Q. phellos* leaves

2 *Q. phellos* fruit

3 *R. arboreum* flowers

3 *R. arboreum* very young fruit

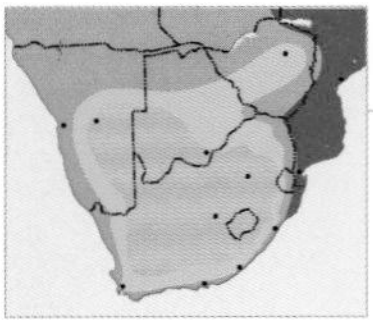

- Drought 2
- Spring
- Evergreen

1 *Solanum betaceum* (= *Cyphomandra betacea*) SOLANACEAE

Tree Tomato, Tamarillo; Boomtamatie

OTHER LANGUAGES: Shufanqie (Chinese); Boomtomaat (Dutch); Arbre à Tomates (French); Baumtomate (German); Tomate-de-árvore (Portuguese); Palo de Tomate (Spanish)

Colombia to Bolivia Small, spreading tree of indefinite shape, **malodorous** throughout; twigs hairy. Leaves with petiole hairy, 40–80mm long; blade 100–350 × 40–120mm, **egg-shaped**, with a drip-tip; base **heart-shaped**; surface usually hairless above. Stipules **absent**. Inflorescences **hanging**. Flowers white or pink; petals free or joined. Fruit fleshy, ellipsoid, yellow to red or purple, hairless, 50–100 × 40–50mm. Seeds whitish.

Thought to be possibly extinct in the wild, tree tomatoes are grown for their fruit. This may be eaten fresh, preserved or cooked in various ways. Although the fruits bear some resemblance to tomatoes, they are sweeter and this influences their uses. Grown in Angola, Zimbabwe and in South Africa, where it is a declared Category 3 invader in the Eastern Cape, KwaZulu-Natal, Mpumalanga and Limpopo provinces.

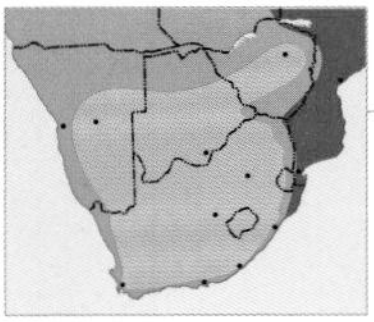

- Drought 2
- Spring
- Deciduous

2 *Terminalia bellirica* (= *Myrobalanus bellirica*) COMBRETACEAE

Bedda Nut Tree, Bastard Myrobalan, Beach Almond; Beddaneutboom

OTHER LANGUAGES: Baheda (Bengali); Pi li le (Chinese); Baherabaum (German); Baheraa (Hindi); Jaha (Malay); Bahuvirya (Sanskrit); Akkam (Tamil); Samo phi phek (Thai); Bahera (Urdu)

India and southern China to Malaysia, Sri Lanka, Indonesia and northern Australia Medium-sized to large tree; trunk buttressed when large; bark black, **deeply fissured**, flaking; buds and twigs hairy. Leaves often **crowded at ends of branches**; petiole hairy, **30–90mm long**; blade 60–160 × 50–105mm, widest beyond the middle; tip and base **rounded**; lower surface **hairy when young**. Inflorescences erect, 30–150mm long, appearing with the leaves. Flowers small, yellow. Fruit a woody, brown, **hairy, 5–8-angled**, **wingless** nut 20–30 × 15–25mm. Seeds about 12 × 5mm.

The fruits are used in tanning and dyeing but the wood is little esteemed other than for making dugout canoes. Used in Ayurvedic medicine. The seeds, known as bedda nuts, have mind-altering qualities. Grown as specimen trees in Durban Botanic Gardens and Maputo, formerly grown in forestry trials in Limpopo and KwaZulu-Natal.

1 *S. betaceum* leaves

GEOFF NICHOLS

1 *S. betaceum* flowers

GEOFF NICHOLS

1 *S. betaceum* fruit

2 *T. bellirica* leaves

MOHANDEP / FLICKR

2 *T. bellirica* flowers

JOLOEI / SHUTTERSTOCK.COM

WORRAKET / SHUTTERSTOCK.COM

2 *T. bellirica* green fruit; inset: dried fruit

1 *Terminalia catappa* *(= Buceras catappa, T. dichotoma)* COMBRETACEAE

Indian Almond, Myrobalan; Ketapboom, Oos-Indiese Amandel

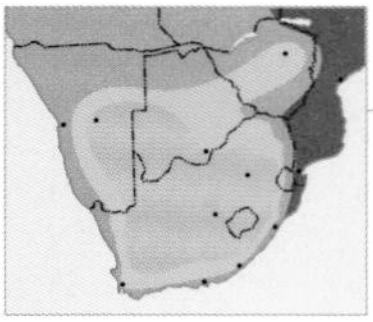

- Drought 2
- Spring
- Evergreen

OTHER LANGUAGES: Bangla badam (Bengali); lanrenshu (Chinese); Amandier des Indes (French); Indischer Mandelbaum (German); Baadaam (Hindi); Amendoeira da India (Portuguese); Almendro de la India (Spanish); Inkuti (Tamil); Hu kwang (Thai); Baadaam (Urdu); Bàng (Vietnamese)

Tropical Asia Medium-sized to large tree with a **layered**, rounded or spreading crown and **red autumn colours**; buds and twigs hairy. Leaves with petiole hairy, 5–12mm long; blade **80–250 × 40–140mm**, egg-shaped, **widest beyond the middle**, with tiny **pit-domatia** in axils of principal lateral veins below; tip rounded; base **narrowed and heart-shaped**. Inflorescences stiff or arching, 80–150mm long. Flowers small, white. Fruit fleshy, reddish, hairless, 2-winged, 30–70 × 20–50mm.

Grown in warm parts of our region as an ornamental or a street tree. The wood is red, easy to work and durable in water but susceptible to termites and is used for boat-building, construction and furniture. The leaves and bark are rich in tannins and so are used to tan leather and to make ink. They are also used by aquarists to condition water in fish tanks. Medicinal uses are recorded.

2 *Theobroma cacao* MALVACEAE

Chocolate, Cacao, Cocoa; Sjokolade, Kakao

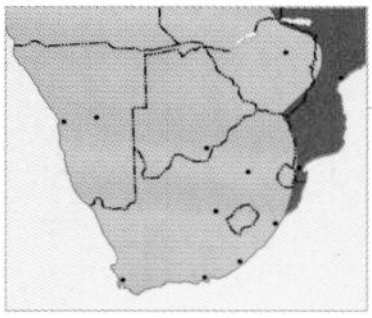

- Drought 1
- Spring
- Evergreen

OTHER LANGUAGES: Cacaoyer (French); Kakaobaum (German); Kakaw (Maya); Cacahuatl (Nahuatl); Caçao (Portuguese); Cacaotero (Spanish)

Southeastern Mexico to the Amazon basin Small tree with a rounded to spreading crown; twigs hairless. Leaves with petiole hairless; blade 100–400 × 50–200mm, **widest beyond the middle** or elliptic, with a **drip-tip**; base narrowly rounded. Inflorescences hanging, **on old wood**. Flowers whitish purple, inconspicuous. Fruit a yellow to orange, hairless, ellipsoid capsule, not splitting open, 150–300 × 80–100mm. Seeds reddish brown to midbrown.

Will only grow in the warmest and wettest parts along the east coast of southern Africa and it therefore grows in the open in Durban Botanic Gardens but not in the 'Outer West' suburbs of Durban. It would probably survive in Richards Bay but not in Maputo, which is drier. The seeds, suitably prepared, are the source of cocoa and chocolate enjoyed by all.

3 *Triplaris weigeltiana* *(= Blochmannia weigeltiana, T. surinamensis)* POLYGONACEAE

Weigelt Ant Tree, Long John Woodsmoke; Weigelt-se-mierboom

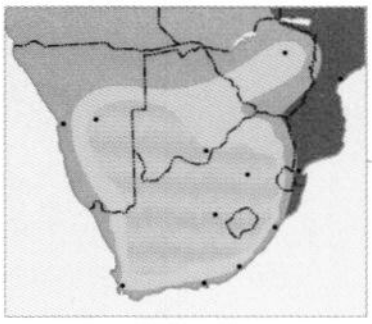

- Drought 2
- Spring
- Deciduous

OTHER LANGUAGES: Pau Formiga, Tachi (Portuguese); Palo Maria (Spanish)

Northern and western South America and Brazil Large tree with a pyramidal crown; trunk with **small buttresses**; buds and twigs hairless. Leaves with petiole hairless, 12–20mm long; blade 175–370 × 70–130mm, oblong, with a drip-tip; base broadly rounded; lower surface sometimes hairy, **veins densely hairy**. Inflorescences erect, 60–100mm long. Flowers with males and females on different trees, males small, white, females larger, pink to purple, persistent. Fruit a nut 8–10 × 4–6mm, **enclosed in the remains of the flower**.

Occasionally grown as a garden ornamental. The timber is used for rough construction, boxes and matchsticks. Medicinal uses are recorded. Compare *T. americana* (p.124).

1 *T. catappa* leaves; inset: autumn leaves

1 *T. catappa* fruit

2 *T. cacao* leaves

2 *T. cacao* flowers

2 *T. cacao* fruit

3 *T. weigeltiana* flowers (male)

3 *T. weigeltiana* fruit

GROUP 11

Raisinbush group

Leaves simple, alternate or in tufts, not bilobed; blade prominently 2–7-veined from base. Latex absent.

See also Group 2: *Carica papaya* (p.44) and *Trevesia palmata* (p.68); Group 3: *Araucaria columnaris* (p.70), *A. cunninghamii* (p.70) and *A. heterophylla* (p.72); Group 4: *Cecropia peltata* (p.104); Group 6: *Cochlospermum vitifolium* (p.126) and *Jatropha multifida* (p.128); Group 10: *Brachychiton populneus* (p.198); Group 39: *Manihot esculenta* (p.400), *M. glaziovii* (p.402) and *Tetrapanax papyrifer* (p.406).

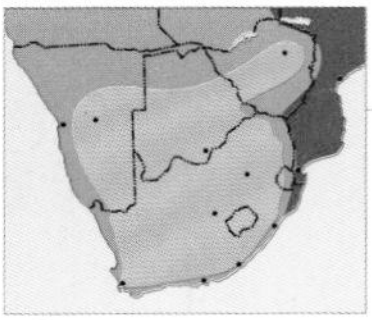

- Drought 3
- Spring
- Deciduous

1 *Abroma augustum*

MALVACEAE

Devil's Cotton; Duiwelskatoen

India to Malaysia Large, narrow to spreading shrub or small tree; stems **covered with irritant, star-shaped hairs**; bark smooth. Leaves with petiole hairy; blade about 150mm long, lance- or egg-shaped, simple or shallowly **palmately 3–5-lobed**; tip drawn out; base **heart-shaped**; surface covered with **star-shaped hairs**; margin smooth or toothed. Inflorescences erect. Flowers white or purple; petals 5, about 25mm long, with a purple or white basal mark and honey guides. Fruit a smooth **5-angled** capsule.

Rarely grown as a specimen tree in our region. The flowers are quite unusual, with their peculiar drooping petals and spreading calyx. The star-shaped hairs are often irritant. The fibre has various uses ranging from fishing nets to false hair.

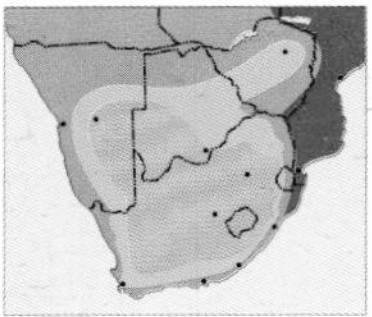

- Drought 2
- Winter–Spring
- Evergreen

2 *Acacia cyclops*

FABACEAE

Red Eye, Cape Coast Wattle; **Rooikrans,** Stinkboontjies

Western Australia Large, dense shrub or small tree; twigs brown or **green**, sometimes **angled**. 'Leaves' 30–90 × 6–15mm, elliptic to oblong, **straight**, sometimes widest beyond the middle, with 3–5 main veins from the base. Inflorescences erect; peduncle up to 7mm long. Flowers yellow, in **round heads**. Fruit a **curved**, smooth, woody, brown pod 60–100 × 8–12mm. Seeds black, 5–7 × 3–4mm, **ringed with a red aril**.

Red eye has become a serious invader wherever it has been planted. In South Africa it is a declared Category 1b invader but the wood is widely and enthusiastically used for firewood. Seed remains viable for a long time in the ground; unsupported stories suggest that it may last in this way for 160 years or more.

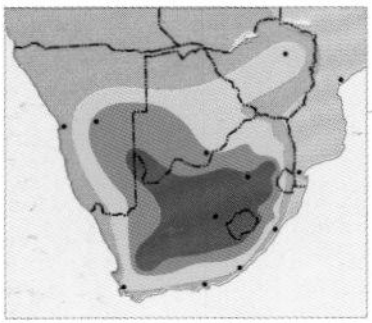

- Drought 2
- Winter–Spring
- Evergreen

3 *Acacia longifolia*

FABACEAE

Sallow Wattle, Sydney Golden Wattle; **Bleekwattel**

OTHER LANGUAGES: Mimosa à feuilles longues (French); Sydney Goldgeflecht (German)

Australia Large shrub or small tree with a spreading crown and often a gnarled trunk; buds **hairy**; twigs hairless, brown or green. 'Leaves' 50–150 × 5–20mm, **lance-shaped** to oblong, with 3 main veins from the base. Inflorescences erect **spikes**, 37–50mm long; peduncle **absent**. Fruit a curved pod 50–150 × 4–8mm, **constricted between seeds**. Seeds 4–6mm long.

The flowers, seeds and pods are reportedly edible. The wood is tough and strong. Invasive in South Africa, where it is a declared Category 1b invader, and in Portugal.

MOKKIE, WIKIMEDIA COMMONS, CC BY SA 4.0

1 *A. augustum* flowers

1 *A. augustum* fruit

2 *A. cyclops* flowers

2 *A. cyclops* fruit

BRAAM VAN WYK

3 *A. longifolia* flowers

GEOFF NICHOLS

3 *A. longifolia* flowers and galls

BRAAM VAN WYK

3 *A. longifolia* insect galls

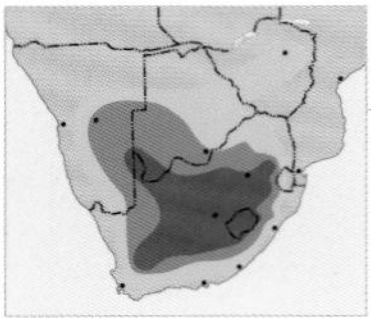

- Drought 2
- Winter–Spring
- Evergreen

1 *Acacia melanoxylon* FABACEAE

Blackwood, Australian Blackwood; Swarthout, Australiese Swarthout

OTHER LANGUAGES: Mimosa à bois noir (French); Ébano-da-Australia (Portuguese); Aromo australiano (Spanish)

Eastern Australia Medium-sized to large tree with a columnar to rounded crown; buds and twigs **hairy**; young growth **angled** or round. 'Leaves' often ending in true, twice-pinnate leaves, especially on young trees, densely hairy, 40–160 × 6–25mm, lance-shaped to elliptic or oblong, with 3–5 main veins from the base. Inflorescences erect groups of **round heads**; peduncle 4.5–13mm long. Flowers usually **creamy white**. Fruit a flat, **twisted** pod 50–125 × 5–10mm. Seeds black, **aril red**, 3–5mm long.

The wood is superficially similar to the indigenous stinkwood (*Ocotea bullata*) and so plantations were established on the fringes of the southern Cape forests, which the alien trees are now invading. The leaves are noteworthy as they quite often show the flattened, leaf-like stalks that supply the reason for including this tree in this group, topped with the twice-compound leaves one expects from an *Acacia*. A pest in southern and East Africa, Portugal, New Zealand, Brazil and California. Although the timber is useful, this tree is a declared Category 2 invader in South Africa.

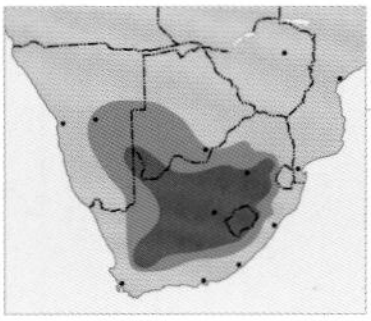

- Drought 2
- Winter–Spring
- Evergreen

2 *Acacia pendula* FABACEAE

Weeping Myall, Boree; Treurwattel

OTHER LANGUAGES: Mimosa pleureur (French)

Eastern Australia Medium-sized tree with a columnar to spreading crown; branches **weeping**; twigs hairy. 'Leaves' **blue-grey**; blade 45–110 × 6–12mm, **narrowly** lance-shaped to elliptic, straight or slightly curved, with 3 main veins from the base; tip sharp; surface hairless or hairy. Inflorescences erect, **round heads**; peduncle 1.5–8mm long. Flowers yellow. Fruit a **densely hairy**, straight to curved pod 40–100 × 10–20mm. Seeds 5–9mm long.

Widely but not commonly grown for ornament in drier gardens but in view of the weedy tendencies of its close relatives, one should probably exercise caution with this species.

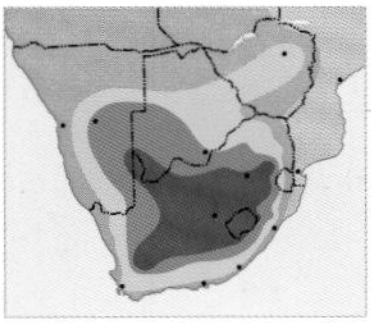

- Drought 2
- Winter
- Evergreen

3 *Acacia podalyriifolia* *(= A. caleyi, A. fraseri)* FABACEAE

Pearl Acacia, Queensland Silver Wattle; Vaalmimosa

OTHER LANGUAGES: Mimose (German), Acácia-mimosa (Portuguese)

Eastern Australia Large shrub or small tree with a usually rounded or spreading crown; twigs hairy, **grey**. 'Leaves' **short and wide**, 20–40 × 15–30mm, **grey** or blue-grey, egg-shaped to oblong; tip with a sharp point; surface hairy or hairless. Inflorescences erect, **30–110mm long**; peduncle 5–10mm long. Flowers yellow. Fruit a grey-brown or purplish, hairy or hairless pod 60–100 × 15–25mm. Seeds black, 6–7.5mm long.

Naturalised in South Africa and a declared Category 1b invader. Grown for ornament and supplies material to florists.

1 *A. melanoxylon* flowers

1 *A. melanoxylon* fruit

1 *A. melanoxylon* seeds

2 *A. pendula*

2 *A. pendula* leaves

2 *A. pendula* flowers

3 *A. podalyriifolia* leaves

3 *A. podalyriifolia* flowers

3 *A. podalyriifolia* fruit

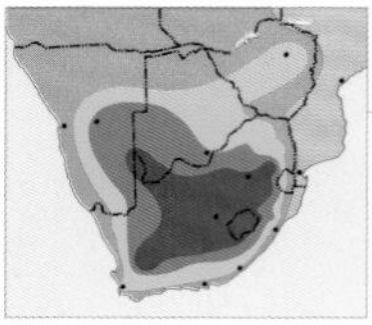

- Drought 2
- Spring
- Evergreen

1 *Acacia saligna* (= *A. cyanophylla*) FABACEAE

Port Jackson Willow, Blue-leaved Wattle, Coojong, Weeping Wattle; Goudwilger

OTHER LANGUAGES: Mimosa bleuâtre (French)

Western Australia Small tree with a vase-shaped to rounded crown; buds and twigs **hairless**; stems angled or round. 'Leaves' 100–250 × 5–50mm, **narrowly lance-shaped, straight**; tip and base **gradually narrowing**. Inflorescences erect, **round heads**; peduncle 5–15mm long. Flowers yellow. Fruit a flat, hairless, almost straight pod 60–120 × 5–6mm. Seeds dark brown to black, 5–6mm long.

Gum has been tested for edibility and is apparently usable. The bark has been used for tanning and the wood for fuel. Port Jackson willow is a particularly noxious weed in the Western Cape and has been declared a Category 1b invader.

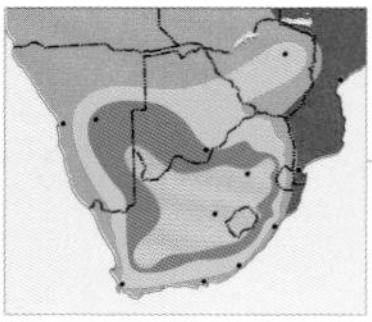

- Drought 2
- Spring
- Evergreen

2 *Agathis australis* (some sources regard *A. brownii* as a synonym, but the application of that name is not certain) ARAUCARIACEAE

Giant Kauri; Reusekauri

New Zealand Very large tree with a columnar to spreading crown and columnar (not tapering) bole; bark smooth, **blue-grey**; buds and twigs hairless. Leaves alternate or almost opposite; petiole **absent or up to 2mm** long, hairless; blade 15–80 × 8–15mm, **lance-shaped to oblong**, with many parallel veins; base rounded to squared. Cones solitary, stalked; males and females on the same tree, males cylindrical, 20–50mm long, about 10mm in diameter, females round, 60–80 × 60–80mm, with many scales about 18mm long, with 1 seed each.

These majestic trees grow relatively fast and yield an exact substitute for yellowwood in half the time taken by indigenous *Podocarpus* to grow to the same size. The largest trees in New Zealand, in fact, contain more usable timber than even a giant redwood of the same height, because the trunk does not taper. Giant kauri is second only to *Eucalyptus regnans* in the amount of carbon a given number of trees can sequester. However, this species has the potential to become invasive.

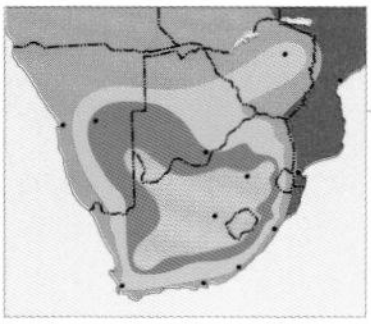

- Drought 2
- Spring
- Evergreen

3 *Agathis robusta* (= *A. palmerstonii*) ARAUCARIACEAE

Queensland Kauri; Queenslandse Kauri

Queensland, Australia Very large tree with a columnar to rounded canopy and tall, straight bole; bark grey with **orange-brown patches**; twigs hairless. Leaves with petiole hairless, **3–10mm long**; blade 50–130 × 10–40mm, strap-shaped to **elliptic**, with many parallel veins, subopposite to **opposite on secondary branches**; base rounded. Cones solitary; males and females on the same tree, males cylindrical, 40–85 × 7–9mm, females **cylindrical** to round, 90–150 × 80–105mm, with 340–440 scales, each 34–41mm long and bearing 1 seed.

This species is not invasive and yields good timber and a valuable resin. Many of the notes for *A. australis* (above) apply here too. Queensland kauri is an exceptionally beautiful tree in a large, old garden. It is believed that the kauris have survived almost unchanged since the early age of the dinosaurs, some 190 million years ago. This and the preceding species are widely but not commonly grown in our region.

1 *A. saligna* flowers

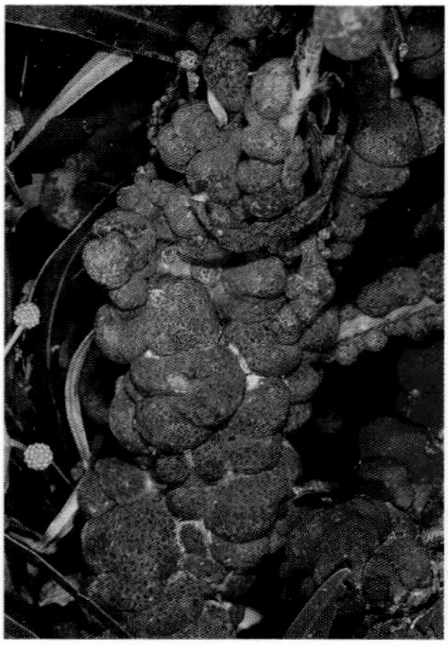

1 *A. saligna* fungal galls

1 *A. saligna* fruit

2 *A. australis* cone (male)

2 *A. australis* cones (female)

3 *A. robusta* leaves

3 *A. robusta* cone (male)

3 *A. robusta* cone (female)

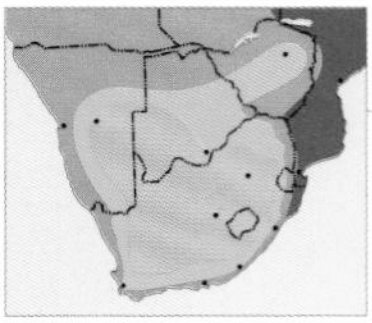

- Drought 2
- Spring
- Evergreen

1 *Bixa orellana*

BIXACEAE

Annatto, Lipstick Tree; Orleaan, Lipstiffieboom

OTHER LANGUAGES: Rocouyer (French); Anattostrauch (German); Achiotl (Nahuatl); Acafroeira da terra (Portuguese); Achiote (Spanish)

Mexico to Bolivia Large, rounded shrub or small tree; twigs **scaly**, brown or purplish. Leaves with petiole hairless, 12–130mm long; blade 50–250 × 33–165mm, **egg-shaped**, with a drip-tip and **5 main veins** from the **heart-shaped** base; margin smooth. Inflorescences erect, 110–150mm long; peduncle 70–80mm long. Flowers pale pink; petals 15–30 × 16–32mm, without markings. Fruit **bristly**, egg-shaped, leathery, brown, 32–35 × 19–23mm. Seeds covered with waxy **red** aril, about 4 × 3 × 2mm.

The conspicuous pale pink flowers make this tree an asset in any garden warm enough for it to survive. The red, hairy fruits are also attractive until they dry out and go brown. The pulp surrounding the seeds of this tree yields the yellow-orange to red dye, called 'annatto' or 'bixin', which is used to colour cheese, butter, margarine, chocolate and, surprisingly, lipstick. It is used in tropical America and the Caribbean as a condiment in the local variant of yellow rice and other dishes, where its vitamin A content forms a useful supplement to the diet.

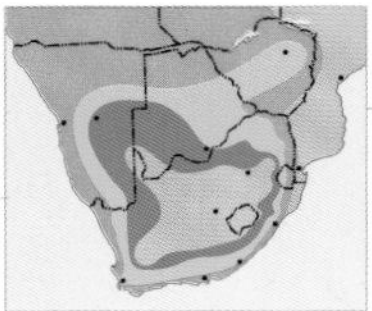

- Drought 2
- Spring–Summer
- Evergreen

2 *Brachychiton acerifolius* (= *Sterculia acerifolia*)

MALVACEAE

Australian Flame Tree, Illawarra Flame Tree; Australiese Vlamboom

OTHER LANGUAGES: Flammender Flaschenbaum (German); Árbol del fuego (Spanish)

Eastern Australia Large tree with a columnar to pyramidal crown; bark grey, narrowly fissured; twigs hairless. Leaves with petiole hairless, 50–200mm long; blade 100–250mm long, ovate, simple or **palmately 3–5-lobed**; tip **rounded**; base rounded to heart-shaped, with **3 or more main veins** from the base; margin smooth. Inflorescences erect. Flowers red, **bell-shaped**; pedicels red. Fruit a dark brown, ellipsoid to spindle-shaped pod 70–120mm long, with **dangerously irritant hairs inside**. Seeds midbrown.

Commonly grown ornamentals in large gardens in Mozambique, South Africa and Zimbabwe. The seeds can be roasted and eaten but care needs to be taken to avoid the dangerous hairs in the pod. The light, soft wood can be used for plywood and model-making. When attacked by insects, the tree produces a mucilage that can lift the paint from cars parked underneath, therefore probably not suitable for parking lots.

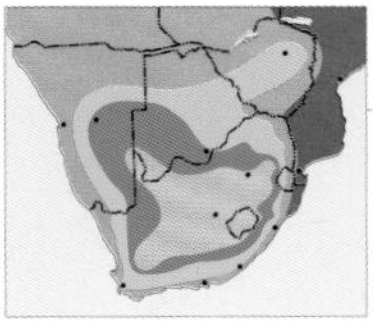

- Drought 2
- Summer
- Deciduous

3 *Brachychiton discolor*

MALVACEAE

Pink Flame Tree, Queensland Lacebark; Pienkvlamboom

Northeastern Australia Medium-sized tree with a pyramidal to rounded crown; bark green or grey, smooth or narrowly fissured; twigs hairy. Leaves with petiole **hairy**, 80–180mm long; blade 80–180mm long, egg-shaped, **palmately 3–7-lobed**; tip **pointed or drawn out**; base heart-shaped, with **more than 3 main veins** from the base; surface glossy above, **woolly below**; margin smooth. Inflorescences erect. Flowers pink, tubular or bell-shaped, hairy, 5-parted. Fruit a **sausage-shaped, densely hairy**, woody, pale brown pods 100–150 × 30–50mm. Seeds buff or midbrown, surrounded by **irritant hairs**.

Grown as an ornamental, recorded from public and private gardens in Mozambique, South Africa and Zimbabwe. The capsule contains dangerously irritant hairs and great care should be taken when seeds are removed.

1 *B. orellana* leaves

CHALLIYAN, WIKIMEDIA COMMONS, CC BY SA 3.0

1 *B. orellana* flowers

1 *B. orellana* fruit; inset: staining

BIDGEE, WIKIMEDIA COMMONS, CC BY SA 3.0 AU

2 *B. acerifolius* flowers

STEVE AND ALISON PEARSON

2 *B. acerifolius* dehisced fruit

GEOFF NICHOLS

3 *B. discolor* flowers

GEOFF NICHOLS

3 *B. discolor* fruit

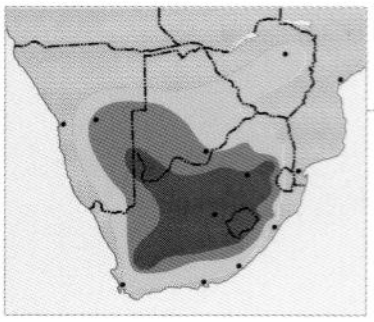

- Drought 3
- Spring
- Deciduous

1 *Celtis australis*

CELTIDACEAE

Nettle Tree, European Hackberry; Netelboom

OTHER LANGUAGES: Koprivić (Croatian); Micicoulier (French); Zürgelbaum (German); Bagolaro (Italian)

Southern Europe and Western Asia Medium-sized to large tree with a rounded crown; buds and twigs **hairy**. Leaves with petiole hairy, 5–15mm long; blade 50–120 × 15–35mm, narrowly egg-shaped, with a **drip-tip** and 3 main veins from the oblique base; lower surface minutely hairy; margin **toothed**. Inflorescences hanging; pedicels 15–25mm long. Flowers inconspicuous, appearing with the leaves. Fruit fleshy, round, hairless, 10–12mm in diameter, yellow-white, turning **purple-black** when ripe.

Both this species and the following are wind-pollinated and believed to hybridise freely with each other and the indigenous white stinkwood *(C. africana)* in Gauteng, rendering specific identification dubious at best. It is often planted as an ornamental or street tree because it is resistant to atmospheric pollution. In South Africa it is a declared Category 3 invader. The fruits are edible and the tough, flexible, durable wood is used for turnery and walking-sticks. Medicinal uses are recorded.

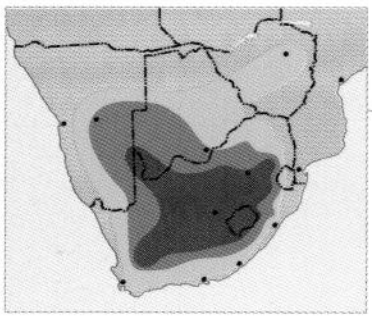

- Drought 3
- Spring
- Deciduous

2 *Celtis sinensis*

CELTIDACEAE

Chinese Nettle Tree; Chinese Netelboom

OTHER LANGUAGES: Po shu (Chinese)

China, Korea and Japan Medium-sized tree with a rounded crown; buds **hairless**; twigs hairy. Leaves with petiole hairy, 3–10mm long; blade 30–100 × 35–60mm, egg-shaped, with a drip-tip and 3 main veins from the oblique base; surface hard, **glossy**; margin **scalloped or bluntly toothed only in top third**. Flowers borne singly, hanging. Fruit fleshy, glabrous, round, **orange**, 5–8mm in diameter.

The leaves of this species are similar to those of *C. laevigata* in being of a hard texture, with glossy upper surfaces, but differ in having at least some marginal teeth. They are also more narrowly elliptic. Planted as an ornamental or street tree for the same reasons as the nettle tree (above). The fruits are said to be edible.

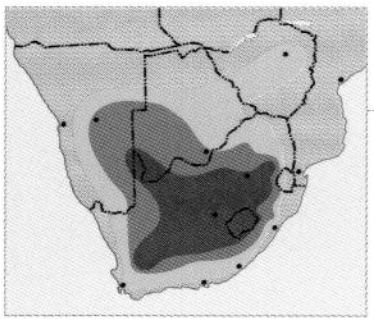

- Drought 2
- Spring
- Deciduous

3 *Cercis siliquastrum*

FABACEAE

Judas Tree; Judasboom

Mediterranean region Small tree with a rounded or spreading crown; buds hairless; twigs hairless, **purple**. Leaves with petiole hairless, 30–40mm long; blade 60–100 × 80–140mm, egg-shaped to **round**, with **7 main veins** from the base; tip rounded or indented; base **heart-shaped**; margin smooth. Inflorescences erect, 40–60mm long. Flowers pink-purple, appearing **before** the leaves; petals 15–20mm long. Fruit a hairless pod 80–120 × 14–20mm, reddish when young.

The wood is hard, with a beautiful grain; it takes a good polish and can be used for veneers. Flowers and pods are edible but trees are usually planted for ornament, in scattered places in South Africa and Mozambique in our area. There is no support for the long-standing myth that Judas Iscariot (hence the common names) hanged himself from a tree of this species.

1 *C. australis* flowers

1 *C. australis* fruit

2 *C. sinensis* leaves

2 *C. sinensis* flowers (female)

2 *C. sinensis* fruit

3 *C. siliquastrum* leaves

3 *C. siliquastrum* flowers

3 *C. siliquastrum* fruit

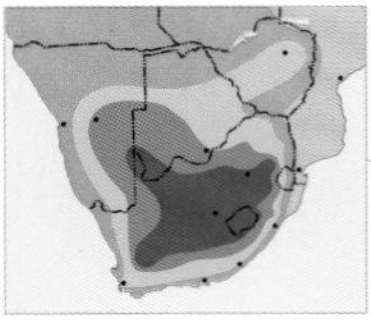

- Drought 2
- Spring
- Evergreen

1 *Cinnamomum camphora* (= *Camphora officinarum, Laurus camphora*)

LAURACEAE

Camphor Tree; Kanferboom

OTHER LANGUAGES: Zhang (Chinese); Camphrier (French); Kampferbaum (German); Kapur (Hindi); Kusunoki (Japanese); Arvore da camphora (Portuguese); Árbol del alcanfor (Spanish); Karabun (Thai)

Malaysia to Japan Large tree with a rounded to spreading crown; bark rough, gnarled, brown; buds **hairless**; twigs **hairy**. Leaves alternate to almost opposite; petiole hairless, 10–25mm long; blade 75–100 × 30–40mm, elliptic, with a **drip-tip** and 3 main veins from the base; margin smooth. Fruit a black berry 6–10mm in diameter.

Source of camphor wood and, before a synthetic substitute was invented, camphor. It has been declared a Category 1b invader in South Africa's Limpopo, Mpumalanga, KwaZulu-Natal and Eastern Cape provinces, and Category 3 in the Western Cape. However, a row of these trees planted by Willem Adriaan van der Stel at Vergelegen (Somerset West, Western Cape) in about 1700 is a National Monument and is therefore exempted from the weed-control legislation. The impressive camphor trees in Kirstenbosch National Botanical Garden, Cape Town, are a remnant of an avenue of trees planted by Cecil John Rhodes in 1898.

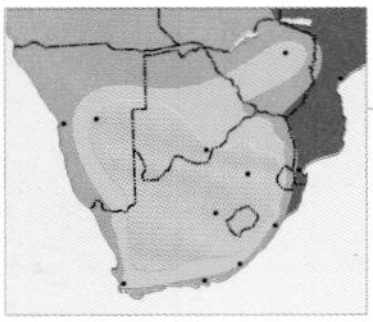

- Drought 2
- Spring
- Evergreen

2 *Cinnamomum verum*

LAURACEAE

Cinnamon; Kaneel

OTHER LANGUAGES: Quarfa (Arabic); Canellier de Ceylan (French); Ceylonzimtbaum (German); Tuj (Gujarati); Daalacinii (Hindi); Albero della Canella (Italian); Caneleiro (Portuguese); Ilavangam (Tamil)

India and Sri Lanka Large tree with a spreading to rounded crown (but trees for commercial production are coppiced and kept small); buds **hairy**; twigs **hairless**, green, slender. Leaves alternate to almost opposite; petiole hairless, 10–20mm long; blade 70–180 × 30–80mm, **lance-shaped to elliptic**, with 3 main veins from the base; tip narrowed; margin smooth. Inflorescences erect, 100mm long or more. Flowers cream, inconspicuous. Fruit a roundish, purple berry up to 12.5 × 9–12mm.

This tree is the source of real cinnamon, which is prepared from the bark and has been used as a spice in food and religious ceremonies for at least 3,000 years. It is mentioned in the earliest books of the Hebrew Bible, among other places. Medicinal uses are recorded. Some trees in the Durban area are showing signs of becoming naturalised. Also seen in other warm parts of South Africa and Mozambique.

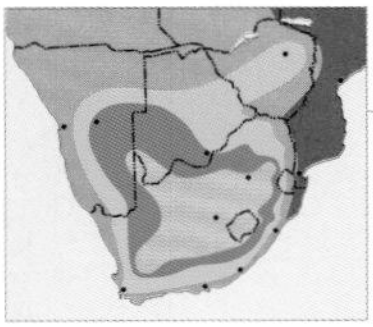

- Drought 2
- Spring
- Evergreen

3 *Dombeya cacuminum*

MALVACEAE

Strawberry Snowball Tree; Pienksneeubalboom

Madagascar Medium-sized tree with a rounded crown; bark grey, smooth; twigs hairy; lenticels smooth and conspicuous. Leaves alternate; petiole **hairless**, up to 250mm long; blade 100–260mm long, up to 220mm wide, round, **shallowly palmately 3-lobed**; tip long **drawn out**; base heart-shaped, usually with 7 **main veins** from the base; surface dull, hairless above, with **star-shaped hairs below**. Inflorescences erect or hanging, up to 150mm long. Flowers pink to red; petals 5, up to 45 × 35mm, with a white basal mark. Fruit a densely hairy, ellipsoid capsule about 13mm long. Seeds 2.5mm long.

Occasionally grown as an ornamental in our region. In Madagascar, the bark yields a fibre used for rope, weaving and barkcloth.

GEOFF NICHOLS

1 *C. camphora* flowers

BRAAM VAN WYK

1 *C. camphora* fruit

2 *C. verum* flowers

2 *C. verum* fruit

3 *D. cacuminum* flowers

BRAAM VAN WYK

3 *D. cacuminum* fruit

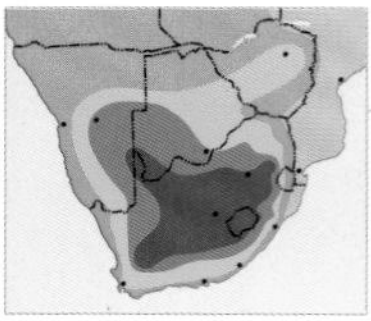

- Drought 2
- Spring
- Deciduous

1 *Firmiana simplex* (= *F. platanifolia, Sterculia platanifolia*) MALVACEAE

Chinese Parasol-tree, Phoenix Tree; Chinese Sambreelboom

OTHER LANGUAGES: Wu tong (Chinese)

Japan to Vietnam Medium-sized tree with a pyramidal crown; bark green or grey, smooth; twigs **hairless**. Leaves alternate; petiole hairless, 100–300mm long; blade 150–300mm long and wide, egg-shaped to round, **palmately 3–5-lobed**, with a drip-tip; base heart-shaped, with about 7 main veins from the base; surface dull, hairless or hairy; margin **smooth**. Inflorescences erect, 200–500mm long, appearing after the leaves. Flowers small, yellow-green; males and females separate, on the same tree. Fruit soon splitting into **4 or 5 papery segments** 60–110 × 15–25mm, with seeds **attached to the edges**. Seeds buff, 4–7mm long and wide.

The wood is used for the soundboards of several Chinese musical instruments. Grown in Mozambique and South Africa as specimen trees and ornamentals. It has become invasive in parts of North America.

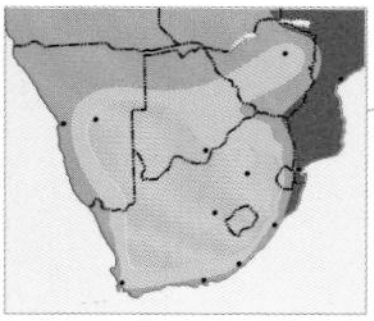

- Drought 2
- Spring
- Evergreen

2 *Guazuma ulmifolia* MALVACEAE (OR BYTTNERIACEAE)

West Indian Elm, Bastard Cedar; Wes-Indiese Olm

OTHER LANGUAGES: Bois de hêtre (French); Mutamba-verdadeira (Portuguese); Cualote (Spanish)

Mexico to Paraguay Small to medium-sized tree with a rounded to spreading crown; twigs **hairy**. Leaves with petiole **hairy**, 8–25mm long; blade 70–160 × 20–80mm, **oblong**, with 3 or more main veins from the base; tip drawn to a point; base rounded to squared; lower surface **hairy**; margin **saw-toothed**. Inflorescences erect, 30–50mm long; peduncle 7–25mm long. Flowers small, yellow. Fruit a round, **warty**, woody, densely hairy capsule 5–20 × 5–20mm. Seeds about 2.5mm long.

Leaves and fruits are used for stock feed. In our region, known from a specimen tree in Durban Botanic Gardens and others in Namibia and further afield.

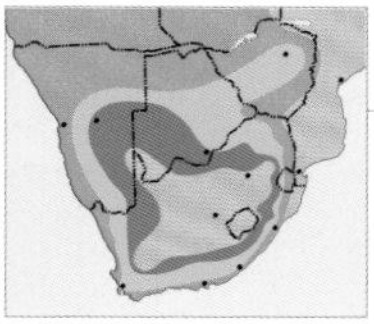

- Drought 2
- Spring
- Evergreen

3 *Hibiscus rosa-sinensis* MALVACEAE

Hibiscus, Chinese Cotton Rose; Chinese Stokroos, Hibiskus, Vuurblom

OTHER LANGUAGES: Kembang Sepatu (Bahasa Indonesia); Zhu jin (Chinese); Hibiscus de Chine (French); Gurhal (Hindi); Fusou (Japanese); Chinesischer Roseneibisch (German); Rosa della Cina (Italian); Bunga raya (Malay); Rosa da China (Portuguese); Clavel japonés (Spanish); Gunamela (Tagalog); Sembaruthi (Tamil)

Tropical Asia and China Large rounded shrub or small, spreading tree, form determined by pruning; twigs hairy. Leaves with petiole **hairless**, 5–20mm long; blade 40–150 × 20–50mm, **egg-shaped**, with more than 3 main veins from the base; tip drawn out to a point; base rounded to squared; lower surface **hairless**; margin saw-toothed. Inflorescence a **hanging, single** flower; stalk hairless, 30–70mm long in flower. Flowers showy, white, yellow, red or any intermediate colour; petals 50–120 × 30–70mm, without markings. Fruit a woody, hairless, egg-shaped capsule 20–25mm long, not often seen.

This is the national flower of Malaysia and the commercial 'totem' flower of the Lower South Coast of KwaZulu-Natal. Very popular as a garden ornamental and for hedging. The flowers are used in tropical countries for personal adornment and are reportedly edible.

1 *F. simplex*

KENPEI, WIKIMEDIA COMMONS, GFDL 1.2

1 *F. simplex* flowers

BRAAM VAN WYK

1 *F. simplex* fruit and seeds

FRANZ XAVER, WIKIMEDIA COMMONS, GFDL 1.2, CC BY SA 3.0

2 *G. ulmifolia* flowers

JOÁS MEDEIROS, WIKIMEDIA COMMONS, CC BY SA 2.0

2 *G. ulmifolia* fruit

3 *H. rosa-sinensis* leaves

BRAAM VAN WYK

3 *H. rosa-sinensis* flowers

GROUP 11 — Raisinbush group

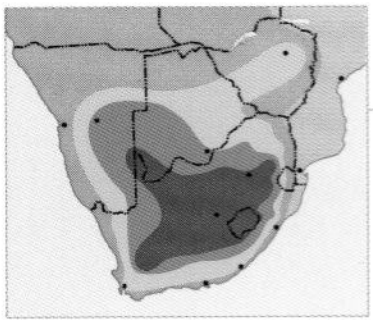

1 *Hibiscus syriacus* — MALVACEAE

Rose of Sharon; Roos-van-Saron

- Drought 2
- Summer
- Deciduous

OTHER LANGUAGES: Mu jin (Chinese); Ketmie des jardins, Mauve de Syrie (French); Syrischer Roseneibisch (German); Mugunghwa (Korean); Hibisco (Portuguese); Rosa de Siria (Spanish)

Tropical and subtropical Asia Columnar to vase-shaped **shrub or small tree**; bark grey, smooth; twigs hairy, red or green; stems angled or round. Leaves alternate; petiole hairy, 6–30mm long; blade 25–100 × 15–50mm, egg-shaped, shallowly **palmately 3-lobed**; tip pointed; base rounded to heart-shaped, with **5 main veins** from the base; veins with or without star-shaped hairs on lower surface; surface glossy; margin **toothed, sometimes deeply**. Inflorescences an erect, single flower. Flowers white, pink to red or purple; petals 5, these 30–50 × 20–35mm, with white, red or purple marks or stripes. Fruit a papery, brown, hairy capsule 15–20 × 10–12mm. Seeds 2–4mm long.

National flower of South Korea. Grown in Mozambique, South Africa and Zimbabwe for ornament or hedging. The leaves and flowers are edible and the leaves can be made into a hair shampoo.

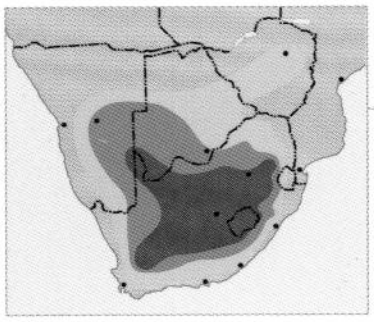

2 *Hovenia dulcis* — RHAMNACEAE

Japanese Raisin Tree; Japanse Rosyntjieboom

- Drought 2
- Spring
- Deciduous

OTHER LANGUAGES: Hūfīniyā Ḥulwat al-thamar (Arabic); Bei zhi ju (Chinese); Raisinier de Chine (French); Japanischer Rosinenbaum (German); Albero dell'uva passa (Italian); Kenpo nashi (Japanese); Bananinha-do-japão, Caju-do-japão (Portuguese); Konfertnoe derevo (Russian); Pasa japonesa (Spanish); Şeker ağacı (Turkish)

East Asia Small to medium-sized tree with an open, elliptic crown and hairy twigs. Leaves with petiole hairless, 20–45mm long; blade 100–175 × 75–150mm, **egg-shaped**, with a **drip-tip and squared base**, ovate to elliptic or oblong, with 3 main veins from the base; lower surface hairy or hairless, veins **hairy**; margin toothed. Inflorescences erect; peduncle about 25mm long. Flowers yellow-green, inconspicuous. Fruit **dry** when mature, black, hairless, ellipsoid, 6.5–7.5mm in diameter; inflorescence axes red, **swollen, sweet, juicy** when ripe. Seeds dark brown to black or purplish, 5–5.5mm wide.

Usually grown as an ornamental in our region, where it may be seen in various parts of South Africa and Zimbabwe. The fleshy inflorescence axes are edible, sweet and fragrant, tasting like raisins. The wood is used to make fine furniture.

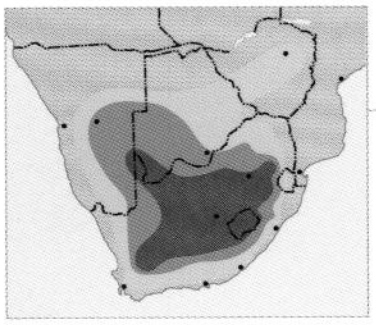

3 *Liquidambar styraciflua* — HAMAMELIDACEAE (OR ALTINGIACEAE)

Sweet Gum, Red Gum; Amberboom, Rooigomboom, Storaksboom

- Drought 3
- Spring
- Deciduous

USA to Central America Large tree with a tall, pyramidal to rounded crown and yellow, **red or purple autumn colours**; bark grey, fissured, forming narrow ridges; buds and twigs hairless. Leaves alternate; petiole hairless, 60–100mm long; blade 120–150mm long and wide, deeply **palmately 5-lobed, lobes not lobed**; tip drawn out; base heart-shaped; surface glossy above, with **tufts of hairs below**; margin **minutely** toothed. Inflorescences male catkins and female hanging balls, on the same tree. Fruit a **ball of capsules**.

Widely grown as an ornamental. The wood is one of the more important commercial timbers of the southeastern USA and has many uses. The resin is collected for a variety of uses. Styrene, the hydrocarbon from which polystyrene plastic is made, was originally prepared from this species.

1 *H. syriacus* flower

1 *H. syriacus* fruit

2 *H. dulcis* flowers

2 *H. dulcis* fruit

3 *L. styraciflua* leaves (see also p.26)

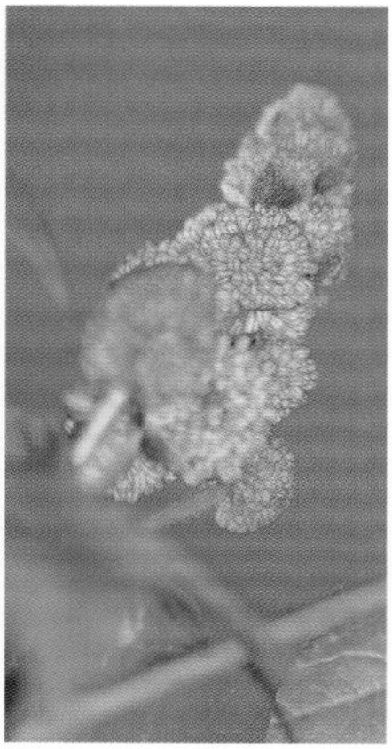

3 *L. styraciflua* flowers

3 *L. styraciflua* fruit

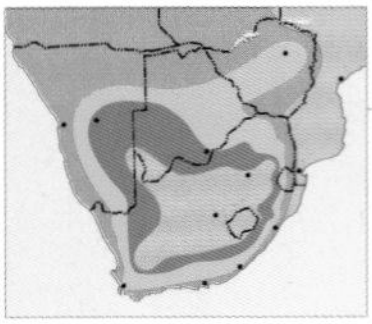

- Drought 2
- Spring
- Evergreen

1 *Melaleuca quinquenervia* MYRTACEAE

Cajeput Tree, Broad-leaved Paperbark, Punk Tree; Kajapoetboom

Australia and New Guinea Medium-sized to tall tree with a narrow to vase-shaped crown; bark **grey and tan, peeling in layers**; twigs **hairy**, slender, brown. Leaves with **petiole** hairless, 4–10mm long; blade 40–90 × 6–25mm, lance-shaped, **secretory cavities** present (**aromatic** when crushed), with more than 3 main veins from the base; tip narrowed; base **gradually narrowing**; margin smooth. Inflorescences erect, 30–85mm long. Flowers white, scented; stamens **conspicuous**, 8–12mm long. Fruit a brown or grey, roundish, woody capsule 3.5–4 × 4–5mm.

Oil distilled from the leaves is used in cosmetics and the flowers yield honey. The timber is used for construction but is not easily worked. Regarded as invasive in parts of Florida, USA. In South Africa, it is a declared Category 1b invader except for National Heritage and National Monument trees.

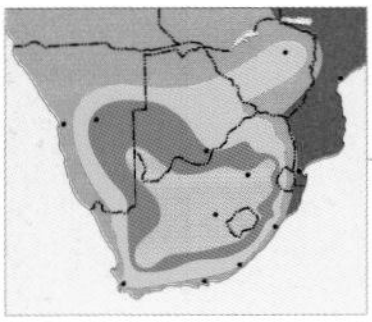

- Drought 2
- Spring
- Evergreen

2 *Melaleuca styphelioides* MYRTACEAE

Prickly Paperbark, Australian Paperbark, Paperbark Myrtle, Prickly-leaved Paperbark; Papierbasmirt

Eastern Australia Medium-sized to large tree with a rounded crown; bark **whitish**, spongy, **peeling off in large sheets**; twigs **hairless**, pinkish. Leaves **without petiole**; blade 15–20 × 2.5–6mm, lance-shaped, **twisted, secretory cavities** present (**aromatic** when crushed), with more than 3 main veins from the base; tip with a **sharp point**; base squared; margin smooth. Inflorescences erect, 20–50mm long. Flowers white; stamens **conspicuous**, 7–8mm long. Fruit a grey, egg-shaped, woody capsule 2–4mm in diameter.

Grown as an ornamental and street tree (rarely in our region) but its vigorous root system may be a hazard to underground pipes.

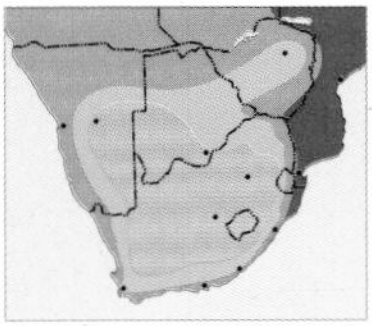

- Drought 1
- Spring
- Deciduous

3 *Ochroma pyramidale* (= *O. lagopus*) MALVACEAE

Balsa Wood, Balsa; Balsahout

OTHER LANGUAGES: Bois de balsa (French); Balsaholz (German); Madera de balsa (Spanish)

Mexico to Bolivia Medium-sized to large tree with a **straight** bole and pyramidal crown; bark brown, smooth; buds and twigs hairy. Leaves alternate; petiole hairy, **200–370mm long**; blade up to 300mm long and wide, **egg-shaped or round**, shallowly **palmately 5–7-lobed**; tip **rounded**; base heart-shaped, with 5–7 main veins from the base; surface glossy and with star-shaped hairs above, whitish hairy below; margin entire. Stipules soon falling. Inflorescences an erect, single flower; stalk 50–100mm long. Flowers white to yellow; petals 5, oblong, up to 150mm long. Fruit a spindle-shaped, **densely hairy**, woody, brown capsule up to 300 × 30mm. Seeds whitish or buff, 3–4mm long.

This extremely light timber is well known to model-builders, both hobbyists and professionals, as an ideal material for their craft. It is particularly well suited to model aircraft that are expected to fly and was even used to make the full-sized World War II De Havilland Mosquito. It can also be used to make rafts, life-belts, insulation and core stock for composites of many kinds, such as wind-turbine blades and boat decks. The wood has been carved into calligraphy nibs of forms not normally available. A specimen tree can be seen in Durban Botanic Gardens.

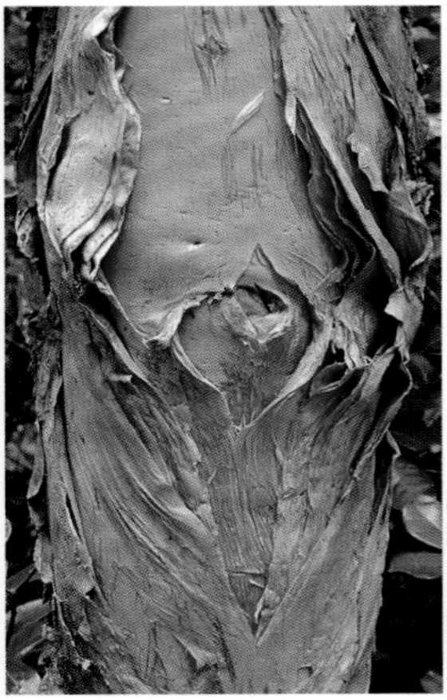

FOREST AND KIM STARR

1 *M. quinquenervia* bark

1 *M. quinquenervia* flowers

FOREST AND KIM STARR

1 *M. quinquenervia* fruit

CASLIBER, WIKIMEDIA COMMONS, CC BY SA 3.0

2 *M. styphelioides* bark

DADEROT, WIKIMEDIA COMMONS, PUBLIC DOMAIN

2 *M. styphelioides* leaves

MELBURNIAN, WIKIMEDIA COMMONS, CC BY SA 3.0

2 *M. styphelioides* flowers

REINALDO AGUILAR

3 *O. pyramidale* flowers

3 *O. pyramidale* fruit

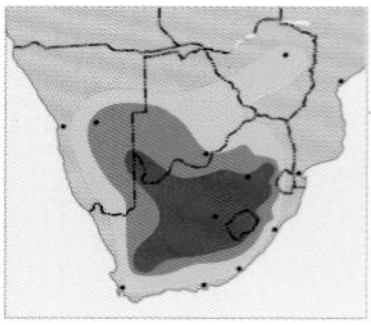

- Drought 2
- Spring
- Deciduous

1 *Platanus × hispanica* (= *P. × acerifolia*)

PLATANACEAE

London Plane; Gewone Plataan

Artificial hybrid raised in Europe Large tree with a pyramidal to rounded crown and yellow to brown autumn colours; bark **smooth, peeling, mottled, underbark yellowish**; buds and twigs hairy; lenticels warty, conspicuous. Leaves with petiole **hairless**, 50–80mm long, base enlarged; blade 100–200 × 120–250mm, kidney-shaped, shallowly **palmately 3–5-lobed**; tip pointed; base squared or heart-shaped; lower surface **woolly** and with star-shaped hairs; margin **coarsely toothed**. Inflorescences **hanging**, a pair of balls, 100–150mm long, appearing after the leaves; peduncle 80–120mm long; males and females separate but on the same tree. Fruit of 2 or 3 **balls of many small, dry fruits (achenes) on the same peduncle**, each 25–30mm in diameter.

Commonly planted ornamental and street tree in many parts of South Africa, well able to withstand urban pollution and root compaction. Quarter-sawn timber has an attractive figure and is sold as Lacewood; it is suitable for cabinet work.

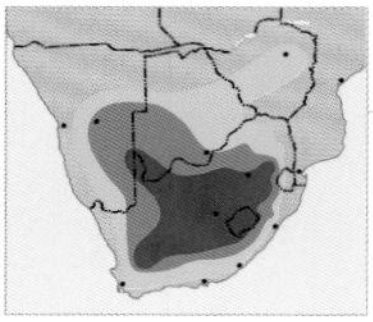

- Drought 2
- Spring
- Deciduous

2 *Platanus occidentalis*

PLATANACEAE

American Plane, Buttonwood; Amerikaanse Plataan

USA Large tree with a pyramidal to rounded crown and yellow to brown autumn colours; bark **smooth, peeling, mottled, underbark white**; buds hairless; twigs hairy, **zigzag**; lenticels smooth but conspicuous. Leaves with petiole **hairy**, 70–130mm long, base enlarged; blade 100–180mm long, up to 300mm wide, kidney-shaped, **palmately 3-lobed**; tip drawn out; base squared to heart-shaped; surface dull, hairless above, **woolly** and with star-shaped hairs below; margin toothed. Inflorescences a **single**, **hanging** ball, appearing after the leaves; peduncle 70–150mm long; males and females separate on the same tree. Fruit a **single ball of many small, dry fruits (achenes)**, 25–30mm in diameter.

Formerly widely planted as a shade tree but more susceptible to anthracnose than London plane (above) and apparently now only grown in Pietermaritzburg. The wood has been extensively used for butchers' blocks and can also be used for making boxes, furniture and musical instruments.

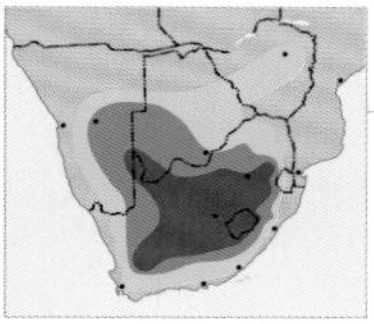

- Drought 2
- Spring
- Deciduous

3 *Platanus racemosa*

PLATANACEAE

Californian Plane; Kaliforniese Plataan

OTHER LANGUAGES: Aliso (Spanish)

Southwestern USA Large tree with a conical to rounded crown and coppery autumn colours; bark **smooth, peeling, mottled, underbark creamy**; buds and twigs **hairless**; lenticels minute. Leaves with petiole hairy, base enlarged; blade 170–320 × 150–300mm, kidney-shaped, **palmately 5-lobed**; tip drawn out; base rounded to heart shaped; surfaces dull, **hairless throughout** except veins below; margin sparsely toothed. Inflorescences hanging, a group of **3–7 balls**, appearing after the leaves; peduncle 80–100mm long; males and females separate, on the same tree. Fruit a **ball of many small, dry fruits (achenes)**, 30–40mm in diameter. Seeds buff, 6–8mm long, 1–1.2mm wide and deep.

Planted for shade but susceptible to anthracnose (a type of plant canker) and only recorded from Johannesburg and Bloemfontein in our region. The wood is hard to split and work but has been used for butchers' blocks. Some birds eat the seeds. The pollen and hairs cause allergic reactions in some people.

1 *P. × hispanica* bark

1 *P. × hispanica* flowers

2 *P. occidentalis* flowers

2 *P. occidentalis* fruit

3 *P. racemosa* flowers

3 *P. racemosa* fruit

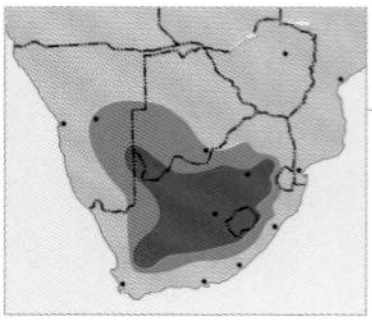

- Drought 1
- Spring
- Deciduous

1 *Populus × canescens* SALICACEAE
Grey Poplar; Vaalpopulier

Eurasia Medium-sized to large tree with a narrow to conical crown; bark **whitish**, rarely fissured; buds and twigs hairy. Leaves alternate; petiole hairless, 12–75mm long; blade 30–120 × 45–115mm, egg-shaped or triangular, sometimes **shallowly palmately 1–5-lobed**; tip pointed or drawn out; base squared; surface **glossy** above, **woolly** below. Stipules soon falling. Inflorescences with males and females on separate trees, appearing before or with the leaves, only females known in our region, **hanging**, 40–100mm long. Fruit a capsule.

Originally introduced to stabilise dongas, this tree is now a declared Category 2 invader in South Africa. The wood is soft but resistant to abrasion. Medicinal uses are recorded.

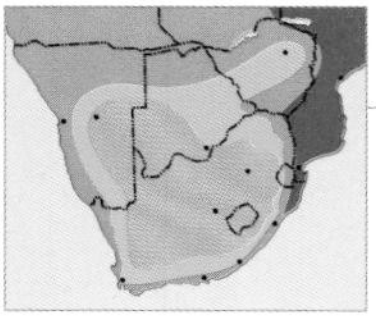

- Drought 2
- Spring
- Evergreen

2 *Pterospermum acerifolium* MALVACEAE (OR PENTAPETACEAE)
Karnikara Tree, Dinner-plate Tree, Maple-leaved Bayur Tree; Karnikaraboom

OTHER LANGUAGES: Muskanda (Bengali); Kanak Champa (Hindi); Vennangu (Tamil)

India to Myanmar Medium-sized tree with an irregularly rounded crown; buds and twigs hairy. Leaves with petiole hairless, 70–150mm long; blade **230–380 × 140–300mm**, egg-shaped to elliptic or oblong, sometimes shallowly 3–7-lobed, with more than 3 main veins from the base, the latter **heart-shaped, eared or surrounding the petiole**; lower surface hairy; margin smooth or toothed. Inflorescences an erect, single flower or sprays. Flowers showy; sepals fleshy, yellowish; petals 70–95 × 6–9mm, white, without markings. Fruit a brown, warty, woody capsule 100–300 × 30–60mm. Seeds midbrown, 10–20 × 10–15mm.

Usually grown for ornament or shade, in our region recorded only from the KwaZulu-Natal coast. The flowers are scented and have been used to perfume linen. Medicinal uses are recorded.

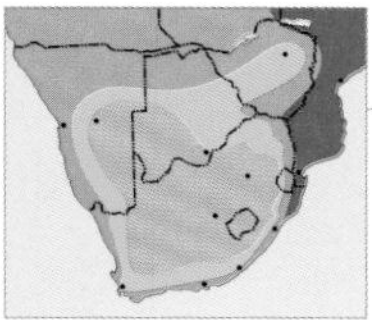

- Drought 2
- Spring
- Evergreen

3 *Reutealis trisperma* *(= Aleurites trispermus)* EUPHORBIACEAE
Philippine Tung; Filippynse Tungboom

OTHER LANGUAGES: San zi tong (Chinese); Balukanag (Tagalog)

The Philippines Medium-sized tree with a rounded to spreading crown; buds and twigs hairy, the latter maroon-brown, **5-angled**. Leaves with petiole hairless, **45–250mm long**; blade 80–160 × 70–150mm, egg-shaped, with 3–7 main veins from the base and a drip-tip; base usually heart-shaped, rarely squared, with **a pair of glands at the top of the petiole**; margin smooth. Inflorescences erect, 80–200mm long. Flowers white to pink; petals with a **spur**, 6–14 × 2.2–5mm, without markings. Fruit a 3- or 4-angled capsule 35–55 × 30–50mm. Seeds 22–32 × 22–28 × 17–20mm.

The whole plant is poisonous but ingestion of seeds is involved most often in human exposures. Seeds were formerly used to make a soap popular among sailors because it lathered in sea water. Grown in our region as a garden curiosity. Compare *Aleurites moluccanus* (p.112) and *Vernicia fordii* (p.264).

1 *P.* × *canescens* bark

BRAAM VAN WYK

1 *P.* × *canescens* leaves

BRAAM VAN WYK

1 *P.* × *canescens* flowers (male)

JAVIER MARTIN, WIKIMEDIA COMMONS, PUBLIC DOMAIN

2 *P. acerifolium* leaves

WWW.SHANTIDHAMA.IN

2 *P. acerifolium* flower

POORNIKANNAN, WIKIMEDIA COMMONS, CC BY SA 4.0

2 *P. acerifolium* fruit

3 *R. trisperma* flowers

3 *R. trisperma* fruit

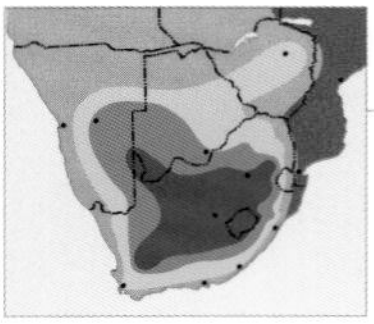

- Drought 3
- Spring
- Evergreen

1 *Ricinus communis* EUPHORBIACEAE
Castor-oil Bean; Kasterolieboom

OTHER LANGUAGES: Févé Castor (French); Gemeiner Wunderbaum (German); Carrapateiro (Portuguese); Higueira del diablo (Spanish); Mbalika (Swahili); Amaanaakku (Tamil)

Tropical Africa Large shrub or small tree with a rounded crown; bark reddish brown, smooth. Leaves alternate; petiole hairless, 80–500mm long; blade 100–750mm long and wide, round, deeply **palmately 7–11-lobed**; tip pointed; base **surrounding the point of attachment of the petiole**; surface sometimes **red-purple, glossy** above, dull below; margin saw-toothed. Stipules **sheathing petiole**. Inflorescences **erect**, 100–400mm long. Flowers small, pale yellow; males and females separate, in the same inflorescence, male pedicels 5–15mm long, female ones 2.5–4.0mm long. Fruit a **spiny**, woody, red or brown capsule 15–25mm long and in diameter. Seeds **buff, mottled black**, 8–15 × 5–7mm.

Invasive throughout the tropics and subtropics, and a declared Category 2 invader in South Africa. Nevertheless, this country was the world's eighth largest producer of castor-oil beans in 2008. Castor oil is an important lubricant for engines and other machinery and has potential as a source of biodiesel. Seeds are poisonous. Medicinal uses are recorded.

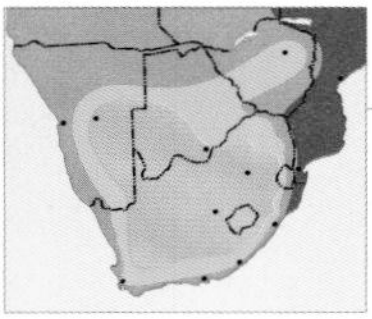

- Drought 2
- Summer
- Evergreen

2 *Stenocarpus salignus* PROTEACEAE
Scrub Beefwood, Red Silky-oak; Witwielboom

Australia Medium-sized tree of indefinite shape; trunk sometimes buttressed; bark brown to grey, smooth; twigs **hairless**, brown to red. Leaves with petiole hairless, 8–20mm long with enlarged base; blade **50–100 × 10–40mm**, elliptic, with **3 main veins from the base**; surface hairless; margin smooth, sometimes wavy. Inflorescences erect; peduncle 25–60mm long. Flowers white, narrow, **twisted**, 10–20mm long. Fruit a leathery, brown, hairless pod 40–60mm long. Seeds about 10–15 × 5mm.

Rare in cultivation in our region and to be found in enthusiasts' collections and a few botanical gardens.

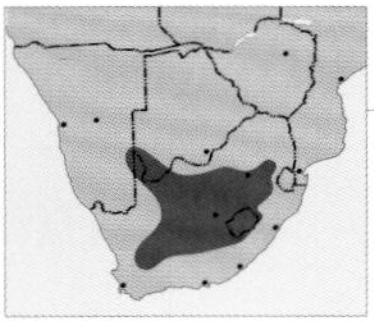

- Drought 2
- Spring
- Deciduous

3 *Tilia cordata* (= *T. parvifolia*) MALVACEAE (OR TILIACEAE)
Small-leaved Linden; Kleinblaarlindeboom

Europe Medium-sized tree with a pyramidal to rounded crown and **yellow autumn colours**; buds **greenish to brown**, hairless; twigs hairless, brown to grey. Leaves with petiole hairless, 25–40mm long; blade 35–75 × 30–80mm, egg-shaped, with 3–5 main veins from the base; tip drawn out to a point; base **symmetrical**, heart-shaped; lower surface **dull blue-green**; margin saw-toothed. Inflorescences hanging, 50–75mm long, with a **prominent bract**. Flowers small, white to yellow. Fruit a roundish, grey-brown nut 6–7 × 4–7mm.

Grown overseas as a street tree. The famous Berlin street *Unter den Linden* commemorates this species. In our region, it is only found as a specimen tree in cool botanical gardens. The wood is excellent for carving and is seen in the works of many famous European workers such as Tilman Riemenschneider and Grinling Gibbons. It is also used for making piano and organ keys as it is dimensionally stable and does not warp. Bees make a highly desirable honey from the nectar and humans eat the leaves and flowers. Medicinal uses are recorded. Small-leaved linden is the national tree of the Czech Republic and Slovenia.

1 *R. communis* leaves

1 *R. communis* flowers

1 *R. communis* fruit

2 *S. salignus* flowers

2 *S. salignus* young fruit

3 *T. cordata* flowers

3 *T. cordata* fruit

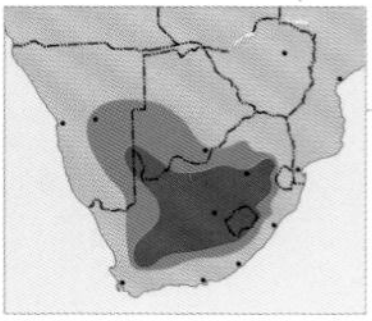

- Drought 2
- Spring
- Deciduous

1 *Tilia × europaea* (*= T. cordata × T. platyphyllos*) MALVACEAE (OR TILIACEAE)

European Linden, Common Lime, Common Linden; Europese Lindeboom

A natural hybrid occurring sporadically in Europe Large tree with a pyramidal to rounded crown, **many burrs and suckers** at the base and inconspicuous autumn colours; buds and twigs hairless, brown. Leaves with petiole hairless, 25–50mm long; blade 50–150 × 35–75mm, **round to egg-shaped**, with 3–5 main veins from the base and a drip-tip; base **obliquely** heart-shaped; lower surface with sparsely hairy veins with **tufts of white hairs in their angles (domatia)**; margin saw-toothed. Inflorescences hanging, appearing after the leaves, 75–100mm long, with a **conspicuous bract**; peduncle 65–75mm long. Flowers yellow; petals about 7mm long. Fruit a densely hairy, woody, brown nut.

Commonly grown overseas as a street tree but only occasionally in cool botanical gardens in our region. It is not ideal in well-populated areas, as trees sucker promiscuously and are often host to heavy aphid populations that drip honeydew.

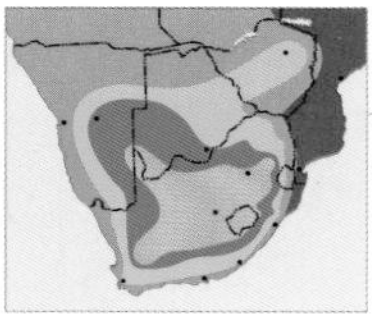

- Drought 2
- Spring
- Deciduous

2 *Vernicia fordii* (*= Aleurites fordii*) EUPHORBIACEAE

Tung Tree, Tung Nut; Tungboom, Chinese Houtolieboom, Tungneutboom

OTHER LANGUAGES: You tong (Chinese); Tungölbaum (German); Árbol del Tung (Spanish)

China Medium-sized to large tree with a pyramidal crown; buds hairless, **10–20mm long at end of a twig**; twigs **hairy**, stout. Leaves with petiole hairless, 50–200mm long, with **a pair of conspicuous dark glands** where it joins the blade; blade 75–250 × 70–220mm, **egg-shaped to triangular**, with 5–7 main veins from the base. Inflorescences appearing **before** the leaves, erect, 80–160mm long. Flowers white; petals 20–35 × 8–20mm, with red lines; males and females separate but in the same inflorescence. Fruit a 3-angled, ellipsoid, brown, woody capsule **40–60 × 30–50mm**. Seeds black, 20–25 × 18–22 × 14–15mm.

The whole plant is poisonous but ingestion of seeds is involved most often in human exposures. The drying oil obtained from the seeds is used in wood finishes, oil paints and printing inks. Invasive in the southeastern USA but usually seen as a specimen tree in botanical gardens in our region. It has also been grown experimentally.

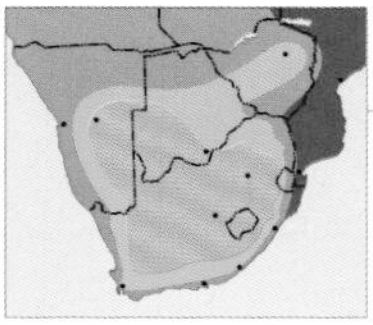

- Drought 2
- Spring
- Deciduous

3 *Ziziphus mauritiana* RHAMNACEAE

Ber (fruit), Indian Jujube, Chinee Apple; Indiese Jujube

OTHER LANGUAGES: Jujubier de l'Inde (French); Filzblättrige Jujube (German); Ber (Hindi); Bidara (Malay); Azufaifo Indio (Spanish); Mkunazi (Swahili); Elandhai (Tamil); Phutsaa (Thai)

Old World tropics Small tree with a spreading crown; buds and twigs glabrous; thorns paired, **one hooked and one straight**. Leaves with petiole hairless, 8–11mm long; blade 30–60 × 15–40mm, lance- or egg-shaped to elliptic, with 3 main veins from the base; tip and base **rounded**; margin **scalloped**. Inflorescences erect, 10–20mm long; peduncle 1–5mm long. Fruit fleshy, roundish, red or black, hairless, 12–25mm long.

Ber fruits are very popular among residents of our region with connections to the Indian subcontinent and are often seen both fresh and dried in shops and markets selling Indian foods. The wood is hard and strong and takes a high polish. It can be used for any purpose where a durable, attractive finish is required. Very similar to and easily confused with the indigenous *Z. mucronata* (buffalo-thorn, Van Wyk & Van Wyk 2013, p.282) but leaves hairless and margin scalloped, not toothed. It is recorded as cultivated in Durban and Réunion.

1 *T.* × *europaea*

1 *T.* × *europaea* flowers

2 *V. fordii* flowers

2 *V. fordii* fruit; glands at base of leaf blade (arrowed)

3 *Z. mauritiana* leaves and flowers

3 *Z. mauritiana* fruit and flowers

GROUP 12

Monkey-orange group

Leaves simple, opposite; blade prominently 3–7-veined from or near base.

See also Group 23: *Acer oblongum* (p.308).

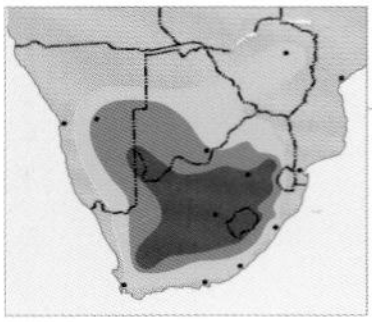

- Drought 2
- Spring
- Deciduous

1 *Acer buergerianum* (= *A. trifidum*)

ACERACEAE (OR SAPINDACEAE)

Chinese Maple, Trident Maple; Chinese Esdoring, Chinese Ahorn

OTHER LANGUAGES: San jiao feng (Chinese); Érable à écorce de dragon (French); Dreispitz-Ahorn (German); Tou kaede (Japanese); Klyon tryokhrazdel'nyj (Russian); Arce tridente (Spanish)

China (subsp. *buergerianum*) and Taiwan (subsp. *formosanum*) Medium-sized tree with a rounded crown and **yellow or red autumn colours**. Leaves with petiole hairless, 25–50mm long; blade 30–100 × 40–60mm, shallowly palmately **3-lobed**, with terminal lobe **shouldered** and sharply tapering (subsp. *buergerianum*) or shallowly lobed to unlobed (subsp. *formosanum*); base square or heart-shaped; margin **entire**. Inflorescences erect, 15–20mm long; peduncle 10–15mm long. Flowers yellow-green, fairly inconspicuous; pedicels hairless, 6–8mm long. Fruit a pair of **hairless winged nuts** 10–30 × 8–10mm, diverging at **90°**, spinning as they fall.

The main means of propagation in southern Africa is by seed. As the leaves turn beautiful shades of red in autumn, it is mainly planted for ornament. It is a common tree in cooler parts of South Africa and Zimbabwe and a declared Category 3 invader in much of South Africa but excluding Gauteng, the Free State and urban areas in other provinces. Several cultivars have been developed in Japan but none are known from southern African cultivation. The leaves are similar in shape to, but smaller than those of *A. rubrum* (p.268). In this species the leaf margins are plain or at most with a few minute teeth, but in *A. rubrum* they are conspicuously, coarsely toothed.

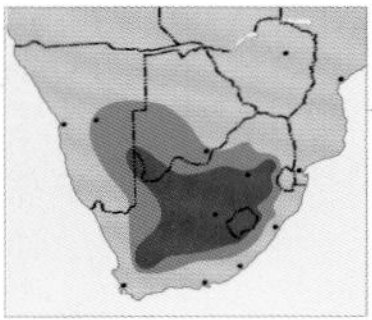

- Drought 1
- Spring
- Deciduous

2 *Acer campestre*

ACERACEAE (OR SAPINDACEAE)

Field Maple, Hedge Maple; Veld-esdoring, Veldahorn

OTHER LANGUAGES: Qayqab (Arabic); Xiàn chăng fēng mù (Chinese); Érable champêtre (French); Feldahorn (German); Kobukaede (Japanese); Bordo-comum (Portuguese); Klyon polevoj (Russian); Arce común (Spanish); Akçaağaç (Turkish)

Europe and Western Asia Medium-sized to large tree with a rounded crown and **yellow autumn colours**. Leaves with petiole hairless, showing **milky sap** when freshly broken; blade 40–60 × 30–60mm, palmately **3–5-lobed**, lobes shouldered and with smooth or coarsely toothed margin; lower surface sometimes hairy, with **densely hairy veins**; base with a **heart-shaped indentation**. Inflorescences erect, 90–100mm long; peduncle 15–25mm long. Flowers inconspicuous; pedicels hairy, 8–10mm long. Fruit a pair of hairless or **sparsely hairy winged nuts** 25–30 × 9–11mm, diverging at 160–180°, spinning as they fall.

Tolerant of moderate shade to full sun. A good tree for large, park-like gardens in the coldest parts of our area. Recorded from Gauteng and KwaZulu-Natal. The timber is relatively soft and is suitable for tool handles, turnery and inexpensive furniture. Numerous cultivars have been developed overseas but none are known from southern African cultivation. Of these cultivars, several have variegated leaves and one ('Schwerinii') has leaves that are purple when young. The leaves of this species are similar to, but smaller than those of *A. saccharum* (p.270). The teeth and lobes are much more rounded than in the latter. The bark of this species is smoother than that of *A. saccharum* and does not flake off.

1 *A. buergerianum* early autumn foliage

1 *A. buergerianum* flowers

1 *A. buergerianum* fruit

2 *A. campestre* leaves

2 *A. campestre* flowers

2 *A. campestre* fruit

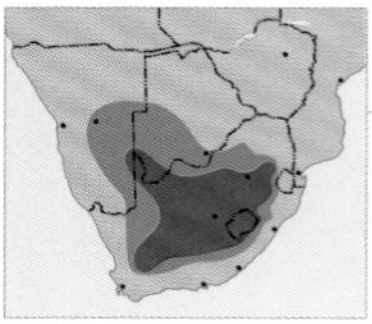

- Drought 1
- Spring
- Deciduous

1 *Acer japonicum* ACERACEAE (OR SAPINDACEAE)

Fullmoon Maple, Downy Japanese Maple; Volmaanesdoring, Volmaanahorn

OTHER LANGUAGES: Yu shan feng (Chinese); Hauchiwa-kaede (Japanese)

Japan (Nagasaki Prefecture) and Korea Small tree with a layered crown and **purple autumn colours**. Leaves with petiole densely hairy, 20–40mm long; base enlarged, often enclosing axillary bud; blade 50–60 × 80–140mm, deeply palmately **7–11-lobed**, terminal lobe **not shouldered**; base **narrowly heart-shaped**; margin **toothed and often ribbon-like**. Inflorescences erect; peduncle 40–50mm long. Flowers **purple**, otherwise inconspicuous; pedicels sparsely hairy. Fruit a pair of **winged nuts, densely to sparsely hairy** when young, 20–25 × up to 7–10mm, diverging at **150–160°**, spinning as they fall.

This species can be confused with *A. palmatum* (below), as there are very similar cultivars in the two species.

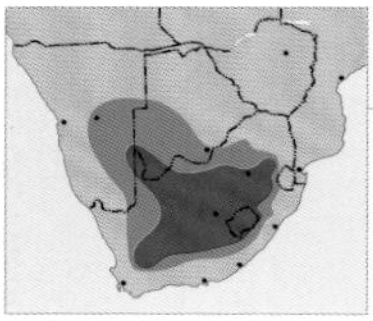

- Drought 2
- Spring
- Deciduous

2 *Acer palmatum* (= *A. polymorphum*) ACERACEAE (OR SAPINDACEAE)

Japanese Maple; Japanse Esdoring, Japanse Ahorn

OTHER LANGUAGES: Ji zhua feng (Chinese); Érable du Japon (French); Fächerahorn (German); Iroha kaede (Japanese); Danpung na mu (Korean); Ácer-japonês (Portuguese); Arce japonés (Spanish)

Japan, Korea and Taiwan Small tree with a spreading crown and **red to purple autumn colours**; bark grey, not striped; buds hairless; twigs hairless, **purple**. Leaves with petiole hairless, 15–45mm long; blade 50–90 × 50–90mm, round overall, deeply **5–7-lobed**, lobes lance-shaped; tip long-pointed; base heart-shaped; margin **saw-toothed**. Inflorescences erect. Flowers reddish, inconspicuous. Fruit a pair of **hairless, winged nuts** 12–14 × 3–5mm, diverging at about 180°, spinning as they fall.

Leaves of the Japanese maple are often and easily confused with those of the fullmoon maple (*A. japonicum*, above). Mainly grown for ornament (recorded from Gauteng and the KwaZulu-Natal midlands in our area) but the leaves have been used as packaging for fruit and vegetables stored over winter.

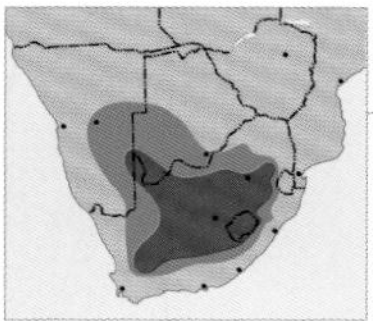

- Drought 1
- Spring
- Deciduous

3 *Acer rubrum* ACERACEAE (OR SAPINDACEAE)

Red Maple; Rooi-esdoring, Rooiahorn

OTHER LANGUAGES: Asfandan ahmar (Arabic); Érable rouge (French); Roter Ahorn (German); Acer-vermelho (Portuguese); Klyon krasnyj (Russian); Arce rojo (Spanish); Kızılakçaağaç (Turkish)

Eastern Canada and USA Medium-sized tree with a pyramidal crown and **red autumn colours**. Leaves with petiole hairless, 25–75mm long, with **clear** sap; blade 75–100 × 50–125mm, shallowly palmately **3–5-lobed**, with terminal lobe shouldered; base square or heart-shaped; surface hairy below; margin coarsely toothed. Inflorescences stalkless clusters or umbels; individual pedicels hairless, 4–13mm long. Flowers brownish grey, inconspicuous. Fruit a pair of **hairless winged nuts** 15–50 × 6–12mm, diverging at 30–85°, spinning as they fall.

At first glance the leaves of the red maple may be taken for those of its Chinese cousin, *A. buergerianum* (p.266). Red maple leaves, however, have the end lobe roughly square, but in the Chinese maple it tapers. Grown for ornament in the colder parts of KwaZulu-Natal and as a specimen tree in the Western Cape (George).

1 *A. japonicum* flowers

1 *A. japonicum* leaves and fruit

2 *A. palmatum* flowers

2 *A. palmatum* fruit

3 *A. rubrum* flowers

3 *A. rubrum* fruit

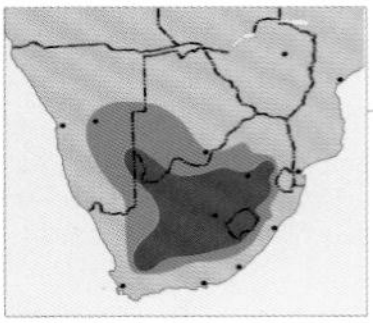

- Drought 1
- Spring
- Deciduous

1 *Acer saccharinum* (= *A. dasycarpum*)

ACERACEAE (OR SAPINDACEAE)

White Maple, Silver Maple; Witesdoring, Witahorn

OTHER LANGUAGES: Asfandan sukkari (Arabic); Érable argenté (French); Silberahorn (German); Eder machsif (Hebrew); Ginyou kaede (Japanese); Arce del Canadá (Spanish)

Eastern Canada and USA Medium-sized to tall tree branching low down, with an irregular, columnar crown and **pale yellow autumn colours**. Leaves with petiole hairless, 35–50mm long, with **clear** sap; blade 75–125 × 70–100mm, **deeply palmately 3–5-lobed**; base square; lower surface **blue-green**, minutely hairy; margin smooth or toothed. Inflorescences hanging, 30–50mm long; peduncle 20–25mm long. Flowers reddish or greenish, inconspicuous; pedicels very short. Fruit a pair of **sparsely hairy winged nuts** (often **only one developing**) 40–80 × 11–20mm, diverging at 90–125°, spinning as they fall.

The leaves are reminiscent of the maple on the Canadian flag but with deeper, narrower lobes. The underside of the leaf is blue-green, unusual in maples. The bark comes off in narrow, thin, loose, vertical flakes. Often only one seed of a pair matures, distinguishing this species from all others in southern Africa while fruit is available.

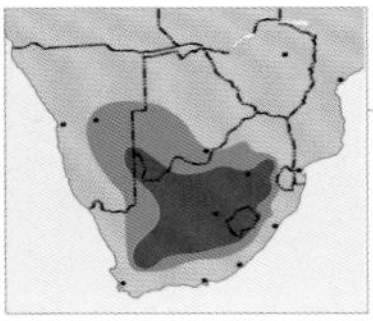

- Drought 1
- Spring
- Deciduous

2 *Acer saccharum*

ACERACEAE (OR SAPINDACEAE)

Sugar Maple; Suikeresdoring, Maselhout, Suikerahorn

OTHER LANGUAGES: Érable à sucre (French); Zuckerahorn (German); Acero da zucchero (Italian); Satou kaede (Japanese); Bordo-açucareiro (Portuguese); Arce del azúcar (Spanish)

Eastern Canada and USA Large tree with a rounded crown and **yellow, orange or red autumn colours**. Leaves with petiole hairy or hairless, with **clear** sap; blade 75–125mm long and about as wide, shallowly palmately **3–5-lobed**, with terminal lobe shouldered; base **square or heart-shaped**; veins hairy below; margin smooth. Inflorescences stalkless, hanging clusters. Flowers yellow-green, inconspicuous; pedicels hairy, 30–37mm long. Fruit a pair of **winged nuts** 23–40 × 6–12mm, diverging at **50–100°**, spinning as they fall.

The rising sap of this species is tapped in spring and boiled down to make maple syrup. The tree seems only ever to have been grown for ornament in Hogsback and there is no record of any attempt to prepare maple syrup in this country. It is reported that this species yields one of the most valuable hardwoods in Canada and is justly famed as the source of expensive 'birdseye' and 'fiddleback' maple veneers. According to some sources, the maple leaf on the Canadian flag is this species but others are on record as stating that the representation there is of no particular species.

1 *A. saccharinum* leaves; inset: lower surface

1 *A. saccharinum* flowers

1 *A. saccharinum* fruit

2 *A. saccharum* leaves

2 *A. saccharum* flowers (male)

2 *A. saccharum* fruit

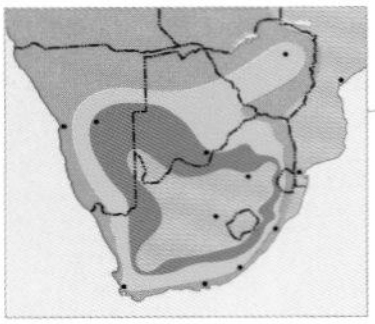

- Drought 2
- Spring–Early Summer
- Deciduous

1 *Gmelina arborea* LAMIACEAE

White Teak, Snapdragon Tree; Witkiaat

OTHER LANGUAGES: Jati putih (Bahasa Indonesia); Gamhar (Hindi); Yemane (Tagalog)

India, Indochina and southern China Medium-sized to large tree with a columnar crown. Leaves with petiole densely hairy, 50–150mm long; blade 100–250 × 50–150mm; base usually square, with **two minute glands** at junction with petiole; surface **densely hairy** below. Inflorescences erect. Flowers with **upper petals brownish-yellow, bottom petal yellow**. Fruit **fleshy**, egg-shaped, hairless, up to 20mm in diameter, yellow-green when ripe.

Although only occasionally grown in Namibia, South Africa and Zimbabwe, it is widely used in Asia, where it grows rapidly, as a street tree and ornamental. Superficially similar to *Tectona grandis* (p.318) but leaves of the latter lack the two glands at the junction of the blade with the petiole.

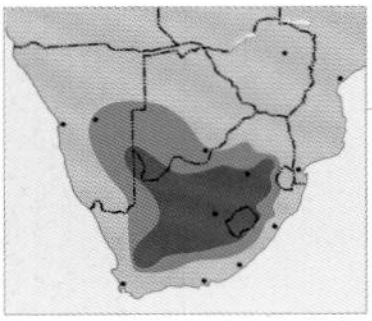

- Drought 2
- Spring
- Semi-deciduous

2 *Paulownia tomentosa* (= *P. imperialis*) SCROPHULARIACEAE (OR PAULOWNIACEAE)

Empress Tree, Princess Tree, Royal Paulownia; Keiserinboom, Prinsesboom

OTHER LANGUAGES: Paulònia (Catalan); Maopaotong (Chinese); Anna Paulowna boom (Dutch); Paulownia d'Anna Pavlovna (French); Blauglockenbaum (German); Kiri (Japanese); Cham o dong na mu (Korean); Paulovnia-real (Portuguese)

China Small to medium-sized tree with a pyramidal to rounded or occasionally spreading crown; bark fairly smooth; buds and twigs **hairy**; lenticels **conspicuous**. Leaves with petiole **hairy**; blade 125–250mm long, up to 1m on coppice growth, 125–250mm wide, **egg-shaped**, shallowly 3-lobed on coppice growth; tip narrowed; base heart-shaped; surface glossy or hairy above, **woolly** below, sticky when young. Inflorescences **erect, pyramidal**, 300–500mm long, appearing before the leaves; peduncle 10–20mm long. Flowers irregular, tubular, lobes 5, these 37–75mm long, about 45mm wide, **purple or blue, without markings**. Fruit a **sticky**, brown, egg-shaped capsule 30–50mm long. Seeds 3.5–4 × 1.5–3mm.

The seeds have been used as packing material around Chinese porcelain and leaked seeds from boxes have caused invasions of this species in Japan and the eastern USA. Grown mainly for ornament and recorded from Lesotho and the cooler parts of South Africa, where it is a declared Category 1a invader.

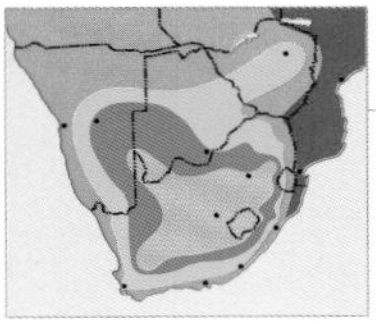

- Drought 2
- Spring
- Evergreen

3 *Tibouchina granulosa* MELASTOMATACEAE

Glory Bush Tree; Gloriebos, Gloriebosboom

OTHER LANGUAGES: Quaresmeira (Portuguese)

Brazil Small, bushy tree; if a shrub then spreading, if a tree then with a rounded crown; young stems **square**. Leaves with petiole densely hairy, 10–30mm long; blade 100–160 × 30–50mm; apex and base sharply tapering; surface **velvety and rough**; margin smooth. Inflorescences erect, 50–150mm long. Flowers **pink** (rarely almost white) **to purple, almost completely covering the crown in a good season**; petals 25–30 × 15–30mm. Fruit a sparsely hairy, ellipsoid capsule about 8 × 6mm, rind rough, leathery, red or yellow.

Very commonly grown in the Durban area but also seen elsewhere in South Africa, Swaziland and Zimbabwe. Its uses are almost exclusively as a decorative horticultural subject. In Brazil, it is noted as useful for planting under power lines and in the rehabilitation of degraded habitats.

1 *G. arborea* flowers

1 *G. arborea* flowers and leaves; inset: fruit

KENPEI, WIKIMEDIA COMMONS, GFDL 1.2, CC BY SA 3.0

2 *P. tomentosa* flowers

HAEFERI, WIKIMEDIA COMMONS, CC BY SA 3.0

2 *P. tomentosa* fruit

MAURO HALPERN

3 *T. granulosa* flowers

3 *T. granulosa* leaves

FOREST AND KIM STARR

3 *T. granulosa* flowers

3 *T. granulosa* fruit

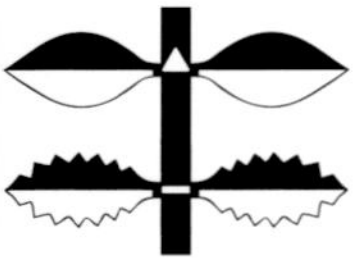

GROUP 13

Sagewood group

Leaves simple, opposite; blade single- or pinnately veined, distinctly discolorous, white or silvery-grey beneath. Interpetiolar stipules, scars or ridge present.

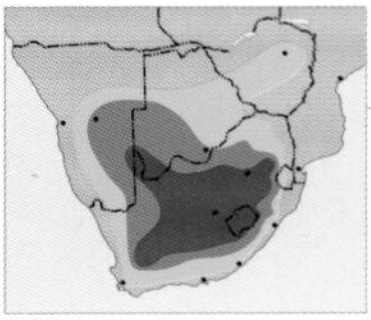

- Drought 2
- Early Spring
- Deciduous

1 *Buddleja asiatica*

BUDDLEJACEAE

Asian Sagewood, Dog's Tail; Asiatiese Saliehout

OTHER LANGUAGES: Bai bei feng (Chinese); Bhimsen pate (Nepalese)

India to China, Indochina, Indonesia and the Philippines Large shrub or small tree of indefinite shape; buds hairy, brown; twigs hairy, **greenish**, with interpetiolar **scars**. Leaves with petiole hairy, 2–15mm long; blade 30–100 × 5–70mm, narrowly **egg-shaped** to elliptic; tip drawn out to a point; base narrowed; upper surface hairless or with star-shaped hairs; lower surface white-woolly; margin **saw-toothed**. Inflorescences erect or arching, 50–250mm long. Flowers small, **white**, sweetly scented. Fruit a hairless, grey capsule 3–5 × 1.5–3mm. Seeds buff, 0.8–1 × 0.3–0.4 × 0.2mm.

Grown in many countries as an ornamental. Recorded in our region from cooler parts of South Africa and Zimbabwe. In Nepal it is used as firewood and fodder and the flowers appear as part of some wedding rituals.

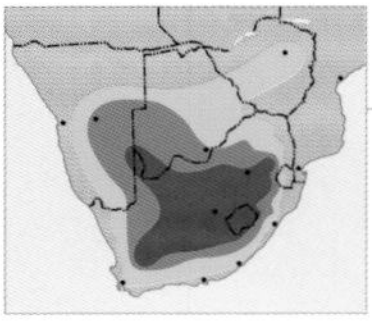

- Drought 2
- Spring
- Deciduous

2 *Buddleja davidii* (= *B. variabilis*)

BUDDLEJACEAE

Chinese Sagewood, Summer Lilac; Chinese Saliehout

OTHER LANGUAGES: Daye zuiyucao (Chinese)

China, records from Japan probably introduced Large, rounded shrub or small tree; buds hairy, brown; twigs **soon losing their hair, brown or purple**, with an interpetiolar **ridge**. Leaves with petiole hairy, 1–5mm long; blade 40–300 × 10–75mm, **lance-shaped**; upper surface dark green, hairless; lower surface white-hairy; margin **toothed**. Inflorescences erect or arching, 150–900mm long. Flowers **blue, lilac, red or black**, often with a **yellow to orange** throat, sweetly scented, small. Fruit a grey, ellipsoid capsule 6–12 × 1.2–2mm. Seeds midbrown, 2–4 × 0.4–0.5 × 0.2–0.4mm.

Grown in many countries for ornament. Recorded from the Eastern Cape, Mpumalanga and Gauteng provinces of South Africa and from Zimbabwe in our area. Naturalised in several temperate areas in both hemispheres. With the exception of sterile cultivars and hybrids, it is a declared Category 3 invader in South Africa. Bees and butterflies are attracted to the nectar of the flowers. The following cultivars are known in southern Africa: 'Black Knight' – petals purple, without markings; 'Royal Red' – petals red; 'White Cloud' – petals white.

RONNIE YEO

1 *B. asiatica* flowers

FOREST AND KIM STARR

1 *B. asiatica* fruit

2 *B. davidii* leaves

2 *B. davidii* flowers

2 *B. davidii* flowers

2 *B. davidii* fruit

GROUP 13 — Sagewood group

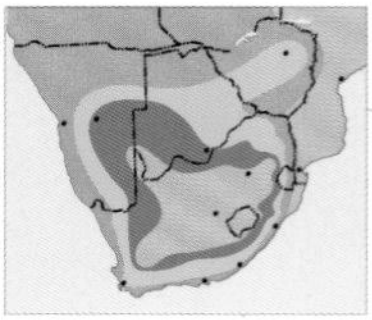

1 *Buddleja madagascariensis* *(= Nicodemia madagascariensis)* BUDDLEJACEAE
Madagascar Sagewood, Smokebush; Madagaskarsaliehout

- Drought 2
- Spring
- Evergreen

OTHER LANGUAGES: Jiangguo zuiyucao (Chinese)

Madagascar Large, rounded shrub or small tree; buds hairy, yellowish to greyish brown; twigs **woolly**, greenish or purple, with an interpetiolar ridge. Leaves with petiole hairy, 5–20mm long, base **enlarged**; blade 40–140 × 15–70mm, egg-shaped to elliptic; lower surface densely hairy; margin **smooth**. Inflorescences erect, 50–250mm long. Flowers **yellow-orange to salmon**, small. Fruit a **blue or orange**, round berry 2.5–5 × 2.5–5mm. Seeds midbrown, 0.6–0.9mm long, 0.4–0.6mm wide and deep.

Widely grown for ornament. Recorded from Namibia, Botswana and South Africa in our area and invasive in many tropical and subtropical countries.

GROUP 14 — Turkeyberry group

Leaves simple, opposite; blade single- or pinnately veined, not distinctly discolorous; margin smooth. Interpetiolar stipules, scar or ridge present. Spines present.

GROUP 15 — Bride's bush group

Leaves simple, opposite; blade single- or pinnately veined, not distinctly discolorous, with blackish bacterial nodules; margin smooth. Interpetiolar stipules, scar or ridge present. Spines absent.

GROUP 16 — Wild-medlar group

Leaves simple, opposite; blade single- or pinnately veined, not distinctly discolorous, without bacterial nodules, densely hairy, at least below; margin smooth. Interpetiolar stipules, scar or ridge present. Spines absent.

There are no trees of Groups 14–16 in this book. If a tree belongs to one of these groups, it is most probably native to southern Africa. Please consult Groups 14–16 in *Field Guide to Trees of Southern Africa* (Van Wyk & Van Wyk 2013).

1 *B. madagascariensis* leaves and flowers

1 *B. madagascariensis* flowers

1 *B. madagascariensis* fruit

GROUP 17

False-gardenia group

Leaves simple, opposite; blade single- or pinnately veined, not distinctly discolorous, without bacterial nodules, smooth or sparsely hairy; margin smooth. Interpetiolar stipules, scars or ridge present. Spines absent.

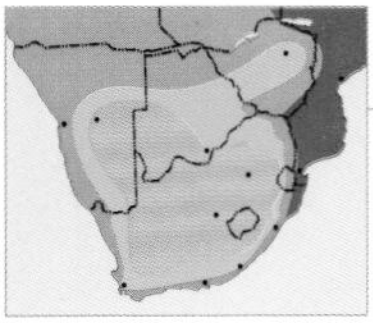

- Drought 2
- After rain
- Evergreen

1 *Coffea arabica*

RUBIACEAE

Arabica Coffee; Koffie

OTHER LANGUAGES: Café Arabica (French); Arabicakaffee (German); Kafes (Greek); Arbusto del Caffè (Italian); Café (Portuguese); Árbol del Café (Spanish); Kahawa (Swahili); Kahvé oghadji (Turkish)

Southwestern Ethiopia, South Sudan and northern Kenya Small tree or large shrub with a **deep root system**, rounded crown and **arching branches**; buds hairless; twigs glossy green, with **interpetiolar ridges**. Leaves with petiole hairless, 5–14mm long; blade 60–180 × 30–80mm, elliptic, with **pit-like domatia** in axils of principal side veins, ending in a **long drip-tip**. Flowers **white**, in clusters along branches, tubular, lobes 5, about 12 × 3–5mm. Fruit **fleshy, red**, hairless, ellipsoid, 12–15 × 8–10mm. Seeds buff, 10–15 × 5–10mm.

This is the main species used in coffees made from ground beans (the seeds of the plant). It is also grown as a garden ornamental. It can be seen grown thus and commercially in the warmer parts of Mozambique, South Africa and Zimbabwe.

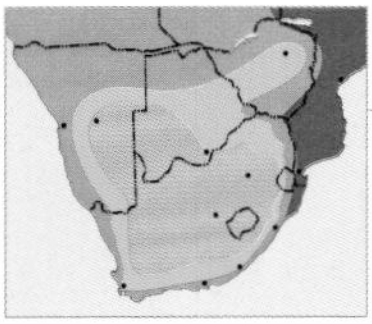

- Drought 2
- Irregular
- Evergreen

2 *Coffea canephora* *(= C. bukobensis, C. robusta)*

RUBIACEAE

Robusta Coffee, Congo Coffee; Robustakoffie

OTHER LANGUAGES: Café Robusta (French); Robustakaffee (German); Caffe di Congo (Italian); Café-robusta (Portuguese); Cafeto Robusto (Spanish)

Western and central Africa Small tree or large shrub with a **shallow root system**, columnar to spreading crown and **arching branches**; buds hairless; twigs glossy green, hairless, with **interpetiolar scars**. Leaves with petiole hairless, 5–18mm long; blade **120–315 × 45–120mm, oblong**, with **pit-like domatia** in axils of principal side veins, ending in a long drip-tip; base narrowed to rounded; lower surface dull, veins hairless; margin sometimes wavy. Flowers **white**, in clusters along branches, tubular, lobes 5, these 8–19 × 2–3mm. Fruit **fleshy, red**, hairless, ellipsoid, 9–17 × 6–12mm. Seeds buff, 7–13 × 5.5–9.5mm.

This is the main species used in instant coffee. It has double the caffeine as arabica and has a heavier, earthier flavour. It has been grown experimentally in Mpumalanga.

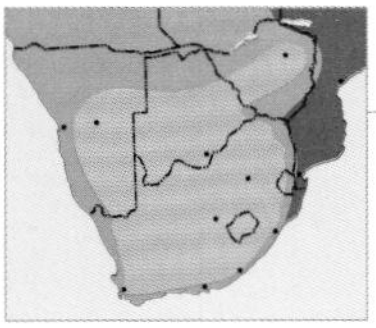

- Drought 2
- Spring
- Evergreen

3 *Coffea liberica*

RUBIACEAE

Abeokuta Coffee, Liberian Coffee; Liberiese Koffie

OTHER LANGUAGES: Café du Libéria (French); Liberiakaffee (German); Caffe liberica (Italian); Café-libérica (Portuguese); Cafeto de Liberia (Spanish)

Liberia Medium-sized tree with a columnar to pyramidal crown and **horizontal** branches; buds hairless; twigs hairless, orange-brown, with **interpetiolar scars meeting as a line**. Leaves with petiole hairless, 8–20mm long; blade 140–380 × **55–205mm, egg-shaped** to elliptic, with a long drip-tip; base narrowed; margin **wavy**. Flowers **white**, in clusters in leaf axils, tubular, lobes 6–9, these 8–16 × 5–10mm. Fruit **fleshy, brown or yellow**, ellipsoid, 20–25 × 17–21mm. Seeds buff, 7–15 × 6–10mm.

This is a minor coffee, mostly grown in Java and the Philippines. Specimen trees can be seen in Durban Botanic Gardens.

1 *C. arabica* flowers

BRAAM VAN WYK

1 *C. arabica* fruit

BRAAM VAN WYK

2 *C. canephora* flowers

GEOFF NICHOLS

2 *C. canephora* fruit

GEOFF NICHOLS

3 *C. liberica* leaves and flowers

CARMEN GALDAMES

3 *C. liberica* flowers

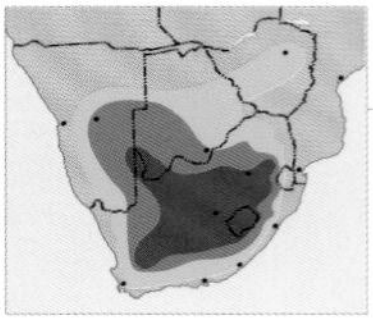

- Drought 2
- Spring
- Evergreen

1 *Gardenia augusta* (= *G. jasminoides*) RUBIACEAE

Common Gardenia, Cape Jasmine; Gewone Katjiepiering, Katjiepiering

OTHER LANGUAGES: Zhizi (Chinese); Kap-Gardenie (German); Gandhraj (Hindi)

China to India and Indochina Large shrub, shape dependent on pruning; buds hairless; twigs hairy, with **interpetiolar ridges**. Leaves with petiole **absent** or very short, hairless; blade 50–150 × 20–70mm, lance-shaped or oblong; tip drawn to a point; base narrowed. Inflorescences an erect, **single** flower. Flowers **strongly scented**, white, tubular; petals 5–8 (more in double flowers), 25–30 × 15–20mm. Fruit a red, dry or fleshy, ellipsoid to ovoid, hairless berry 10–15mm in diameter.

Common gardenia has been grown for ornament in China since the Song Dynasty (960–1279 AD). The fruits yield a yellow dye and the flowers are an important part of lei (traditional adornments such as festive garlands) throughout the Pacific. In our region it is seen in many parts of South Africa and Zimbabwe.

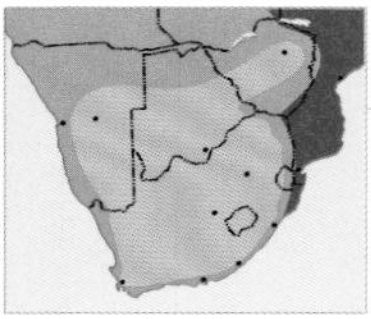

- Drought 2
- Spring
- Evergreen

2 *Gnetum gnemon* GNETACEAE

Gnemon Tree; Gnemonboom

OTHER LANGUAGES: Melindjo (Bahasa Indonesia); Guan zhuang mai ma teng (Chinese); Gnetum à feuilles comestibles (French); Bago (Tagalog); Peesae (Thai)

Malaysia and Indonesia Small to medium-sized tree with a pyramidal crown; twigs **hairless**, glossy, green, with **interpetiolar ridges**. Leaves with petiole hairless, 5–18mm long; blade 75–200 × 25–100mm, elliptic to oblong, with a drip-tip; base **gradually** narrowing; surface glossy above, dull below. Stipules **absent**. Cones with males and females on separate trees, stalked, males cylindrical, **20–60 × 2.5–3mm** (sometimes regarded as a cluster of flowers, each consisting of a stamen and a bract), females yellow to orange or pink, scales with 1 seed each. Seeds **elliptic**, 10–30 × 9–15mm.

Grown in our region as a specimen tree in botanical gardens but in Indonesia it is grown for food and timber. One of us (HG) uses the branches as material in a practical demonstration of the need for close observation when identifying plants – this is a gymnosperm but looks at first and even at second glance like a member of the flowering plant family Rubiaceae.

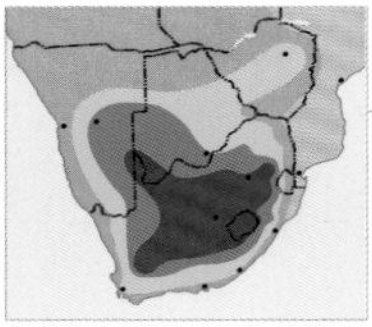

- Drought 2
- Spring
- Evergreen

3 *Hamelia patens* (= *H. erecta, H. nodosa*) RUBIACEAE

Firebush, Hummingbird Bush, Mexican Firecracker; Vuurbos

OTHER LANGUAGES: Fleur-corail (French); Ix-canan (Maya); Doña Julia (Spanish)

Florida (USA) to Argentina Rounded shrub or small tree, shape determined by pruning; twigs **hairy, brown or red**, with interpetiolar scars. Leaves opposite or in **whorls of 3–7**; petiole hairy or hairless, 8–34mm long; blade 55–180 × 26–80mm, egg-shaped to elliptic, **thin-textured**; tip drawn out to a point; base narrowed to rounded; surface glossy and **hairy** above, more densely below. Inflorescences erect or hanging; peduncle 6–42mm long. Flowers yellow or red, **tubular**, lobes 5, egg-shaped, 1.3–25mm long. Fruit a round, red or black, hairless berry 7–10mm long. Seeds 0.6–0.9mm wide.

A quite common ornamental whose flowers attract birds and insects. The fruits are eaten by man and beast. In cooler areas (USDA Zones 8 and 9) plants may die back to ground level in winter and resprout the following spring. In warmer places (Zones 10 and 11) they grow as small trees.

1 *G. augusta* flowers

1 *G. augusta* fruit

2 *G. gnemon* cone (male)

2 *G. gnemon* cones (female)

3 *H. patens* flowers

3 *H. patens* fruit

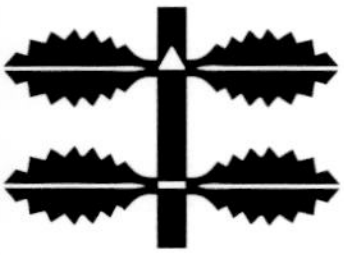

GROUP 18

Onionwood group

Leaves simple, opposite; blade single- or pinnately veined, not distinctly discolorous; margin toothed. Interpetiolar stipules, scar or ridge present.

There are no trees of Group 18 in this book. If a tree belongs to this group, it is most probably native to southern Africa. Please consult Group 18 in *Field Guide to Trees of Southern Africa* (Van Wyk & Van Wyk 2013).

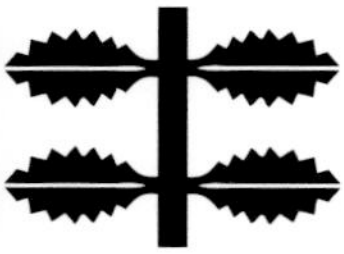

GROUP 19

Spoonwood group

Leaves simple, opposite; blade single- or pinnately veined; margin toothed or lobed. Interpetiolar stipules, scar or ridge absent.

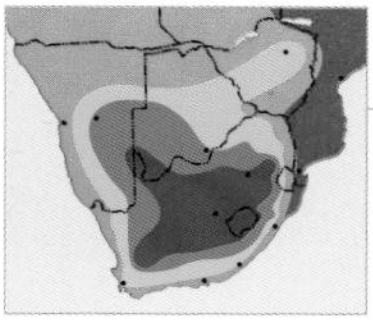

- Drought 2
- Amost all year
- Evergreen

1 *Duranta erecta* (= *D. repens*) VERBENACEAE

Pigeon-berry, Forget-me-not Tree, Golden Dewdrop; Vergeet-my-nie-boom

OTHER LANGUAGES: Xcambocoché (Nahuatl)

Florida and Mexico to Brazil Usually a **large rounded shrub** with weak, arching stems, but can be shaped by pruning; twigs hairless, brown, sometimes with hooked prickles. Leaves with petiole hairless, up to 15mm long; blade 20–65 × 15–35mm, **egg-shaped to elliptic**; margin toothed, mainly in the upper half. Inflorescences erect or arched, 150–200mm long. Flowers irregularly shaped, **blue**, scented, tubular; lobes 5, oblong, 3.5–8mm long, without markings. Fruit fleshy, **round, yellow-orange**, hairless, 5–10mm long and in diameter.

Grown as a garden ornamental but invasive in South Africa, Australia and China. It is a declared invader in South Africa but the regulations are complex.

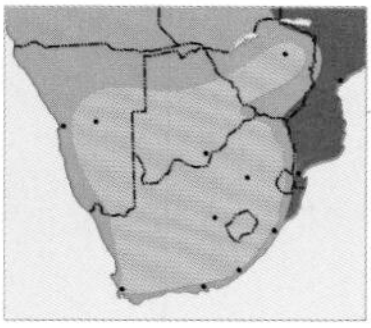

- Drought 2
- Spring
- Semi-evergreen

2 *Maesopsis eminii* RHAMNACEAE

Musizi, Umbrella Tree; Visgraatboom

OTHER LANGUAGES: Msizi (Swahili)

East Africa Tall forest tree with a narrow, rounded crown; bark **pale grey**; buds hairy; twigs with **short, spreading hairs**. Leaves **subopposite**; petiole hairless, 6–12mm long; blade 70–140 × 25–60mm, egg-shaped to elliptic or oblong, with a drip-tip; base rounded to heart-shaped; lateral veins impressed, giving the **upper surface a herringbone appearance**; margin toothed. Inflorescences erect, 15–75mm long. Flowers yellow-green, inconspicuous. Fruit fleshy, purple to black, hairless, ellipsoid, 22–30 × 10–16mm.

Grows large enough to be cropped for timber as fast as many pines and useful for rough work. However, the timber is susceptible to termites and moisture if left untreated. The leaves are used for animal fodder. Trees can be grown for shade, as in coffee plantations, but have become invasive in some tropical countries. Seen in our region as specimen trees in private and experimental collections; an old record from Lubumbashi, Democratic Republic of Congo, indicates that it was used as a street tree.

1 *D. erecta* leaves

BRAAM VAN WYK

1 *D. erecta* flowers

1 *D. erecta* fruit

2 *M. eminii* leaves

2 *M. eminii* flowers

2 *M. eminii* fruit

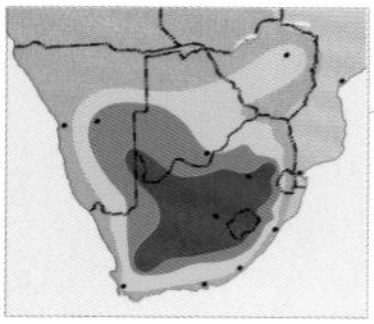

1 *Osmanthus fragrans*

OLEACEAE

Sweet Osmanthus; Soetolyf

- Drought 2
- Autumn
- Evergreen

OTHER LANGUAGES: Mu xi (Chinese); Silang (Hindi); Mokusei (Japanese)

Himalayas to southern China, Taiwan and Japan Small to medium-sized tree with an upright to rounded crown; buds and twigs **hairless**. Leaves with petiole hairless, 7–13mm long; blade 70–150 × 10–50mm, lance-shaped; tip pointed; base narrowed; margin smooth or toothed. Inflorescences **erect**, 20–30mm long. Flowers white or yellow, **strongly and sweetly scented**, tube 10–15mm long, without markings. Fruit **fleshy, purple**, hairless, ellipsoid, 18–24 × 7–10mm.

Grown for its scented flowers in China for many centuries and occasionally offered by nurseries in our region. The cut flowers may be almost invisible in an arrangement but will still perfume the whole room for an evening. They are also used to flavour tea and other sweet-scented products, while in India a preparation of the flowers is used as an insect repellent. The Chinese phrase *changong zhe gui* 'to pluck sweet osmanthus in the Toad Palace' was commonly used until about 1911 to mean that one had passed the Imperial Examinations. Many cultivars are known but the most comprehensive guide to them is in Chinese.

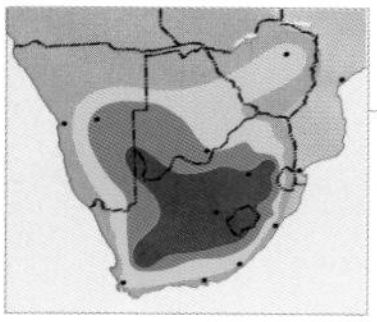

2 *Viburnum odoratissimum*

VIBURNACEAE

Sweet Snowball; Soetsneeubal

- Drought 2
- Spring
- Evergreen

OTHER LANGUAGES: Shan hu shu (Chinese)

India and southern China to Indonesia Small tree or large shrub with a rounded crown; buds hairless; twigs **hairless, red** or green. Leaves with petiole hairless, 12–30mm long; blade 75–200 × 37–100mm, **widest beyond the middle** or elliptic; tip **rounded**; base narrowed; margin smooth, rarely toothed. Inflorescences erect, 55–150mm long; peduncle 40–100mm long. Flowers white, **small, scented, many together**. Fruit **fleshy, red or black**, hairless, ellipsoid, about 8 × 5–6mm.

Common garden ornamental. Can be trimmed into a tall, thick hedge that blocks noise. Fruits attract birds.

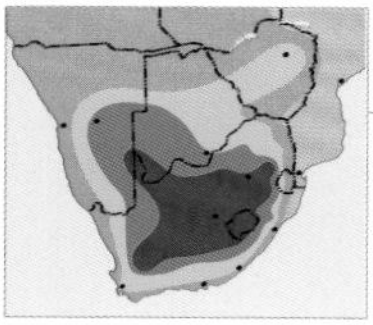

3 *Wigandia urens* (= *W. caracasana*)

HYDROPHYLLACEAE

Caracas Wigandia, Fibreglass Plant; Caracas-wigandia

- Drought 2
- Spring
- Evergreen

OTHER LANGUAGES: Chocon, Ortiga de tierra caliente, Chichicaste (Spanish)

Mexico to Venezuela Large, **coarse**, spreading shrub or small tree with a rounded crown; twigs hairy or **bristly**, some hairs irritant. Leaves with petiole hairless, 20–50mm long; blade **up to 600 × 450mm**, egg-shaped; tip rounded; base **heart-shaped**; surface rough or hairy; margin **scalloped and toothed**. Inflorescencess erect. Flowers irregularly shaped, **blue to purple**, tubular, up to 20mm long, lobes with a white basal mark. Fruit a capsule.

Occasionally grown as an ornamental and recorded from South Africa and Zimbabwe. In the former it is a declared Category 3 invader. Medicinal and ritual uses are recorded in Mexico.

1 *O. fragrans* flowers (yellow form)

1 *O. fragrans* flowers (white form)

2 *V. odoratissimum* flowers

2 *V. odoratissimum* fruit

3 *W. urens*

3 *W. urens* flowers

GROUP 20

Numnum group

Leaves simple, opposite; blade single- or pinnately veined; margin smooth. Interpetiolar stipules, scar or ridge absent. Spines present. Latex present.

See also Group 1: *Pachypodium geayi* (p.38) and *P. lamerei* (p.38).

There are no trees of Group 20 in this book (but see cross references above). If a tree belongs to this group, it is most probably native to southern Africa. Please consult Group 20 in *Field Guide to Trees of Southern Africa* (Van Wyk & Van Wyk 2013).

GROUP 21

Poisonbush group

Leaves simple, opposite; blade single- or pinnately veined; margin smooth. Interpetiolar stipules, scar or ridge absent. Spines absent. Latex present.

See also Group 5: *Plumeria alba* (p.120), *P. rubra* (p.120), *Thevetia peruviana* (p.124).

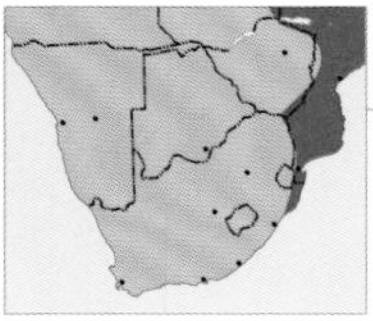

- Drought 2
- Spring
- Evergreen

1 *Calophyllum inophyllum*

CLUSIACEAE (OR CALOPHYLLACEAE)

Alexandrian Laurel; Alexandriese Lourier

OTHER LANGUAGES: Hong hou ke (Chinese); Kamani (Hawaii); Sultan Champa (Hindi); Nag champa (Sanskrit); Mtondoo (Swahili)

Old World tropics Medium-sized to large tree with a spreading crown; trunk usually branching low; buds hairy; twigs stout, **square, glossy**, green, hairless; latex **yellowish**. Leaves with petiole hairless, 10–15mm long; blade 90–190 × 40–90mm, elliptic or oblong; tip **indented**; base narrowed; surface **glossy**. Inflorescences erect, 70–80mm long. Flowers white, scented; petals 7–14mm long. Fruit fleshy, yellow, hairless, ovoid, 17–22 × 25–40mm.

Timber (trade name 'Bintagor') is often scarce but is good for fine decorative work and furniture. The seed oil fulfils US (ASTM D6751) and EU (EN 14214) requirements for use as biodiesel. It is also used as a wood finish and has medicinal uses. No part of the fruit should be ingested as they are poisonous. Trees are grown throughout the Pacific for ornament and shade but require plenty of space; they are resistant to salt spray and pollution. On the Indian Ocean seaboard, recorded from KwaZulu-Natal in South Africa and also from Réunion and the Seychelles.

1 *C. inophyllum*

1 *C. inophyllum* leaves and fruit

1 *C. inophyllum* flowers

1 *C. inophyllum* fruit

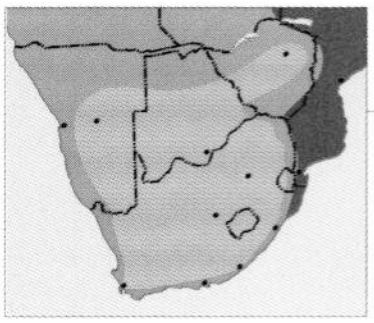

- Drought 2
- Spring
- Evergreen

1 *Calotropis procera* (= *Asclepias procera*) APOCYNACEAE

Giant Milkweed, Apple of Sodom, Calotrope, Mudar Fibre; **Reusemelkbos**

OTHER LANGUAGES: Akanda (Bengali); Oscher (German); Aak (Hindi); Shwetarka (Sanskrit); Algodon Extranjero (Spanish); Mpamba Mwitu (Swahili); Vellerukku (Tamil); Jilledu (Telugu)

Tropical Africa, North Africa and Western and South Asia to Indochina Vase-shaped to rounded shrub or small tree; twigs stout, **round, dull**, hairy; latex white. Leaves with petiole hairless, 3–4mm long, or **appearing to clasp the stem**; blade 90–150 × 55–100mm, **grey-green or grey-blue, dull, waxy**, widest beyond the middle or oblong; tip with a small spine; base heart-shaped or eared; lower surface hairy. Inflorescences erect, up to 100mm long; peduncle 50–85mm long. Flowers tubular, pink, with a white basal mark; lobes 5, egg- or lance-shaped, 6–8mm long, tube slightly shorter, 4–5mm wide. Fruit a pair of egg-shaped pods 60–125 × 30–70mm. Seeds about 8–8.5 × 5mm, with a tuft of white hairs 25–28mm long.

All parts of the plant are at least mildly poisonous. The wood makes good charcoal and fishing floats and the pith is good as tinder. It was formerly grown as an ornamental in Australia but has largely fallen out of favour because of its toxicity and invasive potential. Grown and invasive in Limpopo, Zimbabwe and Mozambique; it is a declared Category 1b invader in South Africa. Medicinal uses are recorded.

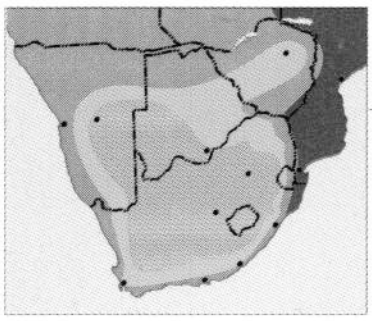

- Drought 2
- Spring
- Evergreen

2 *Clusia major* CLUSIACEAE

Autograph Tree, Balsam Apple, Scotch Attorney; **Wurgbalsemappel**

Florida and the West Indies Medium-sized to large, spreading tree; twigs stout, round, hairless; latex **white to yellowish**. Stems round, unarmed. Leaves with petiole hairless, 10–25mm long; blade 50–200 × 40–100mm, **widest well beyond the middle**; tip **rounded to squared**; base narrowed; margin inrolled. Inflorescences an erect, single flower or a few together; stalk 15–25mm long. Flowers **white**; petals 30–40mm long, with a **pink** basal mark; males and females on different trees. Fruit a dry or fleshy, woody, purple or yellow capsule 35–60 × 50–80mm. Seeds whitish or yellow.

Invasive in several tropical countries but rarely seen in our region, only recorded from Durban. It is a hemi-epiphyte that often starts growth on rocks or other trees, thus resembling a strangling fig. The fruit itself is poisonous but the seeds are popular with birds. Doubtfully distinct from *C. rosea* (below).

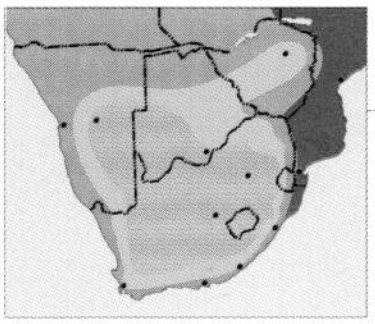

- Drought 2
- Spring
- Evergreen

3 *Clusia rosea* CLUSIACEAE

Balsam Apple, Pitch Apple, Scotch Attorney; **Balsemappel**

OTHER LANGUAGES: Copey (Spanish)

Florida, Mexico and the West Indies Spreading, medium-sized tree; twigs stout, round, green, hairless; latex **yellowish**. Leaves with petiole hairless, 10–25mm long; blade 70–180 × 70–110mm, **widest beyond the middle**; tip **indented**; base narrowed to rounded; margin inrolled. Inflorescences an erect, single flower. Flowers with petals 30–40mm long, **white or pink**; males and females on different trees. Fruit a round, yellow-green, hairless capsule 50–80 × 50–80mm. Seeds reddish brown, about 5mm long.

Rarely grown as an ornamental in our region, only recorded from Durban. Flowers attract bees but the quality of the honey is unknown. The black material surrounding the seeds was formerly used for caulking boats.

BRAAM VAN WYK

1 *C. procera* flowers

BRAAM VAN WYK

1 *C. procera* fruit

2 *C. major* flower

FOREST AND KIM STARR

3 *C. rosea* flower

FOREST AND KIM STARR

3 *C. rosea* fruit

FOREST AND KIM STARR

3 *C. rosea* fruit (dehisced)

1 *Harungana madagascariensis* HYPERICACEAE

Orange-milk Tree, Blood Tree, Haronga, Praying-hands; **Oranjemelkboom**

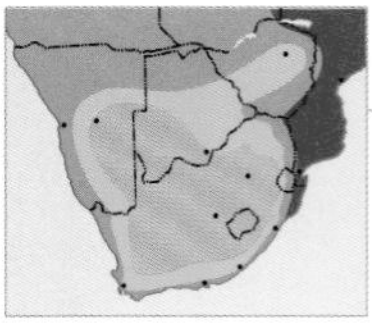

- Drought 2
- Spring
- Evergreen

OTHER LANGUAGES: Mutsotso (Shona); Kumamaji (Swahili)

Tropical Africa and Madagascar Small to medium-sized tree with an irregularly rounded crown; new growth covered with **golden brown, star-shaped hairs** which soon fall off; twigs **round**, stout, dull; latex **orange**. Leaves with petiole **hairy**, about 30mm long; blade 60–200 × 30–120mm, lance- to egg-shaped or elliptic, with a drip-tip; lower surface with **star-shaped hairs**. Inflorescences erect, 80–200mm long. Flowers white, inconspicuous. Fruit fleshy, round, red-orange, hairless, about 4 × 4mm. Seeds reddish brown, about 2mm long.

Grown in our region as specimens in botanical gardens. The wood is used for charcoal and firewood. Although the timber is attractive, it is rarely seen in pieces large enough to be useful. This species is becoming invasive in northern Australia. Medicinal uses are recorded.

2 *Kopsia fruticosa* APOCYNACEAE

Pink Kopsia, Shrub Vinca; **Pienkkopsia**

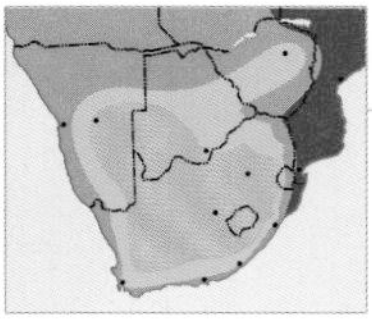

- Drought 2
- Spring
- Evergreen

OTHER LANGUAGES: Hong hua rui mu (Chinese)

India, Thailand, Malaysia, Indonesia, the Philippines and southernmost China Large, spreading shrub or small tree; buds hairless; twigs **minutely hairy**, green; latex white. Leaves with petiole **hairless**, 6–12mm long; blade 100–225 × 40–90mm, elliptic, with a drip-tip; surface glossy above, paler, dull below. Inflorescences erect; peduncle 5–15mm long. Flowers **pink with a red mouth**; tube 25–45mm long, lobes 20–30mm long. Fruit fleshy, usually solitary, 25–30mm long.

Grown for ornament, rarely in our region. All parts of the plant are poisonous. Medicinal uses are recorded.

3 *Mascarenhasia arborescens* APOCYNACEAE

Mascarenhasia; Mascarenhasia

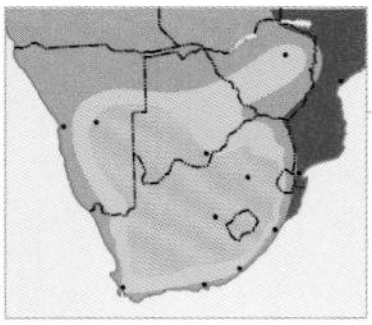

- Drought 2
- Spring
- Evergreen

OTHER LANGUAGES: Barabanja (Malagasy)

Madagascar, Comoros, Seychelles and East Africa Large shrub or small tree with a more or less rounded crown; buds hairless; twigs hairy at first, soon becoming hairless, with **prominent lenticels**; latex white. Leaves with petiole hairless, 1–8mm long; blade 40–180 × 20–70mm, **elliptic or slightly wider beyond the middle**, with a drip-tip; base narrowed; surface glossy; margin **rolled inwards**. Inflorescences erect, 20–40mm long; peduncle 2–5mm long. Flowers white to creamy; tube 5–14mm long, lobes 4–15 × 2–14mm. Fruit a **pair of spindle-shaped**, dark brown to black pods 60–175 × 20–60mm. Seeds dark brown, 10–14 × 2–4 × 0.8–1mm, with **hairs** 10–20mm long.

Formerly a source of rubber in Madagascar. Now seen most often in our region as a specimen tree in botanical gardens in Durban and Harare, it is decidedly ornamental. Medicinal uses are recorded.

1 *H. madagascariensis* growth tip

1 *H. madagascariensis* flowers

1 *H. madagascariensis* fruit

2 *K. fruticosa* leaves and flowers

2 *K. fruticosa* flowers

3 *M. arborescens* flowers

3 *M. arborescens* fruit

GROUP 22

Waterberry group

Leaves simple, opposite; blade single- or pinnately veined, with secretory cavities; margin smooth. Interpetiolar stipules, scar or ridge absent. Latex absent.

See also Group 10: In many species of *Eucalyptus* (eucalypts; *bloekoms*) the leaves are opposite in juvenile plants or on coppice shoots; compare in particular *Eucalyptus diversicolor* (p.212), *E. globulus* (p.214), *E. grandis* (p.214) and *E. saligna* (p.216).

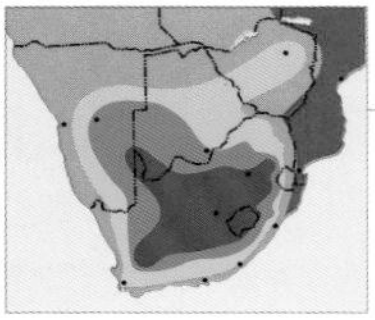

- Drought 2
- Spring
- Evergreen

1 *Acca sellowiana* *(= Feijoa sellowiana)*

MYRTACEAE

Pineapple Guava; Pynappelkoejawel

OTHER LANGUAGES: Goyavier ananas (French); Goiaba do campo (Portuguese); Guayaba del país (Spanish)

Brazil and Uruguay Small tree or large shrub with a rounded crown; bark **smooth, grey**; buds hairy; twigs hairy or hairless; lenticels inconspicuous. Leaves with petiole hairy, up to 6mm long; blade 25–75 × 20–37mm, egg-shaped to elliptic; tip **rounded**; base narrowed; lower surface **woolly**; margin **inrolled**. Inflorescences an erect, single flower; stalk 25–37mm long. Flowers white to pink; petals 4; stamens red. Fruit a berry, **green**, egg-shaped, widest at end, rough-skinned, **up to 50mm** long.

Usually grown as a garden ornamental or a hedge but the fruits are deliciously edible when ripe. For the best flavour the ripe fruit, which remain green, must be allowed to fall from the tree. One source states that it is not fully cold-hardy, though we have seen it fruiting in one of the coldest places in southern Africa. It resists salt-laden winds. Although bees are the chief pollinators, the petals in open flowers often become swollen and are popular with birds. The petals are edible, with a sweet, spicy taste, and can be used is as an addition to salads. Recorded in our region from Mozambique, South Africa and Zimbabwe.

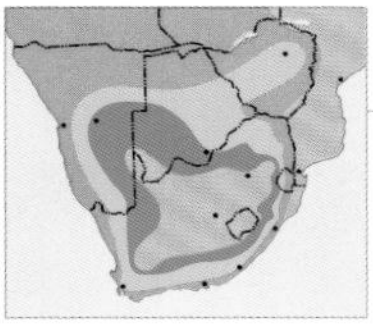

- Drought 2
- Spring–Summer
- Evergreen

2 *Angophora costata* *(= A. lanceolata)*

MYRTACEAE

Smooth-barked Apple, Apple Myrtle; Appelmirt

Eastern Australia Medium-sized to tall tree with a narrow crown; bark brown or grey, **shed in spring** like a gum-tree's; twigs hairless, pale grey. Each pair of leaves **at right angles to preceding pair**; petiole 8–19mm long, hairless; blade 70–175 × 9–50mm, lance-shaped; surface **glossy** above, **dull** below. Inflorescences **erect**; peduncle 12–30mm long. Flowers white; petals about 4 × 3–4mm. Fruit a **5-ribbed**, grey-black, woody, hemispherical **capsule** 9–17mm long and in diameter. Seeds dark brown.

May at first sight be mistaken for a eucalypt but the adult leaves are opposite and the fruits are strongly ribbed. Seen as specimen trees in arboreta. The timber is of relatively limited value. Recorded from Gauteng and Western Cape in our region.

1 *A. sellowiana* leaves

1 *A. sellowiana* flower

1 *A. sellowiana* fruit

2 *A. costata* flower and buds

2 *A. costata* flowers

2 *A. costata* fruit

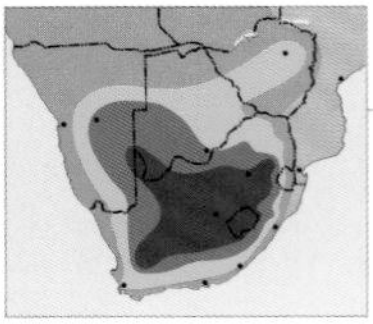

1 *Eucalyptus cinerea* MYRTACEAE

Florist's Gum, Argyle Apple, Silver-dollar Tree; Floristebloekom, Lowerbloekom

- Drought 3
- Spring
- Evergreen

Southeastern Australia Medium-sized tree with a narrow to rounded crown; bark **adhering**, rough even on small branches, grey. Juvenile and intermediate leaves opposite, **grey**; adult leaves rarely if ever produced in cultivation in southern Africa; juveniles **roundish**, up to 80 × 45mm, clasping the stem, base **squared**, tip **rounded**; intermediate leaves egg- to lance-shaped, 50–90 × 20–45mm, base rounded, tip pointed, on petiole 8–14mm long. Flowers **in 3s**, on a pedicel 2–9mm long, white; buds **grey-waxy**, diamond-shaped. Fruit a conical capsule 5–9mm in diameter, rim level, valves **3 or 4**.

A commonly and widely grown ornamental that sometimes seems to be naturalised in colder areas. The leafy stems are widely used by florists, hence the common names, as background foliage for colourful arrangements. They can be dyed or dried.

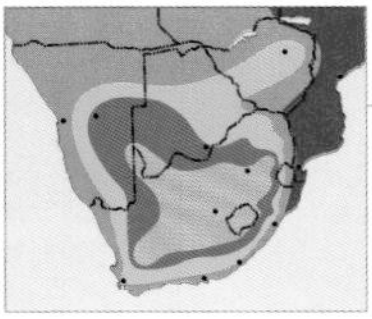

2 *Eugenia uniflora* MYRTACEAE

Surinam Cherry, Brazil Cherry, Pitanga; Surinaamse Kersie

- Drought 2
- All year
- Evergreen

OTHER LANGUAGES: Surinaamse Kers (Dutch); Cerise à Cotes (French); Surinamkirsche (German); Pitanga da Praia (Portuguese); Cereza de Cayena (Spanish)

Brazil and Surinam Small, shrubby tree with a rounded crown; bark smooth, pale; buds and twigs hairy or hairless, the latter **dull brown**. Leaves with petiole hairless, 2–5mm long; blade 20–60 × 12–35mm, **egg-shaped**; tip and base narrowed; surface glossy above, dull below. Inflorescences an erect, **single** flower **or clusters**; stalk 15–20mm or somewhat longer. Flowers white; petals 8–12mm long. Fruit a **many-angled**, red, hairless berry 25–30mm in diameter.

Grown as a hedge or for its fruit in many places in Mozambique, Namibia, South Africa and further north. In the Amazon Valley, the leaves are scattered where villagers walk and the juice of crushed leaves acts as a fly repellent. The tree is invasive in coastal KwaZulu-Natal and some tropical countries, and has been declared a Category 1b invader in South Africa.

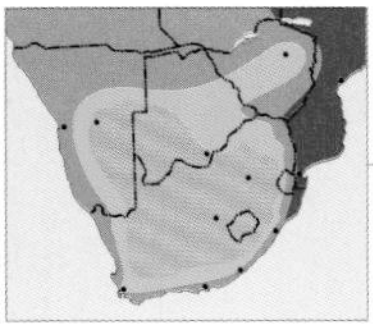

3 *Lophostemon confertus* (= *Tristania conferta*) MYRTACEAE

Brush Box, Australian Box, Brisbane Box, Queensland Box; Australiese Buksboom, Brisbane-kamassie

- Drought 2
- Spring
- Evergreen

Eastern Australia Medium-sized to large tree with an ovoid to rounded crown; bark pale, **rough**, flaking; twigs **hairless**, green. Leaves may appear whorled; petiole hairless, 20–25mm long; blade 100–200 × 25–70mm, **egg-shaped** to elliptic; tip **long drawn out**; base narrowed; upper surface glossy. Inflorescences erect. Flowers white; petals 6–9mm long and wide; stamens in **5 bundles** 10–20mm long. Fruit a **woody**, grey-black, hemispherical capsule 8–12mm long and in diameter. Seeds about 3mm long.

Grown as a street tree as it requires little maintenance. Recorded from KwaZulu-Natal in South Africa and from Zimbabwe, where it is resistant to pollution and other urban hazards. Recommended in Australia as a replacement for camphor tree (p.250). Its invasive potential, though limited, is not zero and it has made some inroads in Hawaii and parts of Australia where it is not native. The wood is good and is used for construction and decorative purposes.

1 *E. cinerea* leaves and flower buds

1 *E. cinerea* fruit

2 *E. uniflora* flower

2 *E. uniflora* fruit

3 *L. confertus* flowers

3 *L. confertus* fruit

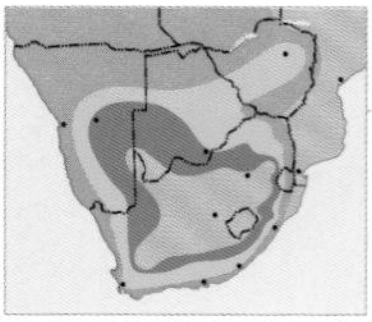

- Drought 2
- Spring
- Evergreen

1 *Melaleuca cuticularis*

MYRTACEAE

Saltwater Paperbark; Soutmirt

Southwestern Australia Small, upright to sprawling tree; bark pale, peeling; buds hairless; twigs hairless, slender, **pale grey**. Leaves **without petiole**; blade 6–11 × 1.5–3mm, **narrowly lance-shaped** to oblong; tip rounded; base **squared**; surface dull. Inflorescences an erect, single flower or clusters. Flowers white. Fruit a **5-angled, woody, grey**, hairless capsule 6–11mm in diameter.

Grown in the Western Cape for hedges and windbreaks. Tolerant of waterlogging and salty wind.

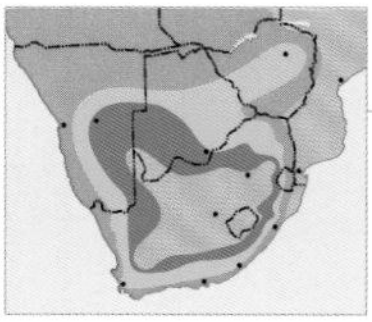

- Drought 2
- Spring
- Evergreen

2 *Melaleuca decora*

MYRTACEAE

White Feather Honeymyrtle; Witpluimheuningmirt

Eastern Australia Small to medium-sized tree with a narrow, rarely rounded crown; bark papery, pale brown; twigs hairy or not, brown. Leaves with petiole hairless and up to 1mm long or absent; blade 8–18 × 1–2mm, **strap-shaped**; tip narrowed; base gradually narrowed; surface **glossy**. Inflorescences erect, **20–90mm long**. Flowers small, white. Fruit a woody, brown, urn-shaped, hairless capsule 2–3mm long and in diameter.

Grown as a screen or ornamental. Recorded from Zimbabwe and the Limpopo, Gauteng and KwaZulu-Natal provinces of South Africa. Known to damage underground services and should not be planted within 6m of water or sewerage pipes.

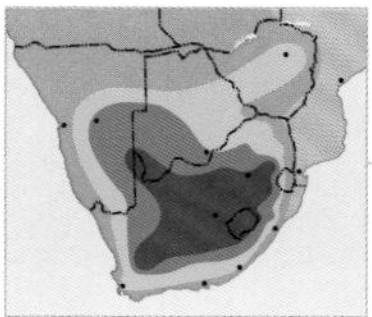

- Drought 2
- Summer
- Evergreen

3 *Metrosideros excelsa*

MYRTACEAE

Pohutukawa, Iron Tree, New Zealand Bottlebrush, New Zealand Christmas-tree; Ysterboom, Nieu-Seelandse Kersboom, Nieu-Seelandse Perdestert

OTHER LANGUAGES: Pohutukawa (Maori)

New Zealand Small to medium-sized, rounded or sprawling, often multistemmed tree; trunks and branches sometimes festooned with matted, fibrous **aerial roots**; twigs hairy, stout, young stems **square**. Leaves with petiole hairy, 5–10mm long; blade **40–90 × 22–40mm**, elliptic, **leathery**; tip and base **narrowed**; lower surface **white-hairy**; margin **bent downwards**. Inflorescences erect, 50–100mm long. Flowers **red**, showy; stamens many, 20–25mm long. Fruit a roundish, woody capsule 8–10 × 7–8mm.

In New Zealand, this tree seems to combine the functions of poinsettia (p.128) and conifers as Christmas trees. There are several cultivars. In our area it is planted mainly in the Western Cape, where it is resistant to salty winds and has become a weed. It is a declared Category 1a invader only in the Overstrand district, South Africa. It is the civic tree of La Coruña, Spain.

STEVE AND ALISON PEARSON

1 *M. cuticularis* flowers

C.T. JOHANSSON, WIKIMEDIA COMMONS, CC BY SA 3.0

1 *M. cuticularis* flowers

2 *M. decora* flowers

2 *M. decora* fruit

KAHUROA, WIKIMEDIA COMMONS, PUBLIC DOMAIN

3 *M. excelsa* flowers

KAHUROA, WIKIMEDIA COMMONS, PUBLIC DOMAIN

3 *M. excelsa* branches with aerial roots

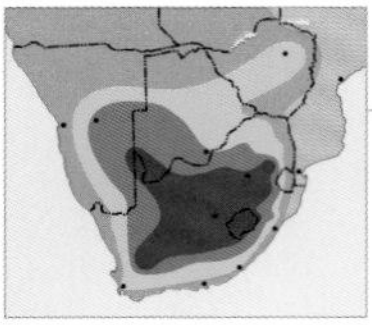

1 *Metrosideros kermadecensis* MYRTACEAE

Kermadec Pohutukawa, Dwarf Pohutukawa; Dwergysterboom

- Drought 2
- All year
- Evergreen

Kermadec Islands, 900km northeast of New Zealand Medium-sized, usually multitrunked tree with a rounded to spreading crown; trunks and branches usually clad with matted, fibrous **aerial roots**; buds and twigs hairy; new stems round. Leaves with petiole hairy, 5–7mm long, densely hairy; blade **20–50 × 10–30mm, almost round to egg-shaped**; tip and base **rounded**; upper surface **hairy when young**, lower **grey-woolly**; margin **flat**. Inflorescences erect. Flowers showy, red to pink; stamens 12–20mm long. Fruit a densely hairy, woody, whitish, egg-shaped capsule about 6mm long.

Similar to the preceding species and used for the same purposes. This pohutukawa has become invasive in Hawaii but not, apparently, in our region where it is recorded from Gauteng and KwaZulu-Natal. A cultivar ('Variegata') with variegated leaves is known.

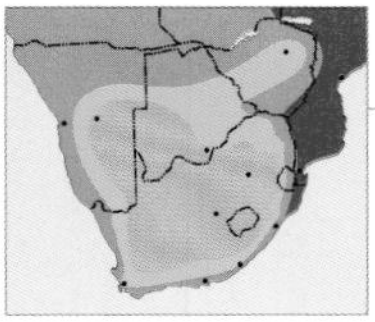

2 *Pimenta dioica* (= *P. officinalis*) MYRTACEAE

Allspice, Pimento; Wonderpeper, Jamaikapeper, Piment

- Drought 2
- Spring
- Evergreen

OTHER LANGUAGES: Piment de la Jamaïque, Toutes-épices (French); Allgewürz (German); Pimenta da jamaica (Portuguese); Pimenta da Jamaica (Spanish)

Mexico to Nicaragua Medium-sized tree with a narrowly elliptic crown; bark smooth, pale brown or grey; twigs hairless, **square** when young. Leaves with petiole hairless, **10–25mm long**; blade 55–170 × 20–65mm, **lance-shaped** to elliptic or oblong; tip and base rounded; margin **rolled inwards**. Inflorescences erect, **50–120mm long**. Flowers white, small; males and females on separate trees but visually similar. Fruit fleshy, round, **5–10mm long and in diameter**. Seeds about 4mm long.

Allspice is the dried, unripe berries of this tree. Fresh leaves can also be used in cookery, treated like bay leaves, when available. The wood is used to make walking sticks and umbrella handles. Medicinal uses for various parts of the plant are recorded. Trees have been grown experimentally with limited success in our region, possibly because seeds need to pass through a bird's digestive tract before they will germinate. Birds spread the trees in Tonga and Hawaii and allspice is invasive in the latter.

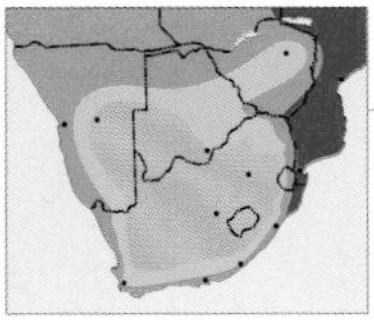

3 *Pimenta racemosa* MYRTACEAE

Bay Rum; Lourierrum

- Drought 2
- Spring
- Evergreen

OTHER LANGUAGES: Bois d'Inde (French); Bayrumbaum (German); Limoncillo (Spanish)

The Caribbean Small to medium-sized tree with a narrow crown; bark smooth, peeling, pale grey; twigs hairless, **round**. Leaves with petiole hairless, **3–10mm long**; blade 30–150 × 12–65mm, **elliptic to round**; tip and base rounded; margin **rolled inwards**. Inflorescences erect, **25–120mm long**. Flowers white, small. Fruit a round, hairless berry 6–12mm long and in diameter. Seeds about 4mm long.

The highly aromatic leaves are used in Caribbean cookery but all other parts of the plant are reputed to be mildly toxic. They are also the source of an essential oil used in various cosmetics. In our region, seen as a few specimen trees in KwaZulu-Natal.

1 *M. kermadecensis* leaves

KAHUROA, WIKIMEDIA COMMONS, PUBLIC DOMAIN

1 *M. kermadecensis* flowers

1 *M. kermadecensis* fruit

TAU'OLUNGA, WIKIMEDIA COMMONS, CC BY SA 3.0

2 *P. dioica* flowers

PETER ZIJLSTRA / SHUTTERSTOCK.COM

2 *P. dioica* fruit

CERLIN NG

3 *P. racemosa* flowers

3 *P. racemosa* fruit

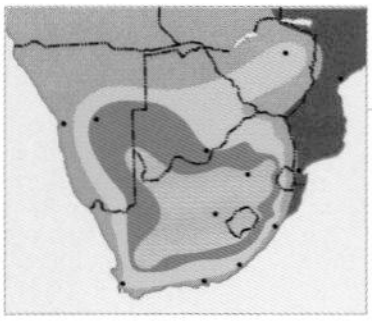

1 *Plinia cauliflora* (= *Myrciaria cauliflora*) MYRTACEAE

Jaboticaba, Brazilian Grape Tree; Jaboticaba

- Drought 2
- Spring
- Evergreen

OTHER LANGUAGES: Jaboticaba (Portuguese); Guapurú, Iba-purú (Spanish)

Brazil, Paraguay and Bolivia Medium-sized tree with a pyramidal crown; bark smooth, flaking; twigs hairless. Leaves with petiole hairy or hairless, 3–5mm long; blade 25–70 × 13–25mm, lance-shaped to elliptic or oblong; tip with a **small point**; surfaces glossy to dull. Inflorescences erect clusters of flowers **on old wood**. Flowers white; petals 3–4mm long and wide; stamens **many**, up to 7mm long. Fruit a **round, black**, hairless berry up to **30mm long** and in diameter, flesh white. Seeds buff.

Usually grown in private gardens as an ornamental and for its delicious fruit. Young trees bear for the first time after about six years. Recorded mainly in KwaZulu-Natal but also in South Africa's Gauteng and Western Cape provinces and in Zimbabwe.

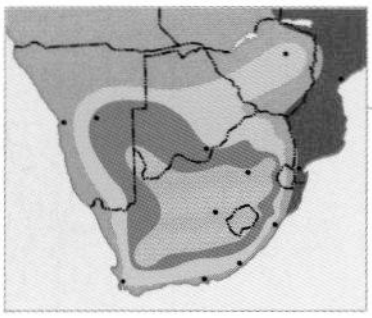

2 *Psidium cattleianum* (= *P. littorale* var. *longipes*) MYRTACEAE

Strawberry Guava; Aarbeikoejawel

- Drought 2
- Spring
- Evergreen

OTHER LANGUAGES: Goyavier-fraise (French); Erdbeerguave (German); Araçaleiro (Portuguese); Guayaba pequeña (Spanish)

Brazil Small, often multitrunked tree with a vase-shaped crown; bark **very smooth**, in various shades of grey, brown or greenish brown; buds and twigs **hairless**. Leaves with petiole hairless, 1–2mm long; blade 50–100 × 10–26mm, usually **widest beyond the middle, leathery**; tip and base narrowed. Inflorescences an erect, **single** flower; stalk hairless, 2–4mm long in flower, up to 8mm in fruit. Flowers with petals thin, about 6 × 4.5mm. Fruit a roundish, **red to purple** berry crowned with persistent sepals, 25–50mm long, about 50mm in diameter. Seeds buff to reddish brown, about 2.5 × 2 × 1.5mm.

Grown for its fruits, which are as delicious as common guavas and can be prepared in the same ways. Strawberry guava has become seriously invasive in many tropical countries, including South Africa, where it is a declared Category 1b invader.

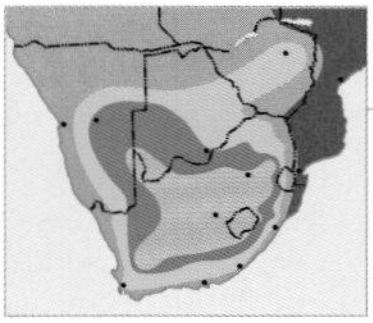

3 *Psidium guajava* MYRTACEAE

Guava; Koejawel

- Drought 2
- Spring
- Evergreen

OTHER LANGUAGES: Gawafa (Arabic); Jambu Padang (Bahasa Indonesia); Guaiaber (Catalan); Fan shi liu (Chinese); Goyavier (French); Echte Guave (German); Araçá-guaçu (Portuguese); Guayaba (Spanish)

Tropical America Small tree or large shrub with a rounded crown; bark **very smooth, flaking, pale brown**; buds hairy; twigs **square, hairy at first**. Leaves with petiole hairy, 37–62mm long; blade 70–150 × 40–70mm, egg-shaped to oblong; surface **sparsely hairy**. Inflorescences an erect, **single** flower; stalk 15–20mm long. Flowers bell-shaped; petals 4 or 5, egg-shaped, 12–20 × 6–10mm, white; stamens many, about 12mm long. Fruit a round to pear-shaped, yellow-green, **hairless berry 25–100mm** long and in diameter, flesh yellow to pink. Seeds buff, 3–3.5 × 1.5–2 × 1.5–2mm.

Widely grown for fruit, which can be consumed fresh, dried, cooked or as juice. The flowers produce copious nectar, from which bees make honey. Wood is hard and moderately strong; it is used for carpentry, turnery, tool handles and posts. Medicinal uses are recorded. Invasive in southern and East Africa, guava is a declared Category 3 (2 in plantations) invader in the Eastern Cape, KwaZulu-Natal, Mpumalanga, Limpopo and North West provinces of South Africa.

1 *P. cauliflora* leaves

1 *P. cauliflora* flowers

1 *P. cauliflora* fruit

GEOFF NICHOLS

2 *P. cattleianum* flowers

2 *P. cattleianum* fruit

BRAAM VAN WYK

3 *P. guajava* bark

3 *P. guajava* flower

BRAAM VAN WYK

3 *P. guajava* fruit

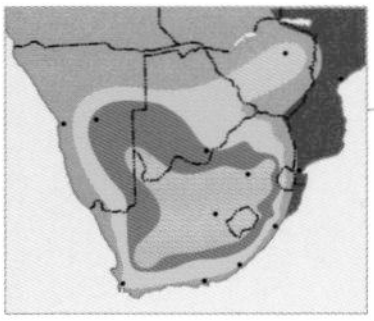

1 *Psidium guineense* MYRTACEAE
Brazilian Guava; Brasiliaanse Koejawel

- Drought 2
- Spring
- Evergreen

OTHER LANGUAGES: Goyavier du Brésil (French); Stachelbeerguave (German); Araçá do Campo (Portuguese); Guyaba Brava (Spanish)

Mexico and the Caribbean to Argentina Large shrub or small, rounded tree; bark **smooth, grey**; buds hairy; twigs **hairy, round**. Leaves with petiole hairy, 10–15mm long; blade 70–120 × 25–80mm, egg-shaped to elliptic; tip shortly pointed; lower surface **hairy**. Inflorescences erect, usually **3** flowers. Flowers white; petals about 15 × 10mm. Fruit a **densely hairy**, yellow-green, egg-shaped berry **15–30mm** long and in diameter. Seeds buff.

Grown for its fruit, which is usually cooked. A declared Category 1b invader in South Africa and known to be invasive in East Africa.

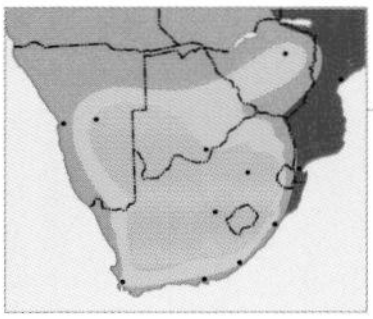

2 *Syncarpia glomulifera* (= *S. laurifolia*) MYRTACEAE
Turpentine Tree; Terpentynboom

- Drought 2
- Spring/Summer
- Evergreen

Eastern Australia Tall tree with a narrow crown; bark **fibrous**, not shed; twigs hairy, green or brown. Leaves opposite, forming pseudo-whorls of 4 leaves near branch tip; petiole hairy, **7–13mm long**; blade 70–100 × 25–45mm, egg-shaped or oblong, leathery; tip pointed; base rounded to squared; upper surface shiny, lower **grey-hairy**; margin **bent downwards**. Inflorescences erect, 7-flowered **fused heads**. Flowers white. Fruit woody, **fused groups of 7 capsules**, grey, 10–20mm in diameter.

Turpentine timber is hard, strong and generally insect-resistant, making it excellent for high-traffic flooring, marine construction and similar uses. Trees are suitable for providing shade and shelter in large parks and gardens and are recorded from forestry and private gardens in Mozambique, South Africa, Swaziland and Zimbabwe. Occasionally grown as windbreaks in banana plantations. Many trees seen in ill-chosen localities in some Durban suburbs.

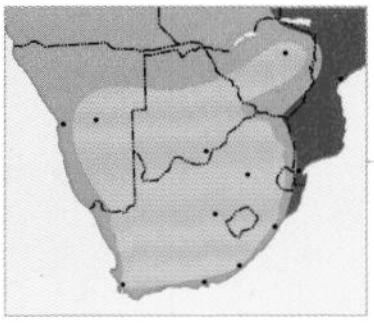

3 *Syzygium aromaticum* (= *Caryophyllus aromaticus*, *Eugenia aromatica*) MYRTACEAE
Cloves; Naeltjies

- Drought 2
- Spring
- Evergreen

OTHER LANGUAGES: Dingxiang (Chinese); Kruidnagel (Dutch); Clous de Girofle (French); Gewürznelke (German); Cravo-da-India (Portuguese); Árbol del clavo (Spanish); Karafuu (Swahili); Garn ploo (Thai); laung (Urdu)

Indonesia (Ternate, Tenasserim) Small tree with a narrow to pyramidal crown; bark **flaking**, forming thin strips; buds and twigs hairless. Leaves with petiole hairless, 20–30mm long; blade 70–130 × 30–60mm, **egg-shaped** to elliptic, with a **drip-tip**; base narrowed; margin **rolled inwards**. Inflorescences erect, about 50mm long; peduncle 3–4mm long. Flowers white or pink; petals round, about 6mm long and wide; stamens many, 5–10mm long. Fruit fleshy, egg-shaped, red, hairless, 25–40 × 12–15mm. Seeds 15–20mm long.

Cloves have been grown away from their natural habitat for some 200 years. The spice is the dried, unopened flower buds and is used in many cuisines around the world. Trees are sometimes grown to shade coconut groves. Medicinal uses are recorded both for whole cloves and the essential oil. In our region, there are clove trees in Durban Botanic Gardens and in Maputo. They are a major crop in Zanzibar.

1 *P. guineense* leaves

1 *P. guineense* flowers

1 *P. guineense* fruit

2 *S. glomulifera* flowers

2 *S. glomulifera* fruit

3 *S. aromaticum* flowers

3 *S. aromaticum* cloves

3 *S. aromaticum* fruit

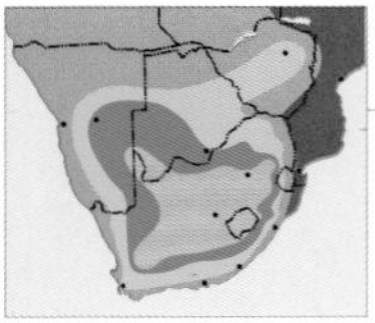

- Drought 2
- Spring
- Evergreen

1 *Syzygium cumini* (= *Eugenia cumini, E. jambolan, S. jambolanum*) MYRTACEAE

Jambolan, Java Plum; Jambolan

OTHER LANGUAGES: Jamblang (Bahasa Indonesia); Wu mo (Chinese); Jambolanier, Jamelonguier (French); Jambolanapflaume (German); Jamun (Hindi); Jamboran (Japanese); Azeitona da Terra (Portuguese); Jambolana, Ciruelo de Java (Spanish); Hwa (Thai)

Malaysia and Indonesia Small to medium-sized tree with a rounded crown; bark pale, peeling in thin scales; buds and twigs hairless. Leaves with petiole hairless, 10–20mm long; blade 75–150 × 35–70mm, **oblong**, with a **drip-tip**; base rounded; margin **flat**. Inflorescences erect, up to 100mm long. Flowers white; petals about 3.5mm long; stamens 4–5mm long. Fruit fleshy, ellipsoid, **purple or black**, hairless, 20–24 × 10–20mm.

Fruits are eaten fresh or are juiced or cooked. The flowers yield copious nectar, which bees make into high-quality honey. Usually grown for ornament and shade but jambolan has become invasive in warm places, including the USA (Hawaii and Florida). It has been declared a Category 1b invader in South Africa.

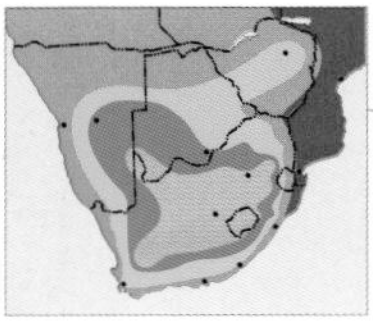

- Drought 2
- Spring
- Evergreen

2 *Syzygium jambos* (= *Eugenia jambos*) MYRTACEAE

Rose Apple, Malabar Plum; Jamboes

OTHER LANGUAGES: Putao (Chinese); Jambosier (French); Jambubaum, Rosenapfel (German); Gulab jamun (Hindi); Futo momo (Japanese); Jambo amarelo (Portuguese); Jambo amarillo (Spanish); Tampoy (Tagalog); Chomphuu namdokmai (Thai); Bô dào (Vietnamese)

Southeast Asia Small tree with an upright to rounded crown; bark smooth, adhering; buds and twigs hairless. Leaves with petiole hairless, 5–13mm long; blade **90–260** × 20–60mm, **lance-shaped** or oblong, with a **drip-tip**; base narrowed; margin flat. Inflorescences erect, 50–100mm long; peduncle 10–35mm long. Flowers white or pink; petals 4, widest beyond the middle, 15–18mm long and wide; stamens **15–40mm long**. Fruit fleshy, **pear-shaped**, **white to pink**, hairless, 25–50 × 25–40mm.

Invasive in several tropical countries, rose apple is a declared Category 3 invader in South Africa. It is grown for its fruit and it produces honey, timber, fuel and fodder as well. Medicinal uses are recorded.

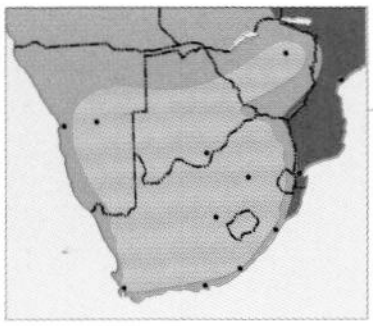

- Drought 2
- Spring
- Evergreen

3 *Syzygium malaccense* MYRTACEAE

Malacca Apple, Pomerac; Maleise Appel

OTHER LANGUAGES: Darsana (Bahasa Indonesia); Thabyo thabyang (Burmese); Ma liu jia putao (Chinese); Jambosier rouge (French); Malacca-Apfel (German); Malay jamun (Hindi); Maree futo momo (Japanese); Jambo vermelho (Portuguese); Manzana de Agua (Spanish); Makopang kalabo (Tagalog); Chom phu daeng (Thai); Cay dao (Vietnamese)

Malaysia, Indonesia and Vietnam Medium-sized to large tree with a broadly pyramidal crown; bark smooth, grey; twigs hairless. Leaves with petiole hairless, 8–20mm long; blade **90–260** × 60–130mm, **egg-shaped to elliptic**, with a drip-tip; base **broadly pointed to rounded**; margin flat. Inflorescences erect, up to 60mm long. Flowers **pink to red**; petals 6–17 × 6–8mm; stamens 10–35mm long. Fruit fleshy, egg-shaped, **red or white**, hairless, 30–80 × 25–75mm. Seeds midbrown, 16–20mm wide.

Grown for its fruit, which is usually eaten fresh but can be stewed. The timber is used for construction and other purposes. Medicinal uses are recorded. Malacca apple is invasive in some tropical countries but is rarely seen in our region.

1 *S. cumini* flowers

GEOFF NICHOLS

1 *S. cumini* fruit

BRAAM VAN WYK

2 *S. jambos* flowers

JOHN RICHFIELD, WIKIMEDIA COMMONS, CC BY SA 3.0

2 *S. jambos* fruit

CRISCO 1492, WIKIMEDIA COMMONS, CC BY SA 3.0

3 *S. malaccense* flower

FOREST AND KIM STARR

3 *S. malaccense* fruit

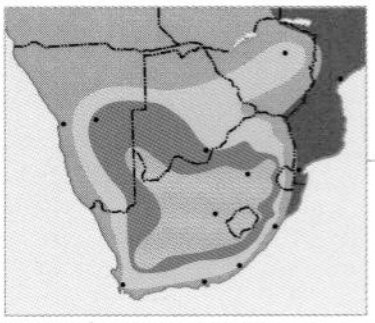

1 *Syzygium paniculatum* (= *Eugenia australis, E. paniculata*) MYRTACEAE

Magenta Lilly Pilly, Australian Brush-cherry, Australian Water-pear; Australiese Waterbessie, Australiese Waterpeer

- Drought 2
- Spring
- Evergreen

OTHER LANGUAGES: Aozhou putao (Chinese); Kirschmyrte (German)

Australia Large shrub or small tree with a pyramidal crown, often shaped by pruning; bark grey, smooth to rough, sometimes flaking; twigs hairless. Leaves with petiole hairless, 3–6mm long; blade 50–90 × 15–25mm, **lance-shaped**; tip long-pointed; base narrowed; surface **copper-coloured when young**. Inflorescences erect. Flowers white. Fruit fleshy, egg-shaped, **red, pink, purple** or white, hairless, 15–25mm in diameter.

Commonly grown for ornament, hedging or bonsai and reportedly becoming naturalised in parts of the Western Cape. The fruits are edible, with a pleasantly sour apple-like flavour; it is eaten fresh or made into jam.

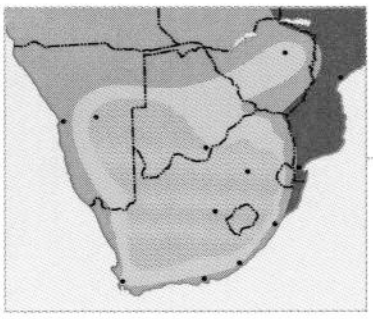

2 *Syzygium samarangense* (= *Eugenia alba, E. javanica, Myrtus samarangensis*) MYRTACEAE

Java Apple, Wax Apple; Javaanse Waterbessie

- Drought 2
- Spring
- Evergreen

OTHER LANGUAGES: Jambu semarang (Bahasa Indonesia); Yang pu tao (Chinese); Curacaose appel (Dutch); Pomme d'eau de Formose (French); Java-Apfel (German); Renbu (Japanese); Jambu air mawar (Malay); Manzana de Java (Spanish); Makopa (Tagalog); Chomphuu (Thai)

Myanmar to New Guinea Small tree with a spreading crown and often multiple trunks; bark grey, smooth; twigs hairless. Leaves with petiole hairless, **2–6mm long**; blade 60–210 × 20–100mm, elliptic, with a **long drip-tip**; base rounded. Inflorescences erect, 90–120mm long. Flowers white; petals 7–12mm long; stamens up to 22mm long. Fruit fleshy, **bell-shaped**, **red or white**, hairless, 25–50mm long. Seeds midbrown, 5–8mm wide.

Grown for its fruit, which is usually eaten fresh. The timber has been used in construction. Medicinal uses are recorded. In our region, usually seen as specimen trees in botanical gardens.

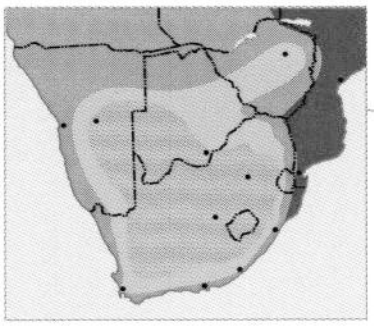

3 *Syzygium smithii* (= *Acmena smithii*) MYRTACEAE

Lilly Pilly; Lillie-pillie

- Drought 2
- Spring
- Evergreen

Northeastern Australia Medium-sized tree with an upright to rounded crown, can be pruned into a hedge; bark **rough**; twigs hairless. Leaves with petiole **hairless**, 4–5mm long; blade 35–90 × 15–40mm, lance- to egg-shaped; tip **pointed**; base rounded; lower surface **hairless**; margin sometimes wavy. Inflorescences erect, about 100mm long. Flowers white, individually small but showy in masses. Fruit a berry, round, hairless, white, pale pink or **purplish pink (mauve)**, 10–20mm in diameter.

Seen in our region as a specimen tree in botanical gardens, as a garden ornamental or a very dense, tall hedge. Recorded from Gauteng, KwaZulu-Natal and the Western Cape. The fruits are edible but not tasty. The timber has been used for construction and flooring.

BRAAM VAN WYK

1 *S. paniculatum* leaves and fruit

BRAAM VAN WYK

1 *S. paniculatum* flowers

BRAAM VAN WYK

1 *S. paniculatum* fruit

PINUS, WIKIMEDIA COMMONS, CC BY SA 3.0

2 *S. samarangense* flowers

2 *S. samarangense* fruit

3 *S. smithii* flowers

ERIC HUNT

3 *S. smithii* fruit

GROUP 23

Bushwillow group

Leaves simple, opposite; blade single- or pinnately veined, without secretory cavities; margin smooth. Interpetiolar stipules, scar or ridges absent. Latex absent.

See also Group 10: *Terminalia bellirica* (p.236); Group 12: *Gmelina arborea* (p.272); Group 19: *Duranta erecta* (p.282) and *Viburnum odoratissimum* (p.284); Group 22, in case secretory cavities in the leaves are obscure, or have been overlooked: particularly *Metrosideros excelsa* (p.296), *M. kermadecensis* (p.298) and *Plinia cauliflora* (p.300).

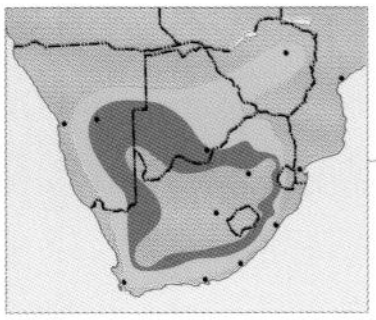

- Drought 2
- Spring
- Evergreen

1 *Acer oblongum*

ACERACEAE (OR SAPINDACEAE)

Evergreen Maple, Himalayan Maple, Kashmir Maple; Immergroenesdoring, Immergroenahorn

OTHER LANGUAGES: Feieshu (Chinese); Pharjanj (Hindi)

Himalayan foothills, Pakistan to China Small to medium-sized tree; bark rough; buds hairless; twigs hairless, reddish brown. Leaves with petiole hairless, 15–40mm long; blade 50–120 × 30–70mm, **egg-shaped or oblong, green** above, **bluish green** below, with a drip-tip; base rounded. Inflorescences erect or hanging. Flowers inconspicuous. Fruit a **pair of winged** nuts about 25mm long, diverging at 90–170°, spinning as they fall.

Juvenile leaves are three-lobed but adult leaves are not. Trees that retain their juvenile foliage throughout their lives and reproduce by seed are known. Uniquely among maples, this species keeps its green leaves over winter. The leaves are used as preservative packaging for crops such as apples and potatoes kept over winter and the timber is used for minor construction, agricultural tools and the like. Recorded only from Cape Town and Johannesburg in our region.

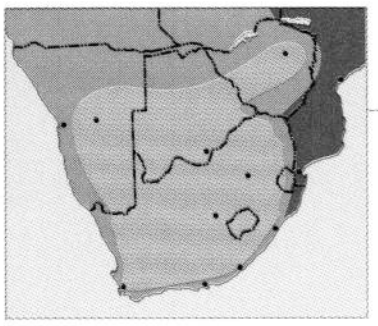

- Drought 2
- Spring
- Evergreen

2 *Anogeissus leiocarpa*

COMBRETACEAE

Ngalama Tree, African Birch; Ngalamaboom, Afrikaberk

OTHER LANGUAGES: Ngalama (Bambara); Bouleau d'Afrique (French)

Tropical Africa from Senegal to Ethiopia Medium-sized tree with a rounded or pyramidal crown; bark flaking **in rectangular pieces**; buds and twigs **hairy**. Leaves with petiole hairy, 1–6mm long; blade up to 75 × 40mm, lance-shaped to elliptic, **silky-hairy when young**. Inflorescences erect. Flowers small, white. Fruit a **2-winged**, reddish brown nut 4–10 × 6–11 × 2–3mm, in **cone-like** groups.

Grown in our region as specimen trees in private collections. In West Africa, various parts of the tree are used for dyeing and tanning. The wood is utilised for fuel. Various medicinal uses are recorded.

1 *A. oblongum*

1 *A. oblongum* leaves

1 *A. oblongum* fruit

2 *A. leiocarpa* leaves and young fruit

2 *A. leiocarpa* flowers

2 *A. leiocarpa* fruit

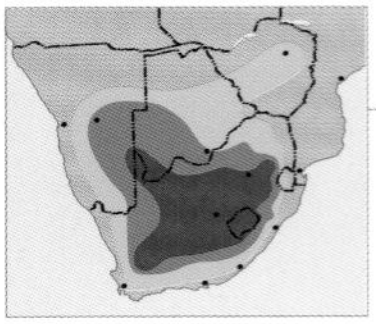

1 *Buxus sempervirens* BUXACEAE
Common Box(wood); Gewone Buksboom

- Drought 2
- Spring
- Evergreen

Europe to Turkey Small tree almost never seen in its natural, rounded shape, at least not in cultivation; bark whitish, smooth; twigs hairless, green, **square**. Leaves opposite, **in two ranks**; petiole hairless, **very short**; blade **12–25 × 5–12mm**, egg-shaped to oblong; cut leaves aromatic or ill-smelling; tip **indented**. Inflorescences erect. Flowers inconspicuous, greenish. Fruit a woody, brown, **3-lobed** capsule about 8mm long. Seeds black.

Box is the classic plant for topiary and clipping into formal hedges and knot gardens. Because it grows slowly, the wood is hard, heavy and dimensionally stable, making it well suited for printing blocks and instruments such as rulers and for engraving. It is much appreciated for turning and cabinet-making. All parts of the plant are poisonous and medicinal uses are recorded. Being inconspicuous, it is probably more widespread in our region than records would suggest.

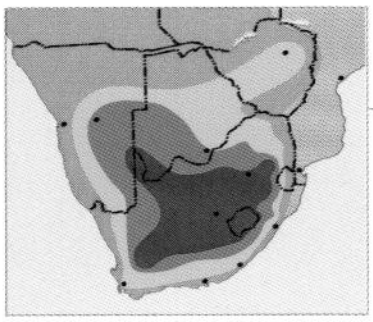

2 *Citharexylum spinosum* *(= C. quadrangulare)* VERBENACEAE
Fiddlewood; Vioolhout

- Drought 2
- Spring–Autumn
- Semi-deciduous

OTHER LANGUAGES: Bois Fidèle (French)

Florida (USA), the West Indies, Guyana, Suriname and Venezuela Medium-sized tree, usually with a **vase-shaped** crown and **bronzy autumn colours**; bark brown; buds hairless; twigs hairless, green or yellowish brown, **square**. Leaves with petiole hairless, 5–30mm long; blade 60–300 × 20–110mm, **elliptic**, with a very short drip-tip. Inflorescences erect or arched, 250–300mm long. Flowers appearing after the leaves, white, scented, tubular, oblong, up to 8 × 5–7mm, without markings. Fruit not seen in our region, fleshy, red or black, about 10mm long.

Trees do not set seed in South Africa, nor do they sucker. The mistaken idea that this species is invasive seems to come from the fact that it is very commonly planted (for windbreaks, shelter belts or ornament) and conspicuous in some places. However, in Hawaii, where it does set fruit, the species is invasive. The English common name comes not from any desirability in making musical instruments, but from a mangled form of the French name; correctly translated, it would be 'faithful wood'.

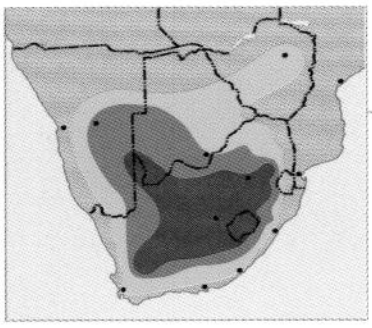

3 *Cornus florida* *(= Benthamia florida, Cynoxylum floridum)* CORNACEAE
Flowering Dogwood, Flowering Cornel; **Blomkornoelie**

- Drought 2
- Spring
- Deciduous

Eastern USA Small tree with a rounded or layered crown and **red to purple autumn colours**; bark **rough**, **flaking**; buds and twigs hairy. Leaves with petiole hairless, 15–25mm long, base enlarged; blade 75–125 × 50–80mm, egg-shaped to elliptic, with a broad drip-tip; lower surface whitish powdery. Inflorescences erect, appearing with the leaves; peduncle 30–40mm long; bracts **4**, 30–150 × 20–30mm, **white or pink**. Flowers individually **minute, inconspicuous**. Fruit **clustered**, fleshy, **red or black**, about 12 × 8mm. Seeds buff, 7–8 × 4–5mm wide and deep.

A spectacular garden ornamental with many cultivars, not as widely grown as it might be, apparently restricted in our area to Gauteng, KwaZulu-Natal and Eastern Cape. It is one of the first flowers of spring and possesses glorious autumn colours. The wood has been used for various purposes and is hard and heavy. Many parts of the plant are poisonous and medicinal uses are recorded.

1 *B. sempervirens* inflorescences; inset: flowers

1 *B. sempervirens* fruit

2 *C. spinosum*

2 *C. spinosum* flowers

3 *C. florida* flowerheads

3 *C. florida* fruit

1 *Cornus nuttallii* CORNACEAE

Pacific Dogwood, Mountain Dogwood; Bergkornoelie

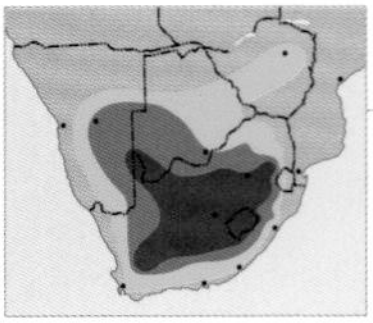

- Drought 2
- Spring
- Evergreen

Western USA Small tree with a rounded crown, whorled branches and **yellow to red autumn colours**; bark **smooth, adhering**; buds hairy; twigs hairy or hairless. Leaves with petiole hairy, 6–15mm long; blade 50–100 × 30–70mm, **egg-shaped**, widest below or beyond the middle; tip often with a sharp point; lower surface **hairy**. Inflorescences erect, 35–40mm long, appearing before the leaves; peduncle 28–32mm long; **bracts 6, white**, 27–44 × 25–35mm. Flowers **tiny, inconspicuous**. Fruit clustered, fleshy, **orange-red**, 8–12mm long. Seeds buff, 9–11 × 5.5–6.5mm wide and deep.

Pacific dogwood is said to be not as frost-hardy as its eastern North American relative, *C. florida* (see p.310). One easily spotted distinguishing character between the two is that *C. nuttallii* usually has six, rarely five, bracts surrounding the inflorescences, while *C. florida* almost always has four. Like those of *C. florida*, the fruits are separate and sometimes orange when ripe. The leaves go yellow and red before falling in autumn. One or two named cultivars are available overseas and there is a hybrid between this species and *C. florida* that is intermediate in hardiness between the two parent species. A good garden ornamental, seen far too rarely. Other uses much as for flowering dogwood (p.310). This is the provincial tree of British Columbia, Canada.

2 *Lagerstroemia speciosa* (= *L. reginae*) LYTHRACEAE

Queen's Crepe-myrtle, Giant Crepe Myrtle; Koningincrêpemirt, Koninginskubliesroos

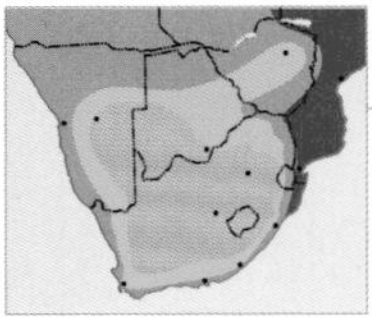

- Drought 2
- Spring
- Deciduous

OTHER LANGUAGES: Bungor Raya (Bahasa Indonesia); Da hua zi wei (Chinese); Jarul (Hindi); Reseda-flor-da-rainha (Portuguese); Banabá (Spanish); Kadali (Tamil); Dtà-bàek dam (Thai); Jarul (Urdu); Bằng lăng (Vietnamese)

China to Australia Medium-sized tree with a rounded to spreading crown; bark **very smooth**, flaking, pale grey; buds hairless; twigs hairless, **dark reddish brown**; stems occasionally with single, straight thorns. Leaves with petiole hairless, 5–10mm long; blade 80–300 × 30–100mm, elliptic or oblong, with a small drip-tip; base narrowed or rounded; surface **grey-green above, brownish below**. Inflorescences erect, 100–400mm long, appearing after the leaves. Flowers white, pink or purple; petals 6, round, 15–30 × 10–20mm. Fruit a roundish, woody capsule 15–25 × 12–23mm.

Widely grown for ornament in the tropics and subtropics. Recorded in our area from a few places in Zimbabwe and in South Africa's Limpopo, Mpumalanga and KwaZulu-Natal provinces. The wood is used for railway sleepers, construction and furniture. Medicinal uses are recorded. Compare *L. indica* (p.220).

1 *C. nuttallii* flowerhead

1 *C. nuttallii* leaves and flowerheads

1 *C. nuttallii* fruit

1 *C. nuttallii* old fruit

2 *L. speciosa* leaves

2 *L. speciosa* flowers

2 *L. speciosa* fruit

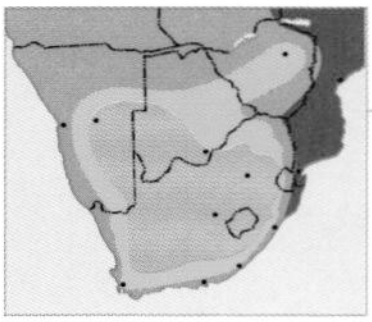

- Drought 2
- Spring
- Evergreen

1 *Lawsonia inermis* (= *L. alba*) LYTHRACEAE

Henna, Egyptian Privet; Henna

OTHER LANGUAGES: Al-Henna (Arabic); Henné (French); Hennastrauch (German); Mehendi (Hindi); Alfeneiro (Portuguese); Alheña (Spanish); Marudaani (Tamil)

North Africa and Southwestern Asia Large shrub or small tree with a vase-shaped to rounded crown, often shaped by pruning; bark smooth; buds and twigs hairless; branches occasionally ending in straight thorns. Leaves opposite, each pair **at right angles to preceding pair**; petiole **absent** or hairless, short, up to 4mm long; blade 13–67 × 5–27mm, **lance-shaped or elliptic**; base narrowing gradually. Inflorescences erect, 50–250mm long. Flowers white, pink or red; petals **4, kidney-shaped**, 1.5–2.5mm long. Fruit an almost round, purplish green capsule 4–6 × 5–8mm. Seeds 2–2.6mm long.

Overwhelmingly, the major use of this species is the preparation of a dyestuff from the leaves, as it has been for at least 6,000 years. In the Middle East and India, and in their diasporas, brides have their hands and feet painted in patterns probably little changed from those seen on wall paintings and statuettes from Ancient Egypt, Ugarit and Minoan Thera thousands of years old. Usually seen as specimen trees in botanical gardens in our area, with one commercial record from Zimbabwe.

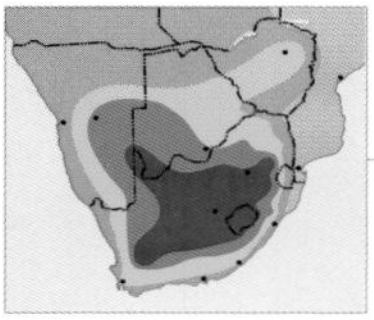

- Drought 2
- Spring
- Evergreen

2 *Ligustrum lucidum* OLEACEAE

Glossy Privet, Broad-leaved Privet, Chinese Privet; Blinkliguster, Chinese Liguster, Glansige Mondhout

OTHER LANGUAGES: Nuzhen (Chinese)

China Large shrub or small tree with a rounded crown, usually shaped by pruning; bark grey, rather smooth; buds and twigs hairless; young stems glossy; lenticels **white, warty, conspicuous**. Leaves with petiole hairless, 10–20mm long; blade **60–120** × 30–50mm, **lance**- to egg-shaped, with a drip-tip; upper surface glossy dark green. Inflorescences erect, on short shoots, 120–160mm long. Flowers small, white, scented. Fruit fleshy, round, **purple to black**, 6–8mm long.

Grown for ornament and hedges. The fruit, which are dispersed by birds, are very messy near buildings, staining walls, patios or walkways purple-black. Invasive in many parts of the world and a declared Category 3 invader in the Free State, Gauteng and Northern Cape, 1b in the rest of South Africa.

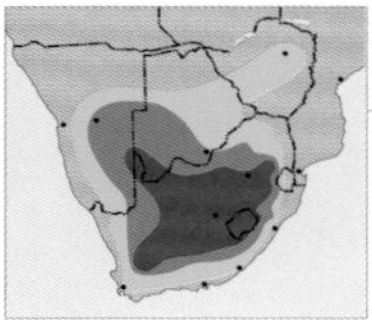

- Drought 2
- Spring
- Evergreen

3 *Ligustrum ovalifolium* OLEACEAE

Oval-leaved Privet; Ovaalblaarliguster, Kaliforniese Liguster

Japan Small tree or large shrub, crown naturally elliptic to rounded, but often shaped by pruning; buds and twigs hairless; young twigs dull; lenticels **smooth, pale**, conspicuous. Leaves with petiole hairless, 2–4mm long; blade **25–50** × 15–30mm, egg-shaped; tip and base narrowed. Inflorescences erect, 40–100mm long. Flowers white, small. Fruit fleshy, black, egg-shaped, about 6mm long.

Said to be one of the world's most popular hedging plants. Invasive in parts of the USA and our region and a declared Category 3 invader in the Free State, Gauteng and Northern Cape, 1b in the rest of South Africa. The cultivar 'Aureum' has variegated leaves. It is commonly known as the golden privet, its oval leaves rich yellow with green centres.

GEOFF NICHOLS

1 *L. inermis* flowers

SWAPAN PHOTOGRAPHY / SHUTTERSTOCK

1 *L. inermis* fruit

2 *L. lucidum* flowers

2 *L. lucidum* fruit

P. GARIN

3 *L. ovalifolium* flowers

BRAAM VAN WYK

3 *L. ovalifolium* 'Aureum'

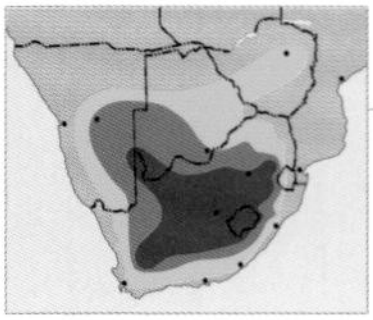

- Drought 2
- Winter–Spring
- Evergreen

1 *Ligustrum sinense* OLEACEAE
Chinese Privet; Chinese Liguster

OTHER LANGUAGES: Xiaola (Chinese)

China and Vietnam Large shrub or small tree, naturally with a rounded crown, but often shaped by pruning; buds hairless; twigs **hairy**, greenish brown; lenticels **warty, conspicuous**, pale. Leaves with petiole **hairy**, 2–4mm long; blade 20–60 × 10–30mm, elliptic; tip rounded; base narrowed or rounded; lower surface **hairy**. Inflorescences erect, 40–80mm long. Flowers small, white. Fruit fleshy, round, black, 4–5mm long and in diameter.

A common hedging plant, invasive in several countries and a declared Category 3 invader in the Free State, Gauteng and Northern Cape, 1b in the rest of South Africa.

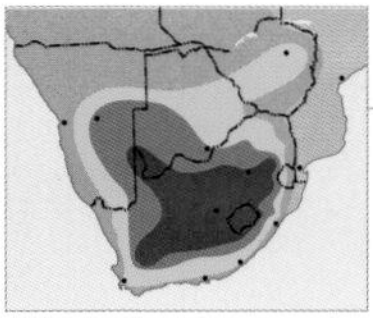

- Drought 2
- Spring
- Evergreen

2 *Olea europaea* OLEACEAE
Olive; Olyf

OTHER LANGUAGES: Zeitoun (Arabic); Maslina (Bulgarian); Olive commun (French); Ölbaum (German); Elia (Greek); Zayit (Hebrew); Oliva (Italian); Azeitona (Portuguese); Aceituna (Spanish); Zeytin (Turkish)

Mediterranean region Small to medium-sized tree with a generally rounded crown and often **gnarled** trunk; buds scaly, yellowish green; twigs hairless, slender. Leaves with petiole hairless, 3–10mm long; blade 30–80 × 8–20mm, **narrowly elliptic**; tip and base narrowed; surface **grey-green above, silvery below**. Inflorescences erect, 10–60mm long. Flowers small, white; petals **4**; stamens **2**. Fruit fleshy, ellipsoid, purple to black, hairless, **20–35 × 10–20mm**.

Archaeological finds in Israel indicate that olives have been eaten for some 20,000 years and cultivated for about a quarter of that time. Mycenaean Linear B tablets from 3,500 years ago include a word for olives (transcribed *e-lai-wa*) that is a direct ancestor of the modern Greek name and the word for oil in most European languages. Olives must be treated before they are eaten, to remove a bitter glycoside; they can be pickled, salted or pressed for oil. Olive wood is hard, durable and highly esteemed by craftsmen. The list of medicinal uses is almost endless.

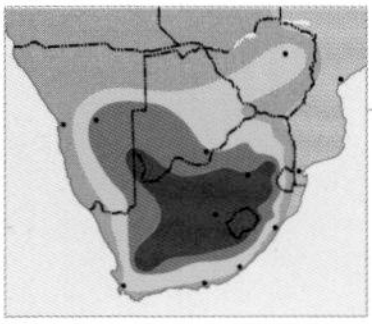

- Drought 2
- Summer
- Deciduous

3 *Punica granatum* PUNICACEAE
Pomegranate; Granaat

OTHER LANGUAGES: Roman (Arabic); Noor (Armenian); Delima (Bahasa Indonesia); Shi liu (Chinese); Anaar (Farsi, Urdu); Grenadier (French); Granatapfelbaum (German); Rodi (Greek); Rimon (Hebrew); Anaar (Hindi); Romãzeira (Portuguese); Granat (Russian); Nar (Turkish)

Turkey to Central Asia Large shrub or small tree with a **vase-shaped to weeping** crown; buds and twigs hairless, the latter sometimes ending in thorns. Leaves with petiole hairless, 2–4.5mm long; blade 25–80 × 8–25mm, **widest beyond the middle**; tip **rounded**, usually ending in a short, **spine-like** point; base narrowed. Inflorescences an erect, single flower. Flowers red; petals 15–20mm long. Fruit roundish, with a brown, rarely black, leathery rind, 50–80 × 60–120mm. Seeds individually surrounded by **red, edible, juicy flesh**.

Usually a garden ornamental, grown for hedging, flowers and fruit, the last sometimes expensively found in greengrocers. The fruit has been treasured in the Middle East since the Early Bronze Age, about 5,000 years ago. It is widely used in cooking and in the long time it has been known, it has attracted at least its fair share of symbolism and medicinal uses. Naturalised in South Africa.

P. GARIN

1 *L. sinense* flowers

DOUG BECKERS

1 *L. sinense* fruit

JAVIER MARTIN, WIKIMEDIA COMMONS, PUBLIC DOMAIN

2 *O. europaea* flowers

B. J. SCHOENMAKERS, WIKIMEDIA COMMONS, PUBLIC DOMAIN

2 *O. europaea* fruit

3 *P. granatum* leaves

BRAAM VAN WYK

3 *P. granatum* flower

BRAAM VAN WYK

3 *P. granatum* fruit

GROUP 23 Bushwillow group

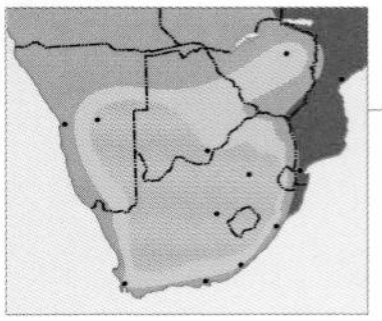

- Drought 2
- Spring
- Evergreen

1 *Santalum album* SANTALACEAE

Sandalwood, Indian Sandalwood, White Sandalwood; Sandelhout

OTHER LANGUAGES: Cendana (Bahasa Indonesia); Tan xiang (Chinese); Santal de l'Inde (French); Echter Sandelholzbaum (German); Sandal (Hindi); Sândalo (Portuguese); Chandanam (Sanskrit); Sándalo (Spanish); Chandanam (Tamil)

Indomalesia Upright to sprawling tree with a narrow to rounded crown, hemiparasitic, attaching to roots of host plants; bark reddish brown to dark grey; twigs hairless. Leaves with petiole hairless, 50–150mm long; blade 40–80 × 20–40mm, oblong, with a **drip-tip**; base rounded; margin **wavy**. Inflorescences erect. Flowers **reddish**. Fruit round, fleshy, red or black, about **10mm long and in diameter**.

Grown for its valuable timber, used for carving and ornaments and for essential oil. In our region, seen as specimen trees in botanical gardens (Durban). The sawdust is a component of incense, particularly Indian formulations. This aromatic tree has many symbolic and ethnomedicinal uses.

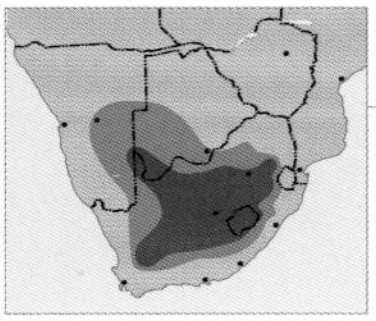

- Drought 2
- Spring
- Deciduous

2 *Syringa vulgaris* OLEACEAE

Common Lilac; Gewone Sering

OTHER LANGUAGES: Jorgovan (Croatian); Lilas (French); Flieder (German); Lillà (Italian)

Balkan Peninsula Narrow, upright shrub or small tree, usually **suckering** and forming thickets; buds and twigs hairless. Leaves with petiole hairless, 18–30mm long; blade 40–90 × 30–50mm, **egg-shaped**, with a drip-tip; base **heart-shaped** or squared; surface dull. Inflorescences erect, 100–200mm long. Flowers scented, white or lilac; tube 8–12mm long, lobes **4**, elliptic, 4–5mm long; stamens **2**. Fruit an ellipsoid **capsule** 8–12mm long.

Grown for ornament in western European gardens since about 1600. State flower of New Hampshire, USA, where it is naturalised. An essential oil is distilled from the flowers and medicinal uses are recorded. Scattered in Lesotho and South Africa but not recommended because of its suckering habit.

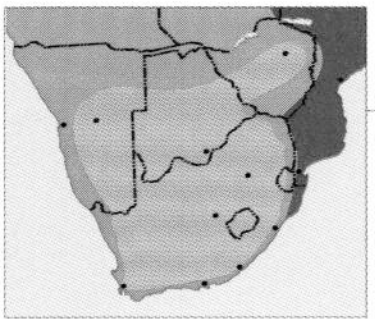

- Drought 2
- Summer
- Deciduous

3 *Tectona grandis* LAMIACEAE

Indian Teak; Indiese Kiaat

OTHER LANGUAGES: Shajarat al saj (Arabic); Deleg (Bahasa Indonesia); Segun (Bengali); Teca (Catalan, Portuguese, Spanish); You mu (Chinese); Arbre à Teck (French); Tiek (German); Sagun (Hindi); Saka (Sanskrit); Teekka (Sinhalese); Dalanang (Tagalog); Potut tēkku (Tamil); Dton maai sak (Thai)

India to Laos Tall tree with a rounded to spreading crown; bark brown, narrowly fissured; buds and twigs **hairy**. Leaves with petiole **hairy, very short**, up to 10mm long; blade **160–700 × 140–440mm**, egg-shaped to elliptic, with a drip-tip; base narrowed to heart-shaped; lower surface **densely hairy**. Inflorescences erect, about 400mm long, appearing after the leaves. Flowers cup-shaped, **small, white**. Fruit thinly fleshy, yellow-brown, round, up to 15 × 15mm.

One of the finest timbers there is, teak is now more often plantation-grown than wild harvested. The wood is so oily that its sawdust can be rubbed onto finished pieces to oil and preserve them. Because of this, it has important uses in marine and dry-land construction, garden furniture and much more. In our region, it is seen as specimen trees in Durban Botanic Gardens and Maputo and it was once tried as a plantation tree in Limpopo.

1 *S. album* flowers

1 *S. album* fruit

2 *S. vulgaris* leaves

2 *S. vulgaris* flowers

2 *S. vulgaris* fruit

3 *T. grandis* flowers and young fruit

FOREST AND KIM STARR

3 *T. grandis* fruit

GROUP 24

Quininetree group

Leaves simple, in whorls of 3 or more. Latex present.

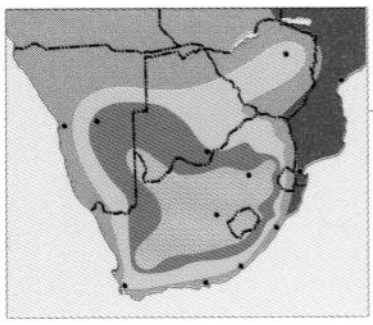

1 *Allamanda blanchetii* (= *A. violacea*)

APOCYNACEAE

Purple Allamanda; Pers-allamanda

- Drought 2
- Spring
- Evergreen

Brazil Large shrub or small tree with a rounded crown; buds hairless; twigs hairy at first but soon hairless, **often climbing**; latex **white**. Leaves in whorls of 2–5; petiole hairless, 8–12mm long; blade 45–120 × 18–55mm, lance-shaped to oblong, with a drip-tip; base rounded; surface **hairy, more so below**; margin **flat**. Inflorescences erect. Flowers tubular, 25–70mm long; lobes 5, **egg-shaped**, 18–45 × 21–40mm, **pink or purple**, without markings. Fruit a **spiny** capsule 45–65 × 35–40mm. Seeds about 35mm long, winged.

Grown as a garden ornamental and recorded from Zimbabwe and South Africa's Limpopo and KwaZulu-Natal provinces in our region. All parts are poisonous and medicinal uses are recorded.

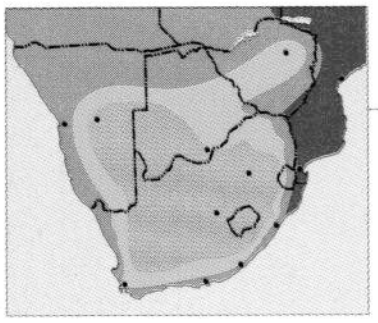

2 *Allamanda cathartica*

APOCYNACEAE

Golden Trumpet; Gouetrompet

- Drought 2
- Spring
- Evergreen

OTHER LANGUAGES: Canario Amarillo, Copa de Oro (Spanish)

Mexico to Brazil and the Caribbean Shrub, small or medium-sized tree or climber; buds hairless; twigs hairless, climbing; latex **white**. Leaves in whorls of 3–5 per node; petiole hairless, up to 5mm long or absent; blade 60–120 × 25–50mm, egg-shaped, widest beyond or below the middle, with a drip-tip; base narrowed; surface glossy above, hairless or hairy below; margin **rolled inwards**. Inflorescences erect; peduncle 10–40mm long. Flowers **funnel-shaped, yellow**, without markings; tube 43–95mm long, lobes 5, these 15–50mm long and wide. Fruit a **spiny**, grey-brown capsule 10–40 × 24–26mm. Seeds winged, 13–16 × 8–10mm.

Quite commonly grown ornamental and the official flower of Canóvanas, Puerto Rico. All parts of the plant are poisonous. Medicinal uses are recorded. It is invasive in northern Queensland, Australia. The cultivar 'Hendersonii' has larger flowers than usual. 'Williamsonii' is a smaller shrub with hairy twigs.

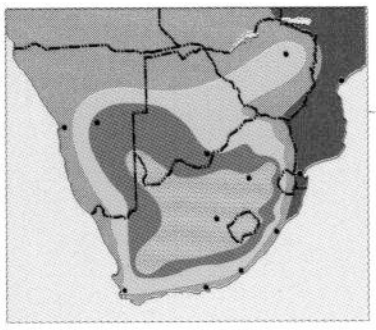

3 *Alstonia venenata*

APOCYNACEAE

Poison Devil-tree; Gifsatansboom

- Drought 2
- Summer
- Evergreen

OTHER LANGUAGES: Raja-adana (Sanskrit); Sinnappalai (Tamil)

India Small tree with a rounded crown; buds and twigs hairless; latex **white**. Leaves in whorls of 4–6; petiole hairless, about 15mm long; blade **100–200** × 10–30mm, **widest beyond the middle**; tip and base narrowing gradually; lower surface **hairless**; margin smooth. Inflorescences erect; peduncle up to 50mm long. Flowers tubular, scented, white; tube **about 25mm long**, lobes 5, oblong, about 15 × 5mm. Fruit a pair of pods **80–130mm** long, about 8mm in diameter. Seeds 8–10mm long.

Recorded in our region from gardens in Gauteng and Mpumalanga provinces and in Zimbabwe. Medicinal uses are recorded but this plant is very poisonous.

1 *A. blanchetii* flower

1 *A. blanchetii* fruit

2 *A. cathartica* flowers

2 *A. cathartica* fruit

DAVID HARTUNG

3 *A. venenata* leaves

DAVID HARTUNG

3 *A. venenata* flowers

DAVID HARTUNG

3 *A. venenata* fruit

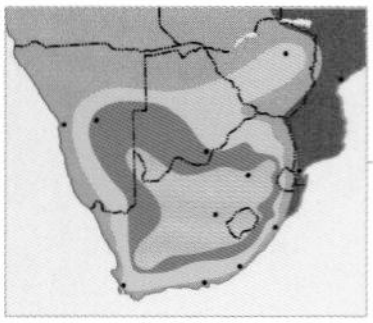

- Drought 2
- Winter
- Evergreen

1 *Euphorbia leucocephala* EUPHORBIACEAE

Snow on the Mountain, Little Christmas Flower, White Poinsettia; Sneeu-op-die-berge

OTHER LANGUAGES: Flor-de-maio, Cabeleira de Velho (Portuguese); Pascuita (Spanish)

Central America **Large shrub or small tree** with a spreading crown; twigs hairless, **green**; latex **white**. Leaves in whorls of **3**; petiole hairless; blade 30–80mm **long, lance-shaped to oblong**. Inflorescences erect; bracts **white**, widest beyond the middle. Flowers **small**, white. Fruit a **3-angled**, hairless capsule about 7 × 8mm.

Widely grown as a garden ornamental in South Africa and Zimbabwe and now declared a Category 1b invader in the former. The latex is poisonous and irritant. Not to be confused with *E. marginata*, a rather similar-looking but low-growing annual plant also called 'snow on the mountain'.

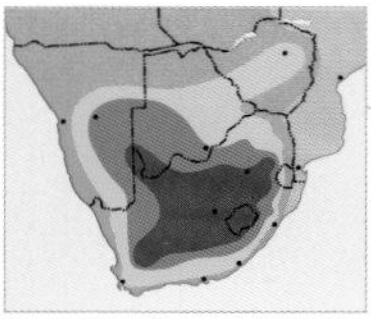

- Drought 3
- Spring
- Evergreen

2 *Nerium oleander* (= *N. indicum*) APOCYNACEAE

Oleander, Rosebay; Selonsroos, Ceylonsroos

OTHER LANGUAGES: Jia zhu tao (Chinese); Kaner (Hindi); Oleandria (Italian); Loendro (Portuguese); Adelfa (Spanish)

Morocco to China, but may be naturalised in much of this range Large shrub or small tree with a rounded crown; buds and twigs hairless, the latter blue-green, without visible lenticels; latex **clear**. Leaves in whorls of **3**; petiole hairless, 3–10mm long, with milky sap in fresh petiole; blade 100–300 × 10–35mm, **narrowly oblong**; tip drawn out to a point; base gradually narrowed; surface dull, hairless; margin **rolled inwards**. Inflorescences erect. Flowers **tubular**, white, yellow, pink or red; tube 12–22mm long, lobes 5, obovate, 13–30 × 8–25mm. Fruit **a pair of smooth**, brown, spindle-shaped pods 75–175 × 10–13mm. Seeds midbrown, 4–7 × 1.5–2 × 1mm, with a **tuft of hairs 9–12mm long**.

This is one of the most toxic plants commonly grown in gardens and all parts of the plant are deadly poisonous. Recorded uses include rat poison, parasiticide and insecticide. Medicinal uses are recorded. Plants naturalise in suitable areas and the species is a declared Category 1b invader in South Africa.

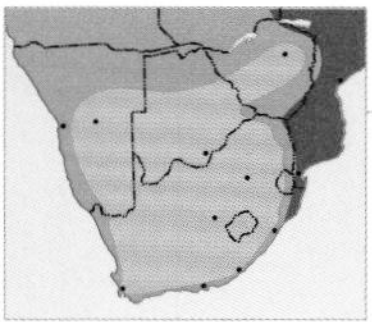

- Drought 2
- Spring
- Evergreen

3 *Ochrosia elliptica* APOCYNACEAE

Bloodhorn, Elliptic Yellowwood, Kopsia, Mangrove Ochrosia; Rooihoring

OTHER LANGUAGES: Gu cheng mei gui shu (Chinese)

Northeastern Australia and New Caledonia Small tree with a spreading crown; buds and twigs hairless; lenticels warty and raised; latex **white**. Leaves in whorls of **4**; petiole hairless, **5–11mm long**; blade up to 170 × 70mm, widest at or beyond the middle, with a **drip-tip**; base narrowed; surface dark green above, pale green below. Inflorescences erect. Flowers tubular, creamy, without markings; tube 5–6mm long, lobes 5, 6–7 × 1.2–1.8mm. Fruit **fleshy, red, elongated**, 50–60 × 20–30mm, borne **in pairs**.

Grown as a garden ornamental in Zimbabwe and South Africa's KwaZulu-Natal, although the fruits (and probably other parts as well) are poisonous. Medicinal uses are recorded.

1 *E. leucocephala* flowers

1 *E. leucocephala* fruit

BRAAM VAN WYK

2 *N. oleander* flower

JÚLIO REIS, WIKIMEDIA COMMONS, CC BY SA 3.0

2 *N. oleander* dehisced fruit and seeds

CERLIN NG

3 *O. elliptica* flower

BILL HIGHAM

3 *O. elliptica* fruit

GROUP 25 Wild-almond group

Leaves simple, in whorls of 3 or more. Latex absent.

1 *Clerodendrum trichotomum* LAMIACEAE

Harlequin Glorybower; Harlekynboom

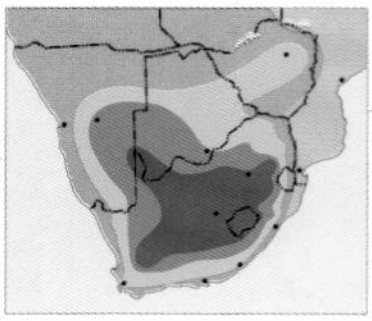

- Drought 2
- Spring
- Deciduous

OTHER LANGUAGES: Haizhou changshan (Chinese)

India, Indochina, China, Taiwan, Korea and Japan Small tree with a rounded to spreading crown; twigs **hairy**; lenticels **warty and raised**, conspicuous. Leaves in whorls of **3**; petiole hairy, **25–100mm long**; blade 100–200 × 50–100mm, egg-shaped, with a drip-tip; base broadly pointed to squared; surface **hairy**; margin smooth or scalloped-toothed. Inflorescences erect, 80–180mm long; peduncle 30–60mm long. Flowers with calyx tubular, lobes 5, triangular, **green, turning red or reddish** in fruit; corolla tubular, white, without markings, lobes 5, oblong, 5–15 × 3–5mm. Fruit fleshy, roundish, ripening from **white through bright to dark blue**, hairless, 5–8 × 6–8mm.

Occasionally grown as a garden ornamental for its fragrant flowers and ornamental berries. Recorded from Gauteng, KwaZulu-Natal and the Eastern Cape in our region. The leaves produce a peanut butter odour when crushed.

2 *Macadamia integrifolia* PROTEACEAE

Smooth-shelled Macadamia, Australian Nut, Queensland Nut; Gladdedopmakadamia, Queenslandneut

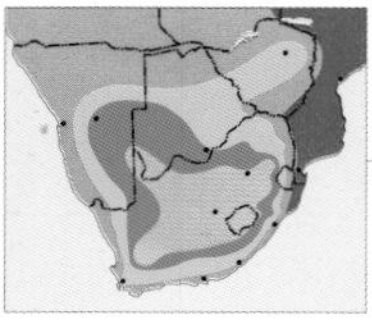

- Drought 2
- Summer–Winter
- Evergreen

OTHER LANGUAGES: Aozhou jianguo (Chinese); Macadamia à coque lisse (French); Glattschalige Macadamia (German); Macadâmia, Nogueira de Australia (Portuguese); Macadamia (Spanish)

Queensland, Australia Medium-sized tree with a rounded crown; bark grey, **narrowly fissured**; twigs hairless. Leaves **in whorls of 3**; petiole hairless, 6–18mm long; blade 65–140 × 20–65mm, narrowly elliptic to oblong; tip **rounded**; base narrowed; margin wavy, spiny in juveniles, **smooth in adult trees**. Inflorescences **hanging, 85–250mm long**. Flowers **white to creamy**, tubular, curled. Fruit a roundish, **smooth**, woody, brown pod 30–40 × 20–45mm. Seeds whitish to buff, 25–31 × 24–30mm.

Seeds are such good eating as to be considered among the world's finest table nuts, though the shells are very hard and difficult to open. The nuts are eaten raw, roasted and salted, or in various forms of confectionery. Trees can also be used for timber. Grown in orchards for the fruit and occasionally in home gardens in South Africa and Zimbabwe.

1 *C. trichotomum* flowers

1 *C. trichotomum* fruit

1 *C. trichotomum* flowers

2 *M. integrifolia* leaves

2 *M. integrifolia* flowers

2 *M. integrifolia* flowers

2 *M. integrifolia* fruit

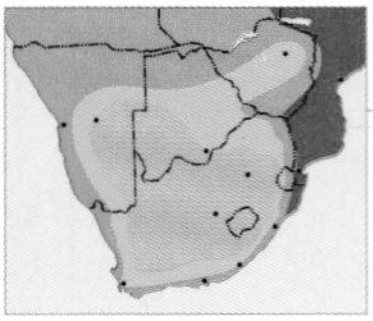

1 *Macadamia ternifolia*

PROTEACEAE

Gympie Nut, Maroochy Nut, Small-fruited Queensland Nut; Gympie-neut

- Drought 2
- Winter–Spring
- Evergreen

Eastern Australia Small tree with a cylindrical to pyramidal crown; bark smooth; twigs hairless; lenticels **warty, conspicuous**. Leaves **in whorls of 3**; petiole hairless, 4–10mm long; blade 90–125 × 20–35mm, widest beyond the middle; tip **pointed, with a spine**; base gradually narrowed; margin toothed, sometimes wavy. Inflorescences **erect**, 50–180mm long. Flowers **pink**, tubular, curled. Fruit a brown, woody, smooth, hairless pod 14–22 × 13–22mm. Seeds buff, about 16 × 12mm.

The seeds are not edible because the kernel is bitter and releases cyanide. Nevertheless, it is occasionally grown in gardens and has been recorded in Mozambique, South Africa and Zimbabwe.

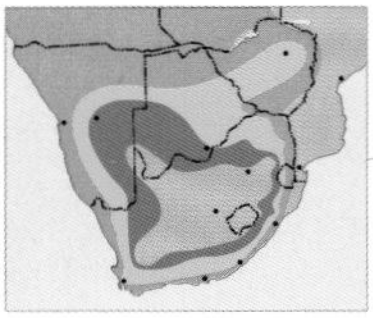

2 *Macadamia tetraphylla*

PROTEACEAE

Rough-shelled Macadamia Nut, Australian Nut, Queensland Nut; Skurwedopmakadamia, Queenslandneut

- Drought 2
- Spring
- Evergreen

OTHER LANGUAGES: Siye aozhou jianguo (Chinese); Macadamia à coque ridée (French); Rauhschalige Macadamia (German); Nogueira-macadâmia (Portuguese); Nogal de Australia (Spanish)

Eastern Australia Small to medium-sized tree with a rounded to pyramidal crown; bark smooth, brown; twigs, hairless, with conspicuous lenticels. Leaves **in whorls of 4**; petiole hairless, up to 4mm long **or absent**; blade 85–275 × 20–60mm, **lance-shaped**; tip more or less rounded; base narrowed to squared; lower surface sometimes sparsely hairy; margin **toothed**. Inflorescences **hanging**, 55–380mm long. Flowers **white or pink**, tubular, curled. Fruit a **rough**, woody, brown pod 24–50 × 15–50mm. Seeds midbrown, 26–50 × 16–24mm.

The seeds are good eating and are so similar to those of *M. integrifolia* (p.324) that they are also grown, sold and used as macadamia nuts. Usually grown commercially but occasionally seen as a garden ornamental, recorded in Zimbabwe and South Africa.

1 *M. ternifolia* leaves

1 *M. ternifolia* flowers

1 *M. ternifolia* fruit

2 *M. tetraphylla*

2 *M. tetraphylla* leaves

2 *M. tetraphylla* flowers

2 *M. tetraphylla* fruit

GROUP 26

Bauhinia group

Leaves simple, bilobed.

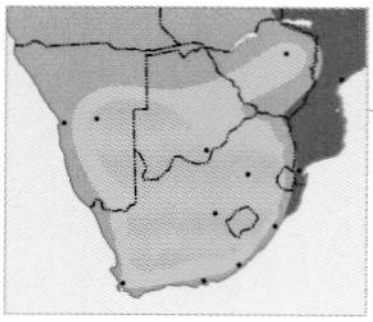

- Drought 2
- Winter–Spring
- Evergreen

1 *Bauhinia × blakeana*

FABACEAE

Hong Kong Orchid Tree, Fragrant Orchid Tree; **Geurorgideeboom**

OTHER LANGUAGES: Honghua yangtijia (Chinese); Árbol orquídea de Hong Kong (Spanish)

An apparently natural hybrid from Hong Kong Small tree with a rounded to spreading crown; bark brown, rough; buds and twigs hairy; lenticels **warty, conspicuous**. Leaves with petiole hairy, 20–50mm long; blade **75–150mm long and wide, oblong** to round; notch between lobes **reaching about a third of the way** to the base; tip of each lobe rounded; base heart-shaped, with 8–10 main veins from the base. Inflorescences erect, about 200mm long. Flowers **purple**; petals 5, free, with darker purple honey guides, 50–80 × 25–30mm; stamens 5 or 6. Fruit not produced.

Floral emblem of Hong Kong, stylised flowers appearing on their flag, coins and coat of arms. Widely grown as a garden ornamental, this plant cannot become invasive as it is completely sterile and must necessarily be reproduced vegetatively, with human intervention.

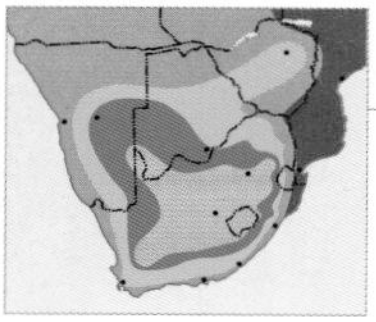

- Drought 2
- Spring
- Evergreen

2 *Bauhinia forficata* (= *B. candicans*)

FABACEAE

Thorny Orchid Tree; Doringorgideeboom

OTHER LANGUAGES: Pata de Vaca (Portuguese); Árbol orquidea (Spanish)

Brazil Small tree with a rounded to spreading crown; buds and twigs hairy; stems with **paired, hooked thorns**; lenticels **smooth, minute**. Leaves with petiole hairy, 15–20mm long; blade **40–90 × 30–80mm**, elliptic to round; notch between lobes **reaching about two thirds of the way** to the base; tip of each lobe rounded; base squared to heart-shaped, with 9–11 main veins from the base; lower surface **hairy**. Inflorescences erect. Flowers **white**; petals 5, free, 80–120 × 11–35mm. Fruit a pod 100–200 × 15–20mm.

Grown as a garden ornamental in Mozambique, South Africa and Zimbabwe, with potential for highway median strips and similar localities. Medicinal uses are recorded.

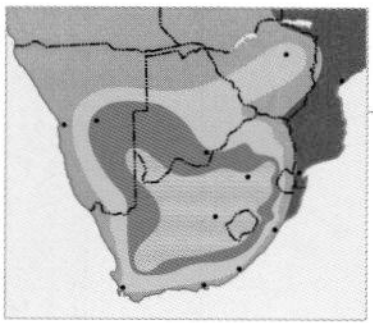

- Drought 2
- Spring
- Evergreen

3 *Bauhinia monandra*

FABACEAE

Madagascar Orchid Tree, Butterfly Flower; **Madagaskarorgideeboom**

OTHER LANGUAGES: Bauhinia à fleurs roses (French); Casco de Mulo (Portuguese); Pata de Vaca (Spanish)

Madagascar Small tree with a spreading crown; buds and twigs **hairless**; lenticels warty, conspicuous. Leaves with petiole **hairless**, 22–60mm long; blade **46–155 × 49–148mm**, egg-shaped; notch between lobes **reaching about halfway to the base**; tip rounded or bluntly pointed; base rounded to squared, with 11 or 12 main veins from the base; lower surface **hairless**. Inflorescences erect, about 60mm long. Flowers pale yellowish at first, pink later; petals 5, free, 35–50mm long, **one of the petals densely speckled pink-purple**. Fruit a brown pod 159–211 × 15–25mm. Seeds black, about 8–10 × 6 × 2–3mm.

Grown in our region as specimen trees in Harare, Johannesburg and Durban, elsewhere as a garden ornamental.

1 *B.* × *blakeana* leaves

BRAAM VAN WYK

1 *B.* × *blakeana* flower

2 *B. forficata* flowers

MARCELO MOYANO, WIKIMEDIA COMMONS, PUBLIC DOMAIN

2 *B. forficata* fruit

3 *B. monandra* flowers

TOBY HUDSON, WIKIMEDIA COMMONS, CC BY SA 3.0

3 *B. monandra* fruit

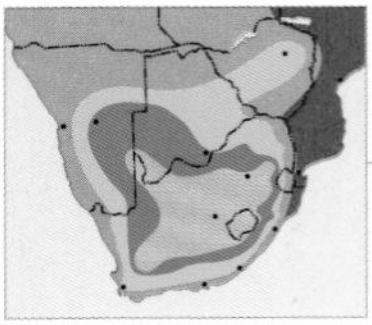

- Drought 2
- Autumn–Winter
- Evergreen

1 *Bauhinia purpurea* FABACEAE

Butterfly Orchid Tree, Indian Camel's Foot; Skoenlapperorgideeboom, Indiese Kameelspoor

OTHER LANGUAGES: Kaniar (Hindi); Pie de cabra (Portuguese); Pata de Vaca (Spanish)

India to China and Malaysia Small tree with a rounded to spreading crown; buds and twigs **hairy**; lenticels smooth, minute. Leaves with petiole **hairless**, 30–45mm long; blade **70–150 × 75–120mm**, elliptic to round; notch between lobes **extending about a quarter of the way** to the base; tip rounded; base squared to heart-shaped. Inflorescences erect, 20–50mm long. Flowers **pink to purple**; petals 5, free, non-overlapping, 40–65 × 15–25mm. Fruit a woody, brown pod up to 250 × 25mm. Seeds dark brown, 10–14 × 7–9mm.

Widely grown as a garden ornamental and reportedly invasive in parts of our region. It is now a declared Category 1b invader in the Eastern Cape, KwaZulu-Natal, Mpumalanga and Limpopo, Category 3 elsewhere in South Africa.

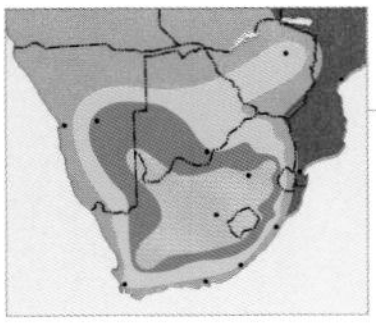

- Drought 2
- Spring
- Evergreen

2 *Bauhinia variegata* FABACEAE

Orchid Tree; Orgideeboom

OTHER LANGUAGES: yang zi jing (Chinese); Kachnar (Hindi)

India and China Small tree with a pyramidal to rounded crown; buds and twigs hairless; lenticels smooth, minute. Leaves with petiole hairless, about 25mm long; blade **50–140 × 60–140mm**, egg-shaped to round; notch between lobes **reaching much less than a quarter of the way** to the base; tip rounded; base squared to heart-shaped, with 11–13 main veins from the base. Inflorescences erect, 70–100mm long. Flowers **white or pink to purple, with purple lengthways stripes**; petals 5, free, 40–60mm long, up to 30mm wide; stamens 5–6, 25–35mm long. Fruit a brown pod up to 300 × 18–25mm.

The cultivar 'Candida' (= *B. alba, B. candida*, white orchid tree; witorgideeboom) is relatively common in cultivation in southern Africa. The species is invasive in parts of our region and is now a declared Category 1b invader in the Eastern Cape, KwaZulu-Natal, Mpumalanga and Limpopo, Category 3 elsewhere in South Africa.

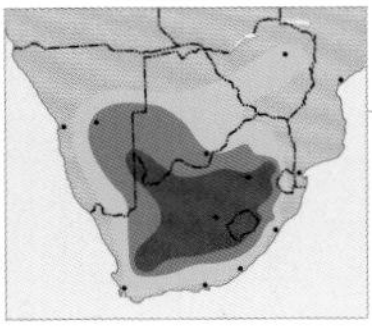

- Drought 2
- Spring
- Evergreen

3 *Ginkgo biloba* GINKGOACEAE

Maidenhair Tree, Ginkgo; Nooienshaarboom, Ginkgo, Ginkgoboom, Vrekboom

OTHER LANGUAGES: Bai guo (Chinese); Arbre aux mille écus (French); Japanischer Tempelbaum (German); Gin kyo (Japanese); Eun-haeng-na-mu (Korean); Nogueira-do-Japão (Portuguese)

China Tall tree with a pyramidal crown in young trees, becoming Y-shaped in the second or third century of growth, and **deep yellow autumn colours**; buds and twigs hairless. Leaves alternate or **in tufts**; petiole hairless, 20–45mm long; blade 60–120 × 50–100mm, **fan-shaped**; notch between lobes **variable**, absent in some leaves, all the way to the base in others, or anything in between; veins **repeatedly dividing into 2, not forming a network**. Cones with males and females on separate trees, males cylindrical, green, about 25mm long, females of a single, naked seed, yellow and **malodorous** when ripe. Seeds whitish.

For centuries ginkgo was thought to be extinct in the wild but is now known to grow in at least two small areas in Zhejiang Province, eastern China. Leaves very similar to those of ginkgo have been found in Permo-Carboniferous deposits (dating from about 300 million years before present) in South Africa. Grown in much of the world, including scattered places in our region, as a curiosity and ornamental.

1 *B. purpurea* leaves

1 *B. purpurea* flowers

J. M. GARG, WIKIMEDIA COMMONS, GFDL 1.2

1 *B. purpurea* fruit

BRAAM VAN WYK

2 *B. variegata* flowers

BRAAM VAN WYK

2 *B. variegata* fruit

BRAAM VAN WYK

3 *G. biloba* seeds

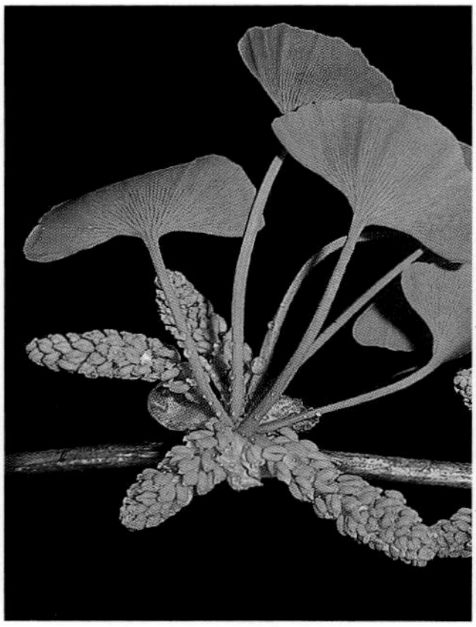

GINKGOB, WIKIMEDIA COMMONS, CC BY SA 3.0

3 *G. biloba* cones (male)

H. ZELL, WIKIMEDIA COMMONS, CC BY SA 3.0

3 *G. biloba* seeds

GROUP 27

Mopane group

Leaves compound, with 2 leaflets (bifoliolate).

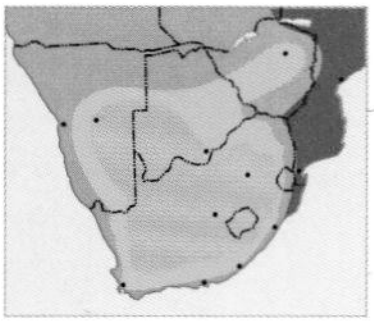

- Drought 2
- Spring
- Evergreen

1 *Hymenaea courbaril*

FABACEAE

Brazilian Copal, West Indian Locust; Brasiliaanse Kopaalboom

OTHER LANGUAGES: Courbaril (French); Jatobá (Portuguese); Guapinol (Spanish)

Mexico to Brazil Large tree with a columnar to spreading crown; bark grey-brown, **smooth**; buds and twigs hairless; lenticels **conspicuous**. Leaves with petiole hairless, 10–20mm long; leaflets with blade 40–100 × 20–50mm, **widest beyond the middle** or oblong, with a **drip-tip**; base oblique; surface **bronze-red when young**; margin smooth. Inflorescences erect. Flowers white to creamy; petals 5, free, about 20 × 9mm; stamens 10, free, 25–40mm long. Fruit a **rough**, woody, dark brown **pod 80–140** × 40–60mm. Seeds 20–30mm long.

Wounds in the tree exude an aromatic gum that softens at blood heat and is used in varnish and incense. The wood is highly esteemed for flooring and quality indoor work, formerly also for railway sleepers, though it is difficult to work because of its hardness. Specimen trees can be seen in Harare, Maputo and Durban Botanic Gardens. Medicinal uses are recorded for the gum.

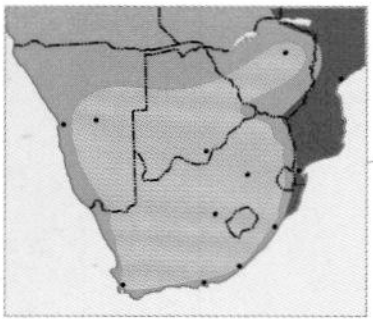

- Drought 2
- Spring
- Evergreen

2 *Hymenaea verrucosa* (= *Trachylobium verrucosum*)

FABACEAE

Zanzibar Copal, East African Copal, Madagascar Copal; Zanzibarkopal, Oos-Afrika-kopaal

OTHER LANGUAGES: Mtandarusi (Swahili)

East Africa, Madagascar and the Mascarenes Small to large tree with a rounded crown; bark pale grey, **smooth**; buds and twigs hairless; lenticels **conspicuous**. Leaves with petiole hairless, 8–18mm long; leaflets with blade 30–120 × 20–60mm, **egg-shaped to elliptic**; tip pointed; base obliquely rounded; margin smooth. Inflorescences erect, up to 300mm long. Flowers white; petals 5, free, 3 of these almost round, 15–20 × 8–10mm, 2 scale-like; stamens 10, free, about 25mm long. Fruit a reddish to dark brown, woody, **warty pod 25–50** × 15–30mm. Seeds dark brown, 13–18 × 9–12mm, about 8mm deep.

Formerly grown for its resin, which was replaced for a time by synthetic resins but is now again becoming popular as a natural floor sealant, this tree is now more important for its timber. Planted as ornamentals and specimen trees in Maputo and Durban.

1 *H. courbaril* leaves

1 *H. courbaril* flowers

1 *H. courbaril* fruit

2 *H. verrucosa* leaves

GEOFF NICHOLS

2 *H. verrucosa* flowers

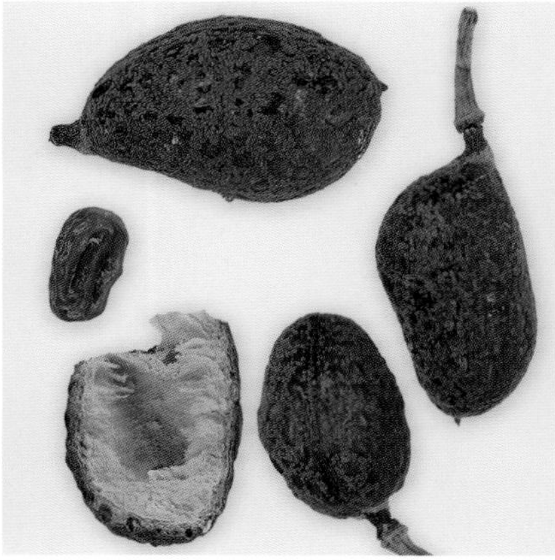

2 *H. verrucosa* fruit and seed

GROUP 28 Corkwood group

Leaves compound, with 3 leaflets (3-foliolate/trifoliolate). Latex present.

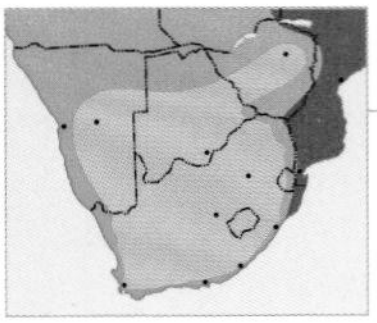

- Drought 2
- Spring
- Evergreen

1 *Hevea brasiliensis* EUPHORBIACEAE

Rubber Tree, Pará Rubber; Rubberboom

OTHER LANGUAGES: Kayu getah (Bahasa Indonesia); Caoutchouc de Para (French); Parakautschukbaum (German); Caucho (Spanish); Mpira (Swahili)

Brazil and Colombia Medium-sized tree with a narrow, rarely rounded crown; bark pale grey; buds and twigs hairless; latex **white**. Leaves alternate; petiole hairless, **60–200mm long**; leaflets with blade 70–200 × 30–80mm, widest beyond the middle, with a drip-tip; base rounded; margin **smooth**. Inflorescences erect, up to 200mm long. Flowers inconspicuous; males and females separate, on the same tree. Fruit a woody, **3-angled** capsule about 40 × 45mm. Seeds pale grey with darker mottles and streaks, 23 × 15mm.

This is the classic rubber of commerce, grown on a vast scale in Malaysia. Frost is disastrous to the crop as it renders the rubber brittle after purification. Timber from felled trees is used to make furniture and the seeds yield an oil used in making paint. There is a specimen tree in Durban Botanic Gardens.

1 *H. brasiliensis*

1 *H. brasiliensis* leaves

1 *H. brasiliensis* fruit

1 *H. brasiliensis* flowers

GROUP 29

Coraltree group

Leaves compound, with 3 leaflets (3-foliolate/trifoliolate). Stipules present. Latex absent.

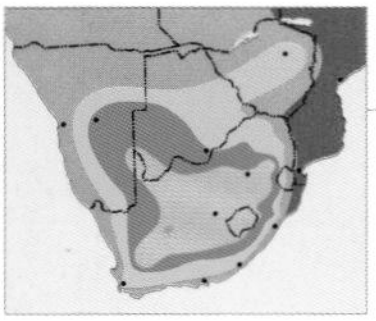

- Drought 2
- Spring
- Deciduous

1 *Butea monosperma* (= *B. frondosa*)

FABACEAE

Flame-of-the-forest; Vlam-van-die-bosse

OTHER LANGUAGES: Ploso (Bahasa Indonesia); Zi kuang (Chinese); Arbre à laque (French); Lackbaum (German); Dhak (Hindi); Samidha (Sanskrit); Palasham (Tamil); Tong gwaao (Thai)

Pakistan to Indochina Medium-sized tree with an upright to spreading crown; bark grey, smooth; twigs **hairy**; stems **unarmed**. Leaves alternate; petiole hairy, 40–75mm long; rachis **flattened**; leaflets with blade 80–250 × 60–200mm, lance- to egg-shaped; tip **rounded and indented**; base broad; lower surface hairy, at least on veins; margin **smooth**. Inflorescences erect, 15–40mm long, **appearing before** the leaves. Flowers yellow or red, without markings; petals 5, free, 40–60 × 20–40mm. Fruit a red or brown pod 100–170 × 30–50mm. Seeds 25–40 × 20–30mm.

Wood is off-white and soft but durable under water and therefore useful in constructing wells. The gum has various uses and the flowers supply a dyestuff or act as a mosquito trap. In our region it is recorded from Gauteng, Mpumalanga and KwaZulu-Natal.

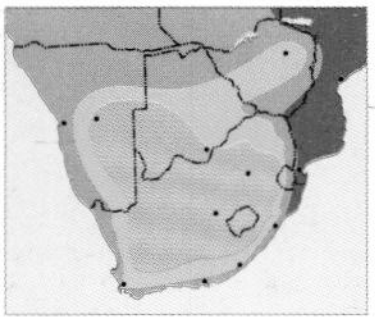

- Drought 2
- Spring
- Evergreen

2 *Ceratopetalum gummiferum*

CUNONIACEAE

Australian White Alder, Christmas Bush; Australiese Witels

Australia Large shrub or small tree with a rounded to pyramidal crown; buds hairless; twigs hairy. Leaves **opposite**; petiole hairless, 12–36mm long; leaflets with blade 30–70 × 6–14mm, **narrowly oblong**; tip rounded; base narrowed; margin **toothed**. Stipules soon falling, **interpetiolar**. Inflorescences erect; peduncle 10–35mm long. Flowers with sepals 5, free, elliptic-oblong, **red, persistent**; petals 5, free, 3-lobed, 2–3mm long, white flushed pink, soon falling. Fruit a small capsule surrounded by the red sepals.

Grown for ornament, in scattered localities in our region.

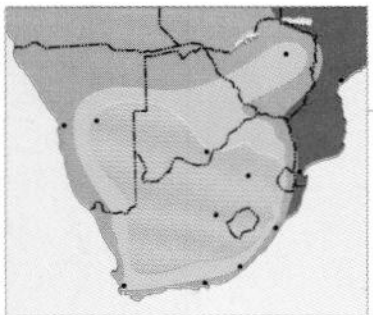

- Drought 2
- Spring
- Deciduous

3 *Erythrina abyssinica*

FABACEAE

Red-hot-poker Tree, Ethiopian Coral Tree; Vuurpylkoraalboom, Ethiopiese Koraalboom

OTHER LANGUAGES: Érythrine d'Abyssinie (French); Mutiti (Shona); Mbamba ngoma (Swahili)

East Africa to Zimbabwe Small tree with a rounded crown; bark deeply furrowed, **corky**, often spiny; buds hairy; twigs hairy when young, with large, triangular prickles. Leaves alternate; petiole hairy, 80–170mm long; central leaflet with blade 50–140 × 45–135mm, egg-shaped to round; tip **rounded and indented**; base **obliquely** squared; surface hairless or hairy to velvety; margin smooth. Stipules soon falling. Inflorescences erect, 90–360mm long, appearing before leaves; peduncle 40–160mm long. Flowers red; calyx with **long, slender lobes at apex**; petals 5, these 11–40 × 6–15mm. Fruit a woody, brown or black, hairy pod 48–160 × 12–24mm, **deeply constricted** between seeds. Seeds **red**, 7–12 × 5–7 × 3–5mm.

Increasingly grown for ornament; the flowers are visited by bees in search of nectar. The timber is soft and woolly and of only minor usefulness. Medicinal uses are recorded. The seeds are used for decoration.

1 *B. monosperma* flowers

1 *B. monosperma* fruit

2 *C. gummiferum* leaves

2 *C. gummiferum* flowers

3 *E. abyssinica* flowers

3 *E. abyssinica* fruit

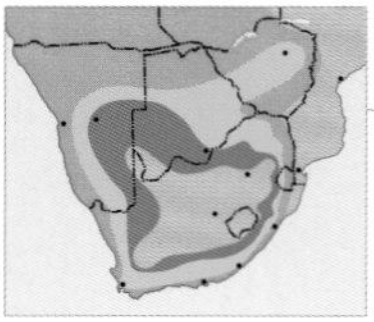

1 *Erythrina corallodendron* FABACEAE

West Indian Coral Tree; Wes-Indiese Koraalboom

OTHER LANGUAGES: Arbre corail de la Jamaique (French); Árvore-coral (Portuguese); Palo de pito (Spanish)

Southern USA Small tree with a rounded to spreading crown and **gnarled** trunk; bark smooth or with narrow fissures, flaking; twigs hairless, with large, hooked prickles. Leaves alternate; petiole **hairless**; leaflets with blade 50–120mm long, lance- to egg-shaped, with a **drip-tip**; base squared; surface **hairless**; margin smooth. Inflorescences erect, 400–600mm long, appearing **before** the leaves; peduncle about 300mm long. Flowers red; petals 5, up to about 75 × 10mm. Fruit a necklace-like, hairless pod 150–250mm long. Seeds **red**.

- Drought 2
- Spring
- Deciduous

Occasionally grown in KwaZulu-Natal as a garden ornamental. Medicinal uses are reported.

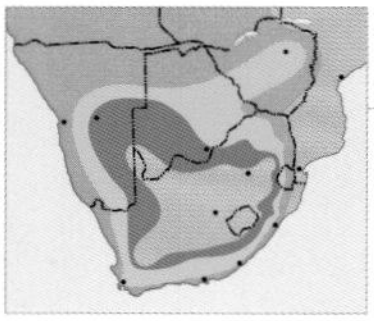

2 *Erythrina crista-galli* FABACEAE

Cockspur Coral Tree; Hoenderspoorkoraalboom

OTHER LANGUAGES: Érythrine crête de coq (French); Corticeira (Portuguese); Bucaré (Spanish)

Brazil to Argentina **Small** tree with a spreading crown and thick trunk; bark **deeply fissured**; buds and twigs hairless, the latter with single, **stout, curved thorns**. Leaves alternate; petiole hairless, 50–100mm long; leaflets with blade 30–150 × 20–50mm, egg-shaped; tip **pointed**; base **rounded**; surface dull, hairless; margin smooth. Inflorescences erect, **80–300mm long**, appearing **after** the leaves. Flowers red; petals 5, these 10–50mm long. Fruit a slightly curved, green to black pod 80–220mm long, slightly constricted between seeds. Seeds black.

- Drought 2
- Summer
- Deciduous

National tree of Argentina; national flower of Argentina and Uruguay. A common garden ornamental, naturalised in southeastern USA, eastern Australia and in parts of our region. The butterfly-shaped flowers are very characteristically twisted through 180° so that the largest petal (the 'standard') is arranged in the lower part, a phenomenon known as 'resupination'.

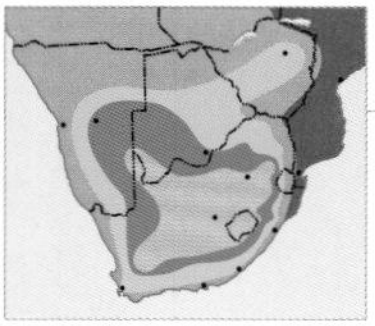

3 *Erythrina falcata* FABACEAE

Brazilian Coral Tree; Brasiliaanse Koraalboom

OTHER LANGUAGES: Bico de pato, Suinã (Portuguese); Ají de Chilicchi, Seibo de Jujuy (Spanish)

Peru to Argentina Medium-sized tree with a rounded to **spreading** crown; bark grey to black, rough; buds and twigs hairless; stems with single, **curved prickles**. Leaves alternate; petiole hairless; leaflets with blade 20–60 × 18–32mm, egg-shaped to oblong; tip **rounded**; base **broadly pointed**; margin smooth. Inflorescences **drooping, 200–300mm long**, appearing **before** the leaves. Flowers red; petals 5, these 25–35 × 7–32mm. Fruit a brown, hairless pod 20–30mm in diameter. Seeds **dark brown**, about 15 × 8–10mm.

- Drought 2
- Spring
- Deciduous

Garden ornamental recorded from a few sites in Gauteng, with some reported medicinal uses.

1 *E. corallodendron* leaves

1 *E. corallodendron* flowers

2 *E. crista-galli* bark

2 *E. crista-galli* flowers

2 *E. crista-galli* fruit

3 *E. falcata*

3 *E. falcata* flowers

3 *E. falcata* fruit

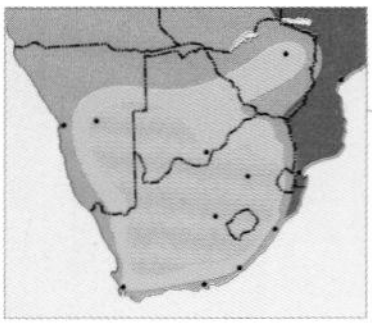

- Drought 2
- Spring
- Deciduous

1 *Erythrina fusca* FABACEAE

Purple Coral Tree; Perskoraalboom

OTHER LANGUAGES: Bois immortel (French); Eritrina-de-baixa (Portuguese); Ahuijote (Spanish)

Pantropical – the only coral tree found naturally in both the Old and New World Large tree with a round to spreading crown; bark with narrow fissures; twigs hairless, with single, **curved prickles**. Leaves alternate; petiole hairless, 10–190mm long; leaflets with blade **100–190** × 14–115mm, egg-shaped to elliptic; tip **pointed**; base rounded; surface hairless above, **velvety below**; margin smooth. Inflorescences erect, 100–430mm long; peduncle 25–130mm long, appearing **before** the leaves. Flowers yellow to red; petals 5, these 25–68 × 30–58mm. Fruit a flat, black, hairless pod **140–330** × 14–18mm. Seeds **dark brown**, 12–18mm long, 5–8mm wide and deep.

Usually grown as a garden ornamental, only recorded from Durban in our region. Also used for shade in cocoa and coffee plantations. Medicinal uses are recorded. The seeds are buoyant, allowing them to disperse across oceans, thus accounting for its wide distribution.

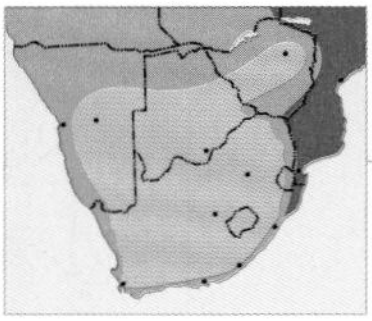

- Drought 2
- Spring
- Deciduous

2 *Erythrina livingstoneana* FABACEAE

Aloe Coral Tree, Mozambique Coral Tree; Aalwynkoraalboom, Mosambiekse Koraalboom

Tropical Africa Medium-sized tree with an ascending, vase-shaped crown; bark yellowish to brown, **deeply fissured**, forming broad ridges; twigs hairless, grey, with single, curved thorns. Leaves alternate; petiole hairless, 50–195mm long; leaflets with blade 60–200 × 65–190mm, **triangular**, shallowly **3-lobed**; base squared; surface hairless; margin smooth. Inflorescences **erect, 125–300mm long**, appearing **before** the leaves; peduncle 65–142mm long. Flowers red; petals 5, these 15–48 × 10–35mm. Fruit a yellow-brown, hairless pod 110–390mm long, constricted between and inflated over seeds, there 25–35mm in diameter. Seeds **red and black**, 12–15 × 6–10 × 5–6mm.

The seeds are poisonous, more so than those of most coral trees. Nevertheless, it is grown as a garden ornamental, recorded from gardens in Durban.

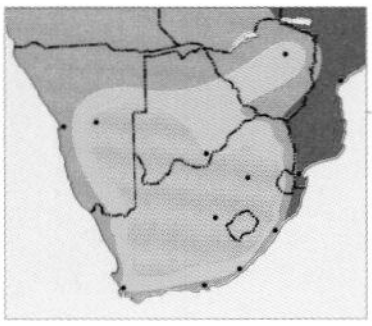

- Drought 2
- Spring
- Deciduous

3 *Erythrina pallida* FABACEAE

Pink Coral Tree; Pienkkoraalboom

Venezuela and the West Indies Small, spreading tree; bark yellow-brown, **smooth**; twigs hairless, with single, curved **prickles**. Leaves alternate; petiole hairless; leaflets with blade 70–100 × 60–90mm, egg-shaped; tip **drawn to a point**; base **broadly pointed**; margin smooth. Inflorescences erect, appearing before the leaves. Flowers **pink**; petals 5, these **10–70 × 5–20mm**. Fruit a hairless, black pod. Seeds **black**, about 10 × 7mm.

Occasionally planted as a garden ornamental. Recorded from a few sites in Durban and also Ofcolaco in Limpopo. The seeds are poisonous.

ROLANDO PÉREZ

1 *E. fusca* leaves and flowers

1 *E. fusca* flowers

GEOFF NICHOLS

2 *E. livingstoneana* flowers

GEOFF NICHOLS

2 *E. livingstoneana* fruit

3 *E. pallida* leaves

GEOFF NICHOLS

3 *E. pallida* flowers

NEIDA AVENDAÑO

3 *E. pallida* flowers

GROUP 30

White-ironwood group

Leaves compound, with 3 leaflets (3-foliolate/trifoliolate). Secretory cavities present. Stipules absent. Latex absent.

See also Group 39: *Casimiroa edulis* (p.398).

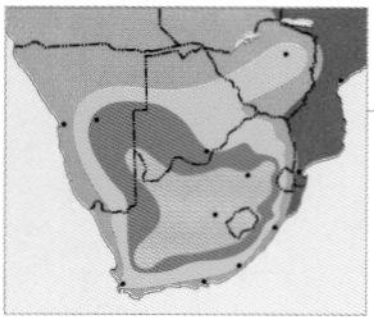

- Drought 2
- Spring
- Deciduous

1 *Aegle marmelos*

RUTACEAE

Bael Fruit, Bengal Quince; Baelvrug

OTHER LANGUAGES: Mu ju (Chinese); Bel indien, Cognassier du Bengal (French); Belbaum, Bengalische Quitte (German); Bel (Hindi); Bel (Marathi, Nepalese); Kuuviram (Tamil); Matum (Thai); Bael (Urdu)

India and Myanmar Medium-sized tree with a narrow to rounded crown; bark **bluish grey**; twigs hairless, green, **slightly zigzag**, sometimes with single or paired thorns, **exuding a gum** resembling gum arabic if wounded. Leaves **evil-smelling** if crushed; petiole hairless, **round**, 20–40mm long; leaflets 25–75 × 16–48mm, egg-shaped to elliptic; margin scalloped. Inflorescences erect, 40–50mm long. Flowers white; petals 4 or 5, about 14 × 8mm. Fruit a woody, greyish berry **50–125mm in diameter**.

Fruit pulp is eaten fresh or variously prepared. The wood is highly aromatic when freshly cut but is not durable; it has various indoor uses. Leaves are poisonous and medicinal uses are recorded for these and for the unripe fruits. Recorded in our region as specimen trees in Mpumalanga.

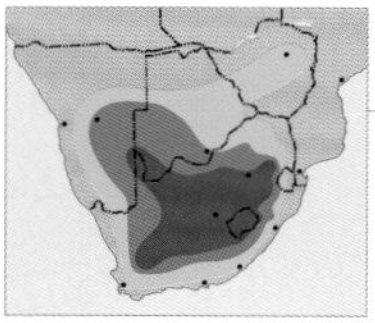

- Drought 2
- Spring
- Deciduous

2 *Poncirus trifoliata*

RUTACEAE

Japanese Bitter Orange, Trifoliate Orange; Japanse Lemoen, Struiklemoen

Korea and northern China Small tree with a columnar to rounded crown; bark **brownish**, with small fissures; twigs hairless, with **many** single, straight thorns. Leaves with petiole **winged**, hairless, 10–25mm long; leaflets 30–60 × 15–25mm, oblong; tip **broadly pointed**; base narrowed; margin **scalloped**. Inflorescences a single, stalkless flower. Flowers white; petals 5, these 18–30 × 8–15mm. Fruit a downy, round to pear-shaped, yellow-green berry 30–50mm in diameter.

Used as a cold-resistant rootstock for grafted citrus trees, more rarely as a tall, thorny hedge plant. Present but usually unseen in much of our region. The fruits are very sour but can be made into marmalade or a soft drink. Medicinal uses are recorded.

1 *A. marmelos* leaves

1 *A. marmelos* flowers

1 *A. marmelos* fruit

2 *P. trifoliata* leaves

2 *P. trifoliata* thorns

2 *P. trifoliata* fruit

GROUP 31

Karee group

Leaves compound, with 3 leaflets (3-foliolate/trifoliolate). Secretory cavities absent. Stipules absent. Latex absent, or if present then watery or cloudy, with flow inconspicuous or inconsistent.

See also Group 40: *Tabebuia roseo-alba* (p.416).

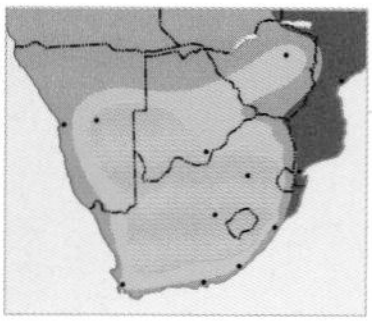

1 *Parmentiera cereifera*

BIGNONIACEAE

Candle Tree; Kersboom

- Drought 2
- Spring
- Deciduous

OTHER LANGUAGES: Kaarsenboom (Dutch); Árbol de Velas, Velario (Spanish)

Panama Small tree with a spreading crown; bark grey, smooth; buds hairless; twigs hairy at first; lenticels warty, conspicuous. Leaves **opposite**; petiole **winged**, hairless, 24–62mm long; leaflets 30–95 × 14–40mm, elliptic, with a drip-tip; base gradually narrowed. Inflorescences an erect single flower or clusters of up to 23 flowers **on old wood**, 25–50mm long. Flowers tubular; lobes 5, white, 37–64mm long. Fruit a fleshy, **candle-shaped**, yellowish, waxy capsule **390–540 × 10–24mm**. Seeds 3–4mm long and wide.

Grown as specimen trees in botanical gardens throughout the world, in Durban, Harare and Maputo in our region, but endangered in the wild. The fibrous fruit is edible, having a sweet flavour reminiscent of sugar cane. It is eaten either raw or cooked and is sometimes made into pickles or preserves.

1 *P. cereifera* leaves

VIRTUAL HERBARIUM / FLICKR

1 *P. cereifera* flowers

GHIR / FLICKR

1 *P. cereifera* fruit (main and inset)

KYLE WICOMB

CYNDY SIMS PARR, WIKIMEDIA COMMONS, CC BY SA 2.0

GROUP 32

Sausage-tree group

Leaves pinnately compound, opposite or whorled. Leaflets more than 3.

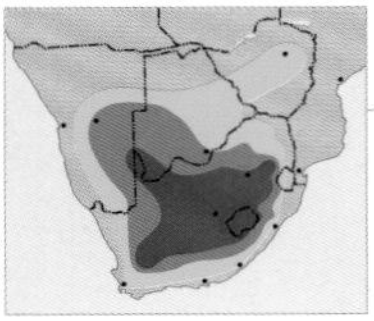

- Drought 2
- Spring
- Deciduous

1 *Acer negundo* (= *Negundo aceroides*)

ACERACEAE (OR SAPINDACEAE)

Boxelder, Ash-leaved Maple; Esseblaar-esdoring, Esseblaarahorn, Kaliforniese Esdoring

OTHER LANGUAGES: Fu ye feng (Chinese); Érable à feuilles de frêne (French); Eschen-Ahorn (German); Tonerikoba-no-kaede (Japanese); Acecintle (Spanish)

Canada to Mexico Medium-sized tree with an irregularly rounded crown; bark **deeply fissured**; buds hairy; twigs hairless; lenticels **warty, conspicuous**. Leaves with petiole hairy or hairless, 50–80mm long; leaflets **usually 3 or 5**, 50–130 × 40–100mm, lance- to egg-shaped or oblong; tip drawn out to a point; base rounded; veins hairy or not below; margin smooth or coarsely toothed. Inflorescences **hanging**, appearing **before or with** the leaves; males and females on different trees. Flowers inconspicuous. Fruit a **pair of winged** nuts 25–46 × 8–12mm, diverging at 50–70°.

Acer negundo is a very frost-hardy but somewhat drought-sensitive ornamental that tolerates poor soil. It is cultivated in many places but is attacked by termites in South Africa. Nonetheless, it is widely used as a street tree, also in Zimbabwe. It is now a declared Category 3 invader in South Africa.

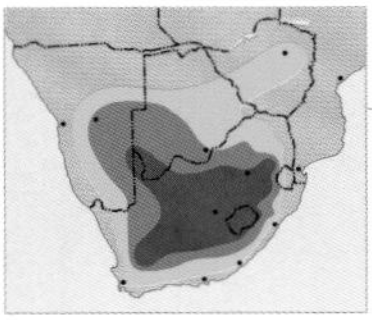

- Drought 2
- Spring
- Deciduous

2 *Fraxinus americana*

OLEACEAE

American Ash, White Ash; Amerikaanse Esseboom

Eastern USA and Canada Large tree with a rounded crown and yellow to purple autumn colours; bark with **interlacing small ridges**; buds hairy; twigs hairless; lenticels **conspicuous**. Leaves with petiole hairless, 35–56mm long; leaflets 40–150 × 23–70mm, lance-shaped to oblong; tip **long drawn out**; lower surface **whitish**; margin **smooth**. Inflorescences **hanging**, 50–70mm long. Flowers inconspicuous. Fruit a **1-winged**, buff-coloured nut 30–50mm long.

This timber is the material of choice for baseball bats, because it is shock-resistant. It can also be used for making furniture, tool handles and other items. Trees are planted for ornament in parks and large gardens in cooler parts of South Africa and Zimbabwe. It is a declared Category 3 invader in South Africa's Eastern Cape, KwaZulu-Natal, Mpumalanga and Limpopo provinces.

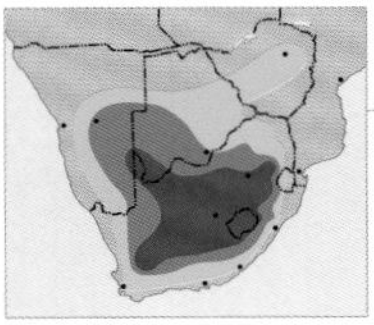

- Drought 2
- Spring
- Deciduous

3 *Fraxinus angustifolia*

OLEACEAE

Algerian Ash, Kabyl Ash; Algeriese Esseboom, Kabylesseboom

Southern Europe, North Africa and Southwestern Asia Large tree with a narrow, rounded crown; bark deeply fissured, forming **prominent broad ridges**; buds hairy; twigs hairless; lenticels **smooth but conspicuous**. Leaves opposite or whorled; petiole hairless, 17–50mm long; leaflets 20–50 × 10–25mm, lance-shaped to elliptic; tip drawn out to a point; surfaces hairless; margin **toothed**. Inflorescences **hanging**, 25–60mm long, appearing with or after the leaves; males and females separate, on the same tree. Flowers inconspicuous. Fruit a **1-winged**, buff-coloured nut 30–50mm long.

Widely planted as a street tree and for shade in parks in Namibia and South Africa, this species has become naturalised in parts of Australia. It is a declared Category 3 invader in the Eastern Cape, KwaZulu-Natal, Mpumalanga and Limpopo provinces of South Africa.

BRAAM VAN WYK

1 *A. negundo* flowers (male)

1 *A. negundo* fruit

DADEROT, WIKIMEDIA COMMONS, PUBLIC DOMAIN

2 *F. americana* leaves

2 *F. americana* flowers

BRAAM VAN WYK

2 *F. americana* fruit

JAVIER MARTIN, WIKIMEDIA COMMONS, PUBLIC DOMAIN

3 *F. angustifolia* flowers

JMK, WIKIMEDIA COMMONS, CC BY SA 3.0

3 *F. angustifolia* leaves and fruit

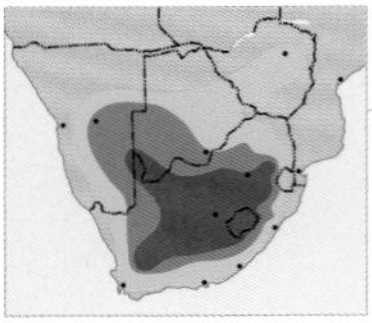

- Drought 2
- Spring
- Deciduous

1 *Fraxinus excelsior* OLEACEAE

European Ash; Europese Esseboom

Southern Europe and Southwestern Asia Large tree with a rounded crown and **yellowish autumn colours**; bark **smooth or with narrow fissures** on old trunks; buds and twigs **hairless**; lenticels **warty**, conspicuous. Leaves with petiole hairless, 30–55mm long; rachis flattened or round; leaflets 30–80 × 15–25mm, lance-shaped; tip drawn out to a long point; base rounded; surfaces hairless; veins hairy below; margin **toothed**. Inflorescences **hanging**, appearing **before** the leaves. Flowers inconspicuous; males and females separate, on the same or different trees. Fruit a **1-winged** nut 25–45mm long.

Ash wood is very shock-resistant and is now used for hockey sticks and billiard cues, and formerly was used to make longbows. It was also used for making the frames of some cars and early aircraft. Green wood is flexible and can be bent into chair backs, walking sticks and the like. In former times trees were coppiced every 10 years for poles and firewood. Medicinal uses are recorded. In Norse mythology the giant tree Yggdrasil stretched up from the Underworld and its crown supported the heavens. In many sources this tree is claimed to have been an ash. However, some scholars now claim that in the past an error had been made in the interpretation of the ancient writings and that the tree is most likely a common yew (*Taxus baccata*, p.100). Formerly more widely planted in our region than at present, it is now only seen in the coldest parts of Mpumalanga and Gauteng.

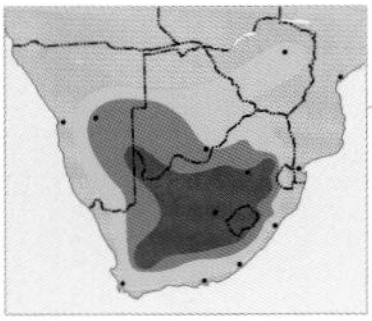

- Drought 2
- Spring
- Deciduous

2 *Fraxinus pennsylvanica* (= *F. lanceolata*) OLEACEAE

Green Ash, Pennsylvanian Ash; Groenesseboom, Pennsilvaniese Esseboom

Eastern USA Large tree with an upright, oval crown and **yellow autumn colours**; bark grey, with **interlacing ridges** in older trees; buds hairy; twigs hairy to hairless; lenticels **warty**, conspicuous. Leaves with petiole hairy to hairless, 10–53mm long; rachis round; leaflets 60–120 × 40–80mm, lance-shaped to elliptic, with a **drip-tip**; base narrowed; lower surface **minutely hairy with hairy veins**; margin **coarsely toothed**. Inflorescences **hanging**, 25–30mm long, appearing with the leaves. Flowers inconspicuous. Fruit a **1-winged**, buff-coloured nut 30–60mm long.

The comments for *F. americana* (p.346) apply here too, and green ash timber is often sold as 'white ash'. It is good for making the bodies of electric guitars. In our region, it is recorded from Lesotho and cooler parts of Namibia, South Africa and Zimbabwe.

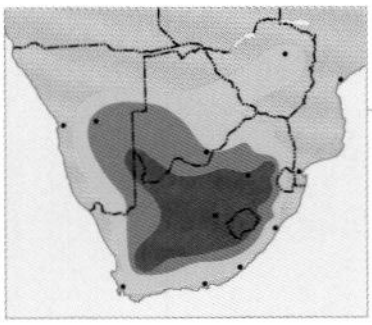

- Drought 2
- Spring
- Deciduous

3 *Fraxinus velutina* (= *F. berlandieriana*) OLEACEAE

Velvet Ash, Arizona Ash, Mexican Ash; Fluweelesseboom, Mexikaanse Esseboom

Southern USA and Mexico Small to medium-sized tree with oval to rounded crown; bark **deeply fissured**; buds and twigs hairy; lenticels **warty**, conspicuous. Leaves with petiole hairy, **20–40mm** long; rachis **channelled**; leaflets 30–80 × 15–40mm, lance-shaped to elliptic, with a drip-tip or tip pointed; base narrowed to rounded; surface glossy above, **velvety below**; margin smooth or saw-toothed. Inflorescences **hanging**, 20–60mm long, appearing with the leaves. Flowers inconspicuous. Fruit a **1-winged**, brownish nut 15–30mm long.

Widely grown in South Africa and Zimbabwe as an ornamental or part of a shelterbelt. The wood has limited value in its native area.

1 *F. excelsior* flowers

1 *F. excelsior* fruit

PETER LINEHAN

2 *F. pennsylvanica* flowers

2 *F. pennsylvanica* leaves and fruit

3 *F. velutina* leaves

3 *F. velutina* fruit

1 *Markhamia lutea* (= *M. hildebrandtii, M. platycalyx*) BIGNONIACEAE

Nile Bellbean, Nile Tulip; Nylklokkiesboontjie

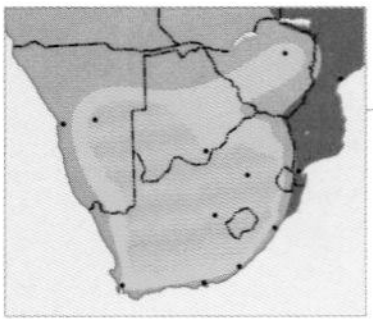

- Drought 2
- Spring
- Evergreen

OTHER LANGUAGES: Siala (Swahili)

East Africa Small to medium-sized tree with a narrow to rounded crown; bark reddish brown; buds hairy; twigs **hairless**; lenticels **smooth but conspicuous**. Leaves with petiole hairless, 50–70mm long; rachis **round**; leaflets 50–90 × 23–35mm, **widest beyond the middle**; tip pointed; base rounded; lower surface minutely hairy. Inflorescences **hanging**, up to 100mm long. Flowers tubular; lobes 5, yellow, 50–80mm long. Fruit a twisted, **flat, narrow pod** 400–800mm long, velvety with **soft, golden hairs**.

Grown in our region for shade and ornament as in Durban Botanic Gardens. The flowers are visited by bees and the wood is used for furniture, boat-building and more. Medicinal uses are recorded.

2 *Sambucus nigra* (= *S. canadensis*) SAMBUCACEAE

Elder; Vlier

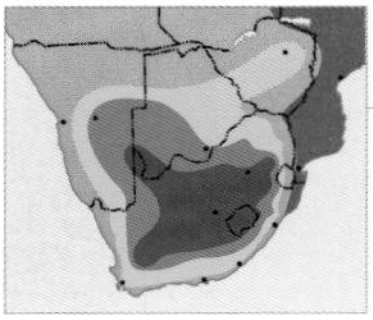

- Drought 2
- Spring
- Deciduous

OTHER LANGUAGES: Sureau Noir (French); Schwarzer Holunder (German); Sambuco Comune (Italian); Sabugueiro (Portuguese); Saúco (Spanish); Sommarfläder (Swedish)

Europe, Western Asia, North Africa and eastern USA **Large shrub or small tree** with a rounded crown; bark grey, adhering, becoming fissured in old specimens; buds and twigs hairless; lenticels **warty**, conspicuous. Leaves with petiole hairless; rachis **channelled**; leaflets 37–125 × 20–50mm, **egg-shaped**; tip drawn out to a point; base rounded; surfaces **glossy**; margin **coarsely toothed**. Inflorescences erect, appearing after the leaves. Flowers small, white, in **large trusses**. Fruit a round, black, hairless berry 5–6mm long and in diameter.

Widely grown in Mozambique, South Africa, Zimbabwe and a surprising number of countries further north as a frost-resistant garden ornamental or screen, though in other areas it has a reputation for weediness. A wine-analogue can be fermented from the flowers (white, often strongly aromatic) and fruits (red). The fruits are edible but need to be cooked to destroy a toxic principle. The wood and pith can be used in various ways. Medicinal uses are recorded. The species is a declared Category 1b invader in South Africa.

3 *Spathodea campanulata* (= *S. nilotica*) BIGNONIACEAE

African Flame Tree, African Tulip Tree, East African Flame Tree; Afrikavlamboom

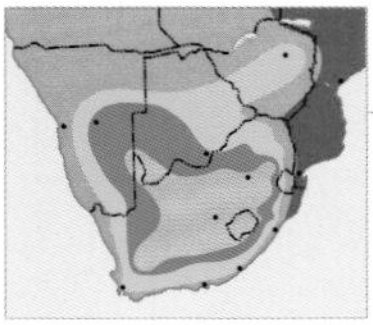

- Drought 2
- Spring
- Deciduous

OTHER LANGUAGES: Tulipier du Gabon (French); Tulipeira-da-África (Portuguese); Kibobakasi (Swahili)

East Africa Large tree with an irregularly rounded crown; bark **smooth**, grey; buds and twigs hairy; lenticels **warty**, conspicuous. Leaves with petiole **hairy**, about 100mm long; rachis round; leaflets up to 150 × 55mm, oblong; tip rounded; base obliquely narrowed; surface glossy above, with **impressed** secondary veins giving a quilted appearance, **woolly** below; margin smooth. Inflorescences erect, 150–200mm long. Flowers tubular; lobes 5, red to orange, **85–90mm long**. Fruit a woody, brown capsule **170–250 × 35–70mm**. Seeds whitish, **winged**, 12–15 × 18–20 × 0.5–1mm.

In Nairobi there is a yellow-flowered variant apparently not grown in southern Africa. The orange form is naturalised in KwaZulu-Natal and has been declared a Category 3 invader in the Eastern Cape, KwaZulu-Natal, Mpumalanga and Limpopo. Elsewhere it has been nominated as one of the 100 'world's worst' invaders.

TATIANA GERUS

1 *M. lutea* flowers

J.M. GARG, WIKIMEDIA COMMONS, CC BY SA 3.0

1 *M. lutea* fruit

BRAAM VAN WYK

2 *S. nigra* flowers

H. ZELL, WIKIMEDIA COMMONS, CC BY SA 3.0

2 *S. nigra* fruit

BRAAM VAN WYK

3 *S. campanulata*

FOREST AND KIM STARR

3 *S. campanulata* flowers and fruit

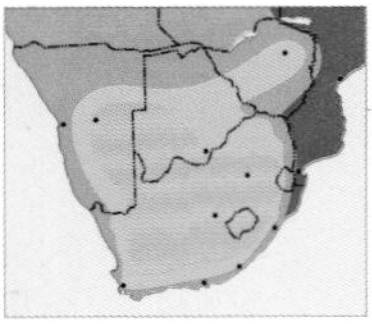

1 *Stereospermum colais* (= *S. personatum*) BIGNONIACEAE
Yellow Snake Tree; Geel-slangboom

- Drought 2
- Spring
- Deciduous

OTHER LANGUAGES: Parul (Bengali); Yuyeqiu (Chinese); Paral (Hindi); Patala (Sanskrit); Patiri (Tamil); Paral (Urdu)

India to China and Indonesia Large tree with an oval crown; bark **deeply fissured**, grey; buds hairy; twigs hairless; lenticels **smooth** but conspicuous. Leaves with petiole hairless, 35–80mm long; rachis **channelled**; leaflets 65–125 × 40–50mm, **elliptic to oblong**, with a drip-tip; base narrowed; surface **dull, hairless on both sides**; margin smooth. Inflorescences erect, up to 400mm long, appearing before or with the leaves. Flowers tubular; lobes 5, these 17–22mm long, creamy to yellow, with **dark red lengthways stripes**. Fruit a 4-angled, **twisted** capsule 80–450 × 8–12mm. Seeds 20 × 5mm.

Occasionally grown for ornament in our region and seen in Mpumalanga and KwaZulu-Natal. Medicinal uses are recorded.

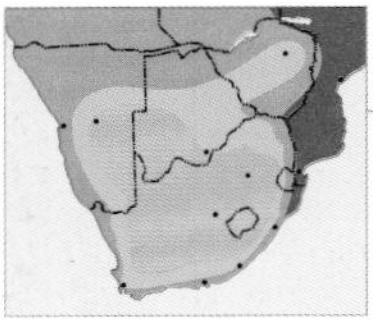

2 *Stereospermum kunthianum* BIGNONIACEAE
Pink Jacaranda; Pienkjakaranda

- Drought 2
- Spring
- Deciduous

Tropical Africa Small to medium-sized tree with a rounded crown; bark pale, **flaking in round patches**; buds hairy; twigs hairless; lenticels **smooth** but conspicuous. Leaves with 4 pairs of leaflets; petiole hairless, 27–90mm long; rachis round; leaflets 50–130 × 20–60mm, ovate, widest below or beyond the middle, **stiff and brittle, snapping audibly in two when folded**; lower surface hairy; margin smooth. Inflorescences erect, 150–480mm long, appearing **before** the leaves. Flowers tubular; lobes 5, these 30–40mm long, **pink, with red streaks**. Fruit a long, thin capsule. Seeds 7 × 20–30mm.

Occasionally grown as an ornamental, in Mpumalanga and KwaZulu-Natal, but hard to obtain. The fruit is used medicinally.

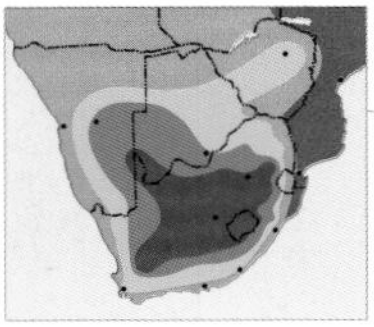

3 *Tecoma stans* (= *Bignonia stans*) BIGNONIACEAE
Yellow Bells, Yellow Elder, Yellow Trumpet Flower; Geelklokkies

- Drought 2
- Spring
- Evergreen/ semi-deciduous

OTHER LANGUAGES: Gele Bignonia (Dutch); Bignone Jaune (French); Gelbe Trompetenblume (German); Amarelinho (Portuguese); Bignonia amarilla (Spanish)

Florida (USA) to Argentina Large, spreading **shrub or small tree**; bark smooth; buds and twigs hairless; lenticels **smooth**, conspicuous, whitish. Leaves with 2–6 pairs of leaflets; petiole hairless, 10–90mm long; rachis round; leaflets 24–150 × 8–60mm, lance-shaped; tip **sharply pointed**; surface bright green above, paler green below; margin **sharply and coarsely toothed**. Inflorescences erect. Flowers trumpet-shaped; lobes 5, these 36–58mm long, yellow **with fine red stripes**. Fruit a flat, brown capsule **70–210 × 5–8mm**. Seeds **winged**, whitish, 3–5 × 24–27mm.

A declared Category 1b invader in South Africa, formerly grown for ornament. Possibly with medicinal uses.

VINAYARAJ, WIKIMEDIA COMMONS, CC BY SA 3.0

1 *S. colais* leaves

BGO PLANT DATABASES / THE BOTANICAL GARDEN ORGANIZATION

1 *S. colais* flowers

2 *S. kunthianum* leaves

WARREN McCLELAND

2 *S. kunthianum* flowers

BRAAM VAN WYK

3 *T. stans* leaves

BRAAM VAN WYK

3 *T. stans* flowers

BRAAM VAN WYK

3 *T. stans* fruit

GROUP 33

Boerbean group

Leaves pinnately compound, alternate or in tufts. Leaflets more than 3, terminal one absent (paripinnate). Stipules present.

See also Group 3: *Parkinsonia aculeata* (p.84).

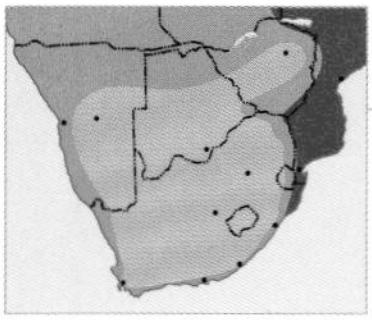

- Drought 2
- Spring
- Deciduous

1 *Baikiaea plurijuga*

FABACEAE

Zambezi Teak; Zambezikiaat

OTHER LANGUAGES: Mukusi (Lozi); Mokusi (Tswana)

Tropical Africa Medium-sized to large tree with a dense, spreading crown; bark grey-brown, smooth; buds and twigs **hairy**. Leaves with petiole hairy, 10–20mm long; leaflets 35–70 × 20–25mm, elliptic to oblong; tip **slightly indented, with a short bristle**; base squared; veins hairy below; margin smooth. Inflorescences **erect**, up to 300mm long; buds **brown, velvety**. Flowers pink to mauve or purple; petals 5, these 20–30 × 10–15mm. Fruit a **velvety-hairy**, brown pod 90–130 × 35–50mm, opening explosively. Seeds dark reddish brown, about 20 × 15mm.

The wood is dark red-brown, hard, strong and durable. Trees are grown as ornamentals, suitable for parks and large gardens. Medicinal uses are recorded.

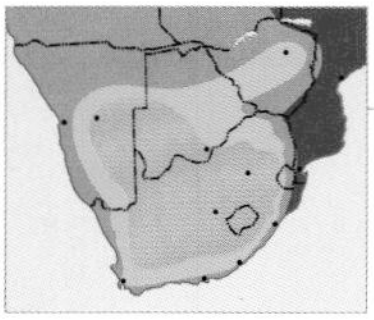

- Drought 2
- Spring
- Deciduous

2 *Brachystegia boehmii*

FABACEAE

Mufuti, Prince-of-Wales' Feathers; Skoensoolpeul

OTHER LANGUAGES: Mufuti (Shona)

Tropical Africa Small to medium-sized tree with a spreading, **flat-topped** crown; bark grey-brown, rough; buds and twigs hairless. Leaves **feathery**; petiole hairless, 3–10mm long; rachis V-shaped; leaflets **14–28 pairs** per leaf, **30–60 × 10–15mm**, oblong; tip rounded, indented; base obliquely rounded; surface **pink to brick-red when young**, hairless above, minutely hairy below; margin smooth. Stipules long, narrow, **shrivelled when leaves are mature**. Inflorescences erect, up to 100mm long. Flowers inconspicuous. Fruit a woody, brown, hairless pod up to 150 × 50mm, upper margin with a **broad, flat ridge**.

Grown as a specimen tree in botanical gardens and, in Zimbabwe, for ornament. The bark is used for tanning and inner bark yields a strong fibre used for ropes. Heartwood is used for railway sleepers after preservative treatment.

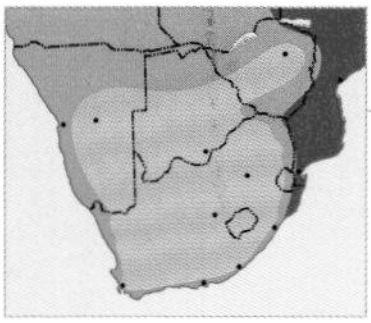

- Drought 2
- Spring
- Deciduous

3 *Cassia ferruginea*

FABACEAE

Imperial Cassia; Keiserkassia

OTHER LANGUAGES: Cassia Imperial (Portuguese)

Brazil Small tree with a rounded crown; bark rough, grey; twigs hairless. Leaves with **many pairs** of leaflets; petiole hairless; rachis round; leaflets small, **oblong**, hairless; tip and base **rounded**. Inflorescences **hanging**. Flowers yellow, large; stamens 10, of two different lengths, long ones S-shaped. Fruit a cylindrical, woody pod about **300mm long**. Seeds many, hard.

Very ornamental but rarely grown in our region, in Zimbabwe and in KwaZulu-Natal, South Africa. The flowers are visited by bees and indirectly yield honey. Seeds have strong dormancy and are difficult to germinate.

1 *B. plurijuga* leaflets

1 *B. plurijuga* flowers

2 *B. boehmii* flowers

2 *B. boehmii* new growth

2 *B. boehmii* fruit

3 *C. ferruginea* leaves and flowers

3 *C. ferruginea* flowers

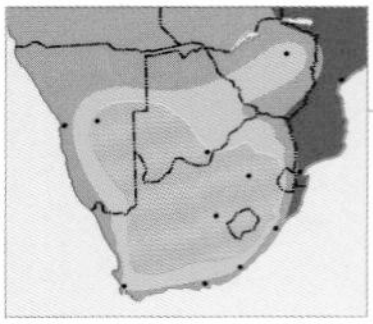

- Drought 2
- Spring
- Deciduous

1 *Cassia fistula* FABACEAE

Golden Shower, Indian Laburnum, Pudding Pipe Tree; Gouereën, Indiese Laburnum

OTHER LANGUAGES: Trengguli (Bahasa Indonesia); Douche d'or (French); Amaltas (Hindi); Lluva de oro (Spanish); Aragvadhamu (Tagalog); Konrai (Tamil); Dok khun (Thai); Bò Cạp Nước (Vietnamese)

India and Southeast Asia Small to medium-sized tree with an upright to spreading crown; bark grey; lenticels **warty**, conspicuous. Leaves with **3–8 pairs** of leaflets; petiole hairless, 40–110mm long; rachis round; leaflets 60–140 × 35–70mm, **lance- or egg-shaped** or elliptic; tip **pointed**; base rounded; margin **wavy**. Inflorescences **hanging, 200–400mm long**; peduncle 20–100mm long. Flowers golden yellow; petals 5, these 12–25 × 10–18mm. Fruit a woody, cylindrical, almost black pod **300–600** × 20–25mm.

A commonly planted ornamental and street tree in warmer parts of South Africa and Zimbabwe, and national flower of Thailand and state flower of Kerala, India. Bees collect pollen and nectar from the flowers. The timber is reddish, quite heavy and used in cabinet-making, inlay work and rough carpentry.

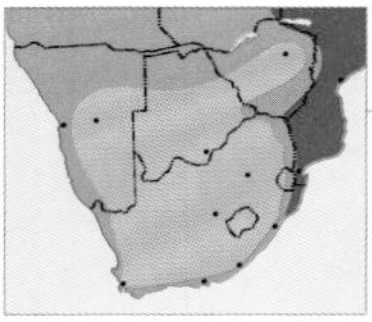

- Drought 2
- Spring
- Deciduous

2 *Cassia javanica* (= *C. nodosa*) FABACEAE

Pink Shower, Apple-blossom Cassia, Java Shower; Pienkreën

OTHER LANGUAGES: Bobondelan (Bahasa Indonesia); Zhao wa jue ming (Chinese); Cassie à fleurs roses (French); Anahuhan (Tagalog); Muồng hoa đào (Vietnamese)

India to New Guinea Medium-sized tree with an open, spreading crown; buds hairy; twigs hairy at first, later hairless, **ribbed**. Leaves with many pairs of leaflets; petiole hairless, 15–40mm long; rachis round; leaflets 25–55 × 15–35mm, oblong; tip **pointed**; base rounded; veins **hairy below**; margin smooth. Inflorescences **hanging, 50–180mm long**; peduncle 20–30mm long. Flowers **pink to red**; petals 5, these 25–35 × 7–8mm. Fruit a woody, black pod **200–700** × 10–20mm. Seeds buff, 6.5–8 × 6.5–8 × 4–5mm.

Commonly grown in the tropics as a garden ornamental, seen in our area as specimen trees and ornamentals in Mozambique, South Africa and Zimbabwe. The timber is used for cabinet work, furniture and construction.

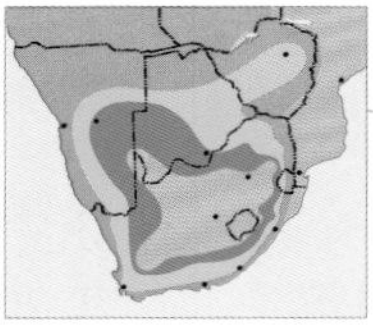

- Drought 2
- Spring
- Evergreen

3 *Ceratonia siliqua* FABACEAE

Carob, Locust Tree, St. John's Bread; Karob, Johannesbroodboom

OTHER LANGUAGES: Kharrûb (Arabic); Chang jiao dou (Chinese); Caroubier (French); Echter Johannisbrotbaum (German); Kharoupiá (Greek); Haruv matzuy (Hebrew); Guainella (Italian); Alfarrobeira (Portuguese); Algarrobo (Spanish); Harrub (Turkish)

Mediterranean region Small tree with a rounded or spreading crown; bark grey, smooth; lenticels warty, conspicuous. Leaves with **3–5 pairs** of leaflets; petiole hairless, 15–30mm long; leaflets 30–70 × 30–40mm, **egg-shaped**; tip rounded or indented; margin smooth, often **wavy**. Stipules **absent or apparently so**. Inflorescences erect, 50–130mm long. Flowers small, pink, tubular; males and females usually on different trees. Fruit a dry or fleshy, flattish, purple-brown pod **100–300 × 15–25mm, flattened**.

Grown throughout our region as a garden ornamental and street tree. Seeds of this tree are very uniform in size and were once used as a weight standard, giving us the word 'carat' as the unit by which diamonds are weighed. Once dried and roasted, the pulp is ground into carob flour/powder. It is similar to cocoa powder in colour and can be substituted one-for-one in recipes.

GEOFF NICHOLS

1 *C. fistula* flowers

GEOFF NICHOLS

1 *C. fistula* flowers

1 *C. fistula* fruit

2 *C. javanica* flowers

2 *C. javanica* fruit

BRAAM VAN WYK

3 *C. siliqua* leaves

3 *C. siliqua* flowers (male)

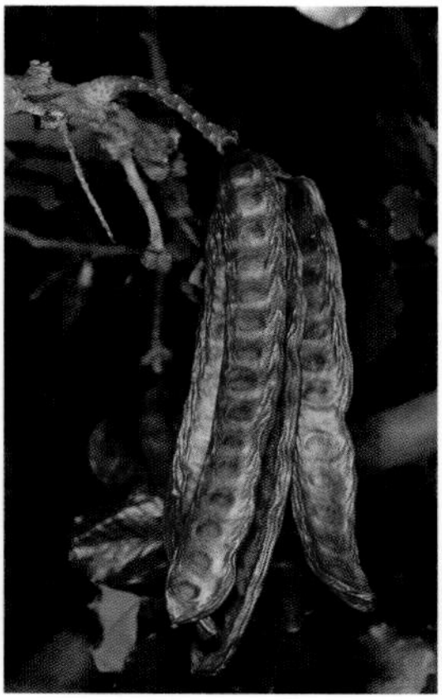

BRAAM VAN WYK

3 *C. siliqua* fruit

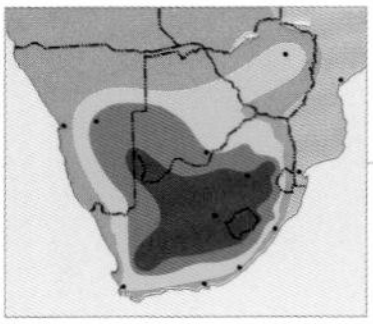

- Drought 2
- Spring
- Deciduous

1 *Gleditsia triacanthos* FABACEAE

Honey Locust, American Three-thorn, Sweet Locust; Soetpeulboom, Amerikaanse Driedoring

Eastern USA Medium-sized to large tree with a rounded to spreading crown and **yellow autumn colours**; bark variable; buds and twigs hairless; twigs and trunks with **persistent, straight thorns, usually with at least one pair of thorns at right angles to the main thorn**; lenticels warty, conspicuous. Leaves once- or twice-pinnate, with **7–15 pairs** of leaflets; petiole minutely hairy, 9–18mm long; rachis round; leaflets 15–35 × 5–15mm, lance-shaped to oblong; tip bluntly pointed; base obliquely rounded; veins **hairless below**; margin smooth to scalloped, wavy. Inflorescences **hanging, 50–70mm long**, appearing with the leaves. Flowers yellow or green; petals 5, oblong to narrowly triangular; males and females separate, on the same or different trees. Fruit a **flattened, woody, dark brown pod** 300–450 × 25–40mm.

The pulp on the inside of the pods is edible, sweet, with a honey flavour. Grown for fodder and, in a spectacular piece of bad planning (considering the vicious thorns on the trunk), as a street tree in a residential suburb in Johannesburg. This tree is a declared Category 1b invader in South Africa and must (by law) be removed in the many places where it is naturalised.

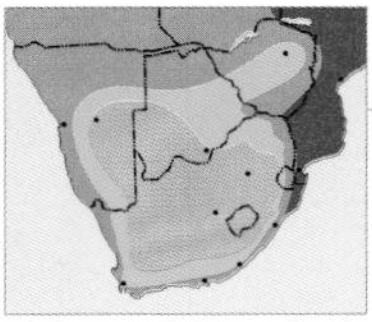

- Drought 2
- Spring
- Evergreen

2 *Saraca asoca* FABACEAE

Ashoka Tree, Asoc, Asoka; Ashoka-boom

OTHER LANGUAGES: Sita Ashok (Hindi); Asogam (Tamil)

India, Myanmar and Sri Lanka Small tree with a vase-shaped to rounded crown; bark grey, narrowly fissured; twigs hairless, almost black; lenticels **warty**, conspicuous. Leaves with 3–6 pairs of leaflets; petiole hairless, **1–3mm long**; young foliage **limp, very pale**; mature leaflets 35–250 × 10–90mm, **stiffly leathery**, lance-shaped or oblong, with a drip-tip; margin smooth. Inflorescences erect, **on old wood**, 15–150mm long. Flowers tubular; lobes 4, bright **orange-yellow, aging to red**. Fruit a flattened pod 45–150 × 20–45mm, up to 15mm thick, **red** when young, black when mature.

Grown as specimen trees in botanical gardens in South Africa's KwaZulu-Natal and in the Seychelles but would be a superb ornamental. It is sacred to Hindus and Buddhists. Medicinal uses are recorded.

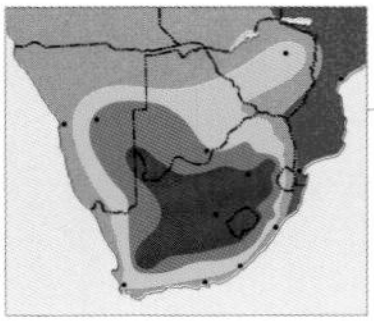

- Drought 2
- Spring
- Evergreen

3 *Senna alata* (= *Cassia alata*) FABACEAE

Candlebush, Ringworm Bush; Kerspeulbos

OTHER LANGUAGES: Yì bing jue míng (Chinese); Épis d'or (French); Kerzenstrauch (German); Mangerioba-do-pará (Portuguese); Flor del Secreto (Spanish)

Brazil and Venezuela Spreading shrub or small tree; bark smooth, grey; twigs hairy, green; lenticels minute. Leaves with **6–14 pairs** of leaflets; petiole **hairless**, 20–30mm long; rachis **5-angled**; leaflets 50–150 × 30–70mm, oblong; tip rounded; base **obliquely** obtuse; margin smooth. Stipules persistent. Inflorescences **erect, 200–500mm long**; peduncle 70–140mm long. Flowers yellow; petals 5, these 16–24 × 10–15mm. Fruit a **4-winged**, woody, black pod 100–150 × 15–20mm. Seeds 7–8 × 5–8mm.

Grown as a garden ornamental in Zimbabwe and in KwaZulu-Natal, South Africa, but has considerable potential to become invasive in warm areas.

1 *G. triacanthos* thorns

1 *G. triacanthos* flowers

1 *G. triacanthos* fruit

2 *S. asoca* leaves

2 *S. asoca* young leaves

2 *S. asoca* flowers

3 *S. alata* flowers

3 *S. alata* fruit

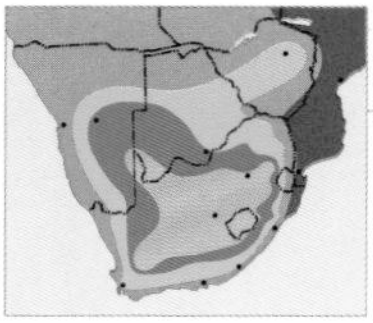

- Drought 2
- Spring
- Evergreen

1 *Senna didymobotrya* (= *Cassia didymobotrya*) FABACEAE
Peanut Butter Cassia, Chemagro, Oatmeal Cassia; Grondboontjiebotterkassia

Tropical Africa Spreading shrub or small tree, **unpleasantly scented**; bark pale grey, smooth; buds hairy; twigs sparsely hairy; lenticels minute. Leaves with 8–18 pairs of leaflets; petiole **hairy**, 20–50mm long; rachis **round**; leaflets 20–50 × 8–20mm, elliptic to oblong; tip rounded to squared, **spine-tipped**; base rounded; both surfaces **hairy**; margin smooth. Inflorescences **erect, 150–350mm long**. Flowers yellow; petals 5, these 10–25mm long. Fruit a dark brown, sparsely hairy, **flattened** pod 60–120 × 15–25mm. Seeds grey-brown.

Most parts of the plant are unpleasantly scented, sometimes reminiscent of peanut butter and hence the common names. A declared Category 1b invader in the Western and Eastern Cape, Kwa-Zulu-Natal, Mpumalanga and Limpopo, South Africa, and invasive in many other countries. It can be used as a green manure. Medicinal uses are recorded.

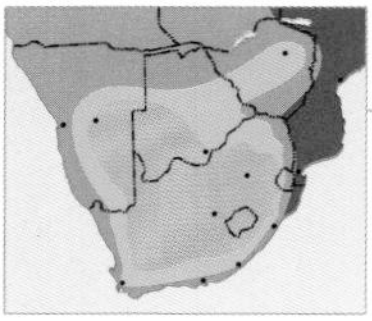

- Drought 2
- Spring and Summer
- Evergreen

2 *Senna multiglandulosa* (= *Cassia multiglandulosa, C. tomentosa*) FABACEAE
Woolly Senna, Woolly Cassia; Wolpeulbos

OTHER LANGUAGES: Retama, Parral (Spanish)

Mexico and Guatemala Spreading **shrub or small tree**; bark grey, almost smooth; buds and twigs hairy; lenticels **warty**, conspicuous. Leaves with 6–8 pairs of leaflets; petiole hairy, 2–12mm long; rachis round; leaflets 20–40 × 5–12mm, oblong; tip indented and spine-tipped; base obliquely rounded; lower surface **hairy**; margin **rolled inwards**. Stipules soon falling. Inflorescences **erect**, 30–100mm long; peduncle 20–30mm long. Flowers yellow; petals 5, these 10–20mm long. Fruit a **papery, pale brown, densely hairy** (sparser with age) pod 60–120 × 6–10mm. Seeds midbrown.

Grown occasionally as an ornamental in Mozambique and South Africa. A weed in Australia and New Zealand.

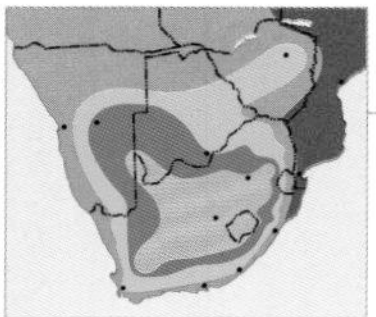

- Drought 2
- Spring
- Evergreen

3 *Senna multijuga* (= *Cassia multijuga*) FABACEAE
Brazil Shower; Brasilreën

OTHER LANGUAGES: Pau-cigarra (Portuguese)

Brazil Medium-sized tree with a rounded crown; bark smooth; buds hairy, twigs hairless, round, **ribbed**; lenticels **warty**, conspicuous. Leaves with **18–44 pairs** of leaflets; petiole hairless, 5–30mm long; rachis **flat or channelled** above, with **glands** between at least some leaflet pairs; leaflets 15–45 × 3–8mm, **narrowly** oblong, **hair-tipped**; base obliquely obtuse; lower surface **much paler** than upper; margin smooth. Inflorescences **erect**, 100–250mm long; peduncle 20–40mm long. Flowers yellow; petals 5, these 14–30mm long. Fruit a **papery**, dark brown, **flattened** pod 80–200 × 13–20mm. Seeds midbrown, about 6mm long.

Timber is of limited usefulness but it makes good charcoal. The main value of this tree is as an ornamental. Recorded from Mpumalanga, KwaZulu-Natal, Gauteng and the Eastern Cape.

1 *S. didymobotrya* leaves

BRAAM VAN WYK

1 *S. didymobotrya* flowers

BRAAM VAN WYK

1 *S. didymobotrya* flowers and fruit

STAN SHEBS, WIKIMEDIA COMMONS, CC BY SA 3.0

2 *S. multiglandulosa* flowers and leaves

STAN SHEBS, WIKIMEDIA COMMONS, CC BY SA 3.0

2 *S. multiglandulosa* flowers

3 *S. multijuga* flowers

FOREST AND KIM STARR

3 *S. multijuga* fruit

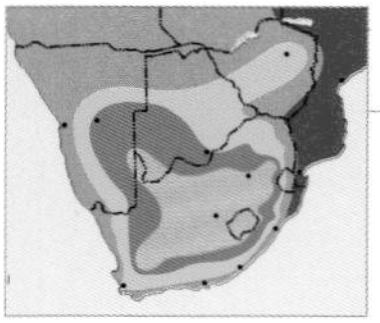

- Drought 2
- All year
- Evergreen

1 *Senna pendula* *(= Cassia coluteoides, C. pendula)* FABACEAE

Easter Senna, Easter Cassia, Wood Creeper; Paaspeul

OTHER LANGUAGES: Fedegoso (Portuguese); Valamuerto (Spanish)

South America Spreading **shrub or small tree** with a rounded crown; bark dark grey; buds and twigs **minutely hairy**; lenticels minute. Leaves with 3–6 pairs of leaflets; petiole hairless, 15–30mm long; leaflets 20–50 × 10–20mm, often **widest beyond the middle**; tip **rounded and indented**; base obliquely rounded; lower surface **sparsely hairy**; margins smooth, **yellow**. Stipules soon falling. Inflorescences **erect**, 30–100mm long; peduncle 30–60mm long. Flowers golden to orange yellow; petals 5, these 10–25mm long. Fruit a **papery**, dark brown pod 50–100 × 8–14mm. Seeds dark brown, 4–6mm long.

A declared Category 1b invader in South Africa, particularly bad in the warm, wet east of our region. Also invasive in other tropical and subtropical areas such as Australia and the southern USA. Grown for ornament.

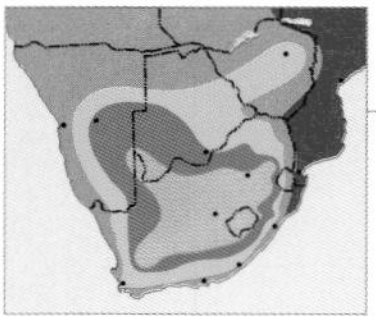

- Drought 2
- Spring
- Evergreen

2 *Senna septemtrionalis* *(= Cassia laevigata, C. septemtrionalis)* FABACEAE

Smooth Senna, Arsenic Bush, Dooley Weed; Gladdepeul

OTHER LANGUAGES: Carbonero (Spanish)

Mexico to Peru Small tree with a rounded crown; bark rough; buds and twigs **hairless**; young stems **faintly ribbed**; lenticels minute. Leaves with 3–5 pairs of leaflets; petiole hairless, 25–50mm long; rachis round; leaflets 45–90 × 15–35mm, **lance-shaped**; tip **drawn to a long point**; base rounded; surface dull, hairless; margin **bent downwards**. Stipules soon falling. Inflorescences **erect**, 50–100mm long; peduncle 20–40mm long. Flowers bright yellow; petals 5, these 10–20mm long. Fruit a smooth, **papery**, brown pod 60–100 × 10–15mm. Seeds olive, 5–6mm long.

A garden ornamental that has become invasive throughout the tropics and a declared Category 1b invader in South Africa. Medicinal uses are recorded.

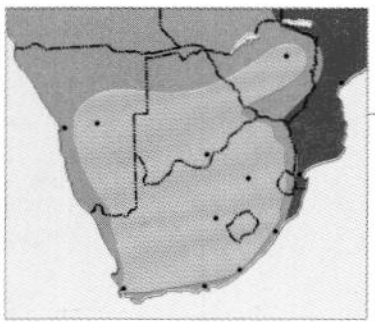

- Drought 2
- Spring
- Evergreen

3 *Senna siamea* *(= Cassia siamea)* FABACEAE

Kassod Tree, Siamese Shower; Kassodboom

OTHER LANGUAGES: Tie dao mu (Chinese); Bois perdrix (French); Kassodbaum (German); Kassod (Hindi); Flamboyán amarillo (Spanish); Khilek (Thai)

Myanmar and Thailand Medium-sized tree with a rounded to spreading crown; bark grey, rough; buds **hairy**; twigs becoming hairless; lenticels **warty**, conspicuous. Leaves with **8–13 pairs** of leaflets; petiole minutely, sparsely hairy, 20–30mm long; rachis round; leaflets 50–80 × 15–30mm, elliptic; tip **rounded, indented**; base rounded; surface **glossy above**, dull below; margin smooth. Stipules tiny, soon falling. Inflorescences erect, 70–200mm long; peduncle 50–70mm long. Flowers yellow; petals 5, these 10–20 × 5–10mm. Fruit a **flattened** pod 150–250 × 10–15mm. Seeds buff, 20–25 × 5–6mm.

Leaves, young pods and seeds are edible if boiled and the water discarded three times to remove toxins. The wood (trade name 'Pheasantwood') is hard and blunts tools quickly but is used for musical instruments, carving and small turned items. Grown for ornament but naturalised in many parts of the tropics.

GEOFF NICHOLS

1 *S. pendula* flowers

FOREST AND KIM STARR

1 *S. pendula* fruit

BRAAM VAN WYK

2 *S. septemtrionalis* flowers

BRAAM VAN WYK

2 *S. septemtrionalis* fruit

3 *S. siamea* leaves

3 *S. siamea* flowers and fruit

GROUP 33 Boerbean group

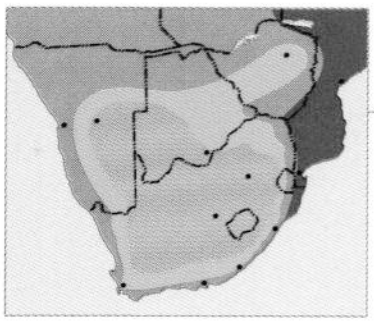

- Drought 2
- Spring
- Deciduous

1 *Senna spectabilis* *(= Cassia carnaval, C. speciosa, C. spectabilis)* FABACEAE

Scented Senna/Cassia, Calceolaria Cassia, Crown-of-gold Tree; Lekkerruiksenna

OTHER LANGUAGES: Cássia-do-nordeste (Portuguese); Mucuteno (Spanish); Mhoba (Swahili)

Mexico to Brazil Medium-sized tree with a rounded crown; bark grey, becoming fissured with age; buds and twigs **hairy**; lenticels conspicuous. Leaves with 4–15 pairs of leaflets; petiole **hairy**, 30–50mm long; rachis round; leaflets 30–60 × 15–25mm, lance-shaped to elliptic; tip **sharply pointed**; base obliquely rounded; lower surface **hairy**; margin smooth. Stipules soon falling. Inflorescences **erect**, 150–300mm long. Flowers yellow; petals 5, these 10–35mm long. Fruit a round to **4-angled**, papery or woody, dark brown pod 200–300 × 10–20mm. Seeds buff, 4.5–5.5 × 3.5–4mm.

Grown for ornament and shade in South Africa and Zimbabwe. The wood is of limited use as timber, more so for charcoal. Flowers are visited by bees. Naturalised in parts of Africa, Malaysia and southern USA.

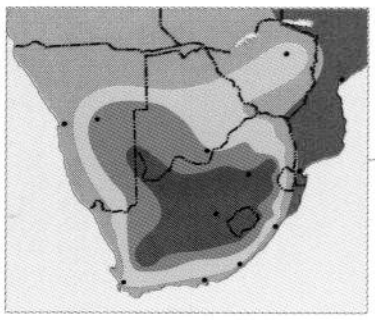

- Drought 2
- Summer
- Deciduous

2 *Sesbania punicea* *(= Daubentonia punicea)* FABACEAE

Red Sesbania, Brazilian Glory Pea, Scarlet Wisteria Tree; Rooisesbania, Brasiliaanse Glorie-ertjie

OTHER LANGUAGES: Flamboyant d'Hyères (French); Scharlach Strauchwisterie (German)

Brazil to Argentina **Small tree or shrub** with a rounded crown; bark grey, smooth; twigs hairless; lenticels **warty**, conspicuous. Leaves with 7–16 pairs of leaflets; petiole **hairless**; rachis round; leaflets about 25mm long, **narrowly oblong**; tip rounded, **hair-tipped**; base rounded or squared; surfaces hairless; margin smooth. Inflorescences **hanging**, up to 250mm long. Flowers orange-red, 15–20mm long. Fruit a **4-angled**, brown pod 50–100mm long, up to 10mm in diameter. Seeds midbrown.

A noxious weed in the USA and a declared Category 1b invader in South Africa. Formerly grown for ornament, with no other known uses. All parts of the plant are poisonous.

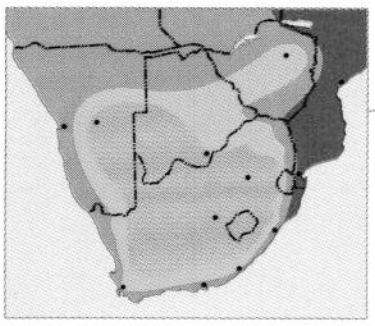

- Drought 2
- Spring
- Evergreen

3 *Tamarindus indica* FABACEAE

Tamarind; Tamarinde

OTHER LANGUAGES: Tamar-el-Hindi (Arabic); Kemal (Bahasa Indonesia); Suan dou (Chinese); Tamarinier des Indes (French); Indische Dattel (German); Imalii (Hindi); Amilii (Nepalese); Tamarindeira (Portuguese); Tamaríndo de la India (Spanish); Mkwaju (Swahili); Kalamagi (Tagalog)

India to tropical Africa (Zambezi Valley) Medium-sized to tall tree with an **irregularly vase-shaped** crown; bark pale grey, rough; buds and twigs hairless; lenticels minute. Leaves with 10–20 pairs of leaflets; petiole hairy, 4–8mm long; rachis round; leaflets 12–32 × 3–11mm, oblong; tip rounded; base **obliquely** squared; margin smooth. Stipules soon falling. Inflorescences **erect**, 10–150mm long. Flowers yellow or pink with red veins; petals 5, of which 3 are well developed, 2 minute, large ones 10–13mm long. Fruit a **velvety, fleshy pod** 100–180 × 15–30mm, shell brittle, rusty brown. Seeds midbrown, 11–17 × 10–12mm.

Fruits are an essential feature of Indian and Southeast Asian cookery. The pulp is also used in East Asia for cleaning brassware. The wood is prized for making furniture and charcoal and for other uses. This is the provincial tree of Phetchabun, Thailand. Medicinal uses are recorded. Recorded from South Africa's Limpopo and KwaZulu-Natal provinces, Mozambique and tropical Africa.

1 *S. spectabilis* leaves

1 *S. spectabilis* flowers

1 *S. spectabilis* fruit

2 *S. punicea* leaves

BRAAM VAN WYK

2 *S. punicea* flowers

GEOFF NICHOLS

2 *S. punicea* fruit

FOREST AND KIM STARR

3 *T. indica* flowers

FOREST AND KIM STARR

3 *T. indica* fruit

GROUP 34

Soapberry group

Leaves pinnately compound, alternate or in tufts. Leaflets more than 3, terminal one absent (paripinnate). Stipules absent.

See also Group 3: *Parkinsonia aculeata* (p.84).

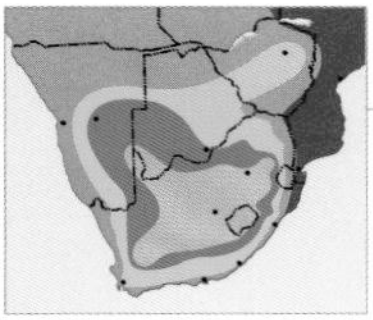

- Drought 2
- Spring
- Deciduous

1 *Khaya anthotheca* (= *K. nyasica*)

MELIACEAE

Red Mahogany, East African Mahogany; Rooimahonie, Oos-Afrikamahonie

East Africa to Zimbabwe and Mozambique **Large to very large** tree with a columnar to rounded crown; bark grey-brown, smooth, forming plate-like scales; buds and twigs hairless; new growth **red**. Leaves with 2–7 pairs of leaflets; petiole hairless; rachis round; leaflets up to **170 × 70mm**, oblong, with a **drip-tip**; base rounded; surface dark green, glossy above, dull, paler below; margin smooth. Inflorescences erect, up to 250mm long. Flowers small, white; males and females separate but on the same tree. Fruit a round, woody, grey capsule **30–50mm in diameter**. Seeds 10–20 × 15–30mm.

Grown in South Africa and Zimbabwe experimentally and as specimen trees in botanical gardens but makes a fine shade tree in a large garden. The wood is dark red, fine-grained and suitable for furniture, flooring and boat-building.

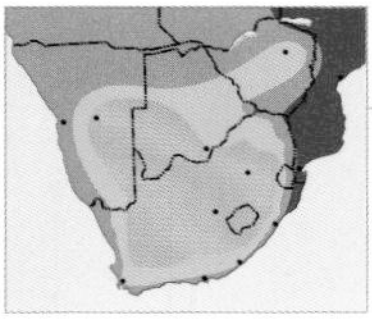

- Drought 3
- Summer
- Evergreen

2 *Khaya senegalensis*

MELIACEAE

Senegal Mahogany; Senegalmahonie

OTHER LANGUAGES: Bois rouge (French)

Senegal to Uganda and Gabon **Medium-sized** tree, with a rounded to spreading crown; new growth **yellowish brown**. Leaves with 2–7 pairs of leaflets, petiole long, hairless, with enlarged base; leaflets narrowly oblong; base rounded: margin smooth. Inflorescences erect, up to 200mm long. Flowers small, white, fragrant; males and females separate but on the same tree. Fruit a round, woody, grey to black capsule **up to 50mm in diameter**.

Rarely grown in our region and most often seen as specimen trees in private collections. The timber has many uses and it has been over-exploited in its natural habitat. This species is sometimes used as a street tree in West Africa.

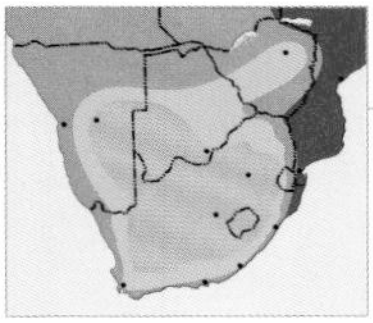

- Drought 2
- Spring
- Evergreen

3 *Litchi chinensis* (= *Nephelium litchi*)

SAPINDACEAE

Litchi, Lychee; Lietsjie

OTHER LANGUAGES: Kalengkeng (Bahasa Indonesia); Li zhi (Chinese); Cerisier de Chine (French); Lichi (Hindi, Marathi); Litschibaum (German); Lechia (Portuguese, Spanish); Alupag-amo (Tagalog); Linchi (Thai); Cây vải (Vietnamese)

China to Cambodia Small tree with a **spreading to rounded** crown; buds hairy; twigs becoming hairless. Leaves with 2–4 pairs of leaflets; petiole hairless, 20–45mm long; leaflets 80–110 × 17.5–40mm, **elliptic**, with a drip-tip; base narrowed; surface glossy above, dull below; margin smooth. Inflorescences erect, 150–300mm long. Flowers small, white. Fruit fleshy, round, about 35 × 30mm, rind **rough and warty**, leathery, red or brown. Seeds black, 20–25mm long, 10–15mm wide and deep, covered by a **layer of sweet, translucent white flesh**.

Grown as a fruit tree for the last 4,000 years and appreciated by western visitors to its native area very early on. The main cultivar grown in our region, recorded from South Africa and Swaziland, is 'Mauritius' but there are many others elsewhere.

1 *K. anthotheca* flowers

1 *K. anthotheca* fruit

2 *K. senegalensis* flowers

2 *K. senegalensis* fruit

3 *L. chinensis* flowers

3 *L. chinensis* fruit

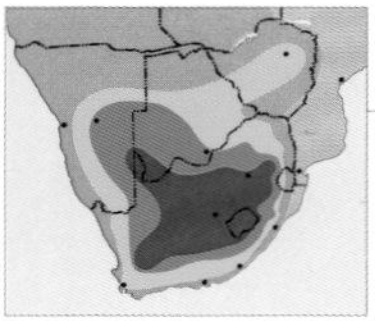

- Drought 2
- Spring
- Evergreen

1 *Sapindus saponaria* SAPINDACEAE

Wing-leaved Soapberry, False Dogwood, Western Soapberry; **Vlerkblaarseepbessie**

OTHER LANGUAGES: Jaboncillo (Spanish)

Florida to Argentina Small tree with a rounded crown; bark pale grey, flaking; buds hairy; twigs hairless; lenticels **smooth**, conspicuous, **in rows**. Leaves with 3–10 pairs of leaflets; petiole **hairless**, 20–70mm long; rachis usually **flattened or winged**; leaflets 70–130 × 30–50mm, lance-shaped to elliptic, with a drip-tip; base **obliquely** narrowed; surface dull both sides; margin smooth. Inflorescences erect, **up to 360mm long**. Flowers small, white. Fruit fleshy, yellow-green, ellipsoid, about 25 × 15–20mm, becoming **translucent and wrinkled** when mature. Seeds black, 12mm wide.

Resistant to coastal environments if grown as an ornamental. Fruits are poisonous but can be used as a soap substitute. Medicinal uses are recorded. The wood splits into thin strips suitable for basket-making. Recorded from scattered places in Mozambique, South Africa and Zimbabwe.

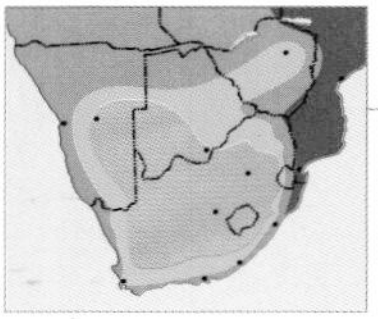

- Drought 2
- Spring
- Deciduous to semi-evergreen

2 *Swietenia mahagoni* MELIACEAE

Spanish Mahogany, West Indies Mahogany; **Spaanse Mahonie,** Mahonie

OTHER LANGUAGES: Tao hua xin mu (Chinese); Acajou de Cuba (French); Amerikanisches Mahagoni (German); Aguano (Spanish)

Florida to Hispaniola Medium-sized to large tree with a rounded crown; bark smooth grey, becoming brown, flaking in older trees; twigs hairless; lenticels **warty**, conspicuous. Leaves with 4–10 pairs of leaflets; petiole hairless, with enlarged base; leaflets **50–60 × 25–30mm**, lance-shaped to elliptic; tip long drawn out; base narrowed or rounded; surface **glossy**; margin smooth. Inflorescences erect, 80–150mm long. Flowers pale greenish cream, small. Fruit a woody, dark brown to black, egg-shaped to roundish capsule **60–100 × 30–60mm**. Seeds chestnut to dark brown, 20–50mm long, **winged**.

National tree of the Dominican Republic. Grown in our region as a specimen tree in Durban Botanic Gardens and would do well as an ornamental shade tree in a warm, large garden. Used in the Victorian period for making fine furniture (commanding high prices today), scientific instruments and their cases. Used until about World War II to make high-end large-format cameras. Medicinal uses are recorded.

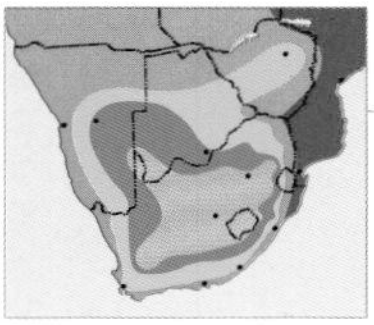

- Drought 2
- Spring
- Deciduous

3 *Toona ciliata* *(= Cedrela toona, T. australis, T. microcarpa)* MELIACEAE

Toon Tree, Indian Mahogany; **Toonboom,** Indiese Mahonie

OTHER LANGUAGES: Suren kapar (Bahasa Indonesia); Hong chun (Chinese); Cèdre rouge d'Australie (French); Australisches Mahagoni (German); Tuun (Hindi); Tunnah (Sanskrit); Danupra (Tagalog)

India to Australia Large tree with an irregularly rounded to columnar crown; bark grey or brown, deeply fissured; buds hairy; twigs hairless; lenticels **warty**, conspicuous. Leaves **drooping**, with 5–14 pairs of leaflets; petiole hairless, **60–110mm long**, with enlarged base; leaflets 90–128 × 32–50mm, lance- to egg-shaped, with a **drip-tip**; base **oblique**; margin smooth. Inflorescences **hanging**, up to 550mm long. Flowers small, creamy white. Fruit a woody, reddish brown, **5-angled** capsule **15–20** × 5–7mm. Seeds 11–19 × 2.5–4.5mm.

Invasive in South Africa, Zimbabwe, Tanzania and Kenya. A declared Category 3 invader in South Africa. In Australia, the timber is highly prized and in Asia wood fragments are used as a substrate for growing shiitake mushrooms.

1 *S. saponaria* leaves

JOÃO MEDEIROS, WIKIMEDIA COMMONS, CC BY SA 2.0

1 *S. saponaria* flowers

DAVID EICKHOFF, WIKIMEDIA COMMONS, CC BY SA 2.0

1 *S. saponaria* fruit

LALITHAMB, WIKIMEDIA COMMONS, CC BY SA 2.0

2 *S. mahagoni* flowers

FOREST AND KIM STARR

2 *S. mahagoni* fruit

BRAAM VAN WYK

3 *T. ciliata* flowers

PETER WOODARD, WIKIMEDIA COMMONS, PUBLIC DOMAIN

3 *T. ciliata* fruit and seeds

BRAAM VAN WYK

3 *T. ciliata* dehisced fruit

GROUP 35

Peppertree group

Leaves pinnately compound, alternate or in tufts. Leaflets more than 3, terminal one present (imparipinnate); margin toothed or lobed. Latex present, but may only show as a stickiness at the freshly broken end of a petiole.

Species of introduced trees that appear to fit in this group often seem closer to Group 37, and are treated there. If a tree is not found in the latter group, it may well be native to southern Africa. Please consult Group 35 in *Field Guide to Trees of Southern Africa* (Van Wyk & Van Wyk 2013).

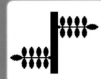

GROUP 36

Knobwood group

Leaves pinnately compound, alternate or in tufts. Leaflets more than 3, terminal one present (imparipinnate); margin toothed or lobed. Latex absent.

See also Group 37: *Pistacia terebinthus* (p.378), *P. vera* (p.378) and *Toxicodendron succedaneum* (p.380); Group 38: *Ailanthus altissima* (p.382).

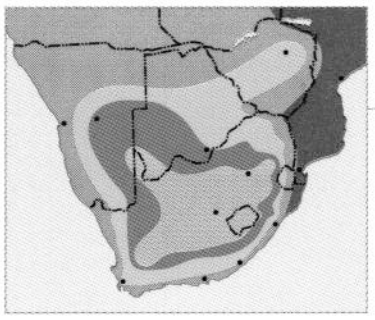

- Drought 2
- Spring
- Evergreen

1 *Azadirachta indica*

MELIACEAE

Neem, Margosa; Neemboom

OTHER LANGUAGES: Nim (Arabic); Nim des Indes (French); Neem (Hindi); Nimbak (Sanskrit)

Myanmar Medium-sized tree with a rounded crown similar to that of syringa (*Melia azedarach*, p.442); bark reddish brown to grey, fissured; buds and twigs hairless, the latter **reddish**; lenticels **minute**. Leaves with 10–16 pairs of leaflets; petiole hairless, 30–70mm long; leaflets 50–90 × 15–35mm, lance-shaped; tip **long-pointed**; base **oblique**; margin coarsely toothed. Inflorescences erect, up to 300mm long. Flowers small, **white**. Fruit fleshy, yellow-green, 10–20mm long.

Official tree of Sindh Province, Pakistan. Seen in our region only in Mozambique and in South Africa in Mpumalanga and KwaZulu-Natal. It is invasive in much of the Middle East and tropical Africa and should be planted with caution. Preparations of the fruit are widely used on crop plants as a form of pest control.

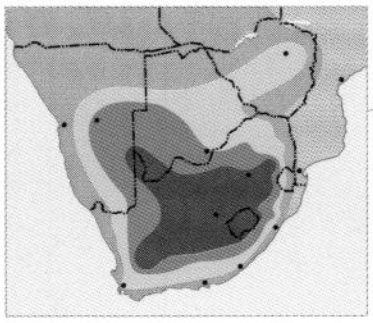

- Drought 2
- Spring
- Evergreen

2 *Bersama abyssinica*

MELIANTHACEAE

Wing-leaved White-ash; Gevleuelde Witessenhout

OTHER LANGUAGES: Munyahawa (Shona); Mwangwakwao (Swahili)

Tropical Africa Medium-sized to large tree with a rounded crown; bark smooth, brown; buds and twigs **hairy**. Leaves with 5–10 pairs of leaflets; petiole about 80mm long; rachis **usually winged**; leaflets 80–140mm long, up to 50mm wide, egg-shaped to elliptic, with a short drip-tip; base narrowed or rounded; side veins **sunken above, raised below**; margin smooth or toothed. Inflorescences erect, up to 350mm long. Flowers white, creamy, yellow, pink or green; petals 5, these 10–22mm long. Fruit a round, **smooth**, woody, brown capsule about 25mm long and in diameter. Seeds about 10–11 × 8mm.

Grown as specimen trees in botanical gardens in Zimbabwe and in Mpumalanga, South Africa. All parts are poisonous. Medicinal uses are recorded.

1 *A. indica*

1 *A. indica* leaves

GEOFF NICHOLS

1 *A. indica* flowers

KEVINSOORYAN, WIKIMEDIA COMMONS, CC BY SA 3.0

1 *A. indica* fruit

BRAAM VAN WYK

2 *B. abyssinica* leaf

PIET VAN WYK

2 *B. abyssinica* flowers

PIET VAN WYK

PIET VAN WYK

2 *B. abyssinica* fruit; inset: dehisced fruit

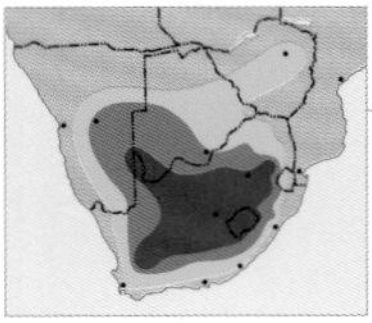

1 *Carya illinoinensis* (= *C. oliviformis, C. pecan, Hicoria pecan*) JUGLANDACEAE
Pecan Nut; Pekanneut

- Drought 2
- Spring
- Deciduous

OTHER LANGUAGES: Bao ke shan he tao (Chinese); Pacanier (French); Pekannussbaum (German); Nogueira-peca (Portuguese); Pecanero (Spanish)

Southern USA Large tree with a columnar to rounded crown and **yellow autumn colours**; bark grey, forming rectangular flakes; buds and twigs **hairy**; lenticels **warty**, conspicuous, orange. Leaves with 4–8 pairs of leaflets; petiole hairless, 40–80mm long; rachis **flattened**; leaflets 50–175 × 25–75mm, lance-shaped or elliptic; tip **long-pointed**; base rounded; surface hairy or hairless; margin **finely toothed**. Inflorescences **hanging**, appearing before the leaves; males and females separate but on the same tree, males up to 180mm long. Fruit a fleshy, smooth, brown, **4-ridged** nut 25–60 × 12–25mm. Seeds midbrown.

Widely grown commercially and for ornament in South Africa and Zimbabwe. Seeds are the pecans of commerce and are eaten as is or cooked. The wood is not particularly valuable but has been used for agricultural implements and firewood. Medicinal uses are recorded.

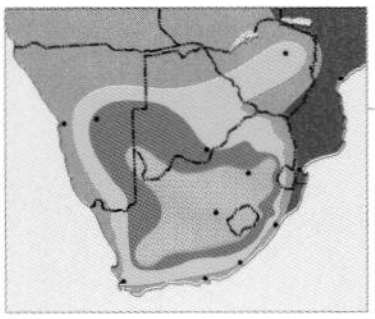

2 *Grevillea banksii* PROTEACEAE
Australian Crimson Oak; Australiese Rooi-eik

- Drought 2
- Spring
- Evergreen

Eastern Australia Large shrub or small tree with a rounded to spreading crown; prostrate forms are known; bark brown, narrowly fissured; twigs **hairless**. Leaves with **3–6 pairs** of leaflets, sometimes not completely separated; petiole hairless; leaflets 50–180 × 5–15mm, linear, sometimes deeply pinnately lobed, with **4–12 lobes**; tip pointed; base narrowed; lower surface hairy; margin **rolled inwards**. Inflorescences **erect, 50–200mm long**. Flowers tubular, red, rarely creamy. Fruit a woody, brown, densely hairy, egg-shaped pod 15–25mm long. Seeds buff.

Widely grown in Mozambique, South Africa, Swaziland, Zimbabwe and tropical Africa as an ornamental or as a windbreak but a declared Category 1b invader in South Africa. Wood used only for fuel.

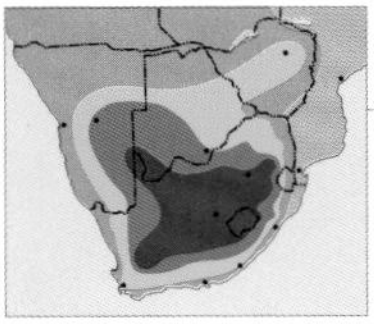

3 *Grevillea robusta* PROTEACEAE
Australian Silky Oak, Silky Oak; **Australiese Silwereik,** Silwereik

- Drought 2
- Spring
- Evergreen

Queensland, Australia Large tree with a narrow, pyramidal crown; bark grey, fissured; buds and twigs **hairy**, the latter **almost black**; lenticels **warty**, conspicuous. Leaves with **11–21 pairs** of leaflets, these themselves pinnately **1–4-lobed**; petiole hairy, 25–35mm long; rachis channelled or flattened; leaflets 70–80 × 10–20mm, elliptic; tip pointed, **spine-tipped**; base narrowed; lower surface hairless; margin smooth. Inflorescences erect, 100–150mm long; peduncles 35–45mm long. Flowers tubular, orange, with abundant **brownish nectar**. Fruit an ellipsoid pod 15–20mm long.

Grown in shelterbelts and as an ornamental but invasive in many places. This species is a declared Category 3 invader in South Africa. Timber makes beautiful furniture with a 'guineafowl' figure but the sawdust is known to be irritant. The flowers are among the richest known sources of nectar.

GEOFF NICHOLS

1 *C. illinoinensis* flowers

TONY RODD

1 *C. illinoinensis* fruit

BRAAM VAN WYK

2 *G. banksii* flowers

MAURO HALPERN

2 *G. banksii* flowers and fruit

3 *G. robusta* leaves

BRAAM VAN WYK

3 *G. robusta* old flowers

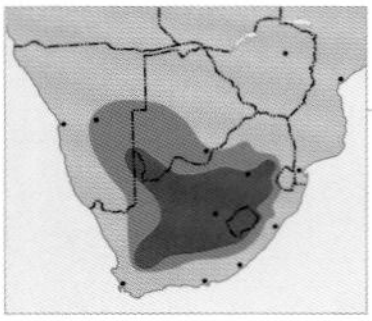

- Drought 2
- Summer
- Deciduous

1 *Koelreuteria paniculata* SAPINDACEAE

Pride-of-China, Golden Rain, Varnish Tree; Trots-van-China, Gouereënboom

OTHER LANGUAGES: Luanshu (Chinese)

China Small to medium-sized tree with an upright to spreading crown and **yellow to golden-orange autumn colours**; bark grey to black, rough; buds and twigs hairless; lenticels **minute**. Leaves with 3–7 pairs of leaflets; petiole hairless, 35–60mm long; rachis flattened; leaflets 48–107 × 38–69mm, egg-shaped to elliptic; tip drawn out; base narrowed or squared; surface glossy above, dull below; margin **coarsely scalloped or saw-toothed** throughout. Inflorescences erect, 250–300mm long. Flowers yellow becoming orange-red; petals 4, oblong, 4.5–7 × 1.5–2mm, with a spur. Fruit an **inflated, triangular** capsule, ripening orange to pinkish, eventually brownish when dry, 43–69 × 25–32mm. Seeds dark brown to black, 6–7mm long, 6.5–8mm wide and deep.

Grown as a street tree and garden ornamental in Lesotho and cooler parts of South Africa. Reported as invasive in some parts of the USA. The inflated, bladder-like pods are produced in great masses and render the trees very attractive and conspicuous. Seeds can be used for personal ornament but are poisonous. Medicinal uses are reported. Compare *K. bipinnata* (p.438) and *K. elegans* (p.440).

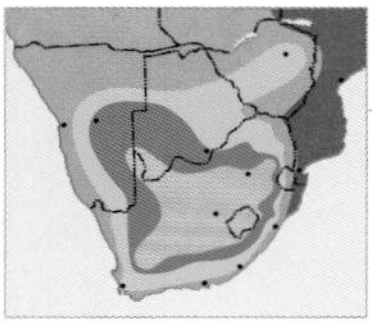

- Drought 2
- Spring
- Evergreen

2 *Murraya koenigii* RUTACEAE

Curry Leaf, Kurripulya Leaf; Kerrieblaar

OTHER LANGUAGES: Warak al kari (Arabic); Daun kari (Bahasa Indonesia); Tiao liao jiu li xiang (Chinese); Arbre à feuilles de curry (French); Curryblätter (German); Karipatta (Hindi); Folhas de Caril (Portuguese); Hojas de Curry (Spanish); Kari vempu (Tamil); Hom khaek (Thai); Kariapat (Urdu); Lá cà ri (Vietnamese)

India to China Small, shrubby tree with a spreading crown; bark **grey**; buds and twigs hairy; lenticels **smooth** but conspicuous. Leaves with 5–15 pairs of leaflets; petiole **hairless**, 12–15mm long; rachis round; leaflets 10–40 × 8–15mm, lance-shaped to oblong, **with secretory cavities**; tip pointed; base oblique; surfaces hairless throughout; margin smooth or finely saw-toothed. Inflorescences erect, about 60mm long. Flowers **fragrant**; petals 5, white, 4–8 × 0.8–1.7mm. Fruit a **round, blue-black** berry up to 11mm in diameter. Seeds green.

Recorded in our region from Mozambique and South Africa's Mpumalanga and KwaZulu-Natal provinces. Leaves are used in Indian and Indo-Chinese cuisine. Medicinal and ritual uses are recorded. *Murraya siamensis* is frequently confused with *M. koenigii* and grown for that reason. Trees tend to be larger, with black bark, and the leaves have a hairy petiole. The aroma of the leaves is coarser and hints that the suggestion arising from DNA studies that the group of species to which it belongs would be better placed in *Clausena* (horsewood), is well founded. Compare also *M. paniculata* (p.390).

1 *K. paniculata* leaves

1 *K. paniculata* flowers

MAURO HALPERN

1 *K. paniculata* fruit

FOREST AND KIM STARR

2 *M. koenigii* leaves

MUHAMMAD MAHDI KARIM, WIKIMEDIA COMMONS, CC BY SA 2.5

2 *M. koenigii* flowers

GEOFF NICHOLS

2 *M. koenigii* fruit

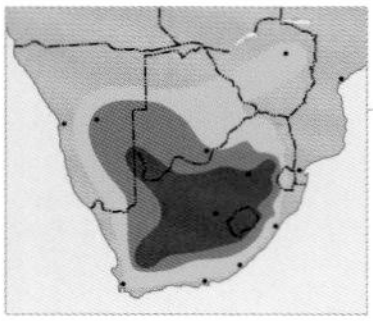

- Drought 2
- Spring
- Deciduous

1 *Pterocarya fraxinifolia*

JUGLANDACEAE

Caucasian Wingnut; Kaukasiese Vleuelneut

Caucasus and Iran Medium-sized to large tree with a rounded crown; bark deeply fissured; buds and twigs **hairless**; lenticels **smooth** but conspicuous. Leaves with 3–13 pairs of leaflets; petiole hairless, 25–50mm long, with enlarged base; rachis **round**; leaflets 80–95 × 26–45mm, oblong to lance-shaped; tip **long drawn out**; base **oblique**; veins densely hairy with **star-shaped hairs** on lower surface; margin saw-toothed. Inflorescences **hanging**, appearing with the leaves; males and females on the same tree, males 75–125mm long, females 300–500mm long. Flowers individually inconspicuous. Fruit a **1-winged**, brown nut 18–22 × 5–7mm.

Grown occasionally in Gauteng and KwaZulu-Natal for ornament and shade. The inner bark provides a fibre that can be woven and the wood has minimal uses. Medicinal uses are recorded.

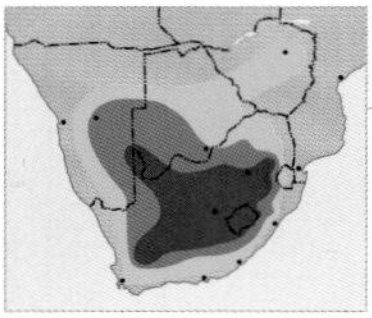

- Drought 2
- Spring
- Deciduous

2 *Pterocarya stenoptera*

JUGLANDACEAE

Chinese Wingnut; Chinese Vleuelneut

OTHER LANGUAGES: Feng yang (Chinese)

China Medium-sized to large tree with a rounded crown; bark not as deeply fissured as in *P. fraxinifolia* (above); buds and twigs **hairy**; lenticels **warty**, conspicuous. Leaves with 5–10 pairs of leaflets; petiole sparsely hairy, 20–36mm long, with enlarged base; rachis **winged**; leaflets 40–100 × 15–42mm, oblong; tip **rounded**; margin saw-toothed. Inflorescences **hanging**, appearing with the leaves; males and females on the same tree, males 30–60mm long, females about 200mm long. Flowers individually inconspicuous. Fruit a **2-winged**, brown nut 18–25mm long, 7–12mm across the wings.

Grown for ornament, especially in classical East Asian gardens. Recorded in our region from Limpopo, Gauteng and KwaZulu-Natal. The leaves are insecticidal and medicinal uses are recorded.

1 *P. fraxinifolia*

1 *P. fraxinifolia* leaves

1 *P. fraxinifolia* flowers

1 *P. fraxinifolia* fruit

2 *P. stenoptera*

2 *P. stenoptera* leaves

2 *P. stenoptera* fruit

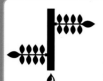

GROUP 37

Marula group

Leaves pinnately compound, alternate or in tufts. Leaflets more than 3, terminal one present (imparipinnate); margin smooth. Latex present, but may only show as a stickiness at the freshly broken end of a petiole.

The species below may sometimes key out in Group 35.

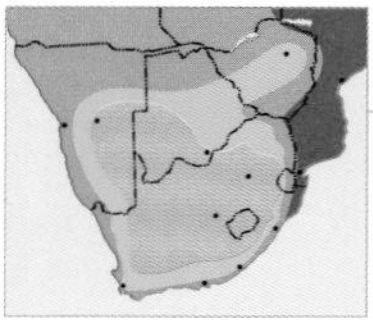

- Drought 2
- Spring
- Evergreen

1 *Owenia acidula*

MELIACEAE

Emu Apple, Sour Plum; Emoe-appel

Eastern Australia Small tree with an upright to spreading crown; bark black, very rough; buds hairy; twigs becoming hairless, dark purple; lenticels **warty**, conspicuous; latex **white**. Leaves with **many pairs of leaflets**; petiole hairy; rachis **often winged**; leaflets 10–50 × 3–9mm, **narrowly** elliptic; tip rounded, **spine-tipped**; base obliquely narrowed. Inflorescences erect, 45–120mm long. Flowers small, creamy. Fruit **fleshy, red-purple, 22–38** × 18–30mm, skin with **lengthways creases**.

Grown as a street tree in parts of Durban and very rarely as a garden ornamental elsewhere. The fruits are edible but hardly palatable.

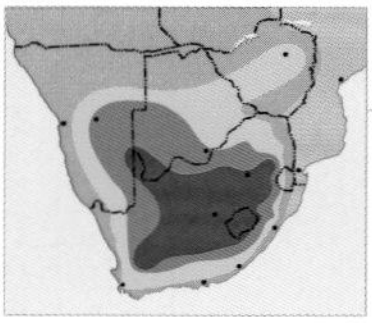

- Drought 2
- Spring
- Deciduous

2 *Pistacia terebinthus*

ANACARDIACEAE

Terebinth, Turpentine Tree; Terpentynboom

OTHER LANGUAGES: Térébinthe (French); Comalheira (Portuguese); Terebinto (Spanish)

Mediterranean region Small tree or large shrub with a spreading crown; twigs **hairless**; lenticels warty, **minute, rusty orange**. Leaves with 3–6 pairs of leaflets; petiole **hairless**, 30–80mm long; rachis **round**; leaflets 30–50 × 20–40mm, egg-shaped; tip spine-tipped. Inflorescences **erect**; males 60–100mm long, female 150–200mm long, on different trees. Flowers inconspicuous. Fruit **fleshy**, red, later brown, widest beyond the middle, 5–7 × 5–6mm.

Terebinth has been cultivated for millennia and is believed to be the plant called *ki-ta-no* in some Mycenaean Linear B texts. Fruits are edible and are particularly a part of Cretan cuisine. This is the original source of turpentine, and resins from the tree have numerous uses.

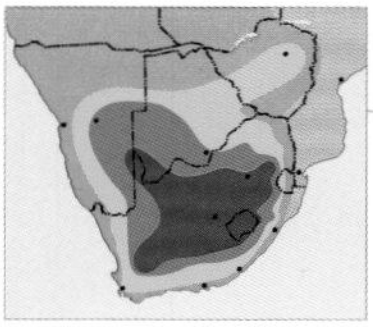

- Drought 2
- Spring
- Evergreen

3 *Pistacia vera*

ANACARDIACEAE

Real Pistachio, Pistachio Nut; Pistasieneut, Pimperneut

OTHER LANGUAGES: Fustuq (Arabic); Pistah (Farsi); Pistachier (French); Pistazienbaum (German); Pistacheira (Portuguese); Fistashka (Russian); Pistachero (Spanish); Fistik (Turkish); Pistaa (Urdu, Farsi)

Iran to Central Asia Small tree with a spreading crown; twigs **hairy**; lenticels **warty, conspicuous**. Leaves with 1–4 pairs of leaflets; petiole **hairy**, 50–100mm long; rachis **winged**; leaflets 50–120 × 30–60mm, broadly **lance-shaped to round**; tip **spine-tipped**; surface glossy above, paler below. Inflorescences erect; males and females on different trees, males 50–80mm long. Fruit with a buff, **woody shell**, 16–29 × 6–12mm.

The earliest archaeological traces of pistachio shells and nut-cracking tools have been dated to 78,000 BP. The seeds are eaten fresh, salted or prepared in numerous ways. Although they contain an oil, it is seldom extracted because the seeds are too valuable in other forms. Mature trees produce a high-quality resin. In our region found as a specimen tree at the University of Pretoria and recorded from the Free State and also from the Northern Cape, where it is now grown commercially.

STEVE AND ALISON PEARSON

1 *O. acidula* flowers

STEVE AND ALISON PEARSON

1 *O. acidula* fruit

RAM EISENBERG, WIKIMEDIA COMMONS, CC BY SA 3.0

2 *P. terebinthus* flowers

JAVIER MARTIN, WIKIMEDIA COMMONS, PUBLIC DOMAIN

2 *P. terebinthus* fruit

STAN SHEBS, WIKIMEDIA COMMONS, CC BY SA 3.0

3 *P. vera* fruit

TOM GRUNDY / SHUTTERSTOCK.COM

3 *P. vera* nuts

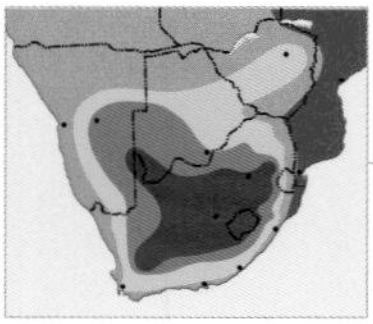

- Drought 3
- Spring
- Evergreen

1 *Schinus molle* ANACARDIACEAE

Pepper Tree, Californian Pepper Tree, Peruvian Mastic Tree; Peperboom, Kaliforniese Peperboom

OTHER LANGUAGES: Jia zhou hu jiao (Chinese); Faux Poivrier (French); Peruanischer Pfefferbaum (German); Aroeira-vermelha (Portuguese); Aguaribay (Spanish)

Mexico to Argentina Small to large tree with **weeping** branches and foliage; bark grey-brown, **fissured**; buds hairless; twigs becoming hairless. Leaves with **up to 18 pairs** of leaflets; petiole hairless, 20–30mm long; rachis flattened to winged; leaflets **40–90 × 6–10mm, narrowly** lance-shaped; surface hairless; margin smooth or toothed. Inflorescences **drooping**, 100–200mm long. Flowers small, yellowish green. Fruit **thinly fleshy, deep pink**, round, 6–10mm long and in diameter.

Naturalised in South Africa. Grown in dry areas of Botswana, Namibia and South Africa for shade and ornament. The red fruits have a peppery taste and are sold as 'pink peppercorns'. Both these and the leaves are eaten in curries.

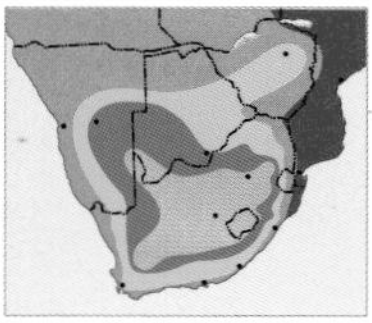

- Drought 2
- Spring
- Evergreen

2 *Schinus terebinthifolius* var. *acutifolius* ANACARDIACEAE

Brazilian Pepper Tree, Christmas-berry Tree; Brasiliaanse Peperboom

OTHER LANGUAGES: Ba xi hu iao mu (Chinese); Faux Poivrier du Brésil (French); Brasilianischer Pfefferbaum (German); Aroeirinha preta (Portuguese); Pimienta de Brasil (Spanish)

Brazil Small tree with a spreading crown of **horizontal** branches; bark dark brown, smooth, becoming fissured later; buds and twigs hairless; lenticels **warty**, conspicuous. Leaves with **3 or 4 pairs** of leaflets; petiole hairless, 20–30mm long; rachis partly winged; leaflets **15–100 × 10–30mm, elliptic**; tip and base rounded; margin smooth or scalloped. Inflorescences erect, 30–100mm long. Flowers very small, creamy white. Fruit round, **fleshy, red**, 3.5–5mm in diameter.

Grown for ornament, hedging and shade. A declared Category 1b invader in the Eastern Cape, KwaZulu-Natal, Mpumalanga and Limpopo, Category 3 elsewhere in South Africa.

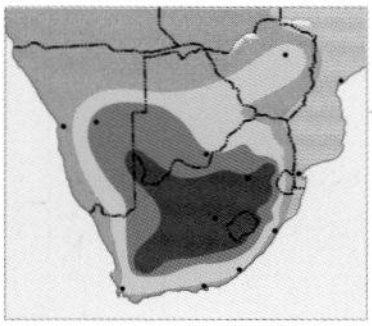

- Drought 2
- Spring
- Evergreen

3 *Toxicodendron succedaneum* (= *Rhus succedanea*) ANACARDIACEAE

Wax Tree; Wasboom

OTHER LANGUAGES: Ye qi (Chinese); Sumac Cirier (French); Japanischer Wachsbaum (German); Hazenoki (Japanese); Iaponskoye voskovoye derevo (Russian); Árbol de la cera (Spanish)

East Asia Small tree with a rounded to spreading crown and **red autumn colours**; bark smooth; buds and twigs hairless; lenticels **warty**, conspicuous. Leaves with 4–7 pairs of leaflets; petiole hairless, 40–60mm long; rachis round; leaflets 60–120 × 13–30mm, lance-shaped to oblong, with a **drip-tip**; base **obliquely** narrowed. Inflorescences erect, 80–150mm long. Flowers yellow-green, inconspicuous. Fruit fleshy, egg-shaped, tan, **7–9mm in diameter**.

A declared Category 1b invader in South Africa and a noxious weed in parts of Australia. All parts of the plant can cause severe skin irritation on contact, especially in sensitive people. Medicinal uses are recorded. The sap is used in the preparation of lacquer.

FOREST AND KIM STARR

1 *S. molle*

BRAAM VAN WYK

1 *S. molle* flowers

BRAAM VAN WYK

1 *S. molle* fruit

2 *S. terebinthifolius* leaves

BRAAM VAN WYK

2 *S. terebinthifolius* flowers

BRAAM VAN WYK

2 *S. terebinthifolius* fruit

3 *T. succedaneum* flowers

PIERIA, WIKIMEDIA COMMONS, PUBLIC DOMAIN

3 *T. succedaneum* fruit

GROUP 38

Kiaat group

Leaves pinnately compound, alternate or in tufts. Leaflets more than 3, terminal one present (imparipinnate); margin smooth. Latex absent.

See also Group 3: *Parkinsonia aculeata* (p.84); Group 4: *Artocarpus altilis* (p.102); Group 9: *Stenocarpus sinuatus* (p.188); Group 10: *Grevillea hilliana* (p.218); Group 36: *Bersama abyssinica* (p.370), *Murraya koenigii* (p.374) and *M. siamensis* (p.374); Group 37: *Owenia acidula* (p.378), *Pistacia terebinthus* (p.378), *P. vera* (p.378) and *Toxicodendron succedaneum* (p.380).

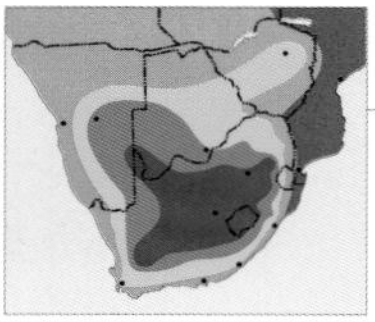

- Drought 2
- Spring
- Deciduous

1 *Ailanthus altissima*

SIMAROUBACEAE

Tree of Heaven; Hemelboom

OTHER LANGUAGES: Chou chun (Chinese)

China Medium-sized to large, **freely suckering, evil-smelling** tree with a columnar to rounded crown; bark grey, deeply fissured; buds hairy; twigs hairless; lenticels **smooth** but conspicuous. Leaves with **5–20 pairs** of leaflets; petiole hairless; rachis round; leaflets 100–170 × 25–30mm, lance-shaped; tip long drawn out; base rounded; lower leaflets often with 1–3 pairs of blunt teeth near the base, each with a **small gland** (extrafloral nectary) on the lower surface; surface glossy. Inflorescences erect, up to 500mm long. Flowers small, white; some bisexual and others either male or female on different trees. Fruit a **reddish brown, 2-winged** nut 30–40mm long, greatest width 7–9mm.

Invasive almost wherever it has been planted and a declared Category 1b invader in South Africa. The wood is flexible and used in China for making kitchen steamers. It has also been used for cabinet work. In its native range, the leaves feed a moth that produces an inferior grade of silk. Many medicinal uses are recorded.

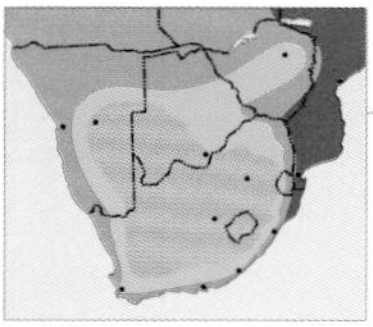

- Drought 2
- Spring
- Evergreen

2 *Averrhoa carambola*

OXALIDACEAE

Star-fruit, Caramba, Carambola; Stervrug, Karambola

OTHER LANGUAGES: Belimbing manis (Bahasa Indonesia, Malay); Yang tao (Chinese); Carambolier doux (French); Sternfrucht (German); Karmal (Hindi); Karanbora (Japanese); Caramboleira (Portuguese); Carambola, Caramba (Spanish); Belimbing (Tagalog); Ma fuang (Thai); Khế (Vietnamese)

South Asia Small, multistemmed tree with a spreading crown; bark reddish brown; buds and twigs hairy. Leaves **drooping**, with 3–5 pairs of leaflets; petiole hairy, 12–35mm long, base enlarged; leaflets **15–35 × 10–20mm**, egg-shaped, with a drip-tip; base rounded or squared; surface **glossy** above, **whitish** below. Inflorescences erect, sometimes **on old wood**, 40–80mm long; peduncle to 10mm long. Flowers violet, with white margin; petals 5, each with a spur, 6–9 × 1.5–3mm. Fruit a yellow to orange, **5-angled berry** 50–125 × 50–60mm, star-shaped in section. Seeds up to 12 × 6mm.

Recorded from a few places in South Africa, Zimbabwe and Réunion and grown for its fruit. It would also make an attractive garden ornamental on account of its flowers. The fruit is eaten fresh on its own or in salads, cooked in jams and chutneys or processed into juice. Medicinal uses are recorded. The high concentration of oxalates in some fruits may render them toxic to certain individuals.

1 *A. altissima* leaves

1 *A. altissima* flowers

1 *A. altissima* fruit (see also p.14)

2 *A. carambola* leaves

2 *A. carambola* flowers

2 *A. carambola* fruit

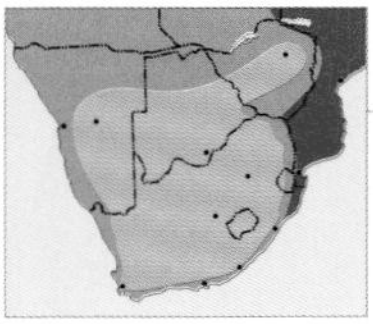

1 *Brownea grandiceps* (= *B. ariza*) FABACEAE

Rose-of-Venezuela, Scarlet Flame Bean; Roos-van-Venezuela

- Drought 2
- Spring
- Evergreen

OTHER LANGUAGES: Palo de la Cruz (Spanish)

Venezuela to Peru Small, spreading tree; buds hairless; twigs **hairy**; lenticels **warty**, conspicuous. Leaves with 4–13 pairs of leaflets; petiole **hairy at the base**, 11–60mm long; young foliage **limp, brown as if dead**; mature leaflets 50–170 × 20–60mm, widest below or beyond the middle, with a drip-tip; base obliquely rounded or **heart-shaped**. Inflorescences **hanging** on side branches, 110–200mm long; peduncle 40–110mm long. Flowers red; petals 5, these 50–67 × 17–24mm. Fruit a hairy, **flat, woody** pod 210–400 × 60–80mm. Seeds 30–42 × 25–35 × 5–15mm.

A showy ornamental for a tropical garden, recorded in our region only from Durban Botanic Gardens. Medicinal uses are recorded.

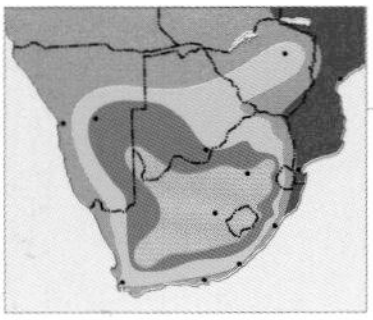

2 *Castanospermum australe* FABACEAE

Australian Chestnut, Moreton Bay Chestnut; Australiese Kastaiing

- Drought 2
- Spring
- Evergreen

Eastern Australia Large tree with a rounded crown; bark flaking; twigs **hairless**; lenticels warty, conspicuous. Leaves with **4–8 pairs** of leaflets; petiole hairless, 30–60mm long; leaflets **100–200** × 30–50mm, elliptic to oblong, with a **drip-tip**; base narrowed; upper surface glossy. Stipules soon falling. Inflorescences erect, 50–150mm long, often **borne directly on the trunk and older branches**. Flowers **bicoloured**; petals 5, yellow, changing to orange-red with age, 30–40mm long. Fruit a cylindrical, woody, brown, hairless **pod 100–200** × 40–60mm. Seeds reddish brown, **up to 30mm long**.

Grown as a street tree or for ornament in larger gardens and recorded from scattered localities in Mozambique and South Africa. Bees visit the flowers for nectar and pollen. These trees provide one of the most sought-after timbers in Australia. It is used for carvings, furniture, joinery, plywood, veneer and more. The very large seeds are poisonous but medicinal uses are recorded for the tree.

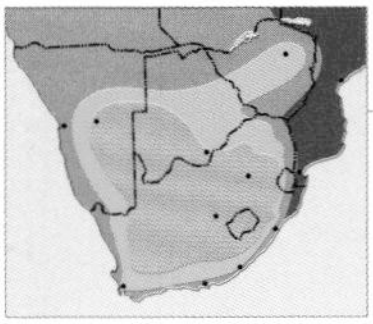

3 *Cedrela odorata* MELIACEAE

West Indian Cedar, West Indian Mahogany; Rooiseder, Wes-Indiese Mahonie

- Drought 2
- Spring
- Deciduous

OTHER LANGUAGES: Cèdre acajou (French); Westindische Zedrele (German); Cedro colorado (Spanish)

Mexico to Ecuador, and the West Indies Large tree with a rounded crown; bark greyish brown to black, **deeply fissured**, forming broad ridges; buds hairy; twigs hairless; lenticels **warty**, conspicuous. Leaves with 6–12 pairs of leaflets; petiole hairless; leaflets 70–150 × 30–50mm, **lance- to egg-shaped**, with a drip-tip; base obliquely narrowed to squared. Inflorescences **hanging**, 200–400mm long, appearing with the leaves. Flowers greenish white; petals 5, oblong, 7–8 × 1.5–2mm; males and females separate but on the same tree. Fruit a **woody, warty, grey, ellipsoid capsule** 20–35mm long. Seeds reddish brown to midbrown, **2-winged**, 20–30mm long.

This is the timber traditionally used to make cigar boxes. It is also the traditional choice for making the neck of classical and flamenco guitars. The aromatic timber repels insects, is easily worked and has many uses. Bees visit the flowers for nectar. Medicinal uses are recorded. Planted in Zimbabwe and the warmer eastern parts of South Africa.

1 *B. grandiceps* leaves

GEOFF NICHOLS

1 *B. grandiceps* flowers

FOREST AND KIM STARR

2 *C. australe* flowers

JMK, WIKIMEDIA COMMONS, CC BY SA 3.0

2 *C. australe* fruit

ARTHUR CHAPMAN, WIKIMEDIA COMMONS, CC BY SA 2.0

2 *C. australe* fruit with seed

GEOFF NICHOLS

3 *C. odorata* flowers

ANTONIO SERGIO FARIAS CASTRO

REINALDO AGUILAR

3 *C. odorata* fruit; inset: dehisced fruit

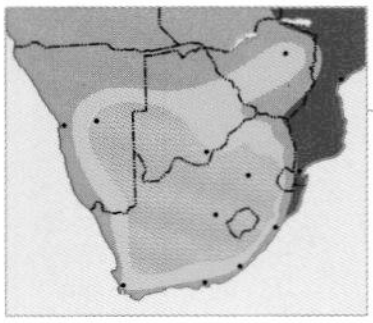

- Drought 2
- Spring
- Evergreen

1 *Dimocarpus longan* *(= Euphoria longan)*

SAPINDACEAE

Longan, Dragon's Eye; Longanboom

OTHER LANGUAGES: Mata Kuching (Bahasa Indonesia); Long-yan (Chinese); Longanbaum (German); Rongan (Japanese); Kelengkeng (Malay); Longana (Portuguese); Lamyai (Thai); Long nhan (Vietnamese)

India to New Guinea Large tree with a rounded crown; bark dark, fissured; buds and twigs hairy; lenticels warty, conspicuous. Leaves with **4–10 pairs** of leaflets; petiole almost hairless, 20–100mm long; leaflets 30–190 × 15–65mm, elliptic to oblong; tip pointed; base **obliquely** narrowed. Inflorescences erect, 80–400mm long. Flowers yellow to brown; petals 5, oblong, 1.5–6 × 0.6–2mm. Fruit a berry, roundish, 20–25 × 12.5–15mm, rind **warty, yellow-brown**. Seeds dark brown, surrounded by a layer of **translucent** flesh.

Grown for its edible fruit, which is seldom seen for sale though almost as well regarded as the litchi (Group 34, p.366), which it much resembles. In our region, seen only in KwaZulu-Natal, and there rarely. The Chinese name means 'dragon's eye' and refers to the fruit – the dark seed visible through translucent flesh looks like an eye with its pupil.

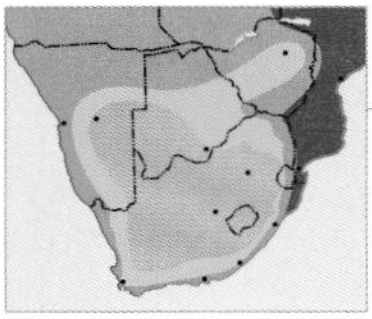

- Drought 2
- Spring
- Evergreen

2 *Gliricidia sepium*

FABACEAE

Gliricidia, Mexican Lilac, Quick Stick; Glirisidia

OTHER LANGUAGES: Madriado, Cacahuananche (Spanish)

Mexico to Guyana Small to medium-sized tree with a vase-shaped crown; bark rough, forming **broad ridges**; twigs hairy or hairless. Leaves with **6–10 pairs** of leaflets; petiole hairless, 3–6mm long; rachis round; leaflets 30–65 × 15–35mm, egg-shaped to elliptic; tip pointed; base narrowed. Inflorescences erect, 50–150mm long. Flowers **pink, with a white to yellow** basal mark; petals 5, these12–20 × 5–20mm. Fruit a **flat**, woody, brown pod 75–150 × 14–16mm. Seeds dark brown, 6–10 × 5–9mm.

Regarded as the second most important multipurpose tree after *Leucaena leucocephala* (Group 43, p.440). Like that tree, its roots fix nitrogen. Grown as specimen trees in arboreta and botanical gardens in KwaZulu-Natal.

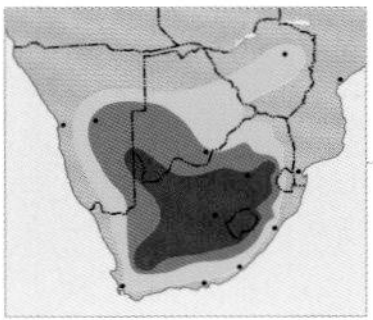

- Drought 1
- Summer
- Deciduous

3 *Juglans regia*

JUGLANDACEAE

Walnut, English Walnut, European Walnut, Persian Walnut; Okkerneut, Europese Okkerneut

OTHER LANGUAGES: Noguer comú (Catalan); hú táo (Chinese); Noyer commun (French); Echter Walnussbaum (German); Perusha gurumi (Japanese); Nogueira-comum (Portuguese)

Central Asia, from Xinjiang (China) to Turkey Large, spreading tree; bark pale grey, **smooth** or fissured with age; buds and twigs hairy. Leaves with petiole sparsely hairy and its base enlarged; leaflets **2–4 pairs**, 60–120 × **40–75mm**, egg-shaped to oblong; tip pointed. Inflorescences **hanging**, male spikes 50–100mm long. Fruit an **egg-shaped nut** with a greenish to brown, leathery husk, **up to 50 × 40–50mm**. Seeds buff.

Grown for ornament, nuts and oil in many parts of South Africa and Zimbabwe but nowhere common. Trees grow slowly, giving rise to the Flemish folk-saying 'Boompje groot, plantertje dood' – the grower will not live to see the mature tree. Walnut timber often has unusual figures and is highly prized for top-quality furniture, musical instruments, flooring, gunstocks and veneer. The nuts are highly allergenic. Medicinal uses are recorded.

1 *D. longan* leaves

1 *D. longan* flowers

1 *D. longan* fruit

2 *G. sepium* flowers

2 *G. sepium* fruit

3 *J. regia* flowers (male)

3 *J. regia* flowers (female)

3 *J. regia* fruit

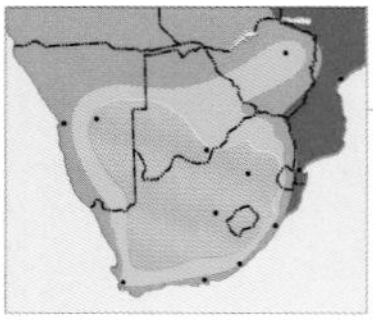

1 *Millettia dura*

FABACEAE

East African Millettia; Oos-Afrikamillettia

- Drought 2
- Spring
- Deciduous

Ethiopia, Kenya, Tanzania and Uganda **Small** tree with a vase-shaped crown; bark grey, smooth; twigs **brownish hairy**. Leaves with 5–12 pairs of leaflets; petiole hairless, 30–50mm long; rachis round; leaflets up to 90 × 30mm, oblong; tip drawn out to a point; base oblique; surface dull, hairless above in adult leaves, **hairy below**. Inflorescences erect or hanging, **up to 150mm long**; peduncle up to 50mm long, often appearing before the leaves. Flowers purple; petals 5, these19–28 × 7–18mm. Fruit a **flat, woody**, brown pod 140–200mm long, up to 21mm wide, opening explosively.

Timber is tough and durable, used for tool handles and poles. Grown in our region as a specimen tree in botanical gardens but has potential as an ornamental.

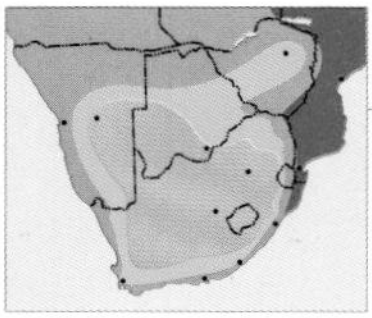

2 *Millettia pinnata* (= *Pongamia pinnata*)

FABACEAE

Indian Beech, Pongam; Pongamboom

- Drought 2
- Spring
- Briefly deciduous to evergreen

OTHER LANGUAGES: Karanj (Hindi); Naktamāla (Sanskrit); Coqueluche (Spanish); Pungai (Tamil)

Malaysia to the Pacific islands Small to medium-sized tree with a spreading crown; bark grey, smooth; buds and twigs **hairless**. Leaves with 2–4 pairs of leaflets; petiole hairless, 50–60mm long; rachis round; leaflets 40–200 × 18–100mm, **egg-shaped**; tip long drawn out or at least pointed; base rounded to heart-shaped; lower surface **hairless**. Stipules soon falling. Inflorescences erect, **100–200mm long**; peduncle 40–50mm long. Flowers white or pink, with a yellow basal mark; petals 5. Fruit a **flat, brown** pod 35–80 × 10–30mm. Seeds 17–22 × 16–18 × 7–8mm.

A decorative tree for ornament and shade, seen in our region almost exclusively as specimen trees in Durban and Maputo. Timber is of poor quality because it splits and warps while drying. The seeds contain a high proportion of 'pongam oil' with many industrial uses. This oil contains a toxic principle but medicinal uses are recorded.

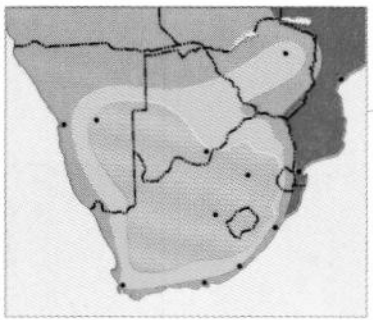

3 *Millettia stuhlmannii*

FABACEAE

Panga-panga; Patryshout

- Drought 2
- Spring
- Deciduous

OTHER LANGUAGES: Panga-panga (French); Jambire (Portuguese); Mpande, Mpangapanga (Swahili); Muangaila (Venda)

Tropical Africa Medium-sized to large tree with a spreading crown; bark yellowish or grey, **smooth**; twigs **hairy**; lenticels **warty**, conspicuous. Leaves with 3 or 4(6) pairs of leaflets, each pair with two **minute, hair-like stipels at the base**; petiole hairless, up to 100mm long; rachis round; leaflets 90–130 × 40–90mm, egg-shaped to elliptic; tip rounded and indented; base broadly pointed to rounded; surface **pale green** above, **blue-green** below. Inflorescences erect or hanging, up to 350mm long. Flowers white, creamy or lilac, with lilac honey guides; petals 5, these 22–25 × 11–25mm. Fruit a **flat, woody**, brown pod 250–500 × 35–47mm, **velvety at first**. Seeds mid- to dark brown, about 20–23 × 17–19 × 4mm.

Panga-panga is one of the most important export timbers of Mozambique. It is dark brown to almost black, fine-grained and durable and is used for furniture, flooring, veneer and other purposes. Medicinal and magical uses are recorded for the roots. Grown in our area as specimen trees in botanical gardens but would make a good ornamental in private gardens.

1 *M. dura* flowers

1 *M. dura* fruit

TATIANA GERUS

2 *M. pinnata* flowers

DR.S.SOUNDARAPANDIAN, WIKIMEDIA COMMONS, PUBLIC DOMAIN

2 *M. pinnata* fruit

3 *M. stuhlmannii* flowers

PIET VAN WYK

3 *M. stuhlmannii* fruit

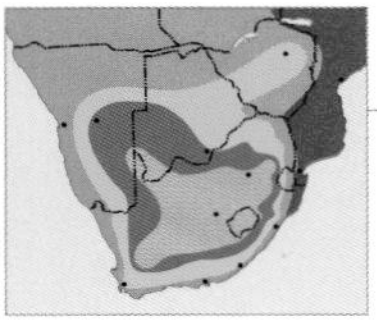

- Drought 2
- All year
- Evergreen

1 *Murraya paniculata* *(= M. exotica)* RUTACEAE

Orange Jessamine, Cosmetic Bark Tree, Satinwood; Lemoenjasmyn

OTHER LANGUAGES: Jiu li xiang (Chinese); Orange-jessamine (French); Madhukamini (Hindi); Naranjo jasmín (Spanish); Kamuning (Tagalog)

Southeast Asia Large shrub or small tree with a vase-shaped to rounded crown, often shaped by pruning; bark **whitish**; buds and twigs **hairy**. Leaves with **1–4 pairs** of leaflets; petiole hairless, 10–20mm long; rachis **flattened** or round; leaflets with **secretory cavities**, 28–70 × 12–20mm, egg-shaped, with a drip-tip; base rounded; surface **glossy**. Inflorescences erect; peduncle 10–20mm long. Flowers **scented**; petals 5, white, 13–21 × 4–6mm. Fruit an **orange**, egg-shaped berry 13mm long. Seeds greyish olive-brown, about 10 × 5–6mm.

Very commonly grown garden ornamental in Mozambique, Namibia, South Africa and Zimbabwe. It is invasive in Australia and southern Florida, USA. In South Africa, it is a declared Category 1b invader in KwaZulu-Natal, Mpumalanga and Limpopo. Bee farmers grow orange jessamine as shelterbelts for their hives. Medicinal uses are recorded from the Far East. See also *M. koenigii* (p.374).

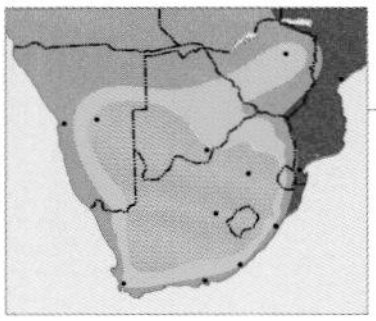

- Drought 2
- Spring
- Evergreen

2 *Myroxylon balsamum* FABACEAE

Balsam of Peru, Balsam of Tolú, Santos Mahogany (timber); Balsem-van-Peru

Mexico to Colombia Medium-sized to large tree with a tall, straight bole and vase-shaped crown; bark grey, smooth; buds hairy; twigs **hairless**; lenticels **warty**, conspicuous. Leaves with **2–6 pairs** of leaflets; petiole hairless, 30–40mm long; rachis round; leaflets 40–140 × 15–55mm, egg-shaped to elliptic, with a drip-tip; base **rounded**. Inflorescences erect, up to 200mm long. Flowers white to creamy; petals 5, these 8–10 × 3–9mm. Fruit a brown, hairless, **winged nut** 10–110 × 10–20mm.

Grown in our region as a specimen tree in Durban Botanic Gardens. The timber is used for furniture, railway sleepers, flooring and more. Gums from these trees, also known as 'Balsam of Peru', are used mainly as flavourants of food and drink, and in perfumes and toiletries for fragrance. Medicinal uses are recorded.

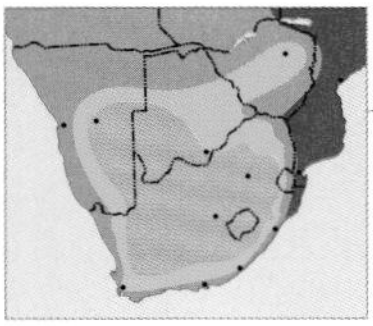

- Drought 2
- Summer–Autumn
- Evergreen

3 *Ormocarpum kirkii* *(= O. mimosoides)* FABACEAE

Curled Caterpillar-pod; Krulruspeboontjie

OTHER LANGUAGES: Kapurupuru (Shona)

Tropical and southern Africa Large shrub or small tree with a spreading crown; bark **rough, deeply fissured**; buds hairy; twigs hairy or **bristly**. Leaves with 3–6 pairs of leaflets; petiole hairy, 5–13mm long; rachis round; leaflets **6–24 × 3–10mm**, elliptic or oblong; tip **indented** and **spine-tipped**; base narrowed or rounded; surface hairless or velvety; margin rolled inwards. Inflorescences erect, up to 15mm long; peduncle absent or up to 10mm long. Flowers pink, with a **purple basal mark**; petals 5, these 12–26 × 15–29mm. Fruit a **densely hairy, ellipsoid** pod about 20 × 3–5mm. Seeds buff, about 3–4 × 2–2.5 × 1.5mm.

Grown occasionally as a specimen tree or ornamental.

1 *M. paniculata* flowers

1 *M. paniculata* fruit

2 *M. balsamum* leaves

2 *M. balsamum* fruit

3 *O. kirkii* flowers

3 *O. kirkii* fruit

GROUP 38 Kiaat group

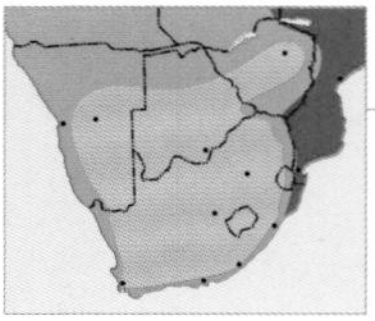

1 *Picrasma excelsa* SIMAROUBACEAE

Bitter Wood, Bitter Ash, Quassia; Bitterhout, Kwassiehout

- Drought 2
- Spring
- Evergreen

OTHER LANGUAGES: Bois noyer (French); Bitterholz (German); Madera de la Cuasia (Spanish)

The West Indies and Venezuela Small to medium-sized tree with a rounded crown; bark **almost smooth**, with a network of small ridges; buds hairy; twigs **hairless except when very young**. Leaves with about 6 pairs of leaflets; petiole minutely hairy; leaflets 70–135 × 30–46mm, **lance-shaped or elliptic** to oblong, with a drip-tip; base obliquely rounded; surface **glossy** above, minutely hairy below. Inflorescences erect, up to 100mm long. Flowers small, yellow-green. Fruit fleshy, red to purple, **round, 7–9mm long**. Seeds 4–6mm long.

Vulnerable in its natural habitat and the specimen tree in Durban has been felled but the species is recorded from Maputo. The wood is very bitter. Medicinal uses are recorded.

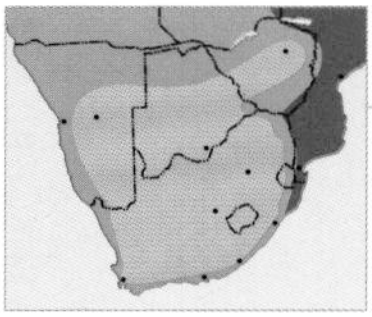

2 *Piscidia piscipula* (= *P. erythrina*) FABACEAE

Jamaica Dogwood, Fish-fuddle Tree, Florida Fishpoison; Jamaikaanse Kornoelie

- Drought 2
- Spring
- Deciduous

Mexico to Ecuador Small tree with an irregular crown; bark grey, smooth; buds hairy; twigs hairless; lenticels **warty**, conspicuous. Leaves with 2–5 pairs of leaflets; petiole hairless, 80–100mm long; rachis round; leaflets 40–100 × 30–60mm, egg-shaped to elliptic, with a **small, short drip-tip**; base **rounded to squared**; lower surface **hairy**. Inflorescences erect, about **120mm long**; peduncle about 25mm long. Flowers pea-like; petals 5, pink to red, 13–15mm long, up to 12mm wide. Fruit a **4-angled**, leathery, brown pod 30–90mm long.

Suitable as a garden ornamental but seen in our region as a specimen tree in botanical gardens. The wood is used for boat-building, carving and poles. Most, if not all parts of the tree are poisonous and have been used as aids in catching fish. Medicinal uses are recorded.

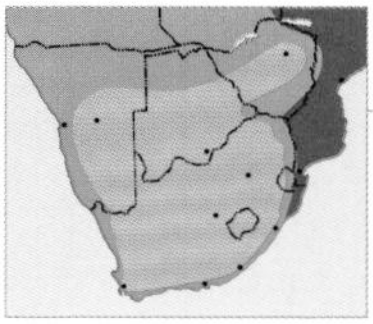

3 *Pterocarpus indicus* FABACEAE

Burmese Rosewood; Burmese Rooshout

- Drought 2
- Spring
- Deciduous

OTHER LANGUAGES: Sonokembang (Bahasa Indonesia); Angsana (Malay); Narra (Tagalog)

Myanmar to the Solomon Islands Large tree with a spreading, rounded crown and **drooping** branches; bark narrowly fissured; buds and twigs hairy; lenticels conspicuous. Leaves with 2–5 pairs of leaflets; petiole hairless, 20–60mm long; rachis round; leaflets 50–150 × 30–80mm, egg-shaped, with a **drip-tip**; veins **hairless**. Inflorescences erect, 60–200mm long, appearing after the leaves. Flowers **pea-like**; petals 5, yellow, 10–20 × 7–15mm. Fruit a **1-winged, flat**, brown pod 40–70 × 6–9mm, '**flying-saucer-shaped**'. Seeds dark brown, 8–10 × 2–5mm.

National tree of the Philippines and provincial tree of Chonburi and Phuket, Thailand. The timber is highly prized for cabinet work; the burl form, called Amboyna, is one of the world's most expensive veneers. Planted in Malaysia as a shade and ornamental tree but in our area a specimen tree in botanical gardens in Durban and Maputo. Medicinal uses are recorded.

ROLAND SPOHN

1 *P. excelsa* flowers

ROLAND SPOHN

1 *P. excelsa* fruit

HOMER EDWARD PRICE

2 *P. piscipula* leaves

CHRISTIAN TUN

2 *P. piscipula* flowers

VIRTUAL HERBARIUM / FLICKR

2 *P. piscipula* fruit

RUSSEL CUMMING

3 *P. indicus* flowers

3 *P. indicus* fruit

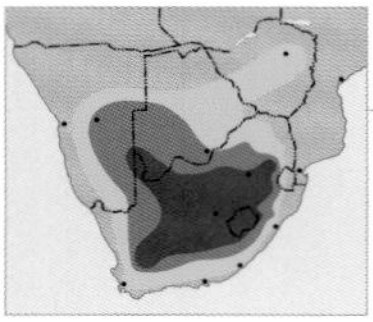

- Drought 2
- Spring
- Deciduous

1 *Robinia pseudoacacia* FABACEAE

Black Locust, False Acacia; Witakasia

OTHER LANGUAGES: Robinier (French); Robinie (German); Falsa acácia (Portuguese); Falsa acacia (Spanish)

Eastern USA Medium-sized tree with a rounded crown and **yellow autumn colours**; bark black, deeply fissured; twigs hairless; lenticels **warty**, conspicuous; stems round, **with paired, straight thorns**. Leaves with 4–9 pairs of leaflets; petiole hairless; rachis round; leaflets 25–50 × 15–30mm, egg-shaped to elliptic; tip and base **rounded**; surfaces dull, hairless or hairy; veins hairy below. Inflorescences **hanging**, 75–175mm long, appearing after the leaves. Flowers pea-like; petals 5, white, 15–20mm long, with a yellow basal mark. Fruit a **flat**, dark brown pod 60–90 × 12–18mm.

A declared Category 1b invader in South Africa and known to be invasive in North America, Europe and Asia. The wood is prized for flooring, boat-building, furniture and fuel. All parts of the tree except the flowers are poisonous. Medicinal uses are recorded.

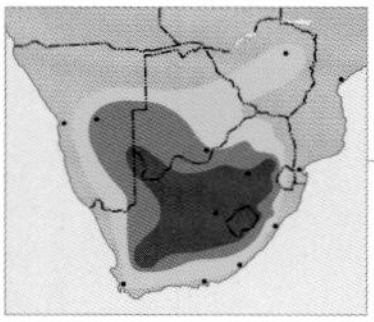

- Drought 2
- Spring
- Deciduous

2 *Styphnolobium japonicum* *(= Sophora japonica)* FABACEAE

Japanese Pagoda Tree, Chinese Scholar Tree, Pagoda Tree; Japanse Pagodeboom, Heuningboom, Pagodeboom

OTHER LANGUAGES: Huai (Chinese)

China and Korea Medium-sized, spreading tree; bark grey to black, fissured and rough; twigs hairy, **olive-green**; lenticels conspicuous, **tan**. Leaves with 4–10 pairs of leaflets; petiole hairless, with enlarged base; rachis round; leaflets 25–60 × 10–30mm, oblong; tip **pointed**; base rounded; lower surface hairy. Stipules soon falling. Inflorescences **hanging**, 150–350mm long. Flowers pea-like; petals 5, creamy white, 10–15 × 4mm or more. Fruit a **fleshy, yellow-green** pod 25–80 × 8–10mm, **narrowed between seeds**. Seeds dark brown to black, about 8 × 4–5mm.

Grown for ornament in scattered places in South Africa and Zimbabwe, often very long-lived. The wood is tough and springy and is used in carpentry, especially for the handles of traditional Japanese adzes. Most parts of the plant are poisonous and many uses in traditional Chinese medicine are recorded.

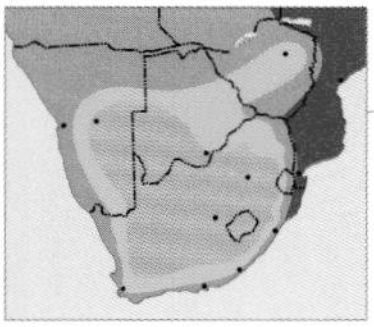

- Drought 2
- Spring
- Evergreen

3 *Swartzia langsdorffii* FABACEAE

Jacaranda Banana; Jakarandapiesang

OTHER LANGUAGES: Pau de Sangre (Portuguese)

Brazil Medium-sized tree with a rounded crown; bark grey, **smooth, with minute fissures**, forming small ridges; twigs **hairless**. Leaves with 2–4 pairs of leaflets; petiole hairless, 15–45mm long; rachis **winged**; leaflets 40–100 × 25–60mm, elliptic; tip pointed; base narrowed. Stipules soon falling. Inflorescences erect, 70–250mm long. Flowers **white**; petal **1, spoon-shaped**, 20–40 × 25–50mm. Fruit a dark brown, ellipsoid or **flat** pod about **80–85** × 45mm.

Grown for ornament, in our region as a specimen tree in Durban Botanic Gardens. The timber is used for cabinet work and construction.

1 *R. pseudoacacia* leaves

1 *R. pseudoacacia* flowers

1 *R. pseudoacacia* fruit

2 *S. japonicum* flowers

2 *S. japonicum* fruit

3 *S. langsdorffii* flower

3 *S. langsdorffii* closed fruit; inset: open fruit

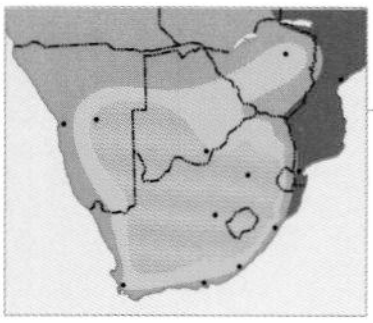

- Drought 1
- Spring
- Deciduous

1 *Sweetia fruticosa* *(= Ferreirea spectabilis)*

FABACEAE

Tapir Bean; Tapirboon

OTHER LANGUAGES: Sucupira (Portuguese)

Brazil to Bolivia Medium-sized tree with a rounded crown; bark brown to grey, narrowly fissured, flaking; twigs hairless; lenticels conspicuous. Leaves with 4–8 pairs of leaflets; petiole hairless, 75–100mm long; rachis round; leaflets **6–25** × 2.5–10mm, egg-shaped to oblong; tip **pointed**; base narrowed; surface glossy above, dull, glabrous below; margin smooth. Inflorescences erect, 50–150mm long, appearing with the leaves. Flowers pea-like, small, creamy to yellow. Fruit a **1-winged, flat**, red or yellow pod.

Grown in our region as a specimen tree in Durban Botanic Gardens. The heavy, hard wood is used for fine cabinet work, veneer, construction, railway sleepers and other purposes. Medicinal uses are recorded.

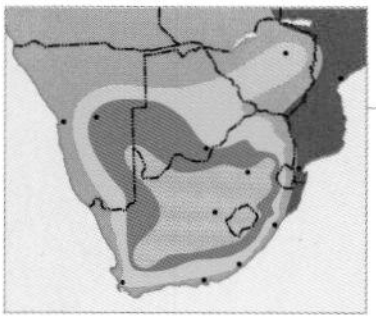

- Drought 2
- Spring
- Evergreen

2 *Tipuana tipu* *(= T. speciosa)*

FABACEAE

Tipu Tree; Tipoeboom, Trots-van-Bolivië

Bolivia and Argentina Medium-sized to large tree with a spreading crown; bark **narrowly fissured or rough**; twigs hairless. Leaves with 1–10 pairs of leaflets; petiole hairless; leaflets 27–75 × 10–20mm, **oblong**; tip **rounded and indented**; base rounded; surface dull, hairless. Inflorescences erect. Flowers pea-like; petals 5, yellow, 17–25mm long, with red honey guides or stripes. Fruit a **1-winged, brown nut 40–70mm long**, spinning as it falls. Seeds red-orange, about 6mm long.

A declared Category 3 invader in South Africa and invasive in Australia. It has an invasive root system and provides a home for spittlebugs, causing the tree to 'rain' certain times of the year, thus making a mess wherever it is planted. Despite all these drawbacks, it is still a very commonly grown ornamental and street tree. The wood is of high quality and the leaves are used for animal fodder.

1 *S. fruticosa*

1 *S. fruticosa* leaves

1 *S. fruticosa* fruit

2 *T. tipu* leaves

2 *T. tipu* flowers

2 *T. tipu* fruit

GROUP 39

Baobab group

Leaves palmately compound, once-divided, alternate. Leaflets more than 3.

See also Group 2: *Carica papaya* (p.44) and *Trevesia palmata* (p.68); Group 4: *Cecropia peltata* (p.104); Group 6: *Cochlospermum vitifolium* (p.126) and *Jatropha multifida* (p.128); Group 11: *Firmiana simplex* (p.252) and *Ricinus communis* (p.262).

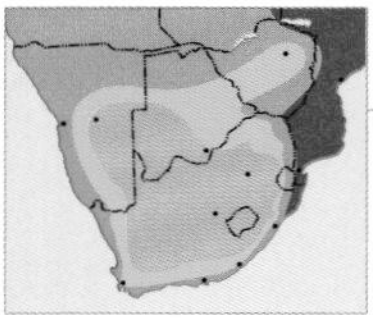

- Drought 2
- Spring
- Evergreen

1 *Bombax ceiba* (= *B. malabaricum*)

MALVACEAE

Red Cotton Tree; Rooikapok

OTHER LANGUAGES: Mu mian (Chinese); Roter Seidenwollbaum (German); Shalmali (Hindi); Simal (Nepalese); Algodoeiro do mato (Portuguese); Árbol capoc (Spanish); Ilavu (Tamil); Ngio pong daeng (Thai)

Tropical Asia Large tree with a rounded crown and **buttressed** trunk; bark green or grey, **spiny**, with narrow fissures forming small ridges; twigs hairless. Leaves with **5–7** leaflets; petiole hairless, up to 250mm long; leaflets up to 250 × 50mm, **elliptic or widest beyond the middle**, with a drip-tip; base narrowed or rounded; surface glossy; margin smooth. Stipules soon falling. Inflorescences a **hanging**, single flower. Flowers creamy or red; petals 5, oblong, up to 120 × 50mm. Fruit a smooth, woody, brown capsule up to 150mm long. Seeds embedded in long **white cotton**.

Grown in scattered parts of our region as an ornamental. Elsewhere the wood is used for matches and coffins. The dried, fallen flowers are eaten in some Thai curries. Medicinal uses are recorded for various exudates.

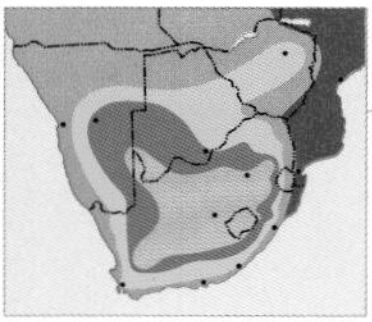

- Drought 2
- Spring
- Evergreen

2 *Casimiroa edulis*

RUTACEAE

White Sapote, Mexican Apple; Witsapot, Mexikaanse Appel

OTHER LANGUAGES: Sapote blanche (French); Weisse Sapote (German); Caccique (Maya); Cochitzápotl (Nahuatl); Sapoti (Portuguese); Zapote blanco (Spanish)

Mexico to Costa Rica Medium-sized tree with a rounded crown; buds hairy; twigs hairless; lenticels **warty, conspicuous**. Leaves with **5** (rarely 3 or 4) leaflets; petiole hairless, 50–75mm long; leaflets with **secretory cavities**, 50–180 × **30–90mm**, egg-shaped to elliptic, with a drip-tip; base narrowed to rounded; margin smooth. Inflorescences erect, 20–50mm long. Flowers small, fragrant, greenish white to yellow. Fruit a fleshy, **whitish yellow or green**, 5-lobed drupe 60–100mm long and in diameter. Seeds whitish to buff, 32–40 × 20–25 × 14–16mm.

Although widespread in our region, being recorded from Namibia, South Africa and Zimbabwe, white sapote fruits deserve to be better known. However, over-indulgence in these is known to cause drowsiness. Indeed, the Nahuatl name can be translated as 'sleep sweet fruit'.

1 *B. ceiba* leaves

1 *B. ceiba* flower

1 *B. ceiba* fruit

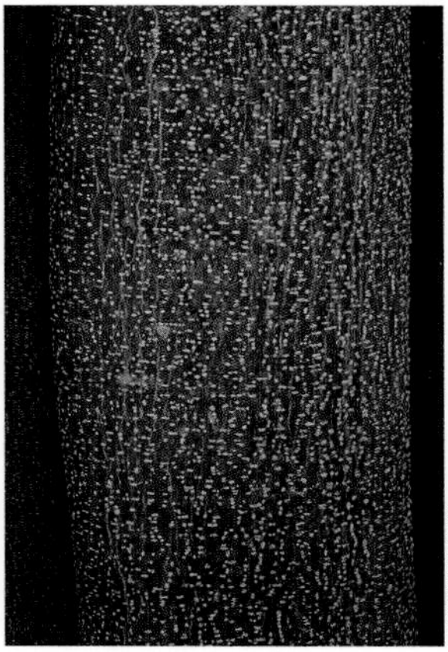

2 *C. edulis* bark

2 *C. edulis* flowers

2 *C. edulis* fruit

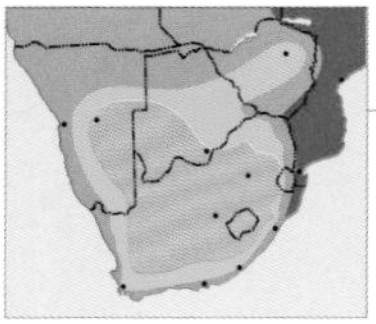

- Drought 2
- Spring
- Evergreen

1 *Ceiba pentandra* *(= Bombax pentandrum, Eriodendron anfractuosum)* MALVACEAE

Kapok Tree, Silk-cotton Tree; Kapokboom

OTHER LANGUAGES: Arbre coton (French); Árbol de la seda (Spanish); Mbuyu (Swahili)

Tropical Americas and West Africa Large to very large tree with a spreading crown and **buttressed** trunk which is sometimes **spiny**; bark grey, smooth; twigs hairless, **with single, straight thorns**. Leaves with (usually) **5** leaflets; petiole hairless, up to 200mm long; leaflets up to 150 × 40mm, elliptic, with a drip-tip; base narrowed; margin **smooth**. Stipules soon falling. Inflorescences an **erect**, single flower or clusters. Flowers **white to creamy**, rarely yellow or pink; petals 5, oblong, 35–40mm long. Fruit a woody, ellipsoid capsule about 150mm long. Seeds embedded in a **mass of whitish wool**.

Usually seen in our region as specimen trees in botanical gardens as it is suited only to the largest private collections. The whitish hairs surrounding the seeds are used as stuffing for pillows and similar items. Being very light, it was until recently used in lifejackets and other naval safety equipment. It is an excellent insulator against heat, cold and noise. The wood is used for plywood and paper pulp. Oil from the seeds is used as a lubricant and in soap. Medicinal uses are recorded.

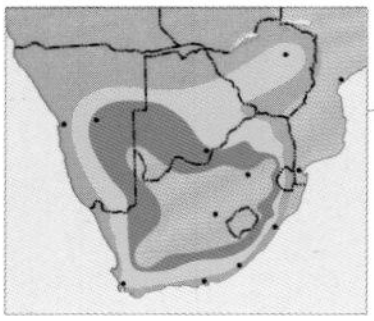

- Drought 2
- Autumn–Spring
- Deciduous

2 *Ceiba speciosa* *(= Chorisia speciosa)* MALVACEAE

Brazil Kapok, Floss-silk Tree; Brasiliaanse Kapok

Paraguay and Brazil Medium-sized tree with a **spiny, stout to bottle-shaped** trunk; bark **green** or grey; buds and twigs hairless; lenticels minute. Leaves with **5** leaflets; petiole hairless, 45–70mm long; leaflets 60–85 × 14–30mm, elliptic or widest beyond the middle; tip pointed; base narrowed; margin **toothed**. Inflorescences an erect, single flower. Flowers with **throat yellow, upper half pink, with purple to brown spots**; petals 5, 60–80 × 18–28mm. Fruit a grey capsule about 200mm long. Seeds embedded in **white woolly hairs**.

Commonly grown as an ornamental in private gardens and parks in South Africa and Zimbabwe. The silk from the pods can be used as stuffing like that of the kapok tree (above) but is of inferior quality. The wood is light, soft and flexible. *C. crispiflora* (2.1) often co-occurs with *C. speciosa*, but flowers in midsummer. It has narrower petals with darker markings and the stamens are completely fused into a tube.

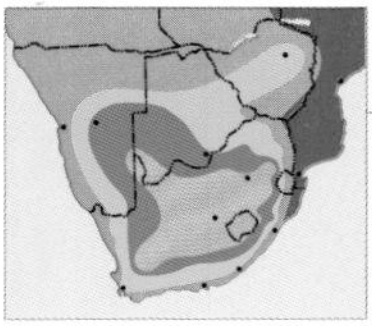

- Drought 2
- Spring
- Evergreen

3 *Manihot esculenta* *(= M. dulcis, M. utilissima)* EUPHORBIACEAE

Cassava, Bitter Cassava, Manioc, Tapioca; Kassawe, Bitter Broodwortel, Maniok

OTHER LANGUAGES: Kaspe, Singkong (Bahasa Indonesia); Manioc, Tapioca (French); Kassava, Maniok (German); Mandioca (Portuguese, Spanish); Mhogo (Swahili)

Wild species, now extinct, evidently from parts of present-day Brazil, Paraguay and Argentina Narrow upright shrub or small tree of indefinite form; buds and twigs hairless; latex **cloudy**. Leaves alternate; petiole hairless, 40–250mm long; blade 65–170 × 60–250mm, **deeply palmately 3–7-lobed**, lobes 15–60mm wide, lance-shaped, widest beyond the middle, with a **drip-tip**; base heart-shaped or surrounding the attachment of the petiole, with 3–7 main veins from the base. Inflorescences erect panicles, 20–110mm long. Flowers small, green. Fruit a greenish, **6-winged**, ellipsoid capsule 13–17 × 13–15mm. Seeds pale grey.

All present varieties of cassava are cultigens (of garden origin). Cassava is the third most important source of dietary carbohydrate in the tropics, after rice and maize. Recorded from Mozambique, South Africa and Swaziland in our region.

1 *C. pentandra* leaves

1 *C. pentandra* flowers

SAKHORN / SHUTTERSTOCK.COM

1 *C. pentandra* dehisced fruit

BRAAM VAN WYK

2 *C. speciosa* flowers

BRAAM VAN WYK

2.1 *C. crispiflora* flower

WOUTER HAGENS, WIKIMEDIA COMMONS, PUBLIC DOMAIN

2 *C. speciosa* fruit

3 *M. esculenta* leaves

3 *M. esculenta* flowers

TON RULKENS

3 *M. esculenta* fruit

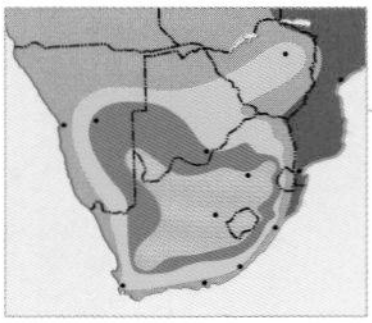

- Drought 1
- Spring
- Deciduous

1 *Manihot glaziovii* (= *M. carthaginensis* subsp. *glaziovii*) EUPHORBIACEAE

Tree Cassava, Ceará Rubber; Boomkassawe

OTHER LANGUAGES: Manicoba (Portuguese)

Brazil **Shrub or small tree** with a vase-shaped crown, or a rounded crown on a relatively long clear bole; bark pale brown or grey, smooth, peeling; buds and twigs hairless; latex **cloudy to white**. Leaves alternate; petiole hairless, 70–200mm long; blade 150–250 × 100–280mm, **deeply palmately 3–5-lobed**, lobes 10–70mm wide, widest beyond the middle; tip **pointed or rounded**; base heart-shaped or surrounding the attachment of the petiole, with 3–5 main veins from the base; surface dull, hairless, **dark bluish green above**, paler below; margin smooth. Stipules soon falling. Inflorescences erect, 20–150mm long. Flowers small, greenish white or yellow with reddish honey guides; males and females separate but on the same tree. Fruit a capsule, **smooth, warty on drying**, spongy and fibrous or woody, buff or grey-green, 15–20 × 14–22mm. Seeds 12–15 × 9–10 × 6–7mm.

Grown in our region as specimen trees in a few places in North West, Limpopo and KwaZulu-Natal. Plants have weedy tendencies, often reseeding themselves in gardens. The seeds are released explosively from the dry capsules. In Brazil, the latex provides a rubber which is usually uneconomic because of the high resin content. The leaves can be used as a famine food or fodder. *Manihot grahamii* (p.15; hardy cassava/tapioca; goossensboom), a shrub or small tree, also has unwinged fruit and weedy tendencies, but its leaves are more reminiscent of *M. esculenta*. It is widely grown for its attractive foliage in gardens on the South African highveld. Said to be the most cold-hardy of the *Manihot* species, it dies to the ground in areas with severe frost, but quickly resprouts in spring. All parts of the plant should be considered poisonous if ingested. The Afrikaans common name honours the botanist, Prof. A.P. Goossens (1896–1972), who is said to have been the first to have introduced the species to gardens in Potchefstroom.

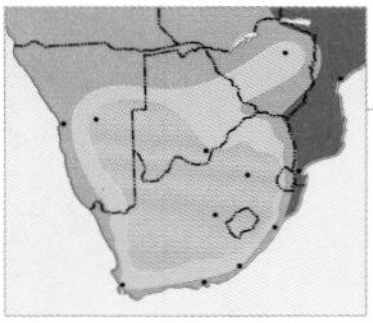

- Drought 2
- Spring
- Evergreen

2 *Pachira insignis* MALVACEAE

False Chestnut; Basterkastaiing

OTHER LANGUAGES: Marronier des Antilles (French); Cacáo-selvagem (Portuguese); Mamorana grande (Spanish)

Puerto Rico to Brazil Large tree with a rounded or layered crown; bark green, smooth; twigs hairless. Leaves with **5–7** leaflets; petiole **hairless**, 90–310mm long; leaflets 60–340 × 28–140mm, egg-shaped to elliptic, **purple at first**; tip **rounded to squared**; base narrowed; lower surface **hairless**; margin smooth, sometimes rolled inwards. Stipules inconspicuous. Inflorescences an erect, **single** flower; stalk hairy, 10–70mm long. Flowers **red**; petals 5, narrowly oblong, 175–340 × 11–25mm; stamens many, 160–300mm long, white at the base, top half red. Fruit a **densely hairy**, woody, brown, ellipsoid capsule 140–360 × 80–130mm. Seeds midbrown, 22–26 × 25–35 × 20–24mm.

Grown as specimen trees in Limpopo and Durban in our region. Elsewhere the seeds are eaten. Medicinal uses are recorded.

1 *M. glaziovii* leaves

FOREST AND KIM STARR

1 *M. glaziovii* fruit

2 *P. insignis* leaf

CERLIN NG

2 *P. insignis* old flower

MAURO HALPERN

2 *P. insignis* flower

CERLIN NG

2 *P. insignis* fruit

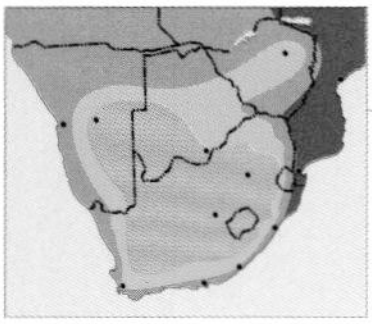

- Drought 2
- Spring
- Deciduous

1 *Pseudobombax ellipticum* *(= Bombax ellipticum, Pachira fastuosa)* MALVACEAE
Shaving-brush Tree; Skeerkwasboom

OTHER LANGUAGES: Árbol de señoritas (Spanish)

Mexico to Nicaragua Small to medium-sized tree with a **succulent** trunk, branching quite low down into a vase-shaped to rounded crown; bark grey, **deeply fissured**, forming broad ridges; twigs hairless. Leaves with **5** leaflets; petiole hairless, up to 350mm long; leaflets up to 300 × 80mm, egg-shaped, **widest beyond the middle**, **coppery** when young; tip pointed; base narrowed; lower surface hairless. Inflorescences an erect, **single** flower, appearing before the leaves; stalk hairless, about 35mm long. Flowers **white or pink**; petals 5, narrowly oblong; stamens many, white or pink, up to 130mm long. Fruit a **densely hairy**, woody, yellow-green, ellipsoid capsule up to 150mm long.

Grown in Zimbabwe and in South Africa's Mpumalanga and KwaZulu-Natal provinces as specimen trees. In the New World, the wood is used for firewood and carving and the seeds are edible if toasted. Medicinal uses are recorded.

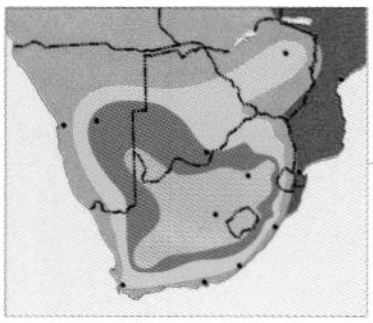

- Drought 2
- Spring
- Evergreen

2 *Schefflera actinophylla* *(= Brassaia actinophylla)* ARALIACEAE
Octopus Tree, Australian Cabbage Tree, Australian Umbrella Tree, Queensland Umbrella Tree; Seekatboom, Australiese Kiepersol

OTHER LANGUAGES: Arbre ombelle (French); Schefflere (German); Árbol pulpo (Spanish)

New Guinea Small, **multistemmed** tree usually with a vase-shaped crown; bark grey, smooth, with **conspicuous leaf scars**; twigs hairless. Leaves with **7–16** leaflets; petiole hairless, 150–800mm long, with enlarged base; leaflets 80–300 × 40–80mm, oblong; tip **pointed**; base **narrowed**; surface glossy; margin smooth. Stipules inconspicuous, attached to the petiole. Inflorescences **erect, with spreading branches 0.6–2m long**. Flowers **pink to red**, small. Fruit fleshy, **red or black**, ellipsoid, 3–5mm long.

Often grown for ornament or as an indoor plant but has a very aggressive root system and has become an invader in several warm, humid areas, including the east coast of our region. It is a declared Category 1b invader in the Eastern Cape, KwaZulu-Natal, Mpumalanga and Limpopo.

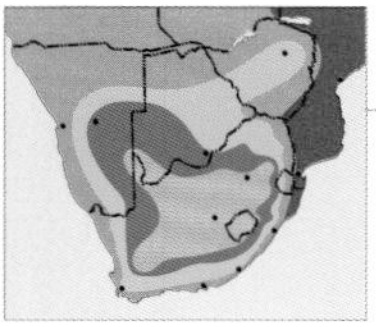

- Drought 2
- All year
- Evergreen

3 *Schefflera arboricola* *(= Heptapleurum arboricola)* ARALIACEAE
Dwarf Umbrella Tree; Dwergkiepersol

OTHER LANGUAGES: Ezhangteng (Chinese); Parasol (French); Kleine Strahlenaralie (German)

Hainan and Taiwan **Multistemmed** large shrub or small tree with a columnar to vase-shaped crown; bark grey, smooth; buds and twigs hairless; lenticels **warty**, conspicuous. Leaves with **7–9** leaflets; petiole hairless, 60–300mm long, with enlarged base; leaflets 60–200 × 10–100mm, egg-shaped or oblong; tip **rounded**; base **broad to rounded**; surface **glossy**; margin smooth. Inflorescences **erect, about 200mm long**. Flowers small, white. Fruit fleshy, roundish, **usually orange**, about 5 × 4–5mm.

Commonly grown for ornament and as an indoor plant, this species sets fruit and is therefore potentially invasive in warm, moist places. Plants will not flower when grown indoors in cooler areas such as the Highveld. It is a declared Category 3 invader in the Eastern Cape, KwaZulu-Natal, Mpumalanga and Limpopo. All parts of the plant contain calcium oxalate crystals and may cause poisoning, especially in pets. Several cultivars with variegated leaves are commonly grown.

JFDUFFEK, WIKIMEDIA COMMONS, CC BY SA 3.0

1 *P. ellipticum* flowers

FOREST AND KIM STARR

1 *P. ellipticum* fruit

2 *S. actinophylla* flowers

WENDY CUTLER

2 *S. actinophylla* fruit

3 *S. arboricola* flowers

GEOFF NICHOLS

3 *S. arboricola* fruit

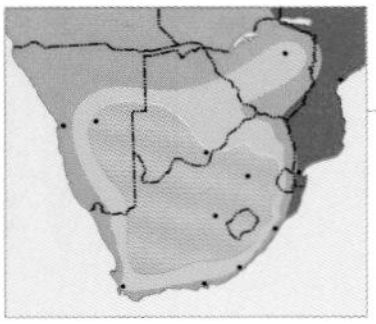

- Drought 2
- Spring
- Evergreen

1 *Schefflera elegantissima* (= *Dizygotheca elegantissima*) ARALIACEAE

False Aralia, Lacy Umbrella Plant; Vals-aralia, Rietpalmpie

OTHER LANGUAGES: Schefflera à feuilles découpées (French); Falsa aralia (Spanish)

New Caledonia **Multistemmed** small tree or large shrub with a vase-shaped crown; bark grey, narrowly fissured; twigs hairless; lenticels smooth but conspicuous. Leaves with **7–10** leaflets; petiole hairless, with enlarged base; leaflets up to 230 × 30mm, **narrowly oblong**, adult blade **wider**, juveniles **shallowly to deeply lobed, very narrow, purple to grey-green**; margin smooth, **toothed or incised**. Inflorescences erect; peduncle about 300mm long. Flowers inconspicuous, yellow-green. Fruit fleshy, black, ellipsoid.

The juvenile form is sometimes grown as a house-plant. In this capacity, one source describes it as a 'supermodel' because it is 'fussy, high-maintenance, tall', with skinny leaves, stems and petioles. More rarely, adult trees are seen as specimens in botanical gardens. It is a declared Category 3 invader in the Eastern Cape, KwaZulu-Natal, Mpumalanga and Limpopo.

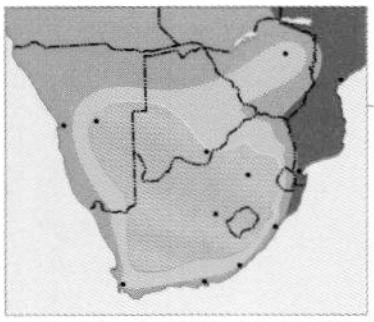

- Drought 2
- Spring
- Deciduous

2 *Sterculia foetida* MALVACEAE

Java Star-chestnut, Java Olive; Javaanse Sterkastaiing

OTHER LANGUAGES: Kepoh (Bahasa Indonesia); Xiang ping po (Chinese); Arbre puant (French); Jangli badam (Hindi); Anacagüita (Spanish); Kalumpang (Tagalog)

Tropical Africa to Australia Large tree with a rounded to spreading crown; bark smooth; buds and twigs hairless. Leaves with **5–9** leaflets; petiole hairless, 100–300mm long; leaflets 100–300 × 25–80mm, **lance-shaped**; tip pointed; base rounded; margin **smooth**. Inflorescences erect, up to 300mm long. Flowers yellow or reddish, **evil-smelling**; males and females sometimes separate on the same tree. Fruit of **5 reddish**, egg-shaped, sparsely hairy **pods** up to 100mm long and in diameter. Seeds black.

Grown occasionally in larger, warm gardens for shade and ornament. Recorded from Mpumalanga and KwaZulu-Natal. Some reports indicate that the seeds are poisonous, others that they are edible. Oil expressed from the seeds meets requirements for biodiesel. Medicinal uses are recorded.

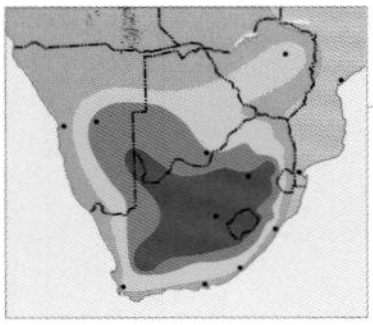

- Drought 2
- Spring
- Evergreen

3 *Tetrapanax papyrifer* (= *Aralia papyrifera, Fatsia papyrifera*) ARALIACEAE

Rice-paper Tree; Ryspapierboom

OTHER LANGUAGES: Tongtuomu (Chinese); Aralie à papier de Chine (French); Kami yatsude (Japanese); Tong tal mok (Korean); Planta del papel de arroz (Spanish)

Taiwan **Large shrub or small tree** with a rounded to spreading crown, often **branched from the base** or suckering; bark whitish or brown, smooth; twigs hairy, stout; lenticels warty, conspicuous. Leaves alternate; petiole hairless, up to 500mm long; blade **500–750mm long and wide**, round, **deeply palmately 5–11-lobed**, central lobes sometimes Y-forked; tip pointed; base heart-shaped; lower surface **white** with dense star-shaped hairs; margin smooth. Stipules attached to the petiole. Inflorescences erect, complex, up to 1m long; peduncle 10–15mm long. Flowers individually very small. Fruit fleshy, round, purple or yellow, about 4 × 4mm.

As this plant spreads by suckering, it is considered to be a weed in eastern Australia. In our region, it is grown occasionally in South Africa and Zimbabwe as a garden ornamental. The pith of younger stems is used to make rice paper.

1 *S. elegantissima* flowers

1 *S. elegantissima* fruit

GEOFF NICHOLS

2 *S. foetida* flowers

2 *S. foetida* fruit

3 *T. papyrifer* leaves and young inflorescences

MARGARET DONALD

3 *T. papyrifer* flowers

GEOFF NICHOLS

GROUP 40

Fingerleaf group

Leaves palmately compound, once-divided, opposite or whorled. Leaflets more than 3.

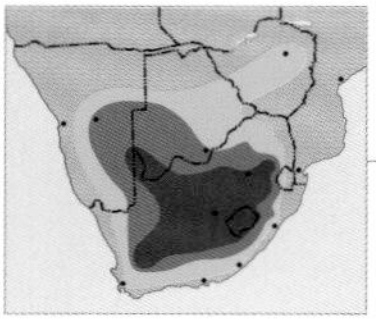

- Drought 2
- Spring
- Deciduous

1 *Aesculus × carnea* (= *A. hippocastanum × A. pavia, A. rubicunda*)

HIPPOCASTANACEAE (OR SAPINDACEAE)

Red Horse-chestnut; Rooiperdekastaiing

OTHER LANGUAGES: Rotblühende Rosskastanie (German)

Raised in Germany Small to medium-sized tree with a pyramidal to rounded crown; twigs **hairy**; lenticels **warty**, conspicuous. Leaves with **5–7** leaflets; petiole hairless, 80–140mm long; leaflets 75–150 × 40–55mm, egg-shaped or oblong, with a **drip-tip**; base narrowed; upper surface dull; margin **scalloped or toothed, wavy**. Inflorescences erect, 150–180mm long; peduncle 40–120mm long. Flowers pink; petals 5, these 15–18 × 7–9mm, each with a yellow basal mark. Fruit an egg-shaped capsule 40–60 × 30–40mm. Seeds reddish brown.

An artificial hybrid raised in Germany, probably before 1820. Grown all too rarely as a garden ornamental. Recorded from the Western and Eastern Cape. The seeds can be used as a soap substitute. Medicinal uses are recorded.

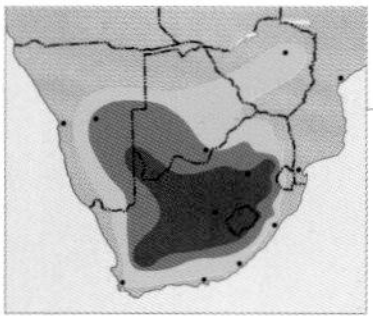

- Drought 2
- Summer
- Evergreen

2 *Aesculus hippocastanum*

HIPPOCASTANACEAE (OR SAPINDACEAE)

White Horse-chestnut, Common Horse-chestnut; Gewone Perdekastaiing

OTHER LANGUAGES: Marronier d'Inde (French); Rosskastanie (German); Agriokastania (Greek); Castagna amara (Italian); Castanheiro-da-Índia (Portuguese); Castaño de Indias (Spanish)

Southeastern Europe Medium-sized to large tree with a spreading crown; bark **purple-grey**; lenticels **warty and raised**, conspicuous. Leaves with **5–7** leaflets; petiole 65–125mm long, **woolly** at the enlarged base; blade 50–150 × 15–70mm, widest near the tip; veins **densely hairy below**, with a drip-tip; margin **saw-toothed**; base gradually narrowed. Inflorescences erect, 150–300mm long; peduncle 100–140mm long. Flowers white; petals 4 or 5, these 13–15 × 10mm, each with a yellow to red basal mark. Fruit an egg-shaped capsule 60–65mm in diameter. Seeds reddish or midbrown.

Recorded in our region from gardens in Gauteng, the Western and Eastern Cape.

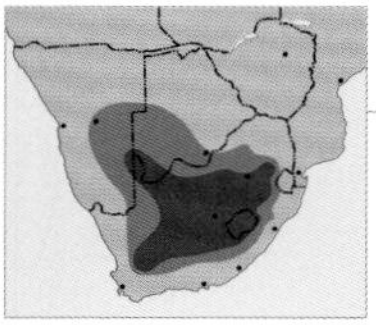

- Drought 2
- Spring–Summer
- Deciduous

3 *Aesculus indica*

HIPPOCASTANACEAE (OR SAPINDACEAE)

Indian Horse-chestnut; Indiese Perdekastaiing

OTHER LANGUAGES: Karu (Nepali)

Himalayas of India and Pakistan Large, spreading tree with a rounded crown; bark **grey-green**, smooth, flaking; twigs **hairless**, greenish brown; lenticels **smooth** but conspicuous. Leaves with **5–9** leaflets; petiole minutely hairy, 50–150mm long, with enlarged base; leaflets 70–150 × 30–60mm, elliptic, with a drip-tip; surface coppery at first, later apple green. Inflorescences erect, 300–400mm long; peduncle 40–125mm long. Flowers white or pink; petals 4, these 15–20 × 6–10mm, with yellow to red basal marks. Fruit a brownish, egg-shaped capsule 50–75mm long. Seeds nearly black, 26–30mm long, wide and deep.

The seeds remain viable for only about three weeks after ripening and trees need a definite cold season to prosper, remaining stunted and juvenile on the KwaZulu-Natal coast. Rarely grown in our region and apparently only successful in Gauteng, but a fine shade and ornamental tree for a large garden. The seeds are poisonous.

1 *A.* × *carnea* flowers

1 *A.* × *carnea* fruit

2 *A. hippocastanum* flowers

2 *A. hippocastanum* fruit

3 *A. indica* flowers

3 *A. indica* fruit and seeds

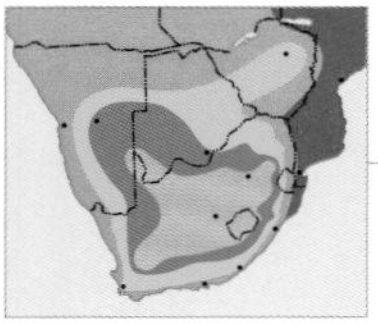

- Drought 2
- Spring
- Deciduous

1 ***Handroanthus impetiginosus*** *(= Tabebuia avellanedae, T. impetiginosa, T. ipe* var. *integra)* BIGNONIACEAE

Pink Trumpet Tree; Pienktrompetboom

OTHER LANGUAGES: Groenhart (Dutch); Arbre sacré des Incas (French); Lapachobaum (German); Tawiyo (Nahuatl); Ipê Rosa (Portuguese); Canafistula, Lapacho Rosado, Polvillo (Spanish)

Mexico to Argentina Medium-sized tree with a narrow to rounded crown; bark grey, **smooth or shallowly fissured**; buds and twigs hairy; lenticels **warty**, conspicuous. Leaves with **5** leaflets; petiole **hairy, scaly**, 40–130mm long; leaflets 50–190 × 15–80mm, **egg-shaped to elliptic**, with a drip-tip; base rounded; lower surface **hairy**; margin smooth or saw-toothed. Inflorescences erect. Flowers trumpet-shaped, 40–75mm long, **magenta with a yellow throat**; lobes 5. Fruit a purplish brown capsule **120–560 × 13–26mm**. Seeds buff, 10–16 × 34–80 × 1–2mm.

National tree of Paraguay. The wood is over-harvested in Brazil to make flooring and decking. It is widely planted as an ornamental and a street tree, recorded from Durban, Johannesburg and Pretoria. Medicinal uses are recorded.

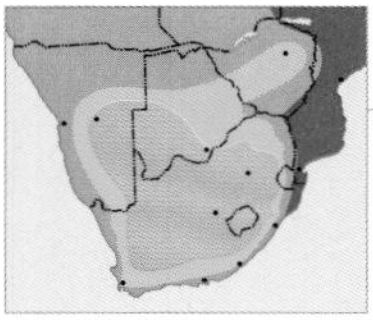

- Drought 2
- Summer
- Evergreen

2 ***Tabebuia aurea*** *(= Tabebuia argentea, Tecoma caraiba)* BIGNONIACEAE

Silver Trumpet Tree, Caribbean Trumpet-tree, Tree-of-gold; Silwertrompetboom

OTHER LANGUAGES: Carabeira (Portuguese); Alchornoque (Spanish)

Surinam to Argentina Small tree with an irregular crown; bark grey-brown, fissured; buds and twigs hairy; lenticels **warty**, conspicuous. Leaves with **5–7** leaflets; petiole hairless, 65–140mm long; leaflets 50–150 × 20–70mm, **narrowly** elliptic to oblong; tip rounded; base rounded to shallowly heart-shaped; surface dull, **hairless**. Inflorescences erect. Flowers trumpet-shaped, 55–90mm long, **yellow**; lobes 5. Fruit a strap-shaped capsule **85–150 × 17–30mm**. Seeds about 20 × 45–55mm including wings.

Occasionally grown as a garden ornamental, seen only in Durban Botanic Gardens.

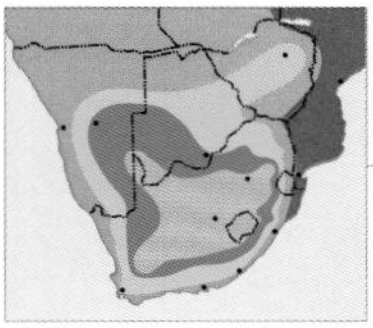

- Drought 2
- Spring
- Deciduous

3 ***Tabebuia chrysantha*** *(= Bignonia chrysantha, Tabebuia rufescens, Tecoma chrysantha)* BIGNONIACEAE

Yellow Poui; Geelpoui

OTHER LANGUAGES: Roble Amarillo (Spanish)

Mexico to Peru Small tree with an open, rounded crown; bark grey, **fissured**; buds hairy; twigs with star-shaped hairs, becoming hairless, almost square; lenticels minute. Leaves with **5** leaflets; petiole **hairy**, **30–90mm long**; leaflets up to 170 × 90mm, widest beyond the middle, with a **prominent drip-tip**; base rounded to squared; surface with **star-shaped hairs**; margin smooth or saw-toothed. Inflorescences erect, appearing **before** the leaves. Flowers trumpet-shaped, **yellow** with red lines, 40–65mm long; lobes 5. Fruit a very hairy, long, flat, brown capsule **150–500 × 8–20mm**. Seeds whitish to buff, 4–9 × 14–33mm.

National tree of Venezuela. The wood is hard and can be used for cabinet work, making bows and other articles. Medicinal uses are recorded. Grown for ornament in Harare, Pretoria and Johannesburg.

1 *H. impetiginosus* leaves

MAURO HALPERN

1 *H. impetiginosus* flowers

2 *T. aurea* young plant

GEOFF NICHOLS

2 *T. aurea* flowers

FOREST AND KIM STARR

2 *T. aurea* dehisced fruit

3 *T. chrysantha* leaves

3 *T. chrysantha* flowers

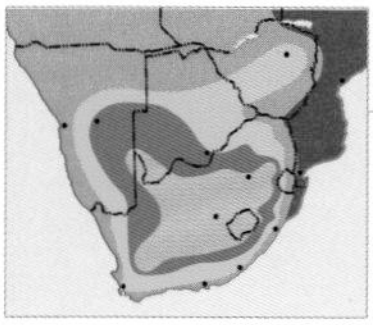

1 *Tabebuia chrysotricha* (= *Tecoma chrysotricha*) BIGNONIACEAE
Yellow Trumpet Tree; Geeltrompetboom

- Drought 2
- Spring
- Evergreen

OTHER LANGUAGES: Goldtrompetenbaum (German); Ipê Amarelo (Portuguese); Árbol Trompeto Dorada (Spanish)

Brazil to Argentina Small tree; bark **smooth**; buds hairy; twigs with star-shaped hairs, becoming hairless, almost square; lenticels minute. Leaves with **5** leaflets; petiole hairy, **10–25mm long**; leaflets 20–110 × 17–55mm, widest beyond the middle, with a short drip-tip; base rounded to squared; upper surface **becoming hairless**, lower with **star-shaped hairs**; margin smooth. Inflorescences erect **spikes**. Flowers trumpet-shaped, **yellow**, 40–75mm long, with red lines; lobes 5. Fruit a curved, brown, very hairy capsule **110–380 × 8–12mm**. Seeds 6–9 × 17–29mm.

National tree of Brazil. Grown for ornament in scattered parts of our region but has been seen to display invasive tendencies.

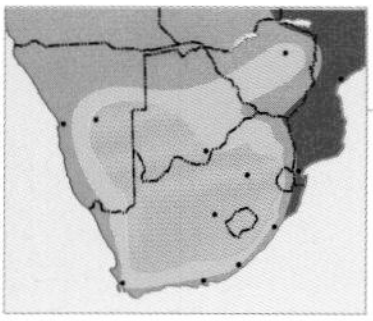

2 *Tabebuia donnell-smithii* (= *Cybistax donnell-smithii*) BIGNONIACEAE
White Mahogany; Witmahonie

- Drought 2
- Spring
- Deciduous

OTHER LANGUAGES: Ipê-do-México (Portuguese); Primavera (Spanish)

Mexico to Venezuela Tall tree with a rounded crown on a **long, straight** bole; bark smooth; twigs hairless, almost square. Leaves with **3–7** leaflets; petiole **hairless**, up to 260mm long; leaflets up to 280 × 140mm, elliptic to oblong, with a drip-tip; base squared; upper surface hairless, with **impressed veins**, lower minutely hairy; margin smooth or saw-toothed. Inflorescences erect **panicles or clusters**. Flowers trumpet-shaped, 45–60mm long, **yellow**, without markings. Fruit a very hairy capsule **250–450 × 14–30mm, 8–12-ribbed**. Seeds 9–12 × 16–21mm.

Timber is used in Guatemala to make furniture. Grown in our region as a specimen tree in Durban Botanic Gardens.

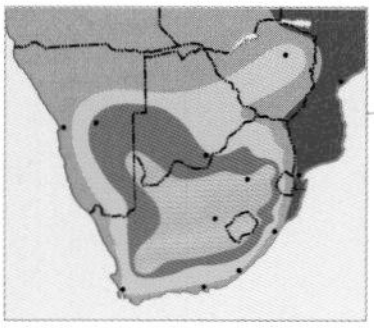

3 *Tabebuia heptaphylla* (= *Tabebuia ipe, Tecoma heptaphylla*) BIGNONIACEAE
Mauve Trumpet Tree; Perstrompetboom

- Drought 2
- Spring
- Deciduous

OTHER LANGUAGES: Ipê-rosa, Ipê roxo (Portuguese); Lapacho negro (Spanish)

Brazil to Bolivia Small to large tree with an irregularly rounded to spreading crown; bark **pale grey, fissured**; buds hairless; twigs becoming hairless; lenticels **warty**, conspicuous. Leaves with **5–7** leaflets; petiole hairless, 40–110mm long; terminal leaflet 30–160 × 17–60mm, laterals progressively smaller, broadly **lance-shaped** to oblong; tip **long drawn out**; base narrowed to squared; surface hairless, glossy above, dull below but veins hairy; margin **saw-toothed**. Inflorescences erect. Flowers trumpet-shaped, **magenta**, with a basal yellow mark. Fruit a smooth, black capsule **90–470 × 7–17mm**. Seeds whitish, 5–9 × 18–32mm, 2-winged.

Grown as a specimen tree in parks and gardens in Durban and as a street tree in Pretoria. Medicinal uses are recorded.

ADISAK INTACHAI / SHUTTERSTOCK

1 *T. chrysotricha* flowers

1 *T. chrysotricha* fruit

FOREST AND KIM STARR

2 *T. donnell-smithii* leaves

2 *T. donnell-smithii* flowers

3 *T. heptaphylla* flowers

3 *T. heptaphylla* fruit

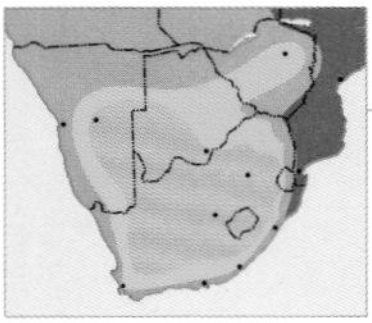

1 *Tabebuia heterophylla* (= *T. pentaphylla, T. riparia*)

BIGNONIACEAE

Lilac Trumpet Tree, Pink Manjack, Whitewood; Lilatrompetboom

- Drought 2
- Spring
- Deciduous

OTHER LANGUAGES: Tabébuia à cinq feuilles (French); Pau d'arco Branco (Portuguese); Roble Blanco (Spanish)

Honduras to Trinidad Medium-sized tree with a **pyramidal** to rounded crown; bark grey-brown, **rough, flaking**; buds and twigs hairless; lenticels **warty**. Leaves with **3–5** leaflets; petiole hairless, 5–80mm long; leaflets 7–160 × 3–75mm, **leathery**, widest beyond the middle; tip and base **rounded**; upper surface glossy; margin smooth. Inflorescences erect. Flowers trumpet-shaped, 35–70mm long, **whitish to pale magenta with a yellow throat**; lobes 5. Fruit a smooth, brown capsule **70–200 × 6–10mm**. Seeds whitish, 7–9 × 20–30mm.

Grown as a garden ornamental in South Africa and as a street tree in Mozambique. In the Caribbean, the wood is used for cabinet work, flooring, veneer and many other purposes.

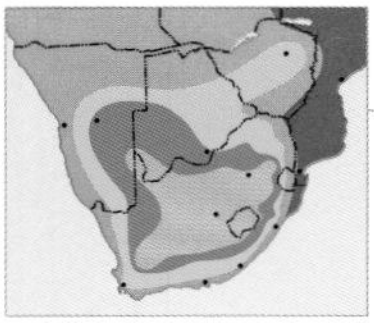

2 *Tabebuia ochracea*

BIGNONIACEAE

Gold Trumpet Tree, Cortez, Corteza; Gouetrompetboom

- Drought 2
- Spring
- Evergreen

OTHER LANGUAGES: Ipê Macaco (Portuguese); Corteza Amarilla (Spanish)

Honduras to Brazil Small tree with a rounded to spreading crown; bark grey, deeply fissured; buds hairy; twigs almost square, with star-shaped hairs; lenticels minute. Leaves with **5** leaflets; petiole **25–120mm long**, with **star-shaped hairs**; leaflets 30–130 × 23–90mm, **broad**, widest beyond the middle, with a short drip-tip; base rounded to squared; upper surface **becoming hairless**, lower with star-shaped hairs; margin **saw-toothed**. Inflorescences erect. Flowers trumpet-shaped, **yellow**, 45–90mm long, with red stripes; lobes 5. Fruit a very hairy, brown, spindle-shaped capsule **120–300 × 15–22mm**. Seeds whitish, 8–110 × 22–33mm.

Planted as a specimen tree in botanical gardens in Durban and Pretoria in our region. Very similar to *T. chrysotricha* (p.412). Timber is used in its native range for flooring, railway sleepers, furniture and more. Medicinal uses are recorded.

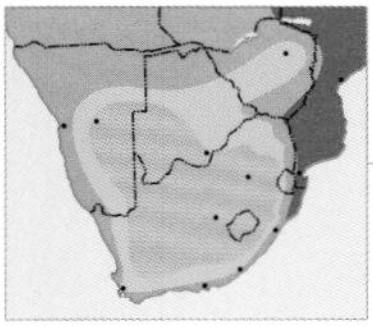

3 *Tabebuia pallida* (= *T. dominicensis*)

BIGNONIACEAE

Cuban Pink Trumpet Tree, Lilac Trumpet Tree, White Cedar; Kubaanse Pienktrompetboom

- Drought 2
- Spring
- Deciduous

OTHER LANGUAGES: Poirier Blanc (French); Roble Blanco (Spanish)

The West Indies Large tree (often smaller in cultivation) with a columnar trunk; bark grey, flaking; buds and twigs hairy; lenticels **warty**, conspicuous. Leaves with **3–5** leaflets; petiole **scaly**, 8–70mm long; leaflets 40–200 × 30–120mm, elliptic to oblong; tip **rounded**; base rounded to squared; surface **apparently hairless**. Inflorescences erect. Flowers trumpet-shaped, **pale lavender-pink**, 50–80mm long; lobes 5. Fruit a capsule **110–230 × 8–11mm**. Seeds 5–8 × 20–25mm.

Very similar to *T. heterophylla* (above) and invasive in Réunion and Mauritius. In our region, it is only seen as specimen trees in Durban Botanic Gardens.

GEOFF NICHOLS

1 *T. heterophylla* flowers

1 *T. heterophylla* fruit

2 *T. ochracea* flowers

Y. S. YEOH

2 *T. ochracea* fruit

3 *T. pallida* flowers

GEOFF NICHOLS

3 *T. pallida* dehisced fruit

1 *Tabebuia rosea* BIGNONIACEAE

Rose Trumpet Tree; Roostrompetboom

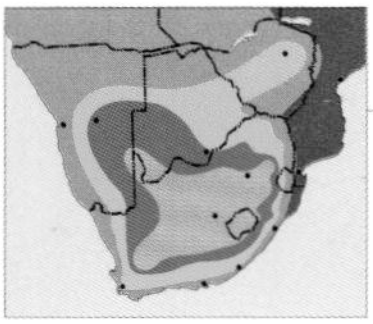

- Drought 2
- Spring
- Deciduous

OTHER LANGUAGES: Tabébuia Rose (French); Ipê Rosa (Portuguese); Roble Colorado, Roble de Sabana (Spanish)

Mexico to Ecuador and Brazil Medium-large tree with a rounded to spreading crown; bark dark grey to black, fissured; buds hairy; twigs almost square, **scaly**; lenticels smooth but conspicuous. Leaves with **5** leaflets; petiole **scaly**, 50–320mm long; leaflets 80–350 × 30–180mm, elliptic, with a **drip-tip**; base narrowed or rounded; surfaces with **star-shaped hairs**; margin smooth. Inflorescences erect, appearing before the leaves. Flowers trumpet-shaped, **lavender to magenta**, 50–100mm long, with a basal yellow mark becoming white; lobes 5. Fruit a spindle-shaped capsule **220–380 × 9–15mm**. Seeds 7–10 × 28–44mm.

National tree of El Salvador and state tree of Cojedes, Venezuela. Grown as specimen trees in botanical gardens in South Africa and street trees in Mozambique. The timber is used to make furniture. Medicinal uses are recorded.

2 *Tabebuia roseo-alba* (= *T. odontodiscus*) BIGNONIACEAE

White Trumpet Tree, White Ipê; Wittrompetboom

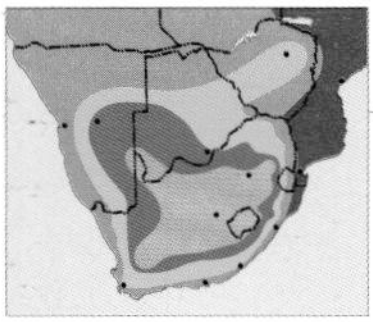

- Drought 2
- Spring
- Deciduous

OTHER LANGUAGES: Ipê Branco (Portuguese); Lapacho Blanco (Spanish)

Peru to Brazil and Argentina Small to medium-sized tree with a pyramidal to rounded crown; buds hairy; twigs **scaly**; lenticels **warty**, conspicuous. Leaves with **3–5** leaflets; petiole **scaly**, 15–90mm long; leaflets 20–150 × 12–100mm, egg-shaped to elliptic, with a **small** drip-tip; lower surface **hairy**. Inflorescences erect, appearing briefly before the leaves. Flowers trumpet-shaped, **white or pink**, 25–70mm long; lobes 5. Fruit a spindle-shaped capsule **130–240 × 5–7mm**. Seeds 5–6 × 25–30mm.

Grown in its native area for ornament and honey, in our region as a specimen tree in Durban Botanic Gardens, though peak flowering only lasts for two to four days. The timber is used for indoor finishes.

3 *Vitex agnus-castus* LAMIACEAE

Chaste Tree, Abraham's Balm, Monk's Pepper; Monniksboom

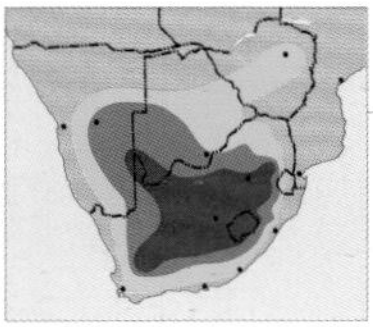

- Drought 2
- Spring
- Deciduous

OTHER LANGUAGES: Agnocast (Catalan); Konopljika (Croatian); Kuisboom (Dutch); Arbre au poivre (French); Mönchspfeffer (German); Agno casto (Italian); Anho-casto (Portuguese); Ayit (Turkish)

Southern Europe **Shrub or small tree** with a rounded to spreading crown; bark dark brown, fissured; twigs hairy, **square** or round. Leaves with **5–7** leaflets; petiole hairless; leaflets 35–110 × 7–20mm, elliptic; tip **drawn out**; base narrowed; lower surface **hairy**; margin smooth. Inflorescences erect, 100–300mm long, appearing after the leaves. Flowers irregular, tubular, **7–10mm long, pink or purple**; lobes 5. Fruit **fleshy**, brown, 2–3mm long and in diameter.

Widely grown as an ornamental and recorded from South Africa and Zimbabwe. Medicinal uses of this plant have been recorded as long ago as the 4th century BC.

1 *T. rosea* flowers

1 *T. rosea* fruit

2 *T. roseo-alba* flowers

2 *T. roseo-alba* flowers

3 *V. agnus-castus* leaves

3 *V. agnus-castus* flowers

3 *V. agnus-castus* fruit

GROUP 41

Hook thorn group

Leaves bipinnately compound (twice-divided). Spines present, at least some, if not all, recurved.

Also see Group 43: *Caesalpinia pulcherrima* (p.434).

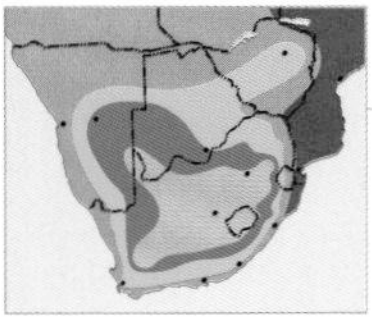

- Drought 2
- Spring
- Evergreen

1 *Caesalpinia decapetala*

FABACEAE

Mauritius-thorn; Kraaldoring

OTHER LANGUAGES: Mauritiusdorn (German); Ralan (Hindi); Setjang lembut (Malay); Ufenisi (Zulu)

India and Southeast Asia Robust, evergreen **scrambling shrub or climber**, usually forming dense, **impenetrable thickets**, invading forest margins and gaps, commercial plantations, roadsides and watercourses. Branchlets with numerous, **randomly scattered, straight to hooked spines**. Leaves with leaflets up to 8mm wide, dull dark green above, paler green below. Inflorescences elongated, **erect, axillary racemes**. Flowers pale yellow. Pods woody, flattened, unsegmented, brown, hairless, **sharply pointed** at apex.

Cultivated for security hedging and ornament. This is a declared Category 1b invader in South Africa and is a particular problem in Gauteng and also in KwaZulu-Natal and Mpumalanga. It is recorded as invasive in much of Africa, the Mascarenes and a number of Pacific islands.

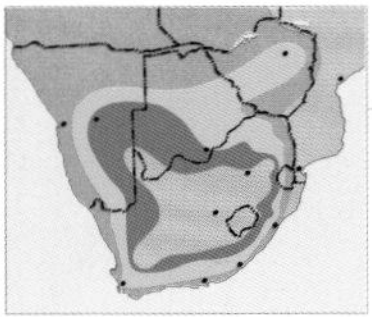

- Drought 2
- Spring
- Evergreen

2 *Caesalpinia spinosa* (= *Tara spinosa*)

FABACEAE

Tara Tree, Spiny Holdback, Tara; Taraboom, Doringpronkstert

OTHER LANGUAGES: Flamboyant petit (French); Tara (Quechua); Guaranga, Tara (Spanish)

Venezuela to Argentina Small tree with a **densely leafy**, vase-shaped to spreading crown. Leaves alternate, bipinnate, with **recurved prickles**; leaflets 15–45 × 6–20mm, **glossy green**, hairless; base obliquely rounded; tip indented. Inflorescences **terminal**, sparsely prickly, **upright to horizontal** racemes, 100–200mm long. Flowers yellow to orange. Pods brown or red, woody, flattened, hairless, 50–95 × 10–25mm, **broadly pointed**.

Cultivated for ornament in many parts of South Africa and Namibia as well as many places outside our region. It is recorded as naturalised in California. The bark can be used in tanning leathers used for automotive and furniture upholstery. The seeds yield a gum used as thickening in the food industry. Medicinal uses are recorded.

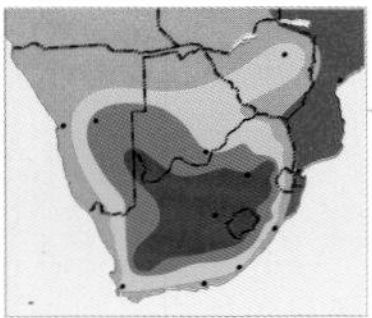

- Drought 2
- Spring
- Deciduous

3 *Parkinsonia aculeata*

FABACEAE

Jerusalem Thorn, Ratama; Mexikaanse Groenhaarboom

OTHER LANGUAGES: Jerusalemdorn (German); Espinho de Jerusalem (Portuguese); Palo verde (Spanish)

Southern USA and adjacent Mexico Small, **thinly leaved** tree or large shrub with a vase-shaped to spreading crown; bark brown, narrowly fissured; buds hairy; twigs hairless, yellow-brown or greenish yellow; stems with **paired thorns** (modified stipules). Leaves alternate, **twice-pinnate, drooping**; petiole hairless; rachis flattened, **ending in a spine**; leaflets 2–6 × 1–2mm, elliptic; tip rounded and tapering to an abrupt point; base obliquely narrowed. Inflorescences erect, up to 200mm long. Flowers yellow; petals 5, these 8–14mm long. Fruit a papery, brown, flattened pod 30–120 × 5–8mm. Seeds 5–9 × 4–6 × 1.5–2.5mm.

Invasive in Australia, Africa, Pakistan and the Pacific islands. A declared Category 1b invader in South Africa. Grown for fodder. The pulp of the pods is edible and sweet. There are reports that the foliage is poisonous. Medicinal uses are recorded.

1 *C. decapetala* flowers

1 *C. decapetala* flowers and fruit

1 *C. decapetala* old fruit

2 *C. spinosa* flowers

2 *C. spinosa* fruit

3 *P. aculeata* leaves

3 *P. aculeata* flowers

3 *P. aculeata* fruit

GROUP 42

Sweet-thorn group

Leaves bipinnately compound (twice-divided). Spines present, all straight.

See also Group 41: *Parkinsonia aculeata* (p.418); Group 33: *Gleditsia triacanthos* (p.358); Group 43: *Caesalpinia echinata* (p.430).

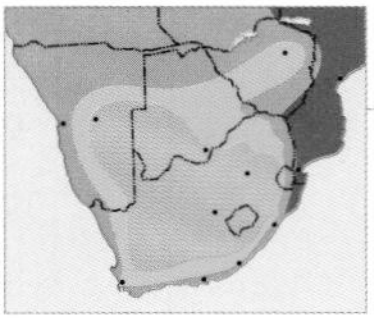

- Drought 2
- Spring
- Deciduous

1 *Pithecellobium dulce*

FABACEAE

Manila Tamarind, Madras Thorn; Manila-tamarinde, Madrasdoring

OTHER LANGUAGES: Tamarin de l'Inde (French); Camambilarinde (German); Guayamochil, Guama Americano (Spanish)

Mexico, Central America and northern South America Medium-sized tree with a columnar to rounded crown; bark **grey, smooth or narrowly fissured**; buds hairless; twigs hairy or hairless, with paired spines; lenticels warty, conspicuous. Leaves alternate; petiole hairless, 10–15mm long; rachis round; leaflets **up to 25 (rarely 60)** × 9mm (rarely 32mm), egg-shaped to oblong; tip rounded; base oblique; upper surface **glossy**; margin smooth. Inflorescences hanging, up to 220mm long; peduncle 4–20mm long. Flowers small, white. Fruit a more or less cylindrical, **red** pod 105–165 × 8–19mm, **coiled into a circle** and slightly narrowed between seeds. Seeds dark brown, 8–12 × 6–10 × 2–4mm.

Grown in our area as a specimen tree in botanical gardens in Durban and Maputo, elsewhere for the edible sweet and sour pulp in the fruits. The seed is dispersed by birds that feed on the pulp. Invasive in Hawaii.

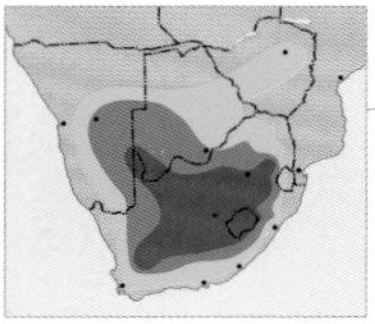

- Drought 3
- Spring
- Deciduous

2 *Prosopis glandulosa* (= *P. juliflora* of some authors)

FABACEAE

Mesquite; Suidwesdoring

OTHER LANGUAGES: Mizquitl (Nahuatl)

Southwestern USA Large shrub or small tree; bark brown to grey, smooth; buds and twigs hairless; stems round, with **often single spines** 10–45mm long. Leaves alternate, with **1, rarely 2 pairs of pinnae**, each pinna with 6–17 pairs of leaflets up to 18mm apart; petiole hairless, 20–150mm long; rachis round; leaflets 20–63 × 1.5–4.5mm, linear, **leathery**; tip bluntly pointed; base oblique; surface dull, hairless; margin smooth. Inflorescences **spikes**, 50–140mm long. Flowers small, creamy to yellow. Fruit a slightly bent, flattened, woody, yellow-brown pod 80–300 × 5–13mm. Seeds midbrown, 6–7mm long.

All species of *Prosopis* hybridise freely among themselves. Invasive wherever it is seen, even in its natural range. In South Africa, a declared Category 1b invader in the Western and Eastern Cape, Free State and North West (Category 3 in the Northern Cape). Leaves are used for fodder and the pods are eaten by man and beast. Wood is a prized fuel for smoking foods and for other purposes, the timber good for woodworking. Bees use the flowers to make abundant honey. Medicinal uses are recorded. *Prosopis chilensis* (Chilean mesquite) is similar but has paired spines and several pairs of pinnae with widely separated leaflets. Its uses and range in our region are similar to those of *P. glandulosa*.

1 *P. dulce*

1 *P. dulce* leaves

FOREST AND KIM STARR

1 *P. dulce* flowers

B. NAVEZ, WIKIMEDIA COMMONS, CC BY SA 3.0

1 *P. dulce* fruit

2 *P. glandulosa*

2 *P. glandulosa* leaves

BRAAM VAN WYK

2 *P. glandulosa* flowers

BRAAM VAN WYK

2 *P. glandulosa* fruit

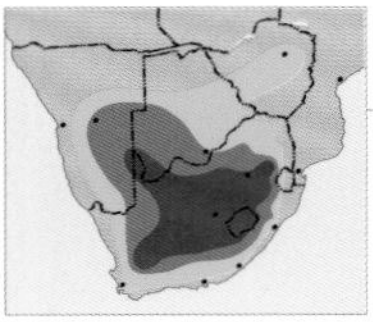

1 *Prosopis pubescens* FABACEAE
Screw-bean; Skroefboontjie

- Drought 3
- Spring
- Deciduous

OTHER LANGUAGES: Tornillo (Spanish)

Southwestern USA and adjacent Mexico Large shrub or small tree with a vase-shaped crown; bark brown or grey to black, narrowly fissured or rough, forming stringy scales; buds and twigs **hairless**; stems round, with paired spines 10–30mm long. Leaves alternate, usually with **1 pair of pinnae, rarely 2 or 3**, each pinna with **5–8 pairs of leaflets**; petiole hairless; rachis round; leaflets **4–12** × 2–4mm, elliptic to oblong; tip rounded; base rounded or squared; surface **hairy**; margin smooth. Inflorescences **spikes**, 50–80mm long; peduncle 10–15mm long. Flowers small, yellow. Fruit a **tightly spirally coiled** pod 25–55 × 5–6mm. Seeds 3–3.5mm long.

All species of *Prosopis* hybridise freely among themselves. Invasive in South Africa. The tightly twisted pods very much resemble turned screws, hence the common names. Native Americans have traditionally ground the pods to meal and eaten it for centuries. The timber is good for construction, woodwork and fuel.

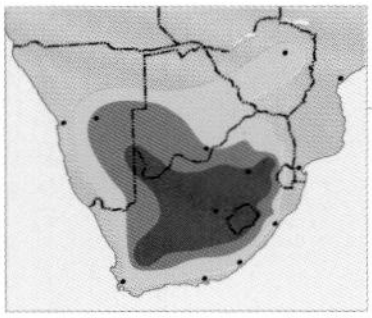

2 *Prosopis velutina* FABACEAE
Velvet Mesquite; Fluweelboontjie

- Drought 3
- Spring
- Deciduous

Mexico and Central America Small to medium-sized, multistemmed tree with a rounded crown; bark brown to grey, narrowly fissured, flaking; buds and twigs **hairy**; stems round, with paired spines up to 25mm long. Leaves alternate, with **1 pair of pinnae**, each pinna with **14–30 pairs** of leaflets; petiole hairy, 6–60mm long; rachis round; leaflets 4–13 × 2–4mm, oblong; tip rounded; base squared; surface **velvety**; margin hair-fringed. Inflorescences **spikes**, 50–150mm long, appearing after the leaves. Flowers small, creamy to yellow. Fruit a flat, curved to U-shaped, brown, hairy pod 80–160 × 6–10mm. Seeds reddish brown, 5–7mm long.

All species of *Prosopis* hybridise freely among themselves. A Federal Noxious Weed in the USA and invasive in many other places, including South Africa where it is a declared Category 1b invader in the Western and Eastern Cape, Free State and North West, and a Category 3 invader in the Northern Cape. The pods are used for forage.

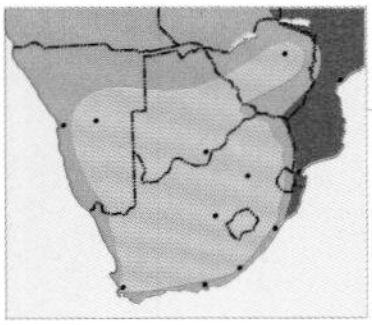

3 *Vachellia seyal* (= *Acacia seyal*) FABACEAE
Gum Arabic Thorn, Shittah Tree; Arabiese Gomdoring

- Drought 3
- Spring
- Deciduous

OTHER LANGUAGES: Sayyaal (Arabic); Talha (French); Gummi-Akazie (German); Shittah (Hebrew)

Tropical Africa to Egypt Small tree with an umbrella-shaped crown; bark **yellowish green or brown, powdery**; twigs hairless; stems with paired, long, straight spines sometimes inflated at the base, with resident colonies of ants. Leaves alternate; petiole **hairless**, 5–20mm long; leaflets 3–6 × 0.7–2mm, narrowly oblong; tip rounded; base **obliquely** rounded to squared; surface dull, hairless; margin smooth. Inflorescences **globose heads**. Flowers yellow, individually small. Fruit a flat, brown pod 70–220 × 5–9mm, **bent into a U-shape and narrowed between the seeds**. Seeds olive-brown, 7–9 × 4.5–5mm.

The wood is the 'shittim' of the Old Testament. Greatest use of this species today is the bark, which is used for fodder; the exudate from wounds is sold as gum arabic. Grown in a few places in South Africa and Zimbabwe as a specimen tree.

CURTIS CLARK, WIKIMEDIA COMMONS, CC BY SA 2.5

1 *P. pubescens* flowers

STAN SHEBS, WIKIMEDIA COMMONS, GFDL 1.2

1 *P. pubescens* fruit

SUE IN AZ, WIKIMEDIA COMMONS, GFDL 1.2

2 *P. velutina* flowers

PAUL B. MOORE / SHUTTERSTOCK.COM

2 *P. velutina* fruit

STEFAN DRESSLER

3 *V. seyal* leaves and flowers

MIKE BINGHAM

3 *V. seyal* flowers

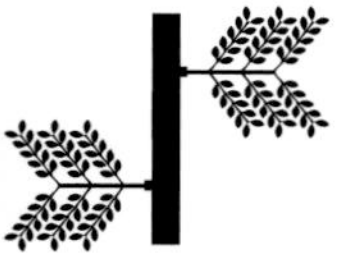

GROUP 43

False-thorn group

Leaves at least bipinnately compound (twice- or more times divided). Spines absent.

See also Group 11: *Acacia melanoxylon* (p.242).

1 *Acacia baileyana*

FABACEAE

Bailey's Wattle, Cootamundra Wattle; Bailey-se-wattel

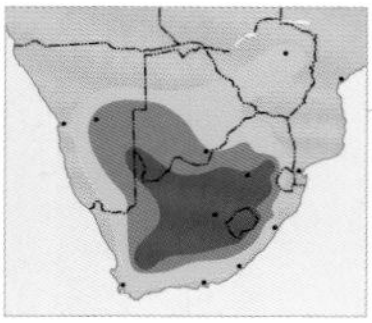

- Drought 2
- Spring
- Evergreen

OTHER LANGUAGES: Mimosa de Bailey (French, Spanish); Cootamundra-Akazie (German)

New South Wales, Australia Small tree with a spreading crown; bark grey, **smooth**; buds hairless; twigs hairy; lenticels minute. Leaves alternate; petiole hairless, 4–10mm long; rachis flattened or round, **with 2–6 pinnae**; leaflets 4–8 × 0.8–1.5mm, linear; tip pointed; base squared; surface **hairless, blue-green**; margin smooth. Inflorescences **globose heads**, yellow. Fruit a flat, straight, blue-grey to red-brown pod 50–75 × 10–15mm. Seeds black, about 6 × 3mm.

Naturalised in parts of Australia outside its range and in New Zealand, California and South Africa, where it is a declared Category 3 invader. It has limited use in the cut flower industry, mainly as foliage. The abundant pollen is food for bees in the production of honey.

2 *Acacia dealbata*

FABACEAE

Silver Wattle; Silwerwattel

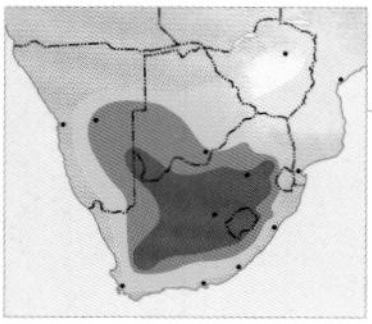

- Drought 2
- Spring
- Evergreen

OTHER LANGUAGES: Mimosa des fleuristes (French); Silberakazie (German); Acácia-prateada (Portuguese); Acacia de hoja azul (Spanish)

Southeastern Australia Small to medium-sized tree with a rounded crown and a tendency to sucker; bark brown or grey to black, **smooth**; buds and twigs hairy; lenticels minute. Leaves alternate; petiole hairless, 5–20mm long; rachis round, with **10–30 pinnae**; leaflets 2–5.5 × 0.4–0.7mm, linear; tip pointed; base squared; surface **hairy**, **grey-green**; margin smooth, sometimes hair-fringed. Inflorescences **globose heads**, yellow. Fruit a flat, slightly twisted, blue-grey or brown pod 40–90 × 7–13mm. Seeds dark brown to black, 5–6 × 3–3.5mm.

A declared Category 2 invader in South Africa. Grown for shelter, shade and firewood. The timber is of limited use in making furniture and the flowers are sometimes used for cut flowers.

3 *Acacia decurrens*

FABACEAE

Green Wattle; Groenwattel

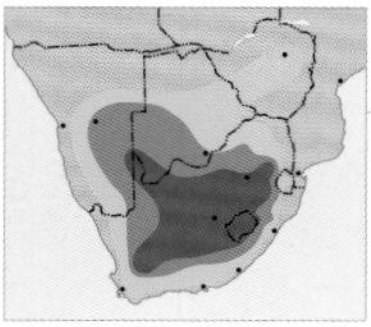

- Drought 2
- Spring
- Evergreen

OTHER LANGUAGES: Schwarze Akazie (German); Mimosa-prateada (Portuguese)

Eastern Australia Medium-sized tree with a pyramidal crown; bark brown to black, smooth or fissured; buds and twigs hairless; lenticels warty, conspicuous; stems with **wings extending below leaves**. Leaves alternate, with 3–15 pairs of pinnae; petiole hairless, 4–28mm long; leaflets **widely separated**, 5–15 × 0.4–1mm, linear; tip pointed to rounded; surface dull, hairless, **bright green**; margin smooth. Inflorescences **globose heads**, yellow. Fruit a flat, brown pod 40–100 × 5–12mm, with **thickened margin**. Seeds dark brown, about 5 × 3.5mm.

Invasive almost everywhere it has been grown and a declared Category 2 invader in South Africa. Grown for shelter, shade and firewood.

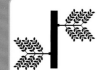

1 *A. baileyana* flowers

1 *A. baileyana* fruit

2 *A. dealbata* flowers

2 *A. dealbata* fruit

3 *A. decurrens* flowers

3 *A. decurrens* flowers

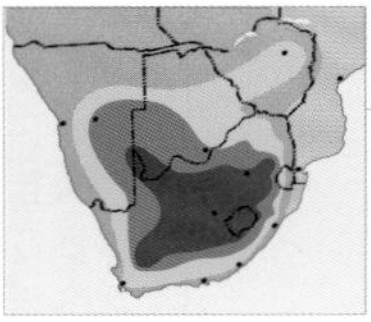

- Drought 2
- Spring
- Evergreen

1 *Acacia elata* *(= A. terminalis)* FABACEAE

Peppertree Wattle, Cedar Wattle, Elata Wattle; Peperboomwattel

Eastern Australia **Medium-sized** tree with a columnar to rounded crown; bark black, fissured or rough, forming plate-like scales; buds hairless; twigs hairy; lenticels minute; stems round. Leaves alternate, with 2–7 pairs of pinnae; petiole hairless, 25–90mm long; rachis round; leaflets **10–60 × 5–13mm, lance-shaped**; tip **drawn out**; base rounded; surface **glossy above**, dull and paler below; margin smooth. Inflorescences **globose heads, creamy or pale yellow**. Fruit a flat, woody, dark brown pod 70–150 × 9–15mm.

Naturalised in South Africa where it is a declared Category 1b invader. The timber is dark, heavy and strong, suitable for turning and carpentry.

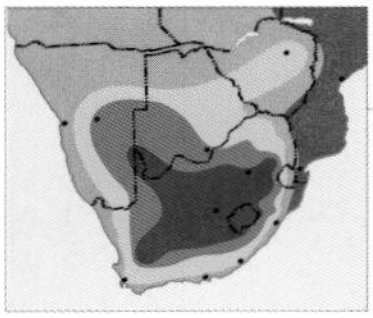

- Drought 3
- Spring
- Evergreen

2 *Acacia mearnsii* *(= A. decurrens* var. *mollis, A. mollissima)* FABACEAE

Black Wattle, Tan Wattle; Swartwattel, Basboom, Looiwattel

OTHER LANGUAGES: Acacia noir (French); Gerberakazie (German); Acácia-negra (Portuguese); Acacia negra (Spanish)

Eastern Australia Small tree with a rounded crown; bark **black**, deeply fissured or rough, forming ridges; buds hairy; twigs minutely hairy, **striped**; lenticels smooth. Leaves with 8–21 pairs of pinnae, densely hairy; petiole hairy, 10–25mm long; rachis channelled; leaflets 1.5–4mm long, up to 1mm wide, oblong, dark olive-green; tip rounded; base rounded to squared; surface dull, sometimes hairy; margin hair-fringed. Inflorescences **globose heads, pale yellow**. Fruit a flat, leathery, purple-black, hairy pod 50–100 × 5–8mm, indented between seeds. Seeds black, about 5 × 3.5mm.

Invasive in North America, Europe, New Zealand and Africa. A declared Category 2 invader in South Africa. Introduced into our region for tanning bark, now used for firewood, shelter, shade and hut-building as well.

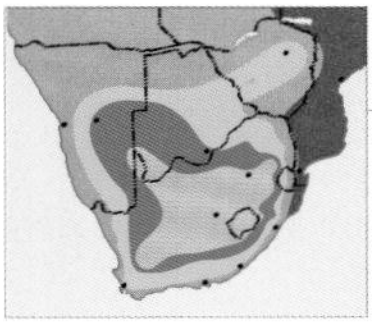

- Drought 2
- Spring
- Deciduous

3 *Acrocarpus fraxinifolius* FABACEAE

Shingle Tree, Pink Cedar; Dakspaanboom

OTHER LANGUAGES: Mandhani (Hindi); Malai-k-konrai (Tamil)

India to Indonesia Tall tree with a columnar crown on a straight, **buttressed** bole; bark whitish, brown or grey, smooth; buds hairy; twigs hairless, green; lenticels warty, conspicuous, brown. Leaves alternate, **coppery to yellow when young**, with 3 or 4 pairs of pinnae, each pinna with 5–7 pairs of leaflets; petiole hairless; rachis round; leaflets 35–110 × 15–50mm, egg-shaped to oblong, with a **drip-tip**; base narrowed to rounded; veins **hairy on lower surface**; margin smooth. Stipules small, soon falling. Inflorescences erect, **up to 320mm long**. Flowers **green**; stamens conspicuous, **red-orange**. Fruit a straight, flat, brown, **1-winged** pod with several seeds, 100–120 × 15–20mm. Seeds about 6.5 × 5mm.

Timber is decorative and used for panelling, furniture and carving. The flowers are a good source of nectar for honey, also popular with nectar-eating birds. Recorded from a few places in South Africa and Zimbabwe.

1 *A. elata* leaves

1 *A. elata* flowers

2 *A. mearnsii* flowers

2 *A. mearnsii* fruit

3 *A. fraxinifolius*

3 *A. fraxinifolius* leaves

3 *A. fraxinifolius* flowers

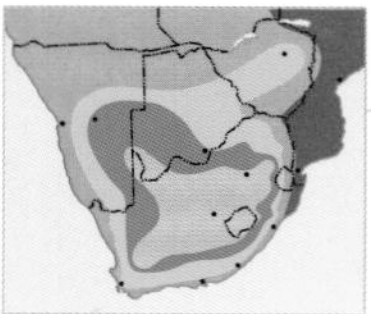

1 *Albizia chinensis* (= *A. stipulata*) FABACEAE

Chinese False-thorn; Chinese Valsdoring

- Drought 2
- Spring
- Deciduous

OTHER LANGUAGES: Sengon (Bahasa Indonesia); Ying shu (Chinese); Albizzie de Chine (French); Kala siris (Hindi); Cilai vakai (Tamil); Kang luang (Thai)

Pakistan to Indonesia Large tree with a **spreading, often flat-topped** crown; bark grey, smooth; buds and twigs hairy; lenticels **warty**, conspicuous; stems angled or round. Leaves alternate, with 4–14 pairs of pinnae; petiole hairy, 30–40mm long; rachis round; leaflets about 7–10 × 3mm, oblong; tip rounded and **spine-tipped**; base obliquely rounded. Stipules **eared, very hairy at first**, soon falling. Inflorescences erect. Flowers with stamens many, showy, white. Fruit a flat, straight, brown pod 100–180mm long.

Grown for shade and soil improvement. In our region experimentally and as a specimen tree in botanical gardens. Recorded from KwaZulu-Natal in South Africa and from Zimbabwe and the Comoros. The wood and bark are poisonous. Invasive in Hawaii and Samoa.

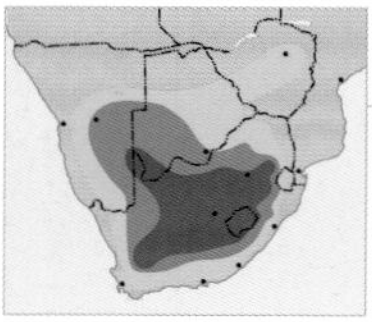

2 *Albizia julibrissin* (= *Acacia julibrissin*) FABACEAE

Silk Tree, Pink Siris; Syboom, Pienksiris

- Drought 3
- Spring
- Deciduous

OTHER LANGUAGES: Shajarat al harir (Arabic); Hé huān shù (Chinese); Gul i abrisham (Farsi); Arbre à soie (French); Seidenbaum (German); Nemu no ki (Japanese); Acacia nemu (Portuguese); Asrakhadira (Sanskrit); Parasol de la China (Spanish); Phu chomphu (Thai); Gülibrişim (Turkish); Rēśama rakha (Urdu)

Ethiopia to Japan Small tree with a spreading crown; bark **greenish grey**, smooth; buds and twigs **hairless**; lenticels **warty**, conspicuous. Leaves alternate, with 6–12 pairs of pinnae, each pinna with 20–30 leaflets; petiole hairless, 40–60mm long; rachis round; leaflets 8–12mm long, up to 3mm wide, oblong; tip rounded and spine-tipped; base oblique; upper surface glossy; veins hairless; margin smooth. Inflorescences erect; peduncle 25–50mm long. Flowers with a mass of stamens up to 25mm long, lower half **white**, upper half **pink**. Fruit a flat, straight, smooth, brown pod 125–150mm long.

Widely grown for dappled shade and ornament. Recorded from Mozambique, Zimbabwe and South Africa but invasive in some parts of the USA. The specific name, *julibrissin*, is a corruption of the Farsi (Persian) word for 'silk flower'. The wood is dense, hard and strong, used for furniture-making. Medicinal uses are recorded.

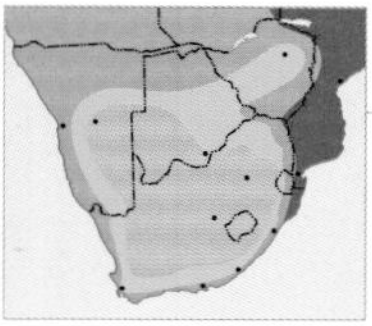

3 *Albizia lebbeck* (= *Acacia lebbeck, Mimosa lebbeck*) FABACEAE

Lebbeck Tree, Siris; Lebbekboom

- Drought 3
- Spring
- Deciduous

OTHER LANGUAGES: Tarisi (Bahasa Indonesia); Sarasa (Hindi); Ébano-oriental (Portuguese); Sirīsa (Sanskrit); Algarroba de olor (Spanish); Aninapala (Tagalog); Vagai (Tamil); Kagoh (Thai); Saras (Urdu)

India to Australia Small to medium-sized, spreading tree; bark grey, **rough, forming rectangular scales**; twigs **hairy**; lenticels **warty**, conspicuous. Leaves alternate, with 2–4 pairs of pinnae, each pinna with **2–11 pairs of leaflets**; petiole hairy or hairless; rachis round; leaflets **15–48** × 6–24mm, oblong; tip rounded; base **rounded to squared**; surface glossy; veins hairless; margin smooth. Inflorescences erect. Flowers with stamens a showy mass, **white**, 15–30mm long. Fruit a straight, flat, pale brown pod 150–330 × 30–55mm. Seeds midbrown, 7–11.5 × 7–9mm.

Naturalised in many tropical and subtropical areas. A declared Category 1b invader in South Africa.

1 *A. chinensis* flowers

1 *A. chinensis* fruit

2 *A. julibrissin* flowers

2 *A. julibrissin* flowers

3 *A. lebbeck* flowers

3 *A. lebbeck* fruit

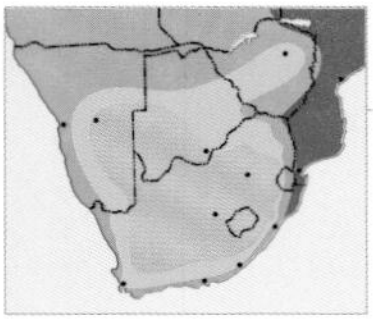

- Drought 3
- Spring
- Deciduous

1 *Albizia procera* FABACEAE

False Lebbeck Tree; Basterlebbekboom

OTHER LANGUAGES: Wangkal (Bahasa Indonesia); Huang dou shu (Chinese); Akleng parang (Tagalog); Thingthon (Thai)

India to the Philippines Medium-sized, spreading tree; bark yellowish or grey, **smooth, forming scales**; twigs hairless, angled or round. Leaves alternate, with 3–5 pairs of pinnae, each pinna with 6–12 pairs of leaflets; petiole hairless; rachis round; leaflets 25–30 × 13–15mm, egg-shaped to oblong, **somewhat leathery**; tip pointed to rounded; base **obliquely** rounded; surface dull; margin smooth. Inflorescences erect; peduncle 15–23mm long. Flowers in individual heads of 15–20; stamens conspicuous, **white**. Fruit a leathery, purple to brown, flat pod 80–150 × 15–20mm.

Naturalised in many tropical and subtropical areas. A declared Category 1b invader in South Africa. Grown for shade and ornament. The timber has many uses and inferior wood can be used for firewood and ethanol production. Medicinal uses are reported.

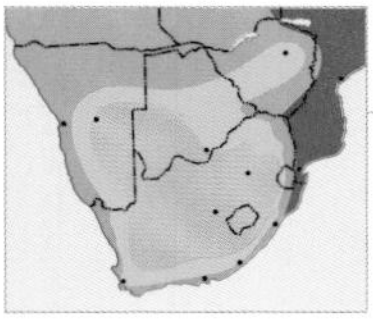

- Drought 3
- Spring
- Semi-deciduous

2 *Albizia saman* (= *Samanea saman*) FABACEAE

Rain Tree, Saman; Reënboom

OTHER LANGUAGES: Arbre à la Pluie (French); Regenbaum (German); Chorona (Portuguese); Cenízaro, Acacia Preta (Spanish)

Mexico to Peru and Brazil Medium-sized to large, spreading tree; bark grey, **fissured and rough**, flaking; buds and twigs hairy. Leaves with 2–6 pairs of pinnae, each pinna with 3–8 pairs of leaflets; petiole **hairy**, 15–40mm long; rachis round; leaflets 20–40 × 10–18mm, rhombic; tip rounded and **indented**; base **obliquely** rounded to squared; surface **glossy above, hairy below**; margin smooth. Inflorescences erect, 90–185mm long; peduncle 50–125mm long. Flowers with stamens long, **pink**, in a cluster. Fruit a flattish, leathery, black pod 100–200 × 13–25mm, **bent into a U-shape**, with thickened margin. Seeds mid- to dark brown, about 8 × 5mm.

Recorded from Mozambique and South Africa in our region. Pods contain a sweet pulp eaten fresh or processed into a drink. The wood is highly prized for carvings, furniture and panelling, waste wood makes good charcoal or firewood.

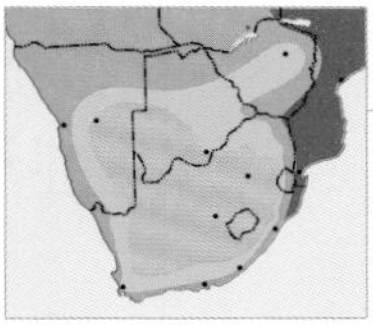

- Drought 2
- Spring
- Deciduous

3 *Caesalpinia echinata* FABACEAE

Brazilwood; Brasiliaanse Hout

OTHER LANGUAGES: Bois rouge du Brésil (French); Brasilholz (German); Pau-Brasil (Portuguese); Palo de Brasil (Spanish)

Brazil Small tree with a pyramidal to rounded crown; bark brown or grey, smooth or rough; twigs hairless; stems with single, **knob-like, straight thorns**. Leaves alternate; petiole **hairy**, 20–25mm long; rachis round; leaflets **12–20** × 4–7mm, oblong; tip rounded; base narrowed; surface **hairy**; margin smooth. Inflorescences erect. Flowers yellow; petals 5, each with a **purple basal mark**. Fruit a **prickly**, flattened, red-brown pod about 70 × 10–20mm.

This is the premier wood for making bows for violins and other stringed instruments. Because trees have been over-exploited for centuries and there are no known plantations, the species is listed on CITES Appendix II and wood is not legally available. National tree of Brazil. Grown as specimen trees in a private collection in our region.

1 *A. procera* flowers

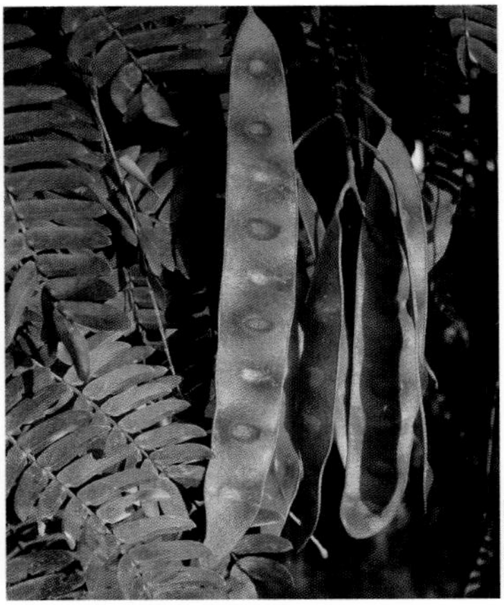

1 *A. procera* fruit

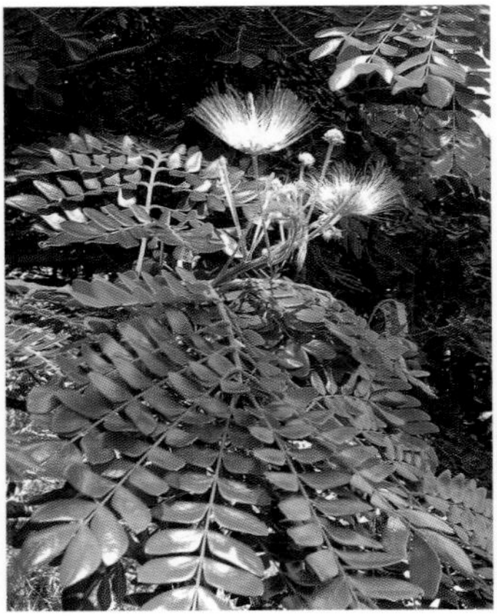

2 *A. saman* leaves

2 *A. saman* flowers

2 *A. saman* fruit and seeds

3 *C. echinata* flowers

3 *C. echinata* fruit

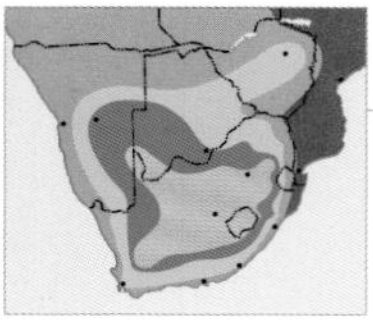

1 *Caesalpinia ferrea* FABACEAE

Leopard Tree, Brazilian Ironwood; Luiperdboom, Brasiliaanse Ysterhout

- Drought 2
- Spring
- Deciduous

OTHER LANGUAGES: Leopardenbaum (German); Pau-ferro (Portuguese); Imyrá-itá (Spanish)

Brazil Small to medium-sized tree with a vase-shaped to rounded crown; bark **very smooth, mottled whitish, brown and grey**, forming thin scales; buds and twigs hairless; lenticels **warty**, conspicuous. Leaves alternate, with about 3 pairs of pinnae, each pinna with 4–9 leaflets; petiole hairless, 15–30mm long; rachis round; leaflets 7–25 × 3–15mm, widest at or **beyond the middle**; tip **rounded or indented**; base oblique or heart-shaped; margin entire. Stipules absent. Inflorescences erect, about 110mm long. Flowers yellow, showy. Fruit a **flattened, shiny**, reddish brown to black pod 50–75 × 14–25mm.

Timber is used for furniture, flooring, gunstocks and musical instruments. The sawdust can cause acute allergic reactions. Grown in South Africa and Zimbabwe as a garden ornamental, elsewhere as a street tree but the roots are aggressive and trees should not be planted near walls or services. Medicinal uses are recorded.

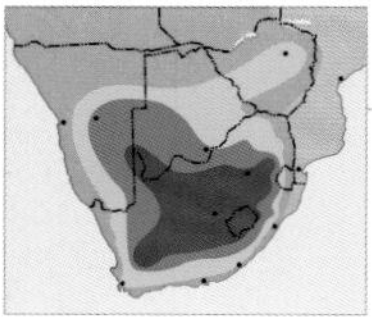

2 *Caesalpinia gilliesii* *(= Poinciana gilliesii)* FABACEAE

Bird-of-paradise Flower; Paradysvoëlblom

- Drought 3
- Spring
- Deciduous or semi-evergreen

OTHER LANGUAGES: Oiseau de Paradis jaune (French); Paradiesvogelbusch (German); Ave del Paraiso (Spanish); Cennet Çalısı (Turkish)

Argentina and Uruguay Unarmed large shrub or small tree of rounded to indefinite shape; new growth **hairy**. Leaves with **7–15 pairs of pinnae**, each pinna with 7–12 pairs of leaflets; petiole hairless; leaflets **2–8 × 1–2.5mm**, elliptic-oblong. Inflorescences erect, terminal. Flowers **yellow**; petals 5, these 17–32mm long; stamens **bright red**, 50–100mm long. Pods more or less oblong, 60–100 × 16–21mm, pale brown when ripe, covered with dark brown to black glands when young. Seeds flattened.

Grown for ornament in Botswana, Namibia, many parts of South Africa, Zimbabwe and further north. It is recorded as invasive in the southwestern USA and parts of Spain. The fruits and seeds are poisonous. Medicinal uses are recorded.

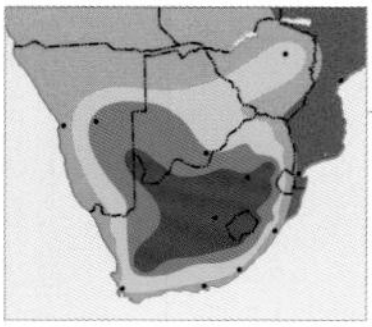

3 *Caesalpinia pluviosa* *(= C. peltophoroides)* FABACEAE

False Brazilwood, Sibipiruna; Vals Brasiliaanse Hout

- Drought 3
- Spring
- Deciduous

OTHER LANGUAGES: Sibipiruna (Portuguese)

Brazil Medium-sized tree with a rounded to spreading crown; bark brown or grey, **fissured or rough**; buds hairy; twigs **hairless**; lenticels **warty**, conspicuous. Leaves alternate, with **8 or 9 pairs of pinnae**, each pinna with 11–13 pairs of leaflets; petiole hairy; rachis round; leaflets 8–20 × 5–10mm, elliptic to oblong; tip rounded and indented; base **rounded to squared**; veins **hairy on lower surface**; margin smooth. Inflorescences erect. Flowers yellow; petals 5, these 2–11 × 10–11mm. Fruit a woody, brown, flattened, hairy pod 85–95 × 28–30mm. Seeds buff.

Timber is used for construction, furniture and more. Trees are grown for ornament and as street trees, in our region as specimen trees in Durban and Kimberley.

BRAAM VAN WYK

1 *C. ferrea* bark

TATIANA GERUS

1 *C. ferrea* flowers

TATIANA GERUS

1 *C. ferrea* fruit

BRAAM VAN WYK

2 *C. gilliesii* flowers

BRAAM VAN WYK

2 *C. gilliesii* fruit

3 *C. pluviosa* flowers

MAURO HALPERN

3 *C. pluviosa* fruit

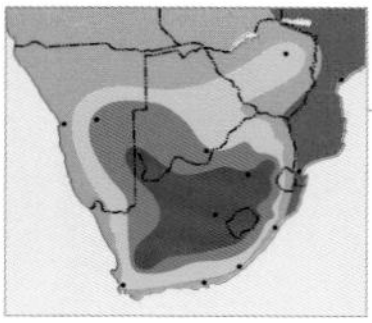

- Drought 2
- Spring
- Evergreen

1 *Caesalpinia pulcherrima* FABACEAE

Barbados Pride, Peacock Flower, Pride of Barbados; Poublom, Trots-van-Barbados

OTHER LANGUAGES: Faux flamboyant (French); Pfauenstrauch (German); Pequeño flamboyant (Spanish)

The West Indies **Large shrub or small tree** with a rounded crown; bark brown, **smooth**; buds and twigs hairless; stems sometimes with **single, hooked thorns**. Leaves alternate, with 3–10 pairs of pinnae, each pinna with 6–10 pairs of leaflets; petiole hairless, 33–65mm long; rachis round; leaflets 5–30 × 4–15mm, elliptic to oblong; tip rounded and indented; base **obliquely** rounded; margin smooth. Inflorescences erect, 200–500mm long; peduncle 25–60mm long. Flowers with sepals **5, red**; petals **5, yellow or red**, 10–25 × 6–20mm; stamens 10, **red**, 50–75mm long. Fruit a flat, red-brown, scimitar-shaped pod 70–120 × 18–22mm. Seeds dark brown to black, 8–10 × 6–8mm.

National flower of Barbados. Barbados pride is a widely grown ornamental in private and public gardens in Mozambique, South Africa and Zimbabwe. The seeds are poisonous unless knowledgeably prepared. Medicinal uses are recorded.

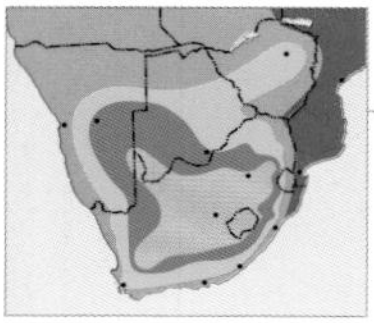

- Drought 2
- Mostly Autumn and Winter
- Evergreen

2 *Calliandra haematocephala* FABACEAE

Red Powder Puff; Rooipoeierkwas

OTHER LANGUAGES: Faux flamboyant (French); Pequeño flamboyant (Spanish)

Tropical South America Large shrub or small tree of rounded to indefinite shape. Leaves hairless, **glossy**, with 1 pair of pinnae, each pinna with 5–10 pairs of leaflets; petiole 10–25mm long; leaflets **coppery red when young**, later dark glossy green, **20–40 × 7–15mm**; tip **rounded**; base oblique; margins smooth. Inflorescences axillary heads, round or hemispherical, 30–75mm in diameter. Flowers with **conspicuous red stamens**, though pink and white forms are known. Pods woody, 60–110mm long, very narrow.

Both red- and white-flowered forms are grown for ornament in Gauteng and KwaZulu-Natal in South Africa and in Zimbabwe in our area, and widely in warm places elsewhere. It is not recorded as invasive. *Calliandra tweedii* (Mexican flame bush; Mexikaanse vlambos) has similar-looking red flowers but it is usually a shrub up to 2m high, with much finer and more crowded leaflets. Widely cultivated in gardens.

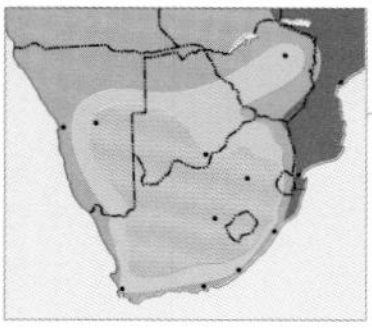

- Drought 2
- Spring
- Evergreen

3 *Calliandra surinamensis* FABACEAE

Surinam Powder Puff; Surinaamse Poeierkwas

OTHER LANGUAGES: Salsa (Spanish)

Brazil and Ecuador Shrub or small tree with a spreading crown; bark brown or grey, smooth or rough; twigs **hairy**. Leaves alternate, with 1 or few pairs of pinnae, each pinna with 6–10 pairs of leaflets; petiole hairless; rachis round; leaflets 8–25 × 2–18mm, **lance-shaped** or oblong; tip **pointed**; base rounded to squared; surface **glossy above**, dull below; margin smooth. Inflorescences erect; peduncle 7–20mm long. Flowers with conspicuous stamens, these **white below, red above**, 24–50mm long. Fruit a flat, brown to black, woody pod 45–110 × 7–14mm, with thickened margin. Seeds midbrown, 7.5–10.5 × 0.45–0.7mm.

Grown as a garden ornamental, in our region as a specimen tree in botanical and private gardens in South Africa and Zimbabwe. *Calliandra brevipes* (pink powderpuff; pienkpoeierkwas) has very similar-looking flowers. It is usually a small to medium-sized shrub rather than a tree and widely planted in gardens in our region.

BRAAM VAN WYK

1 *C. pulcherrima* flowers

FOREST AND KIM STARR

1 *C. pulcherrima* fruit

2 *C. haematocephala* leaves

BRAAM VAN WYK

2 *C. haematocephala* flowers (red form); inset: flowers (white form)

BRAAM VAN WYK

3 *C. surinamensis* flowers

FOREST AND KIM STARR

3 *C. surinamensis* flowers and fruit

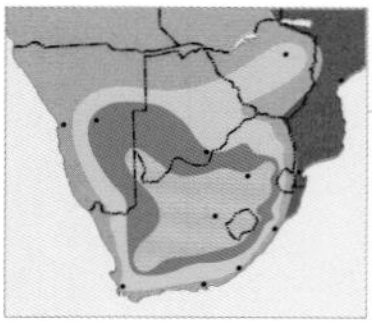

- Drought 2
- Spring
- Deciduous

1 *Colvillea racemosa* FABACEAE

False Flamboyant; Valsflambojant

Madagascar Medium-sized tree with a rounded crown; bark smooth, flaking; buds and twigs hairy; lenticels warty, conspicuous, orange. Leaves alternate, with up to **30 pairs of pinnae**, each pinna with up to about 30 pairs of leaflets; petiole hairy, up to about 120mm long; rachis channelled; leaflets up to 15 × 5mm, elliptic to oblong; tip rounded; base **obliquely** rounded; surface **glossy** dark green above, dull, paler below; veins hairy on lower surface; margin **rolled inwards**. Inflorescences **hanging**, up to about **800mm long**. Flowers **orange, with red veins**; petals 5, one free, the others joined, 26–33 × 8–12mm. Fruit a flat, woody, brown pod up to 280 × 45mm. Seeds mottled green and midbrown, about 14 × 8 × 2.5mm.

A spectacular ornamental tree grown as a street tree in parts of Durban, as specimens in botanical gardens and all too rarely in private gardens. Recorded from warmer parts of Gauteng and from KwaZulu-Natal and Mpumalanga.

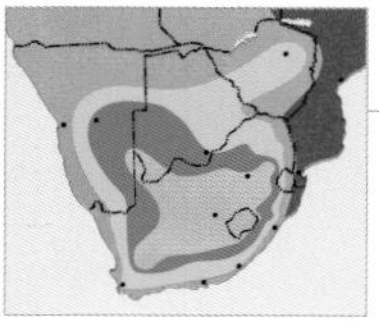

- Drought 2
- Summer
- Deciduous

2 *Delonix regia* (= *Poinciana regia*) FABACEAE

Flamboyant, Peacock Flower, Royal Poinciana; Flambojant

OTHER LANGUAGES: Gulmohar (Hindi); Llama del Bosque (Spanish); Phượng vĩ (Vietnamese)

Madagascar Small or medium-sized tree with a spreading crown; bark pale grey, smooth, **crumbling**; buds hairy; twigs hairless, lenticels **warty**, conspicuous. Leaves alternate, with 10–25 pairs of pinnae, each pinna with 15–30 pairs of leaflets; petiole hairless, 20–70mm long, base enlarged; leaflets 4–12 × 1.5–5mm, oblong; tip rounded and **spine-tipped**; base rounded; surface **dull**, upper hairless, dark green, lower **hairy**, paler; margin smooth. Stipules **pinnate**. Inflorescences erect, appearing before or with the leaves. Flowers with petals 5, **spoon-shaped, one enlarged**, pink, white or yellow streaked with red, the others bright scarlet, 50–70 × 25–47mm. Fruit a **flattened**, woody, dark brown pod **400–700 × 40–63mm**. Seeds 17–23 × 5–7 × 4–5mm.

A yellow-flowered form is occasionally seen. The red form is a commonly grown ornamental in the warmer parts of our region where it is seen in all countries except Lesotho. It is recorded as invasive in a relatively few tropical places where it has been introduced.

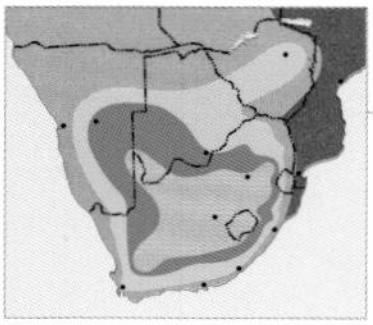

- Drought 2
- Spring
- Deciduous

3 *Enterolobium contortisiliquum* FABACEAE

Black Ear, Ring-Pod; Swartoor

OTHER LANGUAGES: Tamboril (Portuguese); Timbó (Spanish)

Brazil to Bolivia Medium-sized tree with a spreading crown; bark black, rough; buds and twigs hairy. Leaves alternate, with 7–10 pairs of pinnae, each pinna with 10–20 leaflets; petiole hairless; rachis round; leaflets 10–25mm long, about 5mm wide, **lance-shaped**; tip **pointed and spine-tipped**; base obliquely squared; surface **hairless**, glossy above, dull below; margin smooth. Stipules soon falling. Inflorescences erect, appearing after the leaves. Flowers **white**; stamens about 15mm long. Fruit a woody, **black, slightly flattened** pod 50–90 × 50–75mm, **coiled almost into a circle**. Seeds reddish brown, 10–15mm long.

Grown occasionally in eastern South Africa and Zimbabwe as an ornamental or street tree. The seeds are poisonous. Medicinal uses are recorded.

PRIMEJYOTHI, WIKIMEDIA COMMONS, CC BY SA 3.0

1 *C. racemosa* flowers

1 *C. racemosa* fruit

SCOTT ZONA

2 *D. regia* flowers

DICKY SIU

2 *D. regia* flowers

ARVORE.ESPECIES / FLICKR

3 *E. contortisiliquum* flowers

MAURICIO MERCADANTE

3 *E. contortisiliquum* fruit

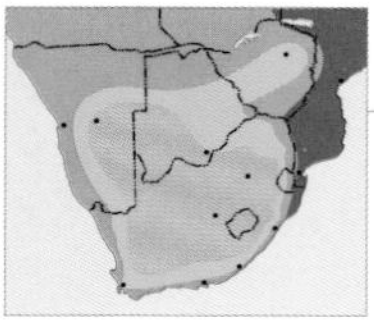

- Drought 2
- Spring
- Evergreen

1 *Heteropanax fragrans* *(= Aralia fragrans, Panax fragrans)* ARALIACEAE
Fragrant Aralia; Geur-aralia

OTHER LANGUAGES: Huangsanfeng (Chinese)

India to southern China, Indochina and Indonesia Large tree with a vase-shaped to spreading crown; bark grey, smooth or rough; twigs hairless. Leaves alternate, **3–5 times pinnately divided**; petiole hairless, 150–450mm long, base enlarged; rachis round; leaflets 30–130 × **15–60mm**, elliptic, with a **drip-tip**; base narrowed; surface glossy; margin wavy. Stipules minute. Inflorescences erect, 300–400mm long; peduncle to 90mm long. Flowers **small, inconspicuous**. Fruit fleshy, egg-shaped to round, 5–7 × 3–5mm.

Uses for ornament, timber and medicine are recorded, without further detail. Grown in our region as a specimen tree in Durban Botanic Gardens.

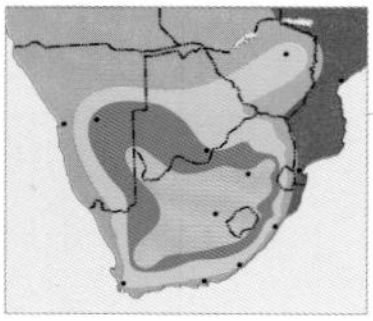

- Drought 2
- Spring
- Deciduous

2 *Jacaranda mimosifolia* *(= J. acutifolia, J. ovalifolia)* BIGNONIACEAE
Jacaranda; Jakaranda

OTHER LANGUAGES: Flambouyant Bleu (French); Neeli gulmohur (Hindi); Jacarandá (Portuguese, Spanish)

Brazil, Bolivia and Argentina Medium-sized tree with a rounded to spreading crown; bark grey or buff, **narrowly fissured**; buds and twigs hairless; lenticels **warty**, conspicuous. Leaves **opposite**, with **13–25 pairs of pinnae**, each pinna with many leaflets; petiole hairless, base enlarged; leaflets 3–12 × 1–4mm, narrowly elliptic; tip sharply pointed; base **narrowed**; margin smooth. Inflorescences erect. Flowers tubular, usually **blue**, rarely white or lilac-pink, 30–40mm long. Fruit a **round**, brownish capsule 32–60mm in diameter. Seeds 9–12 × 11–17mm.

A declared Category 1b invader in the Gauteng, KwaZulu-Natal, Limpopo, Mpumalanga and North West provinces of South Africa (with complex exceptions). Also problematic in East Africa, Australia and warmer parts of the USA. Very commonly grown as an ornamental, so much so that Pretoria is known as 'the Jacaranda City' and the local radio station is called 'Jacaranda FM'. However, displays in Johannesburg, Cape Town, Pietermaritzburg, Harare and Lusaka are hardly less spectacular. Timber is used for carpentry and turnery.

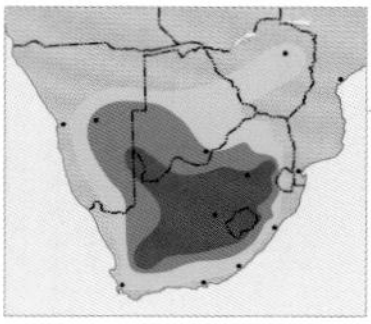

- Drought 2
- Late Summer–Autumn
- Deciduous

3 *Koelreuteria bipinnata* SAPINDACEAE
Chinese Flame Tree; Chinese Vlamboom

OTHER LANGUAGES: Fuyuye luanshu (Chinese)

China Medium-sized tree with a rounded to spreading crown; bark brown to grey, narrowly fissured; buds hairless; twigs hairy or hairless; lenticels **warty**, conspicuous. Leaves alternate, with about **3 pairs of pinnae**, each pinna with 4–8 pairs of leaflets; petiole hairless, 75–110mm long; rachis flattened; leaflets 78–141 × 21–51mm, egg-shaped to elliptic; tip drawn out; base obliquely narrowed; surface glossy above, dull below; margin **saw-toothed near tip**, otherwise smooth. Inflorescences erect, 350–700mm long. Flowers yellow, later orangered; petals 4, these 5.5–9.5 × 1.5–3mm, with a spur. Fruit a **triangular, inflated, lilac or brown capsule** 37–66 × 30–50mm. Seeds dark brown, 5.5–6mm long, 5.5–7.5mm wide and deep.

Grown in KwaZulu-Natal as a garden ornamental or street tree. The seeds are used for personal adornment and the flowers to make a yellow dye. Compare *K. paniculata* (p.374).

1 *H. fragrans* leaves

1 *H. fragrans* fruit

2 *J. mimosifolia* flowers

2 *J. mimosifolia* green fruit

2 *J. mimosifolia* dehisced fruit

3 *K. bipinnata* flowers

3 *K. bipinnata* fruit

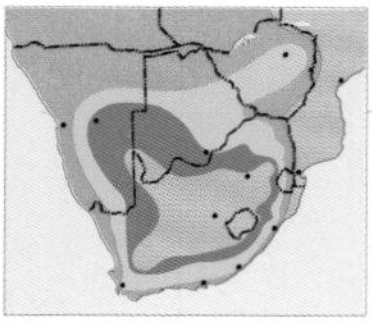

- Drought 3
- Spring
- Deciduous

1 *Koelreuteria elegans*
SAPINDACEAE

Golden Rain Tree; Gouereënboom

OTHER LANGUAGES: Taiwan luanshu (Chinese)

Fiji (subsp. *formosana* in Taiwan) Medium-sized tree with a rounded to spreading crown; bark brown to grey, rough, flaking; buds and twigs hairless; lenticels **warty**, conspicuous. Leaves alternate, with **5 or 6 pairs of pinnae**, each pinna with 2–6 pairs of leaflets; petiole hairless, 50–100mm long; rachis flattened; leaflets 55–92 × 13–30mm, lance-shaped to elliptic, with a drip-tip; base oblique; surface glossy above, dull below; margin **scalloped in upper three quarters**. Inflorescences erect, 300–500mm long. Flowers yellow becoming orange-red; petals 5, oblong, 5.5–7 × 1.5–3.5mm, with a spur. Fruit an **inflated, ellipsoid, pink or brown capsule** 34–50 × 31–46mm. Seeds black, 5.2–5.5mm long, wide and deep.

Commonly grown as a street tree and ornamental in many parts of the world but only recorded from Gauteng and KwaZulu-Natal in our area. Invasive in the warmer parts of Australia and the USA. The inflated, bladder-like pods are produced in great masses, rendering the trees very attractive and conspicuous. Compare *K. paniculata* (p.374).

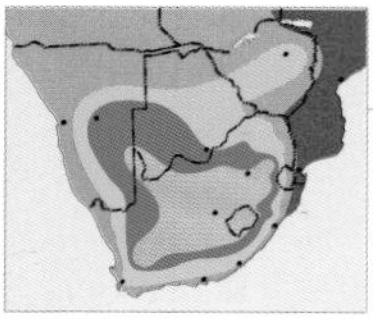

- Drought 2
- All year
- Evergreen

2 *Leucaena leucocephala* (= *L. glauca*)
FABACEAE

Giant Wattle, Giant Leucaena, Lead Tree; Reusewattel

OTHER LANGUAGES: Klandingan (Bahasa Indonesia); Ipil ipil (Malay, Tagalog); Lusina (Swahili)

Mexico and Central America Small tree with a columnar to rounded crown; bark grey, **smooth**; twigs hairy. Leaves alternate, with 4–9 pairs of pinnae, each pinna with 11–22 pairs of leaflets; petiole hairless, 20–47mm long; rachis **channelled**; leaflets 5–20 × 1.5–4mm, narrowly oblong; tip **pointed**; base narrowed, rounded or squared; surface dull, hairless; margin **hair-fringed**. Inflorescences erect; peduncle about 25mm long. Flowers **small, white**. Fruit a flat, straight, leathery, brown pod 80–180 × 16–21mm. Seeds 7.5–9 × 4–5mm.

Naturalised throughout the tropics and invasive in many places. A declared Category 2 invader in South Africa. Considered to be both one of the best forage plants (because it grows fast and luxuriantly) and worst weeds in the world. Although ruminants, such as cattle, can generally eat the foliage and fruits with impunity, this tree can be toxic to other animals as all parts contain mimosine. Timber can be used for fuel, pulp, parquet flooring and other purposes.

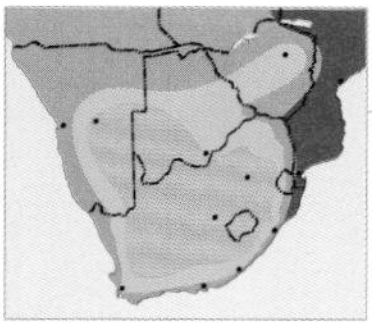

- Drought 2
- Spring
- Deciduous

3 *Lysiloma latisiliquum*
FABACEAE

False Tamarind, Sabicu Wood (timber), Wild Tamarind; Bastertamarinde

OTHER LANGUAGES: Tabernon (French); Tsalam (Náhuatl); Sabíco (Spanish)

Florida and the West Indies Medium-sized tree with a spreading crown; bark grey, **deeply fissured**, flaking; buds and twigs hairless; lenticels **warty**, conspicuous. Leaves alternate, with 2–5 pairs of pinnae, each pinna with 4–10 pairs of leaflets; petiole hairless; rachis **round**; leaflets 8–25mm long, oblong, shiny purple at first; tip and base **rounded**; surface dull, hairless; margin **smooth**. Inflorescences **globose heads, white**. Fruit a flat, straight, grey pod 70–150 × 20–30mm. Seeds dark brown, 6–12mm long.

Grown for shade or as a street tree, in our region mainly in KwaZulu-Natal.

GEOFF NICHOLS

1 *K. elegans* flowers

1 *K. elegans* fruit

2 *L. leucocephala* flowers

2 *L. leucocephala* fruit

SANIBEL-CAPTIVA CONSERVATION FOUNDATION

3 *L. latisiliquum* flowers

ROSS BAYTON

3 *L. latisiliquum* old fruit

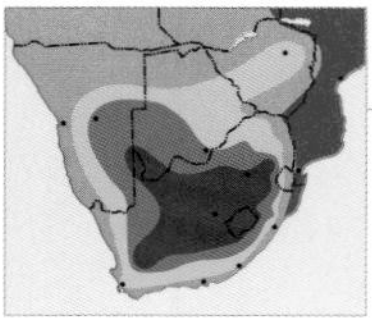

- Drought 3
- Spring
- Deciduous

1 *Melia azedarach* MELIACEAE

Syringa, Persian Lilac, Seringa; Sering, Maksering

OTHER LANGUAGES: Gringging (Bahasa Indonesia); Lian chu (Chinese); Zanzalakht (Farsi); Lilas de Perse (French); Chinesischer Holunder (German); Bakain (Hindi); Amargoseira-do-Himalaio (Portuguese); Mahanimbah (Sanskrit); Flor del paraiso (Spanish); Kattu vembhu (Tamil); Dryk (Urdu)

India and Sri Lanka Medium-sized to large tree with a rounded to spreading crown; bark brown to grey, smooth, with narrow fissures; buds and twigs hairless. Leaves alternate, with 3–5 pairs of pinnae, each pinna with 1–5 pairs of leaflets, **topmost 1 or 2 pinnae not fully separated**; petiole hairless, 80–300mm long, base enlarged; leaflets 30–60 × 10–25mm, lance- to egg-shaped, with a drip-tip; base narrowed to rounded; surface dull, hairless; margin often **saw-toothed in upper half**. Inflorescences erect, 100–220mm long. Flowers white to **lilac or blue**; petals 5, narrowly oblong, 6–10 × 2mm. Fruit fleshy, **yellow to orange**, 20–40 × 10–20mm. Seeds midbrown, about 3.5 × 1.6mm.

Invasive in many places and a declared Category 1b invader in South Africa, Category 3 in urban areas. The timber resembles Indian teak (p.318) but is generally under-appreciated and under-used. Exactly how toxic the fruits are is open to debate but it appears that humans would be poisoned by over-indulgence while birds can eat them with impunity; the leaves are more poisonous. The 'seeds' (stones) were formerly used to make rosaries and other items needing similar beads but have now been replaced by plastic mouldings. Medicinal uses are recorded.

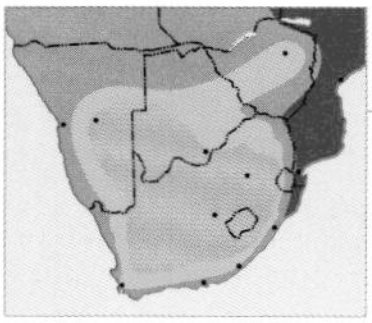

- Drought 3
- Spring
- Deciduous

2 *Moringa hildebrandtii* MORINGACEAE

Madagascar Moringa; Madagaskarpeperwortelboom

OTHER LANGUAGES: Maroserana (Malagasy)

Madagascar Small to medium-sized tree with a narrow, columnar crown; bark **whitish** or grey, **very smooth**; twigs hairless. Leaves alternate, 2 or 3 times pinnate; petiole hairless, 50–100mm long; rachis often **reddish**; leaflets **45–70** × 20–35mm, **egg-shaped**; tip pointed; base rounded; surface dull, hairless, pale apple-green; margin smooth. Stipules absent. Inflorescences erect or arched, up to 250mm long. Flowers **white to creamy**; petals 5, narrowly oblong, 8–9 × 1–2mm. Fruit a pale brown capsule **450–650 × 20–30mm**. Seeds winged, 35–40 × 22–25mm.

Almost extinct in the wild but maintained in villages in western Madagascar. Grown as a curiosity by succulent collectors and rarely seen in botanical gardens.

1 *M. azedarach*

1 *M. azedarach* leaves

BRAAM VAN WYK

1 *M. azedarach* flowers

1 *M. azedarach* fruit

BRAAM VAN WYK

2 *M. hildebrandtii* part of leaf

BRAAM VAN WYK

2 *M. hildebrandtii* part of young leaf showing reddish rachides

RUSSEL CUMMING

2 *M. hildebrandtii* fruit

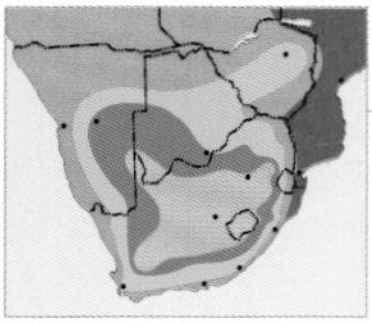

• Drought 3
• Spring
• Deciduous

1 *Moringa oleifera* *(= M. pterygosperma)* MORINGACEAE

Horse-radish Tree, Asparagus-bean Tree, Ben Nut; Peperwortelboom

OTHER LANGUAGES: Kalor (Bahasa Indonesia); Ben oléifère (French); Behennussbaum (German); Senjana (Hindi); Muringueiro (Portuguese); Mboga chungu, Mrongo (Swahili); Murungai maram (Tamil)

Northwestern India Small tree with a narrowly rhombic crown; bark whitish, brown or pale grey, **corky and deeply fissured**, adhering; buds and twigs hairy; lenticels **warty**, conspicuous. Leaves alternate, 2 or 3 times pinnate; petiole hairy, 40–150mm long, base enlarged; leaflets **5–20** × 3–13mm, **widest at or beyond the middle**; tip rounded or indented; base narrowed or rounded; surface apple-green, minutely hairy; margin smooth. Stipules absent. Inflorescences erect, 80–300mm long. Flowers **white to creamy**; petals 5, oblong to spoon-shaped, 10–18 × 3–8mm. Fruit a **9-ribbed**, buff or green capsule **100–500 × 15–26mm**. Seeds buff to grey, winged, 10–14 × 10–14mm.

Grown in private gardens in Mozambique, Namibia, Zimbabwe and the northern parts of South Africa, rarely seen in public places. The leaves, fruits and seeds are edible and eaten in various ways. Shredded roots can be used as a condiment like horseradish but they contain a neurotoxin and need to be used with caution. Oil expressed from the seeds is edible and has many uses. It also has potential as a biofuel, among other things. Medicinal uses are recorded.

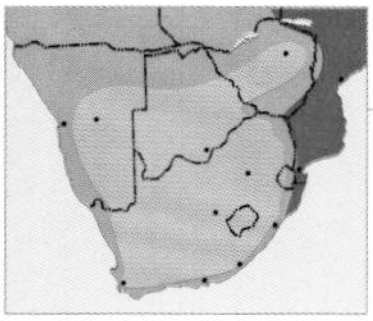

• Drought 3
• Spring
• Deciduous

2 *Moringa stenopetala* MORINGACEAE

African Moringa, Cabbage Tree; Afrikapeperwortelboom

Kenya, formerly also Ethiopia Small tree with a columnar to spreading crown; bark pale grey, **with very fine fissures**; twigs minutely hairy, stout, with large leaf scars. Leaves alternate, 2 or 3 times pinnate; petiole 10–15mm long; leaflets **33–65** × 18–33mm, **egg-shaped to elliptic**; tip bluntly pointed; base broadly rounded; surface apple-green. Inflorescences **hanging**, about 600mm long; peduncle 40–100mm long. Flowers **white to yellow tinged pink**; petals 5, oblong to spoon-shaped, 8–10 × 1.5–2.5mm. Fruit a reddish grey, dagger-shaped capsule **197–500 × 23–40mm**. Seeds cream and buff, winged, 25–35 × 14–20mm.

Rarely grown in our region as specimen trees in botanical gardens. In Ethiopia, the leaves are eaten and the seeds used for water purification. It is also grown as a companion or shade tree for other crops. Medicinal uses are recorded.

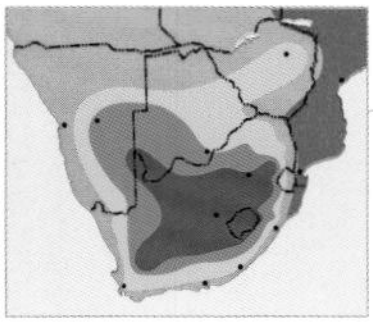

• Drought 3
• Spring
• Evergreen

3 *Paraserianthes lophantha* *(= Acacia lophantha, Albizia lophantha)* FABACEAE

Stink Bean, Australian False-thorn, Plume False-thorn; Stinkboon, Australiese Valsdoring

Western Australia Small tree or large shrub with a narrow (where crowded) or rounded (in the open) crown; bark grey to black, smooth; twigs **hairy**; stems **angled**. Leaves alternate, with 7–14 pairs of pinnae, each pinna with 15–40 pairs of leaflets; petiole hairy, 40–75mm long; rachis round; leaflets 6–13 × 1–4mm, **narrowly oblong**; tip rounded; base obliquely rounded; surface dull, hairless, paler below; margin smooth. Stipules soon falling. Inflorescences erect, **40–80mm long**; peduncle 8–15mm long. Flowers small, creamy to yellow; stamens 12–16mm long. Fruit a flat, woody, brown pod 55–120 × 15–25mm. Seeds dark brown to black, 6–8.5 × 4.5–5.5 × 3–4mm.

Considered a weed in those parts of Australia where it is not indigenous and also in New Zealand, the Canary Islands, Chile and in South Africa, where it is a declared Category 1b invader. Originally grown as an ornamental.

BRAAM VAN WYK

1 *M. oleifera* flowers

BRAAM VAN WYK

1 *M. oleifera* fruit

PLANTNUITY / FLICKR

2 *M. stenopetala* flowers

2 *M. stenopetala* fruit

JOHN TANN, WIKIMEDIA COMMONS, CC BY SA 2.0

3 *P. lophantha* leaves and flowers

BRAAM VAN WYK

3 *P. lophantha* flowers

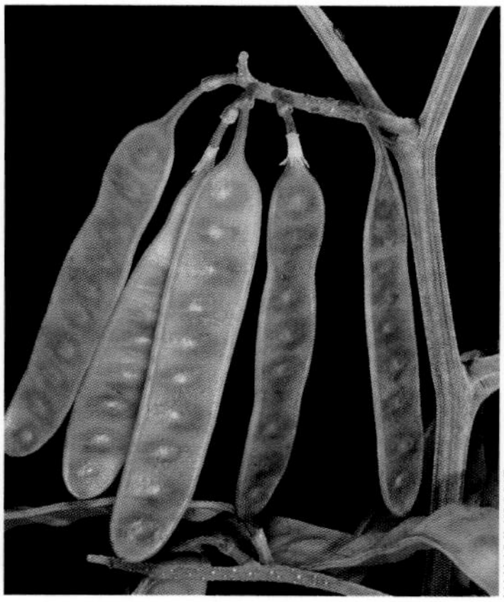
BRAAM VAN WYK

3 *P. lophantha* fruit

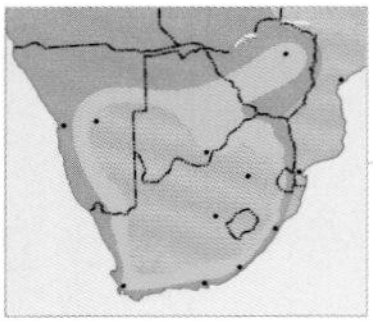

- Drought 2
- Spring
- Deciduous

1 *Peltophorum pterocarpum* (= *P. inerme*)

FABACEAE

Copperpod, Malayan Weeping Wattle, Yellow Flamboyant, Yellow Flame-of-Malaya; Maleise Huilboom

OTHER LANGUAGES: Peela gulmohar (Hindi); Perunkonrai (Tamil)

Sri Lanka and Vietnam to Australia Medium-sized to large tree with a rounded to spreading crown; bark grey, narrowly fissured or rough; blaze **aromatic**; buds and twigs hairy; lenticels **warty**, conspicuous. Leaves alternate, with 8–14 pairs of pinnae, each pinna with 10–20 pairs of leaflets; petiole hairy, 30–75mm long, base enlarged; rachis round; leaflets 8–21 × 3.5–9mm, oblong; tip **rounded and indented**; base obliquely rounded; surface **dull**, hairless or hairy, paler below; margin smooth. Inflorescences **erect, 200–400mm long**; peduncle 60–120mm long, appearing after the leaves. Flowers yellow; petals 5, these 13–23 × 8–13mm. Fruit a **flat**, leathery, copper-brown, **2-winged** pod 40–120 × 16–32mm. Seeds buff, 10–11 × 5–6mm.

Widely grown as a street tree, sometimes alternating with flamboyant (p.436), rarely seen in Mozambique and South Africa's KwaZulu-Natal. The wood is used for cabinet-making and the leaves for fodder. Naturalised in the warmer, wetter parts of the USA.

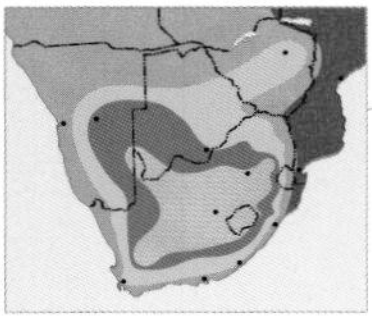

- Drought 2
- Late Spring–Early Summer
- Deciduous

2 *Schizolobium parahyba* (= *S. excelsum*)

FABACEAE

Feather-duster Tree, Sky-duster Tree; Verestofferboom

OTHER LANGUAGES: Guapuru, Pau de vintém (Portuguese)

Brazil Tall tree with a **clean** bole and a cabbage-like to spreading crown; bark green or pale grey, **smooth** except for large leaf scars; buds hairy; twigs hairless; lenticels warty, conspicuous. Leaves alternate, with **15–25 pairs of pinnae**, each pinna with 20–30 pairs of leaflets; petiole hairless, 110–230mm long; rachis channelled; leaflets 12–25 × 6–10mm, oblong; tip rounded; base obliquely squared; surface glossy above, whitish below; margin smooth. Stipules absent or apparently so. Inflorescences erect, **300mm long or more**, appearing with the leaves; peduncle 75–120mm long. Flowers yellow; petals 5, about 12mm long. Fruit a **woody, tadpole-shaped** pod about 100 × 40mm.

Widely grown as an ornamental in gardens and parks in Mozambique, South Africa and Zimbabwe. The wood is used for pulp, the inner layers of plywood, boxes, toys and shoe heels. Seeds are made into beads and buttons. Medicinal uses are recorded.

JANIE R. BEACHY

1 *P. pterocarpum* flowers

TATIANA GERUS

1 *P. pterocarpum* flowers

1 *P. pterocarpum* fruit

2 *S. parahyba*

2 *S. parahyba* leaves

TATIANA GERUS

2 *S. parahyba* flowers

REINALDO AGUILAR

2 *S. parahyba* fruit

GLOSSARY OF TERMS

Numbers in square brackets refer to the line drawings and photographs on p.451 and p.453. Synonyms commonly encountered in botanical works are supplied for some terms, and are given in round brackets at the end of the definition. More information on some of the descriptive terms is provided by Van Wyk & Van Wyk (2007).

alien a plant whose presence in a given area is not natural but due to introduction from elsewhere; this book covers species that are native elsewhere but grown in southern Africa. Compare **invader, native, naturalised**.
alternate applied to leaves borne singly at different heights on a stem [9]. Compare **opposite, whorl**.
anther the part of the stamen containing the pollen; usually borne on a slender stalk (filament) [39].
apex (*adj.* **apical**; *pl.* **apices**) the tip of a plant organ.
aril a fleshy outer covering or appendage that encloses the whole or part of the seed and usually develops from its stalk; often brightly coloured.
armed bearing thorns, spines, barbs or prickles.
axil the upper angle between a leaf and the stem on which it is carried.
axillary in, or arising from, an axil [1].
axis the main stem of a plant, or inflorescence, on which the plant's other organs are borne.
bacterial nodule a swelling or knob containing bacteria [60].
berry a many-seeded fleshy fruit with a soft outer portion, with the seeds embedded in the fleshy or pulpy tissue (e.g. a tomato). Compare **drupe**.
bifoliolate, 2-foliolate with two leaflets [3].
bilobed divided into two lobes [2].
bipinnate, bipinnately compound when the first divisions (pinnae or leaflets) of a leaf are further divided, i.e. with leaflets (pinnules) borne on branches of the rachis [8] (= twice-pinnate). Compare **pinnate**.
blade the flat, expanded part of a leaf [1] (= lamina).
bloom 1. a flower, or process of flowering. 2. a thin layer of white waxy powder on some leaves and fruit.
bole in trees, the part of the trunk below the lowermost branches; the unbranched part of the trunk. Compare **trunk**.
bract a usually small, leaf-like structure, in the axil from which arises a flower or a branch of an inflorescence.
bracteate having bracts.
branchlet a twig or small branch.
calyx collective term for all the sepals of a flower; the outer whorl of most flowers; usually green [39].
capitate head-like, or in a head-shaped cluster, as in the flowers of some species of *Acacia*.
capsule a dry fruit produced by an ovary comprising two or more united carpels and usually opening by slits or pores. Compare **pod**.
carpel one of the leaf-derived, usually ovule-bearing units of a pistil or ovary; sometimes free, but usually united to form a compound pistil or ovary. The number of carpels in a compound pistil is generally difficult to establish, but often equals the number of chambers or stigmatic lobes per pistil.
chamber the cavity of an ovary which contains the ovules [39] (= locule).
clasping applied to a leaf base that partly or completely encloses the stem.
compound consisting of several parts; e.g. a compound leaf has two or more separate leaflets [3–8].
cone a rounded or elongate structure comprising, on a central axis, many overlapping bracts which bear pollen, spores or seeds; characteristic of many gymnosperms.
congested crowded.
coppice, coppicing vegetative shoots at the base of a stem; sprouts arising from a stump; also, pruning trees to encourage the growth of long, slender shoots.
cordate heart-shaped, with the notch at the base [31].
corolla collective term for the petals of a flower; usually coloured [39].
costa (*pl.* **costae**) the midrib of a pinna in ferns.
costule the midrib of a pinnule in ferns.
cyathium a flower-like inflorescence characteristic of the genus *Euphorbia*.
deciduous shedding leaves at the end of the growing season. Compare **evergreen**.
dehiscent opening, as in anthers or fruit.
dichotomous branched or forked into two more or less equal divisions.
discolorous applied to a leaf in which the upper and lower surfaces are of markedly different colours.
domatia (*sing.* **domatium**) small structures in the forks of the midrib and the main lateral veins. They take two main forms: conspicuous tufts of hairs or small pits. These structures formed by the plant act as shelter for mites, who in return help clean the leaf surface and protect it against damage by plant-eating mites [57, 58].
drip-tip a long, gradually tapering tip of a leaf [18] (= tip attenuate).

drooping bending or hanging downwards, but not quite pendulous (= nodding). Compare **pendulous**.
drupe a fleshy, indehiscent fruit with one or more seeds, each of which is surrounded by a hard stony layer formed by the inner part of the ovary wall (e.g. stone fruit such as a peach, olive). Compare **berry**.
ellipsoid a solid body elliptic in long section and circular in cross section.
elliptic with oval and narrowed to rounded ends, widest at or about the middle [26].
entire see **smooth**.
epiphyte a plant that grows on another plant but is not parasitic on it; usually with its roots not in the ground. Compare **parasite**.
even-pinnate see **paripinnate**.
evergreen retaining green leaves throughout the year, even during winter. Compare **deciduous**.
exserted projecting beyond the surrounding parts, as with stamens protruding from a corolla; not included.
felted closely matted with intertwined hairs.
filament see **flower**.
flower the structure concerned with sexual reproduction in flowering plants [39]. Generally interpreted as a short length of stem with modified leaves attached to it. Four sets of modified leaves may be present. The outermost are the **sepals**, usually green, leaf-like, in the bud stage enclosing and protecting the other flower parts, and collectively known as the **calyx**. Within the sepals are the **petals**, usually conspicuous and brightly coloured, collectively known as the **corolla**. Within the petals are the **stamens** which are the male reproductive organs, each comprising a **filament** (stalk) which bears an **anther**, in which pollen grains are produced. In the centre of the flower is the female reproductive organ, the **pistil(s)**. Each pistil consists of an **ovary** (derived from modified leaves called **carpels**) at its base, a slender, more or less elongated projection (more than one in some species) called a **style**, and an often enlarged tip called a **stigma** which acts as the receptive surface for pollen grains. The ovary contains a varying number of **ovules**, which after fertilisation develop into **seeds**. The male and female parts may be in the same flower (**bisexual**) or in separate flowers (**unisexual**). Compare **ovary, perianth**.
foliolate pertaining to or having leaflets; usually used in compounds, such as **bifoliolate** or **trifoliolate** [3, 4].
follicle a dry 1-chambered fruit derived from a single carpel and opening along a single suture to release the seed.
forest a tree-dominated vegetation type with a continuous canopy cover of mostly evergreen trees, a multilayered understorey, and almost no ground layer.
free not joined to each other or to any other organ (e.g. petals not joined to other petals, or stamens not joined to petals). Compare **united**.
fruit the ripened ovary (pistil) and its attached parts; the seed-containing structure. Compare **seed**.
fused see **united**.
gall a localised abnormal growth on a plant induced by a fungus, insect or other foreign agent.
glabrous smooth; hairless.
gland an appendage, protuberance or other structure that secretes sticky, oily or sugary liquid; usually found on the surface of, or within, an organ (e.g. leaf, stem or flower) [55, 56].
gland-dotted with small translucent or coloured dots when viewed against the light, usually descriptive of leaves with secretory cavities in their tissues [59] (= pellucid gland-dotted; glandular-punctate). Compare **secretory cavities**.
glandular hairs hairs terminated by minute glands, often sticky to the touch.
globose spherical; rounded.
glutinous gluey; sticky; gummy; covered with a sticky exudate.
gregarious growing in groups or colonies.
heart-shaped see **cordate**.
heartwood the innermost, generally harder and somewhat darker wood of a woody stem; nonliving (= duramen). Compare **sapwood**.
hemiparasite a parasitic plant that contains chlorophyll and is thus partly self-sustaining, as in the Santalaceae. Compare **epiphyte, parasite**.
imparipinnate applied to a pinnately compound leaf with an odd number of leaflets and with a single terminal leaflet [6] (= odd-pinnate). Compare **paripinnate, bipinnate**.
indehiscent remaining closed; not opening when ripe or mature. Compare **dehiscent**.
inflorescence any arrangement of more than one flower; the flowering portion of a plant, e.g. head, spike, panicle, cyathium, raceme.
interpetiolar between the leaf stalks, as an interpetiolar stipule that extends from the base of one leaf stalk across the stem to the base of the stalk of the opposite leaf (e.g. a feature of many Rubiaceae) [50, 51]. Compare **intrapetiolar**.
intersecondary veins the veins in a leaf blade that interconnect the main lateral veins.
intramarginal vein a vein of constant thickness (but much thinner than the midrib) just inside the margin of the leaf blade, running from the base to the apex. Lateral veins run from the midrib to the intramarginal vein [1].

intrapetiolar between the petiole and the stem, as an intrapetiolar stipule that extends across the axil of the leaf (e.g. in members of the Melianthaceae). Compare **interpetiolar**.

invader a naturalised plant that produces reproductive offspring, often in very large numbers, at considerable distances from the parent plants, thus with the potential to spread over a large area. Compare **alien, naturalised**.

irregular applied to a flower that can be divided into two equal halves (mirror images) along only one plane, i.e. corolla lobes unequal [44] (= zygomorphic). Compare **regular**.

keel (petals) the two loosely united lower petals of the flowers of some Fabaceae [40] (= carina). Compare **standard, wing**.

lanceolate with the shape of a lance or spear; much longer than broad, tapering to the tip from a broad base, with the widest point below the middle [29] (= lance-shaped).

lateral borne on or at the side.

latex in this book used rather loosely for any copious liquid exudate whether watery (clear), milky or any other colour [53, 54].

leaf an aerial outgrowth from a stem, numbers of which make up the foliage of a plant. Characterised by an axillary bud. A leaf typically consists of a stalk (petiole) and a flattened blade (lamina), and is the principal food-manufacturing (photosynthetic) organ of a green plant [1].

leaflet the individual division of a compound leaf, which is usually leaf-like. It has a stalk of its own, but lacks an axillary bud in the axil with the rachis [3–7] (= **pinna**, pinnule).

lenticel a slightly raised, somewhat corky, often lens-shaped area on the surface of a young stem. Lenticels facilitate gaseous exchange between plant tissues and the atmosphere [45].

linear resembling a line; long and narrow, with more or less parallel sides [24]. Compare **oblong**.

lobe a part or a segment of an organ (e.g. leaf, petal) deeply divided from the rest of the organ but not separated; segments are usually rounded.

locule see **chamber**.

midrib the central or largest vein or rib of a leaf or other organ.

monocarpic applied to a plant flowering and producing fruit only once and then dying.

native applied to a plant occurring naturally in a given area and not introduced from elsewhere (= indigenous). Compare **alien, invader, naturalised**.

naturalised applied to a plant introduced from a foreign area (an alien) that has become established and has been sustaining self-replacing populations for at least ten years without direct intervention by humans (or in spite of human intervention). Compare **alien, invader, native**.

nectar the sugary liquid produced by the flowers or other floral parts on which insects and birds feed.

nectary any structure that produces nectar, such as glands or special hairs.

notched with a small V-shaped cut or indentation at the apex; usually referring to leaves [22] (= emarginate).

nut a dry, single-seeded and indehiscent fruit with a hard outer covering, e.g. an acorn, walnut.

nutlet a small nut.

obconic(al) conical or cone-shaped, with the attachment at the narrow end.

ob- a prefix meaning opposite, inverse or against.

obcordate inversely cordate (heart-shaped), with the attachment at the narrow end; sometimes refers to any leaf with a deeply notched apex.

oblanceolate inversely lanceolate (lance-shaped), with the attachment at the narrow end [32].

oblong elongated but relatively wide, two to four times longer than broad with nearly parallel sides [25] (= strap-shaped). Compare **linear**.

obovate inversely egg-shaped, with the broadest end towards the tip [34]. Compare **ovate**.

obtriangular inversely triangular, with the broadest end towards the tip.

odd-pinnate see **imparipinnate**.

opposite applied to two organs (e.g. leaves) growing at the same level on opposite sides of the stem [10], or otherwise opposite each other, or when the one organ arises at the base of another (e.g. a stamen opposite a petal or sepal). Compare **alternate, whorl**.

oval broadly elliptic, the width more than half the length [27].

ovary the hollow basal portion of a pistil which contains the ovules within one or more chambers, and which produces the fruit if pollination and fertilisation have taken place [39]. A **superior ovary** is borne on top of the receptacle and, as the sepals, petals and stamens are attached below its base, is visible when the flower is viewed from above [41]. Fruits from superior ovaries are not tipped by the remains of the perianth and stamens (e.g. avocados, oranges, grapes). An **inferior ovary** is completely enclosed by the receptacle and is usually visible as a swelling of the flower stalk below the attachment of the sepals, petals and stamens [42]. Fruits from inferior ovaries are often tipped by the remains of the perianth, or by a scar if it is deciduous (e.g. apples, guavas, pomegranates).

SIMPLE LEAVES

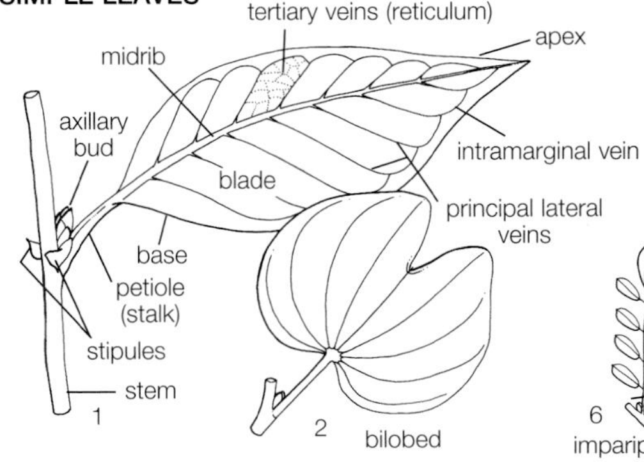

COMPOUND LEAVES

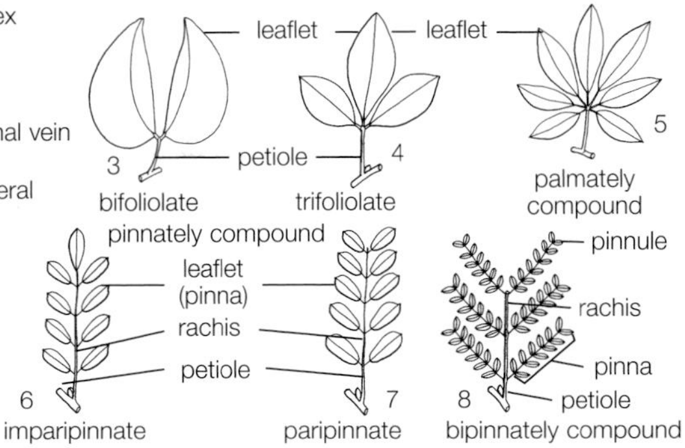

LEAF ARRANGEMENT

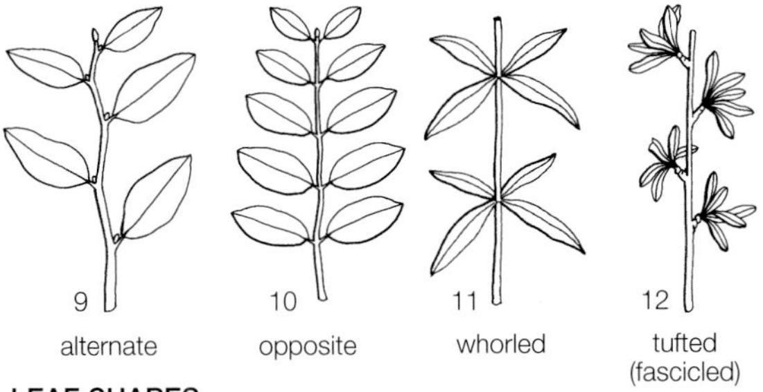

LEAF BASES

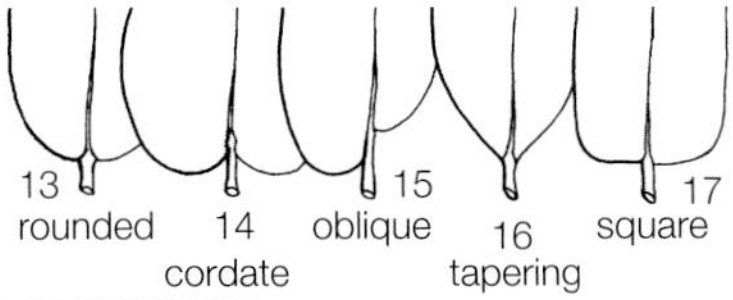

LEAF APICES

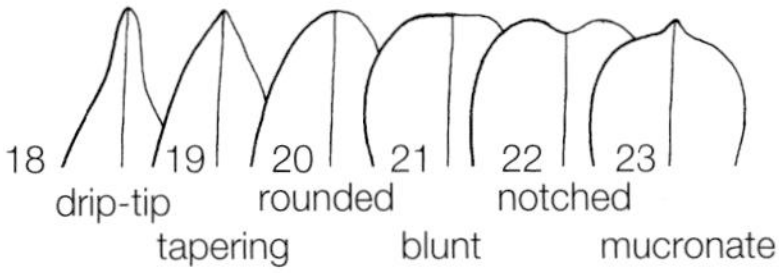

LEAF SHAPES

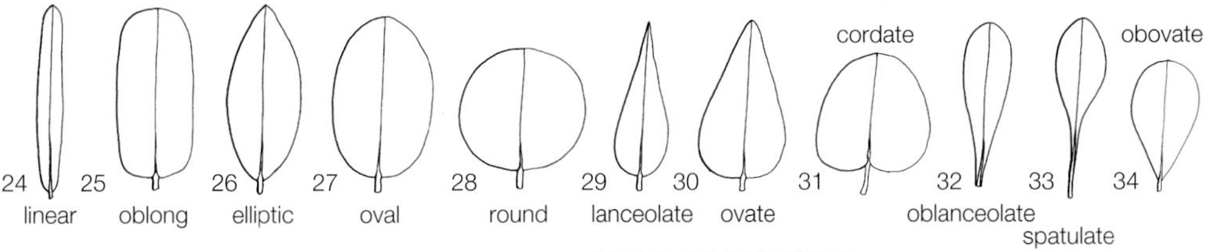

LEAF MARGINS

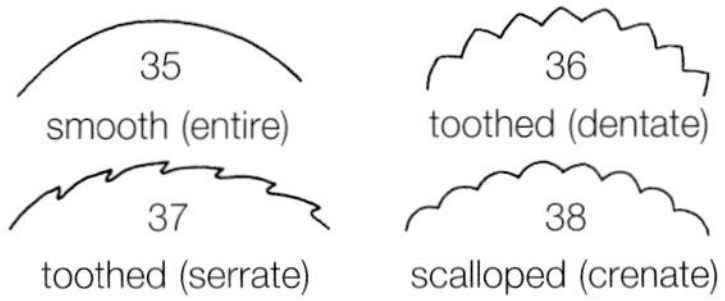

PARTS OF A FLOWER

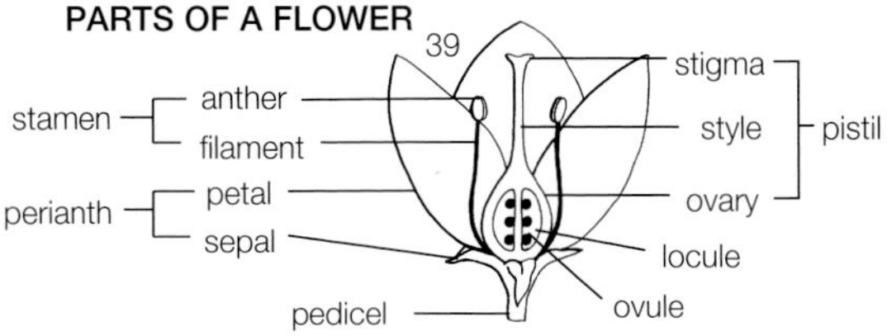

FLORAL STRUCTURE IN FABACEAE

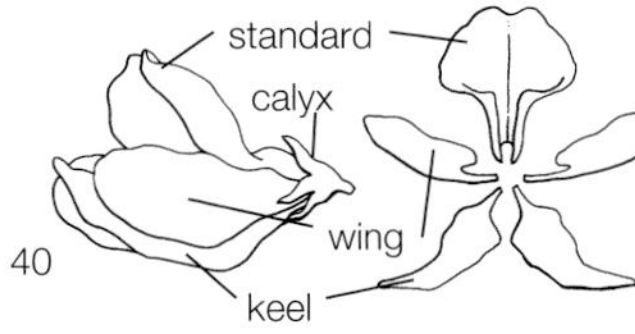

OVARY POSITION

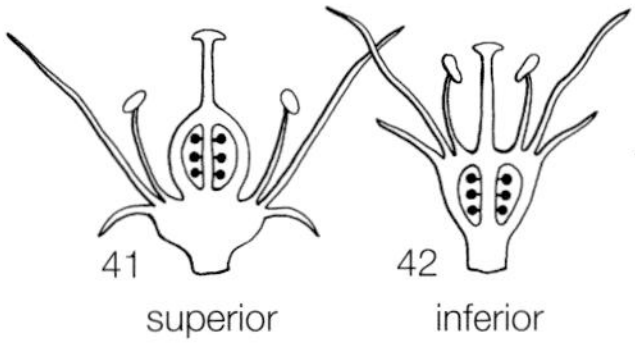

FLOWER SYMMETRY

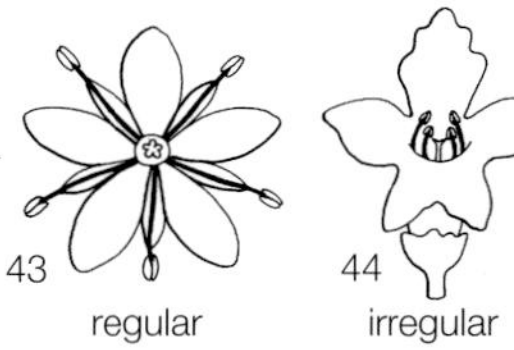

ovate egg-shaped in outline and attached at the broad end (applied to flat surfaces) [30]. Compare **ovoid**.
ovoid egg-shaped (applied to three-dimensional structures). Compare **ovate**.
ovule(s) the minute roundish structure(s) within the chamber of the ovary. The ovule contains the egg cell and, after fertilisation, develops into the seed [39].
palmate with three or more parts arising from a single point and radiating outward like the fingers of an open hand; as in palmately compound leaves [5] or palmate venation [2].
panicle an inflorescence with an axis that can continue to grow and does not end in a flower (i.e. the axis is indeterminate). It has many branches, each of which bears two or more flowers; often loosely applied to any complex, branched inflorescence.
parasite a plant that obtains its food from another living plant (the host) to which it is attached. Compare **hemiparasite**.
paripinnate applied to a pinnately compound leaf with an even number of leaflets and terminated by a pair of leaflets [7] (even-pinnate). Compare **imparipinnate, bipinnate**.
pedicel the stalk of an individual flower [39].
peltate shield-shaped; pertaining to a flat structure borne on a stalk attached to the lower surface (like the handle of an umbrella) rather than to the base or margin; usually used to describe leaves.
pendulous hanging downward (= pendent). Compare **drooping**.
perennial living for three or more years.
perianth collective term for the outer, sterile whorls of a flower, made up of sepals or petals or both [39].
persistent remaining attached and not falling off.
petal see **flower**.
petiolate applied to leaves possessing a stalk (**petiole**).
petiole the leaf stalk [1].
petiolule the stalk of a leaflet of a compound leaf.
pinna 1. the primary division of a pinnate leaf [3–7] (= leaflet). 2. the first series of branches within a bipinnate leaf which bears the pinnules [8].
pinnate, pinnately compound applied to a compound leaf whose leaflets are arranged in two rows along an extension (the rachis) of the leaf stalk [6, 7]. Compare **imparipinnate, paripinnate, bipinnate**.
plane with a flat surface.
pod a general term applied to any dry and many-seeded dehiscent fruit, formed from one unit or carpel. In this book the word is usually applied to a legume which is the product of a single pistil (carpel) usually splitting open along one or both of the two opposite sutures or seams (a character of many Fabaceae). Compare **capsule, follicle**.
prickle a small, sharp-pointed outgrowth of the epidermis or bark. Compare **spine, thorn**.
raceme an inflorescence in which the flowers are borne consecutively along a single (unbranched) axis, the lowest on the axis being the oldest. Each flower has a stalk. Compare **spike**.
rachis (rhachis; ***pl.*** **rachides)** 1. the axis of a compound leaf [6–8]. 2. the axis of an inflorescence.
rank a vertical row; leaves arranged in two ranks are in two vertical rows when viewed from the tip of the shoot.
receptacle the expanded uppermost part of the flower stalk, on which the floral parts are borne.
regular radially symmetrical, as in a flower that can be divided into two identical halves (mirror images) along more than one plane (i.e. the corolla lobes are equal) [43] (= actinomorphic). Compare **irregular**.
sapwood the outer, newer, usually softer and somewhat lighter wood of a woody stem; the wood that is alive and actively transporting water (= alburnum). Compare **heartwood**.
scalloped applied to a leaf margin notched with rounded or broad, blunt teeth or projections [38] (= crenate, crenulate). Compare **toothed**.
secretory cavities roundish cavities within the leaf blade that contain secretions such as resin, mucilage and oil [59]. Compare **gland-dotted**.
seed the ripened ovule containing an embryo. Compare **fruit**.
sepal see **flower**.
sessile attached directly, without a supporting stalk, as in a leaf without a petiole (= stalkless).
shrub a perennial woody plant with, usually, two or more stems arising from or near the ground; differs from a tree in that it is smaller and does not possess a trunk or bole. Compare **tree**.
simple applied to a leaf with only a single blade (= undivided) [1, 2]; the opposite of a compound leaf.
sinuate usually used to describe structures, such as leaf margins, with a number of regular curved indentations or small lobes. Compare **wavy**.
smooth with an even and continuous margin; lacking teeth, lobes or indentations [35] (= entire). Compare **toothed**.
sorus (***pl.*** **sori**) structure bearing or containing groups of spore-producing sporangia (in ferns).
spike an inflorescence with stalkless flowers arranged along an elongated, unbranched axis. Compare **raceme**.
spine a hard and sharp-pointed structure, often long and narrow. Usually a modified leaf or stipule. In this book used as a collective term for all sharp-pointed structures, notably straight ones. Compare **prickle, thorn**.

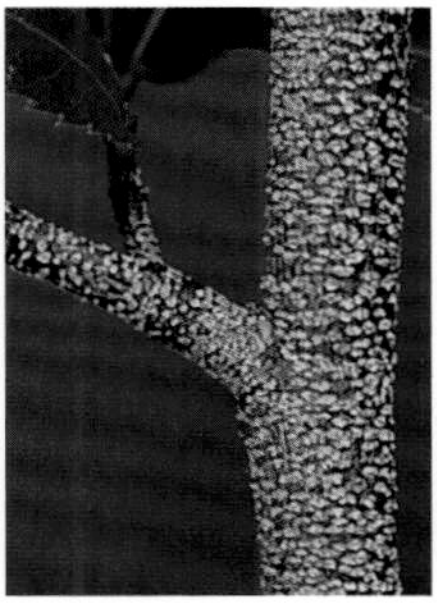
BRAAM VAN WYK

45 lenticels

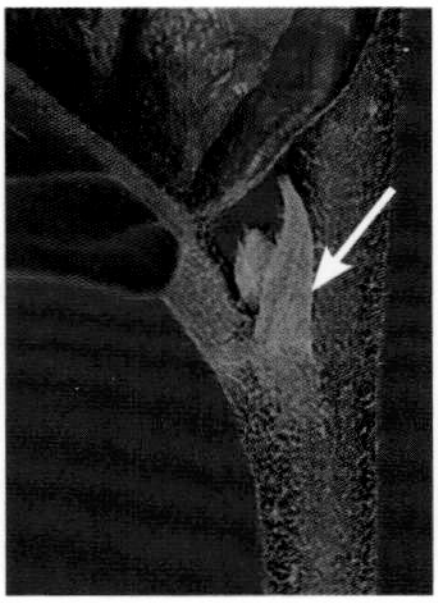
BRAAM VAN WYK

46 stipule

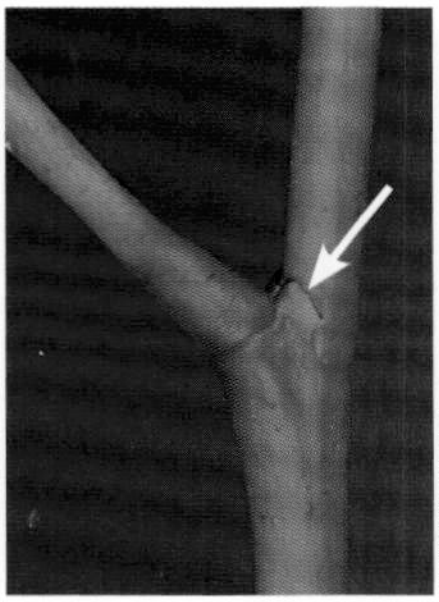
BRAAM VAN WYK

47 stipule

BRAAM VAN WYK

48 stipular scars

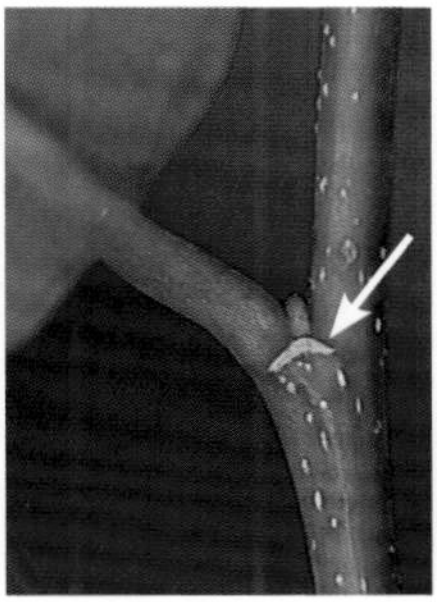
BRAAM VAN WYK

49 stipular scar

BRAAM VAN WYK

50 interpetiolar stipule

BRAAM VAN WYK

51 interpetiolar stipule

BRAAM VAN WYK

52 stipels

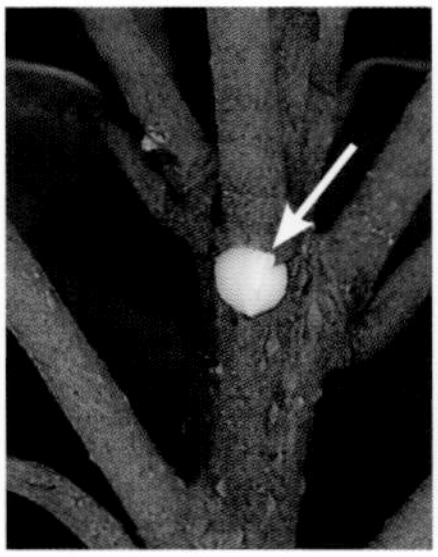
BRAAM VAN WYK

53 milky latex

BRAAM VAN WYK

54 watery latex

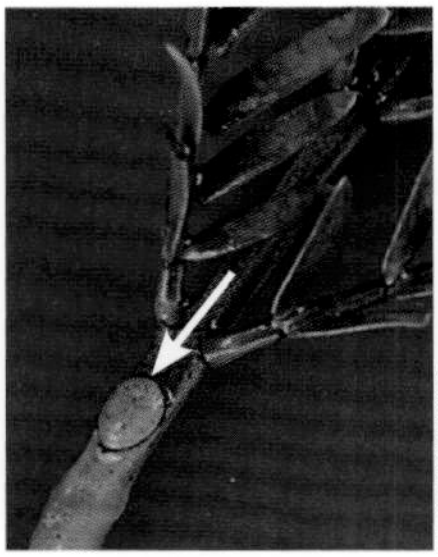
BRAAM VAN WYK

55 extrafloral nectary

BRAAM VAN WYK

56 extrafloral nectaries

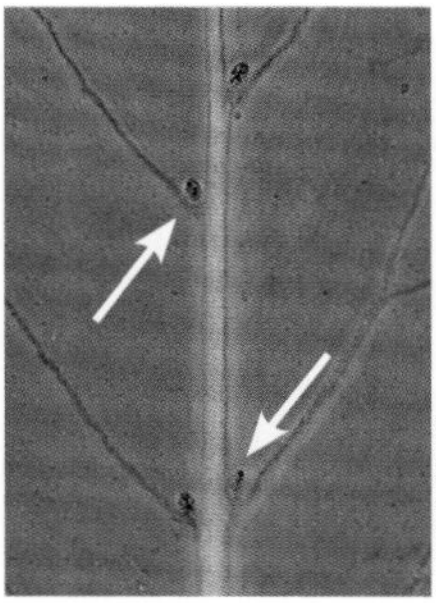
BRAAM VAN WYK

57 pit domatia

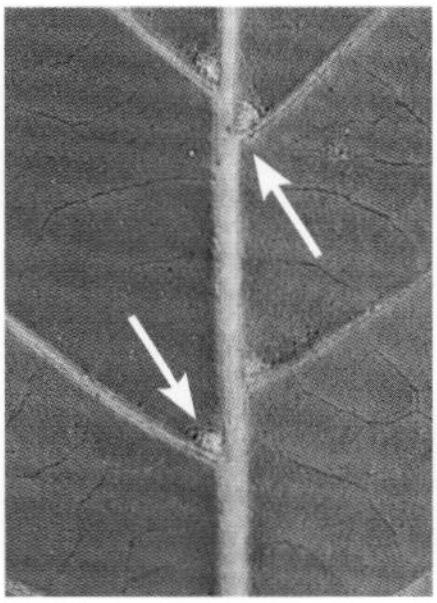
BRAAM VAN WYK

58 hairtuft domatia

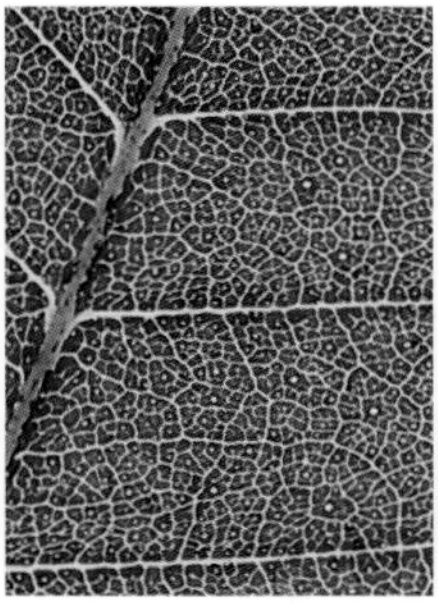
BRAAM VAN WYK

59 secretory cavities

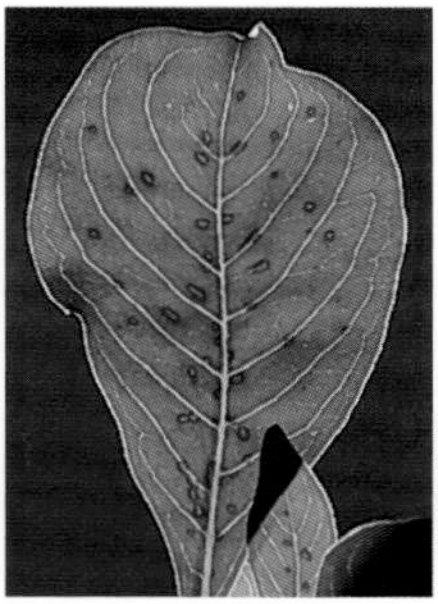
BRAAM VAN WYK

60 bacterial nodules

spray a slender shoot or branch together with its leaves, flowers or fruit.
spreading extending outwards in all directions.
stamen one of the male reproductive organs of the flower, usually made up of a narrow stalk (filament) and an anther in which the pollen is produced [39].
standard the large upper petal of a flower in some Fabaceae [40] (= banner, vexillum). Compare **keel, wing**.
stem the main axis of the plant, or a branch of the main axis, that produces leaves and buds at the nodes. Usually above ground, but sometimes modified and underground (e.g. a rhizome).
stem-clasping see **clasping**.
sterile lacking functional sex organs; a sterile flower produces neither pollen nor functional ovules.
stigma the part of the pistil on which the pollen grains germinate, normally situated at the top of the style and covered with a sticky secretion [39].
stipel (*pl.* **stipellae**) the equivalent of a stipule but found on compound leaves near the point of attachment of leaflet stalks [52].
stipule small scale- or leaf-like appendage at the base of the petiole in some plants; generally found in pairs on each side of the stem at the junction of the leaf stalk and the stem. Stipules often fall off early in life, leaving scars on the stem. They are best seen on young, actively growing shoots [1, 46–51].
stone the hard, seed-containing pit of a drupe (e.g. the so-called 'seed' of a peach, cherry or olive). Compare **drupe**.
style a more or less elongated projection of the ovary that bears the stigma [39].
subtend to be below and close to, as a bract subtending a flower.
taxon (*pl.* **taxa**) a general term denoting a named group of any rank into which living organisms are classified, such as family, genus, species or subspecies.
taxonomy (*adj.* **taxonomic**) the science of the classification of organisms into groups according to relationships. More or less synonymous with the term 'systematics'.
tendril a slender, usually coiling part of a leaf or stem that serves to support the stem; a climbing organ.
thicket 1. a vegetation type characterised by thickly growing (almost impenetrable) deciduous or evergreen shrubs, occasionally with trees rising above, and lacking a conspicuous grassy ground layer; sometimes very thorny or with many succulents. 2. a woody plant with many tall stems, intermediate between a true tree and a shrub, usually growing in thicket vegetation.
thorn 1. technically a sharp-pointed branch. 2. in this book often used in a generalised sense for any sharp-pointed structure, especially a curved or hooked one. Compare **prickle, spine**.
throat the opening of a tubular or funnel-shaped corolla.
toothed used in a generalised sense in this book to refer to leaf margins that are toothed in various ways, including dentate (with coarse sharp teeth perpendicular to the margin), serrate (with sharp, forward-pointing teeth) and crenate (with shallow, rounded teeth) [36–38]. Compare **smooth**.
trifoliolate, 3-foliolate referring to a compound leaf with three leaflets [4].
tree a rooted perennial woody plant with a single (usually) main stem and a distinct upper crown. In this book a broad practical concept of what constitutes a tree has been adopted, namely a woody perennial of 2m or taller. Not only have some marginal species that are technically closer to shrubs, been included, but also robust, woody climbers, the latter having stems that are not always self-supporting. Compare **shrub**.
trunk the main stem of a tree from the roots to where the crown branches; the bole plus the main axis of the crown. Compare **bole**.
umbel an umbrella-shaped inflorescence in which the stalks of the flowers all grow from the top of the main stem; the umbels themselves may be similarly arranged, in an inflorescence that is called a compound umbel.
unarmed lacking spines, thorns or prickles.
undulate with a wavy margin (= wavy).
united joined together (= fused). Compare **free**.
wavy a term used to describe the margin of leaves that are wavy (not flat), but not indented as in sinuate margins (= undulate). Compare **sinuate**.
whorl 1. the arrangement of three or more leaves or flowers at the same node of the axis, forming an encircling ring [11] (= verticil). Compare **alternate, opposite**. 2. the arrangement of three or more of any other organs (e.g. petals, stamens) arising at the same level.
wing 1. any thin, flat extension of an organ, as in winged fruit or seed. 2. each of the two side (lateral) petals of some Fabaceae flowers [40] (= ala, *pl.* alae). Compare **keel, standard**.
woodland an open, park-like vegetation type with scattered trees at least 8m tall, a canopy cover of 40 per cent or more and a grass-dominated ground layer.
woolly with long, soft, rather tangled hairs.

BIBLIOGRAPHY AND CONTACT ADDRESSES

Bean, W.J. 1970–1976. *Trees and Shrubs Hardy in the British Isles.* John Murray, London.

Brickell, C. et al. 2002. *International Code of Nomenclature for Cultivated Plants*, edn 8. Scripta Horticulturae 10: ISHS, Leuven, Belgium. ISBN 9789066056626

Brooker, M.I.H., Slee, A.V., Connors, J.R. & Duffy, S.M. 2002. *EUCLID: Eucalypts of Southern Australia.* CSIRO, Canberra. ISBN 0643068368

Burckhalter, R.E. 1992. The genus *Nyssa* (Nyssaceae) in North America: a revision. *Sida* 15: 323–342.

Burrows, J.E. & Burrows, S.M. 2003. *Figs of Southern and South-central Africa.* Umdaus Press, Pretoria. ISBN 1919766243

Coates Palgrave, M. 2002. *Keith Coates Palgrave's Trees of Southern Africa*, edn 3. Struik, Cape Town. ISBN 1868723895

Crouch, N.R., Klopper, R.R., Burrows, J.E. & Burrows, S.M. 2011. *Ferns of Southern Africa: A Comprehensive Guide.* Struik Nature, Cape Town. ISBN 9781770079106

Daly, C., Widrlechner, M.P., Halbleib, M.D., Smith, J.I. & Gibson, W.P. 2012. Development of a New USDA Plant Hardiness Zone Map for the United States. *Journal of Applied Meteorology and Climatology* 51: 242–264.

Hawksworth, D.L. 2010. *Terms Used in Bionomenclature. The Naming of Organisms (and Plant Communities).* Global Biodiversity Information Facility, Copenhagen. ISBN 8792020097

Heywood, V.H., Brummitt, R.K., Culham, A. & Seberg, O. 2007. *Flowering Plant Families of the World.* Firefly Books, Ontario. ISBN 9781554072064

Immelman, W.F.E., Wicht, C.L. & Ackerman, D.P. 1973. *Our Green Heritage: The South African Book of Trees.* Tafelberg, Cape Town. ISBN 0624003728

Judd, W.S., Campbell, C.S., Kellogg, E.A., Stevens, P.F. & Donoghue, M.J. 2008. *Plant Systematics: A Phylogenetic Approach*, edn 3. Sinauer, Sunderland MA. ISBN 9780878934072

Lawrence, G.H.M. 1951. *Taxonomy of Vascular Plants.* Macmillan, New York.

Maglin, R.R. & Ohmann, L.F. 1973. Boxelder (*Acer negundo*): A review and commentary. *Bulletin of the Torrey Botanical Club* 100: 357–363.

McNeill, J. *et al.* 2012. *International Code of Nomenclature for Algae, Fungi and Plants.* Koeltz Scientific Books, Koenigstein, Germany. ISBN 9783874294256 (electronic version can be consulted at http://www.iapt-taxon.org/nomen/main.php)

More, D. & White, J. 2013. *Illustrated Trees of Britain and Europe.* Bloomsbury, London. ISBN 9781408123669

National Terminology Services of the Department of National Education in collaboration with an Editorial Committee (compilers) 1991. *Dictionary of Horticulture with Plant Names: English–Afrikaans, Afrikaans–English.* Government Printer, Pretoria. ISBN 0621135313

Pearce, F. 2015. *The New Wild: Why Invasive Species will be Nature's Salvation.* Beacon Press, Boston. ISBN 9780807033685

Pienaar, K. 1996. *Kristo Pienaar Introduces the Ultimate Book of Trees and Shrubs for Southern African Gardeners.* Southern Book Publishers, Halfway House. ISBN 1868126773

Polunin, O. 1969. *Flowers of Europe: A Field Guide.* Oxford University Press, London. ISBN 0192176218

Polunin, O. 1980. *Flowers of Greece and the Balkans: A Field Guide.* Oxford University Press, London. ISBN 0192176269

Poynton, R.J. 1979. *Tree Planting in Southern Africa. Vol. 1: The Pines.* Department of Forestry, Pretoria. ISBN 9780621035292

Poynton, R.J. 1979. *Tree Planting in Southern Africa. Vol. 2: The Eucalypts.* Department of Forestry, Pretoria. ISBN 9780621047622

Poynton, R.J. 1984. *Characteristics and Uses of Selected Trees and Shrubs Cultivated in South Africa.* Bulletin No. 39, edn 4. Directorate of Forestry, Pretoria. ISBN 0621084425

Poynton, R.J. 2009. *Tree Planting in Southern Africa. Vol. 3: Other Genera.* Department of Agriculture, Forestry and Fisheries, Pretoria.

Simpson, M.G. 2005. *Plant Systematics.* Elsevier, Amsterdam. ISBN 9780126444605

Smith, G.F. & Pienaar, K. 2011. *The Southern African: What Flower is That?* Struik Lifestyle, Cape Town. ISBN 9781770075269

Spencer, R., Cross, R. & Lumley, P. 2007. *Plant Names: A Guide to Botanical Nomenclature.* CSIRO, Canberra. ISBN 9780643094406

Van Wyk, B., Van den Berg, E., Coates Palgrave, M., Jordaan, M. 2011. *Dictionary of Names for Southern African Trees. Scientific Names of Indigenous Trees, Shrubs and Climbers with Common Names from 30 Languages.* Briza Academic Books, Briza Publications, Pretoria. ISBN 9781920146016

Van Wyk, B. & Van Wyk, P. 2007. *How to Identify Trees in Southern Africa.* Struik Publishers, Cape Town. ISBN 9781770072404

Van Wyk, B. & Van Wyk, P. 2008. *Identifiseer die Bome van Suider-Afrika*. Struik Publishers, Cape Town. ISBN 978177007730
Van Wyk, B. & Van Wyk, P. 2013. *Field Guide to Trees of Southern Africa*, edn 2. Struik Nature, Cape Town. ISBN 9781770079113
Von Breitenbach, F. 1989. *National List of Introduced Trees*, edn 2. Dendrological Foundation, Pretoria. ISBN 0620068507
Whitman, A.H. 1986. *National Audubon Society Pocket Guide: Familiar Trees of North America: East.* Chanticleer Press, New York. ISBN 0394748514
Zomlefer, W.A. 1994. *Guide to Flowering Plant Families.* University of North Carolina Press, Chapel Hill. ISBN 0807844705

WEBSITES

edis.ifas.ufl.edu/topic_landscape_tree_varieties
hort.ifas.ufl.edu/woody/fact-sheets.shtml
plants.ces.ncsu.edu/plants/category/all/
www.anbg.gov.au/abrs/online-resources/flora/main-query-styles.html
www.davesgarden.com
www.efloras.org
www.floridata.com
www.flowersofindia.net
www.plantnames.unimelb.edu.au/Sorting/List_bot.html
www.theplantlist.org
(Various other universities apart from Florida and North Carolina also have good websites with useful tree information; these appear in the first few pages of a Google search for the relevant species.)

HERBARIA

Only those southern African herbaria with significant collections of cultivated plant material are listed here. Many others may have small but useful collections; a complete directory of herbaria worldwide can be consulted at sciweb.nybg.org/science2/IndexHerbariorum.asp. In any event, please remember to make an appointment before visiting a herbarium.

MOZAMBIQUE: Herbario, National Institute of Agronomic Research (IIAM), CP 3658, Mavalane, Maputo 8

NAMIBIA: National Herbarium of Namibia, Ministry of Agriculture, Water and Rural Development, National Botanical Research Institute, Private Bag 13184, Windhoek

SOUTH AFRICA: The best collection of specimens of cultivated trees in southern Africa was assembled between about 1880 and 1990 by the Forestry Department Herbarium, Pretoria. This collection has now passed to the National Herbarium, Pretoria, where it is incorporated in their 'cultivated collection', the foundation ultimately underlying this book.

C.E. Moss Herbarium, Department of Botany, University of the Witwatersrand, Private Bag 3, Wits 2050
H.G.W.J. Schweickerdt Herbarium, Department of Plant Science, University of Pretoria, Pretoria 0002
Hortus Siccus Macmurtrianus, Whytethorne, Mbombela (see below)
KwaZulu-Natal Herbarium, PO Box 52009, Berea Road, 4007
National Herbarium, Private Bag X101, Silverton, Pretoria 0001

ZIMBABWE: National Herbarium, Botanic Garden, PO Box CY550, Causeway, Harare

LIVING TREE COLLECTIONS

The following collections among others, some public and others private, maintain interesting and sometimes rare living trees:

Arderne Gardens, Main Road, Claremont, Cape Town
B&B@Bloem, Jacobs Street, Universitas, Bloemfontein, has a remarkable collection of labelled trees. This is a private collection, so please phone 084 577 3226/051 522 4770 or e-mail info@mjsjordaan.co.za for an appointment.
Durban Botanic Garden, John Zikhali (Sydenham) Road, Durban
Johannesburg Botanic Garden, Olifants Road, Emmarentia, Johannesburg
Lowveld National Botanical Garden, Mbombela
Makaranga Garden Lodge, Igwababa Road, Kloof, Durban. Admission fee to be paid. Contact www.makaranga.com or 031 764 6616.
Manie van der Schijff Botanical Garden, Department of Plant Science, University of Pretoria. Contact the Curator to book a guided tour and parking spot, and for directions: www.up.ac.za/botanical-garden or 012 420 4274.
Paarl Arboretum, Arboretum Avenue, Paarl
Tokai Arboretum, Tokai Road, Tokai, Cape Town
Whytethorne, Mbombela. By appointment only as this is a private collection. Phone Doug MacMurtry or Shane Burns on 013 747 2270.

SOCIETIES

Dendrological Society of South Africa: www.dendro.co.za
Palm Society of South Africa: contact Peter Wunderlin, 031 267 1111
Tree Society of South Africa: www.treesocietysa.org
Tree Society of Zimbabwe: www.lind.org.zw/treesociety

ACKNOWLEDGEMENTS

We are most grateful to Arnia van Vuuren for making a draft of the index to this book. She volunteered her services as a labour of love, even while the book was still no more than an idea in the authors' minds. Di Higginson-Keath has helped in many ways, not least in preparing information for the analysis of origins in the introduction. For permission to use her line drawings, our grateful thanks go to Anne Stadler. We are much indebted to the many people and institutions who kindly allowed us to use their photographs in this book. We would have liked to acknowledge each individually, but there are just too many. Their names are indicated alongside their individual photographs throughout the book. Truly, the pictures make the book, and so a word and more of gratitude to the kind souls who have made images available for downloading via Wikimedia Commons is most definitely in order. There are instances where we have been unable to trace or contact the copyright holder. If notified, the publisher will be pleased to rectify any errors or omissions at the earliest opportunity.

We express our sincere appreciation to Elsa de Jager, Unit Manager: Climate Information, SA Weather Service, for valuable assistance with the demarcation of cold-hardiness zones for southern Africa. Jaco van Wyk made the final maps, based on information from the SA Weather Service and a suggestion from Melissa Glen; to all of them, we are grateful. We are also much indebted to Elsa van Wyk for technical assistance.

Many thanks and much appreciation are due to the team at Struik Nature who worked with us on this book, especially Pippa Parker (Publisher), Helen de Villiers (Managing editor), Emsie du Plessis (Editor), Colette Alves (Project manager), Janice Evans (Design director), Gillian Black (Designer), Deirdré Geldenhuys (Typesetter), Colette Stott (Image library manager) and Tina Mössmer (Proofreader).

INDEX

Not included in the index are scientific and common names mentioned in the 'Family descriptions' (pp.20–33), most casually mentioned names in the rest of the book, as well as common names in languages other than English and Afrikaans.

B

D

E